PEACEMAKING IN
INTERNATIONAL CONFLICT

Methods & Techniques

PEACEMAKING IN INTERNATIONAL CONFLICT

METHODS & TECHNIQUES

Revised Edition

I. William Zartman
Editor

UNITED STATES INSTITUTE OF PEACE
Washington, D.C

UNITED STATES INSTITUTE OF PEACE
1200 17th Street NW, Suite 200
Washington, DC 20036-3011
www.usip.org

First edition 1997, revised edition 2007

Printed in the United States of America

The paper used in this publication meets the minimum requirements of American National Standards for Information Science—Permanence of Paper for Printed Library Materials, ANSI Z39.48-1984.

Library of Congress Cataloging-in-Publication Data
    Peacemaking in international conflict : methods and techniques / I. William Zartman, editor. — Rev. ed.
        p. cm.
    Includes bibliographical references and index.
    ISBN 978-1-929223-66-4 (pbk. : alk. paper) — ISBN 978-1-929223-65-7 (cloth : alk. paper)
    1. Pacific settlement of international disputes. 2. Diplomatic negotiations in international disputes. 3. Mediation, International. 4. Arbitration, Interna-tional. 5. Conflict management—Methodology. I. Zartman, I. William.
    JZ6010.P42 2007
    327.1'72—dc22

                        2007034632

Contents

FOREWORD

The landscape of conflict across the globe has undergone major changes since the original edition of this volume appeared in 1997. Much has also changed in the study of conflict management and resolution, as the various methods and techniques applied to various conflicts have evolved rapidly. Recognizing the need for an updated examination of the approaches to dealing with inter- and intrastate conflict, the United States Institute of Peace presents this revised edition of *Peacemaking in International Conflict: Methods and Techniques*.

In addition to updating the original chapters, editor William Zartman has added several new chapters to address such topics as the use or threat of force in peacemaking, the role of conflict resolution education, and economic tools as innovative peacemaking practices. This revised edition also features a concluding chapter that offers guidelines for determining when a conflict is ready for peacemaking initiatives, which peacemaking tools and methods are most appropriate, and who should wield those tools.

Under the best of circumstances, peacemaking is a complicated and difficult endeavor. Today's peacemaking comprises a great many approaches and methods for understanding, managing, and hopefully resolving conflicts. The variety of methods is a product of the increasing complexity of international conflicts, as well as the experience of the international community in dealing with failed and failing states, separatist and centralist conflicts, and the dwindling instances of interstate conflict. Whereas wars in times past were largely the province of august heads of state and foreign ministers representing powerful nations and grand alliances, conflict in the twentieth and twenty-first centuries has "evolved" to bring destruction and death to mass publics and to threaten stability on a regional and global scale.

Fortunately, we are not helpless in confronting such organized violence and mass social chaos. Ever since nation-states first went to war with each other, scholars in the social sciences and members of the foreign policymaking establishment have developed a vital body of knowledge about how to curb the destructiveness of state-organized aggression. Over time, as international wars became more extensive and destructive, the relevant body of knowledge has become more elaborate, and approaches to peacemaking have become more diversified through their sheer number.

The techniques of making violence-prone adversaries halt their acts of carnage and destruction are not always based on detailed analyses or the invocation of time-honored principles and techniques. In many cases, snap judgments and plain luck guide a peacemaker's tactics and stratagems. Nevertheless, conflict managers today can execute their assignments with an intellectual arsenal of knowledge, theories, and techniques that have proved successful in managing previous conflicts.

Some of the methods explored in this collection are time-honored and well known, such as negotiation, bargaining, and third-party mediation. Some are relatively new to the peacemaking community, such as problem-solving workshops, economic incentives and disincentives for managing conflict, conflict resolution education in zones of conflict, and training in conflict management techniques. All methods aim to combine analytical and prescriptive components in order to form a durable and effective approach in diverse conflict settings.

Editor William Zartman is well known to specialists in conflict and peace studies as a former director of the African Studies Program and director of the Conflict Management Program at Johns Hopkins University's Nitze School of Advanced International Studies, as well as a preeminent scholar on conflict resolution. He brings to this project a lifetime of distinguished scholarship and writing not only on Africa's various national and subnational conflicts but also on the cognitive and policymaking dimensions of peacemaking and conflict resolution.

Readers interested in complementary perspectives on conflict and peacemaking might explore some other volumes published by the U.S. Institute of Peace: *Leashing the Dogs of War: Conflict Management in a Divided World*; *Managing Global Chaos: Sources of and Responses to International Conflict*; *Taming Intractable Conflicts: Mediation in the Hardest Cases*; and *Grasping the Nettle: Analyzing Cases of Intractable Conflicts*, all edited by Chester Crocker, Fen Hampson, and Pamela Aall.

This revised edition of *Peacemaking in International Conflict* represents an important addition to a growing body of analytical and practical writings on approaches to managing and resolving inter- and intrastate conflict. It touches on all the issues that scholars at the United States Institute of Peace explore daily in their efforts to understand and educate professionals engaged in international peacemaking.

Richard H. Solomon, President
United States Institute of Peace

PEACEMAKING IN INTERNATIONAL CONFLICT

Methods & Techniques

INTRODUCTION

Toward the Resolution of International Conflicts

I. William Zartman

In the early years of the twenty-first century the methods of conflict are more brutal and the methods of conflict resolution more sophisticated than ever before, leaving a tremendous gap between conflict and resolution that remains to be filled. Courage and commitment are needed to use the tools required to meet the challenge of moving people away from their proclivity to violence and nations away from the temptation to war. The purpose of this book is to build an awareness of the tools and techniques available to pursue this goal.

Peacemaking in International Conflict concerns conflict both among and within states and nations and therefore deals with power and interests. It thus encompasses conflicts among people, who act in the name of states and nations, and so touches on basic human interactions and reactions. It bridges and unites these two areas of activity—the interactional and the interpersonal—as it looks for lessons that each has for the other. It recognizes the inevitability of conflict among sovereign and nonsovereign groups speaking in the name of peoples or nations, but it presents ways in which that conflict can be first managed, moving it from violent to political manifestations, and then resolved, transforming it and removing its causes. This book presents the state of the art of the subject in descriptions, generalizations, and concepts, organized according to different methods of international conflict resolution, with the aim of emphasizing their usefulness and limitations.

THE CHALLENGES OF THE NEW MILLENNIUM

Conflict in a New World Order

The end of the Cold War was a monumental event, the first global turning point in modern international relations not caused by a major war. However, now we are left without a sense of a dominant structure and system of world order; the post–Cold War era will persist until this uncertainty is resolved (Zartman 2007). Even the negative and destructive globalization inherent in the al-Qaeda attacks of September 11, 2001, did not introduce any new certainty or revised order, only a mirror reflecting the absence of clear norms and structures.

The Cold War had barely become history when observers noted that its passing had opened an era of vicious "little" conflicts, uncontained by superpower restraints and impervious to regional ministrations. Although regional conflicts and national struggles for power were used by the Cold War protagonists for their own purposes (or to thwart their opponent's suspected purposes), these conflicts were kept under careful control, lest they turn into tails that wag the dogs of global war, by the Cold War's system of world order. When these constraints suddenly vanished in the early 1990s, conflicts of many types sprang forth. Many arose over the inheritance of a former communist-supported domestic order—including Angola, Mozambique, Ethiopia, Somalia, Cambodia, Yugoslavia, Armenia, Tajikistan, Afghanistan, Georgia, Moldova, Chechnya, Nicaragua, and others.[1]

Many regimes were artificially protected and ignored at the same time by the previous global balance. As soon as the balance shifted, some governments set about privatizing power and its profits. When justified rebellion broke out, the rebels imposed their own brand of bad government, eventually perpetuating the cycle of greed and grievance. Such is the recent history of Liberia, Sierra Leone, both Congos, all three Guineas, Haiti, Somalia, Cambodia, Burma, Pakistan, Venezuela, Mexico, and others.[2]

Elsewhere (and in some of the same cases), conflicts arose from deep-rooted antagonisms that had lain dormant or been held in check by the old balance of power. Such antagonisms rise and fall according to external conditions. When national systems of order break down, people fall back on ethnic or confessional identities that may exclude others with whom they formerly lived in harmony. When economic conditions worsen and the national resource pie shrinks, people (again, often mobilized by a selective sense of identity) fight over the scraps. International pressures for competitive, pluralist political and economic systems may augment the problem, creating a new context of conflict that societies cannot handle productively. These conditions fostered conflict in Algeria, Rwanda, Burundi, Somalia, Ethiopia, Liberia,

Sierra Leone, Lebanon, Yugoslavia, Albania, Afghanistan, Sri Lanka, India, Guatemala, Haiti, El Salvador, Mexico, Peru, and Colombia.[3] In addition to unsupported authoritarian systems, another inheritance from the Cold War is the sea of arms that has flowed into potential conflict areas. Africa, the former Soviet littoral from Afghanistan to Yugoslavia, Southeast Asia, and Andean and Central America are all awash with arms (Boutwell, Klare, and Reed 1995). In some places, an AK-47 is cheaper than a bucket of grain, and sales of ex-Soviet heavy armaments are a thriving discount business years after the Soviet Union dissolved. Although conflicts are pursued and atrocities are committed using even the most primitive weapons, the widespread availability of modern weaponry has provided the means to make many men and women mass murderers.

The international dimension that ties together these disparate types of internal conflicts is the new terrorism. Scarcely a "war" in any classical sense, and impervious to classical or modern methods of waging war, terrorist conflicts are expressions of desperation and hopelessness, where life is so meaningless that its only use is found in its negation. The source of such conflict is ultimately structural—the impingement of globalization on unwelcoming lives and cultures and unsatisfying spiritual and material conditions at home. But structural causes of conflict are notoriously difficult to work into peacemaking, and conflicts born of desperation are impervious to operational conflict management methods. Conflicts in West and Central Africa, Andean America, and the Middle East are partially rooted in the failure of the promise of contending "isms" of the Cold War, whether communism, native socialism, or capitalism. People who see the control of their individual and collective lives escape from their hands and who are accustomed to searching for solace in isms continue to search. To find comfort, they resort to a millennialist justification of anger and hate against the impingements and impositions of an outside world.

Despite spillover effects and "neighborhood" involvement, the conflicts of the 1990s and 2000s have not been classic interstate conflicts over causes such as boundaries, territory, hostile regimes, or the possession of resources. In the 1990s, only the first Gulf War, between Iraq and Kuwait, involved interstate aggression, making it the last of the Cold War conflicts (see Zartman and Kremenyuk 1995). In the 2000s, the exceptions as of this writing have been the U.S.-led coalition's invasion of Afghanistan in 2001, the U.S.-led invasion of Iraq, which began in 2003, and the Israel-Lebanon conflict in 2006. Indeed, neighbors tend to regard conflicts with apprehension, fearing that there, too, but for the grace of God, go they. Conflicts tend to become regionalized, not by unbridled aggression but by "contamination," where violence overflows boundaries and neighbors seek allies, as in West Africa (Liberia, Sierra Leone, Guinea-Bissau, Ivory Coast), Central Africa (Rwanda, Burundi, Congo, Central African Republic, Congo-Brazzaville, Chad), the Horn of Africa (Ethiopia, Somalia, Sudan), Caucasus (Georgia, Azerbaijan, Chechnya, Ingushetia, Armenia), Eastern Mediterranean (Israel, Palestine, Lebanon, Syria), Central Asia (Afghanistan, Tajikistan, Pakistan, Kurdistan, Iran, Iraq), Central America (Mexico, Guatemala, Nicaragua, El Salvador), and the Balkans.[4]

Although interstate conflict has remained at a low level of frequency, the incidence of intrastate wars peaked in the mid-1990s and then settled down to a "standard" level. But that observation hides both the low-level conflicts of contaminated regions and the long-term intractable conflicts in remission (many of the regional conflict areas noted above; Crocker, Hampson, and Aall 2004, 2005). These conflicts underlie internal and interstate political dynamics, dribbling along below the statistically significant level of one thousand, or even twenty-five, battle-related deaths per year (Wallensteen 2007, 22–27) but ready to flare into incomprehensible outbursts.

The limits of the new situation are being tested everywhere. How much unrestrained conflict and brutality will the international community allow? How much interference in domestic security policies—nuclear, conventional, or counterinsurgent—will the international community permit? How immutable are the existing states and their boundaries? How widespread is the right of self-determination, and who may claim it? How long may a rapacious ruler take his turn at the trough to enrich himself before someone replaces him, and will the replacement be domestically, regionally, or internationally accepted or imposed? Until new and effective systems of world and domestic order are recognized, and until restive populations and ambitious actors have learned the new rules of the international and national communities, conflict over values such as sovereignty, liberty, self-determination, identity, creed, and power will continue to take place.

The conflict over appropriate measures occurs on two levels—opposing sides fight for the specific and the general, the case and the principle, the exception and the precedent. Serbs in Yugoslavia fight for a Greater Serbia against Croats, Bosnians, Montenegrins, and Kosovars battling for recognition of established republics and boundaries. But Serbs also fight to establish an ethnic (nation) state, Bosnians for a multiethnic state with a constructed national identity principle (with Croats putting a foot on each principle), and Kosovars for an independent state based on a neighboring ethnicity. Old limits, criteria, and principles were broken and new ones are being tried. Southern Sudanese wrestle with the advisability of secession, spurred not only by the aggressiveness of the Muslim Sudanese of the north but also by the idea that the new Eritrean precedent for secession might apply to them as well, while the Fur, Beja, Nuba, and other Muslim groups in the north fight for the same autonomy southerners have obtained. While African and Western intellectuals contest the principal of inherited boundaries, Ivory Coast tears itself apart over the principle of *ivoirité* ("Ivoryness"), defined as citizenship based on certain ethnic groups within the colonial boundaries; elsewhere, in Congo and Zambia among others, a nationality principle excludes migrations into the country over the past century. The uncertainty following the passing of the old order allows conflict to break out with such abandon.

Conflict Management

Uncertainty also pervades the norms of response to the conflicts. The lack of consensus about world order and normal conduct within it, and confusion about commitments to enforce norms and limits on deviant behavior, have given rise to conflict in the new era. Not only is the international response to conflict weak, but its very weakness causes an increasingly stronger challenge in a vicious circle of inaction and action. With the lifting of the nuclear balance of terror and the lessening of bipolar tensions, the world's leaders have lost interest in mediation and engagement as ways to impose restraint. This inertia is doubtless caused by a sense of relaxation and relief that follows a half-century of hot-war conflagrations and Cold War tensions, a political demobilization akin to those that characterized the latter half of the 1940s following the decomposition of world order in the two world wars.

This demobilization breaks down into many specific components. The absence of a system of world order has left leaders and their publics without a sense of the shape of the world, without a notion of friends and enemies, even without an idea of friendly and inimical behavior on which to base appropriate reactions. At the domestic level, notions such as "sovereignty as responsibility" turn established principles on their heads in the search for better guidelines for behavior (Deng et al. 1996; Obasanjo 1991; Evans and Sahnoun 2001; United Nations 2004). The search for principles involves testing alternative actions of prevention, management, resolution, and transformation—testing for acceptability and effectiveness that is part of the creation of new order. Thus, there is uncertainty not only about what to do when confronted with conflict but also about what not to do—uncertainty about what is normal and permissible and the limits and constraints in the evolving norms.

At the interstate level, the most striking collapse of order concerns the fragile conventions and norms on nuclear armament. Agreements born in the tensest moments of the Cold War—strategic arms limitation, nonproliferation, and international atomic energy monitoring—have been set aside by signatory great powers and challenged by upstarts such as India, Pakistan, Iraq, Israel, North Korea, and Iran. As a result, only rags restrain aspiring nuclear club members, and concerned states search among a range of diplomatic and military means to manage the problem.

In the absence of a world order to defend, a sense of appropriate solutions is missing. Although most mediators work toward any solution that the parties to a conflict will accept, they usually have some guidelines of appropriateness and some notions of stability. Mediators in the Namibian and Rhodesian conflicts would accept any outcome acceptable to the parties as long as it was independence, and they were ultimately successful; mediators in the Eritrean, Cypriot, Great Lakes, and Sri Lankan conflicts were not so sure where stability lay, and they failed. The absence of clear solutions has dogged the many attempts at mediation throughout much of the former communist world, from Chechnya to Yugoslavia. Mediators and parties alike are still experimenting with stability. Elections are deemed the appropriate mechanism for conflict resolution and the symbolic indication of conflict management from violent to political means, but the aftermath of such elections remains unclear. The Angolan experience of 1992 taught that a winner-take-all outcome was not wise, yet the Mozambican elections of 1994, 1999, and 2004 led to a winner-take-all government. For decades (since 1963) the Organization of African Unity proclaimed the sanctity of colonial boundaries (*uti possidetis*), reaffirmed under strained conditions over the former Italian colony of Eritrea. Yet the 2005 Comprehensive Peace Agreement promised independence as an option to half of Sudan, whereas independence was denied to half of Senegal and a third of Nigeria and to a separate colonial part of Somalia. The international community held the (reinterpreted) line on *uti possidetis* in Yugoslavia by dismantling the state into preexisting republics rather than allowing the established principle of national self-determination to be observed. When norms for management and resolution are malleable, conflicts are hard to resolve.

Because contemporary conflicts tend to be internal, the legitimacy of intervention is questionable. In a democratic age, people are sovereign and they get the government they deserve. In the absence of law-based world rule, violence is still the ultimate means of asserting basic internal rights and values, and so there is a strong argument for letting conflict run its course. Some things are worth fighting for—and against. The weak international law that does exist has protected the sovereignty of states and their internal affairs from foreign interference since the Peaces of Westphalia in 1648, and for good reason: relaxing the inhibitions on internal interference can leave power unrestrained and invite the strong to overrule the weak. The prohibition also protects would-be intervenors from involvement in cultures and arenas that are not their own. Ultimately, all these arguments are half-sound, reasoned justifications for inaction against the trumpeted need for action and responsibility. Yet they are dangerous to populations needing protection against both the incapacity and the rapaciousness of their own governments. The alternative, sovereignty as responsibility, permits intervention under certain conditions to protect populations rather than states. But sovereignty as responsibility, too, is dangerous, removing the license and inviolability of the state. We are still working out the details of the conditions surrounding the new doctrine, in principle, such as in the UN Charter (United Nations 2004), and in action, such as in Iraq.

In the absence of established systems of order and consensus on solutions, one defends one's own interests. Yet there is no clear sense of interest in dealing with the present era's many conflicts. It is clear to decision makers and the public alike that Rwanda does not fall into the geographic area of U.S. interests, and the one outside state that seems concerned—France—is widely decried for its involvement. It is not even clear to many that the former Yugoslavia fits into U.S. interests, because it resides just outside the area of the North Atlantic Treaty Organization's (NATO's) purview; even those European countries that saw themselves concerned—Germany and France—are criticized for their narrow-minded engagement. It is not clear what levels of interest govern the debate between the United States and continental European states over appropriate engagement in Iraq, recognition of genocide in Sudan, or conflict resolution in Cyprus. The compelling interest to become involved in messy internal conflicts or international regime changes, where peacemaking, peacekeeping, and peace enforcement are likely to be viewed as unfriendly behavior by all sides, is nowhere apparent.

The lack of a clear sense of interest and legitimacy results in an absence of public commitment. All these doubts and arguments, repeated authoritatively by world leaders, feed the cautiousness and inaction behind which the leaders hide. Yet many polls have shown that the public is strongly committed to the management and resolution of international conflicts for reasons of both morality and interest, under specific conditions: when leaders show that they know what they are doing, have a plan, explain it confidently, and pursue it deliberately (Yankelovich 1994; Nelson 1992). Conflict prevention, management, and resolution are good politics, good business, and good morality, and need to be sold as such (Zartman 2005). A commitment to these goals allows leaders to turn conflict into an occasion for decisiveness and allows parties to get on with productive activity. It reduces debilitating conflict in three ways: by dealing with the specific conflict; by contributing to the construction of the principles of order; and, in turn, by reducing the ambiguity and uncertainty that give rise to conflict. Such commitment requires courage and compassion, a hard defense of basic interests under dangerous conditions, a contribution to local reconciliation, and global leadership.

This book displays the tools and skills available when a commitment to peacemaking is exercised. It begins with a discussion of how the field of conflict resolution has evolved into such a broad discipline, as described by Louis Kriesberg. The current state of the art has built explicit bodies of knowledge, concepts, and prescriptions out of a number of components, combining politics, psychology, sociology, economics, and historical experience. Both hard-nosed interests and soft-handed charities join in providing insights and inspiration on human behavior. Underlying the concepts of conflict and its management are the social-psychological dynamics of both elements, discussed by Herbert Kelman. Although an understanding of conflict escalation and deescalation alone cannot encompass the specific issues in contention, it does provide the context and atmosphere that admit resolution and transformation into the equation. These insights come together at a time when there is a greater, though incomplete, knowledge about human interaction, and an increased, though imperfectly coordinated, involvement of many levels of society in foreign relations.

Officials undertake three major types of activities to manage and resolve conflicts, as presented by Daniel Druckman, Jacob Bercovitch, and Richard Bilder. Although these activities in international conflict resolution are generally carried out by states and their representatives, the mechanisms, effects, and relations are as applicable in interpersonal relationships and are based on a well-grounded understanding of social and human behavior. Parties undertake bargaining and negotiation to resolve their differences directly, overcoming conflict and establishing cooperation. Parties need specific tactics and strategies to move from conflicting to reconciling mindsets and behavior. When they are unable to do so, they need the involvement of third parties through mediation and conciliation. The introduction of a third party creates a triangle of relationships that complicates—but also helps to facilitate—reconciliation, requiring special tactics and relations. When parties are unable to reconcile or be reconciled, but only plead their antagonistic causes, the reconciling decision is transferred to an arbitrator or adjudicator. In this case, the third party's decision is binding, and the external third party, rather than to the adversaries themselves, is responsible for finding an appropriate solution to the problem.

None of the forms of reconciliation and resolution can function in the absence of incentives and constraints. The chapters by David Cortright, on inducements, and Jane Holl Lute, on force, lay out the gratifications and deprivations closely associated with peacemaking. Parties in conflict need to be shown a better future than the conflicted present, which often is not inherent in resolution but needs to be sweetened by enticements. Parties in conflict need to see that the present course is painful in order to perceive the better future promised by reconciliation, a vision of the present that often involves the use—or at least threat—of force to keep the conflict within limits and to hold the peace afterward. The question of norms is particularly important in controlling the use of counterforce to confront conflict, although inducements, too, have their limits, since another word for "inducements" is "bribery."

In the interstices of these activities lie other approaches to conflict resolution, generally practiced by nonofficials, as presented by Ronald Fisher and Cynthia Sampson. Reconciliation efforts deal with the affective aspects of conflict, which are often more powerful driving forces than the cold items at issue. Interactive conflict resolution uses the third party to help conflicting parties work out the nest of relationships in which the conflict is situated. It presents techniques whereby the third party can take a facilitating role in improving the relations among the parties. Faith-based approaches are often torn between an effort to bring peace and a role of advocacy for the weaker side.

The book closes with a review of education and training in peacekeeping as conducted at home and in the conflict area itself. The notion of education is basic to this or any work on peacemaking. Any skill (and even art) requires training on the use of the tools. Although personality helps, the ability to handle conflict is not inherent, and the skills and tricks of an experienced peacemaker need to be conveyed to avoid eternal reinvention of the wheel and to permit progress. Education and training programs convey these skills and approaches in packages that range from short courses to longer training sessions to higher education programs. In providing education and training, these teachers also practice conflict resolution, building skills and reflexes in preparation for the real thing.

KNOWLEDGE AND PRACTICE

Conflict

The very notion of training is based on a belief, current since the writings of the encyclopedists in the late eighteenth century, that conflict resolution is a skill that can be transmitted, not (as earlier believed) an inborn personality trait (de Felice 1987; de Callières 1963). But myths die slowly, and even today some practitioners believe that peacemaking skills cannot be analyzed or transmitted. Although some personalities are certainly better suited to managing conflict than others, management and resolution comprise such a broad range of activities that there is a role for just about any personality, and everyone can benefit from analysis, training, and the study of seized and missed opportunities. Although any situation, just as any person, has its unique elements, no situation—or person—is unique. Keys to understanding how to deal with a situation come from examining it in a comparative or generalized (conceptual) context.

The knowledge we have about what works and what does not work in conflict resolution is based primarily on studies of what practitioners do. (The only other source of data is experiments, whose relevant results are presented here in Daniel Druckman's chapter.) That information is either examined for regularities, correlations, and causal sequences (i.e., used inductively) or used to test ideas, hunches, and hypotheses (i.e., deductively). Only when information about practitioners' activities becomes ordered and focused does it become knowledge, and only as knowledge—not as isolated anecdotes—can it be useful in the maintenance and improvement of conflict resolution practices. So the cycle runs from practice to knowledge and back again, and that is the only way humanity improves itself in any field.

The knowledge reported in this work is new when seen as an accumulation. Probably none of the isolated acts that provide data for this knowledge is new, however; even the most modern twist on conflict resolution has doubtless been used somewhere in the past, perhaps accidentally, perhaps consciously. Even the first recorded case of negotiation, between Abraham and the Lord over the fate of Sodom (Genesis 18:16–33), carries pertinent conceptual lessons, for example, about formulas and details. What is new is the discovery of regularities, correlations, and causal sequences on the basis of newly accumulated, ordered, and focused information, an aspect of the subject that is every bit as exciting as the resolution of a particular conflict by a practitioner. Indeed, the field of conflict resolution was only identified by name during the interwar period, and the component activity of negotiation was so named (in that meaning) only in the eighteenth century. (Several languages have not named either term yet.) Other components of the field—prenegotiations, conflict management, positive-sum outcomes, ripeness, formulas, to name a few—have been discovered and identified in the past few decades, although, of course, they have existed unnamed as long as there has been human interaction.

Epistemologically, an object does not exist until it has a name, and it cannot be the subject of meaningful communication until its name, with its attendant definition, has been broadly accepted. In this new field, many aspects require definition at the outset (Bercovitch, Kremenyuk, and Zartman 2007; Toolkit 2007). The subject of this work, conflict resolution, refers to removing the causes as well as the manifestations of a conflict between parties and eliminating the sources of incompatibility in their positions. This process is a longterm proposition, for, in the last analysis, only time resolves conflicts. Conflict management refers to eliminating the violent and violence-related means of pursuing the conflict, still unresolved, leaving it to be worked out on the purely political level. Conflict transformation means replacing conflict with positive relationships, such as satisfaction, cooperation, empathy, and interdependence, between parties. Conflict prevention means eliminating the causes of foreseeable conflict, generically or specifically, before it occurs (or reoccurs, so that prevention of a new round may follow a previous outbreak). Each of these levels begs for the next in order to be fully stable, although relations among the parties or the nature of the conflict may be such that stability can be induced simply by norms and rules for the conduct of the conflict at a particular level; for example, elections are a conflict management device, governed by a stable regime, and do not require resolution or transformation. Corresponding peace-related terms are defined by their UN usage: "peacemaking" refers to diplomatic efforts to manage or resolve conflict according to Chapter VI of the UN Charter; "peacekeeping" (not specifically provided for in the charter) refers to forces interpositioned with the parties' consent to monitor a peace agreement; "peace enforcement" refers to military efforts to bring conflicting parties under control, as provided for under Chapter VII; and "peacebuilding" refers to structural measures to prevent a relapse into conflict (Boutros-Ghali 1995, 45–46).

By identifying important questions and seeking appropriate answers, we discover explanations for outcomes produced in the past and prescriptions on how to produce outcomes desired in the future. Such explanations and prescriptions are likely to become more and more complex as we discover variables that intervene between cause and effect. That complexity brings explanations closer to reality but must be balanced against simplicity and directness in order to be useful and nonideosyncratic. More and more knowledge is being created about the methods of conflict resolution; that very knowledge, in turn, opens up more opportunities to ask new questions, create new countermeasures, and find new answers. Such knowledge is not a procrustean bed, a fixed set of rules and regulations, or a body of incontrovertible doctrine and dogma. Rather, it invites creativity and constructive innovation to create better solutions to conflict.

One major objection can be validly raised, however, to the claim that knowledge is accumulating. The claim assumes that, despite changing world conditions, human interactions are similar enough for knowledge to accumulate and be relevant across time. Specifically, many of the lessons about conflict resolution were formulated during the Cold War; therefore, findings from that era are claimed to be applicable to post–Cold War conflict resolution. That claim needs to be examined critically. Where findings about conflict management depend on a structural context defined by two superpowers, those findings should be reevaluated. For example, accepted wisdom on bipolar stability and hegemonic cooperation was the product of its era and needs to be checked against new (and older) conditions. Where the findings are independent of a specific structural context, however, they can be considered relevant and examined for the insights they bring.

Yet, even bipolar confrontations have been studied in comparison with other conflicts and found to yield useful knowledge (Armstrong 1993; Kriesberg 1992). Much of the conflict resolution literature derives from a tradition and an approach independent of the Cold War and offers even more contexts for comparative assessments of conflicts now that the bipolar era has passed. In short, the Cold War was the aberration in international conflict, not in the ongoing efforts at conflict resolution.

No similar body of knowledge has been developed from the post–Cold War context of terrorism, in part because the twenty-first century is not old enough to have yielded much experience. But also it is because the very nature of terrorism seems to have changed, or at least broadened, from the dedication of nationalists and social revolutions in specific countries to a more global application. *Peacemaking in International Conflict* adopts the considered assumption that such changes make peacemaking more difficult, but also that the basic tools developed through experience have not changed and are still applicable. Terrorist conflict borrows the causes and grievances of past local conflicts to anchor itself in local scenes; it makes its principal, specific cause the corruption and inadequacies of local governments and their foreign, globalizing backers; and it draws on alienated populations for a permissive countervailing sea of support. But the tools available to meet terrorist outbursts are both broad and limited, comprising the same array of prevention, management, resolution, and transformation that can be applied to any conflict. If something new is demanded by the new era, it is the need to put greater emphasis on handling structural causes (grievances and alienation) and on pursuing post-conflict reconstruction (peacebulding). Peacemaking measures should be extended to prevention before the conflict erupts into violence and to implementation before the conflict erupts again into violence.

Resolution

Conflict demands resolution, but not because of the evil of its perpetrators—although incorrigibility and venality often make things worse. Were evil alone the problem, exemplars of the international community could band together, level a collective finger against the perpetrators, and ban their nefarious machinations. Such was the prevailing wisdom in a previous era among such seasoned but idealistic statesmen as President Woodrow Wilson, Secretary of State Frank Kellogg, and French premier Aristide Briand, and it failed because its assumptions were false. The experience of the intervening wars has taught us not only something about how to resolve conflicts but also that such earlier hopes were misguided. Conflict is a permanent feature of social and political interaction, and it often occurs for good reasons (Coser 1956; Bernard et al. 1957). The resolution of conflict depends on recognizing the concerns of the parties. "[T]he great secret of negotiation is to bring out prominently the common advantage to both parties of any proposal, and so to link these advantages that they may appear equally balanced to both parties, . . . to harmonize the interests of the parties concerned," wrote François de Callières to Louis XV in one of the first and still authoritative writings on negotiation (de Callières 1963, 110).

Thus, conflict resolution depends on recognition that parties have at least some interest in the conflict, even though they may also be caught up in it beyond their interests, and that these interests need to be met, outweighed, and reduced in order to be reconciled (Udalov 1995; Zartman 1995a). Parties' interests need to be addressed and their interest in reconciliation need to be enhanced. Before this can take place, though, the parties must understand that reconciliation is not surrender (otherwise, conflict resolution would have a deservedly bad name) and interests are not the same as needs. Peacemakers need to realize that parties do not negotiate to commit suicide. Some approaches have suggested that a conflict can be transformed (and as a result disappear) only after the basic human needs of one or both of the sides are satisfied (Burton 1990; Azar and Burton 1986). Yet human needs are ever only temporarily satisfied: those sated today may be hungry tomorrow, the people who know who they are today may wonder tomorrow, those who have found dignity today may lose it tomorrow, and so on. Because only time resolves conflicts, time can also invent or revive conflict. If human agents can aid resolution by providing post-conflict outcomes that at least address the question of durability—producing solutions that are processes and mechanisms, not judgments and awards—they will have made a respectable contribution to the well-being of the conflict's inheritor generation.

Parties to the conflict may be able to produce such outcomes by themselves, although someone—an internal party of "doves," the opponent in the conflict, or a friendly third-party adviser—needs to draw each conflicting party's attention away from the conflict itself as a means of attaining its interests and toward alternative means through reconciliation. If conflicting parties have interests, so do intervening third parties. Some external parties may have an interest in continuing the conflict, others may have an interest in one side in the conflict (Touval and Zartman 1985, 2007). If the intervenors had no interest of their own in resolution, they would be unmotivated and disarmed indeed.

Even "mediators without muscle," humanitarian agencies and good-willed individuals, have an interest in defending their own efforts and profession by bringing conflict away from violence and toward resolution. The Vatican had powerful interests in mediating the Beagle Channel dispute between Argentina and Chile, the Carter Center had strong interests in mediating a cease-fire in southern Sudan, the Kettering Foundation and the Processes of International Negotiation (PIN) Program of the International Institute of Applied Systems Analysis have their interests in promoting dialogue in Tajikistan and the Caspian basin, and the conflict management programs at George Mason University and Johns Hopkins University's School of Advanced International Studies had their own interests in their diverse efforts at reconciliation in the Liberian civil war (see Princen 1992; Touval and Zartman 2007). These interests may be simply in arriving at an agreement, not in any particular agreement, although most third parties also have an idea of what constitutes a stable and durable resolution and thus have an interest in seeing it achieved for the sake of their reputations. They all seek to launch a process that the conflicting parties themselves will take over and make their own, letting the mediators tiptoe away, carrying the wisdom of experience to put to use somewhere else.

Conflict resolution needs all the help it can get. Because parties to a conflict typically are already well entrenched in their conflicting behavior, for reasons they have often repeated to themselves to justify their resistance toward the other party, all the knowledge that can be brought to bear in favor of conflict resolution is badly needed, and all the hands that can be brought to the task can help. The only requirement is that multiple efforts be well coordinated so that they do not work against one another or allow conflicting parties to play the mediators against one another. At the official level, this requirement means cooperation among assisting parties. On a broader level, it means cooperation between official and unofficial efforts.

Although some agencies are better organized for conflict resolution than others and some states are better positioned to handle a particular conflict than others, conflict resolution is everybody's business. It should be part of the role of global leadership and shared among concerned states and international agencies. Above all, because conflict resolution is a crucial component of global leadership, it should be a leading plank in the foreign policy of the state with the widest global interests, the United States, with the backing of other supporting actors in the international community. Conflict resolution can be practiced quietly or assertively, directly or indirectly, unilaterally or cooperatively, as the particular circumstances require. However it is done, U.S. political leaders must always be cognizant of the fact that it is the country's role, part of America's traditions and calling, and expected by other members of the community of nations. The United States invented the peace process in the Middle East and is best placed to help other parties there and elsewhere out of their conflicts. U.S. foreign policy has been at its finest when it has been able to do so.

A cooperative security system that enlists the collaboration of the major powers in conjunction with regional security organizations is needed to meet the challenge of this century (Zartman and Kremenyuk 1995). Conflict management and resolution should be the leitmotif in every major state's foreign policy, helping each other in the process. The U.S.-mediated negotiations at Dayton, which produced the Bosnian peace agreement in Paris, were the occasion for unseemly squabbles among the two host countries and others regarding which one had made the largest contribution to peace. In fact, all were gravely deficient in peacemaking earlier and could claim significant contributions to the peace process only in the end.

States, too, need help in their efforts to resolve conflicts. They need help both in practicing the calling and in focusing on broader, positive-sum benefits rather than on narrow interpretations of their interests. Private parties can prepare and supplement state efforts and may have an advantage in overcoming problems of legitimacy in officials' efforts to deal with internal conflicts. Because private actors are not geared to producing final results in the same sense as official mediation, they can work on the problem longer. The Sant'Egidio community undertook mediation that no state could do in the Mozambican and Algerian conflicts (although it was backed and surrounded by official efforts in the first case), and Herbert Kelman's long efforts to prepare Israelis and Palestinians for the peace process gradually came to fruition in the early 1990s, as analyzed in this volume. Official and unofficial parties need to recognize the legitimate roles the other can play. Once they recognize these roles, they must cooperate.

Dilemmas

It would be fine to end here, with a clarion call for more and better cooperation in resolving conflict according to the state of the art and practice summarized here (see also Raiffa 1982). But that step would come too soon, because a final caveat is needed if the self-righteousness and self-interest that have so often dogged the field are to be avoided. Not only is there a lot that

analysts and practitioners still do not know and practice about conflict resolution, but even when the preaching is well practiced, inherent dilemmas
exist that have no easy answers.

One is the dilemma of legitimacy, addressed in the chapters by Daniel
Druckman and Jacob Bercovitch. How can intervention be justified if it runs
up against the conflicting parties' own interest to pursue the conflict? Is intervention by anyone in the type of conflict that dominated the 1990s—internal
conflict and civil war—legitimate under international law and norms? In response, third parties and the international community can ask whether the
means that conflicting parties use to pursue their interests are justifiable as well,
whether the use of violence to oppress populations or resist government is not
an abuse of a state's or a people's sovereignty. Third parties can arrogate the
right to enter these debates, as thinking world citizens should, but they need
to recognize the preeminent right of parties to set their own goals and interests.

A second dilemma concerns justice, touched on in this volume by Cynthia
Sampson. Peace is sometimes the enemy of justice, and conflict can be ended
only at the price of objectively fair outcomes. Such peace, so the objection
goes, is illusory: there is no lasting peace without justice. But justice has many
referents and is ultimately subjective (Zartman et al. 1996; Kolm 1997; Zartman and Kremenyuk 2005). A conflict resolution that perfectly combines
peace and justice is as rare as other moments of perfection in human action.
Mediators are often—perhaps usually—troubled by the choice between
peace, however temporary, that saves lives and continuing efforts in order to
better reconcile interests. Conflict resolution among consenting parties is
likely to be achieved only at the cost of letting some of the villains go free,
often as the price for their signature. But how much injustice is peace worth?

A third dilemma involves management, discussed by Louis Kriesberg.
Even if the other two dilemmas are avoided, efforts at reducing violence by
managing conflict may impede its resolution. Eliminating violence in the pursuit of conflict may do nothing to resolve the conflict and may even perpetuate it by rendering it economical to do so. Conflicts that cost little have little
reason for settlement; they just simmer along, waiting for the moment when
they can boil over. The best moment for resolution would appear to be when
the parties to the conflict are stalemated at a high level of intensity from which
they cannot unilaterally escalate their way out (Zartman 1989; Zartman and
Faure 2005). But conflict management can actually work to inhibit such
mutually hurting stalemates.

The fourth dilemma is that of force, examined here by Jane Holl Lute.
Conflict resolution is peacemaking and peacebuilding. But it may also be peace

enforcing; even in peacemaking there may be a need for force and threats of force. "*Si vis pacem para bellum* (If you want peace, prepare for war)," said the Romans, who knew something about both. Mediators in the most active phase of intervention (as the best manipulators will tell you) may have to reinforce the stalemate that makes the parties come to terms: it took the 1973 October War to start the peace process in the Middle East, and nothing less than NATO bombing drove Bosnian combatants to peace in 1995. Yet parties cannot be forced to resolve conflicts in the absence of other interests and perceptions. How much force and when to apply it remain dilemmas of foreign policy, unresolved by the good intentions of peacemakers.

The fifth dilemma is that of power, raised by Ronald Fisher. A myth is circulating that peacemaking is the opposite of power (see Burton 1995). Power is an action designed to move another party in an intended direction (Zartman and Rubin 2000; Dahl 1969; Simon 1969; Tawney 1964; Russell 1938). Persuasion is a form of power. Those who inveigh against "power politics" (a redundant term) merely want to put power in their own hands. Conflict resolution requires power in order to work, as does any other effort at changing a party's course. The dilemma arises when conflicting parties' actions are changed, or blocked, without changing their minds. In this case, the mediator or the reconciling party has exercised enough power to accomplish only a postponement—rather than a resolution—of conflict. This dilemma confronted the Camp David peacemakers, who had to wait more than a decade before the next round of the peace process, starting at Madrid, could begin to work. Even in such cases, conflict resolution arouses the nostalgia for conflict, as witnessed in the popularity of Hamas and Likud.

The last dilemma is that of prevention, evoked by Herbert Kelman. The ultimate in conflict resolution, it would seem, is conflict prevention, which recognizes conflict's causes and deals with them before the conflicts have a chance to become violent. Governance is indeed conflict management, and most conflicts at the heart of politics never become violent because they are handled (within states) by politics or (among states) by diplomacy (Zartman 1996). Many conflicts that become crises in international relations could have been prevented had they been the subject of more intense diplomatic attention earlier. But how can the attentions of public and government be mobilized when a potential crisis is still cold? And how can one distinguish a conflict that will become a crisis, and therefore needs prevention, from one that will burn out on its own and blow away without causing damage? The business of conflict resolution, for all its pride of accomplishment, needs humility—and excitement—to recognize that there are many more worlds to discover.

REFERENCES

Armstrong, Tony. 1993. *Breaking the Ice*. Washington, D.C.: United States Institute of Peace Press.

Arnson, Cynthia, and I. William Zartman, eds. 2005. *Rethinking the Economics of War: The Intersection of Need, Creed and Greed*. Baltimore: Johns Hopkins University Press.

Azar, Edward E., and John W. Burton, eds. 1986. *International Conflict Resolution*. Brighton, UK: Wheatsheaf.

Ballentine, Karen, and Jake Sherman, eds. 2003. *The Political Economy of Armed Conflict*. Boulder, Colo.: Lynne Rienner.

Bercovitch, Jacob, Victor Kremenyuk, and I. William Zartman, eds. 2007. *Handbook on Conflict Resolution*. London: Sage.

Berdal, Mats, and David Malone, eds. 2000. *Greed and Grievance: Economic Agendas in Civil War*. Boulder, Colo.: Lynne Rienner.

Bernard, Jessie, T. H. Pear, Raymond Aron, and Robert Angell. 1957. *The Nature of Conflict*. Paris: United Nations Educational, Scientific, and Cultural Organization.

Boutros-Ghali, Boutros. 1995. *An Agenda for Peace*. New York: United Nations.

Boutwell, Jeffrey, Michael Klare, and Laura Reed, eds. 1995. *Lethal Commerce: The Global Trade in Small Arms and Light Weapons*. Cambridge, Mass.: American Academy of Arts and Sciences.

Burton, John W., ed. 1990. *Conflict: Human Needs Theory*. New York: St. Martin's.

―――. 1995. "Conflict Provention as a Political System." In *Beyond Confrontation*, ed. James Vasquez. Ann Arbor: University of Michigan Press.

Collier, John, V. L. Elliott, Håvard Hegre, Anke Hoeffler, Marta Reynal-Querol, and Nicholas Sambanis. 2003. *Breaking the Conflict Trap*. New York: Oxford University Press.

Coser, Lewis. 1956. *The Functions of Social Conflict*. New York: Free Press.

Crocker, Chester, Fen Osler Hampson, and Pamela Aall. 2004. *Taming Intractable Conflicts*. Washington, D.C.: United States Institute of Peace Press.

Crocker, Chester, Fen Osler Hampson, and Pamela Aall, eds. 2005. *Grasping the Nettle*. Washington, D. C. United States Institute of Peace Press.

Dahl, Robert. 1969. "The Concept of Power." In *Political Power*, ed. David Edwards, Roderick Bell, and R. Harrison Wagner. New York: Free Press.

Damrosch, Lori F., ed. 1993. *Enforcing Restraint: Collective Intervention in Internal Conflicts*. New York: Council on Foreign Relations.

de Callières, François. 1963 [1716]. *On the Manner of Negotiating Among Princes*. South Bend, Ind.: University of Notre Dame Press.

de Felice, Fortune Barthelemy. 1987 [1778]. "Negotiations, or the Art of Negotiating." In *The 50% Solution*, ed. I. William Zartman. New Haven, Conn.: Yale University Press.

Deng, Francis, Sadikiel Kimao, Terrence Lyons, Donald Rothchild, and I. William Zartman. 1996. *Sovereignty as Responsibility*. Washington, D.C.: Brookings Institution Press.

Evans, Gareth, and Mohamed Sahnoun, eds. 2001. *The Responsibility to Protect*. Ottawa: International Development Research Center.

Hopmann, P. Terrence. 2001. "Disintegrating States: Separating without Violence." In *Preventive Negotiation*, ed. I. William Zartman. Lanham, Md.: Rowman and Littlefield.

Kolm, Serge C. 1997. *Modern Theories of Justice*. Cambridge, Mass.: MIT Press.

Kriesberg, Louis. 1992. *De-escalation and Transformation of International Conflicts*. New Haven, Conn.: Yale University Press.

Lake, David, and Donald Rothchild, eds. 1998. *The International Spread and Management of Ethnic Conflict*. Princeton, N.J.: Princeton University Press.

Nelson, Joan. 1992. "Poverty, Equity, and the Politics of Adjustment." In *The Politics of Economic Adjustment*, ed. Stephen Haggard and Robert R. Kaufman. Princeton, N.J.: Princeton University Press.

Obasanjo, Olasegun. 1991. *The Kampala Document*. New York: African Leadership Forum.

Princen, Thomas. 1992. *Intermediaries in International Conflict*. Princeton, N.J.: Princeton University Press.

Raiffa, Howard. 1982. *The Art and Science of Negotiation*. Cambridge, Mass.: Harvard University Press.

Russell, Bertrand. 1938. *Power*. London: Unwin.

Simon, Herbert. 1969. "Notes on the Observation and Measurement of Power." In *Political Power*, ed. David Edwards, Roderick Bell, and R. Harrison Wagner. New York: Free Press.

Tawney, R. H. 1964. *Equality*. London: Unwin.

Toolkit. 2007. *The SAIS Conflict Management Toolkit*. Washington, D.C.: Conflict Management Program, School of Advanced International Studies, Johns Hopkins University, www.sais-jhu.edu/CMtoolkit.

Touval, Saadia, and I. William Zartman, eds. 1985. *International Mediation in Theory and Practice*. Boulder, Colo.: Westview.

————. 2007. "International Mediation." In *Leashing the Dogs of War*, ed. Chester Crocker, Fen Hampson, and Pamela Aall. Washington, D.C.: United States Institute of Peace Press.

Udalov, Vadim. 1995. "National Interests and Conflict Reduction." In *Cooperative Security: Reducing Third World Wars*, ed. I. William Zartman and Victor A. Kremenyuk. Syracuse, N.Y.: Syracuse University Press.

United Nations. 2004. *A More Secure World: Our Shared Responsibility. Report of the High-Level Panel on Threats, Challenges and Change*. New York: United Nations.

Wallensteen, Peter. 2007. *Understanding Conflict Resolution*, 2d ed. London: Sage.

Yankelovich, Daniel. 1994. "Shaping a New Communications Strategy." New York: Public Agenda. Mimeograph.

Zartman, I. William. 1989. *Ripe for Resolution*, 2d ed. New York: Oxford University Press.

―――. 1995a. "Systems of World Order and Regional Conflict Reduction." In *Cooperative Security: Reducing Third World Wars*, ed. I. William Zartman and Victor A. Kremenyuk. Syracuse, N.Y.: Syracuse University Press.

―――, ed. 1995b. *Elusive Peace: Negotiating an End to Civil Wars*. Washington, D.C.: Brookings Institution Press.

―――, ed. 1996. *Governance as Conflict Management: Politics and Violence in West Africa*. Washington, D.C.: Brookings Institution Press.

―――. 2005. *Cowardly Lions: Missed Opportunities to Prevent Deadly Conflict and State Collapse*. Boulder, Colo.: Lynne Rienner.

―――, ed. 2007. *Imbalance of Power*. Boulder, Colo.: Lynne Rienner.

Zartman, I. William, Daniel Druckman, Lloyd Jensen, Dean G. Pruitt, and H. Peyton Young. 1996. "Negotiation as a Search for Justice." *International Negotiation* 1 (1): 79–98.

Zartman, I. William, and Guy Olivier Faure, eds. 2005. *Escalation in International Negotiation*. London: Cambridge University Press.

Zartman, I. William, and Victor A. Kremenyuk, eds. 1995. *Cooperative Security: Reducing Third World Wars*. Syracuse, N.Y.: Syracuse University Press.

―――, eds. 2005. *Peace versus Justice: Negotiating Forward- and Backward-Looking Outcomes*. Lanham, Md.: Rowman and Littlefield.

Zartman, I. William, and Jeffrey Z. Rubin, eds. 2000. *Power and Negotiation*. Ann Arbor: University of Michigan Press.

NOTES

1. Conflict management in some of these cases is examined in Hopmann (2001).

2. For analyses of the role of greed and grievance in perpetuating conflict, see Berdal and Malone (2000), Ballentine and Sherman (2003), Collier et al. (2003), and Arnson and Zartman (2005).

3. On conflict resolution measures in some of these conflicts, see Zartman (1995b) and Damrosch (1993).

4. For a good debate on the issue of contamination, see Lake and Rothchild (1998).

PART ONE

MAPPING THE FIELD

1

THE CONFLICT RESOLUTION FIELD

Origins, Growth, and Differentiation

Louis Kriesberg

As the world changes, so does the field of conflict resolution (CR). Moreover, as the techniques of CR develop, CR affects the way the world changes. This chapter traces those interactions.

CR is oriented toward changing conflicts so that they can be conducted constructively, even creatively, in the sense that violence is minimized, antagonism between adversaries is overcome, outcomes are mutually acceptable to the opponents, and settlements are enduring. CR includes long-term strategies, short-term tactics, and actions by adversaries as well as by mediators. It is based on the work of academic analysts and official and nonofficial practitioners. As such, the rapidly expanding CR field is not a narrowly defined discipline but a general approach.[1]

The first part of this chapter examines the major phases in the development of the CR approach, particularly as it relates to international relations. The second part of the chapter discusses current issues in the field and likely future developments.

PHASES IN THE DEVELOPMENT OF CR

CR is a complex field of endeavor, with many interdependent kinds of activities. This is the natural consequence of the many tasks its practitioners seek to accomplish and the diverse sources of its development. This section discusses the contributions made by scholars, practitioners, and organizations within four periods: 1914–45, when ideas and actions prepared the way for the emergence of the CR field; 1946–69, a period of early efforts and basic research; 1970–85, a period of crystallization and expansion; and 1986–present, a time of differentiation and institutionalization.

The periods are not discrete; events and developments in later years have antecedents in earlier periods. The sequence in which matters are discussed indicates their relative salience, not their origins. For a chronological listing of major publications and events in the field, see the appendix. Developments in the United States are given particular attention, partly because of the central role they have played in what is becoming an increasingly global endeavor.

1914–45: Precursors

The outbreak of World War I undermined liberal optimism that spreading democracy and economic expansion would produce a relatively harmonious world in the near future. Wilsonian idealism briefly revived such expectations in the postwar era, but they were short-lived. The Great Depression, the rise of fascism, and the horrors and devastation of World War II further diluted faith in the attainment of enduring peace. These occurrences provided the context for efforts that helped create modern CR.

In the post–World War I period, analyses of the eruption of large-scale conflicts advanced CR's development, including studies of class-based struggles, particularly revolutions, as exemplified in the work of Crane Brinton (1938). Case studies examined the outbreak of wars, and quantitative analyses were made of the incidence of wars, notably in Quincy Wright's monumental study (1942). Another major subject in this period was the analysis of conflicts within organizations, particularly labor-management conflicts. In this regard, the work of Mary Parker Follett (1942) notably helped lay the groundwork for contemporary CR.

The importance of nonrational sources in the outbreak of revolutions and wars was a major theme in some of this work. Thus, research on these matters examined scapegoating and other kinds of displaced feelings, susceptibility to propaganda, personal attributes of leaders, and their manipulation of powerful political symbols (Lasswell 1930). These phenomena were evident in various social movements and their attendant conflicts. For some analysts, the rise of Nazism in Germany exemplified many aspects of these developments.

In addition to analyzing the causes of intense conflicts, work was done on ways in which conflicts can be managed and how their destructive escalation can be avoided. First appearing in the 1930s, these analyses of social-psychological and group processes in ethnic, industrial, family, and other conflicts left a legacy of methods and issues upon which CR scholars have built (Lewin 1948).

To some extent, the nonrational aspects of many conflicts make them amenable to management, because they are not based entirely on a clash of objective interests. The human relations approach to industrial conflict built on this assumption (Roethlisberger and Dickson 1943). Other research about industrial organizations stressed the way struggles based on differences of interests could be controlled by norms and structures if asymmetries in power were not too large. The experience with regulated collective bargaining provided a model for this possibility (e.g., see Jackson 1952 and the National Labor Relations Board, www.nlrb.gov).

1946–69: Early Efforts and Basic Research

In the 1950s and 1960s, rapid growth in many CR-relevant scholarly and practitioner activities provided the foundations for further CR research. Some of the work was spurred by the specter of nuclear annihilation that the Cold War evoked, but many other components of CR had independent origins. Basic research in many academic disciplines helped establish a foundation for the development of CR. An early locus for such work was the University of Michigan, where the *Journal of Conflict Resolution* began publication in 1957 and the Center for Research on Conflict Resolution was established in 1959 (Harty and Modell 1991). The International Peace Research Institute in Oslo (PRIO) was also founded in 1959 (see www.prio.no).

Obviously, social context profoundly affects the course of social conflicts and the way analysts and partisans think about them. For many years after the end of World War II, nations were preoccupied with economic reconstruction and growth. This period was followed by an era largely distinguished by concerns about justice, autonomy, and equality. In the 1960s, national liberation struggles emerged in European colonies in Africa and Asia; the United States was the scene of mass social unrest over civil rights and the country's involvement in Vietnam; and student demonstrations and national revolutions seemed to engulf the world's political landscape. Many analysts as well as activists viewed these struggles as based on valid grievances and worthy of support.

The Cold War profoundly structured world politics and the ways analysts thought about CR for more than four decades, but its character changed significantly over that time. The 1962 Cuban missile crisis was followed by a brief thaw in the Cold War. A longer-lasting transformation began in 1969, aided by three changes. First, the antagonism between the Soviet Union and the People's Republic of China became especially intense, as revealed in the bloody skirmishes along their border. Second, the Social Democratic Party came to power in West Germany and instituted its policy of accommodation with Eastern Europe and the Soviet Union (*Ostpolitik*). Third, Richard Nixon became president of the United States and, partly as a way to end U.S. engagement in the war in Vietnam, undertook a policy of détente with the Soviet Union and of opening of relations with the People's Republic of China.

Spurred by concerns about the possible eruption of nuclear as well as nonnuclear wars, an important body of scholarly work based on quantitative methods flourished from the onset of the Cold War. Systematic data began to be collected in an effort to examine the incidence and correlates of wars (Richardson 1960; Singer 1972). In addition, quantitative data on conflicting and cooperative interactions among nations began to be collected. These data continue to be analyzed, testing CR as well as traditional international relations concepts (McClelland 1983; Isard 1988; Leng 1993; Vasquez 1993).

Another important body of work focused on the ways cooperative activities and institutions provide a basis for increasing international integration that lessens the possibility of destructive conflict. Much of this work consisted of examining variations in the levels of integration and cooperation among countries; it found that highly integrated countries formed communities with little likelihood of war, as documented in the work of Karl Deutsch et al. (1957) and others. Some analysts argued that institutions providing functional integration in limited economic or political spheres would expand and help create the reality of a common interest in peace (Mitrany 1943). Ernst B. Haas (1958) analyzed how integration crested a common interest in peace in the European Coal and Steel Community, established in 1951, which evolved into the present-day European Union.

Game theory also influenced the development of CR. It helped analysts think about the conflict implications of various payoff matrices and the strategies chosen by interacting players (Rapoport and Chammah 1965). The prisoner's dilemma payoff matrix especially has been the basis of much study. Rather than assuming a zero-sum game, in which one side wins what the other loses, the variable-sum or mixed-motive game of the prisoner's dilemma has been the subject of considerable research. In the prisoner's dilemma game, each side can choose to cooperate or to defect (and seek unilateral advantage). In the payoff matrix, if one side cooperates and the other does not, the player who cooperates loses a great deal and the defecting player gains a great deal. If they both cooperate, they both gain something; if they both defect, they both lose much. From the perspective of each party, with no additional information about what the other side will do, the best strategy is to defect; but if both sides do that, they both lose. Many experiments have been conducted to discern what factors affect the likelihood that people will follow one strategy or the other. Thomas Schelling's (1960) influential work, also drawing from game theory, examined the logic of bargaining.

During this period, traditional diplomacy was also subjected to careful analysis, with researchers inferring principles of practice that could be used to create policy in a nuclear age (Iklé 1964). The increasing attention to the new conditions of international politics created by nuclear weapons, especially for the purpose of deterrence, stimulated growing interest in the subjective and nonrational components in foreign policy decision making and crisis behavior (Jervis 1976; Jervis, Lebow, and Stein 1985; Janis 1972).

Considerable research was done in the 1950s and 1960s on factors affecting the relations between potentially contending groups and how overt struggle can be prevented or, failing that, waged constructively and resolved amicably. Research methods included public opinion surveys, field observations, and small-group experimentation. For example, research on race and ethnic relations produced the well-documented finding that equal-status interaction among members of different ethnic groups reduces prejudice and antagonistic behavior among them. Another relevant finding is that the development of superordinate goals can bring contending groups into a cooperative relationship (Sherif 1966). Morton Deutsch (1973) conducted a variety of experiments on constructive and destructive conflict processes, helping to set the agenda for much subsequent work.

Also during this period many sociologists analyzed the processes of industrial, community, ethnic, and other kinds of conflicts (Coleman 1957). Moreover, some analyses treated social conflicts as a generic phenomenon, noting similarities as well as differences among them (Coser 1956). Recognizing the ubiquity of conflicts, many sociologists directed their attention to the functions of conflicts and how conflicts were waged and settled. Some anthropologists studied dispute settlement processes in societies with and without formal legal systems (Nader 1965; Gulliver 1979).

The analysis of nonviolent action provided another significant contribution to the development of CR (Sharp 1973; www.aeinstein.org). As articulated by some leaders of nonviolent campaigns, committing violence made future negotiation and reconciliation much more difficult. Instead, they argued, waging a nonviolent struggle enhanced the likelihood of later attaining an enduring and mutually acceptable outcome.

An additional influence in the growth of CR has been the diverse field of peace research (Stephenson 1999), which makes several kinds of contributions. It draws attention to how people in different cultures and roles are socialized to believe that certain ways of waging conflicts are proper and others are not. Peace research also examines the social and institutional bases of war, including the military-industrial complex and other vested interests influencing the decision to pursue external conflicts; in so doing, this school of research contributes to the demystification of large-scale conflicts. The peace research community's examination of how protracted conflicts may be de-escalated is particularly germane to CR. For example, the idea underlying Graduated Reciprocation in Tension Reduction (GRIT) is that de-escalation of tensions between adversaries can occur if one side announces it is undertaking conciliatory actions, invites reciprocation, and persists in conciliatory moves even when there is no immediate reciprocation (Osgood 1962). This idea has been influential in the CR field, and there is evidence that GRIT has been an effective instrument in peacemaking, under certain conditions, when applied to protracted international conflicts (Etzioni 1967; Goldstein and Freeman 1990).

While much work was being done on the academic front, actual CR practice underwent significant change during 1946–69, when unofficial diplomacy became increasingly important in international affairs. For example, in 1957, nuclear physicists and others engaged in analyzing the possible use of nuclear weapons from the United States, Great Britain, and the Soviet Union began meeting to exchange ideas about reducing the chances that nuclear weapons would be used again (Pentz and Slovo 1981). The first meetings were held at the summer home of Cyrus Eaton in Pugwash, Nova Scotia, and developed into what have come to be called the Pugwash Conferences on Science and World Affairs. From the 1950s through the 1970s, the discussions at these meetings contributed to the signing of the Partial Test-Ban Treaty, the Nuclear Nonproliferation Treaty, the Biological Weapons Convention, and the Antiballistic Missile Treaty. In 1995, the Pugwash Conferences and Joseph Rotblat, their executive director, won the Nobel Peace Prize.

Other regular, nonofficial meetings between well-connected persons from adversarial parties also were significant in opening up new channels of communication to discuss solutions for contentious issues. One important international example is the Dartmouth Conference (Chufrin and Saunders 1993). At the urging of President Dwight D. Eisenhower, Norman Cousins, then editor of the *Saturday Review*, brought together a group of prominent U.S. and Soviet citizens to find an alternate communications channel when official relations were especially strained. The first of many such meetings was at Dartmouth College in 1960.

Practice was also changing in the domestic sphere. Lines of communication among diverse community groups were sustained by ongoing interethnic and interreligious councils or dialogue groups. More particularly, in the United States the civil rights struggle gave new salience to the power of nonviolent action. In response to these actions and to the outbreaks of violence, efforts to mitigate the civil strife associated with the protests and demonstrations included commissions of inquiry and also quiet mediation carried out by the U.S. Justice Department (see http://www.civilrightsmediation.org/).

1970–85: Crystallization and Expansion

During 1970–85, the practice of CR flourished. As new fields of CR activity were cultivated and grew, publications disseminated CR ideas and reports of experience with more and more types of mediation were published. Academic and nonacademic institutions added training in negotiation and mediation to their programs.

A consensus on many of the core ideas of CR crystallized during this period. Part of this consensus included the idea that conflicts often could be restructured and reframed so that partisans would regard the conflict as a shared problem that had mutually acceptable solutions. The consensus did not preclude the option of coercive struggle to help bring about such change. Another core idea was that intermediaries provide many services that assist adversaries to construct mutually acceptable agreements to settle and ultimately resolve their conflicts. Yet another idea was that negotiators and mediators could learn how to improve their skills to manage and settle disputes in ways that would enhance the adversaries' relationships.

The rapid expansion of CR in the United States was in many ways a social movement, whose origins can be traced to the convergence of several other social movements, including the post-1960s appeal of local self-government and community activism (Adler 1987; Scimecca 1991). CR as a social movement was also fostered by the peacemaking and mediation activities of religious organizations, particularly those associated with the Society of Friends (Quakers) and the Mennonites. In addition, the expansion was furthered by the growth of the legal profession, litigation, and the ensuing congestion of the American court system. The emerging alternative dispute resolution (ADR) movement seemed attractive to some lawyers and many nonlawyers as an alternative to adversarial proceedings and an attractive option to some of the judiciary as a way to reduce the burden on the courts (Ray 1982). Also, CR seemed to offer peace movement members, whose numbers soared in the early 1980s, a practical alternative to the nation's reliance on military options (Lofland 1993). Finally, CR ideas arising from research and theory provided a theoretical basis and intellectual justification for CR practices.

During this period, the Cold War underwent profound changes as well. Official détente began to crumble in the mid-1970s and collapsed by the end of the decade. The Cold War intensified again, spurred by the Soviet military engagement in Afghanistan and by the rhetoric and policies of the Reagan administration. But the growing integration of the world economy undermined the premises of the superpower rivalry. Suffering economic stagnation, the Soviet Union began a radical course of reform with Mikhail Gorbachev's accession to power in 1985, which led to the end of the Cold War.

One important development in CR during the 1970–85 period was the expansion of CR work throughout the world. Notable contributions to theory and practice emerged from European peace research. In Germany, several peace and conflict research institutes were established after the Social Democratic Party came to power in 1969. Ideas about nonoffensive defense and how military defense could be structured so that the other side was not threatened spread across the continent; such ideas included a new generation of confidence-building measures. Finally, the work of Gene Sharp (1973) on nonviolent action evolved into the idea of a civilian-based defense.

Feminist theory and research were another source of ideas in the development of CR. Feminist thought provided a critique and an alternative to the prevailing emphasis on hierarchy and coercive power as the essential mode of decision making in social life, including the international realm (Harris and King 1989). The feminist critique, viewing the traditional perspective largely as a product of men's socialization and dominance, emphasized the importance of nonhierarchical social relations and the possibility of reaching integrative agreements through relatively consensual decision-making processes. Feminist theory also highlighted the many contributions of women in public as well as private life, even in a patriarchal world. In many ways, these feminist ideas were congenial with CR and contributed to its growth.

Additional contributions during this period stemmed from further scholarly investigations of game theory. For example, Snyder and Diesing (1977) analyzed international crises and found that the variation in representative payoff matrices of the crises helped explain their outcomes. Another body of work was based on the payoff matrix for the prisoner's dilemma game. Computer simulations and other evidence indicated that cooperation would result if one party followed a tit-for-tat strategy in an extended series of reiterated games (Axelrod 1984). In an analysis of interactions among the Soviet Union, the United States, and the People's Republic of China, however, the GRIT model seemed to provide a better fit with movement toward de-escalation and cooperation than did tit-for-tat (Goldstein and Freeman 1990).

An extensive body of social-psychological theory and research also made important contributions to CR. In testing a variety of theories pertaining to cognition, interaction, and personality, the research methodology has been predominantly small-group experimentation. Some work, for example, focused on how entrapment (persisting in behavior because of previous investment in the behavior) contributes to escalating conflicts and how the process can be interrupted (Brockner and Rubin 1985). A great deal of work in many disciplines during this period focused on the negotiation process (Druckman 1977; Zartman 1978).

Another important contribution to the growth of CR is the considerable research and theorizing about social movements (Tilly 1978; Toch 1965). The resource-mobilization approach stresses not only the importance of grievances as a source of social movement activity, but also the belief that such grievances can be redressed. The emergence and transformation of large-scale conflicts, therefore, can be regarded as a function of the apparent weakness of the opposition, the capabilities of the social movement's members, and the leaders' formulation of credible goals.

Peace movement actions during 1970–85 manifested themselves in traditional ways, such as mass public demonstrations, but they also took on new forms, such as innovative kinds of civil disobedience. The anti–Vietnam War demonstrations and resistance ended as U.S. military forces were withdrawn from Vietnam. After years of quiescence, peace movement actions were renewed in the early 1980s, with new goals and different forms, including demonstrations and political mobilization in the United States in favor of a bilateral freeze on the production, testing, and deployment of nuclear weapons (Marullo and Lofland 1990; Meyer 1990). In many Western European countries, protest demonstrations and political pressure were directed at preventing the deployment of the North Atlantic Treaty Organization's (NATO's) cruise and Pershing II missiles in their countries. In addition, a groundswell of people-to-people diplomacy occurred during this period, as large numbers of U.S. citizens visited the Soviet Union and U.S. cities developed ties with Soviet counterparts (Lofland 1993).

Also during this period, interactive problem-solving workshops were increasingly undertaken. In this method of CR, a convenor (in most cases, an academic) brings together a few members from the opposing sides to guide and facilitate discussions about their conflict (Kelman 1992). The participants typically have ties to the leadership of their respective sides or have the potential to become members of the leadership in the future. The workshops usually go on for several days, moving through several distinct stages.

John Burton, Leonard Doob, Herbert Kelman, Edward Azar, Ronald Fisher, and others are responsible for developing the workshop concept as a method of CR (Fisher 1996). Workshops typically have been held in relation to protracted internal and international conflicts, such as those in Northern Ireland, Cyprus, and the Middle East.

The workshops' participants themselves sometimes become quasi-mediators upon returning to their adversary group, but as workshop participants, they do not attempt to negotiate agreements (Kriesberg 1995). Sometimes they later become negotiators, as was the case in the negotiations between the Palestine Liberation Organization (PLO) and the Israeli government in the early 1990s (Kelman 1995).

Problem-solving workshops are one channel in what is often referred to as track-two diplomacy in international relations (Montville 1991). Track one consists of the mediation, negotiation, and other official exchanges between governmental representatives. Track two includes more than problem-solving workshops and is best viewed as multitrack (McDonald 1991). Among the many unofficial channels are transnational organizations within which members of adversarial parties meet and discuss matters pertaining to the work of their common organizations. Another track includes ongoing dialogue groups, with members from the adversary parties discussing contentious issues between their respective countries, communities, or organizations (Weiner 1998; Smock 2002; also see www.coexistence.net).

Finally, the practice of ADR also greatly expanded during this period, as community dispute resolution centers were established in many parts of the United States (see the Conflict Resolution Information Source, www.crinfo.org). CR was also increasingly used in public disputes over environmental issues, such as disposal of radioactive waste, water usage, and landfills (Susskind and Cruickshank 1987).

1986–Present: Differentiation and Institutionalization

Since the mid-1980s, the nature and the context of large-scale conflicts have changed in significant ways. The end of the Cold War at the close of the 1980s profoundly transformed the international system and greatly affected intrastate conflicts. For example, conflicts among groups identifying themselves in terms of ethnicity, religion, language, and similar attributes, rather than ideology, became more salient (Gurr 2000, for documentation on the Minorities at Risk project, see www.cidcm.umd.edu/mar; for information about specific ethnic conflicts see www.incore.ulst.ac.uk). The globalization of the world due to technological advances and the increased integration of the global market has also transformed international and intrastate conflicts, for example, by raising the likelihood of external intervention into large-scale domestic as well as international conflicts and by the transnational mobilization of people in non-governmental organizations (NGOs) using Internet technologies (Ronfeldt et al. 1998).

All these changes have affected CR ideas and practices. The rise of complex communal, environmental, and socioeconomic conflicts—often without clear right and wrong sides—has enhanced the pertinence of the CR approach to finding and maximizing mutual benefits for all groups that find themselves in conflict with one another. Moreover, some of these conflicts, particularly those involving ethnic and religious differences, have been especially brutal and destructive. These developments have also directed increased attention to cultural attributes as the source of intercommunal conflicts and their management (Rubinstein and Foster 1988; Cohen 1997; Faure and Rubin 1993; Ross 1993; Lederach 1995; Zartman 1996; Avruch 1998; Salem 1997; Johnston and Sampson 1994; Gopin 2000, 2002).

In addition, recent developments have renewed attention to the emotional factors in conflicts and their resolution (Scheff 1994). Memories of past atrocities and humiliations often arouse the desire for revenge to regain lost honor and ease emotional traumas. Several academics and practitioners have developed CR methods that incorporate alternative ways of addressing such feelings (Volkan 1988). These emotional factors also affect the formation and transformation of ethnic, religious, and other collective identities (Herb and Kaplan 1999; Coy and Woehrle 2000).

CR research has continued to be directed at the use and effects of different kinds of mediation in international and other types of conflicts (Mitchell and Webb 1988; Kressel and Pruitt 1989; Princen 1992; Bercovitch 1996, 2002). Research examining the conditions that lead to de-escalating efforts, whether mediated or not, has also expanded. Many elements must converge for conflicts to undergo a transition to de-escalation, including the adversaries' belief that they cannot gain what they want unilaterally or that efforts to do so would be too painful. Another important element is the possibility of an agreement among the adversaries, offering a mutually acceptable alternative (Touval and Zartman 1985). Policy-relevant research is often framed in terms of discerning the right time to undertake various kinds of de-escalating strategies (Zartman 1985; Kriesberg and Thorson 1991).

In addition to mediation and negotiation, CR analysts and practitioners have expanded their work to include more and more phases of conflicts. Thus, increasing attention has been devoted to the prenegotiation phase, or the process of getting adversaries to the table (Stein 1989). Work at even earlier phases, before a conflict escalates, is also gaining attention, as is work in the postsettlement phase, involving the development of stable political structures and methods of reconciliation between the conflict's adversaries. All this research is part of viewing conflicts in a long-term perspective, including the avoidance of intractable conflicts, the transformation of protracted conflicts into tractable ones, and the establishment of a stable peace, and perhaps reconciliation, between former adversaries.

The expansion in CR activities has led to considerable differentiation within the field. From the outset, interpersonal and intergroup conflicts were distinguished, as were domestic and international conflicts. However, more

and more specific arenas of CR work have emerged that address conflicts that
vary according to the context, the issues at stake, the nature of the adversaries, and the CR methods employed. For instance, CR research and practice may focus on school settings, family relations, public disputes over environmental issues, ethnic relations, interreligious struggles, interstate border
disputes, and fights about the allocation of scarce resources.

Significantly, too, specialization has developed relating to various phases
of a conflict. Thus, a great deal of attention has been given to early warning
and preventing the eruption of large-scale violence within and between states,
often emphasizing the efforts of official and nonofficial interveners (Ackerman 2000; Lund 1996; Carnegie Commission 1997). Many CR practitioners
and analysts have begun to pay more attention to institutional arrangements
for managing recurrent conflicts before they become protracted and destructive. Their work applies in a variety of conflict-prone venues, ranging from
large industrial enterprises to multiethnic societies (Ury, Brett, and Goldberg
1988; Hechter 2000).

Other practitioners and analysts focus on ways to stop the escalation of a conflict, for example, by managing crises (Brecher 1993), by initiating de-escalation
(Kriesberg 1992; Mitchell 2000), by conducting peacekeeping interventions,
and by applying sanctions (Brecher 1993; Cortright and Lopez 2000). Finally,
CR practitioners and scholars are giving increasing attention to posthostilities
peacebuilding, including research into sustaining peace agreements, promoting reconciliation, and developing cultures of peace (Hampson 1996; Boulding 2000; Weiner 1998; Lederach 1997; Kacowicz et al. 2000; Walter 2002).

In addition to becoming increasingly differentiated, CR is becoming more
institutionalized. In the United States, its practice is legislatively mandated
in certain circumstances, for example, in the development of certain federal
regulations and in child custody divorce cases in some jurisdictions. In 1998,
the U.S. congress established the U.S. Institute for Environmental Conflict
Resolution to assist parties in resolving environmental, natural resource, and
public lands conflicts. That same year, the U.S. congress enacted the federal
Alternative Dispute Resolution Act, requiring federal trial courts to promote
the use of ADR.

Institutionalization is also evident in the establishment of many research
centers, several of the more prominent ones being based at universities and
originally funded by the William and Flora Hewlett Foundation. In addition,
many universities provide graduate training in conflict analysis and resolution, including certificate programs within professional schools and graduate
degree programs, as well as MA and PhD programs in CR. Many independent
and university-based centers also provide training and consulting services in

CR and mediation. Training and practice in mediation are increasingly evident at all levels of education, in private corporations, and in government agencies. CR techniques are being introduced in more and more areas of the world—for example, in Eastern Europe and the former Soviet Union, as illustrated by the activities of Partners for Democratic Change, based in the United States. Finally, comprehensive syntheses of the field as it relates to large-scale conflicts have been published (Kriesberg 2007; Ramsbotham, Woodhouse, and Miall 2005; Wallensteen 2002).

The practice of CR has continued to evolve. In the domestic arena, applications have increased in areas relating to deeply rooted ethnic and other communal antagonisms, often exacerbated by immigration, and to deeply held value differences, such as those relating to abortion in the United States. These issues often require long-term strategies to build mutually respectful relations and legitimate institutionalized procedures to manage conflicts and to achieve a sense of justice for all parties involved.

In the international realm, the engagement of outside unofficial intermediaries in the conflicts within and among countries has greatly increased. The CR method requires considerable sensitivity to elicit and adapt local approaches rather than to impose methods developed in another setting (Lederach 1995). This type of international response to conflict has been accompanied by a parallel increase in conventional interventions by international governmental organizations and individual governments into the internal affairs of other countries, particularly in cases of humanitarian crises and extreme violations of human rights, as evident in Somalia, Iraq, Haiti, Rwanda, the former Yugoslavia, Indonesia, Sierra Leone, and elsewhere during the 1990s. Such governmental actions raise profound questions about the existence of shared standards and conceptions regarding sovereignty and human rights (Damrosch 1993; Deng et al. 1996). Moreover, human rights violations may be used selectively to justify interventions for self-aggrandizing purposes of the intervening state.

CURRENT AND FUTURE ISSUES

Having considered the evolution of the CR field, we can now examine areas of consensus and of disagreement within the field and also how international relations theory and practice and CR are converging and complementing each other. We then suggest how the diversity of CR activities provides opportunities for more effective efforts.

Many technological, cultural, political, economic, and social changes in recent decades have already been noted; some of them combine to generate new challenging concerns. These include the increasing number and power of nonstate transnational actors, including multinational corporations, transnational social reform organizations, criminal groups, and organizations relying on terrorist methods. Although the CR approach may have particular adaptability for conflicts involving nonstate actors, it may seem particularly inappropriate for conflicts involving a reliance on terrifying and intimidating violence. Even in such cases, however, the approach may have some value (Kriesberg 2002). CR analysis demonstrates that relying on such violent methods is often counterproductive, whether exercised by challenging groups or repressive states. The CR approach also may provide alternative and constructive methods to challenge authorities or for authorities to isolate challenging groups resorting to terrorist methods.

Consensus and Dissensus within the CR Field

As CR activities have evolved, crystallized, and become institutionalized, some elements of consensus have emerged among those working in the field. Yet the great variety of conflicts to which CR is applied and the diverse sources of CR ideas make universal agreement on CR precepts and techniques unlikely.

Matters of Consensus. There is general agreement, at least in principle, that specific CR strategies and tactics fit particular kinds of conflicts and conflict stages. Thus, long-term strategies that combine a variety of methods typically are required to prevent a conflict from escalating destructively. Attention has been devoted to the various methods that are appropriate for intermediaries trying to hasten de-escalation at different stages of a conflict, referred to as the "contingency approach" (Keashly and Fisher 1995; also see Kriesberg 1996).

There is also widely shared recognition that more evaluation of CR methods is needed. The difficulties in conducting assessments of different CR methods in various settings are increasingly recognized and ways of overcoming them are being developed. More evaluation research using quantitative methods and case study approaches is being undertaken. Practitioners are more often reflective about their work in order to improve their efforts (see, e.g., the work of the Reflecting on Peace Project, www.cdainc.com). Research is often directed at the study of particular methods to limit, de-escalate, or end destructive conflicts, including economic sanctions, mediation, confidence-building measures, negotiations, and interposition of peacekeeping forces (Cortright and Lopez 2000, 2002; Kressel and Pruitt 1989; Bercovitch 2002; Walter and Snyder 1999; O'Leary and Bingham 2003).

In addition, the CR community generally recognizes the important influence adversaries have on each other in both escalating and de-escalating a conflict. Partisans, however, frequently attribute the cause and course of a conflict to the other side's internally driven characteristics or to characteristics within the larger social system that they cannot readily affect (Jervis 1976; Kelley and Michela 1980). The CR approach stresses that both sides impact the relationship and emphasizes what each party can do to influence the course of a struggle (Kriesberg 2007).

Finally, there is growing recognition among CR practitioners that every social conflict involves many parties and issues (Putnam 1988; Kriesberg 1992; Colaresi 2005). Viewed as such, social conflicts share certain elements and are thus interlocked. The changing salience of one conflict relative to another serves as a source of escalation and de-escalation; consequently, reframing a conflict so that its salience is reduced often promotes its settlement and resolution. Emphasizing a threatening common enemy is a frequent reframing device.

Matters of Dissensus. CR analysts and practitioners, as well as others outside the field, debate many aspects of the field. Thus, CR workers vary in the emphasis they place on "conflicts" versus "disputes" and on their settlement, resolution, or transformation. "Dispute" sometimes refers to contestations over matters that are negotiable and contain the elements of compromise, whereas "conflict" is about issues that involve deep-rooted human needs (Burton 1990). According to this view, "conflict resolution" means solving the problems that led to the conflict, and "transformation" means changing the relationships between the parties to a conflict; "conflict settlement" refers to suppressing the conflict itself, without dealing with deeper causes and relations. Not all CR analysts and practitioners make such a sharp distinction; many generally regard some types of contestations as more limited than conflicts but recognize that disputes may also be episodes in a larger conflict. The settlement of disputes, then, may contribute to changes in the relationship between adversaries and the gradual transformation of their conflict. A related question persists: to what extent is attaining justice and satisfying basic needs for the contending parties crucial for an enduring peace?

CR analysts and practitioners also differ in the importance they accord to coercion and violence in the way conflicts are conducted and settled or resolved. Some analysts reason that any reliance on coercion is antithetical to a problem-solving resolution of a conflict. Traditional "realists," on the other hand, tend to assume that all conflicts are ultimately resolved by coercion. Many people working in the CR field, believing that power differentials are an inescapable fact of all relationships, take a middle ground. They stress the varieties of power, such as the ability to impose positive and negative sanctions, normative or persuasive inducements, and altruism and shared identity (Boulding 1989). They also emphasize how conflicts are reframed and the parties' self-identity is redefined in the course of a struggle and efforts to resolve it.

Some observers argue that the dominant party in a conflict may use CR as an instrument of control. Without taking sides in this debate, we must concede that insofar as parties are unequal in status, power, or other resources, the weaker party tends to give up more in a mediated or negotiated agreement (Gulliver 1979; Nader 1991; Mitchell 1995, 25–57). But this is perhaps even more likely to be true if the dispute is settled by other procedures.

Finally, practitioners disagree about when various methods of conflict de-escalation and resolution may be appropriate (Laue and Cormick 1978). Some would not try to mediate or otherwise facilitate a settlement between parties in a highly asymmetrical relationship. Indeed, many feminists and others criticize CR practitioners for their tendency to ignore power differences in their haste to employ CR techniques (Taylor and Miller 1994). However, others in the field believe that mediation should still be undertaken, although thoughtfully, because conflict parties rarely are equal in their resources and capabilities. These CR practitioners may even regard facilitating the adversaries' recognition and acceptance of the realities of their relationship as contributing to a settlement.

One way to resolve the dilemmas these views pose is to incorporate constructive methods of waging a struggle into the adversaries' strategic repertoire (Kriesberg 2007). Thus, some CR analysts and practitioners emphasize ways of redressing power imbalances without denying the grievances or interests of the opposition, which is the appeal of nonviolent action for many people (Wehr, Burgess, and Burgess 1994; Sharp 2005). However, CR also refers to strategies and tactics to help balance asymmetrical parties in negotiations (Deutsch 1973; Zartman and Rubin 1996; Zartman 1987).

Convergence and Complementarity between CR and International Relations

The fields of CR and international relations (IR) overlap and are increasingly converging, in part because of the radically changing nature of the world and of social conflicts. Also, practitioners and academics in each field have sought to build links to the other community. Professional associations, foundation-supported meetings, and the efforts of many academic and nonacademic institutions, such as the United States Institute of Peace (www.usip.org), have facilitated interchanges and this convergence.

However, CR and conventional international relations theory and practice will and should remain somewhat divergent. Traditional IR thinking tends to be "realist" in its emphasis on sovereign states, the centrality of power seeking by political leaders, and the importance of military force. CR can provide a corrective to inappropriate reliance on these views (Galtung et al. 2000). Conversely, traditional IR approaches can provide a corrective to overreliance on good intentions as the basis to resolve conflicts. Although much current IR thinking and practice are converging with many kinds of CR work, the continuing differences can provide a sound basis for complementary work.

Convergence. Many CR ideas have gone beyond the confines of academia to the general public and official and unofficial practitioners. One notable example is the idea that adversaries can achieve win-win outcomes. Thus, the transmission of German and other European peace researchers' ideas about nonoffensive defense to Soviet leaders in the early and mid-1980s played an important role in Gorbachev's "new thinking" and its acceptance within the Soviet foreign policy bureaucracy (Kriesberg 1992). Furthermore, a variety of CR practices have become widely accepted in coping with conflicts. These practices include establishing informal dialogue groups, incorporating brainstorming periods in negotiations, and using mediators.

Innovative ideas and practices in IR have contributed to some noteworthy CR developments, resulting in useful and enduring syntheses. For example, analyses of actual cases of mediation in international conflicts have broadened the concept of the mediator's role and mediation activities. When officials of major states serve as mediators, their access to economic, military, and status resources and their interests in the outcome of the mediation all contribute to the process (Princen 1992). Despite the widespread belief that mediators must strive for neutrality and minimize assertiveness, information about mediation in many arenas reveals that mediators are often active in shaping both the process used and the agreement reached (Kolb 1994). The great variety of mediation activities that can be combined differently in manifold roles and the diversity of persons who provide some of those services—inside as well as outside those roles—are increasingly being explored (Bercovitch 1996).

Another example of synthesis derives from the attention traditional IR has devoted to the study of institutions. Recent analyses of normative regimes and an array of other formal and informal institutional arrangements, which have been negotiated to resolve problems related to weapons, human rights, environmental protection, and many other issues, enrich the repertoire of options adversaries can consider for various ways out of a destructive conflict. Increasingly, CR practitioners focus not only on the processes of de-escalation and negotiation, but on the fairness and durability of the outcomes as well.

Such attention fosters consideration of formulas that cannot only settle a dispute, but also settle it in a way that makes its recurrence unlikely.

Finally, the profound changes in the nature of the world system, noted at the outset of this chapter, have impelled convergence. This convergence may be seen in the increasingly crucial role of non-governmental agents as both partisans and intermediaries in many transnational conflicts (Chatfield, Pagnucco, and Smith 1996). The many factors supporting convergence reinforce each other, as is evident in the evolution of sanctions as a way to nonviolently control conflicts and bring about constructive outcomes. Cortright and Lopez (2002) analyze the many factors shaping this evolution, including the increasing role of NGOs; the interactions among researchers, advocates, and diplomats; the changing international environment; and the blending of persuasive and positive inducements as well as negative sanctions.

Complementarity. Peacemaking practices of CR and of traditional IR often complement one another, whether sequentially or simultaneously. Many examples of sequential complementarity can be cited, usually when the CR practice involves nonofficial or track-two methods that precede the more traditional diplomatic approaches, because track-two diplomacy may prepare the groundwork for official negotiations. At other times, negotiations are initiated in a track-two channel and then handed off to an official negotiating forum. Sometimes, the traditional diplomatic channel reaches an impasse and a new track is opened informally. When progress is made, the negotiations are then transferred back to the official channel, as was the case in the 1993 negotiations between Israelis and PLO representatives in Oslo, Norway (Kriesberg 2001).

Another example is the work deriving from one of the task forces established in 1982 under the auspices of the Dartmouth Conference. Following the deterioration of U.S.-Soviet détente, members of the conference established task forces on (1) arms control and (2) regional conflicts to examine what had gone wrong. Reflection on the process and the phases of the conference's development provided the basis for two members of the regional conflicts task force, Gennady Chufrin and Harold Saunders, to cochair the Inter-Tajik Dialogue (Saunders 1995). The dialogue brought together a wide range of Tajiks in 1993, following the first round of a vicious civil war that erupted after the Soviet Union dissolved and Soviet Tajikistan became independent. Meeting several times a year, the dialogue group's members moved through five stages: (1) deciding to engage in dialogue to resolve mutually intolerable problems; (2) coming together to map out the elements of the problems and the relationships that perpetuate the problems; (3) uncovering the underlying dynamics of the relationships and beginning to see ways to change them; (4) planning steps together to change the relationships; and (5) devising ways to implement their plan. In practice, participants may remain at one stage for several meetings and even return to an earlier stage when circumstances change.

Some of the Tajiks from different factions participated in the official negotiations that began in 1994, after the Inter-Tajik Dialogue had met several times (Saunders 1999). Changes in the government and the opposition, as well as in Russia, Iran, and other engaged countries, contributed crucially to the conduct of the negotiations and to reaching the final agreement, signed in 1997. In addition, the United Nations and the Organization for Security and Cooperation in Europe, in a subsidiary way, provided mediating services. The activities of all these parties and of the unofficial dialogue group were well coordinated (Saunders 1999; Iji 2001).

In some instances, organizers of short-term problem-solving workshops have turned the workshops into a series, constituting a continuing workshop with the same participants, as was the case with the continuing Israeli-Palestinian workshop organized by Rouhana and Kelman (1994). Meeting four times between November 1990 and July 1992, the workshops lasted three or four days and followed ground rules designed to facilitate analytical discussion of the issues that encouraged joint thinking about the conflict. The third-party facilitators steered the participants through two major phases: first, the presentation of concerns and needs; second, joint thinking about satisfying them and overcoming barriers to doing so.

These and earlier workshops involving Israeli Jews and Palestinian Arabs contributed in several ways to the later official negotiations between the Israeli government and the PLO (Kelman 1995). For example, the understandings about each other's points of views and concerns and possible ways to reconcile them provided the basis for officials on each side to believe a mutually acceptable formula could be found. However, the breakdown in negotiations in the fall of 2000 indicates that the support for the negotiations needed to be much wider and deeper, that the agreements previously reached needed to be more completely implemented, and that mutual reassurances about the needs of both being understood needed to be more clearly articulated (Kriesberg 2002).

CR efforts sometimes complement relatively traditional IR activities when they are carried out simultaneously, as may occur when unofficial tracks parallel official negotiating tracks, such as in the case in the Pugwash and Dartmouth meetings during the years of U.S.-Soviet negotiations regarding arms control.

The multiplicity of intermediary efforts, however, can also hamper effective de-escalation and the achievement of enduring, mutually acceptable agreements in several ways. Too many uncoordinated efforts can undermine one another because they convey different messages to the adversaries about what different intermediaries have in mind regarding the future course of the conflict. Or one or more of the adversaries may try to play one intermediary off against another. In addition, intermediaries may compete for attention and strain the capability of the adversaries' representatives to provide an adequate response.

Nevertheless, in large-scale conflicts, various intermediaries and approaches generally need to be combined in order to be effective. If they are well coordinated, their effectiveness enhances the efforts of any one approach. Such coordination includes actions pursued simultaneously and sequentially, as exemplified in the 1989–92 peace process that ended Mozambique's war (Hume 1994). In the course of its missionary and humanitarian work in Mozambique, the Community of Sant'Egidio, a Catholic lay order based in Rome, had developed ties with both the government of Mozambique and the insurgent Mozambican National Resistance (Renamo) forces. Both sides found various international governmental organizations to be unacceptable mediators, even as they both began to consider ways of ending the war. Yet Sant'Egidio was accepted to act as a facilitative mediator. Because it was not a state actor, it could facilitate negotiations, minimizing issues about the status of the adversaries.

A four-person mediation team consisted of two members of Sant'Egidio, the archbishop of Beira, and a member of the Italian parliament who had previous foreign ministry service. During the negotiations, representatives of many governments also assisted in the peace process. The Italian government helped with the arrangements and consulted with the negotiating parties. Representatives of the governments of France, Portugal, the United Kingdom, and the United States and representatives of the United Nations consulted with the mediators and with representatives of Renamo and the Mozambican government; in 1992, the representatives joined the formal negotiations as observers. In addition, the governments of neighboring countries contributed to the process. For example, President Robert Mugabe of Zimbabwe helped arrange the first meeting and handshake between President Joaquim Chissano of Mozambique and Renamo leader Afonso Dhlakama. In addition, NGOs, including those providing humanitarian assistance, actively consulted during the negotiations. As the process evolved, the various intermediaries consulted with one another and coordinated their efforts. A peace agreement was signed in Rome on October 4, 1992.

CONCLUSION

Some disagreements about what can and should be done regarding specific conflicts arise from strongly held values. People assign different priorities to alternative values, such as between achieving freedom or securing economic well-being and between advancing social justice or avoiding deadly violence. The priority given to such alternatives affects preferences about the timing of de-escalation and peacemaking efforts, for example, whether to equalize the power differential between belligerents before trying to settle the conflict. Values also affect preferences about which parties should participate in negotiating a settlement; for example, in deciding whether to exclude especially hard-line factions on one or more sides.

At present, when so many peoples in the world seek to realize their own values, difficult choices may be necessary between conflicting values. Such trade-offs inevitably pose moral dilemmas. For example, how much pain and suffering should be borne (and by whom) to continue fighting to perhaps gain a better settlement later? The CR approach cannot solve such moral dilemmas. However, CR tends to favor long-term processes and outcomes that take into account all sides of a conflict and that maximize the participation of the people directly affected. In addition, the process of problem-solving ways of waging and ending struggles foster creative and constructive options. Consequently, attaining at least some measure of a wide range of values is increased.

CR is a vigorous, evolving field of endeavor, encompassing a great variety of perspectives and methods; its many advocates are familiar with interdisciplinary strife as well as cooperation. The diversity is natural and even beneficial, because no single perspective or method suits every conflict during every phase of its course. Familiarity with the many methods of CR is valuable because proper policymaking in response to conflict requires a large repertoire of possible strategies and techniques. Some are suitable for one person or organization and not another, and rarely can any single person or group transform a conflict or resolve it. Many people contribute a bit, and in this new globalized era of relative political instability among and within nation-states, many people must combine their efforts if destructive conflicts and oppressive outcomes are to be avoided or reduced. Since the end of the Cold War, there have been notable declines in various indicators of large-scale violence (Human Security Centre 2006; Marshall and Gurr 2005; Wallensteen 2002). The expanding and evolving CR field is one of the many developments accounting for those declines.

APPENDIX

Chronology of Publications, Developments, and Events Relevant to Conflict Resolution

Year	Publications Pertaining to Conflict Resolution	Institutional Developments in Conflict Resolution and Global Political Events
1942	M. P. Follett, *Dynamic Administration* Quincy Wright, *A Study of War*	National War Labor Board established in United States
1945	J. P. Chander, *Teachings of Mahatma Gandhi*	World War II ends
1947		U.S. Federal Mediation and Conciliation Service established British sovereignty over India ends
1948		Universal Declaration of Human Rights adopted by the General Assembly of the United Nations signed
1956	L. Coser, *The Functions of Social Conflict*	Successful ending of civil rights bus boycott in Montgomery, Alabama
1957	K. Deutsch et al., *Political Community and the North Atlantic Area*	*Journal of Conflict Resolution* begins publishing, University of Michigan Pugwash Conferences begin, in Canada
1959	R. Dahrendorf, *Class and Class Conflict in Industrial Society*	Center for Research on Conflict Resolution established, University of Michigan International Peace Research Institute (PRIO) founded, Oslo, Norway
1960	L. Richardson, *Statistics of Deadly Quarrels* T. Schelling, *The Strategy of Conflict*	Dartmouth Conferences begin
1961	T. F. Lentz, *Towards a Science of Peace*	

Year		
1962	K. Boulding, *Conflict and Defense*; C. E. Osgood, *An Alternative to War or Surrender*	Cuban missile crisis
1964		*Journal of Peace Research* begins publishing, based at PRIO; International Peace Research Association founded
1965	A. Rapoport and A. Chammah, *The Prisoner's Dilemma*	J. W. Burton and others organize problem-solving workshop with representatives from Malaysia, Indonesia, and Singapore
1966	M. Sherif, *In Common Predicament*	
1968		Centre for Intergroup Studies established in Capetown, South Africa
1969	J. W. Burton, *Conflict and Communication*	
1970	L. Doob, *Resolving Conflict in Africa*	Peace Research Institute Frankfurt established in Germany
1971	A. Curle, *Making Peace*	Department of Peace and Conflict Research established at Uppsala Universitet, Sweden
1972	J. D. Singer and M. Small, *The Wages of War, 1816–1965*	Détente reached between Soviet Union and United States; Treaty on the Limitation of Anti-ballistic Missile Systems signed
1973	M. Deutsch, *The Resolution of Conflict*; G. Sharp, *The Politics of Nonviolent Action*; L. Kriesberg, *The Sociology of Social Conflicts*	Department of Peace Studies established, University of Bradford, United Kingdom; Society of Professionals in Dispute Resolution (SPIDR) initiates conference
1975		Helsinki Final Act signed, product of the Conference on Security and Cooperation in Europe
1977		Panama Canal Treaty signed

Chronology of Publications, Developments, and Events Relevant to Conflict Resolution

Year	Publications Pertaining to Conflict Resolution	Institutional Developments in Conflict Resolution and Global Political Events
1979	P. H. Gulliver, *Disputes and Negotiations: A Cross-Cultural Perspective*	Egyptian-Israeli Treaty, mediated by President J. Carter Iranian revolution
1981	R. Fisher and W. Ury, *Getting to YES*	
1982		Carter Center established in Atlanta, Georgia National Conference on Peacemaking and Conflict Resolution (NCPCR) initiated in United States Search for Common Ground established in Washington, D.C. United Nations Convention on the Law of the Sea adopted
1984	R. Axelrod, *The Evolution of Cooperation*	United States Institute of Peace founded in Washington, D.C. The William and Flora Hewlett Foundation initiates grant program supporting conflict resolution theory and practice International Association for Conflict Management founded
1985	S. Touval and I. W. Zartman, eds., *International Mediation in Theory and Practice* I. W. Zartman, *Ripe for Resolution: Conflict and Intervention in Africa*	The Network for Community Justice and Conflict Resolution established in Canada
1986	C. W. Moore, *The Mediation Process* (1st ed.)	International Alert founded in London
1987	L. Susskind and J. Cruickshank, *Breaking the Impasse: Consensual Approaches to Resolving Public Disputes*	

Year	Publications	Events
1989	K. Kressel and D. G. Pruitt, eds., *Mediation Research* H. W. van der Merwe, *Pursuing Justice and Peace in South Africa* L. Kriesberg, T. A. Northrup, and S. J. Thorson, eds., *Intractable Conflicts and Their Transformation*	Berlin Wall falls Partners for Democratic Change founded, linking university-based centers in Sofia, Prague, Bratislava, Budapest, Warsaw, and Moscow
1990		Organization for Security and Cooperation in Europe, 55-state institution, originated with the Charter of Paris for a New Europe Association of Southeast Asian Nations (ASEAN) begins informal workshops
1992	W. Isard, *Understanding Conflict and the Science of Peace*	Instituto Peruano de Resolución de Conflictos, Negociación, y Mediación (IPRECONM) established in Peru Government of El Salvador and the Frente Farabundo Martí para la Liberación Nacional sign peace agreement
1993	M. H. Ross, *The Management of Conflict*	PLO and Israel sign Declaration of Principles European Union established
1994	D. Johnston and C. Sampson, eds., *Religion, the Missing Dimension of Statecraft* A. Taylor and J. B. Miller, eds., *Conflict and Gender*	Nelson Mandela elected president of South Africa UN Security Council creates the International Criminal Tribunal for Rwanda
1995	J. P. Lederach, *Preparing for Peace*	U.S. brokers end of war in Bosnia International Crisis Group established in Brussels
1996	F. O. Hampson, *Nurturing Peace* Michael S. Lund, *Preventing Violent Conflicts*	South African Truth and Reconciliation Commission established
1997	P. Salem, ed., *Conflict Resolution in the Arab World*	

APPENDIX (cont.)

Chronology of Publications, Developments, and Events Relevant to Conflict Resolution

Year	Publications Pertaining to Conflict Resolution	Institutional Developments in Conflict Resolution and Global Political Events
1998	E. Weiner, ed., *The Handbook of Interethnic Coexistence*	U.S. Federal Alternative Dispute Resolution Act enacted Good Friday Agreement reached for Northern Ireland International Criminal Court established by Rome statute; entered into force in 2002
1999	H. H. Saunders, *A Public Peace Process* B. F. Walter and J. Snyder, eds., *Civil Wars, Insecurity, and Intervention*	People of East Timor vote for independence from Indonesia Peace Agreement between the Government of Sierra Leone and the Revolutionary United Front of Sierra Leone
2000	E. Boulding, *Cultures of Peace* J. Galtung et al., *Searching for Peace* T. R. Gurr, *Peoples versus States*	Second intifada begins between Palestinians and Israelis
2001		September 11 terror attacks on United States
2002	D. Cortright and G. A. Lopez, *Sanctions and the Search for Security* D. R. Smock, ed., *Interfaith Dialogue and Peacebuilding*	
2003	R. O'Leary and L. Bingham, eds., *The Promise and Performance of Environmental Conflict Resolution* E. Uwazie, ed., *Conflict Resolution and Peace Education in Africa*	U.S. and allied forces invade Iraq

2004	Y. Bar-Siman-Tov, ed., *From Conflict Resolution to Reconciliation* R. Paris, *At War's End*	Australian Centre for Peace and Conflict Studies founded at University of Queensland, Brisbane Peace agreement signed between government of Sudan and Sudan People's Liberation Army
2005	C. A. Crocker, F. O. Hampson, and P. Aall, eds., *Grasping the Nettle* D. Druckman, *Doing Research: Methods of Inquiry for Conflict Analysis*	PhD program in peace and conflict studies established at University of Manitoba, Canada
2006	Human Security Centre, *Human Security Report 2005* T. A. Borer, *Telling the Truths*	Full diplomatic relations restored between United States and Libya

REFERENCES

Ackermann, Alice. 2000. *Making Peace Prevail: Preventing Violent Conflict in Macedonia*. Syracuse, N.Y.: Syracuse University Press.

Adler, Peter S. 1987. "Is ADR a Social Movement?" *Negotiation Journal* 3 (1): 59–66.

Avruch, Kevin. 1998. *Culture and Conflict Resolution*. Washington, D.C.: United States Institute of Peace Press.

Axelrod, Robert. 1984. *The Evolution of Cooperation*. New York: Basic Books.

Bar-Siman-Tov, Yaacov, ed. 2003. *From Conflict Resolution to Reconciliation*. New York: Oxford University Press.

Bercovitch, Jacob, ed. 1996. *Resolving International Conflicts: The Theory and Practice of Mediation*. Boulder, Colo.: Lynne Rienner.

Bercovitch Jacob, ed. 2002. *Studies in International Mediation: Essays in Honor of Jeffrey Z. Rubin*. New York: Palgrave/Macmillan.

Borer, Tristan Anne. 2006. *Telling the Truths: Truth Telling and Peace Building in Post-Conflict Societies*. Notre Dame, Ind.: University of Notre Dame Press.

Boulding, Elise. 2000. *Cultures of Peace: The Hidden Side of History*. Syracuse, N.Y.: Syracuse University Press.

Boulding, Kenneth. 1962. *Conflict and Defense*. New York: Harper and Row.

———. 1989. *Three Faces of Power*. Beverly Hills, Calif.: Sage.

Brecher, Michael. 1993. *Crises in World Politics: Theory and Reality*. New York: Pergamon.

Brinton, Crane. 1938. *The Anatomy of Revolution*. New York: W. W. Norton.

Brockner, Joel, and Jeffrey Z. Rubin. 1985. *Entrapment in Escalating Conflicts*. New York: Springer-Verlag.

Burton, John W. 1969. *Conflict and Communication: The Use of Controlled Communication in International Relations*. London: Macmillan.

———. 1990. *Conflict: Resolution and Prevention*. New York: St. Martin's.

Carnegie Commission on Preventing Deadly Conflict. 1997. *Final Report of the Carnegie Commission on Preventing Deadly Conflict*. New York: Carnegie Corporation.

Carnevale, Peter J., and Tahira M. Probst. 1997. "Conflict on the Internet." In *Culture of the Internet*, ed. S. Kiesler. Mahwah, N.J.: Erlbaum.

Chander, Jag Parvesh. 1945. *Teachings of Mahatma Gandhi*. Hyderabad: Indian Printing Works.

Chatfield, Charles, Ronald Pagnucco, and Jackie Smith, eds. 1996. *Solidarity beyond the State: The Dynamics of Transnational Social Movements*. Syracuse, N.Y.: Syracuse University Press.

Chufrin, Gennady I., and Harold H. Saunders. 1993. "A Public Peace Process." *Negotiation Journal* 9 (2): 155–77.

Cohen, Raymond. 1997. *Negotiating across Cultures*, rev. ed. Washington, D.C.: United States Institute of Peace Press.

Colaresi, Michael P. 2005. *Scare Tactics: The Politics of International Rivalry*. Syracuse, N.Y.: Syracuse University Press.

Coleman, James. 1957. *Community Conflict*. New York: Free Press.

Cortright, David, and George Lopez, with Richard W. Conroy, Jaleh Dashti-Gibson, and Julia Wagler. 2000. *The Sanctions Decade: Assessing UN Strategies in the 1990s*. Boulder, Colo.: Lynne Rienner.

Cortright, David, and George A. Lopez. 2002. *Sanctions and the Search for Security*. Boulder, Colo.: Lynne Rienner.

Coser, Lewis. 1956. *The Functions of Social Conflict*. New York: Free Press.

Coy, Patrick G., and Lynne M. Woehrle, eds. 2000. *Social Conflicts and Collective Identities*. Lanham, Md.: Rowman and Littlefield.

Crocker, Chester A., Fen Osler Hampson, and Pamela Aall, eds. 2005. *Grasping the Nettle: Analyzing Cases of Intractable Conflicts*. Washington, D.C.: United States Institute of Peace Press.

Curle, Adam. 1971. *Making Peace*. London: Tavistock.

Dahrendorf, Ralf. 1959. *Class and Class Conflict in Industrial Society*. Stanford, Calif.: Stanford University Press.

Damrosch, Lori F. 1993. *Enforcing Restraint: Collective Intervention in Internal Conflicts*. New York: Council on Foreign Relations Press.

Deng, Francis, Sadikiel Kimaro, Terrence Lyons, Donald Rothchild, and I. William Zartman. 1996. *Sovereignty as Responsibility*. Washington, D.C.: Brookings Institution Press.

Deutsch, Karl, Sidney A. Burrell, Robert A. Kann, Maurice Lee Jr., Martin Lichterman, Raymond Lindgren, Francis L. Loewenheim, and Richard W. Van Wagenen. 1957. *Political Community and the North Atlantic Area*. Princeton, N.J.: Princeton University Press.

Deutsch, Morton, 1973. *The Resolution of Conflict: Constructive and Destructive Processes*. New Haven, Conn.: Yale University Press.

Doob, Leonard W., ed. 1970. *Resolving Conflict in Africa: The Fermeda Workshop*. New Haven, Conn.: Yale University Press.

Druckman, Daniel, ed. 1977. *Negotiations: Social-Psychological Perspectives*. Beverly Hills, Calif.: Sage.

Druckman, Daniel. 2005. *Doing Research: Methods of Inquiry for Conflict Analysis*. Thousand Oaks, Calif.: Sage.

Etzioni, Amitai. 1967. "The Kennedy Experiment." *Western Political Quarterly* 20 (June): 361–80.

Faure, Guy Olivier, and Jeffrey Z. Rubin, eds. 1993. *Culture and Negotiation*. Beverly Hills, Calif.: Sage.

Fisher, Roger, and William Ury. 1981. *Getting to YES: Negotiating Agreement without Giving In*. Boston: Houghton Mifflin.

Fisher, Ronald F. 1996. *Interactive Conflict Resolution: Pioneers, Potential, and Prospects*. Syracuse, N.Y.: Syracuse University Press.

Follett, Mary Parker. 1942. *Dynamic Administration: The Collected Papers of Mary Parker Follett*. New York, London: Harper and Brothers.

Galtung, Johan, Carl G. Jacobsen, Kai Frithjof Brand-Jacobsen, and Finn Tschudi. 2000. *Searching for Peace*. Sterling, Va.: Pluto.

Goldstein, Joshua S., and John R. Freeman. 1990. *Three-Way Street: Strategic Reciprocity in World Politics*. Chicago: University of Chicago Press.

Gopin, Marc. 2000. *Between Eden and Armageddon: The Future of Religion, Violence, and Peacemaking*. New York: Oxford University Press.

———. 2002. *Holy War, Holy Peace: How Religion Can Bring Peace to the Middle East*. New York: Oxford University Press.

Gulliver, P. H. 1979. *Disputes and Negotiations: A Cross-Cultural Perspective*. New York: Academic Press.

Gurr, Ted Robert. 2000. *Peoples versus States: Minorities at Risk in the New Century*. Washington, D.C.: United States Institute of Peace Press.

Haas, Ernst B. 1958. *The Uniting of Europe*. Stanford, Calif.: Stanford University Press.

Hampson, Fen Osler. 1996. *Nurturing Peace: Why Peace Settlements Succeed or Fail*. Washington, D.C.: United States Institute of Peace Press.

Harris, Adrienne, and Ynestra King, eds. 1989. *Rocking the Ship of State: Toward a Feminist Peace Politics*. Boulder, Colo.: Westview.

Harty, Martha, and John Modell. 1991. "The First Conflict Resolution Movement, 1956–1971: An Attempt to Institutionalize Applied Interdisciplinary Social Science." *Journal of Conflict Resolution* 35 (4): 720–58.

Hechter, Michael. 2000. *Containing Nationalism*. New York: Oxford University Press.

Herb, Guntram H., and David H. Kaplan, eds. 1999. *Nested Identities: Nationalism, Territory, and Scale*. Lanham, Md.: Rowman and Littlefield.

Human Security Centre. 2006. *Human Security Report 2005*. New York: Oxford University Press.

Hume, Cameron. 1994. *Ending Mozambique's War*. Washington, D.C.: United States Institute of Peace Press.

Iji, Tetsuro. 2001. "International Mediation in Tajikistan: The 1997 Peace Agreement." Paper presented at the annual convention of the International Studies Association, Chicago.

Iklé, Fred Charles. 1964. *How Nations Negotiate*. New York: Harper and Row.

Isard, Walter. 1988. *Arms Races, Arms Control, and Conflict Analysis: Contributions from Peace Science and Peace Economics*. New York: Cambridge University Press.

Isard, Walter. 1992. *Understanding Conflict and the Science of Peace*. Cambridge, Mass., and Oxford, UK: Blackwell.

Jackson, Elmore. 1952. *Meeting of Minds: A Way to Peace through Mediation*. New York: McGraw-Hill.

Janis, Irving L. 1972. *Victims of Groupthink*. Boston: Houghton Mifflin.

Jervis, Robert. 1976. *Perception and Misperception in International Politics*. Princeton, N.J.: Princeton University Press.

Jervis, Robert, Richard Ned Lebow, and Janice Stein. 1985. *Psychology and Deterrence*. Baltimore: Johns Hopkins University Press.

Johnston, Douglas, and Cynthia Sampson, eds. 1994. *Religion, the Missing Dimension of Statecraft*. New York: Oxford University Press.

Kacowicz, Arie M., Yaacov Bar-Siman Tove, Ole Elgstrom, and Magnus Jerneck, eds. 2000. *Stable Peace among Nations*. Lanham, Md.: Rowman and Littlefield.

Keashly, Loraleigh, and Ronald J. Fisher. 1995. "Complementarity and Coordination of Conflict Interventions: Taking a Contingency Perspective." In *Resolving International Conflicts*, ed. Jacob Bercovitch. Boulder, Colo.: Lynne Rienner.

Kelley, Harold, and John Michela. 1980. "Attribution Theory and Research." *Annual Review of Psychology* 31: 457–501.

Kelman, Herbert C. 1992. "Informal Mediation by the Scholar Practitioner." In *Mediation in International Relations*, ed. Jacob Bercovitch and Jeffrey Z. Rubin. New York: St. Martin's.

———. 1995. "Contributions of an Unofficial Conflict Resolution Effort to the Israeli-Palestinian Breakthrough." *Negotiation Journal* 11 (1): 19–27.

Kolb, Deborah M. 1994. *When Talk Works: Profiles of Mediators*. San Francisco: Jossey-Bass.

Kressel, Kenneth, and Dean G. Pruitt, eds. 1989. *Mediation Research*. San Francisco: Jossey-Bass.

Kriesberg, Louis. 1973. *The Sociology of Social Conflicts*. Englewood Cliffs, N.J.: Prentice-Hall.

———. 1992. *International Conflict Resolution: The U.S.-USSR and Middle East Cases*. New Haven, Conn.: Yale University Press.

———. 1995. "Varieties of Mediating Activities and of Mediators." In *Resolving International Conflicts*, ed. Jacob Bercovitch, 219–33. Boulder, Colo.: Lynne Rienner.

———. 1996. "Preventing and Resolving Destructive Communal Conflicts." In *The International Politics of Ethnic Conflict: Theory and Evidence*, ed. Patrick James and David Carment. Pittsburgh: University of Pittsburgh Press.

———. 2001. "Mediation and the Transformation of the Israeli-Palestinian Conflict." *Journal of Peace Research* 38 (3): 373–92.

———. 2002. "The Relevance of Reconciliation Actions in the Breakdown of Israeli-Palestinian Negotiations." *2000 Peace and Change* 27 (4): 546–71.

———. 2007. *Constructive Conflicts: From Escalation to Resolution*, 3rd ed. Lanham, Md.: Rowman and Littlefield.

Kriesberg, Louis, Terrell A. Northrup, and Stuart J. Thorson, eds. 1989. *Intractable Conflicts and Their Transformation*. Syracuse, N.Y.: Syracuse University Press.

Kriesberg, Louis, and Stuart J. Thorson. 1991. *Timing the De-escalation of International Conflicts*. Syracuse, N.Y.: Syracuse University Press.

Lasswell, Harold D. 1930. *Psychology and Politics*. Chicago: University of Chicago Press.

Laue, James, and Gerald Cormick. 1978. "The Ethics of Intervention in Community Disputes." In *The Ethics of Social Intervention*, ed. Gordon Bermant, Herbert C. Kelman, and Donald P. Warwick. Washington, D.C.: Halsted.

Lederach, John Paul. 1995. *Preparing for Peace: Conflict Transformation across Cultures*. Syracuse, N.Y.: Syracuse University Press.

———. 1997. *Building Peace: Sustainable Reconciliation in Divided Societies*. Washington, D.C.: United States Institute of Peace Press.

Leng, Russell J. 1993. *Interstate Crisis Behavior, 1816–1980*. New York: Cambridge University Press.

Lentz, Theodore F. 1961. *Towards a Science of Peace*. New York: Bookman Associates.

Lewin, Kurt. 1948. *Resolving Social Conflicts*. New York: Harper and Brothers.

Lofland, John. 1993. *Polite Protesters: The American Peace Movement of the 1980s*. Syracuse, N.Y.: Syracuse University Press.

Lund, Michael S. 1996. *Preventing Violent Conflicts: A Strategy for Preventive Diplomacy*. Washington, D.C.: United States Institute of Peace Press.

Marshall, Monty G., and Ted Robert Gurr. 2005. *Peace and Conflict, 2005*. College Park, Md.: Center for International Development and Conflict Management (University of Maryland).

Marullo, Sam, and John Lofland, eds. 1990. *Peace Action in the Eighties*. New Brunswick, N.J.: Rutgers University Press.

McClelland, Charles A. 1983. "Let the User Beware." *International Studies Quarterly* 27: 169–78.

McDonald, John W. 1991. "Further Explorations in Track-Two Diplomacy." In *Timing the De-escalation of International Conflicts*, ed. Louis Kriesberg and Stuart J. Thorson. Syracuse, N.Y.: Syracuse University Press.

Meyer, David S. 1990. *A Winter of Discontent*. New York: Praeger.

Miall, Hugh, Oliver Ramsbotham, and Tom Woodhouse. 1999. *Contemporary Conflict Resolution: The Prevention, Management, and Transformations of Deadly Conflict*. Cambridge, UK: Polity.

Mitchell, Christopher R. 1995. "Asymmetry and Strategies of Regional Conflict Reduction." In *Cooperative Security: Reducing Third World Wars*, ed. I. William Zartman and Victor A. Kremenyuk. Syracuse, N.Y.: Syracuse University Press.

Mitchell, Christopher. 2000. *Gestures of Conciliation: Factors Contributing to Successful Olive Branches*. New York: St. Martin's.

Mitchell, Christopher R., and K. Webb. 1988. *New Approaches to International Mediation*. Westport, Conn.: Greenwood.

Mitrany, David. 1943. *A Working Peace System: An Argument for the Functional Development of International Organization*. New York: Oxford University Press. (Reprinted in 1966 as *A Working Peace System*. Chicago: Quadrangle Books.)

Moore, Christopher W. 1986. *The Mediation Process*. San Francisco: Jossey-Bass.

Montville, Joseph V. 1991. "Transnationalism and the Role of Track-Two Diplomacy." In *Approaches to Peace: An Intellectual Map*, ed. W. Scott Thompson and Kenneth M. Jensen. Washington, D.C.: United States Institute of Peace Press.

Nader, Laura, ed. 1965. "The Ethnography of the Law." Special issue, *American Anthropologist* 67 (6): part 2.

———. 1991. "Harmony Models and the Construction of Law." In *Conflict Resolution: Cross-Cultural Perspectives*, ed. Kevin Avruch, Peter W. Black, and Joseph A. Scimecca. New York: Greenwood.

O'Leary, Rosemary, and Lisa Bingham, eds. 2003. *The Promise and Performance of Environmental Conflict Resolution*. Washington, D.C.: Resources for the Future Press.

Osgood, Charles, 1962. *An Alternative to War or Surrender*. Urbana: University of Illinois Press.

Paris, Roland. 2004. *At War's End: Building Peace after Civil Conflict*. Cambridge, UK: Cambridge University Press.

Pentz, Michael J., and Gillian Slovo. 1981. "The Political Significance of Pugwash." In *Knowledge and Power in a Global Society*, ed. William M. Evan. Beverly Hills, Calif.: Sage.

Princen, Thomas. 1992. *Intermediaries in International Conflict*. Princeton, N.J.: Princeton University Press.

Putnam, Robert. 1988. "Diplomacy and Domestic Politics: The Logic of Two-Level Games." *International Organization* 42 (summer): 427–53.

Ramsbotham, Oliver, Tom Woodhouse, and Hugh Miall. 2005. *Contemporary Conflict Resolution*, 2nd ed. Cambridge, UK, and Malden, Mass.: Polity.

Rapoport, Anatol, and Albert M. Chammah. 1965. *The Prisoner's Dilemma: A Study in Conflict and Cooperation*. Ann Arbor: University of Michigan Press.

Ray, Larry. 1982. "The Alternative Dispute Resolution Movement." *Peace and Change* 8 (summer): 117–28.

Richardson, Lewis. 1960. *Statistics of Deadly Quarrels*. Pittsburgh: Boxwood.

Roethlisberger, Fritz Jules, and William J. Dickson. 1943. *Management and the Worker*. Cambridge, Mass.: Harvard University Press.

Ronfeldt, David, John Arquilla, Graham E. Fuller, and Melissa Fuller. 1998. *The Zapatista Social Netwar in Mexico*. Santa Monica, Calif.: RAND.

Ross, Marc Howard. 1993. *The Management of Conflict: Interpretations and Interests in Comparative Perspective*. New Haven, Conn.: Yale University Press.

Rouhana, Nadim N., and Herbert C. Kelman. 1994. "Promoting Joint Thinking in International Conflicts: An Israeli-Palestinian Continuing Workshop." *Journal of Social Issues* 50 (1): 157–78.

Rubenstein, Robert A., and Mary LeCron Foster, eds. 1988. *The Social Dynamics of Peace and Conflict*. Boulder, Colo.: Westview.

Salem, Paul, ed. 1997. *Conflict Resolution in the Arab World: Selected Essays*. Beirut: American University of Beirut.

Saunders, Harold H. 1995. "Sustained Dialogue on Tajikistan." *Mind and Human Interaction* 6: 123–35.

———. 1999. *A Public Peace Process: Sustained Dialogue to Transform Racial and Ethnic Conflicts*. New York: St. Martin's.

Scheff, Thomas J. 1994. *Bloody Revenge: Emotions, Nationalism, and War*. Boulder, Colo.: Westview.

Schelling, Thomas. 1960. *The Strategy of Conflict*. Cambridge, Mass.: Harvard University Press.

Scimecca, Joseph A. 1991. "Conflict Resolution in the United States: The Emergence of a Profession?" In *Conflict Resolution: Cross-Cultural Perspectives*, ed. Kevin Avruch, Peter W. Black, and Joseph A. Scimecca. New York: Greenwood.

Sharp, Gene. 1973. *The Politics of Nonviolent Action*. Boston: Porter Sargent.

Sharp, Gene. 2005. *Waging Nonviolent Struggle: 20th Century Practice and 21st Century Potential*. Boston: Porter Sargent.

Sherif, Muzafer. 1966. *In Common Predicament*. Boston: Houghton Mifflin.

Singer, J. David. 1972. "The Correlates of War Project: Interim Report." *World Politics* 24 (2): 243–70.

Singer, J. David, and Melvin Small. 1972. *The Wages of War, 1816–1965: A Statistical Handbook*. New York: John Wiley.

Smock, David R., ed. 2002. *Interfaith Dialogue and Peacebuilding*. Washington, D.C.: United States Institute of Peace Press.

Snyder, Glenn Herald, and Paul Diesing. 1977. *Conflict among Nations: Bargaining, Decision Making, and System Structure in International Crises*. Princeton, N.J.: Princeton University Press.

Stein, Janice Gross, ed. 1989. *Getting to the Table: The Processes of International Prenegotiation*. Baltimore: Johns Hopkins University Press.

Stephenson, Carolyn M. 1999. "Peace Studies: Overview." In *Encyclopedia of Violence, Peace, and Conflict*, vol. 2, ed. L. Kurtz, 809–20. San Diego, Calif.: Academic Press.

Susskind, Lawrence, and Jeffrey Cruickshank. 1987. *Breaking the Impasse: Consensual Approaches to Resolving Public Disputes*. New York: Basic Books.

Taylor, Anita, and Judi Beinstein Miller, eds. 1994. *Conflict and Gender*. Cresskill, N.J.: Hampton.

Tilly, Charles. 1978. *From Mobilization to Revolution*. Reading, Mass.: Addison-Wesley.

Toch, Hans. 1965. *The Social Psychology of Social Movements*, 2d ed. New York: Bobbs Merrill.

Touval, Saadia, and I. William Zartman, eds. 1985. *International Mediation in Theory and Practice*. Boulder, Colo.: Westview.

Ury, William L., Jeanne M. Brett, and Stephen B. Goldberg. 1988. *Getting Disputes Resolved*. San Francisco: Jossey-Bass.

Uwazie, Ernest, ed. 2003. *Conflict Resolution and Peace Education in Africa*. Lanham, Md.: Lexington Books.

van der Merwe, Hendrik. 1989. *Pursuing Justice and Peace in South Africa*. London and New York: Routledge.

Vasquez, John A. 1993. *The War Puzzle*. New York: Cambridge University Press.

Volkan, Vamik D. 1988. *The Need to Have Enemies and Allies*. Northvale, N.J.: Jason Aronson.

Wallensteen, Peter. 2002. *Understanding Conflict Resolution: War, Peace and the Global System*. London: Sage.

Walter, Barbara F. 2002. *Committing to Peace: The Successful Settlement of Civil Wars*. Princeton, N.J.: Princeton University Press.

Walter, Barbara F., and Jack Snyder, eds. 1999. *Civil Wars, Insecurity, and Intervention*. New York: Columbia University Press.

Wehr, Paul, Heidi Burgess, and Guy Burgess. 1994. *Justice without Violence*. Boulder, Colo.: Lynne Rienner.

Weiner, Eugene, ed. 1998. *The Handbook of Interethnic Coexistence*. New York: Continuum.

Wright, Quincy. 1942. *A Study of War*. Chicago: University of Chicago Press.

Zartman, I. William. 1987. *Positive Sum: Improving North-South Negotiations*. New York: Transaction.

———. 1985. *Ripe for Resolution: Conflict and Intervention in Africa*. New York: Oxford University Press.

———, ed. 1978. *The Negotiation Process: Theories and Applications*. Beverly Hills, Calif.: Sage.

———, ed. 1996. *Elusive Peace: Negotiating an End to Civil Wars*. Washington, D.C.: Brookings Institution Press.

Zartman, I. William, and Jeffrey Z. Rubin. 1996. *Power and Asymmetry in International Negotiations*. Laxenburg, Austria: International Institute of Applied Systems Analysis.

NOTE

1. Web sites are important sources of information about different approaches to the field and various arenas of research and practice (Carnevale and Probst 1997, 235–55). They also provide channels to the views of contending adversaries. Moreover, new information and communication technologies have significant implica-

tions for international conflict management, which are being assessed in the Virtual Diplomacy Initiative, sponsored by the United States Institute of Peace (see www.usip.org/oc/virtual_dipl.html; for access to a broad range of relevant material, see also the Conflict Resolution Information Source, www.crinfo.org).

2

SOCIAL-PSYCHOLOGICAL DIMENSIONS OF INTERNATIONAL CONFLICT

Herbert C. Kelman

Social-psychological concepts and findings have entered the mainstream of theory and research in international relations. Explorations of the social-psychological dimensions of international politics go back at least to the early 1930s (see Kelman 1965 for a review of the earlier history and a series of contributed chapters on various topics in the field; see also Kelman and Bloom 1973; Kelman 1991; Tetlock 1998 for reviews of later developments). Research on foreign policy decision making and the cognitive, group, and organizational factors that help to shape it (see Holsti 1989; Fischhoff 1991; Farnham 1992), negotiation and bargaining (see Druckman and Hopmann 1989; Rubin, Pruitt, and Kim 1994), enemy images (see Holt and Silverstein 1989), public opinion in the foreign policy process (see Russett 1989), deterrence and other forms of influence in international politics (see Stein 1991), and reconciliation (see Bar-Siman-Tov 2004) draws extensively on social-psychological research and theory.

Paralleling these theoretical and empirical developments, a new form of practice of international conflict resolution, anchored in social-psychological principles, has evolved over the past forty years. The approach derives from the pioneering work of John Burton (1969, 1979, 1984). My colleagues and I have used the term *interactive problem solving* to describe the approach (Kelman 1986, 1992a, 1996; Rouhana and Kelman 1994). Ronald Fisher and other scholars in the field have referred to it as *third-party consultation* (e.g., Fisher 1983, 1989) and more recently as *interactive conflict resolution* (Fisher 1997).

Under the latter title, Fisher reviews the history, central features, and procedures of this approach in his contribution to this volume.

This chapter offers a social-psychological perspective on the analysis and resolution of international conflict—a perspective based in social-psychological theory and research that, in turn, informs the practice of interactive conflict resolution described in chapter seven. A social-psychological analysis provides a special lens for viewing international relations in general and international conflict in particular. It is a different lens than that provided by the realist or the neorealist schools of international relations or other more traditional approaches that focus on structural or strategic factors. It may, therefore, help to explain certain phenomena for which other approaches cannot adequately account or introduce dimensions that these approaches have not considered. But a social-psychological approach is primarily designed to complement other approaches rather than substitute for them. It focuses on only some of the dimensions of what is clearly a large, multidimensional landscape.

Thus, I do not advocate a social-psychological theory of international relations or international conflict as a comprehensive alternative theory for the field. What is needed is a general theory of international relations, one in which analysis of the social-psychological dimensions is not merely an appendage, but an integral part. Several assumptions underlie this view.

First, psychological factors are pervasive in international conflict and international relations generally. Psychological processes at the individual and collective levels constitute and mediate much of the behavior of nations. Any general theory of international relations that fails to take them into account is therefore incomplete. Indeed, political analysts and actors invariably make assumptions about such psychological processes—for example, when they talk about risk taking, decision making, intentions, reactions to threats or incentives, or the role of public opinion. Psychological analysis addresses such assumptions explicitly, critically, and systematically.

Second, the most relevant contributions of psychological analysis are at the social-psychological level. To be sure, general psychological processes—such as those concerned with cognitive functioning, reactions to stress, or the behavioral effects of reward and punishment—explain the behavior of decision makers and other individual actors in international affairs; but these individuals act within organized social structures. Social psychology provides the appropriate framework for analyzing such behavior because it focuses on phenomena at the intersection of psychological and institutional processes: social interaction and the relationship of individuals to social systems.

Third, "psychological" is not the opposite of "real." Psychological analysis of a conflict in no way implies that the conflict is unreal, a mere product of misperception or misunderstanding. In examining the emotional or cognitive processes in a conflict relationship, one does not presume that these processes are unrealistic or irrational. The degree of realism or rationality varies from situation to situation. Indeed, psychological analysis is often concerned with enhancing the realism of perception (e.g., White 1984) or the rationality of decision making (e.g., Janis 1982). On the other hand, psychological analysis is based on the assumption that subjective factors play a role in the perception and interpretation of events. In a conflict relationship, such subjective elements may exacerbate the conflict by generating differences in the way the parties perceive reality and by imposing constraints on the rational pursuit of their interests.

Fourth, though pervasive and important, psychological factors must always be understood in context. International conflict and its resolution must be conceived as societal and intersocietal processes that come about through the actions and interactions of large numbers of individuals who, in turn, function through a variety of groups and organizations and who are propelled by collective moods and states of consciousness with deep historical and ideological roots. Historical, geopolitical, and structural factors provide the context and set the constraints for the operation of psychological factors.

Finally, therefore, the contribution of a social-psychological perspective to understanding international conflict depends on identifying the appropriate points of entry for psychological analysis—those points in a theory of international relations where social-psychological propositions may provide particularly relevant levers for theoretical explanation. But it always must be kept in mind that these are points of entry into a larger theoretical framework that is multidimensional. A parallel assumption, at the level of practice, underlies interactive problem solving or similar social-psychologically based forms of unofficial diplomacy. Such approaches can make significant contributions to conflict resolution and ought to become integral parts of a comprehensive model of diplomacy. They do not, however, provide an alternative to official diplomacy or a substitute for binding negotiations. Their value depends on identifying the appropriate points of entry into the larger diplomatic process where they can make a relevant contribution—for example, by providing opportunities for nonbinding exploration of options or creative reframing of issues.

Proceeding on the above assumptions, this chapter undertakes two tasks. It begins with a discussion of several propositions about the nature of international conflict that flow from a social-psychological perspective and that have clear implications for conflict resolution. It then describes social-psychological processes characteristic of conflict interaction that contribute to the escalation and perpetuation of conflict and that must be reversed if the conflict is to be resolved.

THE NATURE OF INTERNATIONAL CONFLICT

A social-psychological perspective suggests certain propositions about the nature of international conflict that expand on the view of the phenomenon emerging from more traditional approaches, such as the realist school of international relations. The four propositions discussed in this section are particularly relevant to existential conflicts between identity groups—conflicts in which the collective identities of the parties are engaged and in which the continued existence of the group is seen to be at stake. Thus, these propositions apply most directly to ethnic and ideological conflicts, but they also apply to more mundane interstate conflicts insofar as issues of national identity and existence come into play—as they often do.

- First, international conflict is a *process driven by collective needs and fears*, rather than entirely a product of rational calculation of objective national interests on the part of political decision makers.
- Second, international conflict is an *intersocietal process*, not only an interstate or intergovernmental phenomenon.
- Third, international conflict is a a *multifaceted process of mutual influence*, not only a contest in the exercise of coercive power.
- Fourth, international conflict is an *interactive process with an escalatory, self-perpetuating dynamic*, not merely a sequence of actions and reactions by stable actors.

Thus, without denying the importance of objectively anchored national interests, the primacy of the state in the international system, the role of power in international relations, and the effect of structural factors in determining the course of an international conflict, a social-psychological perspective enriches the analysis of international relations in a variety of ways: by exploring the subjective factors that set constraints on rationality; by opening the "black box" of the state as a unitary actor and analyzing the processes within and between societies that underlie state action; by broadening the range of influence processes (and, indeed, of definitions of power) that play a role in international politics; and by conceiving of international conflict as a dynamic process, shaped by changing realities, changing interests, and changing relationships between the conflicting parties.

Conflict as a Process Driven by Collective Needs and Fears

International or ethnic conflict must be conceived as a process in which collective human needs and fears are acted out in powerful ways. Such conflict is typically driven by nonfulfillment or threats to the fulfillment of basic needs.

These needs include not only obvious material ones, such as food, shelter, physical safety, and physical well-being, but also psychological needs, such as identity, security, recognition, autonomy, self-esteem, and a sense of justice (Burton 1990). "Need," as used here, is an individual-level concept; needs are attributes of individual human beings. But insofar as these needs become driving forces in international and intergroup conflict, they are needs of individuals articulated through important identity groups. The link of needs to groups—their collective aspect—is an important and almost ubiquitous feature of human needs. The fulfillment of needs takes place to a considerable extent within the context of groups of different sizes. The ethnic group, the national group, and the state are among the collectivities that serve as important vehicles for fulfilling and protecting fundamental needs.

Closely related to these basic needs in intergroup conflict situations are fears about the denial of such needs—fears focusing, for example, on perceived threats to security or identity. In protracted conflicts between identity groups, such fears often take on an existential character, turning the conflict into a struggle over group survival. The Israeli-Palestinian conflict, for example, can be described as an existential conflict between two parties, each of which sees its very existence as a national group at stake in the conflict (Kelman 1987, 2001).

Identity, security, and similarly powerful collective needs, and the fears and concerns about survival associated with them, are often important causal factors in intergroup and intercommunal conflict. The causes of conflict generally combine objective and subjective factors, which are related to each other in a circular fashion. Conflicts focusing, for example, on issues such as territory and resources almost invariably reflect and further magnify underlying concerns about security and identity. But, whatever their role in the causation of a conflict, subjective forces linked to basic needs and existential fears contribute heavily to the conflict's escalation and perpetuation. Such needs and fears create a resistance to change even in situations in which both parties, or significant elements of both parties, have concluded that it is in their best interests to end the conflict. Despite this perceived interest, the parties are often unable to extricate themselves from the escalatory dynamic in which they are caught up.

Exploration of collective needs and fears is particularly helpful in understanding why it is so difficult for parties to change course in conflicts that have become increasingly destructive and detrimental to their interests. Although the parties may recognize that it is to their advantage to find a negotiated solution, they are afraid to go to the negotiating table. Or, having reluctantly gone to the table, they are afraid to make the necessary concessions or accommodations for the negotiations to move forward. They worry that once they enter negotiations, or—having entered negotiations—once they make certain concessions, they will find themselves on a slippery slope: that they will inexorably be moving, concession after concession, toward an outcome that will leave their very existence compromised. In short, the sense that their identity, security, and existence as a national group are at stake contributes heavily to their resistance to negotiation or to accommodation in the course of negotiations.

The role of such existential fears and needs is more pronounced in ethnic conflicts than in the kinds of interstate conflicts with which traditional theories of international politics have been concerned. But collective needs and fears play a part in all international conflicts and lie behind what are usually described as national interests—essentially the interests perceived by elites who control the operative definition of the national interest. These perceptions are heavily influenced by objective factors. The fact that a state, for example, lacks certain essential resources, or has an ethnically divided population, or has no access to the sea, obviously plays a role in how the elites define the state's interests. But such objective factors always combine with subjective factors to determine how different segments of a society perceive state interests and what ultimately becomes the national interest as defined by the dominant elites. The subjective determinants of perceived national interests are the collective needs and fears of the society, as interpreted by the political leadership and other elites.

Similarly, it can be assumed that all conflicts represent a combination of rational and irrational factors. Ethnic conflicts, though often portrayed as uniquely irrational, resemble conflicts between states and even between superpowers in that regard. Moreover, across cases within each type of conflict, the mix of rational and irrational elements may vary. Some ethnic conflicts may be preponderantly rational, just as some interstate conflicts may be preponderantly irrational.

In all international conflicts, the needs and fears of populations are mobilized and often manipulated by the leadership. Collective needs and fears are typically linked to individual needs and fears. For example, in ethnic conflicts characterized by a high level of violence, the fear of annihilation of one's group is often (and for good reason) tied to a fear of personal annihilation. Insofar as these personally tinged collective needs and fears are mobilized, they become the focus of collective action within a society. The mobilization and manipulation of collective needs and fears vary in the degree of demagoguery and cynicism they involve, but they are always seen as necessary tasks of leaders in a conflict situation. Furthermore, though mobilized and often manipulated, collective needs and fears must be viewed as real and authentic reactions within the population.

What does this conception of conflict as a process driven by collective needs and fears imply for conflict resolution? First, it follows from this view that genuine conflict resolution must address these needs and fears. If a conflict is to be resolved, in the sense of leading to a stable peace that both sides consider just and to a new relationship that is mutually enhancing and contributes to the welfare and development of the two societies, the solution must satisfy the fundamental needs and allay the deepest fears of the affected populations. The objective of conflict resolution is not to eliminate the conflict entirely, which is neither possible nor desirable as a general goal (because conflicts are potentially constructive forces within a society or region and serve as the basis for essential social change); rather, it is to eliminate the violent and otherwise destructive manifestations of conflict. But even these destructive elements cannot be made to disappear overnight in conflicts that have been pursued for many years—in some cases, for generations—and are marked by accumulated memories that are constantly being revived by new events and experiences. Conflict resolution does not imply that past grievances and historical traumas have been forgotten and a consistently harmonious relationship has been put in place. It simply implies that a process has been set into motion that addresses the central needs and fears of the societies and establishes continuing mechanisms to confront them.

From a normative point of view, the ultimate criterion for a successful, mutually satisfactory solution of a conflict is that it address the fundamental needs of both parties. Thus, what negotiation theorists mean by a win-win solution in a protracted conflict between identity groups is a solution that has, in fact, spoken—however imperfectly—to such needs and the fears associated with them: a solution in which neither side is required to sacrifice what it considers to be a vital need and both are reassured with respect to their deepest fears. It is in the search for such solutions that justice enters the picture in nonadversarial approaches to conflict resolution, such as interactive problem solving. Problem-solving workshops, for example, are governed by a no-fault principle, which eschews efforts to establish who is right and who is wrong from a legal or a moral standpoint. Although the parties' differing views of rights and wrongs must be discussed because they contribute significantly to the dynamics of the conflict, the assumption is that the parties cannot find a solution by adjudicating these differing views. Rather, they must move toward a solution by jointly discovering mutually satisfactory ways of dealing with the issues that divide them. Insofar as they arrive at a solution that addresses the fundamental needs of both parties, justice is being done—not perfect justice, but enough to ensure the prospects for a durable peace. Thus, commitment to a solution that is responsive to the basic concerns of the two parties is the operationalization of justice in a problem-solving approach (Kelman 1996).

An interesting implication of a human-needs orientation, first noted by John Burton (1988), is that the psychological or ontological needs on which it focuses—needs such as identity, security, or recognition—are not inherently zero-sum. One party need not gain its identity or security at the expense of another. In fact, much of the new thinking about security, exemplified by the concept of common security, is based on the proposition that each party's security is enhanced by the security of the other. Similarly, in a context of mutual recognition, the identity of one is enhanced by the identity of the other (Kelman 1987, 358). In intense conflicts, of course, there is a strong tendency to see these needs as zero-sum and to assume that one's own security and identity can be protected or enhanced only by depriving the other of security and identity. But because these needs are not by nature mutually exclusive, addressing them may offer possibilities for a mutually satisfactory solution. If the parties can probe behind their incompatible positions and explore the underlying needs that engender these positions, they may be able to shape an integrative solution that satisfies both sets of needs. Once such underlying needs have been addressed, issues such as territory or resources—which are more inherently zero-sum in nature (although also susceptible to creative reframing)—can then be settled through distributive bargaining.

A final implication of the view that conflict is driven by collective needs and fears relates to the question of when the individual becomes the appropriate unit of analysis in international relations. Though the needs and fears that drive conflict are collectively expressed and must be satisfied at the collective level, they are experienced at the level of individual human beings. To address such needs and fears, therefore, conflict resolution must, at some stage, provide for certain processes that take place at the level of individuals and the interaction between individuals. One such process is realistic empathy (White 1984), or taking the perspective of the other, which is essential to any effort to move toward an accommodation that takes into account the needs and fears of both parties. Empathy develops in the interaction between individuals, and it is in the minds of individuals that the perspective of the other has to be represented somehow. Creative problem solving is another example of a process essential to conflict resolution that takes place in the minds of individuals and in the interaction between them as they move from analyzing the causes of a conflict to generating new ideas for resolving it. Insight and learning are further examples of individual-level processes that need to be part of a larger effort at conflict resolution. Problem-solving workshops and similar conflict-resolution activities provide a setting in which such processes can occur. They contribute to the larger process of conflict resolution by creating, through the interaction between the participating individuals, new insights and ideas that can be exported into the political debate and the decision-making processes within the conflicting societies. Thus, a problem-solving workshop can be thought of as a laboratory—indeed, as a workshop in the literal sense of the word—where a product is being created for export. Essentially, workshops represent a special microprocess that provides inputs into the macroprocess of conflict resolution.

Conflict as an Intersocietal Process

A focus on the needs and fears of the populations involved in conflict readily brings to mind a second social-psychological proposition: that international conflict is not merely an intergovernmental or interstate phenomenon, but an intersocietal phenomenon. The conflict, particularly in the case of protracted ethnic struggles, becomes an inescapable part of daily life for the members of the opposing communities. The conflict pervades the whole society and its component elements—not only when it takes the form of explicit violence, but even when the violence is muted. Thus, analysis of conflict requires attention not only to its strategic, military, and diplomatic dimensions, but also to its economic, psychological, cultural, and social-structural dimensions. Interactions along these dimensions, both within and between the conflicting societies, shape the political environment in which governments function. Intrasocietal and intersocietal processes define the political constraints under which governments operate and the resistance to change that these produce. For example, leaders' attempts to respond to public moods, to shape public opinion, and to mobilize group loyalties often feed the conflict and reduce the options for conflict resolution.

A view of conflict as a process that occurs between two societies immediately prompts us to examine what happens within each society. In particular, this view alerts us to the role of internal divisions within each society. Although theories of international relations often treat states as unitary actors, the societies that states or other political organizations represent are never monolithic entities. Every political community is divided in various ways, and these internal divisions often play a major role in exacerbating or even creating conflicts between such political communities. The course of an intergroup conflict typically reflects the intragroup conflicts within both conflicting groups, which impose constraints on the political leaders. Leaders pursuing a policy of accommodation must consider the reactions of opposition elements, who may accuse them of betraying the national cause or jeopardizing the nation's existence. They also must be responsive to the anxieties and doubts within the general population, which opposition elements foster and from which they draw support. In all these ways, internal divisions introduce severe constraints on efforts at conflict resolution.

Although the intersocietal nature of conflict contributes to its perpetuation, it also creates certain necessities and opportunities for conflict resolution. The internal divisions within each society do indeed impose serious constraints on decision makers in the pursuit of peaceful solutions, but they also provide them with potential levers for change. Such divisions challenge the monolithic image of the enemy that parties in conflict tend to hold and enable parties to deal with each other in a more differentiated way. They can come to recognize that even in a community mobilized for violent conflict, there may be elements amenable to an alternative approach who are potential partners for negotiation. This reality provides the opportunity, for example, of forming coalitions across conflict lines—coalitions between elements on each side that are interested in negotiation. Indeed, problem-solving workshops and related activities can be conceptualized as part of a process of forming precisely such a coalition (Kelman 1993). A coalition across the conflict line, however, must of necessity remain an uneasy coalition. If it becomes overly cohesive, its members will lose their ability to influence the political decision making within their respective communities. By becoming too closely identified with their counterparts on the other side, coalition members might become alienated from their own conationals, lose credibility at home, and hence forfeit their political effectiveness and ability to contribute to another important precondition for conflict resolution: the development of a new consensus for a negotiated solution within their own community. If coalitions across conflict lines remain sensitive to the need to maintain the members' separate group identities and credibility at home, they represent a potentially effective way to capitalize on the divisions within the conflicting societies in the interest of conflict resolution, peacemaking, and, ultimately, building a new relationship between the former enemies.

Another implication of an intersocietal view of conflict is that negotiations and third-party efforts ideally should be directed not merely to a political settlement of the conflict in the form of a brokered political agreement, but to its resolution. A political agreement may be adequate for terminating relatively specific, containable interstate disputes, but it is inadequate for conflicts that engage the collective identities and existential concerns of the societies involved. Conflict resolution in this deeper, more lasting sense implies arrangements and accommodations that emerge out of the interactions between the parties themselves, that address the needs of both parties, and to which the parties feel committed. An agreement that is not widely accepted within the two societies is unlikely to lead to a durable peace. What is required, in short, is a gradual process conducive to change in structures and attitudes, to reconciliation, and to the transformation of the relationship between the two societies—the development of a new relationship that recognizes the interdependence of the conflicting societies and is open to cooperative, functional arrangements between them. The real test of conflict resolution in deep-rooted conflicts is how much the process by which agreements are constructed and the nature of those agreements contribute to transforming the relationship between the parties (Kelman 1999a).

Finally, a corollary of an intersocietal analysis of conflict is a view of diplomacy as a complex mix of official and unofficial, formal and informal efforts with complementary contributions. The peaceful termination or management of conflict requires binding agreements that can be achieved only at the official level. But insofar as we think of conflict as not only an interstate but also an intersocietal affair, many different sectors of the two societies must be fruitfully involved in a more elaborate, integrated process of diplomacy. In this context, unofficial, noncommittal interactions can play a complementary role by exploring ways of overcoming obstacles to conflict resolution and helping to create a political environment conducive to negotiation and other diplomatic initiatives (Saunders 1988).

Conflict as a Multifaceted Process of Mutual Influence

Much of international politics entails mutual influence, whereby each party seeks to protect and promote its own interests by shaping the behavior of the other. Conflict occurs when these interests clash: when attainment of one party's interests (and fulfillment of the needs that underlie them) threatens, or is perceived to threaten, the interests (and needs) of the other. In pursuing the conflict, therefore, the parties engage in mutual influence, designed to advance their own positions and block the adversary's. Similarly, in conflict resolution—by negotiation or other means—the parties exercise influence to induce the adversary to come to the table, to make concessions, to accept an agreement that meets their interests and needs, and to live up to that agreement. Third parties, too, exercise influence in conflict situations by backing one or the other party, mediating between them, or maneuvering to protect their own interests.

The typical influence process in international conflict relies on a mixture of threats and inducements, although the balance between negative and positive incentives varies considerably from case to case. Political analysts and decision makers often rely heavily, if not exclusively, on the use and threat of force to exert influence on adversaries. Thus, the U.S.-Soviet relationship during the Cold War was framed largely in terms of an elaborate theory of deterrence—a form of influence designed to keep the other side from doing what you do not want it to do (see George and Smoke 1974; Jervis, Lebow, and Stein 1985; Schelling 1963; and Stein 1991). In other conflict relationships, the emphasis may be on compellence—a form of influence designed to make the other side do what you want it to do. Such coercive strategies are part of the repertoire of influence processes in all domains of social life, but they entail serious costs and risks, and their effects may be severely limited. For example, they are likely to be reciprocated by the other side and thus lead to escalation of the conflict, and they are unlikely to change behavior to which the other is committed.

Thus, the effective exercise of influence in international conflict requires broadening the repertoire of influence strategies, at least to the extent of combining "carrots and sticks"—of supplementing the negative incentives that typically dominate international conflict relationships with positive incentives (see, e.g., Baldwin 1971; Kriesberg 1981, 1982). Positive incentives may take the form of economic benefits, sharing essential resources, international approval, integration in regional or global institutions, or a general reduction in the level of tension. They are particularly effective if they meet the other's interests or respond to the other's security concerns that are at the heart of the conflict, and if they are part of a concerted strategy that invites reciprocation. An example of an approach based on the systematic use of positive incentives is Osgood's (1962) Graduated Reciprocation in Tension Reduction (GRIT) strategy. In his 1977 trip to Jerusalem, Egyptian president Anwar Sadat used a variant of this strategy by undertaking a unilateral initiative based on the expectation (partly prenegotiated) of Israeli reciprocation (Kelman 1985). But unlike the GRIT strategy, which starts with small concessions and gradually builds on them, Sadat's strategy in effect started at the end: "He made a massive, fundamental concession by accepting the basic principles of Israel's position . . . in the anticipation that negotiations would fill in the intervening steps" (Kelman 1985, 216). GRIT, the Sadat initiative, and other strategies based on positive incentives have the potential of transforming a conflict into a new relationship in which both parties' needs and interests are met and continuing differences are resolved by peaceful means.

The view of influence as a multifaceted process emphasizes positive inducements as a useful complement to the negative inducements that predominate in international conflict—as a strategy that often entails smaller short-term risks and greater long-term benefits than the use or threat of force.

But it goes further: it also provides a framework for identifying the *types* of positive inducements that are most likely to be effective. Effective use of positive incentives requires more than offering the other party whatever rewards, promises, or confidence-building measures seem most readily available. It requires actions that address the fundamental needs and fears of the other party. Thus, the key to an effective influence strategy based on the exchange of positive incentives is responsiveness to the other's concerns. The parties influence each other by actively exploring ways in which they can help meet each other's needs and allay each other's fears. Responsiveness also implies sensitivity to the other's constraints. It requires that both parties explore ways to help each other overcome the constraints within their respective societies against taking the actions that each wants the other to take. Responsiveness to the other's needs and fears is a fairly common form of influence in normal social relations. It is not, however, a strategy that parties in conflict are normally inclined to use, because it requires them to explore and carry out actions designed to benefit the adversary.

The advantage of a strategy of responsiveness is that it alerts parties to ways of exerting influence on the other through their own actions—through positive steps (not threats) that are within their own capacity to take. The process is greatly facilitated by communication between the parties to identify actions that are politically feasible and perhaps not even especially costly to one party, but are likely to have an impact on the other. Ultimately, the effectiveness of a strategy of responsiveness depends on careful adherence to the principle of reciprocity. One-sided responsiveness cannot sustain itself for long.

A key element in an influence strategy based on responsiveness is *mutual reassurance*, which is particularly critical in any effort to resolve an existential conflict. For example, how can the parties to such a conflict be induced to come to the negotiating table and, once there, to make the concessions necessary to reach an agreement? For parties afraid that negotiations and concessions might jeopardize their national existence, mutual reassurance is a major motivating force—along with a mutually hurting stalemate and mutual enticements.

Negative incentives clearly play a significant role. The negotiation literature suggests that parties are often driven to the table by a mutually hurting stalemate, which makes negotiations more attractive than continuing the conflict (Zartman and Berman 1982; Touval and Zartman 1985, 16). Thus, one way of inducing an adversary to negotiate is to make the conflict more painful through the use of threats, military pressure, or other coercive means. But reliance on such negative incentives has many liabilities: it may push the parties to the table, but does not necessarily make for productive negotiations once they get there; and it may reduce the likelihood of achieving an agreement that is mutually satisfactory and desirable. Therefore, negative incentives must at least be complemented by positive ones through what Zartman has called "mutual enticement" (see, e.g., Zartman and Aurik 1991).

But parties engaged in existential conflicts are afraid to move to the negotiating table and make concessions even when the status quo has become increasingly painful and they recognize that a negotiated agreement is in their interest. They worry that negotiations may lead to ever more costly concessions that will ultimately jeopardize their security, their national identity, and their very existence. To advance the negotiating process under such circumstances, it is at least as important to reduce the parties' fears as it is to increase their pain.

Mutual reassurance can take the form of acknowledgments, symbolic gestures, or confidence-building measures. To be maximally effective, such steps need to address the other's central needs and fears as directly as possible. When President Sadat spoke to the Israeli Knesset during his dramatic visit to Jerusalem in November 1977, he acknowledged that in the past Egypt had rejected Israel, refused to meet with Israelis, refused to exchange greetings. By clearly acknowledging the past hostility and thus validating the Israelis' own experiences, he greatly enhanced the credibility of the change in course that he was announcing. These remarks helped to reassure the Israeli public that his offer was sincere and not just a trick to extract concessions that would weaken Israel's position in the continuing confrontation.

At the opening of this visit, Sadat offered a symbolic gesture that had an electrifying effect on Israelis: as he stepped off the plane, he engaged in a round of cordial handshakes with the Israeli officials who had come to greet him. The refusal of Arab officials to shake the hands of their Israeli counterparts had been profoundly disturbing to Israelis throughout the years of the conflict. It symbolized Arab denial of Israel's legitimacy and the very humanity of its people. Sadat's gesture spoke directly to this deep hurt and signaled the beginning of a new relationship (cf. Kelman 2005).

Confidence-building measures may consist of any acts that respond to the other's demands or accrue to the other's benefit. Again, however, they are particularly effective when they address major grievances and demonstrate sensitivity to the other's fundamental concerns. Thus, for example, the dismantling of settlements or the closing of military installations and withdrawal of Israeli troops anywhere in the occupied territories—even if they are limited in scope—are concrete indicators to Palestinians that the peace process might ultimately lead to an end to the occupation and thus reassure them that their leaders have not embarked on a course that threatens their national aspirations.

Acknowledgments often have a powerful psychological impact in opening the way to negotiation and accommodation, even though they are verbal statements that may not be immediately translated into concrete actions (Pearson 1990). "Acknowledgment" in this context refers to a party's public acceptance or confirmation of the other party's view of its status, its experience, its reality. Thus, one party may acknowledge the other's humanity, nationhood, national rights, suffering, grievances, interpretation of its history, authentic links to disputed lands, or commitment to peace. Such acknowledgments do not constitute acceptance of the other's position or accession to its claims, but at least they serve to recognize that there is some legitimacy to these positions and claims and some basis for them in the other's experience. Acknowledgments have such a potentially powerful impact because the history of a conflict is often marked by the systematic denial of the other's experience, authenticity, legitimacy, and even membership in the human family. These denials create profound fear and insecurity because they undermine the very foundations of the other's claim to nationhood and challenge the other's right to national existence. Acknowledgment of what was heretofore denied is thus an important source of reassurance to the recipients, because it signals that the other side, having accepted the legitimacy of their claims, may indeed be ready to negotiate an agreement that addresses their fundamental concerns. Under these circumstances, the parties are likely to feel safer about entering negotiations, despite the risks and uncertainties, and to make significant concessions. An example of this kind of acknowledgment was Israel's and the Palestine Liberation Organization's (PLO) mutual recognition in the September 1993 Oslo Accords, which helped create a breakthrough in Israeli-Palestinian negotiations (which, at the time of this writing, are unfortunately derailed).

Apart from persuading the parties that their fundamental concerns will be addressed in the negotiations, acknowledgments may play a more subtle role in reassuring parties that it is now safe to end the conflict even if major concessions are required. Acknowledgments do this insofar as they confirm the parties' "national narratives." A central element of the Palestinian narrative, for example, is that the establishment of Israel constituted a profound injustice to the Palestinian people, who were displaced, dispossessed, dispersed, and deprived of their society and their future. An Israeli acknowledgment of that injustice, by confirming the Palestinians' national narrative, might allow them to let go of the conflict and accept a compromise solution even though it would not fully remove the injustice they feel. Ultimately, the acknowledgment would vindicate the Palestinians' view of history, thus providing a justification for accepting a pragmatic approach so they can end the struggle and go on with their lives. By contrast, a central element of the Israeli national narrative holds that the establishment of Israel was an act of historical justice that enabled the Jewish people to return to its ancestral homeland after centuries of dispersion and persecution. A Palestinian acknowledgment of the Jewish people's historic roots in the land, by confirming the Israelis' national narrative, might enable them to let go of their claim to exclusive ownership of the land and accept a formula for sharing it with the Palestinians. Again, the acknowledgment would vindicate their view of history and thus provide a justification for accepting the reality of the Palestinian presence and putting an end to the conflict.

In sum, acknowledgments provide reassurance at the levels of both security and identity. By signaling acceptance of the other's legitimacy, each party reassures the other that negotiations and concessions no longer constitute mortal threats to its security and national existence. By confirming the other's national narrative, each reassures the other that a compromise does not represent an abandonment of its identity, which is articulated by its national narrative.

Acknowledgments with the capacity to reassure the other are difficult to formulate because national narratives of the conflicting parties typically clash. In confirming the narrative of the other, each party risks undermining its own narrative. Therefore, the parties often need to "negotiate" their acknowledgments with each other (perhaps in the context of a problem-solving workshop)—that is, engage in a joint process of formulating statements that will reassure the recipient without threatening the issuer (Kelman 1992b, 2001). The effectiveness of other forms of mutual reassurance, such as symbolic gestures and confidence-building measures, may be similarly enhanced if they are generated through such an informal "negotiation" process, in which the impact on the recipient and the constraints of the issuer can be considered jointly and balanced. A critical criterion for the maximal effectiveness of acknowledgments, gestures, and confidence-building measures is careful adherence to the principle of reciprocity. Reassuring the other is rarely cost free; the reassurance involves some concession—or at least is perceived to do so—and it often generates some domestic criticism. Thus, it is important that reassurance occur in a context in which the initiator receives a visible return. Reciprocity itself is a source of mutual reassurance in that it signals to the parties that their concessions will not simply be pocketed by the other, but are likely to advance their own interests.

An influence strategy based on responsiveness to each other's needs and fears and the resulting search for ways of reassuring and benefiting each other has important advantages from a long-term point of view. It does not merely elicit specific desired behaviors from the other party, but it can contribute to a creative redefinition of the conflict, joint discovery of mutually satisfactory solutions, and transformation of the relationship between the parties. In terms of my earlier distinction among three processes of social influence (Kelman 1961; Kelman and Hamilton 1989; see also Rubin 1989), a strategy of mutual responsiveness is likely to have an impact that goes beyond compliance, inducing changes at the level of identification and potentially at the level of internalization.

Positive incentives per se have an advantage over negative incentives in that they create an atmosphere more conducive to negotiation and provide greater opportunities for building a new relationship. But if promises, rewards, and confidence-building measures are offered randomly—essentially as "bribes"—without reference to the recipient's underlying needs and fears, they are likely to induce change only at the level of compliance (i.e., a relatively unstable change in public behavior without accompanying changes in private beliefs).

On the other hand, if positive incentives are used as part of a systematic strategy of responsiveness and reciprocity, they help develop a working trust and a valued relationship between the parties—a relationship that can be described as a pragmatic partnership. The relationship becomes an incentive in its own right, in that the parties will be inclined to live up to each other's expectations in order to maintain and extend their new relationship. In this case, the resulting influence can be said to be at the level of identification: the parties are likely to change not only their public behavior, but also their private attitudes and beliefs—at least as long as the relationship remains salient. Identification-based attitudes, however, tend to develop alongside the old attitudes without being fully integrated into a new worldview. Thus, the new relationship remains vulnerable to changes in interests, circumstances, and leadership, which may trigger the old attitudes—including fundamental distrust of the other—in their full force (Kelman 2004, 2006).

As parties develop a relationship based on responsiveness and reciprocity, they become better able to approach their conflict as a shared dilemma that requires joint efforts at analysis and problem solving. A joint problem-solving approach is conducive to agreements that are inherently satisfactory to the parties because they meet their fundamental needs, and are lasting because they create a sense of ownership and commitment. The negotiation and implementation of such agreements can be characterized as changes at the level of internalization: changes in behavior and beliefs that are congruent with the parties' own values and are relatively stable and enduring. The gradual transformation of the parties' relationship, which makes these changes possible, becomes a key element of the mutually satisfactory and stable (i.e., "internalized") outcome of a successful negotiation.

Change at the level of internalization becomes more likely insofar as the process and outcome of negotiations include significant elements of reconciliation. Reconciliation, as defined here, goes beyond conflict resolution in that it represents a change in each party's identity (Kelman 2004). The main feature of that change in identity is removal of the negation of the other as a central component of the group's own identity—i.e., revision of each group's narrative so that it can accommodate the identity of the other. "Reconciliation, with its attendant change in the group's identity and revision of its narrative, becomes possible only if the core of each group's identity is confirmed in the process" (Kelman 2006, 23). This is the essence of the process of "negotiating" the mutual acknowledgment of the other's identity (Kelman 1992b, 2001). If the groups can overcome the negative interdependence of their identities—the negation of each other's identity—they can build on the positive interdependence of their identities that often characterizes groups living in close proximity to each other (Kelman 1999b). As a consequence, their new relationship will be less vulnerable to situational changes.

Conflict as an Interactive Process with an Escalatory, Self-Perpetuating Dynamic

Conflict is an interactive process, in which the parties change as they act and react in relation to each other. In intense conflict relationships, the natural course of the interaction tends to reinforce and deepen the conflict, rather than reduce and resolve it. The interaction is governed by a set of norms and guided by a set of images that create an escalatory, self-perpetuating dynamic. This dynamic can be reversed through skillful diplomacy, imaginative leadership, third-party intervention, and institutionalized mechanisms for managing and resolving conflict. But in the absence of such deliberate efforts, the spontaneous interaction between the parties is likely to increase distrust, hostility, and the sense of grievance.

The needs and fears of parties engaged in intense conflict impose perceptual and cognitive constraints on their processing of new information, with the resulting tendency to underestimate the occurrence and the possibility of change. In normal human relations, social interaction is the way in which people determine what others need and expect, assess the occurrence and possibility of change in these needs and expectations, and adjust their own behavior accordingly. By accommodating to each other's needs and expectations, both participants are able to advance the achievement of their respective goals. An essential feature of social interaction is the effort to take account of the other's purposes, perceptions, intentions, and expectations by implicitly taking the role of the other on the assumption that the other has a mind like one's own, with similar kinds of purposes, perceptions, intentions, and expectations. In intense conflict relationships, this ability to take the role of the other is severely impaired. Dehumanization of the enemy makes it even more difficult to acknowledge and gain access to the other's perspective.

The inaccessibility of the other's perspective contributes significantly to some of the psychological barriers to conflict resolution described by Ross and Ward (1995). The dynamics of conflict interaction tend to entrench the parties firmly in their own perspectives on history and justice. Conflicting parties manifest particularly strong tendencies to seek out evidence that confirms their negative images of each other and to resist evidence that counters these images. Thus, interaction not only fails to contribute to a revision of the enemy image, but actually helps to reinforce and perpetuate it. The combination of demonic enemy images and virtuous self-images leads to the formation of mirror images (see, e.g., Bronfenbrenner 1961; White 1965), which greatly contributes to the escalatory dynamic of conflict interaction, as exemplified by the classic pattern of an arms race. When one side increases its arms and takes other actions that it considers defensive, the other interprets these steps as preparation for aggression and proceeds to increase its arms—presumably in defense against the other's intended aggression. The first side, however, interprets these steps in turn as preparation for aggression and further increases its arms, which further persuades the second party of the other's aggressive intentions—and thus a conflict spiral is set into motion. Interaction guided by such mirror images of enemy and self creates self-fulfilling prophecies by inducing the parties to engage in the hostile actions they expect from one another.

Self-fulfilling prophecies are also generated by the conflict norms that typically govern the interaction between parties engaged in an intense conflict. Expressions in word and action of hostility and distrust toward the enemy are not just spontaneous manifestations of the conflict, but are normatively prescribed behaviors. Both leaders and publics operate under norms that require them to be militant and unyielding vis-à-vis the other side, accuse the other of misdeeds, remain suspicious of their intentions, and deny all justice to their cause. Political leaders assume that their public's evaluation of them depends on their adherence to these norms and may go out of their way to avoid appearing weak or gullible. These tendencies are reflected in the leaders' tactical and strategic decisions, the way they approach negotiations with the other side, their public pronouncements, and, ultimately, the way they educate their own publics. For the public, in turn, adherence to these norms is often taken as an indication of group loyalty; those who acknowledge that there may be some justice on the other side or propose a conciliatory posture may expose themselves to accusations of treason or at least naiveté.

In short, the discourse in deep-rooted conflicts is marked by mutual dele-gitimization and dehumanization. Interaction governed by this set of norms—at the micro- and the macrolevels—contributes to escalation and perpetua-tion of the conflict. Parties that systematically treat each other with hostility and distrust are likely to become increasingly hateful and untrustworthy.

The dynamics of conflict interaction create a high probability that oppor-tunities for conflict resolution will be missed. As realities change in the inter-national, regional, or domestic environment, the parties in a long-standing conflict may well become amenable to compromise. There may be possibilities for resolving the conflict in ways that are mutually satisfactory—or at least preferable to continuing the struggle. But parties caught up in the conflict dy-namics, whose interaction is shaped by the norms and images rooted in the history of the conflict, are systematically constrained in their capacity to re-spond to the occurrence and possibility of change. The nature of their inter-action makes it difficult to communicate the changes that have occurred on their own side or to notice the changes on the other side, and to explore the possibilities for change that would serve both sides' interests. Conflict resolu-tion efforts, therefore, require promotion of a different kind of interaction, capable of reversing the escalatory and self-perpetuating dynamics of conflict: an interaction conducive to sharing perspectives, differentiating enemy images, and developing a language of mutual reassurance and a new discourse based on the norms of responsiveness and reciprocity.

The remainder of this chapter discusses in somewhat greater detail the social-psychological processes that contribute to the escalation and perpetua-tion of international conflict; the chapter concludes with a comment on how these processes might be reversed in the interest of conflict resolution.

Social-Psychological Processes Promoting Conflict

The four propositions about the nature of international conflict discussed so far—especially the view of conflict as a process driven by collective needs and fears—suggest the important role of social-psychological factors in *gener-ating* conflict. But social-psychological analysis can be particularly helpful in explaining why and how, once a conflict has started, powerful forces are set into motion that promote the *escalation* and *perpetuation* of that conflict. The role of social-psychological processes in creating or intensifying barriers to conflict resolution is most apparent in deep-rooted conflicts over identity and security. By the same token, social-psychological analysis, in helping to iden-tify and understand these barriers, can also suggest ways of overcoming them.

The discussion of social-psychological factors that promote international and ethnic conflict focuses on two sets of processes introduced in the preceding section: normative processes and perceptual processes. The term "normative" is used to refer to social processes that provide expectations, support, and pressure to hold on to the conflict, affirm it, and engage in conflictive behavior. The term "perceptual" is used to refer to cognitive processes that help to interpret and organize conflict-related information, particularly information bearing on the image of the enemy and each party's self-image in relation to the conflict. Normative and perceptual processes are clearly interrelated. As we shall see, for example, the normatively prescribed behavior in a conflict relationship is heavily influenced by the image of the enemy; and the enemy image, in turn, is itself normatively prescribed. Nevertheless, these two sets of processes are conceptually separable and provide a convenient basis for organizing the discussion of social-psychological processes. What both sets of processes have in common is that they create a dynamic that inhibits the perception and occurrence of change: despite changing circumstances and interests, parties engaged in an intense conflict tend to underestimate the degree to which change has taken place and further change is possible, and to act in ways that reduce the likelihood of change in their relationship.

The normative and perceptual processes that promote conflict can best be understood in the context of the four propositions about the nature of international conflict presented in the first part of the chapter:

- First, conflict norms and images are rooted in the collective needs and fears that drive the conflict.
- Second, given its intersocietal nature, conflict is shaped by the norms and images at the level of both the political leadership and the general public and by the mutual effect of these two levels on each other.
- Third, conflict norms and images severely limit the range and character of influence processes employed by the parties.
- Finally, and most directly, the conflict norms and images on both sides create the escalatory, self-perpetuating dynamic that characterizes conflict interaction.

Normative Processes

A variety of interaction processes occurring at the mass and elite levels within societies engaged in conflict play an important role in the evolving course of the conflict: formation of collective moods, mobilization of group loyalties, decision-making processes, negotiation and bargaining processes, and processes of structural and psychological commitment. All these processes are governed by a set of powerful social norms that, in an intense conflict relationship, typically encourage actions and attitudes conducive to the generation, escalation, and perpetuation of conflict, and inhibit the perception and occurrence of change in the direction of tension reduction and conflict resolution.

Formation of Collective Moods. Public opinion on issues relating to a protracted conflict (and on foreign policy issues generally) is marked by shifts in collective mood. At different times, the general mood may be characterized by optimism or pessimism, defiance or resignation, anger or conciliation. Moods may shift dramatically in response to major events. Thus, for example, within the Israeli public, the assassination of Prime Minister Rabin in November 1995 created, along with national shock and mourning, a mood of determination to continue the peace process that had cost the prime minister his life. Several months later, in February and March 1996, the series of deadly bombings in Jerusalem and Tel Aviv shifted the public mood in Israel to one of widespread wariness about the course of the peace process. Such moods have a significant effect on political leaders' sense of how far they can go in the pursuit of peace or what they must do to demonstrate their continued commitment to pursue the conflict.

Periodic shifts in collective mood underscore the general role of public opinion as both a resource and a constraint for political leaders in the foreign policy process. Public opinion may work both ways: public support can be a valuable resource in the leaders' pursuit of an aggressive policy as well as in their search for peaceful alternatives. Similarly, public opposition or skepticism may constrain leaders from taking hostile initiatives as well as from making conciliatory moves toward the enemy. In an intense, protracted conflict, however, the prevailing norms are more likely to encourage leaders to choose hostile actions over conciliatory ones. Leaders find it easier to mobilize public support for escalatory than de-escalatory steps; in fact, according to conventional wisdom, leaders at times initiate external aggression in order to distract the public from internal failures and boost their popular support. By the same token, leaders are more constrained in the pursuit of conciliatory policies than in the pursuit of aggressive policies—or at least they believe they are. The relationship between leadership and public opinion is often circular: decision makers play an important role in shaping public opinion about a conflict, framing the issues, and defining the limits of acceptable action. Public opinion then takes on a life of its own, and at some future time, when the leaders contemplate a change in policy, they feel constrained by the very views they previously helped shape. When they pronounce, rightly or wrongly, that "our public will never accept" this or that action, they may well be referring to actions that they themselves had publicly declared unacceptable earlier.

Apart from transitory moods, certain pervasive states of consciousness underlie public opinion in a society engulfed in a deep-rooted conflict. These states of consciousness reflect the existential concerns and the central national narratives that are widely shared within the population. In the Israeli-Palestinian conflict, for example, an underlying theme in both peoples' national consciousness is a profound concern, rooted in their respective historical experiences, about survival of the group and loss of the homeland. At the heart of Israelis' strong emphasis on security is their experience of rejection by their neighbors, who have regarded the establishment of Israel as an illegitimate intrusion of outsiders into the region—in contrast to the Israeli narrative of returning to the ancestral homeland after centuries of exile. The resulting sense of vulnerability is magnified by the Jewish historical memories of exclusion and persecution, culminating in the Holocaust. At the heart of Palestinians' strong emphasis on independent statehood is their experience of displacement, dispossession, dispersion, and occupation, and the resulting sense that they have been stripped not only of their homeland but of their identity as a people. The historical trauma at the center of Palestinian consciousness is *al-naqba* (the catastrophe), the Palestinians' term for the war of 1948 and its consequences for their society.

In most intense, protracted conflicts—for example, in the former Yugoslavia, Northern Ireland, and the Middle East—historical traumas serve as the points of reference for current events. There is no question that ambitious, often ruthless, nationalist leaders manipulate memories in order to whip up public support for their projects. But the fact remains that these memories—and the associated sense of injustice, abandonment, and vulnerability—are part of the people's consciousness and available for manipulation. Moreover, although political leaders may be cynical in using these public sentiments for their own purposes, they generally share the existential concerns that underlie pervasive states of national consciousness. Differences between leaders and publics—and, for that matter, between hawks and doves—diminish in importance when threats to group survival and identity are touched off.

The effect of such collective moods is to bring to the fore powerful social norms that support escalatory actions and inhibit moves toward compromise and accommodation. When fundamental concerns about survival and identity are tapped, national leaders are more prone to resort to hostile speech and action, and, if necessary, to go to war in defense of what they see as their society's threatened values and way of life. And they do so in the full expectation that the public will support them, despite the risks entailed. By contrast, these pervasive moods—especially when aroused by dramatic events, such as bombings or expulsions—inhibit the readiness to take risks for peace. This tendency appears consistent with the proposition derived from prospect theory that people are more reluctant to take risks for the achievement of gains than the avoidance of losses (see Levy 1992). Pervasive existential concerns within a society create a strong inclination to remain vigilant, distrust the enemy, and avoid any action that might weaken the nation's defenses. When these existential concerns are at issue, the prevailing norms support extreme caution. Political leaders, the general public, and even the political opposition reinforce one another in adhering to the old, established formulas. Change itself comes to be seen as dangerous; there is great reluctance to experiment with the nation's very existence.

Beyond contributing to escalation and inhibiting change in the direction of conflict resolution, the activation of collective fears about national survival and identity may lead to the extremes of violence and hostility that have marked some of the recent ethnic conflicts. Unscrupulous and fanatical leaders, taking advantage of opportunities to expand their power and fulfill their nationalist ambitions—such as the opportunity presented to Serbian leaders with the breakup of Yugoslavia—may manipulate collective memories of humiliation and revive old fears (and manufacture new ones) to instigate and justify hostile acts, which may set an escalatory process into motion. With active incitement by the leadership, a new set of norms takes over, whereby members of the other group—including former neighbors—come to be seen as the reincarnation of historic enemies who are planning to dominate one's own group, destroy its way of life, and annihilate its members. Harassing, expelling, and killing them thus come to be seen as justified acts of self-defense and patriotic duty. Small steps, even the silence of bystanders who may not approve of what is happening but are not prepared to take an active stand against the conflict norms that have taken hold, may initiate a continuum of destruction (Staub 1989) that ends with the kind of ethnic cleansing and genocide witnessed in Bosnia and elsewhere. Such actions are planned and orchestrated by political leaders who believe—or persuade themselves, along with their citizenry, to believe—that they are saving their people from imminent destruction. And they are carried out at various levels of command, with varying mixtures of motivation: obedience to authority, conformity to social pressures, and immersion in the collective sense of threat to national and personal survival and hostility against the purported source of that threat.

Mobilization of Group Loyalties. Public support is an essential resource for political leaders engaged in a conflict relationship. Leaders need assurance that the public is prepared to accept the costs and risks that their policies will inevitably entail. Furthermore, assurance of public support enhances the credibility of the threats and promises leaders issue to the other side. The primary means of gaining public support is the mobilization of group loyalties.

The arousal of nationalist and patriotic sentiments is a powerful tool in mobilizing public support. The display of national symbols evokes a strong emotional reaction, developed in the course of early and continuing socialization, which often translates into automatic endorsement of the policies and actions the leadership defines as necessary. When leaders invoke national security and national survival as the issues at stake in the conflict, people are often prepared to make enormous sacrifices that cannot be entirely understood in terms of rational calculations of costs and benefits. The nation generates such powerful identifications and loyalties because it brings together two central psychological dispositions: the need for self-protection and the need for self-transcendence (Kelman 1969, 1997).

In principle, group loyalties should be just as available to mobilize support for policies that entail risks for the sake of peace as for aggressive policies that entail risks of war. In practice, however, the dynamics of intense conflict generally favor efforts to mobilize support for intransigent, hostile actions. An appeal to defend the nation against an imminent attack is more compelling than an appeal to seize a promising opportunity. This phenomenon represents a special case of the central observation of prospect theory: where the expected utilities are equal, people tend to be risk-acceptant to avoid losses and risk-averse to achieve gains (see Farnham 1992; Levy 1992). Also, an appeal to defend the nation against imminent attack elicits almost unanimous response among members of the population. Even doves are not immune to such appeals in the short run, although they may believe that conciliatory policies are more conducive to national security and survival in the long run. On the other hand, an appeal to take advantage of an opportunity for peace holds no attraction to that segment of the population that equates peace with surrender. Furthermore, proposals for aggressive actions can more easily rely on the vocabulary of nationalism, which characteristically marks off the in-group from the out-group to the detriment of the latter. Proposals for conciliatory actions, even if they are in one's own interest, may offend nationalist thinking simply because they are seen as extending some benefits to the enemy or acknowledging a degree of justice in the enemy's positions.

A central element of group loyalty is adherence to the group's norms. In an intense conflict relationship, these norms call for a militant, unyielding, uncompromising, and suspicious attitude toward the enemy. There is a special taboo against any position that implies that the enemy may not be as implacable as had been assumed or may be undergoing change. Those who take such positions expose themselves to the charge that they are being naive, if not treasonous, weakening national unity and resolve, and opening the way to surrender. Militancy and intransigence become the measures of loyalty. Those most militant and unyielding become the reference points against which all positions are evaluated. Hence, particularly in situations of perceived national crisis, the militants wield disproportionate power and often exercise a veto over official actions and policies. They impose severe constraints on the ability of leaders to explore peaceful options. Even the society's dovish elements are constrained and cautious in their analyses and proposals, lest they expose themselves to the accusations of endangering national security and survival.

When national security and survival are seen to be at stake in a society, there are strong pressures to conform to the dominant conflict norms. Dissent is considered an act of disloyalty under these circumstances and is often penalized by exclusion, rejection, and ostracism. To dissent at a time of national crisis is seen as tantamount to excluding oneself from the group, to separating one's fate from that of fellow members—a cardinal sin in the nationalist doctrine. One of the dualities of nationalism is the readiness to accept fellow nationals unconditionally, as long as they identify themselves as part of the group, but to reject them totally if they are seen as separating themselves from the group. The resulting inhibition of dissent on matters that touch on national security and survival may create a state of pluralistic ignorance that further intensifies conformity: because people with reservations about the dominant policy are reluctant to speak out, and those who do speak out are quickly marginalized, potential dissenters are discouraged from expressing their views because they see themselves as a tiny minority confronting a near-unanimous consensus.

In sum, processes of group loyalty in a conflict situation create barriers to change in the relationship. The criteria by which loyalty is measured, the disproportionate power of the militant elements in setting the national agenda, and the suppression of dissent undermine the exploration of peaceful alternatives and reduce the options for conflict resolution. The militants on the two sides reinforce each other by creating self-fulfilling prophecies—a phenomenon described more fully in the discussion of perceptual processes below. Each confirms the other's worst expectations and creates realities that extend and intensify the conflict.

Decision-making Processes. There are historical instances of creative decision making in dangerous crisis situations—such as the Cuban missile crisis (Allison 1971; Lebow 1981)—but conflict norms generally impose serious burdens on the decision-making process. Decision makers in a conflict situation are often inhibited in the search for alternatives and the exploration of new possibilities, particularly when they are operating in an atmosphere of crisis.

A major source of reluctance to explore new options are the domestic constraints under which decision makers labor. In view of the political divisions within their society, they are constantly looking over their shoulders to make sure they are not opening themselves up to disabling attacks from the opposition. In an intense conflict situation, adherence to the conflict norms tends to be seen as the safest course of action. For reasons already discussed, decision makers are likely to see themselves most vulnerable if their policies and actions move toward compromise or even communication with the adversary. Because hawkish opposition elements are often effective in appropriating the definition of group loyalty and national security and are able to appeal to the collective memories and fears of wide segments of the population, they tend to exercise stronger constraints on policy than do dovish opposition elements. Cautious decision makers assume that they are less vulnerable domestically if they stay with the conflict's status quo, adhere to a discourse of hostility and distrust vis-à-vis the other side, or threaten escalatory actions than if they take steps toward accommodation and compromise.

The search for alternatives and the exploration of new options in response to changing realities are further inhibited by institutionalized rigidities in the decision-making apparatus. Decision makers and decision-making bureaucracies operate within a certain framework of assumptions about the choices available to them, the effectiveness of different strategies, and the expectations of different constituencies; such assumptions are rarely questioned and therefore reduce the range of options that are likely to be considered. In longstanding conflicts, these decision-making frameworks are shaped by the prevailing conflict norms. Thus, decision makers may take it for granted, for example, that the two parties' interests are inherently incompatible, that the other side responds only to force, or that their own public demands a militant posture. Operating under unquestioned assumptions of this kind, decision makers are unlikely to recognize the occurrence and possibility of change and to initiate policies aimed at resolving the conflict.

Furthermore, decision-making bureaucracies tend to operate with certain established procedures and technologies; the actions they consider are those that they are equipped to carry out. In conflict situations, the discourse, skills, and technology for pursuing the conflict are much more readily available than those geared toward resolving it. The prime example is the military establishment, which has the weapons systems, personnel, and operational plans in place and is ready to go into action when the need arises. Decision makers are, therefore, more inclined to resort to military options at moments of crisis than to less developed and untried alternatives.

Finally, the microprocesses of action and interaction in crisis decision making inhibit the exploration of new options. At the individual level, the stress that decision makers inevitably experience in situations of crisis—when consequential decisions must be made under severe time pressures—has the effect of limiting the number of alternatives they consider and impelling them to settle quickly on the dominant response. In intense conflicts, the dominant response, dictated by the habits and norms of the conflict, is likely to be aggressive and escalatory (Holsti 1972; Lebow 1987). At the level of decision-making groups, crisis decision making often leads to what Janis (1982) calls "groupthink" processes. To maintain the cohesiveness of the group, the members studiously avoid any actions that might break the evolving consensus. Thus, they are reluctant to raise questions, offer criticisms, or propose different approaches and alternative solutions to the problem. The group's members reinforce each other in affirming the correctness and righteousness of the course of action on which their deliberations are converging. The decision-making process under these circumstances is much more likely to produce policies and actions that perpetuate and escalate the conflict than innovative ideas for conflict resolution.

Negotiation and Bargaining Processes. Negotiation is possible only when both parties define the situation, at least at some level, as a win-win, mixed-motive game. To engage in the process, each must be able to conceive of some outcome that would be better than the status quo. Thus, negotiation is based on the parties' recognition that they have both competitive and cooperative goals. They are competing in that each is trying to maximize interests that are—or at least are perceived to be—incompatible with the other's interests; but they must cooperate in order to continue the "game" and eventually achieve an agreement that advances both their interests. Even in a narrow bargaining process that focuses strictly on the distribution of fixed, limited resources, the parties have a common interest in consummating the exchange. They must cooperate in devising an outcome that gives each party enough to make the agreement worth its while.

Win-win solutions are particularly difficult to attain in protracted identity conflicts. Depending on the circumstances, a mutually satisfactory outcome might be devised by fractionating the conflict (Fisher 1964), which may help the parties move gradually toward an overall settlement by first achieving agreements on a series of less contentious issues; transcending the conflict as they focus on superordinate goals that can be achieved only through joint efforts (Sherif 1958); or redefining the conflict and reframing the issues in ways that make them amenable to solutions that address the needs and fears of both parties (Kelman 1996). Ultimately, success in negotiating a win-win solution depends on mutual responsiveness, as described in the earlier discussion of influence processes. In effect, while pursuing its own interests, each party must actively seek out ways in which the adversary can also win and appear to be winning. But this is precisely the kind of effort that is discouraged by the conflict norms; the approach to negotiation is dominated by zero-sum thinking. Success in how much one's own side is winning and appears to be winning is often measured by how much the other side is losing and appears to be losing.

At the microlevel, negotiators around the table serve as instructed representatives. In an intense conflict, they evaluate their performance by the forcefulness with which they present their own case and by their effectiveness in warding off pressures to compromise. They are not in a listening mode; they are unlikely to pay attention to what the other side needs and how they could help the other side achieve its goals. Indeed, to do so would violate the conflict norms and might subject the negotiators to criticism from their own constituencies and particularly from the domestic opposition that they are "soft" on the enemy and selling out the national cause. Nor are they likely to present their own positions in ways that convey what they need and how the other side can help them achieve it. The interaction does not usually allow the parties to learn something new or to gain a better understanding of the other's perspective. Rather, it tends to confirm old images and to keep the conflict alive. Clearly, it does not contribute to the search for ways in which each party can help the other make valuable and visible gains. Such a search is further undermined by public reports on the progress of negotiations. To appeal to its own constituencies, each side may stress how much it is winning—at the other side's expense. Such pronouncements impose further burdens on the continuing negotiations. In this respect, secret negotiations have a considerable advantage, although their disadvantage is that they usually offer no opportunity to prepare the public for the changes in the relationship that are being negotiated.

At the macrolevel, the overall strategy for negotiations is often marked by zero-sum thinking. Even when the parties recognize their common interest in negotiating certain specific issues, they tend to keep an eye on how the negotiations may affect their relative power advantage. They want to make sure that, at the end of the day, their own position will be strengthened and the adversary's will be weakened. Such strategic considerations may undermine the purpose of the negotiations. A strategy that weakens one's negotiating partners may reduce both their incentive for concluding an agreement and their ability to mobilize their own public's support for whatever agreement is negotiated. It is a strategy that limits the other's opportunity to make valuable and visible gains.

As a description of international negotiations in general, the picture presented here is exaggerated, to be sure. Skilled and experienced negotiators know that if the process is to succeed, the other side must achieve substantial and visible gains and its leadership must be strengthened. But the norms governing political behavior in long-standing conflicts strongly encourage zero-sum thinking, which equates the enemy's loss with one's own gain. As a result, even when the parties have concluded that negotiations are in their own best interest, their actions inside and outside of the negotiating room often undermine the process, causing delays, setbacks, and repeated failures.

Processes of Structural and Psychological Commitment. Conflict creates certain structural and psychological commitments, which then take on a life of their own (see Pruitt and Gahagan 1974; Rubin, Pruitt, and Kim 1994). The most obvious sources of commitment to the conflict and its perpetuation are the vested interests in the status quo. A conflict of long standing and significance to a society—such as that in Northern Ireland (see George 1996)—inevitably becomes a focal point for the lives of various individuals, groups, and organizations within that society. They benefit in a variety of ways from the existence and prosecution of the conflict; ending it threatens to deprive them of profit, power, status, or raison d'être. Such vested interests can be found, for example, in the armaments industry, the military establishment, paramilitary and guerrilla organizations, defense-related research laboratories, and political groups organized to pursue the conflict. A vested interest in maintaining the conflict may also develop, to different degrees, in individuals whose careers are built around the conflict, including political leaders who have played a prominent role in pursuing the struggle and "conflict professionals"—scholars, writers, and journalists who have specialized in chronicling, analyzing, and perhaps even resolving the conflict.

There is another source of commitment that is based not on a vested interest in maintaining the conflict as such, but on an interest in forestalling a compromise solution. Two rather different examples can be cited from the Israeli-Palestinian case. Israeli settlers in the occupied territories generally have been opposed to the peace process because they are convinced that a negotiated agreement would spell the end of their settlement project. Many Palestinians in the refugee camps in Lebanon and Syria opposed the Oslo peace process because they saw it as leading to an agreement that would not address their particular needs and grievances.

Vested interests do not necessarily manifest themselves in a direct, calculated way. There are, of course, those who deliberately undermine efforts at conflict resolution because they do not want to give up the power and privilege that depend on continuation of the status quo (although even they may persuade themselves that they are acting for the good of the nation). In many cases, however, the effects of vested interests are indirect and subtle. People's commitment to the perpetuation of the conflict may motivate their interpretation of ambiguous realities and their choice among uncertain alternatives. Thus, they may be predisposed to dismiss changes or possibilities of change on the other side that might make negotiations promising, and they may be risk-averse in evaluating initiatives for peace but risk-acceptant in their support for aggressive policies that might lead to war.

Vested interests and similar structural commitments to the conflict are bolstered by psychological commitments. People involved in a long-standing and deep-rooted conflict tend to develop a worldview that includes the conflict as a central component. Elements of this worldview may be passed on from one generation to the next, and attitudes and beliefs about the conflict may become firmly embedded in the entire structure of one's thinking and feeling. In this way, people become committed to the continuation of the conflict because ending it would jeopardize their entire worldview; it would force them to revise the way they think and feel about significant aspects of their national and personal lives. Resistance to change is likely to be more pronounced the more elaborate the cognitive structure or ideology in which the view of the conflict is embedded, because changing this view would have wider ramifications.

The image of the enemy is often a particularly important part of the worldview of people engaged in an intense conflict; it has implications for their national identity, their view of their own society, and their interpretation of history. Thus, for Palestinians to revise their view of Israelis as Western intruders in the Middle East who will eventually leave just as the Crusaders did, or for Israelis to revise their view of Palestinians as implacable enemies committed to the destruction of Israel, raises many troublesome issues about their own past, present, and future. Images of the enemy are therefore highly resistant to change and contribute to the escalatory and self-perpetuating dynamic of conflict.

Perceptual Processes

Perceptual and cognitive processes play a major role in the escalation and perpetuation of conflict, and create barriers to redefining and resolving the conflict despite changing realities and interests. Two perceptual processes that characterize mutual images of parties in conflict can account for this effect: the formation of mirror images and the resistance of images to contradictory information. When both parties, in mirror-image fashion, perceive the enemy as harboring hostile intentions in the face of their own vulnerability, their interaction produces a self-fulfilling dynamic; under these circumstances, it is difficult to discover common and complementary interests. Further, conflict-based interactions—within and between the parties—inhibit the perception and the occurrence of change in the other, and thus the opportunity to revise the enemy image. These two processes are discussed in this section.

Formation of Mirror Images. Social psychologists writing about U.S.-Soviet relations (Bronfenbrenner 1961; White 1965) first noted the phenomenon of mirror image formation as a characteristic of many conflict relationships. Both parties tend to develop parallel images of self and other, except with the sign reversed; that is, the two parties have similarly positive self-images and similarly negative enemy images. The core content of mirror images is captured by the good-bad dimension: each side sees itself as good and peaceful, arming only for defensive reasons and fully prepared to engage in open give-and-take and compromise. The enemy, by contrast, is seen as evil and hostile, arming for aggressive reasons and responsive only to the language of force.

A typical corollary of the good-bad image in protracted conflicts is the view that the other side's aggressiveness is inherent in its nature: in its ideology (e.g., Zionism or PLO nationalism), in its system (e.g., capitalist imperialism or communist expansionism), in its religion, or in its national character. On the other hand, if one's own side ever displays aggressiveness, it is entirely reactive and defensive. In the language of attribution theory, the tendency on both sides is to explain the enemy's aggressive behavior in dispositional terms and one's own in situational terms (see Jones and Nisbett 1971). To perceive the enemy's evil action as inherent in its nature is tantamount to demonization and dehumanization of the other, with all the dangerous consequences thereof. Once a group perceived as threatening one's own welfare is excluded from the human family, almost any action against it—including expulsion, dispossession, torture, rape, genocide, and ethnic cleansing in its various forms—comes to be seen as necessary and justified (see Kelman 1973).

Another common corollary of the good-bad image—one that derives from the virtuous self-image—is the assumption on each side that the enemy knows very well "we" are not threatening them. Our own basic decency and peacefulness, and the provocation to which we have been subjected, are so obvious to us that they must also be obvious to the other side (see the discussion of naive realism in Ross and Ward 1995). Thus, the assumption is that they see us as we see *ourselves*—when in fact they see us as we see *them*. As I argue below, this feature of the mirror image process contributes significantly to the escalatory dynamic of conflict interaction.

Another, though less common element of the mirror image is the "evil-ruler" image, which White (1965, 1968) describes in the context of U.S.–Soviet relations. A distinction is made between the masses and the elites on the "enemy's" side: the people are basically decent but have been misled, brain-washed, or intimidated by their rulers. By contrast, there is complete harmony between rulers and citizens on "our" side. A related element, often found in mirror images—as, for example, in the Israeli-Palestinian case—is the view that, in contrast to the genuine unity on one's own side, the enemy's unity is artificial and sustained only by its leaders' effort to keep the conflict alive.

Apart from such generic features of mirror images, which arise from the dynamics of intergroup conflict across the board, mirror images in any given case may reflect the dynamics of the specific conflict. Thus, a central feature of the Israeli-Palestinian conflict over the years has been mutual denial of the other's national identity, accompanied by efforts to delegitimize the other's national movement and claim to nationhood (see Kelman 1978, 1987). Other mirror images that have characterized the Israeli-Palestinian and other intense ethnic conflicts (such as those in Bosnia and Northern Ireland) include:

- mutual fear of national and personal annihilation, anchored in the view that the project of destroying one's group is inherent in and central to the other's ideology;
- a mutual sense of victimization by the other side, accompanied by a tendency to assimilate the images of the current enemy to the image of the historical enemy and the current experience of victimization to the collective memories of past experiences; and
- a mutual view of the enemy as a source of the negative components of one's own identity, such as the sense of humiliation and vulnerability.

Although mirror images are an important and central feature of the dynamics of conflict, the concept requires several qualifications, particularly because it is often taken to imply that conflicts are necessarily symmetrical—an idea vehemently rejected by the parties engaged in conflict. The mirror image concept implies that *certain* symmetries in the parties' reactions arise from the very nature of conflict interaction, and that it is important to understand them because of their role in escalating the conflict. There is no assumption, however, that *all* images of self and enemy are mirror images. In the Israeli-Palestinian conflict, for example, both sides agree that Israel is the more powerful party (although Israelis point out that their conflict has been not only with the Palestinians but with the entire Arab world and much of the Muslim world). Furthermore, there is no assumption that the images on the two sides are equally inaccurate. Clearly, the mirror image concept implies that there is some distortion, because the two views of reality are diametrical opposites and thus cannot both be completely right. It is also presumed that there is probably some distortion on each side because both sides' perceptions are affected by the conflict dynamics. This does not mean, however, that both sides manifest equal degrees of distortion.

A third qualification is that the mirror image concept does not imply empirical symmetry between the two sides. There is no assumption that the historical experiences or the current situations of the two sides are comparable on all or even the most important dimensions. To take one dimension as an example, many conflicts are marked by asymmetries in power between the parties, which have significant effects on the parties' perceptions of the conflict (Rouhana and Fiske 1995). Finally, the mirror image concept does not imply moral equivalence in the positions of the two parties. To note the symmetry in the two sides' perceptions of their own moral superiority is not to postulate moral symmetry in their claims or their actions. Thus, for example, one can point to many mirror images in the relationship between Serbs and Muslims in Bosnia and still make the moral judgment that it was the Serbian side that committed genocide.

With these qualifications in mind, one can trace the common tendency among parties in conflict to form mirror images to the dynamics of the conflict relationship itself. Since each party is engaged in the conflict and subject to similar forces generated by that engagement, parallelism in some of their images is bound to develop. Parallel images arise out of the motivational and cognitive contexts in which parties in conflict generally operate. Motivationally, each side is concerned with "looking good" when blame for the conflict events is being apportioned; political leaders, therefore, feel a strong need to persuade themselves, their own people, the rest of the world, and future historians that the blame rests with the enemy—that their own cause is just and their own actions have been entirely defensive in nature. Cognitively, each side views the conflict from its own perspective and—painfully aware of its own needs, fears, historical traumas, grievances, suspicions, and political constraints—is convinced that it is acting defensively and with the best intentions. Furthermore, each side assumes that these circumstances are so self-evident, they must be equally clear to the enemy; signs of hostility from the enemy must therefore be due to its aggressive intent.

When both sides are motivated to deflect blame from themselves and are convinced that their own good intentions are as clear to the other as to themselves, mirror images are formed. Mirror images increase the danger of escalation, as illustrated in the earlier discussion of arms races. They produce a spiraling effect because each side interprets any hostile action by the other as an indication of aggressive intent against which it must defend itself, but its own reactions—whose defensive nature, it assumes, should be obvious to the enemy—are taken by the other as signs of aggressive intent. The effect of mirror images is accentuated insofar as the enemy's ideology or national character is perceived to be inherently aggressive and expansionist, because this essentialist view provides a stable framework for explaining the other's behavior. In addition to their escalatory effect, mirror images tend to make conflicts more intractable because the sharp contrast between the innocent self and the aggressive other makes it difficult to break out of a zero-sum conception of the conflict.

The concept of mirror images may be a useful tool in conflict resolution. Under the proper circumstances—such as those that problem-solving workshops try to create—the parties may gradually come to recognize the conflict-induced parallelisms in their views. The first and relatively easy step is to discover that one's own actions are perceived differently by the other side than they are by oneself. This discovery can open one up to the possibility that the reverse may be true: that one's perceptions of the other's actions may be different from the other's self-perceptions. Thus, the parties may gain access to each other's perspective and insight into the effects that such two-directional differences in perception can have on the course of the conflict. Such discoveries may encourage the parties to focus on the need for mutual reassurance about each other's intentions and set a de-escalatory process in motion.

Resistance of Images to Contradictory Information. Conflict images are highly resistant to new information that challenges their validity. The persistence of these images inhibits the perception of change and the expectation of future change that might create possibilities for conflict resolution, and thus helps to perpetuate the conflict.

A great deal of social-psychological theorizing and research has addressed the general phenomenon of the persistence of attitudes and beliefs in the face of new information that, from an observer's point of view, is clearly contradictory—information that should at least call the existing attitudes into question but is somehow neutralized or ignored. This is not to say that attitudes never change; indeed, there is considerable evidence that individuals' and societies' attitudes constantly change—sometimes gradually, sometimes drastically—in response to new events and experiences. But change always occurs in the face of some resistance: the continuing struggle between forces for stability and forces for change is one of the hallmarks of attitudes. Resistance is motivated in the sense that people tend to hold on to their attitudes because those attitudes perform certain important functions for them. Beyond that, however, resistance is built into the very functioning of attitudes: since attitudes help shape our experiences and the way new information is organized, they play a role in creating the conditions for their own confirmation and for avoiding disconfirmation. Research has focused on several types of mechanisms that account for resistance to contradictory information: selectivity, consistency, attribution, and the self-fulfilling prophecy.

The concepts of selective exposure, selective perception, and selective recall all point to the fact that our attitudes help determine the kind of information that is available to us. Our political attitudes, for example, determine the organizations we join, the meetings we attend, and the publications we receive. Consequently, we are more likely to be exposed to information that confirms our views than to information that contradicts them. We also tend to seek out confirmatory information because we enjoy it more, trust it more, and find it more useful—for example, to support our position in subsequent discussions. Furthermore, we are more likely to perceive the information to which we are exposed in a way that is congruent with our initial attitudes, because these attitudes create expectations for what we will find and provide a framework for making sense of it. Finally, we are more likely to remember confirmatory information because we have a preexisting framework into which it can be fit and because we are more likely to find it useful. These selectivity processes also operate in interpersonal and intergroup relations. We are less likely to communicate with people whom we dislike; as a result we have less opportunity to make new observations that might conceivably lead to a revision in our attitudes (Newcomb 1947). Similarly, our initial attitudes—sometimes based on first impressions or group labels—create expectations that affect our subsequent observations and provide a framework for how we perceive the person's behavior and what we recall about it.

Cognitive consistency has received a great deal of attention in experimental social psychology. Among the different models explored in numerous studies, the two most influential ones have been Heider's (1958) theory of cognitive balance and Festinger's (1957) theory of cognitive dissonance. The general assumption of the various consistency models is that inconsistency between different cognitive elements (e.g., between feelings and beliefs about an object, between our attitudes and our actions, or between our attitudes and the attitudes of important others) is an uncomfortable psychological state. It creates tension, which we seek to reduce by whatever means are most readily available to restore consistency.

The role of consistency mechanisms in reaction to new information is rather complex. Inconsistent information is often an important instigator of change in attitudes and behavior, provided the information is compelling and challenging and situational forces motivate the person to seek out new information. At other times, however, consistency mechanisms serve to reinforce selective exposure, perception, and recall: people screen out information that is incongruent with their existing attitudes and beliefs and thus maintain cognitive consistency. This reaction is especially likely when the existing attitudes are strongly held and have wide ramifications—as is the case with enemy images.

Attribution theory has been another central focus for research on social cognition. This theory addresses the ways in which people explain their own and others' behavior—how they assess the causes of behavior. One of the key distinctions in the field has been between dispositional and situational attributions: the perceived cause of a particular action may be placed in the actor's character and underlying nature, or in situational forces (Jones and Nisbett 1971). When observing the behavior of others, people have a strong tendency to make dispositional attributions—to commit what has been called "the fundamental attribution error" (Ross 1977). On the other hand, when explaining the causes of their own behavior, people are much more likely to make situational attributions, because they are aware of the many pressures and constraints that affect their behavior at any given time and place. As it turns out, however, in both interpersonal and international relations, these attributional tendencies depend on the nature of the actor and the action. When people explain their own behavior or that of friends and allies, they tend to make dispositional attributions for positive acts and situational attributions for negative acts; when they explain the behavior of enemies, they are inclined to do the reverse (Heradstveit 1981; Rosenberg and Wolfsfeld 1977; Rouhana 1997). Thus, attribution mechanisms—like consistency mechanisms—promote confirmation of the original enemy image. Hostile actions by the enemy are attributed dispositionally and thus provide further evidence of the enemy's inherently aggressive, implacable character. Conciliatory actions are explained away as reactions to situational forces—as tactical maneuvers, responses to external pressure, or temporary adjustments to a position of weakness—and therefore require no revision of the original image.

The concept of the self-fulfilling prophecy refers to the effect of expectations about another person or group on the other's actual behavior. Our expectations are communicated, perhaps subtly and unconsciously, in the way we approach others in the course of interaction. In doing so, we often create conditions that cause others to behave in line with our expectations—to take on the roles in which we have cast them (Weinstein and Deutschberger

1963). For example, a party that enters negotiations with the expectation that the other side will be unyielding may be particularly tough in its own demeanor and present proposals that the other is bound to reject, thus living up to the original expectations and confirming the original attitudes. When the interaction between conflicting parties is characterized by mirror images and mutual expectations of unprovoked hostility, it produces self-fulfilling prophecies that escalate the conflict, as described earlier.

The mechanisms that account for resistance to disconfirming information—selectivity, consistency, attribution, and self-fulfilling prophecy—are particularly powerful in a conflict relationship for several reasons. First, images of the enemy and conflict-related self-images are central aspects of the national consensus. The earlier discussion of the normative processes that operate in a society engaged in an intense conflict points to the strong social pressures toward maintaining uniformity of opinion, especially in a crisis atmosphere. These pressures prevail in both small decision-making groups and the larger society. Softening the image of the enemy breaks the consensus and invites accusations of disloyalty. The militant elements resist a revision of the enemy image because they see it as weakening the national resolve, lowering defenses, and signaling a readiness for hazardous compromise. Their objections may have a broad appeal because the assumption that the risks of underestimating the enemy's hostility are more dangerous than the risks of overestimating it (and thus underestimating the opportunities for peace) is widely shared—and only the former invokes the charge of disloyalty. In sum, the mechanisms of resistance to disconfirming information are reinforced by normative pressures in a conflict situation.

Second, enemy images are especially resistant to disconfirmation because, in a conflict relationship, the opportunities for taking the perspective of the other are limited, and the capacity for doing so is impaired. In normal social interaction, participants' mutual attitudes often change in response to new information they acquire and/or evaluate by taking each other's perspective. However, interaction among parties in conflict—if it occurs at all—is governed by the conflict norms. Under these circumstances, the empathy required for taking the other's perspective is difficult to achieve and is, in fact, frowned upon. As a result, each party's analysis of the enemy's society is dominated by its own perspective. In the Arab-Israeli case, for example, both parties tend to overestimate how much the other knows about their own intentions and concerns: parties' estimates of what the other knows are based on what they themselves know (an important source of the escalatory effect of mirror images, as noted earlier). Other consequences of looking at the other primarily from one's own perspective are:

- a lack of differentiation among various strata and segments of the other society and a tendency to categorize it in terms of one's own concerns (e.g., pro-PLO versus anti-PLO Palestinians, Zionist versus anti-Zionist Israelis) rather than the society's internal dynamics;

- a self-centered view of the other side's opposition groups, equating them with supporters of one's own cause (which is bound to lead to disappointment once one discovers that even the dovish opposition elements have not switched sides); and

- a self-centered view of the other's ideology that perceives the destruction of one's own national existence as the entire meaning and sole purpose of the other side's national movement.

These and similar failures to take account of the other's perspective reduce the impact of potentially new information. Lacking the appropriate context, the parties may not notice or adequately appreciate the varieties, changes, and signs of flexibility in the other side's views.

Third, the resistance of enemy images to disconfirmation is magnified by strong beliefs concerning the unchangeability of the enemy. Such beliefs are typically part of the mirror image, which regards the enemy's hostility as inherent in its ideology and character (i.e., the mirror image attributes such hostility to dispositional causes). Thus, for many years, both Israelis and Palestinians insisted that there had been no real change in the enemy's position, only tactical maneuvers; that view changed over the years—especially after the Oslo agreement in 1993—but, with the failure of the Camp David talks in 2000 and the outbreak of the new intifada, it reemerged in full force. One reason for underestimating the amount of change on the other side is that the two parties use different anchors in assessing movement. The side taking a given action measures the amount of change it represents in terms of how far it has moved from its original position; the other side measures it in terms of how close it has come to its own position. Thus, in the Palestinian view, the 1974 decision of the Palestine National Council to accept a "national authority" on any part of Palestine that is liberated represented a major change—one that was bitterly contested and divided the movement, because it was seen as a step toward a two-state solution. Israelis, however, saw no significance in this move because it was still a long way from recognizing Israel and ending the armed struggle. To take a more recent example, Israelis perceived Prime Minister Barak's offer to the Palestinian side at the 2000 Camp David talks as very generous, because his concessions went considerably further than those made by any previous Israeli government. Palestinians, however, perceived the offer as inadequate, because it did not meet their minimal requirements for a viable Palestinian state and for a final settlement of the conflict (Kelman 2007).

Not only do parties in conflict—starting from different reference points—find it difficult to perceive change in the enemy, they often believe that there will not and cannot be any change in the enemy's position. They give greater credence to history and formal documents than to the ongoing and evolving political process. They therefore consider it dangerous or even treasonous to propose that the enemy has changed or will change, and see no way to exert influence and encourage change other than by force—"the only language the enemy understands." Such beliefs are not easily penetrated by new information suggesting that there has been change in the enemy camp and that further changes are in the offing.

Despite all the reasons why conflict images are particularly resistant to contradictory information, they are not immutable. Social-psychological evidence suggests that they can change, and historical evidence shows that they do change. The challenge for scholars and practitioners of international conflict resolution is to devise the means to overcome their resistance to change.

CONCLUSION

Social-psychological analysis can contribute significantly to the study of international relations by providing a framework for conceptualizing change in the world system and in the relationships among its various components. To be sure, powerful forces—historical, geopolitical, structural, and institutional—lend stability and continuity to the interests of nation-states and their alliances, and hence to the conflicts that result from the clashes of interests between such states or alliances. Indeed, as the preceding section argues, social-psychological processes contribute in their own way to the resistance to change characteristic of international conflict by entrapping the parties in a pattern of interaction with an escalatory, self-perpetuating dynamic. Nevertheless, despite the forces that continually feed conflicts and keep them alive, international conflict is in essence a dynamic phenomenon. The relationships between nations have always been subject to change, but in recent decades change has become more rapid and all-encompassing. Technological, demographic, economic, and environmental factors have contributed to the creation of new interests, new alliances, new actors, and new institutions at the national, international, and global levels. These changing circumstances represent many possibilities, not only for generating new conflicts but also for resolving old ones.

By focusing on the social-psychological dimensions, one can often gain insight into the causes of change, the impact of change, and the ways of promoting change at the level of the national and international systems, precisely because it becomes possible to approach these systemic processes at a different level of analysis. The psychological processes by which decision makers and political elites define national interests and frame the issues in conflict, by which the public develops a collective readiness for pursuing war or pursuing peace, and by which both leaders and the public on the two sides in interaction with each other create an atmosphere and discourse conducive to mutual hostility or mutual accommodation illuminate the precise ways in which changes in public policy and state action may be resisted, facilitated, or deliberately induced. The motivations, cognitions, and emotions characterizing the behavior and interaction of individual actors at any given time are, of course, heavily determined by the necessities and opportunities created by events and changes at the macrolevel. But analysis of these microlevel processes in turn provides a basis for understanding and predicting when and how change at the macrolevel is likely to occur and what kind of change it is likely to be, and for creating the conditions that promote change in the direction of conflict resolution.

Creating these conditions requires a reversal of the social-psychological processes that promote conflict, through changes in the habitual ways of thinking, acting, and interacting in any given conflict and, indeed, in the international system as a whole:

- expanding collective consciousness to include a shared vision of a peaceful world;
- redefining the criteria for group loyalty;
- counteracting the pressures that make militancy and aggressive posturing the politically "safest" course for decision makers to follow;
- moving from zero-sum thinking to a win-win approach in negotiation and bargaining;
- creating structural and psychological commitments to a peaceful, cooperative relationship;
- breaking the conflict spirals initiated by mirror images; and
- developing communication patterns to allow new information to challenge old assumptions.

Promoting such changes is the task of diplomacy in all its varieties, of public education, and of institutional development. It is not an easy task, but the possibilities for change are always present, given the dynamic character of international conflict.

Conflict resolution efforts must be geared toward discovering the possibilities for change, identifying the conditions for change, and overcoming the resistances to change. Such an approach to conflict resolution calls for best-case analyses and an attitude of strategic optimism (Kelman 1978, 1979), "not because of an unrealistic denial of malignant trends, but as part of a deliberate strategy to promote change by actively searching for and accentuating what-ever realistic possibilities for peaceful resolution of the conflict might be on the horizon. Optimism, in this sense, is part of a strategy designed to create self-fulfilling prophecies of a positive nature, balancing the self-fulfilling prophe-cies of escalation created by the pessimistic expectations and the worst-case scenarios often favored by more traditional analysts" (Kelman 1992a, 89).

The barriers to conflict resolution are strengthened by the escalatory, self-perpetuating dynamic that characterizes the interaction between conflicting parties. To overcome these barriers requires the promotion of a different kind of interaction, one that is capable of reversing this conflict dynamic. At the microlevel, problem-solving workshops and similar approaches to conflict resolution can contribute to this objective by encouraging the parties to pen-etrate each other's perspective, to differentiate their image of the enemy, to develop a de-escalatory language and ideas for mutual reassurance, and to engage in joint problem solving designed to generate ideas for resolving the conflict that are responsive to the fundamental needs and fears of both sides. At the macrolevel, reversal of the conflict dynamic depends on the establish-ment of a new discourse among the parties, characterized by a shift in empha-sis from power politics and threat of coercion to mutual responsiveness, reci-procity, and openness to a new relationship.

REFERENCES

Allison, Graham T. 1971. *Essence of Decision: Explaining the Cuban Missile Crisis.* Boston: Little, Brown.

Baldwin, David. 1971. "The Power of Positive Sanctions." *World Politics* 24 (Octo-ber): 19–38.

Bar-Siman-Tov, Yaacov, ed. 2004. *From Conflict Resolution to Reconciliation.* Ox-ford and New York: Oxford University Press.

Bronfenbrenner, Urie. 1961. "The Mirror Image in Soviet-American Relations: A Social Psychologist's Report." *Journal of Social Issues* 17 (3): 45–56.

Burton, John W. 1969. *Conflict and Communication: The Use of Controlled Com-munication in International Relations.* London: Macmillan.

———. 1979. *Deviance, Terrorism, and War: The Process of Solving Unsolved Social and Political Problems.* New York: St. Martin's.

———. 1984. *Global Conflict: The Domestic Sources of International Crisis.* Brighton, Sussex, UK: Wheatsheaf.

————. 1988. "Conflict Resolution as a Function of Human Needs." In *The Power of Human Needs in World Society*, ed. Roger A. Coate and Jerel A. Rosati. Boulder, Colo.: Lynne Rienner.

————, ed. 1990. *Conflict: Human Needs Theory*. New York: St. Martin's.

Druckman, Daniel, and P. Terrence Hopmann. 1989. "Behavioral Aspects of Negotiations on Mutual Security." In *Behavior, Society, and Nuclear War*, vol. 1, ed. Philip E. Tetlock, Jo L. Husbands, Robert Jervis, Paul C. Stern, and Charles Tilly. New York: Oxford University Press.

Farnham, Barbara, ed. 1992. "Prospect Theory and Political Psychology." *Political Psychology* 13 (2): 167–329.

Festinger, Leon. 1957. *A Theory of Cognitive Dissonance*. Stanford, Calif.: Stanford University Press.

Fischhoff, Baruch. 1991. "Nuclear Decisions: Cognitive Limits to the Thinkable." In *Behavior, Society, and Nuclear War*, vol. 2, ed. Philip E. Tetlock, Jo L. Husbands, Robert Jervis, Paul C. Stern, and Charles Tilly. New York: Oxford University Press.

Fisher, Roger. 1964. "Fractionating Conflict." In *International Conflict and Behavioral Science*, ed. Roger Fisher. New York: Basic Books.

Fisher, Ronald J. 1983. "Third-Party Consultation as a Method of Intergroup Conflict Resolution: A Review of Studies." *Journal of Conflict Resolution* 27 (2): 301–34.

————. 1989. "Prenegotiation Problem-Solving Discussions: Enhancing the Potential for Successful Negotiations." In *Getting to the Table: The Processes of International Prenegotiation*, ed. Janice Gross Stein. Baltimore: Johns Hopkins University Press.

————. 1997. *Interactive Conflict Resolution*. Syracuse, N.Y.: Syracuse University Press.

George, Alexander L., and Richard Smoke. 1974. *Deterrence in American Foreign Policy: Theory and Practice*. New York: Columbia University Press.

George, Terry. 1996. "Lost without War in Northern Ireland." *New York Times*, July 17.

Heider, Fritz. 1958. *The Psychology of Interpersonal Relations*. New York: Wiley.

Heradstveit, Daniel. 1981. *The Arab-Israeli Conflict: Psychological Obstacles to Peace*, 2d ed. Oslo: Universitetsforlaget.

Holsti, Ole R. 1972. *Crisis, Escalation, War*. Montreal: McGill-Queens University Press.

————. 1989. "Crisis Decision Making." In *Behavior, Society, and Nuclear War*, vol. 1, ed. Philip E. Tetlock, Jo L. Husbands, Robert Jervis, Paul C. Stern, and Charles Tilly. New York: Oxford University Press.

Holt, Robert R., and Brett Silverstein, eds. 1989. "The Image of the Enemy: U.S. Views of the Soviet Union." *Journal of Social Issues* 45 (2): 1–175.

Janis, Irving L. 1982. *Groupthink*, 2d ed. Boston: Houghton Mifflin.

Jervis, Robert, Richard Ned Lebow, and Janice Gross Stein. 1985. *Psychology and Deterrence*. Baltimore: Johns Hopkins University Press.

Jones, Edward E., and Richard E. Nisbett. 1971. "The Actor and the Observer: Divergent Perceptions of the Causes of Behavior." In *Attribution: Perceiving the Causes of Behavior*, ed. Edward E. Jones, David E. Kanouse, Harold H. Kelley, Richard E. Nisbett, Stuart Valins, and Bernard Weiner. Morristown, N.J.: General Learning Press.

Kelman, Herbert C. 1961. "Processes of Opinion Change." *Public Opinion Quarterly* 25 (Spring): 57–78.

———, ed. 1965. *International Behavior: A Social-Psychological Analysis*. New York: Holt, Rinehart and Winston.

———. 1969. "Patterns of Personal Involvement in the National System: A Social-Psychological Analysis of Political Legitimacy." In *International Politics and Foreign Policy: A Reader in Research and Theory*, rev. ed., ed. James N. Rosenau. New York: Free Press.

———. 1973. "Violence without Moral Restraint: Reflections on the Dehumanization of Victims and Victimness." *Journal of Social Issues* 29 (4): 25–61.

———. 1978. "Israelis and Palestinians: Psychological Prerequisites for Mutual Acceptance." *International Security* 3 (1): 162–86.

———. 1979. "An Interactional Approach to Conflict Resolution and Its Application to Israeli-Palestinian Relations." *International Interactions* 6 (2): 99–122.

———. 1985. "Overcoming the Psychological Barrier: An Analysis of the Egyptian-Israeli Peace Process." *Negotiation Journal* 1 (3): 213–34.

———. 1986. "Interactive Problem Solving: A Social-Psychological Approach to Conflict Resolution." In *Dialogue toward Interfaith Understanding*, ed. William Klassen. Tantur, Jerusalem: Ecumenical Institute for Theological Research.

———. 1987. "The Political Psychology of the Israeli-Palestinian Conflict: How Can We Overcome the Barriers to a Negotiated Solution?" *Political Psychology* 8 (3): 347–63.

———. 1991. "A Behavioral Science Perspective on the Study of War and Peace." In *Perspectives on Behavioral Science: The Colorado Lectures*, ed. Richard Jessor. Boulder, Colo.: Westview.

———. 1992a. "Informal Mediation by the Scholar/Practitioner." In *Mediation in International Relations: Multiple Approaches to Conflict Management*, ed. Jacob Bercovitch and Jeffrey Z. Rubin. New York: St. Martin's.

———. 1992b. "Acknowledging the Other's Nationhood: How to Create a Momentum for the Israeli-Palestinian Negotiations." *Journal of Palestine Studies* 22 (1): 18–38.

———. 1993. "Coalitions across Conflict Lines: The Interplay of Conflicts within and between the Israeli and Palestinian Communities." In *Conflict Between People and Groups*, ed. Stephen Worchel and Jeffry A. Simpson. Chicago: Nelson-Hall.

———. 1996. "Negotiation as Interactive Problem Solving." *International Negotiation: A Journal of Theory and Practice* 1 (1): 99–123.

———. 1997. "Nationalism, Patriotism, and National Identity: Social-Psychological Dimensions." In *Patriotism in the Lives of Individuals and Nations*, ed. Daniel Bar-Tal and Ervin Staub. Chicago: Nelson-Hall.

_____. 1999a. "Transforming the Relationship between Former Enemies: A Social-Psychological Analysis." In *After the Peace: Resistance and Reconciliation*, ed. Robert L. Rothstein. Boulder, Colo.: Lynne Rienner.

_____. 1999b. "The Interdependence of Israeli and Palestinian National Identities: The Role of the Other in Existential Conflicts." *Journal of Social Issues* 55 (3): 581–600.

———. 2001. "The Role of National Identity in Conflict Resolution: Experiences from Israeli-Palestinian Problem-Solving Workshops." In *Social Identity, Intergroup Conflict, and Conflict Reduction*, ed. Richard D. Ashmore, Lee Jussim, and David A. Wilder. New York: Oxford University Press.

_____. 2004. "Reconciliation as Identity Change: A Social-Psychological Perspective." In *From Conflict Resolution to Reconciliation*, ed. Yaacov Bar-Siman-Tov. Oxford and New York: Oxford University Press.

_____. 2005. "The Psychological Impact of Sadat's Visit on Israeli Society." *Peace and Conflict: Journal of Peace Psychology* 11 (2): 111–36.

_____. 2006. "Interests, Relationships, Identities: Three Central Issues for Individuals and Groups in Negotiating Their Social Environment." *Annual Review of Psychology* 57 (January 2006): 1–26.

_____. 2007. "The Israeli-Palestinian Peace Process and Its Vicissitudes: Insights from Attitude Theory." American Psychologist 63 (4): 287–303.

Kelman, Herbert C., and Alfred H. Bloom. 1973. "Assumptive Frameworks in International Politics." In *Handbook of Political Psychology*, ed. Jeanne N. Knutson. San Francisco: Jossey-Bass.

Kelman, Herbert C., and V. Lee Hamilton. 1989. *Crimes of Obedience*. New Haven, Conn.: Yale University Press.

Kriesberg, Louis. 1981. "Non-Coercive Inducements in U.S.-Soviet Conflicts: Ending the Occupation of Austria and Nuclear Weapons Tests." *Journal of Military and Political Sociology* 9 (Spring): 1–16.

———. 1982. "Non-Coercive Inducements in International Conflict." In *Alternative Methods for International Security*, ed. Carolyn M. Stephenson. Lanham, Md.: University Press of America.

Lebow, Richard Ned. 1981. *Between Peace and War*. Baltimore: Johns Hopkins University Press.

———. 1987. *Nuclear Crisis Management: A Dangerous Illusion*. Ithaca, N.Y.: Cornell University Press.

Levy, Jack S. 1992. "Prospect Theory and International Relations: Theoretical Applications and Analytical Problems." *Political Psychology* 13 (2): 283–310.

Newcomb, Theodore M. 1947. "Autistic Hostility and Social Reality." *Human Relations* 1 (1): 69–86.

Osgood, Charles E. 1962. An *Alternative to War or Surrender*. Urbana: University of Illinois Press.

Pearson, Tamra. 1990. *The Role of "Symbolic Gestures" in Intergroup Conflict Resolution: Addressing Group Identity*. PhD diss., Harvard University.

Pruitt, Dean G., and James P. Gahagan. 1974. "Campus Crisis: The Search for Power." In *Perspectives on Social Power*, ed. James T. Tedeschi. Chicago: Aldine.

Rosenberg, Shawn W., and Gadi Wolfsfeld. 1977. "International Conflict and the Problem of Attribution." *Journal of Conflict Resolution* 21 (1): 75–103.

Ross, Lee. 1977. "The Intuitive Psychologist and His Shortcomings: Distortions in the Attribution Process." In *Advances in Experimental Social Psychology*, vol. 10, ed. L. Berkowitz. New York: Academic Press.

Ross, Lee, and Andrew Ward. 1995. "Psychological Barriers to Dispute Resolution." In *Advances in Experimental Social Psychology*, vol. 27, ed. Mark P. Zanna. New York: Academic Press.

Rouhana, Nadim N. 1997. *Palestinian Citizens in an Ethnic Jewish State: Identities in Conflict*. New Haven, Conn.: Yale University Press.

Rouhana, Nadim N., and Susan T. Fiske. 1995. "Perception of Power, Threat, and Conflict Intensity in Asymmetric Intergroup Conflict." *Journal of Conflict Resolution* 39 (1): 49–81.

Rouhana, Nadim N., and Herbert C. Kelman. 1994. "Promoting Joint Thinking in International Conflicts: An Israeli-Palestinian Continuing Workshop." *Journal of Social Issues* 50 (1): 157–78.

Rubin, Jeffrey Z. 1989. "Some Wise and Mistaken Assumptions about Conflict and Negotiation." *Journal of Social Issues* 45 (2): 195–209.

Rubin, Jeffrey Z., Dean G. Pruitt, and Sung Hee Kim. 1994. *Social Conflict: Escalation, Stalemate, and Settlement*, 2d ed. New York: McGraw-Hill.

Russett, Bruce. 1989. "Democracy, Public Opinion, and Nuclear Weapons." In *Behavior, Society, and Nuclear War*, vol. 1, ed. Philip E. Tetlock, Jo L. Husbands, Robert Jervis, Paul C. Stern, and Charles Tilly. New York: Oxford University Press.

Saunders, Harold H. 1988. "The Arab-Israeli Conflict in a Global Perspective." In *Restructuring American Foreign Policy*, ed. John D. Steinbruner. Washington, D.C.: Brookings Institution Press.

Schelling, Thomas C. 1963. *The Strategy of Conflict*. Cambridge, Mass.: Harvard University Press.

Sherif, Muzafer. 1958. "Superordinate Goals in the Reduction of Intergroup Conflict." *American Journal of Sociology* 63 (4): 349–56.

Staub, Ervin. 1989. *The Roots of Evil: The Origins of Genocide and Other Group Violence*. New York: Cambridge University Press.

Stein, Janice Gross. 1991. "Deterrence and Reassurance." In *Behavior, Society, and Nuclear War*, vol. 2, ed. Philip E. Tetlock, Jo L. Husbands, Robert Jervis, Paul C. Stern, and Charles Tilly. New York: Oxford University Press.

Tetlock, Philip E. 1998. "Social Psychology and World Politics." In *Handbook of Social Psychology*, 4th ed., vol. 2, ed. Daniel Gilbert, Susan T. Fiske, and Gardner

Lindzey. New York: McGraw-Hill.

Touval, Saadia, and I. William Zartman, eds. 1985. *International Mediation in Theory and Practice*. Boulder, Colo.: Westview.

Weinstein, Eugene A., and Paul Deutschberger. 1963. "Some Dimensions of Altercasting." *Sociometry* 26 (4): 454–66.

White, Ralph K. 1965. "Images in the Context of International Conflict: Soviet Perceptions of the U.S. and the U.S.S.R." In *International Behavior: A Social-Psychological Analysis*, ed. Herbert C. Kelman. New York: Holt, Rinehart and Winston.

————. 1968. *Nobody Wanted War: Misperception in Vietnam and Other Wars*. New York: Doubleday.

————. 1984. *Fearful Warriors: A Psychological Profile of U.S.-Soviet Relations*. New York: Free Press.

Zartman, I. William, and Johannes Aurik. 1991. "Power Strategies in De-escalation." In *Timing the De-escalation of International Conflicts*, ed. Louis Kriesberg and Stuart J. Thorson. Syracuse, N.Y.: Syracuse University Press.

Zartman, I. William, and Maureen R. Berman. 1982. *The Practical Negotiator*. New Haven, Conn.: Yale University Press.

PART TWO

APPROACHES TO PEACEMAKING

3

Negotiating in the International Context

Daniel Druckman

According to Webster's New Collegiate Dictionary, to negotiate is "to hold intercourse with a view to coming to terms; to confer regarding a basis of agreement." Despite its apparent straightforwardness, this definition has taken on a variety of meanings, especially during the past thirty years. Some view the process of negotiating as a puzzle to be solved, others see it as a bargaining game involving an exchange of concessions, some consider it a way of reconciling differences within and between organizations, and still others think of it as a means for implementing governmental policies.[1] These views have developed into distinct frameworks for research, with their own community of researchers who develop specialties in the fields of game theory, social psychology, organizational behavior, and international relations, respectively. Each field has contributed important insights into the process of negotiating.

These insights apply to a wide range of circumstances in which negotiation takes place. National leaders often make demands or exchange proposals from a distance. Well-known historical examples include the bilateral exchanges between the United States and the Soviet Union over the 1948–49 blockade of Berlin, between Kennedy and Khrushchev in 1962 over Soviet missile bases in Cuba, and between Carter and Khomeini concerning the American hostages in Iran in 1979–80. Leaders and their representatives also often confront each other face to face to discuss their conflicting interests over security, monetary and trade, or environmental issues. These meetings usually consist of formal summits, such as the meeting between Reagan and Gorbachev in 1986 at Reykjavík, or more protracted sessions, such as the long series of talks between their countries' representatives over arms control, beginning with the Strategic Arms Limitation Talks (SALT) and winding up with the Strategic Arms Reduction Talks. They also occur between allies concerning shared and conflicting interests on bilateral trade or military issues.

Other examples include talks among more than two nations. Sometimes they occur between blocs, such as the North Atlantic Treaty Organization (NATO)–Warsaw Pact discussions during the 1970s over mutual and balanced force reductions. They may take the form of trilateral discussions at which simultaneous bilateral negotiations take place. A current example is the discussion among Iceland, Norway, Russia, and the Faroe Islands over fishing rights in the North Atlantic: While Icelandic negotiators rejected the Russo-Norwegian offer, they reached an agreement with the Faroes; the Norwegians protested this agreement. Talks may also occur in multilateral conference settings, where representatives from many nations gather for discussions of regional, continental, or global issues. Notable examples are the Uruguay Round of the General Agreement on Tariffs and Trade (GATT), the negotiations establishing the European Community (referred to as the Single European Act), the ongoing discussions among members of the Organization for Security and Cooperation in Europe and among members of the UN Security Council, the talks that led to the Montreal Protocol on ozone depletion, and the discussions that resulted in the Rio Declaration on Environment and Development.

These examples demonstrate that international negotiation takes many forms. It consists of communications exchanged from a distance or face-to-face. It occurs between two or more nations' representatives in bilateral, trilateral, and multilateral forums. It concerns matters in a great variety of issue-areas that may have local, regional, or global consequences. Although some basic insights apply widely to the many forms, there are also obvious differences of context and scope. These differences complicate the search for a general theory of negotiation. They account for the emergence of alternative perspectives and serve as interesting variables whose impact on negotiating behavior can be ascertained. This chapter examines these perspectives, as well as the general patterns that characterize many types of negotiations through a survey of the literature on negotiating in the international context. Four dominant approaches to the study of negotiation are summarized, followed by a discussion of some important ideas about the distinct rhythms and patterns of negotiations found in these different approaches. Cases of arms control and environmental negotiations illustrate how these ideas have been used in the analysis of complex negotiations. Many of these analyses have been done in the context of large projects on international negotiation developed at such institutions as the U.S. Foreign Service Institute (FSI), the International Institute of Applied Systems Analysis (IIASA), and the Harvard Program on Negotiation (PON). Yet, despite the advances in knowledge about this topic, there remains a gap between research and practice. Some progress in bridging this gap is discussed before concluding the chapter with a look back at what has been accomplished and a look forward to promising directions for research and application.

The literature has expanded since the first version of this chapter appeared in 1997. Much of the recent literature is included in this revised version of the chapter. However, the chapter's organizing framework remains the same: the new studies are incorporated into the original chapter.

THINKING ABOUT NEGOTIATION: FOUR PERSPECTIVES

Four ways of thinking about negotiation have become dominant frameworks for research and theory development. These approaches differ in terms of their emphasis and complexity, but they also differ according to the particular processes they focus on—moves and preferences, communication processes, intra- and interorganizational processes, and an international system of diplomatic politics. Each approach is summarized briefly in the following sections.

Negotiation as Puzzle Solving

Game and decision theorists think about negotiation as a puzzle to be solved and prescribe "solutions" based on the parties' preferences. The key question for game theorists is, How do people make optimal choices when these choices are contingent on what other people do? According to the classical theory advanced by Von Neumann and Morgenstern (1944), players choose strategies, or courses of action, that determine an outcome. In its original form, the theory is static because it says little about the processes by which players' choices unfold to yield an outcome.

Brams (1993) adds a dynamic element to the classical theory. His "theory of moves" takes into account the tendency of players to look ahead before making a move or decision. By doing so, the theory seems to capture several aspects of actual strategic encounters between antagonists and allows for the possibility that players have only incomplete information. As such, Brams's theory assumes that players can rank outcomes in terms of preferences but cannot necessarily attach utilities to them, and allows for the use of threats and cycling of moves to wear down an opponent.

©1993 by Tom Dunne. Reproduced from Brams (1993) with permission of the artist.

Figure 3.1. The Prisoner's Dilemma. The Prisoner's Dilemma has been used to model behavior in a variety of strategic situations. The model involves two suspected criminals who face the following consequences: If one confesses and the other remains silent, the confessor goes free (the best payoff of 4) and the silent suspect gets a ten-year sentence (the worst payoff of 1). If both confess, they each get five-year sentences (the next-worst payoff of 2). If both remain silent, they get one-year sentences (the next-best payoff of 3). Four possible outcomes are represented in the two-by-two matrix: compromise, conflict, and a "win" for either of the two suspects.

The most prominent puzzle for game theorists is the well-known prisoner's dilemma game, which involves two suspected criminals who face the following consequences: If one confesses and the other remains silent, the confessor goes free and the silent suspect gets a ten-year sentence; if both confess, they each get five-year sentences; if both remain silent, they get one-year sentences. Four possible outcomes are represented in a two-by-two matrix: compromise, conflict, and a "win" for either of the two suspects (see figure 3.1). In classical game theory, both suspects have dominant strategies of confessing, resulting in the conflict outcome. Brams's (1993) theory of moves shows how the same dilemma can lead to the compromise outcome. By taking foresight into account, Brams shows that most initial states (compromise, one or the other suspect wins) produce the compromise outcome. However, he also allows for

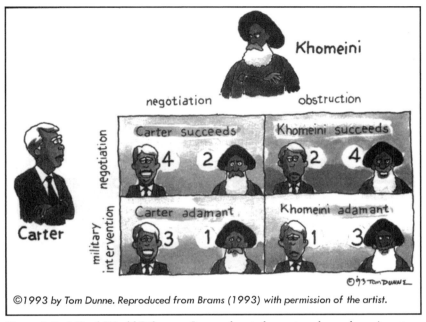

©1993 by Tom Dunne. Reproduced from Brams (1993) with permission of the artist.

Figure 3.2. A Real-World Dilemma. Incomplete information about players' motives leads to misperception and faulty assessments of their strategies. In the Iran hostage crisis, President Carter incorrectly assessed Iran's internal politics, believing that selecting the option of military intervention would force Ayatollah Khomeini to select negotiation to improve his payoff. Yet in the real payoff matrix shown above, Khomeini could not be swayed from his dominant strategy of selecting obstruction. The outcome, shown in the lower right box, gave Khomeini his next-best payoff of 3 and Carter his worst payoff of 1.

the possibility that players possess incomplete information, which can lead to misperception. For example, in the Iran hostage crisis, President Carter believed that choosing the option of military intervention would force Ayatollah Khomeini to select negotiation in order to improve his payoff, at which point Carter could also choose negotiation to obtain his best payoff in the compromise outcome, which was also better for Khomeini. This was not the case. Brams shows that in the real (correctly perceived) payoff matrix, Khomeini could not be swayed from his dominant strategy of selecting obstruction. In fact, the outcome of the crisis reflected the initial preferences, namely, Carter's choice of negotiation and Khomeini's choice of obstruction. The outcome was more favorable to Khomeini than to Carter. Eventually, however, the hostages were released (see figure 3.2).

Brams (1993) uses his formulation to demonstrate some consequences of actions taken by players who move simultaneously. He does not document the consequences of strategies used by opponents when they play the game. Evidence is provided from Axelrod's (1984) studies of the prisoner's dilemma game. He concludes that although no one strategy is optimal, the tit-for-tat approach fares best over the long term, when the value of future payoffs is important and when the other players' strategies are not known. Such an approach is successful, according to Axelrod, because it avoids provocation, makes exploitation impossible, is forgiving, and is simple. Brown (1986) notes, however, that the strategy may be viewed as an attempt to coerce rather than an effort to stimulate cooperation and may, in fact, lead to downward spirals in relations between nations. A more effective strategy, according to Brown, is to "follow two tracks: a tough responsive strategy on substantive issues, and an unconditionally cooperative policy on process issues" (381). This approach sends two messages to an adversary, namely, that we encourage a stable working relationship but we will not be exploited.

Another class of problems connected with negotiation concerns decision making under conditions of uncertainty in noninteractive, noncompetitive situations. Raiffa (1982) and his colleagues at Harvard developed an approach, known as decision analysis, that takes these conditions into account in its applications to negotiation. Like game theory, decision analysis concentrates on players' preferences for alternative outcomes. Unlike game theory, it analyzes decisions one player at a time (i.e., it does not derive from a premise of interdependence among the decision makers). The solution to the puzzle is to use each player's stated preferences to arrive at outcomes acceptable to both (all) parties. This type of analysis has been used during the preparation stage to assist negotiators in deciding where to offer a compromise or concession and where to remain adamant.

Ulvila (1990) illustrates decision analysis in a five-step procedure applied to the Philippines base-rights talks. First, the positions of Philippine and U.S. delegations were identified on each of six issues (including command and control, compensation, and criminal jurisdiction). Second, the impact of each issue on both delegations' key interests (e.g., sovereignty, economic development, and security) was estimated. Third, possible compromise options, located between the parties' initial positions, were identified (e.g., $1.1 billion in compensation, a figure between the U.S. position of $.7 billion and the Philippine position of $1.5 billion). Fourth, the options were expressed in numerical terms, where various compromises were scaled (at 50 for a true compromise) in relation to either delegation getting its own way (assigned a score of 100); this step enables an analyst to evaluate alternative package deals. For example, it was shown that the United States came out best if it compromised on three of the issues (command and control, jurisdiction, and number of facilities), obtained its own position on the security issue, and yielded to the Philippines on the compensation and human rights issues. Finally, the alternative packages were evaluated in terms of payoffs to each delegation and were represented graphically in order to highlight the one package that would produce the largest joint gain. In this case, the package that proved best for the United States was also shown to be the one that resulted in the greatest joint gains; a somewhat better package for the Philippines, but not for the United States, entailed settling four issues on the Philippine delegation's terms, two on the U.S. delegation's terms, and no compromises. For other case applications of this approach, see Raiffa (1982), Ulvila and Snyder (1980), and Spector (1994).

Negotiation as a Bargaining Game

Another way of thinking about negotiation is in terms of a process influenced by forces that promote or detract from agreements. Negotiation is thus viewed as a bargaining game in which opponents exchange concessions and where the exchange is influenced by the situation in which it takes place. This approach is descriptive: Laboratory situations are created to explore hypothesized determinants of bargaining behavior. Starting roughly with the seminal work of Siegel and Fouraker (1960), experimentalists in social psychology have sought an understanding of the conditions that drive the bargaining process. According to this view, negotiation is a process by which parties move gradually from their own initial positions toward the positions of others. In its simplest form, this process occurs between a single buyer and a unique seller who have total control over their interaction; the field of microeconomics refers to this situation as "bilateral monopoly." In their research on bilateral-monopoly bargaining, Siegel and Fouraker found that the best outcomes occur when (1) there is a prominent optimal outcome; (2) there is complete information so that the prominent outcome can be identified; (3) each party has veto power, ensuring that the outcome is mutually acceptable; and (4) only two are parties involved. Further analyses of this approach by Kelley and Schenitzki (1972) show that maximum joint profits can be attained only when bargainers make concessions in a systematic manner.

What happens, however, when there is no prominent optimal outcome or when it is difficult to find? Who concedes first? Which party makes the larger concession? The bargaining becomes a contest of wills between tactical adversaries, each trying to pressure the other into conceding first or more frequently. A good deal of the research on two-party bargaining has focused on this situation, and the findings have identified tactics that could tilt the contest in favor of one or the other bargainer. Examples are commitment tactics, alternating from initially tough to subsequently soft postures, the tactical use of deadline pressures, and distinguishing between "white-hat" (good guy) negotiators and "black-hat" (bad guy) constituents. Tactics such as these could lead to an agreement that favors the more effective tactician. Used effectively by both parties, however, the tactics could produce a deadlock. Other work in this area includes Rubin and Brown (1975) and Pruitt and Carnevale (1993).

Negotiation as Organizational Management

Organizational theorists view negotiation as a process of building consensus among diverse constituencies with stakes in the outcome. Key constituencies are the principals or power holders within the organizations represented in the negotiation. The process is dynamic, consisting of two- (or multi-) way communication among negotiators, constituents, and principals before and during the interparty negotiations. This conception renders negotiation a two- (or multi-) tiered process, also referred to as a two-level game (Putnam 1988): An intraparty (or domestic) negotiation occurs simultaneously with the interparty (or international) negotiation.

This view of negotiation recognizes its complexity. In particular, it recognizes the negotiator's dilemma of being caught between the often conflicting expectations of his or her constituents at home and those of the negotiation's other parties. This dilemma, known as "boundary-role conflict," was identified initially by Walton and McKersie (1965, chapter 8) in the context of labor-management negotiations. These authors highlight both the conditions for internal conflict and the tactics that may be used to resolve the dilemma. Two applications of this concept to international negotiations are Druckman's (1977a) formal model of dual responsiveness and Hopmann's (1977) analysis of the Mutual and Balanced Force Reduction (MBFR) talks. The former depicts the way a representative constructs a negotiating package that is acceptable to the other party, while taking into account the various bureaucratic agencies that seek to influence the contents of that package. The latter demonstrates how the multiple layers of bargaining within and between alliances were partially responsible for the long-term stalemate that entrapped the talks. Boundary roles are examined further in the section on rhythms and patterns.

The importance of bureaucratic politics in negotiation is made evident in both journalistic (Talbott 1979, 1984; Smith 1980) and analytical (Jonsson 1979; Jensen 1988) treatments of arms-control negotiations. By taking into account the organizational "embeddedness" of international negotiators' positions and performances, Kahn (1991) suggests a number of ways organizational theory can contribute to an understanding of negotiations among representatives of nation-states. There seems to be little doubt that negotiators "are motivated in large part by organizationally mediated rewards and penalties, the hope of organizational preferment, organizationally generated feelings of solidarity with others, identification with organizationally defined missions, and organizationally determined standards and values" (Kahn 1991, 149). Similarly, Winham's (1977) conceptualization of negotiation as a management process and Lax and Sebenius's (1986) depiction of management as a negotiation process illustrate clearly how well organizational phenomena reflect the complexity of negotiations between nations. These analyses urge us to pay more attention to the influence of role demands on the process and outcomes of negotiation.

Negotiation as Diplomatic Politics

A fourth perspective views negotiation as another setting for playing the game of international politics. Viewed as such, negotiations are microcosms of international relations, where parallel interactions or cross-linkages among many types of diplomatic activities occur, each influencing the other. This is the perspective of policy analysts and international relations scholars who are interested in how a particular negotiation fits into a broadly conceived foreign policy. The actors are governments whose actions are driven by policy prerogatives and structural elements of the international system.

By placing negotiation in the context of international relations, the analyst develops an appreciation for a variety of objectives served by negotiation, precedents or predilections that constrain negotiators, the linkages established among different negotiating venues, and the influence of external events on the negotiating process. Iklé (1964) illustrates how the type of agreement sought—for example, whether to extend an earlier agreement or to normalize a relationship—influences the main characteristics of the negotiating process. Of particular interest is his discussion of negotiating for side effects, where the parties seek to bolster a relationship, obtain intelligence, or affect the actions of third parties, rather than seeking an agreement. Kelleher (1976) shows that the legacy of past agreements often determines the way nations negotiate, especially when domestic constituencies emphasize the logic of precedent. Attempts to link an ongoing negotiation to others in progress or completed illustrate the connectedness of talks within an issue-area. Linkages are also often used tactically to break or create impasses, as shown in Tollison and Willett's (1979) analysis of economic negotiations and in Jensen's (1988) treatment of arms-control talks.

More generally, international negotiators are influenced by specific external events, as demonstrated by the research reported by Hopmann and his colleagues (Hopmann and King 1976; Hopmann and Smith 1978). They are also influenced by relational contexts as demonstrated by Donohue and Hoobler's (2002) findings. They show that negotiations in escalatory contexts lead to disappointments and resentments, whereas those that occur in de-escalatory settings are more likely to produce enduring agreements. These influences support the view that negotiations are embedded within an international system that has different institutional features than many domestic systems.[2]

Whereas the other approaches concentrate on the process of negotiating, this perspective focuses primarily on the international politics surrounding the negotiation. For the scholar of international relations, negotiation is one type of interaction among national representatives that impinges on the relationship between their nations. For the policymaker, negotiation is only one of several tools for implementing and developing foreign policies; others include official and unofficial diplomatic communications, ministerial meetings, meetings of international organizations, and summitry. For both scholar and practitioner, negotiation is a dynamic process that complements other activities initiated (or participated in) by governments. The results of these activities are evaluated in relation to broad policy objectives (e.g., Rubin 1981; Zartman 1989). They can also be understood in terms of recursive processes set in motion by the way external events impinge on negotiating interactions that, in turn, have shaping influences on those events and activities.[3]

RHYTHMS AND PATTERNS OF NEGOTIATION

Research on negotiation processes has sought to determine whether a particular pattern characterizes most negotiations and has produced an interesting debate about stages: Does negotiation proceed in a linear fashion? If so, through how many distinct stages? If not, what other model best describes the process? Researchers have construed transitions from one stage to another in terms of turning points, and their chief interests revolve around identifying the occurrence of turning points and the circumstances that bring them about. The "circumstances" can be regarded as influences that drive the process toward or away from agreement. This section presents alternative conceptions of stages and turning points and summarizes the research on key variables that influence the process.

Stages and Turning Points

Credit for introducing the concept of stages is usually given to Douglas (1957), who suggested that industrial negotiations pass through three stages: establishing the bargaining range, reconnoitering the range, and precipitating the decision crisis. More detailed renditions of the concept appear in the literature. Gulliver's (1979) eight stages are the most elaborate model proposed to date. Druckman's (1983, 1986b) model consists of five stages: an agenda debate, a search for guiding principles, defining the issues, bargaining to arrive at an acceptable concession change, and a search for implementing details. Even more refined models have been suggested; Pruitt's (1981) distributive/coordinative distinction may be the most basic (see also Morley and Stephenson 1977; Walton and McKersie 1965).

Certain elements are found in each of the schemes: (1) sequential progression, in chronological and conceptual time; (2) alternating antagonistic and coordinative behavior within and across stages; (3) interconnected and overlapping stages rather than rigid and precise steps to an outcome; and (4) synchronization problems between the bargainers. Although disagreement exists on whether the stages are prescriptions for getting agreements or descriptions of processes observed in many cases, they tend to be both, reflecting how it is done and how it is done well.

The stage concept can be a useful device for negotiators and analysts: it can be used to chart progress, to identify disjunctures in the process, and to provide a recognized pattern of expectations and behavior. Gulliver (1979) and Pruitt (1981) note the necessity of experiencing stages to know what is possible and to evaluate alternative agreements. According to Gulliver (1979, 177), "The parties need to experience the process and gain the experience of each other and of themselves so that they come to accept a particular outcome as satisfactory." The stage concept is also a tool for managing cognitive complexity, a function of particular relevance to international negotiations.

Applied to international negotiations, the stage concept has been used to describe a process that moves from the general to the specific. Pruitt (1981) explains the progression as having two functions: to organize the intellectual efforts of the bargainers and to deal efficiently with basic differences in outlook. International negotiators are often required to consider several issues simultaneously. To do this effectively, they must consider ways to simplify the intellectual task. One procedure is to identify a set of general issues and principles on which they agree. This procedure is the first stage of Zartman's (1975) two-stage model of negotiation: development of an abstract formula followed by the details needed to implement this formula.[4] One study that tests this model against concession/convergence behavior is Hopmann and Smith (1978).

As the negotiation passes through stages, momentum builds toward a conclusion, referred to as the endgame. It is useful to think about the progression in terms of turning points, defined as events or processes that mark the passage from one stage to the next, signaling progress from earlier to later phases. This concept has been used to depict progress in such diverse negotiations as the base-rights talks between the United States and Spain (Druckman 1986b), the North American Free Trade Agreement (NAFTA) negotiations (Tomlin 1989), the Intermediate-Range Nuclear Forces (INF) talks (Druckman, Husbands, and Johnston 1991), and eleven cases of multilateral environmental negotiations that took place from 1972 to 1992 (Chasek 1997). Examples are resolving impasses, signing framework agreements, developing formulas and then bargaining over details, and absorbing events outside the talks by either changing evaluations of the terms on the table or resolving the decision dilemma in the endgame. Defined more precisely, turning points have been shown to be useful analytical devices for assessing relationships between aspects of the verbal exchanges and key events (e.g., Druckman 1986b). Similar concepts have been used productively to capture transitions in team development, especially when major "jumps in progress" occur (Gersick 1988) or when shared perspectives have been achieved (Dechant and Marsick 1992).

More recently, Druckman (2001a) developed a framework for the comparative analysis of turning points. He distinguishes between precipitants as external, substantive, or procedural; process departures as relatively abrupt or nonabrupt; and consequences as escalatory or de-escalatory in the short and long term. This framework was used to analyze thirty-four international negotiation cases divided into the three issue-areas of security, political (including environmental), and trade or economic negotiations. The results highlight a distinction between security negotiations on the one hand and political and trade talks on the other: process departures or turning points were precipitated by external events (such as third-party interventions) in security talks; they were precipitated by internal decisions in the political and trade cases. These findings illuminate the risk-averse and reactive orientations taken by governments in the area of security policy.[5] Further analyses showed some differences between the international cases and a set of eleven domestic negotiations in the airline industry. Unlike any of the international cases, the domestic talks were characterized by repeated escalations before a settlement was reached. This pattern can be understood in terms of differences between the institutional contexts in which the talks take place. The repeated escalation is actually encouraged by the domestic, legal institutional structure in which the airline negotiations are embedded. That structure has no counterpart in the international context.

Another recent application of the turning-points framework is the study of NAFTA by Cameron and Tomlin (2000). They applied the concept to the prenegotiation process, showing that "deadlock in the policy process (impasse) or intensification in the problem that gave rise to the onset of the problem (crisis) may prevent or promote movement through the successive stages toward negotiation" (56). They identified events or conditions that influenced progress through the turning points (process departures) of the stages of pre-negotiation leading to NAFTA. Their depiction of aspects of the negotiation process suggests a path from precipitants (procedural) to departures (abrupt) to consequences (de-escalatory) similar to the aggregated path obtained for the trade cases in Druckman's (2001b) study. Other analyses of this case illuminate the importance of the monitoring function in negotiation, where negotiators adjust their moves based on their interpretation of the difference in previous moves made by them and their opposite numbers (Druckman 1978; Stoll and McAndrew 1986).

The research on turning points has been extended in several directions by a study group at Harvard's Program on Negotiation (PON). That group is exploring the meaning of such concepts as tipping points (Gladwell 2000), frame-breaking changes (Druckman, Husbands, and Johnston 1991), shifts in the direction of the negotiation process, the quality of the relationship, or power dynamics; moves and turns; openings and first moves; surprises that change the game; and contests between alternative scripts or frames. Working with case material, PON has concluded that moments might be visibly manifested by anything from changes in the rules of the game to challenges to social positions to scripts that are enacted (see Leary 2004). Further, a larger literature on the turning-point concept calls attention to the emotional, cognitive, and relational aspects of the concept as well as the connections between micro- and macrolevels of analysis (see Druckman 2004). This is a topic that will no doubt continue to capture the attention of the scholarly community.

Issues of timing occur with regard to the decision to negotiate. The question of interest arises when the parties are ready to negotiate or to seek mediation. Fisher's (1990) conflict stages are instructive. He depicts the way international conflicts escalate in terms of four stages: discussion, polarization, segregation, and destruction. At each stage, the relationship between disputants changes. The preferred method of conflict management becomes increasingly competitive, going from joint decision making in stage one to attempts at destruction in stage four. Intervention activities also change: assisting communication through negotiation in the first stage, improving relationships through consultation in the second stage, controlling hostility through "muscled" mediation in stage three, and controlling violence through peacekeeping in stage four. Less is known about the right time to intervene or to undertake an effort to make a desired change—whether early, when the costs are low, or late, when the moment is "ripe."

One well-known approach emphasizes the importance of a "mutually hurting stalemate" (Touval and Zartman 1985). Parties are more likely to come to the table when they are offered the prospect of a way out of a situation of increasing costs, coupled with decreasing prospects of winning.[6] However, other factors may also lead parties to make de-escalatory moves. Kriesberg (1991) identifies three conditions for de-escalation. One concerns relations between the adversaries, including relative power, level of cooperative exchanges, and extent of shared interests and values. Another involves domestic circumstances, including support for reducing antagonism, changes in government leadership, economic difficulties, and changes in support for a military-based security regime. A third condition is the international context, which consists of the impacts of other conflicts and the readiness of various governmental and non-governmental actors to serve as intermediaries in the conflict. These factors are likely to combine in various ways to make the situation conducive (or nonconducive) to de-escalation. Kriesberg also mentions the prospect of positive benefits from de-escalation. Getting to the table is one challenge for conflict reduction. Staying at the table until a satisfactory agreement is reached is another. These may be regarded as two forms of ripeness. The former may depend on an evaluation of costs, the mutually hurting stalemate. The latter is likely to depend on discovering a solution to the parties' dispute. This situation is referred to as a mutually enticing opportunity (MEO) (Zartman 2000). When discovered, an MEO emerges as a turning point in the talks, enhancing the chances for agreements.

Hurting stalemates and enticing opportunities are only two of the many variables that influence incentives to negotiate, the timing of negotiation, and the methods that lead to agreement. In a recent work on escalation and negotiation, Zartman and Faure (2005) identify a number of other variables; these include fear and fatigue, changes in stakes, parties, attitudes and values, disengagements, confidence and security-building measures, learning, and reaffirmed relationships. These are some of the changes that may occur in the context of the larger conflict. To the extent that they influence escalation (or de-escalation) dynamics, they can provide openings to negotiation.

Less is known about the relationship between the dynamics of conflict and the stages through which negotiations proceed. Although conditions may be conducive to entering into negotiation, the negotiation process itself may facilitate or hinder the relationship between the adversaries, leading either to further de-escalation or to the next stage in Fisher's (1990) ladder of escalation. It facilitates the relationship to the extent that it proceeds through the negotiation stages outlined above. It hinders the relationship to the extent that the process is characterized by frequent impasses rather than turning points.

Whether the process gathers momentum toward agreement or ends in stalemate depends on many of the factors discussed in this chapter as well as the kinds of strategies of de-escalation—based on parties, inducements, and issues—proposed by Kriesberg (1991). Further research is needed to increase our understanding of the role played by negotiation in resolving international conflicts as well as the impact of those conflicts on the negotiation process.

Constraints: Boundary Roles

The international negotiator occupies several roles simultaneously. As a representative of his or her government's interests, the negotiator must be responsive to its demands or requests. The negotiator must also take into account the interests of the other governments involved in the talks. Referred to as a "boundary-role conflict" (Walton and McKersie 1965; Frey and Adams 1972; Druckman 1977a; Walton, Cutcher-Gershenfeld, and McKersie 1994), this dilemma often confounds the main objective of the negotiator, who must try to resolve the different interests in order to attain an agreement. The dilemma is further complicated by a lack of consensus within the negotiator's own government and by the presence of multiple parties, including alliance partners, opponents, and third parties and their own interests in particular agreements. Another aspect of this dilemma is the frequent absence of key stakeholders, particularly in negotiations that involve governments and intranational actors that may lack legitimacy. Multilateral negotiations magnify the dilemma further, placing the negotiator in a managerial role that requires consensus building, leadership, and horse trading much in the manner of a lobbyist. Putnam (1988) and Evans and colleagues (Evans, Jacobson, and Putnam 1993) analyzed negotiation as a linked, two-level process, in which the key to international agreement lies in the concordance of proposals with domestic interest coalitions.

Boundary roles place complex information-processing and tactical demands on the negotiator. With regard to information processing, negotiators monitor other sides' moves for evidence of position change. They also monitor their own side for evidence of changes in positions on issues or preferences for various parts of the negotiation package. These monitoring activities have been conceived in different ways: the former as concession-making functions, the latter as utility functions. Neither type of function is simple, and both depend on the results of monitoring. Negotiators have been shown to adjust their strategies (making more or fewer concessions) following an evaluation of the others' moves, as depicted, for example, by Coddington's (1968) model. They alter (or maintain) their positions also in response to changes in agency or constituent evaluations: the more accountable they are to those agencies, the more likely they are to respond to these changing preferences (Druckman 1978).

At the same time, negotiators are not passive observers of the process. They are also tacticians who attempt to bring about change in both directions, influencing both their opponents and their constituents or principals. This "art" of impression management is described by Walton and McKersie (1965) in terms of three types of tactics. One type is intended to increase the negotiator's flexibility, for example, by limiting constituent participation in the formulation of proposals. Another type is intended to reduce constituents' aspirations by invoking rational arguments or using tacit communication to elicit the opponent's cooperation. A third set of tactics serves to reduce the discrepancy between constituents' expectations and performance. These tactics include limiting opportunities for surveillance, obscuring concessions, and exaggerating the level of achievement. The successful execution of these tactics depends on the extent to which negotiators have both control over the process and complete information about their side's preferences and strategies. By reducing the negotiators' latitude through scripting and monitoring and by withholding information, the principals can limit the negotiators' control over the process. To the extent that negotiation is a two- (or multi-) sided struggle for control, the negotiators are also limited by their opponents' control over the process.

The end of the Cold War widened the domains and structures for negotiation. More issues, more actors, and new formats have increased the complexity of international negotiations. These changes have implications for monitoring and control over the process. With regard to monitoring, the negotiator must keep track of many more positions and changed preferences. With regard to control, negotiators have less influence over decisions made in multilateral forums, but they also have more flexibility in developing positions and strategies due to the enlarged negotiating agendas facing governments. In light of these developments, the challenge is less a matter of dealing with conflicting demands of constituents or principals and opponents, and more a matter of keeping track of ongoing developments. Negotiation is becoming more like the management-process metaphor proposed by Winham (1977).

Preparing: Strategizing or Studying

Preparing for the negotiation is a central activity during the prenegotiation phase. Experimental evidence suggests that prenegotiation activities affect both the prospects for entering negotiations and the ease with which parties negotiate. Thibaut (1968) demonstrated the delicate balance of power among the parties needed to preserve a common interest in negotiation. Parties are more likely to enter into a negotiation when the talks can help them avoid a breakdown in their relationship; for example, when one party is in a better position to be exploitative, as in the case of a powerful nation demanding a high price for armaments from a weaker ally, and when another party is in a better position to be disloyal, as in the case of the weaker nation threatening to leave an alliance. Results indicate that most protective contracts were entered into when these threats were highest.

Bass (1966) and Druckman (1968) demonstrated the impact of the way bargaining teams prepare before negotiation. Bargaining was facilitated to the extent that parties avoided intensive strategy preparation and focused on the issues during prenegotiation caucuses. Moreover, it made little difference whether the caucuses were unilateral (teammates only) or bilateral (members of opposing teams). Informal, issue-oriented discussion was more effective than both tactical preparation and no prenegotiation communication among teammates or with opponents (see also Klimoski 1972). The effects on indicators of flexibility or the willingness to compromise are particularly strong: among ten variables analyzed in a meta-analysis of bargaining experiments, type of preparation produced the second-strongest effect size (Druckman 1994). Issue-oriented discussions may further increase the level of cooperation during the process and produce even better outcomes if they include efforts to understand the underlying values that divide the parties (Druckman, Broome, and Korper 1988). However, whether these results are due primarily to increased understanding or camaraderie among the negotiators remains to be explored; further research is needed to distinguish effects between the cognitive and the emotional aspects of planning (see Druckman and Broome 1991).

These results have implications for Dean's (1986) analysis of the preparation of U.S. negotiators for arms-control talks with the Soviet Union. He stresses the importance of bringing the negotiator "into the U.S. concept at the outset." However, such training should be done as part of informal and issue-oriented discussions. Although negotiators' participation in the development of national positions may give them a better understanding of the country's position, it may also enhance their commitment to those positions. Development of a negotiating concept would also benefit from exploratory discussions with the other side before the formal talks. Dean recognizes the importance of such nonbinding exchanges for the formulation of opening positions, taking into account differences and similarities in the parties' objectives.

Prenegotiation activities may also contribute to the "atmospherics" of the negotiation. For example, attention must be paid to the physical setting of the talks, including both their symbolic significance and the facilities used, and to the provision of adequate logistical support. Changes in the way parties interact may lay the foundation for constructive negotiation; alternative channels of communication may be opened for sending up trial balloons and for widening the range of options under consideration. Effective use of prenegotiation preparations may spell the difference between successful and unsuccessful outcomes.

More broadly, the prenegotiation phase has taken on increasing importance as nations discuss complex issues in global forums where difficult conceptual problems must be resolved before bargaining can occur. Chasek's (1997) comparative analysis of multilateral environmental negotiations makes clear that the prenegotiation phase is not simply preparatory in the narrow sense of planning for an eventual negotiation but contributes, in a larger sense, to developing a framework that can make agreement possible. As such, prenegotiation activities are indeed a part of the negotiation process, as Saunders (1984) proposed. They fill important functions, clarifying the agenda, parties, supports, budgets, costs and risks, and other requirements that are necessary before negotiations can begin (Stein 1989).

Framing: Developing Sets and Orientations

Pruitt (1965) highlighted the importance of the ways international actors define or perceive their situation. Of particular relevance for negotiation are perceptions of the task as being either competitive (win-lose) or cooperative (problem solving). A number of experimental studies have demonstrated that these perceptions are heavily influenced by the situation and, in turn, influence the negotiating process and outcome (Druckman 1968; Zechmeister and Druckman 1973; Druckman, Broome, and Korper 1988). For example, in the Druckman study (1968), strategic planning before the negotiation produced competitive perceptions that resulted in frequent deadlocks. Similar correlates of negotiating behavior have been found for perceptions such as whether the negotiating climate is viewed as futile, productive, tolerant, or hostile and whether the opponent is seen as fair or unfair, trusting, or suspicious (Druckman, Broome, and Korper 1988).

In a number of bargaining experiments, the investigator induced the negotiator's orientation through instructions from the experimenter or from constituents (e.g., Summers 1968; Organ 1971). In some studies, orientation was "selected" by recruiting subjects who indicated cooperative or competitive attitudes before the experiment (e.g., Wall 1975; Lindskold, Waters, and Koutsourais 1983). Taken together, these experiments show strong effects for this variable: of ten variables compared in a meta-analysis (Druckman 1994), orientation had the strongest impact on compromise behavior. The impacts were considerably stronger for studies that induced orientations than for those that selected for them.

Orientations toward negotiation may be induced in subtle ways. A series of experiments (Neale, Huber, and Northcraft 1987; Neale and Bazerman 1985) showed that negotiating behavior can be affected by simply framing the bargaining task in terms of "gains to be realized" (potential profits) or "losses to be avoided" (potential costs). Negotiators with a gains orientation typically complete more transactions or conclude more agreements than those with a losses orientation. They do so, however, largely because they are willing to make larger compromises, not because they arrive at integrative agreements that result in high joint profits. Additionally, the larger compromises are thought to be due to an aversion to taking risks (e.g., escalating the conflict or causing impasses) induced by the gains orientation. Indeed, risk aversion may account for the plethora of compromise agreements arms-control negotiators have achieved over the years (Jensen 1988).

At a somewhat deeper level, negotiators may be influenced by the metaphors that are evoked by negotiating situations. For example, subjects who viewed a simulated conflict in ideological terms also perceived the bargaining process as resembling an arms race, and this perception correlated with their being less willing to compromise and less satisfied with the outcome.[7] The arms-race metaphor illustrates the importance of mental models in negotiation. Some models, or analogies, may lead subjects to cooperate in seeking an agreement, while others may lead them to compete for advantage. We need to learn more about the way such imagery influences conflict behavior, leading toward or away from satisfactory agreements. Moreover, negotiation may be more effective to the extent that negotiators develop a shared model of the task and their roles in it. Research on the way teams develop shared mental models seems particularly relevant, especially in the context of the new problem-solving formats of global environmental conferences. Orasanu and Salas (1993, 7) found that effective (compared to ineffective) teams were characterized by "[shared] knowledge enabling each person to carry out his or her role in a timely and coordinated fashion, helping the team to function as a single unit with little negotiation of what to do and when to do it." When asked to account for a team's success, coaches will often say that the team members play well together or that they anticipate each other's moves. These sorts of shared understandings developed among team members may also develop among negotiators from different countries, especially as they continue to interact in long-term conferences.

Bargaining and Concessions

Bargaining and concession making are common features of most, if not all, negotiations. Although the term "bargaining" is often used interchangeably with negotiation, it can also refer to one phase in a process that consists of many other activities (Druckman 1983). Bargaining occurs during the discussions over details, where parties exchange concessions or trade items of value (Zartman 1975). This section examines several aspects of bargaining that have received attention in the research literature: the concession-making "dance," negative spirals and starting mechanisms, driving factors, and the role of values.

The Concession-Making Dance. Since the publication of the study by Siegel and Fouraker (1960), students of bargaining behavior have devoted considerable attention to the effects of alternative concession-making strategies for eliciting concessions from an opponent. A tough strategy, recommended by Siegel and Fouraker, is likely to work if it produces concessions from the opponents, for example, when they are under time pressure and have weak alternatives to a settlement; it will not work if it leads opponents to reciprocate toughness, as when they worry about being exploited or perceive an unfair advantage. Similarly, a softer approach, recommended by Osgood (1962), will work if it produces reciprocation from the opponent who is anxious to conclude a fair agreement; it will not work if the opponent responds with fewer concessions in an attempt to exploit the other's softness. Central to these strategies is the issue of responsiveness: Do bargainers reciprocate, exploit, or ignore the other's concessions (Bartos 1978; Pruitt 1981)? This question has been addressed in analyses of international negotiations.

These analyses sought to ascertain the extent to which international bargainers reciprocate each other's concessions. In his analysis of base-rights talks between the United States and Spain, Druckman (1986b) discovered a pattern in which, following a comparison of mutual concessions in the initial round, negotiators attempted to "close the gap" in the next round by reducing their concessions when the other side failed to concede (i.e., they reciprocated each other's tough postures). A similar pattern, referred to as "comparative responsiveness," was found by Stoll and McAndrew (1986) in the ten years of talks between the Soviet Union and the United States over limiting strategic weapons (SALT I and II). In addition, analyses of seven international negotiations for which concession data were available (including the Nuclear Test Ban talks, SALT I and II, and postwar disarmament talks), conducted by Druckman and Harris (1990), demonstrated that among the ten models of reponsiveness examined (namely, simple tit-for-tat, five variants on monitoring trends in the other's concessions, and four variants on comparing previous mutual concessions), the comparative pattern best depicted the way negotiators responded to each other's moves. Negotiators evaluate the size of the difference between their own positions and those of other sides and then respond. This pattern resembles Coddington's (1968) bargaining cycle of expectations-evaluations-adjustments, also known as "threshold adjustment."[8] Although the adjustments can be made in the direction of either increased toughness or increased softness, the cases examined were characterized by moves that increased mutual toughness, often leading to impasses. Of interest is the challenge of reversing this pattern, moving the negotiation down a path toward agreement rather than stalemate.

The way that offers are communicated is also important. Research presented at the annual meetings of the International Association for Conflict Management (IACM) highlights the value of framing offers in terms of interests rather than concessions, clarifying the connection between the offer and one's needs, emphasizing the value-creating rather than value-claiming features of an offer—a distinction originally made by Lax and Sebenius (1986)— and making a generous offer on one issue in a package.[9] With regard to packages, Medvec and Galinsky (2005) make an intriguing suggestion. They propose that making multiple equivalent simultaneous offers (MESOs) can produce better agreements: MESOs consist of alternative packages of perceived equal value. The alternatives provide an opportunity to compare and then choose which, in turn, may enhance the value of the choice made by the opposing negotiator. MESOs also provide a bargainer with a level of control that might otherwise be elusive at the table.

Negative Spirals and Starting Mechanisms. Only one case analyzed in the Druckman and Harris (1990) study showed a pattern in which bargainers adjusted their moves in the direction of the "softer" opponent. This case occurred during the final two years of discussion between the Soviet Union and the United States over a partial nuclear test ban and resulted in an agreement (Hopmann and Smith 1978). The agreement was marked by President Kennedy's 1963 announcement of a suspension of U.S. nuclear tests and an appeal for a relaxation of East-West tension. Regarded as a unilateral initiative, the announcement broke an impasse in negotiations that lasted from 1958 to 1963. Laboratory and historical case studies have identified some conditions under which unilateral initiatives are likely to produce the desired cooperative responses.

The laboratory evidence suggests that such initiatives are likely to be more effective when the initiator clarifies the intention behind the move, when reciprocity is not required too soon, when it is rewarded, and when it is diffi-cult for the other party to explain away the initiatives (Lindskold, Betz, and Waters 1986). Favorable circumstances include perceived dependence of the intended recipient on the initiator, a perception that the initiating party can-not be exploited, and the recipient's judgment that the benefits of coopera-tion outweigh those of competition. Historical evidence presented by Rose (1988) adds other favorable conditions: a clear signaling of demands by the initiating party, no internal bureaucratic conflicts within the recipient, and no threats to political status, security, economic, or military capabilities. Of these conditions, the most important concern was risk to security; a nation that perceived itself at risk did not reciprocate its adversary's coopera-tive move.

Unilateral initiatives are actions usually taken outside of negotiation. They can be used as starting mechanisms to get talks back on track or to break im-passes (note Osgood's 1973 proposal of Graduated Reduction in Tensions for Mutual and Balanced Force Reduction). They can also be used as alternatives to formal negotiations, such as Adelman's (1984–85) proposed strategy for achieving arms control without treaties. The former is directed primarily toward getting agreements; the latter is intended to improve relationships. In some cases, both purposes are served by one party's initiatives; one example is Gorbachev's stream of unilateral moves leading to the INF agreement and to a markedly changed relationship between the superpowers. The extraordi-nary events that preceded the fall of the Soviet Union have provoked ana-lysts to reexamine their assumptions about the benefits of formal negotiation, at least in the area of arms control (see Ramberg 1993).

Driving Factors in Bargaining. The research discussed above concentrates pri-marily on the effects of the other party's concession making, demonstrating that bargainers respond to each other's moves. However, such responsiveness is only one of several factors that drive the bargaining process. Many other variables have been found in experimental studies to affect bargaining. These effects are summarized in a meta-analysis of the literature in which ten aspects of the bargaining situation were compared for their relative impacts on com-promise in bargaining (Druckman 1994). Beyond a competitive or cooperative orientation, the strongest effects were obtained whether bargainers strate-gized or studied before bargaining, whether the bargaining occurred under a deadline, and whether the distance between initial positions was large or small. The weakest effects were obtained for whether the issue was considered "large" or "small" and whether audiences were present during the bargaining session. It appears that the way bargainers define their task, as a competitive contest or problem to be solved, has a particularly strong influence on their attempts to secure an agreement.

Further analyses of the experimental findings suggest insights into the way different aspects of the situation combine to produce various effects. The question most frequently asked in this regard is: When do bargainers stick to their positions? The answers are varied: when they prepare strategies in cohesive groups for a negotiation in which few issues are being contested and no deadline exists; when competitive orientations are induced during the bargaining by bureaucratic superiors and are linked explicitly to bargaining strategies; when they negotiate in the presence of an audience that creates strong face-saving pressures; and when there are no time limits to reach agreement and no strike costs while the bargaining takes place. These are some of the conditions for intransigence; as such, they are aspects of the situation that can be manipulated as part of a tactical approach to negotiating beneficial agreements.

The accumulated experimental research on negotiation has made evident the importance of situational influences on negotiating behavior. These results suggest a metaphor of "situational levers" that has become a basis for several studies of simulated negotiation (Druckman 1993a; 1995; see also Druckman 2003b for a survey of research on the role of situations in conflict). More recently, attempts have been made to explore the effects of altering aspects of the immediate setting in which discussions take place. Based on earlier research on formal versus informal communication structures (Collins and Raven 1969), it was thought that more agreements would occur in informal than in formal situations. One way of defining formality is in terms of the way negotiations occur between parties facing each other behind tables. This configuration may encourage a competitive approach to negotiation. Of interest is the question of what would happen if the tables were removed from the room, leaving the chairs arranged in a circle: Facing each other in full view without the barrier of a table between them, would negotiators be more cooperative?

This hypothesis was evaluated in a preliminary way with eighteen replications of a simulated multilateral negotiation over territorial and environmental issues. Interestingly, all nine tables groups did not reach an agreement, whereas eight of the nine chairs groups did agree. Self-reported perceptions indicated that the tables groups viewed the situation as less open and more competitive than the chairs groups. However, when this experiment was conducted with actual mediators in the District of Columbia's Small Claims Court, the hypothesized differences between the configurations did not occur. An explanation for the different results is in terms of emotional involvement. The claimants were evidently more emotional about their issues than were the student role players. Strong emotions—also termed "emotional flooding—can reduce attention to aspects of the situation, including seating arrangements.[10]

The Role of Values in Bargaining. Bargaining interactions are also influenced by the types of issues under discussion. In international negotiations, parties typically discuss their interests in matters of security, territory, or trade. These issues are usually well-defined, allowing for the sorts of exchanges characteristic of bargaining over tangible items. Were it this simple, however, the record would show many agreements emerging from a fairly predictable process in many ways akin to collective bargaining in labor-management disputes. Unfortunately, this is seldom the case in international negotiation. Impasse is a major concern in international negotiations, and the process does not exhibit a predictable pattern from one case to another. In part, this situation is due to the role values play in defining the issues at stake.

Differences in values enter the discussions in several ways. One is when government representatives address issues concerning their countries' relationship, as occurs often in regions undergoing political transformation (Druckman 1980). Another is when agendas are expanded to deal with larger issues, as, for example, when Spain demanded that the United States broker its entry into NATO during the course of the 1975–76 talks about renewing base rights (Druckman 1986b). A third example is when issues of national sovereignty are raised in talks about establishing trade or security regimes, economic unions, or regional organizations; the new entities provoke anxieties about the extent to which independence must be sacrificed for the advantages of interdependence (Zartman 1991). Finally, a fourth example is when parties are divided along ideological lines, as in negotiations to resolve internal conflicts between insurgent groups asserting their claims for power and regimes bent on preserving the political order (Zartman 1995).

These issues are rarely the direct subjects of negotiation. They are often regarded as non-negotiable, as issues to be discussed but not compromised. As such, these issues exacerbate the conflict by making it difficult for parties to resolve their differences over interests, especially when the link between value differences and interests or positions is made explicit by one or another party, as illustrated in a series of experiments by Druckman and colleagues. The experimental results showed that conflicts were easier to resolve when value differences were either not introduced or essentially delinked from interests (Druckman, Rozelle, and Zechmeister 1977). However, they also showed that when values were separated from interests, the negotiating process was more competitive than when value differences were confronted and discussed in prenegotiation sessions (Druckman, Broome, and Korper 1988). Further experiments showed that the facilitating effects of the prenegotiation discussions were due to the increased camaraderie and familiarity gained during those meetings (Druckman and Broome 1991). These results underscore an important contribution of prenegotiation sessions, namely, to acknowledge differences of values without letting those differences hinder subsequent talks over specific interests (Stein 1989).

Over the longer term, there may be a broader interplay between values and interests that produces cycles of polarized and depolarized conflicts between parties. The cycles reflect diverging and converging positions owing to repeated attempts to resolve conflicting interests; agreements serve to reduce value differences, which, in turn, makes it easier to negotiate future conflicts. Similarly, stalemates can exaggerate value differences, serving to hinder future negotiations. Earlier theoretical work has described the process in the form of propositions (Druckman and Zechmeister 1973), which were later usefully applied to depict the bargaining and related interactions between conflicting groups in the Philippines (Druckman and Green 1995).

The Use of Content Analysis. Many of the studies reviewed in this section consist of content analyses of laboratory or field data, the preferred approach for analyzing negotiation scripts or texts. Of the many coding systems that have been used, none has been more popular than bargaining process analysis. Harris (1996) showed that this system satisfied most of the criteria of validity, reliability, theoretical relevance, and ease of use. Several applications are reviewed by Druckman and Hopmann (2002). These include an analysis of responsiveness among parties in a multilateral negotiation, an evaluation of the phase movement hypothesis in problem-solving groups, a comparison of simulated with actual historical cases, and the evaluation of alternative models of responsiveness in negotiations conducted in several historical periods. Other content-analysis systems have been designed to probe the relationship between the negotiation process and broader relations between the parties, to provide a more comprehensive analysis of bargaining interactions that involve both verbal and nonverbal behaviors, and to compare national negotiating behaviors. In addition, more complex systems have been designed in order to describe a network of themes and their linkages for identifying a causal sequence (Roberts 1997) or to provide insight into the way a negotiator construes his or her role in influencing events or shaping a negotiation process or outcome (Riessman 1993). These approaches contribute to negotiation analysis by providing additional information about the cognitive and subjective aspects of negotiation interactions.

EXPANDING THE DOMAIN

As noted throughout this chapter, much of our knowledge about negotiation is based on the results of laboratory experiments, supplemented by a rich literature of case studies. An advantage of the experimental approach is that it focuses attention on relationships between precisely defined variables, such as the influence of time pressure on agreements. Such a setting also has the feature of cumulative knowledge, allowing an investigator to compare across experiments the relative impacts of several variables on negotiating behavior (Druckman 1994). A disadvantage of the laboratory approach is a kind of myopic focus that renders the findings only partially relevant to complex cases of international negotiation. The knowledge comes in parts, with each part— a line of experiments—revealing only those aspects of negotiation that are isolated for "microscopic" investigation. A challenge for future research will be to link or synthesize the parts into a broader picture. One way to do this is through the development of frameworks.

Frameworks

A good deal of the conceptual work on negotiation has consisted of identifying the various parts of the process. These are general dimensions that can be used to describe a variety of cases. The primary contributions of this approach are those found in most taxonomic work, namely, to define a field, to distinguish among similar and dissimilar cases, and to identify connections or hypothesized relationships among the categories. These functions have been served by the frameworks proposed by Sawyer and Guetzkow (1965), which relates preconditions to processes, conditions, and outcomes, and by Randolph (1966), which organizes the aspects of negotiation into the categories of prenegotiation, negotiation, agreement, and implementation.

Sawyer and Guetzkow (1965) used their framework to organize the empirical work on negotiation done in the 1950s and 1960s. Since then, it has served to guide research and application, including Ramberg's (1977) study of tactics used in the talks over demilitarization of the deep seabed; Bonham's (1971) analysis of factors influencing the 1955 East-West talks in the UN Disarmament Subcommittee; Druckman and Hopmann's (2002) models of the MBFR process; Druckman's (1973, 1977b) efforts to organize the social-psychological literature on bargaining processes and influences; and Weiss's (1994a, 1994b) framework for organizing cross-cultural research on international business negotiations (see also Graham, Mintu, and Rodgers 1994). The Sawyer-Guetzkow framework has also served as a basis for Fisher's (1983) conceptualization and organization of the literature on third-party consultation.

These frameworks do have their shortcomings. By itself, an organizing framework lacks sufficient penetration of details to capture subtle processes in particular cases; it is also, at least initially, a taxonomic, not an analytical, exercise. Recognizing these shortcomings, projects have been undertaken to move beyond the defining and organizing functions of frameworks. A number of projects, conducted as part of the Processes of International Negotiation program at IIASA, are examples of attempts to bridge analysis and synthesis. These projects fall within the initial framework established by the program, analyzing negotiation according to actors, structures, processes, strategies, and outcomes (Kremenyuk 2002).

Framework categories were used in the design of a simulated conference on environmental regulation (Druckman 1993a). The exercise captured processes of international negotiation—as described by frameworks—without forfeiting the essential properties of experimental design. By developing scenarios that resembled the real-world talks (at each of several negotiating stages), role players (scientists and diplomats) were confronted with contingencies similar to those facing the actual delegates. By "unpacking" the key variables in each scenario, using a pair-comparison procedure, participants could compare the relative impacts of those variables (in each stage) on decisions about position movement, tactics, and perceptions. Results were expressed in the form of trajectories of factors that influenced decisions in each stage. For example, a path toward agreement was as follows: friendly relations with other delegations (stage one) → talks held at a peripheral location (stage two) → talks given limited media attention (stage three) → talks given limited media attention (stage four). These factors increased flexibility leading to an agreement at the end of the process. Other factors served to decrease flexibility, leading to stalemate at the end: a lack of familiarity with the other delegations (stage one) → talks held at a central location (stage two) → talks given wide media attention (stage three) → talks given wide media attention (stage four).[11] These factors can also be altered or manipulated for impact—that is, as levers of negotiating flexibility.

Another project used framework categories as interview questions for comparative case analysis (Druckman 1997). Members of Austrian national delegations to a variety of bilateral and multilateral talks were asked about several aspects of the negotiation: its structure, the composition of the delegations, bureaucratic support, the issues, the negotiating situation, the process, the outcomes, and the influence of events outside the negotiation. Building on the computer model developed by Bloomfield and Beattie (1971) for conflict analysis, the research used statistical procedures to discover similarities and dissimilarities among the cases as well as the critical factors that distinguished them. The key distinguishing factor among the cases was conference size. Smaller conferences were more likely to result in binding agreements or treaties than larger, multilateral conferences. Smaller conferences were characterized by low turnover of delegates, private forums, a stage-like process, packaging of issues, and relatively weak deadline pressures. These factors facilitate choosing among the "available terms" (Iklé 1964, 60). As such, they may be a more cost-effective forum for negotiation than large multilateral talks because they have fewer transaction costs and produce better outcomes. Multilateral talks, however, offer other advantages. One is alliance coordination. Another is the creation of communities of opinion that serve as regimes regulating transactions among regional or global actors. These advantages are a result of conference diplomacy, not negotiation intended to create binding agreements.

The differences between bilateral and multilateral structures also have implications for analysis. Zartman (1994) identifies six characteristics of multilateral negotiations, including multiple parties (but not fixed at a given number), many issues that allow for complex trade-offs, a considerable variety of roles among the parties in the negotiation, outcomes that concern rules more than redistributive issues, and the organization of parties into coalitions that often change during the course of the talks. These features complicate analyses of relationships between processes (or strategies) and outcomes and require an expanded framework, drawing on insights provided by game and decision theory, organization theory, small-group analysis, coalition approaches, and leadership analysis. Each of these approaches addresses how parties manage the complexity of the encounter in order to produce an outcome. By emphasizing a particular aspect of the multilateral process, each approach is limited. By combining these aspects into a broader perspective, a synthesis of the approaches provides the range and scope needed to understand the way multilateral processes lead to outcomes. The increasing popularity of multilateral forums in the post–Cold War world encourages further progress in developing a useful analytical paradigm.

A fourth project was designed to evaluate the plausibility of Iklé's (1964) typology of negotiating objectives. Thirty cases, sampled from the collection of Pew Case Studies in International Affairs, were distinguished in terms of five objectives: innovation, redistribution, extension, normalization, and side effects. In addition, a sixth objective was identified as negotiations concerning the creation of multilateral regimes. These cases focused on issues that surfaced on the international agenda during the 1980s. Each type had a relatively distinct profile based on aspects of negotiation described originally in the Sawyer-Guetzkow (1965) framework—number of parties and issues, bargaining strategies, media exposure, stability of the process, and types of outcomes (Druckman et al. 1999). This analysis reinforces the value of the framework for distinguishing among diverse cases. It also demonstrates the value of advanced statistical techniques—multidimensional scaling and discriminant analysis—for empirical evaluations of complex frameworks and contributes to the state-of-the-art in the comparative study of international negotiation.

A fifth project created a computer program for diagnosing parties' flexibility and projecting probable outcomes of ongoing negotiations (Druckman 1993b). Users were asked questions in each of five categories: the issues, the parties, the delegations, the situation, and the process. The questions varied in terms of the extent to which they correlated with flexibility; each question was assigned a weight based on research evidence about its impact on flexibility. The answers and weights were combined by the program to yield a judgment of each party's flexibility. These judgments were then used as estimates of likely outcomes, including optimal agreements for both parties, fair but less-than-optimal agreements, capitulation by one party to another, impasses, and continuation without agreement. Among the program's features is the ability to make comparisons among different cases and among different theories of negotiation. With regard to cases, users can answer the questions for each of several negotiations and compare their location on a flexibility grid; regarding theories, users can compare the flexibility judgments resulting from answers to questions in each of the categories. In a recent application, a very high correspondence was discovered between the hypothesized outcomes of nine completed cases (Panama Canal, nuclear test ban, INF, and acid rain talks, among others) and the actual outcomes obtained in those negotiations, attesting to the validity of the diagnostic (framework) categories (see Druckman 1993b and Druckman, Ramberg, and Harris 2002).

An expanded web-based version of this tool has been used to assist negotiators to resolve impasses. Referred to as a negotiating support system (NSS), the tool provides three mediating functions: diagnosis, analysis, and advice. Results from three experiments, conducted with a simulated bilateral international dispute, showed that negotiators with access to the NSS between rounds achieved more agreements than various alternatives, including reflection, advice only, and live mediation. Further improvements occurred when the NSS tool was used jointly by the opposed negotiators (Druckman, Druckman, and Arai 2004). These findings attest to the value of computer support for international negotiators.

Activities that occur after an agreement has been negotiated are receiving increasing attention. Regarded as a stage in an extended process of negotiation and renegotiation, these activities include ratification, monitoring the parties for compliance with the provisions or verification of the agreement, and continuing negotiation of the terms or issues still to be resolved. In their study of environmental agreements, Spector and Korula (1992) divided postagreement processes into domestic and international aspects. The domestic aspects included ratification, rule making to protect the agreement, implementation and resistance, and monitoring. The international components consisted of the formation, operation, and adjustment of the regimes that come into being as a result of the agreements. Environmental negotiations are embedded within a larger institutional context; complex issue packages and linkages among issue areas and sectors make them difficult to negotiate and sustain.

Less complex, perhaps, is the implementation of bilateral arms-control and base-rights agreements. A key issue for arms control is verification of the agreed reductions, although issues concerning the emergence of security regimes are also relevant (Jervis 1983). Base-rights provisions are often of shorter duration and are renegotiated periodically.[12] Domestic ratification and relational issues are also important in this arena (Druckman 1990). These are examples of activities to be included in an expanded framework of negotiation.

In addition to postnegotiation processes, an enlarged framework should take into account the various activities that precede negotiation, as discussed earlier, as well as the multilateral (and global) structures characteristic of many current venues, discussed above. Such an enlarged framework should also recognize that negotiations occur between various types of identity groups within and independent of nation-states. Although little attention has been paid to these negotiation processes, a good start in developing a framework, based on diverse cases, is made in Zartman's (1995) work on internal negotiations.

The enlarged framework should also take into account connections between the negotiating process and postnegotiation relations among the parties. The difference between problem-solving and distributive approaches to negotiation may well have impacts on long-term relations. Distinguishing between forward- and backward-looking outcomes, Druckman and Lyons (2005) showed that more collaborative processes that focus attention on the future are likely to result in postnegotiation arrangements that produce societal or institutional changes. Comparing the cases of Mozambique with Nagorno-Karabakh, Druckman and Lyons found that when negotiating parties seize opportunities to address underlying political issues (forward looking), as in the 1992 Rome accord in Mozambique, postagreement relations can improve dramatically. When they concentrate only on reaching settlements on cease-fires that stop the violence (backward looking), as in the 1994 Nagorno-Karabakh talks, the outcome is less likely to lead to a resolution of the conflict.[13] The distinction between negotiation processes geared toward obtaining settlements and those aimed at achieving resolutions is relevant to the way agreements are implemented.[14]

Complex Cases

Frameworks also guide qualitative case analyses, as illustrated by the series of case studies done by the Foreign Policy Institute (FPI) at Johns Hopkins University's School for Advanced International Studies and by the Pew Project, based at Georgetown University's Center for the Study of Diplomacy, and those reported in *Negotiation Journal*, edited by Harvard's PON, and in the journal *International Negotiation*, edited by the Washington Interest in Negotiation (WIN) group. The FPI cases are structured in terms of a common framework for analyzing the negotiation process, and their narratives seem to capture the dynamics of complex bilateral and multilateral negotiations. Following a background summary, each case narrative focuses on the parties and their sources of power and interests, leading to a discussion of the underlying and immediate precipitants that brought about negotiation. The next sections deal with that process, beginning with prenegotiations and culminating in a decision on whether to negotiate. The process continues with a search for a formula that provides a basis for working out the details of an agreement, including the tactics and decisions involved in ending the talks with a mutually satisfactory outcome. The authors' attempts to identify turning points and to provide insights into the impacts of pressures exerted by the parties contribute to compelling lessons for negotiating behavior. Examples of bilateral cases are the 1972 Simla talks between India and Pakistan, the 1904–05 peace talks between Russia and Japan, the Panama Canal negotiations, and the Beagle Channel dispute between Chile and Argentina. Analyses of the multilateral cases provide additional insights into the process of managing complexity: for example, the Stockholm Conference on Security and Cooperation in Europe, the Mediterranean Action Plan, the Contadora peace process, and the Convention on Transboundary Air Pollution.

Although not structured in terms of a common framework, the Pew case studies and those reported in *Negotiation Journal* and *International Negotiation* also use guiding concepts to provide insights into the process. In discussing lessons learned from four international cases (the U.S.-Canada Free Trade Agreement, a hostage release following a 1970 skyjacking in Jordan, the 1971 quadripartite agreement on Berlin, and the Washington Naval Conference), Salacuse and Rubin (1990, 316) note that they all "identify phases . . . and point to the importance of timing and ripeness in beginning a negotiation and then moving from one phase to another." The cases illustrate the shaping influence of external events, or the international environment, and the need for negotiators to manage them. They also highlight the technique of linkage, or managing the complexity of different issues by combining them into packages. Other *Negotiation Journal* case studies document the importance of turning points in the life cycle of a negotiation (Druckman, Husbands, and Johnston 1991), making credible conciliatory gestures to signal a willingness to terminate conflict (Mitchell 1991), acting when the moment is ripe (Dupont 1990), and being sensitive to the timing of multilateral conferences (Koh 1990). Cases in a special issue of *International Negotiation* dealing with the former Soviet Union and Eastern Europe show the effects of past styles and images and of current contextual features (*International Negotiation* 1996). Together, the cases analyzed in the journals identify processes and influences that could be the basis for a general framework for analyzing international negotiation.

An important development that has occurred since the original chapter appeared in 1997 has been the success of the journal *International Negotiation*, published by Kluwer Law International. The journal has published special issues on a wide range of topics, including intercultural business negotiations, social exchange theory, the teaching of international negotiation, international economic negotiations, negotiating security, the roles of non-governmental organizations in negotiation, negotiations in the European Union, and issues on case data sets and methods used in negotiation research. Implemented under the editorial direction of the WIN group and published three times each year, the journal provides a bridge between theory and practice in the field. Further, it provides opportunities for both scholars and practitioners to contribute to the development and definition of the field. A long list of planned issues presages the influence of this publishing outlet for some time to come.

An issue of *International Negotiation* on "Negotiating Identity: From Metaphor to Process," edited by Zartman (2001), raises ideas that are becoming increasingly relevant in international relations. The authors discuss the way identity issues are addressed as part of negotiation processes in a variety of regions, including North Africa, France and Germany, Cameroon, and Syria. Concluding articles by Pruitt (2001) and Druckman (2001a) develop implications from negotiation theory for social identity (Pruitt 2001) and from social identity to negotiation theory (Druckman 2001a). Pruitt contributes a variety of negotiation concepts to identity theory, including the importance of tacit bargaining and prominent solutions, ripeness, the impact of relative power (including alternatives to negotiated agreements), strategies for getting integrative agreements, the role of mediation, and the strength of ties between negotiating representatives and constituencies. Druckman contributes a framework for comparative research on national identities. The framework turns on three dimensions from the literature on identity theory. One dimension concerns a dynamic process in which parties' identities influence identities that are themselves shaped by the negotiation process. One refers to the relationship between durability of identities and flexibility of representatives and their constituents. The third dimension concerns the spread of identities in a population, which are shown to influence the credibility of negotiating commitments, the role played by domestic politics in negotiation, and the willingness of national representatives to enter into regional or global agreements. The framework is applied illustratively to an analysis of national identity in four countries: Morocco, Libya, Tunisia, and Algeria. More generally, examples of comparative analyses provide an example of ways in which the domain is expanded, as illustrated in the next section.

Comparative Analyses

Two projects undertaken by FSI's Center for the Study of Foreign Affairs emphasizes comparative analysis in the study of negotiation. The projects' examination of diverse cases for similarities and differences generated some important lessons for the research community. In one project, an attempt was made to derive lessons from the experiences of negotiators in four cases: the Panama Canal treaties, the Falkland/Malvinas Islands dispute, the Cyprus dispute, and negotiating Zimbabwe's independence (Bendahmane and McDonald 1986). The diversity of the cases provided a rich set of lessons about many aspects of negotiation as well as the interplay of local, regional, and international politics. Among the more interesting insights are those concerning formal and informal diplomacy, conditions for negotiation, procedures, endgame tactics, and strategies for sustaining an agreement. Different procedures and tactics were shown to be effective at different stages. As Druckman (1986a, 287) notes, "It was the combination of choice of technique and its skillful use together with a changing political context, recognized as favorable when it became so, that provided the key to success in Panama and in Zimbabwe."

Another FSI project, undertaken in collaboration with members of the WIN group, developed lessons from three cases of separate base-rights negotiations involving the United States and Spain, Greece, and the Philippines (McDonald and Bendahmane 1990), which were noted more for their comparability than for their diversity. The analyses offer insights into the impact of delegation composition, procedural flexibility, the use of certain tactics, and the role played by language in the endgame and in sustaining the agreement. The cases also illustrate the interplay of context and process. Context is highlighted in the earlier cases, rooted as they were in international politics. Process is emphasized in the base-rights cases, where the bilateral relationship is adjusted through periodic negotiations. These projects illustrate the value of inducing lessons from experience. This alternative analytical approach is used as a framework for case analysis. The lessons contribute to the development of frameworks as we go back and forth between inductive and deductive approaches to understanding negotiation processes.

An innovative comparative analysis was undertaken by a group of scholars who examined messages sent between the kingdoms of the ancient near east in the mid-fourteenth century BC. The messages, known as the Amarna Letters and published in English (Moran 1992), provide a window into the origins of diplomacy. The analyses are collected in a volume edited by Cohen and Westbrook (2000). In their depiction of the interactions among rulers of these kingdoms and their emissaries, Cohen and Westbrook reveal that many of the processes discussed by contemporary negotiation theory have a very long history. One example is the importance of reciprocal exchanges. In dealing with each other, usually through messengers, the kings demanded reciprocal trades where reciprocity took the form of quid pro quo or specific rather than diffuse reciprocity. The exchanges provided a mechanism for managing relations among the kings. Another example is the existence of shared cooperative norms. The competitive bartering was conducted within a cooperative normative framework. The pervasive idiom of a brotherhood was seen as a rhetorical device to enable the business of exchange to proceed in a manner similar to the way modern diplomacy is conducted. A third example is the centrality of power and prestige. Kings were engaged in a competitive game for status. Indeed, they relentlessly jockeyed for advantage only to discover that their disadvantaged position in the power hierarchy led over and over again to solutions that favored the Egyptian pharaoh. As in contemporary international relations, the Amarna system was held together by cooperative norms intended to preserve a favorable balance of power (especially for Egypt) and to sustain a shared community of friends and traders. These examples suggest that ancient diplomacy has lessons to teach us about continuity and change in international diplomacy.

THE "GREAT DIVIDE": THE NEGOTIATOR MEETS THE RESEARCHER

In *Bridging the Gap*, Alexander George (1993) writes that "members of these two communities (academic and policymaking) define their interest in international relations somewhat differently; they pursue different professional goals and have difficulty communicating with each other" (135). He then proposes strategies for generating policy-relevant knowledge: include in the research variables over which policymakers have some control, do not define

concepts at too high a level of abstraction, and seek conditional generalizations. With regard to negotiation, Druckman and Hopmann (1989) describe
similar difficulties in the relationship between scholars and practitioners and
suggest approaches for generating relevant knowledge. Although many communication problems still exist, progress has been made in tailoring conceptual knowledge and research to the needs of negotiators or diplomats and
their support staffs, as illustrated by several projects.

The FSI projects described above are examples of attempts by scholars to
gather lessons of value to practitioners. The lessons are insights derived from
past experience and recast as prescriptions or guidelines for action. Although
limited to only a few cases and made in hindsight, the lessons alert practitioners to pitfalls in the negotiation process and may serve as an aid to planning. The FPI case studies, also described above, are examples of scholar-
practitioners analyzing cases in terms of a conceptual framework of negotiation
stages described in some detail by Zartman and Berman (1982). The insights
are derived from using the framework to analyze the details of the various
cases. Although used primarily for teaching, the case studies are valuable for
participating practitioners, who are challenged to think about their cases in
terms of the Zartman-Berman framework. More generally, framework categories help organize the complex set of activities that occur in negotiation and
facilitate comparing cases in terms of similar and dissimilar processes.

Advances in information technology have provided a number of useful tools
for negotiators. The work of Druckman and Hopmann (2002) on content
analysis illustrates how the method can be used to keep track of statements
made throughout the course of a long negotiation (monitoring), to anticipate
key events such as the tabling of a proposal (signaling), to anticipate reactions
to one's own statements or moves (predicting and posturing), and to construct
plausible packages based on areas where compromise is likely. Applications of
decision analysis to several cases illustrate its usefulness as a tool for generating
options and evaluating those options as plausible alternative agreement packages. Examples are the U.S.-Philippines base-rights talks (Ulvila 1990), the
Panama Canal talks (Raiffa 1982), the International Conference on Tanker
Safety and Pollution Protection (Ulvila and Snyder 1980), the Uruguay Round
of the GATT talks (Spector 1994), the Single European Act of the European
Community (Spector 1994), and the UN Conference on Environment and
Development (Spector 1991). The two approaches are complementary, one
(content analysis) focusing on process; the other (decision analysis) focusing
on preferences. They can be used in tandem, first to assess progress and then
to update the configuration of preferences as these change during the course
of negotiation.

Computer programs can also be used as diagnostic aids. Druckman (1993b) describes Negotiator Assistant, a program developed with support from the United States Institute of Peace. The program provides negotiators and analysts with estimates of each party's flexibility and the extent to which alternative outcomes are likely to occur. It is used to compare cases and "theories" about the key influences on negotiation, evaluate alternative scenarios by allowing a user to perform what-if exercises, and provide advice on tactics for impasse resolution. Program diagnoses have been shown to correspond closely to the actual outcomes reached in nine historical cases. Further development of the theoretical model for the program enhances its value for the scholarly community. The construction of a web-based version, discussed above in the section on frameworks, allows for wide use by analysts and practitioners. Earlier work by Hammond and associates (1975) contributed computer aids designed to help negotiators think analytically about the problem, diagnosing their own bases for making judgments and clarifying the sources of differences between the parties. This research was especially useful in clarifying the technical aspects of negotiation and, as such, particularly relevant to negotiations over complex issues. These are only a sampling of decision-support tools available for negotiation. Andriole (1993) calls attention to a wide array of existing or emerging technologies that can support the negotiation process, ranging from electronic mail to group-decision support systems. His effort to match aspects of the process with tasks and tools provides a way to think about tools in relation to negotiation: Different tools should be designed for different negotiating functions. It also brings the engineering technologies into closer contact with the conceptual work on negotiation and, as such, holds promise for bridging the gap between practitioners and researchers in the social sciences.

While computer aids provide analytical support to negotiators, many aspects of negotiation are not analytical, and negotiators learn about them from experience; these include the effects of emotions, value differences, and cultural factors. In these areas, too, research contributes to understanding. With regard to the role of emotions, Johnson's (1971) research calls attention to the way alternating expressions of warmth and coldness influence expectations and concessions. Pearson (1990) found that sincere acknowledgments of the others' perspectives may facilitate the process of obtaining agreements by increasing feelings of affinity (positive affect) and trust among the parties. Also, the research on responsiveness, discussed above, makes clear the importance of synchrony in bargaining exchanges; bargainers seek equivalence in moves made by themselves and others (Druckman and Harris 1990). They may also imitate the others' expressions, as shown in work on socially induced affect (McIntosh 1994).

With regard to values, the studies reviewed above illustrate what happens when value differences are linked to the interests in dispute. They also show that those differences can be addressed in prenegotiation sessions, leading to more satisfactory settlements and improved relationships between the parties. Many studies document the importance of culture in negotiation. For example, in one study, Indian subjects bargained more competitively than cohorts in comparable age groups from other cultures, at least in part because of their early experiences with resource scarcity (Druckman et al. 1976). In another study (Mushakoji 1972), Japanese negotiators used relative-gain and gain-maximizing strategies more often than Americans, perhaps because of more general approaches to conflict management preferred by these cultures (Ohbuchi and Takahashi 1994).

These findings may be limited to intracultural negotiations, however. Adair, Okumura, and Brett (2001) found that when placed in an intercultural context, Japanese negotiators adapted behaviors more common to U.S. negotiators. However, despite the Japanese negotiators' adaptation, the intercultural agreements were less integrative and more distributive than the intracultural ones. Apparently one party's adaptation to the other's normative behaviors is not sufficient to generate integrative agreements. Adair, Okumura, and Brett suggest that negotiators from any culture need to develop an effective means of information sharing and to be motivated to search for agreements that are best for all parties. The intercultural context elicited shared perceptions of conflict; in the case of Japanese and Americans, this context may be the "compromise" versus the "win" frame (Pinkley 1990). This frame is not conducive to getting integrative agreements. In the intracultural context, however, negotiators may rely more on relatively unique frames such as "infringements to self" for Americans and "giri violations" (perceived violation of social bonds of trust) for Japanese negotiators (Gelfand et al. 2001).

A key concept for understanding cultural differences in negotiating behavior is the distinction between individualist and collectivist cultures. Preferences for procedures that reduce animosity, nonbinding procedures, the desirability of compromising, the willingness to delegate control to a mediator, and problem-solving approaches have been shown to turn on this distinction (Leung 1987; Graham, Mintu, and Rodgers 1994). So too are motivations for deceiving. Carnevale and Leung (2001) found that negotiators from collectivist cultures—notably, China—justify lying when it is helpful in maintaining harmony or strong interpersonal relationships. Negotiators from individualist cultures—notably, the United States—resort to lying when it is instrumental to winning. The former reflects a cultural norm; the latter reflects a propensity for competitiveness. Collectivist negotiators dissimulate in order to avoid excessive competitiveness. Individualists shade the truth in order to increase relative advantage. These tactics pull in opposite directions, making intercultural negotiations difficult and risky.

Nonexperimental analyses of national styles further illustrate the importance of culture in a variety of country contexts such as Solomon's (1985) study of Chinese negotiating tactics and Whelen's (1979) study of changing Soviet diplomacy.[15]

The research underscores the tendency to confuse opponents' intentions (often attributed to negative motives) with their customary ways of behaving in negotiation. Taking into account these influences, Janosik (1987) and Weiss (1994a; 1994b) offer frameworks for thinking about several ways in which culture influences process. Druckman and Hopmann (1989) argue that culture is context, not process, and that it shapes behavior but is not synonymous with it. Practitioners could find the frameworks and the findings quite useful and could incorporate them into training packages and role-playing exercises designed to sensitize negotiators to the human dimensions of negotiation. The training techniques used by Danielian (1967) and Brislin (1986) are good examples. By explaining events and behaviors from the other's point of view, these techniques allow a trainee to internalize the values and norms of different cultures. Such exercises could contribute further to bridging the gap between the research and practitioner communities.

It may also be the case, however, that the practitioners themselves define a subculture that influences their negotiating behavior. These subcultures may reduce the impacts of national styles on the negotiating process. As Alger's (1963) study of diplomats interacting within a UN committee and Modelski's (1970) survey of foreign ministers suggest, a common socialization may produce a cadre of diplomats who are more similar to one another than to their compatriots. This is similar to the way negotiators adapt to each other's normative behaviors in intercultural negotiations (Adair, Okumura, and Brett 2001). We are beginning to learn more about this phenomenon or about its significance for national styles of negotiating behavior. It is a topic that needs to be examined further, perhaps in the manner of Schein's (1985) probes of an organization's values and operating assumptions.

Many of these findings have been found to be useful for training. One project, sponsored by the United States Institute of Peace, has developed training exercises based on summaries of research findings in the form of narratives (see Druckman and Robinson 1998). To date, sixteen thematic narratives have been developed on such topics as emotions in negotiation, culture, relationships, third parties, alternatives, time pressure, power, flexibility, two faces, and a number of other tactics. Emphasizing some counterintuitive implications of the findings, the narratives are used as lenses for analyzing and strategizing about actual cases of international negotiation. Trainees, who have included UN officials, civil servants, lawyers, and students in graduate programs from universities in Europe, Asia, and North and South America, perform four tasks: analyzing cases, developing strategies for impasse resolution, role-playing delegates in a simulated conference, and designing training exercises. In each exercise, they show how the findings described in the narratives were used to develop recommendations or reach negotiated agreements. Evaluations of the exercises showed that the narratives made a difference. Comparisons between randomly assigned narrative and control groups (teams that analyzed the cases without the narrative summaries of research) indicated strong differences in the quality of the written reports and what was learned. The narrative teams wrote more subtle and nuanced reports than the control teams.

The United States Institute of Peace project is one of several intended to increase understanding of the pathways between theory and research on the one hand and policy or practice on the other. Other projects sponsored by the United States Institute of Peace program on new approaches to international negotiation and mediation (see Sisk 1999) include computer and role-playing simulations and analyses of internal conflicts. One of the simulation projects found that prior exposure to principles and practices of negotiation through an automated decision support system led participants to generate more effective negotiating strategies (Wilkenfeld and Kraus 1999). An internal conflict project, based on multiple cases, concluded that civil wars can in fact end through negotiation, but the negotiated settlements may not lead to sustainable peace; wars ended at the table often reoccur (Licklider 1999; see also Druckman 2002a for the distinction between settlements and resolutions). These projects were intended to sensitize practitioners to the findings from academic research. As Sisk (1999, 39) notes: "Such training can highlight the complexity of issues, identify implicit assumptions, help craft strategy, and hone practical skills for challenges in which negotiation and mediation are the desired methods of conflict resolution."

LOOKING BACK AND LOOKING FORWARD

This chapter surveys the basic and applied research literatures on negotiating in the international context. At its core is a discussion of the processes and influences on negotiation as it occurs in diverse settings and issue-areas. Negotiation is viewed in terms of four perspectives, each of which contributes to our understanding of the various parts of the broader domain.

Together, the perspectives present a more complete picture than any one taken alone.

Advances in game and decision theory contribute to strategic thinking about negotiation. From game theory, we learn about the immediate and long-term consequences of alternative moves. From decision theory, we learn about the implications of combining preferences to produce desirable, if not optimal, outcomes. Using simple bargaining games as tools for understanding, experimentalists have identified concession tactics that influence others' responses leading toward or away from acceptable outcomes. Expanding "inward," organizational theorists have made evident the importance of boundary dilemmas confronted by negotiators. Negotiation is best construed as a two- (or multi-) level game in which negotiators must address simultaneously often conflicting demands made by those sitting across the table (other national delegations) and those sitting behind them (representatives from agencies of their own government). Expanding outward, international relations scholars have emphasized the negotiating context, particularly the diplomatic politics among nations with stakes in the outcomes and the linkages that are made among issues discussed in different negotiating venues.

To a large extent, our knowledge about these processes has been gained through research stimulated by these perspectives and conducted in laboratory and field settings. Laboratory studies have provided insights into the impact of preparing, framing, and bargaining exchanges as well as constraints imposed by role demands. Case analyses have illuminated sequences of events in terms of stages and turning points, showing how certain contexts and processes create impasses, while other processes provide the momentum needed to forge agreements. The laboratory studies have been useful in documenting various forces impinging on the negotiation process; the case analyses have provided a more detailed understanding of the unfolding processes. Further contributions to knowledge have come from applications of advanced statistical techniques. More precise estimates of impacts have come from meta-analyses; similarities and dissimilarities among processes that occur in different cases have been discovered through the use of multidimensional scaling.

The study of negotiation is characterized more by a variety of approaches and methods than by a grand theoretical structure and methodological orthodoxy. Although different in many ways, the approaches and methods are also complementary. Just as diverse perspectives on a case enrich understanding (Rubin 1981; Zartman 1994), varied methodologies expand the range of topics that can be analyzed. When used together in the same study, the methods enhance comparison and provide a basis for convergent validity (e.g., Hopmann and Walcott 1977; Beriker and Druckman 1996; Druckman and

Green 1995). Progress has been made in delineating the key features of alternative case-oriented approaches (Telhami 2002), including trade-offs in the use of single case studies, time-series analysis, focused case comparisons, and aggregate data analyses (Druckman 2002b, 2005). Multimethods do not, however, solve problems of information availability and inadequate frameworks for analysis. The dual challenge for the analyst is to recover (or discover) primary data on international negotiation that can be studied through the lens of appropriate analytical frameworks.

The analyses' contributions to knowledge are impressive, but to what extent have they contributed to practice? Scholars have developed practical tools; progress has been made in bridging the gap between researchers and practitioners. Working relationships between scholars and professional diplomats have, for example, produced lessons from past experience that will be invaluable to future generations of negotiators. New information technologies have been tailored to assist negotiators in evaluating alternative options and diagnosing various situations. In addition, research on the effects of emotions, values, and cultural factors provides insights into the nonanalytical aspects of negotiation. These and other findings gain further relevance as they are incorporated into the development of training packages.

Looking back, we can applaud the accomplishments made by the community of negotiation scholars. Looking forward, we can offer a rich agenda for further research, both basic and applied. The agenda is shaped in part by changes that have occurred in international relations. A larger number of actors and relationships in the international system has increased the complexity of analysis and practice. Our conceptual frameworks must encompass the trend toward multilateralism in international affairs as well as the burgeoning number of internal conflicts. We are only beginning to develop frameworks to guide research on multilateral negotiations and the wider web of constituencies that complicate the negotiator's boundary role dilemmas (see Zartman 1994). As we focus more on the highly charged negotiations among groups seeking new sources of identity in failed states and countries undergoing profound social and economic change, the role of values and emotions in negotiation will undoubtedly receive more attention (see Zartman 1995). As we encourage comparative case analyses, we must also view negotiation both as a larger process that includes prenegotiation and implementation stages and as part of a larger strategy that includes unilateral initiatives, mediation, multitrack activities, and even elements of coercive diplomacy. Yet these changes in the diplomatic context can be put in perspective when we appreciate some of the similarities in process gleaned from analyses of ancient diplomacy.

REFERENCES

Adair, W. L., T. Okumura, and J. M. Brett. 2001. "Negotiation Behavior When Cultures Collide: The United States and Japan." *Journal of Applied Psychology* 86: 371–85.

Adelman, Kenneth L. 1984–85. "Arms Control with and without Agreements." *Foreign Affairs* 62 (Winter): 240–63.

Alger, Chadwick F. 1963. "United Nations Participation as a Learning Experience." *Public Opinion Quarterly* 27 (Fall): 411–26.

Andriole, Stephen J. 1993. "Information Management Support for International Negotiations." *Theory and Decision* 34 (3): 313–28.

Axelrod, Robert. 1984. *The Evolution of Cooperation*. New York: Basic Books.

Bartos, Otomar J. 1978. "Simple Model of Negotiation: A Sociological Point of View." In *The Negotiation Process: Theories and Applications*, ed. I. William Zartman. Beverly Hills, Calif.: Sage.

Bass, Bernard M. 1966. "Effects on the Subsequent Performance of Negotiators of Studying Issues or Planning Strategies Alone or in Groups." *Psychological Monographs* 80 (6, whole no. 614).

Bendahmane, Diane B., and John W. McDonald, eds. 1986. *Perspectives on Negotiation: Four Case Studies and Interpretations*. Washington, D.C.: Foreign Service Institute.

Beriker, Nimet, and Daniel Druckman. 1996. "Simulating the Lausanne Peace Negotiations, 1922–1923: Power Symmetries in Bargaining." *Simulation and Gaming* 27: 162–83.

Blacker, Michael, Paul Giarra, and Ezra Vogel. 2002. *Case Studies in Japanese Negotiating Behavior*. Washington, D.C.: United States Institute of Peace Press.

Bloomfield, Lincoln P., and Robert Beattie. 1971. "Computers and Policy-Making: The CASCON Experiment." *Journal of Conflict Resolution* 15 (1): 33–46.

Bonham, G. Matthew. 1971. "Simulating International Disarmament Negotiations." *Journal of Conflict Resolution* 15 (3): 299–315.

Brams, Steven J. 1993. "Theory of Moves." *American Scientist* 81 (November/ December): 562–70.

Brislin, Richard W. 1986. "A Culture General Assimilator: Preparation for Various Types of Sojourns." *International Journal of Intercultural Relations* 10 (2): 215–34.

Brown, Scott. 1986. "The Superpowers' Dilemma." *Negotiation Journal* 2 (4): 371–84.

Cameron, M. A., and B. W. Tomlin. 2000. *The Making of NAFTA: How the Deal Was Done*. Ithaca, N.Y.: Cornell University Press.

Carnevale, Peter, and Kwok Leung. 2001. "Cultural Dimensions of Negotiation." In *Blackwell Handbook of Social Psychology*, vol. 3, ed. Michael A. Hogg and R. S. Tindale. Oxford, UK: Blackwell.

Chasek, P. 1997. "A Comparative Analysis of Multilateral Environmental Negotiations." *Group Decision and Negotiation* 6 (5): 437–61.

Coddington, Alan. 1968. *Theories of the Bargaining Process*. Chicago: Aldine.

Cogan, Charles. 2003. *French Negotiating Behavior: Dealing with La Grande Nation*. Washington, D.C.: United States Institute of Peace Press.

Cohen, R., and R. Westbrook. 2000. *Amarna Diplomacy: The Beginnings of International Relations*. Baltimore: Johns Hopkins University Press.

Collins, B. E., and B. H. Raven. 1969. "Group Structure, Attraction, Coalitions, Communication, and Power." In *The Handbook of Social Psychology*, 2d ed., ed. G. Lindzay and E. Aronson. Reading, Mass.: Addison-Wesley.

Danielian, Jack. 1967. "Live Simulations of Affect-Laden Cultural Cognitions." *Journal of Conflict Resolution* 11 (September): 312–24.

Dean, Jonathan. 1986. "MBFR: From Apathy to Accord." *International Security* 7 (4): 116–39.

Dechant, Kathleen, and Victoria J. Marsick. 1992. "How Groups Learn from Experience." Unpublished paper, Teacher's College, Columbia University.

Donohue, William A., and Gregory D. Hoobler. 2002. "Relational Frames and Their Ethical Implications in International Negotiation: An Analysis Based on the Oslo II Negotiations." *International Negotiation* 7 (2): 143–67.

Douglas, Ann. 1957. "The Peaceful Settlement of Industrial and Intergroup Disputes." *Journal of Conflict Resolution* 1 (March): 69–81.

Druckman, Daniel. 1968. "Prenegotiation Experience and Dyadic Conflict Resolution in a Bargaining Situation." *Journal of Experimental Social Psychology* 4 (October): 367–83.

———. 1973. *Human Factors in International Negotiations: Social-Psychological Aspects of International Conflict*. Sage Professional Papers in International Studies, no. 02-020. Beverly Hills, Calif.: Sage.

———. 1977a. "Boundary Role Conflict: Negotiation as Dual Responsiveness." *Journal of Conflict Resolution* 21 (4): 639–62.

———, ed. 1977b. *Negotiations: Social-Psychological Perspectives*. Beverly Hills, Calif.: Sage.

———. 1978. "The Monitoring Function in Negotiation: Two Models of Responsiveness." In *Contributions to Experimental Economics: Bargaining Behavior*, ed. Heinz Sauermann. Tubingen, West Germany: J. C. B. Mohr.

———. 1980. "Social-Psychological Factors in Regional Politics." In *Comparative Regional Systems: West and East Europe, North America, the Middle East, and Developing Countries*, ed. Werner J. Feld and Gavin Boyd. New York: Pergamon.

———. 1983. "Social Psychology and International Negotiations: Processes and Influences." In *Advances in Applied Social Psychology*, vol. 2, ed. Robert F. Kidd and Michael J. Saks. Hillsdale, N.J.: Erlbaum.

———. 1986a. "Four Cases of Conflict Management: Lessons Learned." In *Perspectives on Negotiation: Four Case Studies and Lessons Learned*, ed. Diane B. Bendahmane and John W. McDonald. Washington, D.C.: Foreign Service Institute.

————. 1986b. "Stages, Turning Points, and Crises: Negotiating Military Base Rights, Spain and the United States." *Journal of Conflict Resolution* 30 (2): 327–60.

————. 1990. "Three Cases of Base-Rights Negotiations: Lessons Learned." In *U.S. Bases Overseas*, ed. John W. McDonald and Diane B. Bendahmane. Boulder, Colo.: Westview.

————. 1993a. "The Situational Levers of Negotiating Flexibility." *Journal of Conflict Resolution* 37 (2): 236–76.

————. 1993b. "Statistical Analysis for Negotiation Support." *Theory and Decision* 34 (3): 215–33.

————. 1994. "Determinants of Compromising Behavior in Negotiation: A Meta-Analysis." *Journal of Conflict Resolution* 38 (3): 507–56.

————. 1995. "Situational Levers of Position Change: Further Explorations." *The Annals of the American Academy of Political and Social Science* 542: 61–80.

————. 1997. "Dimensions of International Negotiations: Structures, Processes, and Outcomes." *Group Decision and Negotiation* 6 (5): 395–420.

————. 2001a. "Negotiation and Identity: Implications for Negotiation Theory." *International Negotiation* 6 (2): 281–91.

————. 2001b. "Turning Points in International Negotiation: A Comparative Analysis." *Journal of Conflict Resolution* 45 (4): 519–44.

————. 2002a. "Settlements and Resolutions: Consequences of Negotiation Processes in the Laboratory and in the Field." *International Negotiation* 7 (3): 313–38.

————. 2002b. "Case-Based Research on International Negotiation: Approaches and Data-sets." *International Negotiation* 7 (1): 17–37.

————. 2003a. "Linking Micro- and Macro-Level Processes: Interaction Analysis in Context." *International Journal of Conflict Management* 14 (3/4):177–90.

————. 2003b. "Situations." In *Conflict: From Analysis to Interventions*, ed. Sandra Cheldelin, Daniel Druckman, and Larissa Fast. London: Continuum.

————. 2003c. "Puzzles in Search of Researchers: Processes, Identities, and Situations." *International Journal of Conflict Management* 14 (1): 3–22.

————. 2004. "Departures in Negotiation: Extensions and New Directions." *Negotiation Journal* 20 (2):185–204.

————. 2005. *Doing Research: Methods of Inquiry for Conflict Analysis*. Thousand Oaks, Calif.: Sage.

Druckman, Daniel, Alan A. Benton, Faizunisa Ali, and J. Susana Bagur. 1976. "Cultural Differences in Bargaining Behavior: Argentina, India, and the United States." *Journal of Conflict Resolution* 20 (3): 413–52.

Druckman, Daniel, and Benjamin J. Broome. 1991. "Value Differences and Conflict Resolution: Familiarity or Liking?" *Journal of Conflict Resolution* 35 (4): 571–93.

Druckman, Daniel, Benjamin J. Broome, and Susan H. Korper. 1988. "Value Differences and Conflict Resolution: Facilitation or Delinking?" *Journal of Conflict Resolution* 32 (3): 489–510.

Druckman, Daniel, James N. Druckman, and Tatsushi Arai. 2004. "e-Mediation: Evaluating the Impacts of an Electronic Mediator on Negotiating Behavior." *Group Decision and Negotiation* 13 (6): 481–511.

Druckman, Daniel, and Justin Green. 1995. "Playing Two Games: Internal Negotiations in the Philippines." In *Elusive Peace: Negotiating an End to Civil Wars*, ed. I. William Zartman. Washington, D.C.: Brookings Institution Press.

Druckman, Daniel, and Richard Harris. 1990. "Alternative Models of Responsiveness in International Negotiation." *Journal of Conflict Resolution* 34 (2): 234–51.

Druckman, Daniel, and P. Terrence Hopmann. 1989. "Behavioral Aspects of Negotiations on Mutual Security." In *Behavior, Society, and Nuclear War*, vol. 1, ed. Philip E. Tetlock, Jo L. Husbands, Paul C. Stern, and Charles Tilly. New York: Oxford University Press.

———. 2002. "Content Analysis." In *International Negotiation: Analysis, Approaches, Issues*, 2d ed., ed. Victor A. Kremenyuk. San Francisco: Jossey-Bass.

Druckman, Daniel, Jo L. Husbands, and Karin Johnston. 1991. "Turning Points in the INF Negotiations." *Negotiation Journal* 7 (1): 55–67.

Druckman, Daniel, and Terrence Lyons. 2005. "Negotiation Processes and Post-Settlement Relationships: Comparing Nagorno-Karabakh to Mozambique." In *Peace versus Justice: Negotiating Forward- and Backward-Looking Outcomes*, ed. I. William Zartman and Victor Kremenyuk. Lanham, Md.: Rowman and Littlefield.

Druckman, Daniel, Jennifer Martin, Susan Allen Nan, and Dimostenis Yagcioglu. 1999. "Dimensions of International Negotiation: A Test of Iklé's Typology." *Group Decision and Negotiation* 8: 89–108.

Druckman, Daniel, B. Ramberg, and R. Harris. 2002. "Computer-Assisted International Negotiation: A Tool for Research and Practice." *Group Decision and Negotiation* 11 (3): 231–56.

Druckman, Daniel, and V. Robinson. 1998. "From Research to Application: Utilizing Research Findings in Negotiation Training Programs." *International Negotiation* 3 (1): 7–38.

Druckman, Daniel, Richard Rozelle, and Kathleen Zechmeister. 1977. "Conflict of Interest and Value Dissensus: Two Perspectives." In *Negotiations: Social-Psychological Perspectives*, ed. Daniel Druckman. Beverly Hills, Calif.: Sage.

Druckman, Daniel, and Kathleen Zechmeister. 1973. "Conflict of Interest and Value Dissensus: Propositions in the Sociology of Conflict." *Human Relations* 26 (August): 449–66.

Dupont, Christophe. 1990. "The Channel Tunnel Negotiations, 1984–1986: Some Aspects of the Process and Its Outcome." *Negotiation Journal* 6 (1): 71–80.

Evans, Peter B., Harold K. Jacobson, and Robert D. Putnam, eds. 1993. *Double-Edged Diplomacy: International Bargaining and Domestic Politics*. Berkeley: University of California Press.

Fisher, Ronald J. 1983. "Third-Party Consultation as a Method of Intergroup Conflict Resolution: A Review of Studies." *Journal of Conflict Resolution* 27 (2): 301–34.

————. 1990. *The Social Psychology of Intergroup and International Conflict*. New York: Springer-Verlag.

Frey, Robert L., and J. Stacy Adams. 1972. "The Negotiator's Dilemma: Simultaneous Ingroup and Outgroup Conflict." *Journal of Experimental Social Psychology* 8 (July): 331–46.

Gelfand, Michele. J., L. H. Nishii, K. M. Holcombe, N. Dyer, K-I. Ohbuchi, and M. Fukuno. 2001. "Cultural Influences on Cognitive Representations of Conflict: Interpretations of Conflict Episodes in the U.S. and Japan." *Journal of Applied Psychology* 86 (6): 1059–74.

George, Alexander. 1993. *Bridging the Gap: Theory and Practice in Foreign Policy*. Washington, D.C.: United States Institute of Peace Press.

Gersick, Connie J. G. 1988. "Time and Transition in Work Groups: Toward a New Model of Group Development." *Academy of Management Journal* 31 (1): 9–41.

Gladwell, M. 2000. *The Tipping Point*. Boston: Little, Brown.

Graham, John L, Alma T. Mintu, and Waymond Rodgers. 1994. "Explorations of Negotiation Behaviors in Ten Foreign Cultures Using a Model Developed in the United States." *Management Science* 40 (1): 72–95.

Gulliver, P. H. 1979. *Disputes and Negotiations: A Cross-Cultural Perspective*. New York: Academic Press.

Hammond, K. R., T. R. Stewart, L. Adelman, and N. Wascoe. 1975. "Report to the Denver City Council and Mayor Regarding the Choice of Handgun Ammunition for the Denver Police Department." Report No. 179, Program of Research on Judgment and Social Interaction, University of Colorado, Boulder.

Harris, K. L. 1996. "Content Analysis in Negotiation Research: A Review and Guide." *Behavior Research Methods, Instruments, and Computers* 28 (3): 458–67.

Hopmann, P. Terrence. 1977. "Bargaining within and between Alliances on MBFR: Perceptions and Interactions." Paper presented at the International Studies Association, March 16–20, St. Louis, Mo.

Hopmann, P. Terrence, and Timothy King. 1976. "Interactions and Perceptions in the Test Ban Negotiations." *International Studies Quarterly* 20 (1): 105–42.

Hopmann, P. Terrence, and T. C. Smith. 1978. "An Application of a Richardson Process Model: Soviet-American Interactions in the Test Ban Negotiations, 1962–63." In *The Negotiation Process: Theories and Applications*, ed. I. William Zartman. Beverly Hills, Calif.: Sage.

Hopmann, P. T., and C. Walcott. 1977. "The Impact of External Stresses and Tensions on Negotiations." In *Negotiations: Social-Psychological Perspectives*, ed. D. Druckman. Beverly Hills, Calif.: Sage.

Iklé, Fred C. 1964. *How Nations Negotiate*. New York: Harper and Row.

International Negotiation. 1996. Inaugural issue: "Negotiation Metaphors: Framing International Negotiations Anew." *International Negotiation* 1 (1).

Janosik, Robert J. 1987. "Rethinking the Culture-Negotiation Link." *Negotiation Journal* 3 (4): 385–96.

Jensen, Lloyd. 1988. *Bargaining for National Security: The Postwar Disarmament Negotiations*. Columbia, S.C.: University of South Carolina Press.

Jervis, Robert. 1983. "Security Regimes." In *International Regimes*, ed. Stephen D. Krasner. Ithaca, N.Y.: Cornell University Press.

Johnson, David W. 1971. "Role Reversal: A Summary and Review of the Research." *International Journal of Group Tensions* 1 (October): 318–34.

Jonsson, Christer. 1979. *Soviet Bargaining Behavior: The Nuclear Test Ban Case*. New York: Columbia University Press.

Kahn, Robert L. 1991. "Organizational Theory." In *International Negotiation: Analysis, Approaches, Issues*, ed. Victor A. Kremenyuk. San Francisco: Jossey-Bass.

Kelleher, Catherine. 1976. "Predilections in Negotiations." Unpublished manuscript. University of Maryland, College Park.

Kelley, Harold H., and D. P. Schenitzki. 1972. "Bargaining." In *Experimental Social Psychology*, ed. Charles Graham McClintock. New York: Holt, Rinehart and Winston.

Klimoski, Richard J. 1972. "The Effects of Intragroup Forces on Intergroup Conflict Resolution." *Organizational Behavior and Human Performance* 8 (December): 363–83.

Koh, Tommy. 1990. "The Paris Conference on Cambodia: A Multilateral Negotiation that 'Failed.'" *Negotiation Journal* 6 (1): 81–87.

Kremenyuk, V. A., ed. 2002. *International Negotiation: Analysis, Approaches, Issues*, 2d ed. San Francisco: Jossey-Bass.

Kriesberg, Louis. 1991. "Introduction: Timing Conditions, Strategies, and Errors." In *Timing the De-escalation of International Conflicts*, ed. Louis Kriesberg and Stuart J. Thorson. Syracuse, N.Y.: Syracuse University Press.

Lax, David A., and James K. Sebenius. 1986. *The Manager as Negotiator: Bargaining for Cooperation and Competitive Gain*. New York: Free Press.

Leary, Kimberlyn, ed. 2004. "Critical Moments in Negotiation." *Negotiation Journal* 20 (2): 143–45.

Leung, Kwok. 1987. "Some Determinants of Reactions to Procedural Models for Conflict Resolution: A Cross-National Study." *Journal of Personality and Social Psychology* 53 (5): 898–908.

Licklider, R. 1999. "Negotiating an End to Civil Wars: General Findings." In *New Approaches to International Negotiation and Mediation: Findings from USIP-Sponsored Research*, Peaceworks no. 30, ed. T. D. Sisk. Washington, D.C.: United States Institute of Peace Press.

Lindskold, Svenn, Brian Betz, and Pamela S. Waters. 1986. "Transforming Competitive or Cooperative Climates." *Journal of Conflict Resolution* 30 (March): 99–114.

Lindskold, Svenn, Pamela S. Waters, and Helen Koutsourais. 1983. "Cooperators, Competitors, and Response to GRIT." *Journal of Conflict Resolution* 27 (September): 521–32.

McDonald, John W., and Diane B. Bendahmane, eds. 1990. *U.S. Bases Overseas: Negotiations with Spain, Greece, and the Philippines*. Boulder, Colo.: Westview.

McIntosh, Daniel. 1994. "Socially-Induced Affect." In *Learning, Remembering, Believing: Enhancing Human Performance*, ed. Daniel Druckman and Robert A. Bjork. Washington, D.C.: National Academy Press.

Medvec, Victoria Husted, and Adam D. Galinsky. 2005. "Putting More on the Table: How Making Multiple Offers can Increase the Final Value of the Deal." *Negotiation*, Harvard Business School, Article Reprint no. N0504B.

Mitchell, Christopher R. 1991. "A Willingness to Talk: Conciliatory Gestures and De-escalation." *Negotiation Journal* 7 (4): 405–30.

Modelski, George. 1970. "The World's Foreign Ministers: A Political Elite." *Journal of Conflict Resolution* 14 (June): 135–75.

Moran, W. L. 1992. *The Amarna Letters*. Baltimore: Johns Hopkins University Press.

Morley, Ian E., and Geoffrey M. Stephenson. 1977. *The Social Psychology of Bargaining*. London: Allen and Unwin.

Mushakoji, Kinhide. 1972. "The Strategies of Negotiation: An American-Japanese Comparison." In *Experimentation and Simulation in Political Science*, ed. J. A. Laponce and Paul Smoker. Toronto: University of Toronto Press.

Neale, Margaret A., and Max H. Bazerman. 1985. "The Effects of Framing and Negotiator Overconfidence on Bargaining Behaviors and Outcomes." *Academy of Management Journal* 28 (1): 34–49.

Neale, Margaret A., Vandra L. Huber, and Gregory B. Northcraft. 1987. "The Framing of Negotiations: Contextual versus Task Frames." *Organizational Behavior and Human Decision Processes* 39 (2): 228–41.

Ohbuchi, Ken-Ichi, and Yumi Takahashi. 1994. "Cultural Styles of Conflict Management in Japanese and Americans: Passivity, Covertness, and Effectiveness of Strategies." *Journal of Applied Social Psychology* 15: 1345–66.

Orasanu, Judith, and Eduardo Salas. 1993. "Team Decision Making in Complex Environments." In *Decision Making in Action: Models and Methods*, ed. Gary A. Klein, Judith Orasanu, and R. Calderwood. Norwood, N.J.: Ablex.

Organ, Dennis. 1971. "Some Variables Affecting Boundary Role Behavior." *Sociometry* 34 (December): 524–37.

Osgood, Charles. 1962. *An Alternative to War or Surrender*. Urbana, Ill.: University of Illinois Press.

———. 1973. "GRIT for MBFR: A Proposal for Unfreezing Force-Level Postures in Europe." Testimony to the Subcommittee on Europe of the House Committee on Foreign Affairs, June 26.

Pearson, Tamara. 1990. "The Role of 'Symbolic Gestures' in Intergroup Conflict Resolution: Addressing Group Identity." PhD diss., Harvard University.

Pinkley, R. L. 1990. "Dimensions of Conflict Frame: Relation to Disputant Perceptions and Expectations." *Journal of Applied Psychology* 75: 117–26.

Pruitt, Dean G. 1965. "Definition of the Situation as a Determinant of International Action." In *International Behavior: A Social-Psychological Analysis*, ed. Herbert C. Kelman. New York: Holt, Rinehart and Winston.

————. 1981. *Negotiation Behavior*. New York: Academic Press.

————. 2001. "Negotiation Theory and the Development of Identity." *International Negotiation* 6 (2): 269–79.

Pruitt, Dean G., and Peter J. Carnevale. 1993. *Negotiation in Social Conflict*. Pacific Grove, Calif.: Brooks/Cole.

Putnam, Robert. 1988. "Diplomacy and Domestic Politics: The Logic of Two-Level Games." *International Organization* 43 (3): 427–60.

Raiffa, Howard. 1982. *The Art and Science of Negotiation*. Cambridge, Mass.: Harvard University Press.

Ramberg, Bennett. 1977. "Tactical Advantages of Opening Positioning Strategies: Lessons from the Seabed Arms Control Talks, 1967–1970." *Journal of Conflict Resolution* 21 (4): 685–700.

————, ed. 1993. *Arms Control without Negotiation: From the Cold War to the New World Order*. Boulder, Colo.: Lynne Rienner.

Randolph, Lillian. 1966. "A Suggested Model of International Negotiation." *Journal of Conflict Resolution* 10 (September): 344–53.

Riessman, C. K. 1993. *Narrative Analysis*. Thousand Oaks, Calif.: Sage.

Roberts, C. W., ed. 1997. *Text Analysis for the Social Sciences: Methods for Drawing Statistical Inferences from Texts and Transcripts*. Mahwah, N.J.: Erlbaum.

Rose, William M. 1988. *U.S. Unilateral Arms Control Initiatives: When Do They Work?* Westport, Conn.: Greenwood.

Rousseau, D. L. 2002. "Motivations for Choice: The Salience of Relative Gains in International Politics." *Journal of Conflict Resolution* 46 (3): 394–426.

Rubin, Jeffrey Z., ed. 1981. *Dynamics of Third-Party Intervention: Kissinger in the Middle East*. New York: Praeger.

Rubin, Jeffrey Z., and Bert R. Brown. 1975. *The Social Psychology of Bargaining and Negotiation*. New York: Academic Press.

Salacuse, Jeswald W., and Jeffrey Z. Rubin. 1990. "Negotiation Processes at Work: Lessons from Four International Cases." *Negotiation Journal* 6 (4): 315–17.

Saunders, Harold H. 1984. "The Prenegotiation Phase." In *International Negotiation: Art and Science*, ed. Diane B. Bendahmane and John W. McDonald. Washington, D.C.: Foreign Service Institute.

Sawyer, Jack, and Harold Guetzkow. 1965. "Bargaining and Negotiation in International Relations." In *International Behavior: A Social-Psychological Analysis*, ed. Herbert C. Kelman. New York: Holt, Rinehart and Winston.

Schein, Edgar H. 1985. *Organizational Culture and Leadership*. San Francisco: Jossey-Bass.

Siegel, Sidney, and Lawrence E. Fouraker. 1960. *Bargaining and Group Decision Making: Experiments in Bilateral Monopoly*. New York: McGraw-Hill.

Sisk, T. D., ed. 1999. *New Approaches to International Negotiation and Mediation: Findings from USIP-Sponsored Projects*, Peaceworks no. 30. Washington, D.C.: United States Institute of Peace Press.

Smith, Gerard C. 1980. *Doubletalk: The Story of SALT I*. New York: Doubleday.

Smyser, W. R. 2003. *How Germans Negotiate: Logical Goals, Practical Solutions*. Washington, D.C.: United States Institute of Peace Press.

Snyder, Glenn H., and Paul Diesing. 1977. *Conflict among Nations: Bargaining, Decision-Making, and System Structure in International Crises*. Princeton, N.J.: Princeton University Press.

Snyder, Scott. 1999. *Negotiating on the Edge: North Korean Negotiating Behavior*. Washington, D.C.: United States Institute of Peace Press.

Solomon, Richard H. 1985. "Chinese Political Negotiating Behavior." Report no. R-3295. Santa Monica, Calif.: RAND. (Revised edition published in 1999 as *Chinese Negotiating Behavior: Pursuing Interests through "Old Friends."* Washington, D.C.: United States Institute of Peace Press.)

Spector, Bertram I. 1991. "Preference Adjustment and Opportunities for Agreement: A Contingency Analysis of the UNCED Prenegotiation Process." Working paper. Laxenburg, Austria: International Institute for Applied Systems Analysis.

———. 1994. "Decision Theory: Diagnosing Strategic Alternatives and Outcome Trade-offs." In *International Multilateral Negotiation*, ed. I. William Zartman. San Francisco: Jossey-Bass.

Spector, Bertram I., and Anna R. Korula. 1992. "The Post-Agreement Negotiation Process: The Problems of Ratifying International Environmental Agreements." Report WP-92-90. Laxenburg, Austria: International Institute for Applied Systems Analysis.

Stein, Janice Gross, ed. 1989. *Getting to the Table: The Processes of International Prenegotiation*. Baltimore: Johns Hopkins University Press.

Stoll, Richard J., and William McAndrew. 1986. "Negotiating Strategic Arms Control, 1969–1979." *Journal of Conflict Resolution* 30 (2): 315–26.

Summers, David A. 1968. "Conflict, Compromise, and Belief Change in a Decision-Making Task." *Journal of Conflict Resolution* 12 (June): 215–21.

Talbott, Strobe. 1979. *Endgame: The Inside Story of SALT II*. New York: Harper and Row.

———. 1984. *Deadly Gambits*. New York: Alfred A. Knopf.

Telhami. Shibley, ed. 2002. "Special Issue: Establishing a Data Set on Intrastate and International Negotiation and Mediation." *International Negotiation* 7 (1).

Thibaut, John. 1968. "The Development of Contractual Norms in Bargaining: Replication and Variation." *Journal of Conflict Resolution* 12 (March): 102–12.

Tollison, Robert D., and Thomas D. Willett. 1979. "An Economic Theory of Mutually Advantageous Issue Linkages in International Negotiations." *International Organization* 33 (4): 425–49.

Tomlin, Brian W. 1989. "The Stages of Prenegotiation: The Decision to Negotiate North American Free Trade." In *Getting to the Table: The Processes of International Prenegotiation*, ed. Janice Gross Stein. Baltimore: Johns Hopkins University Press.

Touval, Saadia, and I. William Zartman, eds. 1985. *The Man in the Middle: International Mediation in Theory and Practice*. Boulder, Colo.: Westview.

Ulvila Jacob W. 1990. "Turning Points: An Analysis." In *U.S. Bases Overseas*, ed. John W. McDonald and Diane B. Bendahmane. Boulder, Colo.: Westview.

Ulvila, Jacob W., and Warren D. Snyder. 1980. "Negotiation of International Oil Tanker Standards: An Application of Multiattribute Value Theory." *Operations Research* 28 (1): 81–96.

Von Neumann, John, and Oskar Morgenstern. 1944. *Theory of Games and Economic Behavior*. Princeton, N.J.: Princeton University Press.

Wall, James A. Jr. 1975. "Effects of Constituent Trust and Representative Bargaining Orientation in Intergroup Bargaining." *Journal of Personality and Social Psychology* 31 (6): 1004–12.

Walton, Richard E., and Robert B. McKersie. 1965. *A Behavioral Theory of Labor Negotiations: An Analysis of a Social Interaction System*. New York: McGraw-Hill.

Walton, Richard E., Joel Cutcher-Gershenfeld, and Robert B. McKersie. 1994. *Strategic Negotiations: A Theory of Change in Labor-Management Relations*. Boston: Harvard Business School Press.

Weiss, Stephen E. 1994a. "Negotiating with 'Romans'—Part I." *Sloan Management Review* 35 (2): 51–61.

———. 1994b. "Negotiating with 'Romans'—Part II." *Sloan Management Review* 35 (3): 85–99.

Whelen, Joseph. G. 1979. *Soviet Diplomacy and Negotiating Behavior: Emerging New Context for U.S. Diplomacy*. Report prepared by the Congressional Research Service for the House Committee on Foreign Affairs. Washington, D.C.: Government Printing Office.

Wilkenfeld, Jonathon, and S. Kraus. 1999. "Crisis Negotiation Environment Project." In *New Approaches to International Negotiation and Mediation: Findings from USIP-Sponsored Research*, Peaceworks no. 30, ed. T. D. Sisk. Washington, D.C.: United States Institute of Peace Press.

Winham, Gilbert R. 1977. "Complexity in International Negotiation." In *Negotiations: Social-Psychological Perspectives*, ed. Daniel Druckman. Beverly Hills, Calif.: Sage.

Zartman, I. William. 1975. "Negotiations: Theory and Reality." *Journal of International Affairs* 9 (1): 69–77.

———. 1989. *Ripe for Resolution: Conflict and Intervention in Africa*, 2d ed. New York: Oxford University Press.

———. 1991. "Regional Conflict Resolution." In *International Negotiation: Analysis, Approaches, Issues*, ed. Victor A. Kremenyuk. San Francisco: Jossey-Bass.

———, ed. 1994. *International Multilateral Negotiation*. San Francisco: Jossey-Bass.

———, ed. 1995. *Elusive Peace: Negotiating an End to Civil Wars*. Washington, D.C.: Brookings Institution Press.

———, ed. 2001. "Special Issue: Negotiating Identity: From Metaphor to Process." *International Negotiation* 6 (2).

————. 2000. "Ripeness: The Hurting Stalemate and Beyond." In *International Conflict Resolution After the Cold War*, ed. Paul C. Stern and Daniel Druckman. Washington, D.C.: National Academy Press.

Zartman, I. William, and Maureen R. Berman, eds. 1982. *The Practical Negotiator*. New Haven, Conn.: Yale University Press.

Zartman, I. William, and Guy Olivier Faure, eds. 2005. *Escalation and Negotiation in International Conflicts*. Cambridge, UK: Cambridge University Press.

Zartman, I. William, and Victor Kremenyuk, eds. 2005. *Peace versus Justice: Negotiating Forward- and Backward-Looking Outcomes*. Lanham, Md.: Rowman and Littlefield.

Zechmeister, Kathleen, and Daniel Druckman. 1973. "Determinants of Resolving a Conflict of Interest: A Simulation of Political Decision Making." *Journal of Conflict Resolution* 17 (March): 63–88.

NOTES

1. For other metaphors, see the inaugural issue of *International Negotiation*.

2. For a comparison of processes in international and domestic contexts, see Druckman (2001b); for an extreme statement of system determinants of negotiating behavior, see Kremenyuk (2002).

3. See Druckman (2003a) for a perspective on the relation between micro- and macrolevel processes.

4. Zartman and Berman (1982) extend this model to three stages, adding a diagnostic process before a formula is developed.

5. See also Rousseau's (2002) results showing that survey respondents emphasized relative or competitive gains more for security than for nonsecurity issues.

6. See Zartman (2000) for a more recent evaluation of this idea.

7. This is an unpublished analysis conducted by the author.

8. Snyder and Diesing (1977) provide further elaboration of these cycles.

9. These are examples of findings reported in papers presented at the 2003–5 annual meetings. See the IACM web page (http://www.iacm-conflict.org/) for the programs of those meetings.

10. The results of this unpublished study are discussed in Druckman (2003c).

11. Media attention is the strongest variable in both stages three and four of each of these paths.

12. See Iklé's (1964) discussion of extension negotiations.

13. For more on the issue of forward- and backward-looking negotiation processes, see Zartman and Kremenyuk (2005).

14. For more on this issue, see Druckman (2002a).

15. See Druckman and Hopmann (1989) for an earlier review of the literature and the more recent studies sponsored by the United States Institute of Peace project on national negotiating styles, such as Blacker, Giarra, and Vogel (2002); Cogan (2003); Smyser (2003); and Snyder (1999).

4

MEDIATION IN INTERNATIONAL CONFLICTS

Theory, Practice, and Developments

Jacob Bercovitch

The international environment of the twenty-first century is vastly different from that of the Cold War system in the late twentieth century. That statement seems a truism, as we notice how old practices and alliances have become unstuck, new patterns of relations and institutions emerge, the legitimacy of the state as a primary actor is challenged from within and without, boundaries offer little or no defense against a determined adversary, and issues such as terrorism, weapons proliferation, and ideological fanaticism threaten the very fabric of international relations. Amid all the changes and transformations we have witnessed in the past two decades, it is useful to ponder how states and other actors can deal with the many conflicts they face. Can they still use the same methods of conflict management that have been in existence for hundreds of years, or will new forms of managing conflicts evolve? Will new actors become involved in conflict management, or will states and international organizations continue to dominate this activity? The main argument advanced in this chapter is that despite all the fundamental changes we have witnessed in the international environment, the intervention of diverse third parties remains an important aspect of any international system. We may have seen an explosion of humanitarian interventions, transnational conflict management, and track-two diplomatic efforts, but there is still a long way to go before we can discard the well-tested tool of mediation.

Although states have a legitimate monopoly over the means of violence, and insist that they be permitted to reserve and, indeed, exercise the right to use violence in conflict situations, there is a strong normative expectation regarding non-use of violence and the desirability of managing conflicts peacefully. Article 2(3) of the UN Charter asks that "All member states shall settle their international disputes in such a manner that international peace and security, and justice, are not endangered." In 1982, the UN General Assembly adopted a Declaration on the Peaceful Settlement of Disputes, which emphasized "the need to exert utmost efforts in order to settle any conflict and dispute between States exclusively by peaceful means." And in 1999, the United Nations reaffirmed a commitment to the principles of peaceful settlement of disputes on the anniversary of the Hague Treaty. The principle of peaceful settlement of conflicts is a cornerstone of the relations between states (that its absence is often observed is a cause for soul searching among scholars and practitioners).

The available methods of peaceful settlement of international conflicts are numerous and varied. They are listed in Article 33 of the UN Charter, which requests that the "parties to any dispute, the continuance of which is likely to endanger the maintenance of international peace and security, shall, first of all, seek a solution by negotiation, inquiry, mediation, conciliation, arbitration, judicial settlement, resort to regional agencies or arrangements, or other peaceful means of their choice."

The UN Charter recognizes the existence of three basic methods for the peaceful management of international conflicts: (1) direct negotiation among the conflicting parties; (2) various forms of mediation, good offices, and conciliation; and (3) binding methods of third-party intervention (e.g., arbitration and adjudication). Each method has its own characteristics, strengths, and disadvantages, and each may be suited to different conflicts. One generic approach cannot deal with all conflicts. It behooves us to understand which method or technique to use in which particular conflict. This chapter explores mediation: examines its unique features and how it works, discusses who is likely to undertake mediation activities and the problems mediators typically encounter, and assesses how mediation can contribute to resolving conflicts and preventing their escalation in the new international environment.

MEDIATION: TOWARD A DEFINITION

The study of mediation has suffered from conceptual imprecision and a startling lack of information. Practitioners of formal or informal mediation in the domestic or international arena were keen to sustain its image as a mysterious practice, akin to some art form, taking place behind closed doors. Scholars of mediation did not believe that their field of study was susceptible to a systematic analysis. In short, neither practitioners nor scholars believed that they could discern any pattern of behavior in mediation's various forms, or that any generalizations could be made about the practice in general.

The prevalent agnosticism toward analysis and the desire to maintain the intuitive mystique of mediation are best exemplified in the observations of two noted American practitioners. Arthur Meyer, commenting on the role of mediators, notes, "The task of the mediator is not an easy one. The sea that he sails is only roughly charted, and its changing contours are not clearly discernible. He has no science of navigation, no fund inherited from the experience of others. He is a solitary artist recognizing at most a few guiding stars, and depending on his personal powers of divination" (1960, 160). William Simkin, an equally respected practitioner of mediation, comments in a slightly more prosaic but no less emphatic fashion that "the variables are so many that it would be an exercise in futility to describe typical mediator behavior with respect to sequence, timing or the use or non-use of the various functions theoretically available" (1971, 118).

The mystery and uniqueness of mediation acted like something of a ghost that haunted many of us for too long. There may be little consensus on how best to study or practice mediation, but there is very broad agreement that this particular ghost should be exorcised. Mediation can, should, and must be studied properly, and the lessons derived from such study should serve as signposts in the quest for a better understanding of the process and more effective conflict management.

Etymologically, "mediation" comes from the Latin root to halve, but different definitions of mediation purport to (1) capture the gist of what mediators do or hope to achieve, (2) distinguish between mediation and related processes of third-party intervention (i.e., arbitration), and (3) describe mediators' attributes.

Focusing on what mediators hope to achieve and how they may go about achieving it, Young offers a definition of mediation as "any action taken by an actor that is not a direct party to the crisis, that is designed to reduce or remove one or more of the problems of the bargaining relationship, and therefore to facilitate the termination of the crisis itself" (1967, 34). In much the same vein, Mitchell defines mediation as any "intermediary activity . . . undertaken by a third party with the primary intention of achieving some compromise settlement of the issues at stake between the parties, or at least ending disruptive conflict behavior" (1981, 287). And in a somewhat more detailed fashion, Blake and Mouton define mediation as a process involving "the intervention of a third party who first investigates and defines the problem and then usually approaches each group separately with recommendations designed to provide a mutually acceptable solution" (1985, 15).

Other definitions focus less on the outcome and more on the process. Thus, Ann Douglas defines mediation as "a form of peacemaking in which an outsider to a dispute intervenes on his own or accepts the invitation of disputing parties to assist them in reaching agreement" (1957, 70). Moore defines it as "an extension and elaboration of the negotiation process. Mediation involves the intervention of an acceptable, impartial, and neutral third party who has no authoritative decision making power to assist contending parties in voluntarily reaching their own mutually acceptable settlement" (1986, 6). And Singer defines it as a "form of third-party assistance [that] involves an outsider to the dispute who lacks the power to make decisions for the parties" (1990, 20).

Still other definitions focus on the attribute of neutrality and impartiality as the distinguishing features of mediation. Bingham defines mediation as the "assistance of a 'neutral' third party to a negotiation" (1985, 5). Folberg and Taylor see mediation "as the process by which the participants, together with the assistance of a neutral person or persons, systematically isolate disputed issues in order to develop options, consider alternatives, and reach a consensual settlement that will accommodate their needs" (1984, 7). Moore draws attention to the process of mediation and the neutrality of a mediator in the following definition: "the intervention into a dispute or negotiation by an acceptable, impartial and neutral third party who has no authoritative decision-making power to assist disputing parties in voluntarily reaching their own mutually acceptable settlement of issues in dispute" (1986, 14). Finally, Spencer and Yang see mediation as "the assistance of a third party not involved in the dispute, who may be of a unique status that gives him or her certain authority with the disputants; or perhaps an outsider who may be regarded by them as a suitably neutral go-between" (1993, 195).

These definitions (and they are but a sample) exemplify the enormous scope of mediation. Mediation may take place in conflicts between states, within states, between groups of states, organizations, and between individuals. Mediators enter a conflict to help those involved achieve a better outcome than they would be able to achieve by themselves. Once involved in a conflict, mediators may use a wide variety of behaviors to achieve this objective. Some mediators make suggestions for a settlement, others refrain from doing so. Some mediators are interested in achieving a compromise; others are not. Although some mediators are neutral, others are decidedly not. Former secretary of state Henry Kissinger in the Middle East, Presidents Carter and

Clinton at Camp David, former British and Russian foreign secretaries Robin Cook and Yevgeny Primakov and Ambassador Holbrooke all mediating in Kosovo, Senator Mitchell in Northern Ireland, Secretary of State Rice shuttling to and fro in the Middle East, or the Chinese in North Korea—they may all have been neutral in mediating their various conflicts, but that was hardly the most notable feature of their intervention.

Some consider quibbling over definitions or aspects of neutrality to be a futile exercise in semantic sophistry. It is most emphatically not so. The myriad of possible mediators and the range of mediation roles and strategies are so wide as to defeat attempts to understand, as we seek to do here, the "essence" of mediation. In the absence of a generally accepted definition, there is a tendency to identify mediation with one particular role (e.g., a go-between) or a single strategy (e.g., offering proposals). But assigning an exclusive role or strategy to one kind of mediation overlooks the dynamics of the process. It is also detrimental to the search for common and divergent dimensions of mediation in international and other social contexts and the effort to draw general lessons from mediation experience.

The reality of international mediation is that of a complex and dynamic interaction between mediators, who have resources and an interest in the conflict or its outcome, and the protagonists or their representatives. The most helpful approach to mediation links it to a related approach to conflict, that of negotiation, but at the same time emphasizes mediation's unique features and conditions. The parameters of such an approach were established by Stevens and Schelling. Stevens states that "mediation, like other social phenomena, is susceptible to systematic analysis. The key to analysis is in recognizing that where mediation is employed it is an integral part of the bargaining process. . . . [A]n analysis of mediation is not possible except in the context of general analysis of bargaining negotiations" (1963, 123). In a similar vein, Schelling notes that a mediator "is probably best viewed as an element in the communication arrangements, or as a third party with a payoff structure of his own" (1960, 22).

In any given conflict, mediators may change, their role may be redefined, issues may alter, indeed even the parties involved in the conflict may and often do change. A comprehensive definition seems to be a primary requisite for understanding this complex reality. The following broad definition provides suitable criteria for inclusion (and exclusion) and serves as a basis for identifying differences and similarities. Mediation is here defined as a process of conflict management, related to but distinct from the parties' own negotiations, where those in conflict seek the assistance of, or accept an offer of help from, an outsider (whether an individual, an organization, a group, or a state) to change their perceptions or behavior, and to do so without resorting to physical force or invoking the authority of law.

This definition may be broad, but it can be generally and widely applied. It forces us to recognize that any mediation situation comprises (a) parties in conflict, (b) a mediator, (c) a process of mediation, and (d) the context of mediation. All these elements are important in mediation. Together they determine its nature, quality, and effectiveness, as well as its success or failure.

Mediation is, at least structurally, the continuation of negotiations by other means. Mediation differs from other accommodative strategies such as negotiation (which is dyadic rather than triadic structure) and arbitration (in its nonbinding character). What mediators do, can do, or are permitted to do in their efforts to resolve a conflict may depend, to some extent, on who they are and what resources and competencies they can bring to bear. Ultimately, though, their efforts depend on who the parties are, the context of the conflict, what is at stake, and the nature of their interaction. "Mediation," as Stulberg so rightly notes, "is a procedure predicated upon the process of negotiation" (1981, 87). Mediation is, above all, adaptive and responsive. It extends the process of negotiation to reflect different parties, different possibilities, and a different situation. To assume otherwise is to mistake wishful thinking for reality.

CHARACTERISTICS OF MEDIATION

What, then, are the main features or characteristics of mediation and mediators across levels?

- Mediation is an extension and continuation of peaceful conflict management.
- Mediation involves the intervention of an outsider—an individual, a group, or an organization—into a conflict between two or more states or other actors.
- Mediation is a noncoercive, nonviolent, and, ultimately, nonbinding form of intervention.
- Mediators enter a conflict, whether internal or international, in order to affect it, change it, resolve it, modify it, or influence it in some way.
- Mediators bring with them, consciously or otherwise, ideas, knowledge, resources, and interests of their own or of the group or organization they represent. Mediators often have their own assumptions and agendas about the conflict in question.

- Mediation is a voluntary form of conflict management. The actors involved retain control over the outcome (if not always over the process) of their conflict, as well as the freedom to accept or reject mediation or mediators' proposals.
- Mediation usually operates on an ad hoc basis only.

THE INCIDENCE OF MEDIATION

It is interesting to note just how widespread the resort to mediation really is in international relations. History of mediation is as old as the notion of conflict itself (Wall, Stark, and Standifer 2001), and the practice of mediation can be found in cultures as different as China (Ciamant 2000; Wall and Lynn 1993), Turkey (Kozan and Ergin 1999; Kozan 1997), Malaysia (Provencher 1968), and Japan (Cortazzi 1990), among others. Although mediation may not always be apparent, most international conflicts experience some form of mediation. Several scholarly studies address this issue. Northedge and Donelan (1971) identify fifty international conflicts from 1945 to 1970, finding that some form of mediation was involved in thirty-one (or 62 percent) of these disputes and achieved a successful settlement in seven of these conflicts (or 23 percent of mediated conflicts). A more comprehensive study conducted by Holsti (1983) lists ninety-four international conflicts in the post-1945 period, noting that mediators were involved in forty-two (or 45 percent) of these disputes and that their involvement achieved some measure of success in thirty disputes (71 percent of mediated conflicts). Mark Zacher (1979), who focuses more specifically on the conflict management activities of regional organizations, finds that such organizations were involved in forty international disputes (35 percent of all disputes between 1945 and 1977), and that in twenty-one of these (53 percent), such interventions produced a successful outcome.

Butterworth's study of international conflict resolution (1976) offers an even more complete picture of the extent of third-party mediation in international conflict. He identifies 310 international conflicts between 1945 and 1974 and notes that in 255 of these disputes (or 82 percent) there was some form of mediation. Bercovitch (1996) identifies 241 international disputes in the 1945–90 period and finds that 145 of these disputes (60 percent) were mediated. The total number of mediations in the same period—international and domestic—was tallied at 593 cases; but the actual number of cases is much higher, because so many informal mediation activities undertaken by individuals or non-governmental organizations are simply not reported. A more recent paper (Bercovitch and Houston 2000) identifies 295 international conflicts from 1945 to 1995 with the aim of creating the most inclusive and accurate record possible. These conflicts experienced 2,614 different conflict management attempts; of the 295 disputes, 171 were mediated, for a total number of 1,583 mediation efforts (excluding 189 mediation offers only). When we look at the period 1945–2000, we find more than 300 international conflicts and more than 3,750 separate cases of mediation (see Bercovitch and Fretter 2004).

What all these studies point out quite unmistakably is that, whichever way one looks at it, international mediation can hardly be described as being in a state of disuse; it is frequently resorted to by actors of the most diverse kind. Mediation is, on the face of it, an effective strategy that can deal with all types of conflicts.

The challenges of the post–Cold War era, with its increased risks and uncertainty, changes to many of the accepted rules of the game, and the proliferation of intense ethnic and other identity-based conflicts and nontraditional security threats, will require us to resort to mediation even more often than we have in the past. Mediation may be the closest thing we have to an effective method for dealing with conflicts in the twenty-first century. For this reason alone we must study mediation seriously and systematically. In an interdependent and increasingly fractious world, conflicts affect us all; their proper management is everyone's business.

THE STUDY OF INTERNATIONAL MEDIATION

The literature on international mediation has attracted many scholars and reflects diversity in terms of approaches and perspectives (see Kolb and Rubin 1991). These approaches—and there seems to be an endless variety of them —range from purely scholarly studies to policy implications to the reflections of mediators themselves, and to studies suggesting that academics should act as third parties in mediation efforts. Different scholars categorize studies of mediation under different categories. For instance, Wall (1981) differentiates among "general theories," "context-specific theories," and "extended context theories." Sometimes these approaches offer implications for practical involvement; at other times they focus on descriptions and theory development. There are three main traditions in the study of international mediation:

1. The first group of studies is essentially prescriptive and is devoted to offering advice on what constitutes good conflict management in real-world situations (e.g., Fisher and Ury 1981). These studies, mostly developed by scholars associated with the Program on Negotiation at Harvard University,

generate books and manuals on how mediators and negotiators should behave, what constitutes good negotiation or mediation, and how conflicts, serious or otherwise, can be resolved.

2. Some studies of mediation in a variety of contexts are based on theoretical notions and the participation of academic practitioners in a variety of actual conflicts, with the aim of testing ideas and developing a generic theory for the resolution of social conflicts. These studies use a variety of interaction and problem-solving techniques to combine political action with scientific experimentation and thus contribute to the development of a set of rules that can address all (not just international) conflicts. Some of this research (Burton 1969, 1972, 1984; Doob 1971; Fisher 1983; Kelman 1992; Walton 1969) has generated valuable insights, but much of it is relevant at the microlevel only; its applicability and effectiveness in international relations is still a matter of some debate.

3. The third set of studies is based on actual descriptions and empirical examinations of mediation cases. These studies seek to develop theories and to offer general guidelines through (a) the detailed description of a particular case of international mediation (e.g., Ott 1972; Rubin 1981); (b) laboratory and experimental approaches to mediation (e.g., Bartunek, Benton, and Keys 1975; Rubin 1980) to discover how parties and mediators behave in controlled circumstances; and (c) a contingency framework that relies on large-scale systematic studies. This approach draws on numerous cases of international mediation to formulate and test propositions about effective mediation and to assess the conditions under which mediation can be made to work better (e.g., Bercovitch and Rubin 1992; Touval and Zartman 1985). Contingency approach has its roots in the social-psychological theories of negotiation as developed by Sawyer and Guetzkow (1965) and modified by Druckman (1977).

The contingency approach provides a framework that permits a systematic analysis of the underlying structures and conditions that shape the conflict, events, and complex relationships of the conflict management process. It takes into consideration the individual influences of personal, role, situational, goal, interactional, and outcome variables (Bercovitch 1984; Bercovitch and Houston 2000; Fisher and Keashley 1991; Gochman 1993; Keashly and Fisher 1996, 235–62) as well as their interactive effects within the context, process, and outcome of conflict management (Bercovitch and Houston 2000). This tradition, in many ways the most fruitful approach and the one that can produce the most relevant policy implications for decision makers, forms the basis of this chapter (see Bercovitch 2005).

THE MOTIVES FOR MEDIATION

These different approaches often complement, and sometimes contrast with, one another. They can all, however, provide useful insights on the three most relevant questions in mediation: Why mediate? How does one mediate? When is mediation most likely to be successful? This section examines these questions in detail.

As an instrument of diplomacy and foreign policy, mediation has become almost as common as conflict itself. It is carried out daily by such disparate actors as private individuals; government officials; religious figures; regional, non-governmental, and international organizations; ad hoc groupings; and states of all sizes. Each of these mediators brings to the mediation situation its own interests, perceptions, and resources. Each may adopt behavior that ranges from the very passive, through the facilitative, to the highly active. The form and character of mediation in a particular international conflict are determined by the context of both the international system and the conflict itself (Bercovitch and Jackson 2001; Touval 1985; Kolb 1989a, 1989b), the issues, the parties involved, and the identity of the mediator. The importance of this reciprocal influence can hardly be overemphasized.

As a legitimate form of international peacemaking and an expression of international concern, mediation is particularly appropriate when (a) a conflict is long, drawn out, or complex; (b) the parties' own conflict-management efforts have reached an impasse; (c) neither party is prepared to countenance further costs or loss of life; and (d) both parties are prepared to cooperate, tacitly or openly, to break their stalemate.

When these conditions prevail, the presence of a mediator can secure a peaceful outcome. But why would a mediator wish to intervene in other people's conflicts, and why, for that matter, would states in conflict (or parties in dispute) accept a mediator?

Thus, one of the crucial themes in mediation literature is the motivation of parties to seek assistance to resolve their conflict and the motivation of the mediators to mediate. The parties' motivation and commitment to accept and engage in mediation undoubtedly affect the outcome of mediation. Effective mediation requires consent, high motivation, and active participation. Traditional approaches to mediation assume that conflict parties and a mediator share one reason for initiating mediation: a desire to reduce, abate, or resolve a conflict. To this end, both sides may invest considerable personnel, time, and resources in the mediation. This shared humanitarian interest may be a genuine reason in a few instances of mediation, but normally even this interest intertwines with other, less altruistic motivations (see Greig 2005).

Motives of mediators and parties seeking mediation often differ. For analytical purposes it is useful to look at mediators' motives and parties' motivations separately.

Mediator Motivation

Different mediators have different motives to intervene in a conflict. When the mediator is an unofficial individual (e.g., Adam Curle in the Nigeria-Biafra conflict in 1967–70 or President Carter in North Korea in 1994), the motives for initiating mediation may include a desire to (a) be instrumental in changing the course of a long-standing or escalating conflict, (b) gain access to major political leaders and open channels of communication, (c) put into practice a set of ideas on conflict management, and (d) spread one's own ideas and thus enhance personal stature and professional status. The presence of one or more of these motives (which may be conscious or subconscious) in an opportune situation provides a very strong rationale for an individual to initiate unofficial mediation.

Where a mediator is an official representative of a government or an organization, another set of motives may prevail. Such persons initiate mediation because (a) they have a clear mandate to intervene in disputes, (b) they may want to do something about a conflict whose continuance could adversely affect their own political interests, (c) they may be directly requested by one or both parties to mediate, (d) they may wish to preserve a structure of which they are a part (e.g., the frequent mediation attempts by the United States in disputes between Greece and Turkey, two valued North Atlantic Treaty Organization member-states), or (e) they may see mediation as a way of extending and enhancing their own influence by becoming indispensable to the parties in conflict or by gaining the gratitude (and presumably the political goodwill) of one or both protagonists (e.g., the frequent efforts by the United States to mediate the Arab-Israeli conflict).

Mediators are political actors; they engage in mediation and expend resources because they expect to resolve a conflict and gain something from it. For many actors, mediation is a policy instrument through which they can pursue some of their interests without arousing too much opposition (Touval 1992). The relationship between a mediator and disputants is thus never entirely devoid of political interest. To overlook this aspect is to miss an important element in the dynamics of mediation.

Disputant Motivation

Adversaries in conflict have a number of motives for desiring mediation: (a) mediation may help them reduce the risks of an escalating conflict and get them closer to a settlement; (b) each party may embrace mediation in the expectation that the mediator will actually nudge or influence the other party; (c) both parties may see mediation as a public expression of their commitment to an international norm of peaceful conflict management; (d) they may want an outsider to take much of the blame should their efforts fail; or (e) a mediator can be used to monitor, verify, and guarantee any eventual agreement. One way or another, parties in conflict—and a mediator—have compelling reasons for accepting, initiating, or desiring mediation.

THE MEDIATOR'S ROLES AND BEHAVIOR

Whether we are studying ethnic, internal, or international conflict, we should resist the tendency to think of mediation as an exogenous input, a unique role, or a distinct humanitarian response to conflict in which a well-meaning actor, motivated only by altruism, is keen to resolve a conflict. A mediator, through the very act of mediating, becomes an actor in a conflict relationship. This relationship involves interests, costs, and potential rewards and exemplifies certain roles and strategies. A mediator's role is part of this broad interaction. To be effective, mediators must reflect and be congruent with that interaction—mediation should be seen, studied, and considered in international relations in this context.

Mediation has been a prevalent form of international conflict management for many years. It is linked to the development of international negotiations and diplomacy, and it is embedded in the creation of institutions, regimes, and formal organizations to help states deal with many aspects of their relationships. But what do mediators actually do? Do they change behavior merely by chairing meetings and carrying messages, or do they possess more active roles and functions?

Considerable attention has been devoted to the question of mediator roles, functions, and behavior. Some scholars see these aspects as the most useful criteria by which to evaluate the success of mediation. Activities have been organized conceptually to describe mediator behavior in terms of various pre-ordained roles and tactics (Gulliver 1979; Laure 1990; Mitchell 1993; Rubin 1981; Stulberg 1981) or phases (Folberg and Taylor 1984; Haynes 1982; Mitchell 1981; Moore 1986). In an exhaustive review of the literature, Wall (1981) identified more than one hundred specific mediation functions and behaviors. All these forms of behavior arise from the fact that the negotiators cannot reach an agreement and their stated purpose is to change, modify, settle, or resolve a conflict—the heart of mediation.

To make sense of the many forms of behavior mediators may undertake, a number of role categories that encompass related forms of behavior are suggested. Mediators' roles may be characterized in a number of ways (e.g., Jabri 1990; Princen 1992). Rubin (1981), for instance, offered a set of mediation roles and distinguished between formal mediation (e.g., by the UN secretary-general) and informal mediation (e.g., by academic practitioners such as John Burton and Herb Kelman), individual mediation (e.g., by Lord Owen) and mediation by a representative of a state (e.g., by the U.S. secretary of state), invited mediation and noninvited mediation, advisory mediation and directive mediation, permanent mediation and temporary mediation, and resolution-oriented mediation and relationship-oriented mediation. Each of these types of mediators has different interests, resources, and capabilities, and the behavior of each may lead to different outcomes. Stulberg (1987) lists the following as mediators' roles: (a) catalyst, (b) educator, (c) translator, (d) resource-expander, (e) bearer of bad news, (f) agent of reality, and (g) scapegoat. Susskind and Cruickshank (1987), whose conception of mediation is that of "assisted negotiation," introduce a dynamic element into the discussion by identifying a number of roles (e.g., representation, inventing options, monitoring) and relating these to the various stages of the conflict.

Another, and some would argue a more useful, approach for categorizing what mediators actually do is that of a mediation strategy, which Kolb defines as "an overall plan, approach or method a mediator has for resolving a dispute. . . . [I]t is the way the mediator intends to manage the case, the parties, and the issue" (1983, 24). In essence, the practice of mediation revolves around the choice of strategic behavior (Bercovitch and Houston 2000). Mediators chose a strategic behavior they believe will facilitate the outcome they seek to achieve. Which are the most important mediation strategies, and do different mediators choose different strategies?

There are a number of ways of thinking about mediation strategies. Kolb (1983) distinguishes two kinds of strategies: deal-making strategies (affecting the substance of a conflict) and orchestration strategies (managing the interaction), similar to Rubin's (1981) resolution- and relationship-oriented roles. Stein (1985), in a study of successive American mediations in the Middle East, talks about incremental strategies, or segmenting a conflict into smaller issues, and comprehensive strategies, which deal with all aspects of a conflict. Carnevale (1986) suggests that mediators may choose from among four fundamental strategies: integration (searching for common ground), pressing (reducing the range of available alternatives), compensation (enhancing the attractiveness of some alternatives), and inaction (which, in effect, means allowing the parties to go their own way). Kressel (1972), in one of the most widely used typologies, presents three general strategies: reflexive (discovering issues, facilitating better interactions), nondirective (producing a favorable climate for mediation), and directive (promoting specific outcomes).

Touval and Zartman (1985) identify three discrete categories of behavior on an ascending level of involvement that can describe the full range of mediation techniques. This typology is particularly useful because it is derived deductively from a general framework of mediation relationships that includes information, decision making, and influence. It can also be examined empirically through either observations or postmediation questionnaires. Above all, it includes all dimensions of mediator behavior within three categories: communication, formulation, and manipulation. This typology overcomes many of the limitations of past research and permits us to analyze and understand what mediators actually do when they get involved in a conflict.

The most useful taxonomy of mediator behavior that can be applied to international mediation analysis is based on the identification of three strategies along a continuum ranging from low to high intervention (Bercovitch and Houston 2000). These are communication-facilitation, procedural, and directive strategies (see Bercovitch 1992; Bercovitch and Houston 2000; Bercovitch and Wells 1993; and Bercovitch, Anagnoson, and Willie 1991). These strategies are based on assumptions derived from Sheppard's (1984) taxonomy of mediator behavior that focuses on the content, process, and procedure of conflict management (see table 4.1).

The choice of any form of mediation behavior or strategy is rarely random. Rather, it is influenced by factors particular to the conflict and internal to the mediator. Mediators try to vary their behavior to reflect the conflict at hand. In low-intensity conflicts, for instance, communication strategies may be more effective; high-intensity conflicts may call for more active, manipulative strategies. Time pressure, mediator rank, and previous relations between the parties all may determine the choice of a strategy. To be effective, mediation strategies and behavior must be truly congruent with the nature of a conflict and the objectives and interests of a mediator (see Wilkenfeld, Quinn, and Smarick 2003). Although the parties are key factors in conflict management, Bercovitch and Houston (2000) find the mediation environment the strongest indicator of mediation behavior, followed by the nature of the actual mediation event.

Whichever intervention strategy mediators use, their underlying objectives in any conflict are to change (a) the physical environment of conflict management (e.g., by maintaining secrecy or imposing time limits, as President Carter did at Camp David); (b) the perception of what is at stake (e.g., by structuring an agenda and/or identifying and packaging new issues); and

Table 4.1. Mediation Strategies and Behavior

Strategies	Tactics
Communication-facilitation	Clarify situation
	Develop rapport with parties
	Make parties aware of relevant information
	Rehearse each party in appropriate behavior
	Clarify what parties intend to communicate
	Avoid taking sides
Procedural	Establish protocol
	Delineate forthcoming agenda
	Separate parties
	Strike a power balance
	Provide direction and act as a spokesman for weaker side
	Reduce tension
	Move from simple to more complex issues
	Keep discussion focused on issues
	Summarize the agreement
	Act as sounding board for propositions and tactics
Directive	Help a party undo a commitment
	Suggest trade-offs
	Help parties save face
	Contrive a prominent position
	Reward parties' concessions
	Highlight costs of nonagreement
	Claim authorship for party's proposal
	Offer carrots or threaten with sticks
	Threaten to quit or to bring in an arbitrator
	Bring third-party ultimatums to the interaction/negotiation

(c) the parties' motivation to reach a peaceful outcome by, for example, using subtle pressure. Any international conflict presents opportunities for some form of mediation. To be effective, however, mediation strategies must reflect the reality of the conflict and the resources of the mediator. To that extent, international mediation is truly a contingent and reciprocal political activity.

WHO MAY MEDIATE?

Given the inevitability and omnipresence of conflict, a limited range of widely accepted procedures for dealing with it, and the unwelcome reality of the scope of its potential destructiveness, it is hardly surprising that so many actors, each adopting different strategies and tactics, are keen to mediate and undertake peacemaking activities. In an international environment lacking a centralized authority, the range of mediators and the diversity of mediation are truly immense. In our current world, the most important structural force on the international mediation market seems to be the hegemonic status of the United States; within this international context, international conflict management is largely, but not exclusively, restricted to the members of the Security Council of the United Nations (Bercovitch and Schneider 2000).

To make some sense of the bewildering range of possible mediators, I suggest that we think of them as falling within one of the following three categories: individuals, institutions and organizations, and states. Let us examine the characteristics of each.

Individuals

The traditional image of international mediation, one nurtured by the media and popular accounts, is that of a high-ranking official shuttling from one place to another in an attempt to search for understanding and to restore communication between hostile parties or to help settle their conflict directly. This image is only partly accurate. The individual mediator who engages in such behavior is normally an official representing his or her government in a series of formal interactions with high-level officials from the disputing countries. This image cannot be accurately described as individual mediation.

By individual mediation, I mean mediation that is carried out by individuals who are not government officials or political incumbents. Although individual mediation exhibits greater variety and experimentation than other forms of mediation, it essentially consists of only two kinds: formal and informal.

Informal Mediation. Informal mediation refers to the efforts of mediators who have a long-standing experience of, and a deep commitment to, international conflict resolution (e.g., Carter in North Korea in 1994; the Quakers; see Yarrow 1978) or to the efforts of knowledgeable scholars whose background, attitudes, and professional experience give them the opportunity to engage in mediation with real conflict parties (the efforts of scholars such as Burton, Doob, and Kelman are some notable examples). Such individuals approach a conflict as private citizens, not as official representatives. They use their academic competence, credibility, and experience to facilitate communications, gain a better understanding of the conflict, and work toward its resolution.

The process of informal mediation usually begins when mediators enter a conflict on their own initiative. The format and arrangements of such mediation are, to say the least, novel. Present in a personal capacity only, mediators rely mostly on communication-facilitation strategies; the whole tone of mediation is free and flexible and can serve as a useful input to a more formal mediation. The efforts of two Israeli academics, Ron Pundak and Yair Hirschfeld, as well as Terje Roed-Larsen of Norway, exemplify the potential benefits of informal mediation in paving the way for more formal discussions between the Israeli government and the Palestine Liberation Organization.

Another example of informal mediation is the assistance given to parties in conflict by the International Negotiation Network (INN) at the Carter Center. This initiative was created by President Carter in 1976, with assistance from other international leaders, to fill a mediation gap. Most states and international organizations are prevented from intervening in the internal affairs of another sovereign state. Yet, because the vast majority of recent serious conflicts have been largely internal rather than interstate, a clear need exists for an informal network of prestigious individuals (including former heads of state and UN secretaries-general) to offer additional mediation resources to the disputants. The INN's informal mediation ranges from offering facilities to clarifying issues to providing a face-saving option by bringing parties into mediation or out of a conflict. The INN has been actively involved in mediation and consultation efforts in Ethiopia, Liberia, Cyprus, Zaire, Burma (Myanmar), Cambodia, and Sudan (Spencer and Yang 1993). The INN has shown just how much can be achieved through informal mediation by individuals.

Formal Mediation. Formal mediation, on the other hand, takes place when a political incumbent, a government representative, or a high-level decision maker acts in an individual capacity to mediate a conflict between the official representatives of other states (e.g., Dennis Ross in his role as the U.S. State Department's Special Middle East Coordinator and Richard Holbrooke at Dayton). It invariably occurs within a formal structure, such as a conference, a political forum, or other official arenas, and is much less flexible than informal mediation. Formal mediation is also less susceptible to the impact of personality. Its loss of flexibility, however, is more than matched by its immediacy of access to influential decision makers. As such, formal mediation is often indistinguishable from diplomatic intercourse; its range of roles is more limited than that of informal mediation, but its impact on outcomes is more direct.

Institutions and Organizations

The complexity of the international environment is such that states can no longer facilitate the pursuit of all human interests or satisfy the demands for a shrinking range of public sector goods and services the world over. Consequently, we have witnessed a phenomenal growth in the number of international and transnational organizations, all of which may affect issues of war and peace. These organizations have become, in some cases, more important providers of services than states. They have also become, in the modern international system, very active participants in the search for mechanisms and procedures conducive to peacemaking and conflict resolution. We can expect these organizations to have a greater impact on the mediation of international conflicts.

Three kinds of organizations play an important role in the area of peacemaking and conflict resolution: regional, international, and transnational. Regional and international organizations, such as the Organization of American States (OAS), African Unity (AU), and the United Nations, represent ensembles of states that have signified their intention to fulfill the obligations—including those of formal mediation—of membership as set forth in a formal treaty. Transnational organizations (e.g., Amnesty International) represent individuals from different countries who have similar knowledge, skills, or interests and who meet on a regular basis to promote their common interests through various means, including informal mediation.

Of the international organizations now in existence, none has been more active in resolving conflicts through negotiations and mediation than the United Nations, whose charter specifically commits it to provide the answers to global problems of conflict and security. In the post–Cold War era's outbreaks of low-level violence, civil wars, and ethnic conflicts, the United Nations is often seen as the only actor capable of resolving conflict independently. *The Agenda for Peace*, released by Secretary-General Boutros-Ghali (1995), recognizes the challenges the United Nations is likely to encounter and places emphasis on preventive diplomacy, peacemaking, and post-conflict peacebuilding as priorities for the world organization.

The United Nations is becoming a center for initiating concerted efforts to deal with the deep-rooted causes of conflict—to resolve conflicts, not merely stop them in their tracks—and will undoubtedly use its political latitude to expand its mediation and conflict resolution activities. UN peacemaking efforts in Somalia, Bosnia, Cambodia, Liberia, Afghanistan, Angola, and Rwanda show the extent to which the United Nations—once a largely ineffectual and much-criticized organization—is prepared to involve itself in all kinds of difficult and intractable conflicts. Once involved, the United

Nations can offer a wealth of related resources unavailable to most other mediators, including a forum, skilled support personnel, and the ability to mobilize an international consensus on a particular outcome.

Regional organizations, such as the European Union (EU), the OAS, the AU, and the Arab League, all adhere to the principles of negotiation and mediation as their preferred means of resolving conflicts. Because most conflict occurs between regional neighbors, it is not surprising that these organizations have always had latitude in the field of conflict resolution. Some, such as the EU and the Organization for Security and Cooperation in Europe, have made conflict resolution a major component of their structure. Regional organizations usually engage in collective mediation; their strength undoubtedly is due to their members' common background, culture, and experience. They may not have the capacity or resources of the United Nations, but they are all involved in some peacemaking activities: the EU in Bosnia, the AU in Somalia, the OAS in El Salvador.

Transnational organizations, such as Amnesty International, the Quakers' Friends Peace Committee and Friends World Committee for Consultation, and the International Committee of the Red Cross, operating independently of states, embody many of the elements commonly associated with impartiality. With limited resources and fewer strategies available to them, these organizations often find themselves involved in what are termed *humanitarian interventions* (where the victims are hostages, refugees, prisoners, or civilians). When strict secrecy or a high degree of impartiality is required and when neither governments nor international organizations can gain access to a conflict, transnational organizations come into their own. Organizations such as the London-based International Alert and the Atlanta-based International Negotiation Network exemplify the growing number of institutions and organizations committed to peacemaking, mediation, and conflict resolution.

States

Individual mediation, although significant, is not common at the international level. Most mediation is carried on by states (or, to be more accurate, their representatives) and regional and international organizations.

When a state is invited to mediate a conflict, or when it initiates mediation, the services of one of its top decision makers are normally engaged. In these cases, figures such as Henry Kissinger, Presidents Carter and Clinton, former secretary of state Warren Christopher, former assistant secretary of state Chester Crocker, and Lord Carrington; and special representatives such as Gunnar Jarring and Philip Habeeb all fulfill mediation roles, usually in the full glare of the international media, as representatives of their countries.

Mediation, at any level and in all its guises, is essentially a voluntary process. This dimension is particularly important in the relations between states where any unwelcome intervention may be strenuously resisted. For mediation between states to be effective, even the most highly placed decision makers must be seen as impartial, acceptable to the disputants, and deserving of their trust. The absence of any one of these attributes may lead to a failed mediation. States will submit their conflict to mediation only when they believe that the mediator can act fairly and recognize the importance of their interests.

When we talk about mediation by states, we normally distinguish between small states and large states. Each claims legitimacy and authority on the basis of different attributes. Small states such as Algeria, Switzerland, and Austria (see Slim 1992) have been involved in a disproportionate number of international mediations. Their very size and presumed lack of clout make them appear nonthreatening and ideally positioned to carry out mediations between adversaries. Small states usually wait for an invitation to mediate. When they do intervene, their efforts tend to be confined to regional conflicts, and their strategies tend to be mostly low-profile strategies of dialogue and communication.

Large states, by contrast, often create the opportunity to mediate and use the mediation as a vehicle to protect or promote their own interests (Touval 1992a). Large states have a greater complement of resources and can select from a wider range of strategies. Because of their global interests, large states get involved in many conflicts in various parts of the world. When large states mediate a conflict, they can use their greater resources to wield a variety of carrots and sticks. They can generate and maintain a momentum toward a settlement by offering a neutral environment (e.g., Camp David or Dayton), pressing for concessions, offering proposals, and generally altering the disputants' payoffs and motivations.

Mediation, whether it is conducted by small or large states, is not prescribed by international law. It is unpredictable and ever changing, but it is not a random process. Its precise form and characteristics are negotiated and renegotiated with each passing phase. There is little that is predetermined about the course of outcomes when states mediate a conflict.

TOWARD MORE EFFECTIVE MEDIATION

Given the diversity of conflicts, circumstances, and actors, there cannot possibly be a "right way" to manage or mediate all international conflicts. However, it is possible to generalize from various studies on mediation and to reflect on lessons learned in order to identify some factors and conditions that impede mediation or help it to become more effective.

Mediation is not a panacea to all the social problems and conflicts in the world. It cannot be successful (whatever that means) in each and every conflict. Clearly, it can be effective in some situations and less effective in others. Scholars and practitioners alike have devoted considerable attention to the conditions under which mediation can be more effective.

From the perspective of a would-be mediator, a number of features can be indicative of the parties' genuine motivation and serious commitment to mediation. Foremost among these is the receipt of a joint request. When only one party requests mediation, the chances of a successful outcome are slim. Mediation offers more rewarding opportunities when it is requested by both parties in conflict rather than by one party only or by the mediator. A joint request may well be a condition for effective international mediation (Bercovitch 1984; Hiltrop 1989).

International mediation is also more likely to be effective when certain conditions and circumstances are present. These include relative power parity between the states or other actors in conflict (Young 1967), the absence of ideological issues or those of general principle from the mediator's scope (Bercovitch and Langley 1993), a clear identification of the parties in conflict (which is not always as straightforward as it may appear), the absence of severe internal disorganization or civil war in the country or countries where the conflict is taking place, the exclusion of the nature and history of the parties' previous relationship from the mediation (Bercovitch 1989), and the presence of a ripe moment constituted by a "hurting stalemate" (Greig 2001; Regan and Stam 2000).

Empirical research (Bercovitch 1986) suggests that neither premature nor belated mediations are especially likely to be effective. The most propitious time to initiate mediation is roughly halfway through the life cycle of a conflict, and certainly after the parties' own efforts have failed. At this stage the parties' motivation to settle is at its highest, and so an opportunity is present —a ripe moment. The timing of mediation is a crucial factor affecting the chances of its success. Conflicts, like all other social processes, have their own life cycles (which may stretch across days, months, or years). There are times when a conflict is "ripe for mediation" (Zartman 1985), and times when mediation can only make a conflict worse and harm the credibility of the mediators (Haas 1990).

Assessing when a conflict is ready for mediation may not be easy, varying from case to case and depending on many dynamic factors. Yet the existence of a hurting stalemate (e.g., a military setback, a change in power relations, or a failure to impose a unilateral outcome) remains the best benchmark in a conflict for deciding when to initiate mediation. The parties reach a hurting stalemate when their own efforts to manage the conflict are going nowhere and when the costs, both human and economic, of pursuing the conflict begin to mount. These and other conditions affect the chances of the mediation's success. Being able to identify these conditions may affect mediators' decisions to initiate or forego mediation as well as its likely course and outcome. Knowing when to use mediation may be more important than how often it is used.

The factors that may have the greatest impact on mediation have been studied by many (e.g., Bercovitch 1992, 1–29; Bercovitch and Houston 2000; Bercovitch and Houston 1993, 1996, 11–35; Bercovitch and Langley 1993; Bercovitch and Wells 1993; Kleiboer 1996; Elangovan 1995). They include the issues at stake in a conflict; the type of issues in conflict; the importance of the dispute to each of the parties; the nature of their relationship; the parties' acceptance of mediation and genuine commitment to settlement; the degree of control over the process that parties and the mediator have; time pressures for settlement; the absence of spoilers or others committed to destroying any chances of peace; the expediency of the mediation process; and the expected likelihood of reaching a satisfactory outcome.

These factors can be grouped under three related clusters: preexisting, concurrent, and background dimensions of conflict management. The preexisting dimension of conflict includes the characteristics of the conflict (i.e., intensity of the conflict; Kressel and Pruitt 1989; Fisher and Keashley 1991; Rubin 1980), the type and nature of the issues (Azar 1990; Diehl 1992; Lewicki and Litterer 1985; Vasquez 1983); the characteristics of the parties (i.e., their internal characteristics; Gochman 1993; Brecher 1993); and their international status and relationships (Kriesberg 1982; Northedge and Donelan 1971).

The concurrent mediation context includes the nature of the mediator (i.e., identity, resources, relationships that the mediator brings in, rank and position) and the specific situational context of the mediation process itself (initiation and timing of mediation, mediation environment).

The background context of mediation includes information from previous mediation efforts (i.e., the course, outcome, and effectiveness of past mediation events; Grebe 1994; Pearson and Thoennes 1984; Roehl and Cook 1985) and the mediator's experience with mediation (Burton and Dukes 1990; Carnevale and Pegnetter 1985; Kochan and Jick 1978).

One of the most crucial factors affecting the process and outcome of mediation is the mediator's identity and skills. A mediator's success will be partially dependent on common bonds, shared history, or common experiences with the disputant parties. The identity of a mediator affects the mediator's influence, trust, and legitimacy. Where mediators enjoy high trust of the parties and have a strong claim to legitimacy, the chances for successful mediation are much higher (Bercovitch and Houston 2000).

Scholars and practitioners agree that appropriate mediators possess intelligence, tact, skills in drafting formal proposals, and a sense of humor, in addition to specific knowledge of the conflict at hand. Mediators who possess these attributes are likely to be acceptable to all sides in a conflict and consequently will enhance the parties' motivation to reach a peaceful settlement. These factors determine the mediator's ability to use various types of power, resources, and leverage.

A related aspect of mediator identity that can aid in distinguishing potentially effective from ineffective mediators is that of rank. It is important to note that some high-ranking mediators (such as a president, a prime minister, or a secretary of state) are better able to marshal resources in the course of mediation than mediators of lesser stature. High-ranking mediators can be more persuasive than middle-level officials; they possess leverage and can use social influence that could be crucial in persuading the parties to make concessions or move toward an agreement. This notion is borne out in a series of empirical studies (Bercovitch and Houston 1993) that clearly show the positive association between high rank and successful mediation outcomes.

A related idea is that mediation roles and strategies may affect outcomes. Some scholars (e.g., Burton 1969; Kelman 1992) advocate communication-facilitation strategies as the most appropriate strategy in a wide range of conflicts. Others (e.g., Touval and Zartman 1985) argue for more forceful mediation involving formulation and directive strategies. Although much may depend on the nature and circumstances of a conflict, there is strong evidence (e.g., Bercovitch and Houston 1993) to suggest that more active strategies are more likely to be effective. Strategies that rely on the full gamut of influence, using reward, persuasion, and legitimacy as well as information and communication, can better effect a change in posture and position and are more likely to get the parties to move closer to a settlement.

Mediators may appear to do little more than shuttle from here to there, chair meetings, and clarify issues. In most cases, though, they quickly begin to urge the parties to reach some agreement. Mediators must do more than generate and share information if they are to have a desired impact on a conflict; they must use more active strategies and change the ways the parties think and interact. The process of identifying the range of factors that may make mediation more effective is still in its infancy. Much more work is needed on this crucial issue, but the more we understand the factors that affect mediation, the more we will be able to enhance its effectiveness.

EVALUATING INTERNATIONAL MEDIATION

Whatever it is that mediators do and achieve, we need to find a way of assessing their contribution to any given conflict. That is no easy task. How can mediation outcomes be assessed? How can the impact of a particular mediation be evaluated? If mediation is ultimately about changing or influencing a conflict, or the way parties in conflict behave, can such changes be discerned? Furthermore, if change has been effected and a satisfactory outcome of sorts has been achieved, can this outcome be attributed to the wisdom and experience of the mediator or to the motivation of the parties? Conversely, if the parties show no change whatsoever, should the lack of change be described as mediation failure? How much time should elapse before we can realistically expect results from the mediation? What is the norm? Six months, one year, three years? Will the criteria change depending on the nature of the conflict, the parties, and the mediator? In short, evaluating success and failure in mediation poses serious conceptual and methodological problems.

Because international mediation is not a uniform practice, it seems futile to draw up one set of criteria to cover the many objectives of all mediators. Individual mediators, for instance, may emphasize communication-facilitating strategies, be more concerned with the quality of interaction, and seek to create a better environment for conflict management. States, on the other hand, may seek to change the behavior of those in conflict and achieve a settlement of sorts. Such different objectives cannot be easily accommodated within a single perspective. To answer the question of whether mediation works, we need to know something about the various goals of mediation. Here I suggest two broad criteria, subjective and objective, to assess the effects and consequences of mediation in any conflict.

Subjective Criteria

Subjective criteria refer to the parties' or the mediator's perception (and, to some extent, that of other relevant external actors) that the goals of mediation have been achieved or that a desired change has taken place. Using this perspective, we can suggest that mediation has been successful when the parties feel or express satisfaction with the process or outcome of mediation, or when the outcome is seen as fair, efficient, or effective (Susskind and Cruickshank 1987).

Fairness of mediation, satisfaction with its performance, or improvement in the overall climate of the parties' relationship cannot be easily demonstrated, but they are undoubtedly consequences of successful mediation. They are subjective because they depend on the perceptions of the parties in conflict. Even if a conflict remains unresolved, mediation—in any guise—can do much to change the way the disputants feel about each other and lead, however indirectly, to both a long-term improvement in the parties' relationship and a resolution of the conflict. We can all describe these efforts as successful, even if we are not quite certain how to demonstrate the correlates of such success.

Objective Criteria

Objective criteria for assessing the impact and consequences of mediation offer a totally different perspective. Objective criteria rely on substantive indicators that can be demonstrated empirically. Usually such criteria involve observations of change and judgments about the extent of change as evidence of the success or failure of mediation. Thus, one may consider a particular mediation effort successful if it contributed to a cessation or reduction of violent behavior and the opening of a dialogue between the parties. Or one can call mediation successful when a formal and binding agreement that settles the conflict's issues has been signed. These are tangible results we can all see.

Evaluating the success or failure of international mediation in objective terms is a relatively straightforward task. Here one can measure success or failure in terms of the permanence of the agreement, the speed with which it was achieved, the reduction in the level of hostilities between the disputants, the number of issues on which agreement was achieved, and so forth. On the face of it, objective criteria seem to offer a perfectly valid way to assess the impact, consequences, and effectiveness of international mediation.

However, it would be unwise to rely solely on objective criteria. Different mediators, and indeed different parties in conflict, have different goals in mind when they enter conflict management. Changing behavior could well be only one among many other objectives. Some international mediators may focus on the substance of interactions, others may focus on its climate, setting, and decision-making norms. These goals cannot always be evaluated easily. Mediation should ideally be evaluated in terms of criteria that are significant to each of the participants in the process. Thus, the question of whether mediation works, or how best to evaluate it, can only be answered by finding out as much as we can about each party's goals and objectives, as well as learning to ascertain when positive change had taken place. There are just too many conceptual problems with the issue of evaluation; it seems that, on this question at least, theoretical ambitions must be tempered by the constraints of a complex reality.

CONCLUSION

For a very long time indeed, scholarly attempts to comprehend the nature and sources of human conflict in general, and the manner of its resolution in particular, were all too few in number and rather marginal in character. This situation has changed considerably. The international environment is experiencing a lot more internal conflicts; some are truly intractable, long lasting, and with very high human costs. Major international conflicts, such as those in Iraq, Afghanistan, and Israel-Palestine, are ripe (some would say overripe) and ready for some kind of political termination. Since the end of the Cold War, which had ossified all patterns of behavior, international conflict and its management have become subjects for systematic analysis and serious scholarly work. Scholarly tracts and practitioners' reflections have helped to institutionalize the field and enhance the individual and collective capacity to manage conflicts. The risks, costs, and tragedies of conflicts in the past twenty-five years have forced us to search for better ways to terminate or resolve them. The traditional reliance on power, deterrence, or avoidance is no longer a relevant set of responses in our era. In a truly globlized and interdependent world, negotiation and mediation are emerging as the most appropriate responses to conflict in its myriad forms and to the challenge of building a more peaceful world. But negotiation and mediation do not just happen. They are social roles subject to many influences, and like other roles, they can be learned and improved.

The shared quest for learning the principles and practices of mediation can make sense only if it is conducted within some kind of intellectual framework, one that can explain the logic and reasoning behind this method of conflict management, in which the mediator is neither directly part of a conflict nor totally removed from it. This chapter has sought to provide such a framework and assess its basic dimensions. The framework embodies my conviction that mediation is an aspect of the broader process of conflict management and that, whatever the conflict is about or who the mediators are, mediation involves the intertwining of interests, resources, and positions in an attempt to influence outcomes. This relationship is critical for analyzing the dynamics of conflict and assessing the prospects of successful mediation. I have tried to unravel many aspects of this relationship and point out their influence on mediation. I do not assume that my analysis is exhaustive, but I believe that the foregoing presentation adequately integrates many findings that have a bearing on conflict resolution, and provides answers to questions such as who may mediate conflicts, when mediation should be initiated, how it actually works, and how its impact can be evaluated.

The end of the Cold War and the emergence of an ever-increasing number of ethnic and internal conflicts provide many opportunities for a significant expansion in the use of mediation as an instrument of conflict resolution. The old techniques of power and deterrence seem increasingly less relevant to deal with the problems and conflicts confronting us. Mediation may well offer the most coherent and effective response to these issues. To ensure that it can also be successful, we need to develop a better understanding of the process and offer consistent guidelines to the many actors involved in mediation. This effort is still in its infancy, and many different fields and disciplines can contribute to its development. In this chapter, I have tried to take a few tentative steps in that direction. The challenge confronting us all is to recognize the diversity, strengths, and limitations of mediation and then to use the most effective range of tools where appropriate. Given the amount of destruction resulting from today's conflicts, and tomorrow's potential crises, we cannot afford to ignore this challenge.

ACKNOWLEDGMENTS

An earlier version of this paper was completed during my term as a senior fellow at the United States Institute of Peace in 2002. I am grateful to Ayse Kadayifci for all her help in the preparation of this paper and to John Crist and Peter Pavilionis for their constructive comments.

REFERENCES

Azar, E. E. 1990. *The Management of Protracted Conflict: Theory and Cases.* Aldershot, UK: Dartmouth.

Bartunek, Jean M., Alan A. Benton, and Christopher B. Keys. 1975. "Third Party Intervention and the Behavior of Group Representatives." *Journal of Conflict Resolution* 19 (3): 532–57.

Bercovitch, Jacob. 1984. *Social Conflicts and Third Parties: Strategies of Conflict Resolution.* Boulder, Colo.: Westview.

———. 1986. "International Mediation: A Study of Incidence, Strategies and Conditions of Successful Outcomes." *Cooperation and Conflict* 21 (3): 155–68.

———. 1989. "International Dispute Mediation." In *Mediation Research: The Process and Effectiveness of Third-Party Intervention*, ed. Kenneth Kressel and Dean G. Pruitt. San Francisco: Jossey-Bass.

———. 1992. "The Structure and Diversity of Mediation in International Relations." In *Mediation in International Relations*, ed. Jacob Bercovitch and Jeffrey Z. Rubin. London: Macmillan; New York: St. Martin's.

———. 1996. "Understanding Mediation's Role in Preventive Diplomacy." *Negotiation Journal* 12 (3): 241–59.

———. 2005. "Social Research and the Study of Mediation: Designing and Implementing Systematic Archival Research." *International Negotiation* 9 (3): 415–28.

Bercovitch, Jacob, Theodore Anagnoson, and Donnette Willie. 1991. "Some Conceptual Issues and Empirical Trends in the Study of Successful Mediation in International Relations." *Journal of Peace Research* 28 (1): 7–18.

Bercovitch, Jacob, and Judith Fretter. 2004. *Regional Guide to International Conflict and Its Management*. Washington, D.C.: Congressional Quarterly.

Bercovitch, Jacob, and Allison Houston. 1993. "Influence of Mediator Characteristics and Behavior on the Success of Mediation in International Relations." *International Journal of Conflict Management* 4 (October): 297–321.

———. 1996. "International Mediation: Theoretical Issues and Empirical Evidence." In *Resolving International Conflicts*, ed. Jacob Percovitch. Boulder, Colo.: Lynne Rienner.

———. 2000. "Why Do They Do It Like This? An Analysis of the Factors Influencing Mediation Behavior in International Conflicts." *Journal of Conflict Resolution* 44 (2): 170–202.

Bercovitch, Jacob, and Richard Jackson. 2001. "Negotiation or Mediation? An Exploration of Factors Affecting the Choice of Conflict Management in International Conflict." *Negotiation Journal* 17 (1): 59–77.

Bercovitch, Jacob, and Jeffrey Langley. 1993. "The Nature of the Dispute and the Effectiveness of International Mediation." *Journal of Conflict Resolution* 37 (4): 670–91.

Bercovitch, Jacob, and Jeffrey Z. Rubin, eds. 1992. *Mediation in International Relations*. New York: St. Martin's.

Bercovitch, Jacob, and Gerald Schneider. 2000. "Who Mediates? Political Economy of International Conflict Management." *Journal of Peace Research* 37 (2): 145–65.

Bercovitch, Jacob, and Richard Wells. 1993. "Evaluating Mediation Strategies: A Theoretical and Empirical Analysis." *Peace and Change* 18 (1993): 325.

Bingham, Gail. 1985. *Resolving Environmental Disputes*. Washington, D.C.: Conservation Foundation.

Blake, Robert A., and Jane Srygley Mouton. 1985. *Solving Costly Organizational Conflicts*. San Francisco: Jossey-Bass.

Boutros-Ghali, Boutros. 1995. *An Agenda for Peace*. New York: United Nations.

Brecher, M. 1993. *Crises in World Politics: Theory and Reality*. Oxford: Perganion.

Burton, John W. 1969. *Conflict and Communication*. London: Macmillan.

———. 1972. "The Resolution of Conflict." *International Studies Quarterly* 16 (March): 5–29.

———. 1984. *Global Conflict*. Brighton, Sussex, UK: Wheatsheaf.

Burton, John, and Fred Dukes. 1990. *Conflict: Readings in Management and Resolution*. New York: St. Martin's.

Butterworth, Robert L. 1976. *Managing Interstate Disputes, 1945–1974*. Pittsburgh: University of Pittsburgh Press.

Carnevale, Peter. 1986. "Strategic Choice in Mediation." *Negotiation Journal* 2 (1): 41–56.

Carnevale, Peter, and Richard Pegnetter. 1985. "The Selection of Mediation Tactics in Public Sector Disputes: A Contingency Analysis." *Journal of Social Issues* 41 (2): 65–81.

Ciamant, N. J. 2000. "Conflict and Conflict Resolution in China: Beyond Mediation-Centered Approaches." *Journal of Conflict Resolution* 44 (4): 523–46.

Cortazzi, H. 1990. *The Japanese Achievement.* London: Sidgewick and Jackson.

Diehl, P. F. 1992. "What Are They Fighting For? The Importance of Issues in International Conflict." *Journal of Peace Research* 29 (3): 333–44.

Doob, Leonard W. 1971. *Resolving Conflict in Africa.* New Haven, Conn.: Yale University Press.

Douglas, Ann. 1957. "The Peaceful Settlement of Industrial and Intergroup Disputes." *Journal of Conflict Resolution* 1 (March): 69–81.

Druckman, Daniel, ed. 1977. *Negotiation: Social Psychological Perspectives.* London: Sage.

Elangovan, A. R. 1995. "Managerial Third-Party Dispute Intervention: A Prescriptive Model of Strategy Selection." *Academy of Managerial Review* 20: 800–830.

Fisher, Roger, and William Ury. 1981. *Getting to Yes.* Boston: Houghton Mifflin.

Fisher, Ronald J. 1983. "Third-Party Consultation as a Method of Intergroup Conflict Resolution." *Journal of Conflict Resolution* 27 (2): 301–44.

Fisher Ronald J., and Loraleigh Keashly. 1991. "The Potential Complementarity of Mediation and Consultation within a Contingency Model of Third-Party Intervention." *Journal of Peace Research* 28 (1): 29–42.

Folberg, Jay, and Alison Taylor. 1984. *Mediation.* San Francisco: Jossey-Bass.

Gochman, Charles S. 1993. "The Evolution of Disputes." *International Interactions* 19 (1–2): 49–76.

Grebe, S. 1994. "Building on Structured Mediation: An Integrated Model for Global Mediation of Separation and Divorce." *Mediation Quarterly* 12 (1): 15–35.

Greig, J. Michael 2001. "Moments of Opportunity: Recognizing Conditions of Ripeness for International Mediation Between Enduring Rivals." *Journal of Conflict Resolution* 45 (6): 691–718.

———. 2005. "Stepping into the Fray: When Do Mediators Mediate?" *American Journal of Political Science* 49 (2): 249–66.

Gulliver, P. H. 1979. *Disputes and Negotiations.* New York: Academic Press.

Haas, Richard N. 1990. *Conflicts Unending.* New Haven, Conn.: Yale University Press.

Haynes, J. M. 1982. "Divorce Mediation: Theory and Practice of a New Social Work Role." PhD diss., Union Graduate School.

Hiltrop, Jean M. 1989. "Factors Affected with Successful Labor Mediation." In *Mediation Research: The Process and Effectiveness of Third-Party Intervention*, ed. Kenneth Kressel and Dean G. Pruitt. San Francisco: Jossey-Bass.

Holsti, Kalevi J. 1983. *International Politics: A Framework for Analysis*, 4th ed. Englewood Cliffs, N.J.: Prentice-Hall.

Jabri, Vivienne. 1990. *Mediating Conflict: Decision Making and Western Intervention in Namibia*. Manchester, UK: Manchester University Press.

Keashly, L., and R. J. Fisher. 1996. "A Contingency Perspective on Conflict Interventions: Theoretical and Practical Consideration." In *Resolving International Conflicts: Theory and Practice of Mediation*, ed. Jacob Bercovitch. Boulder, Colo.: Lynne Reinner.

Kelman, Herbert C. 1992. "Informal Mediation by the Scholar/Practitioner." In *Mediation in International Relations*, ed. Jacob Bercovitch and Jeffrey Z. Rubin. New York: St. Martin's.

Kleiboer, M. 1996. "Understanding the Success and Failure of International Mediation." *Journal of Conflict Resolution* 40 (2): 360–89.

Kochan, T. A., and T. Jick. 1978. "The Public Sector Mediation Process. A Theory and Empirical Examination." *Journal of Conflict Resolution* 22 (2): 209–40.

Kolb, Deborah M. 1983. "Strategy and Tactics of Mediation." *Human Relations* 36 (3): 247–68.

———. 1989a. "How Existing Procedures Shape Alternatives: The Case of Grievance Mediation." *Journal of Dispute Resolution* 4 (1): 59–87.

———. 1989b. "Labor Mediators, Managers, and Ombudsmen: Roles Mediators Play in Different Contexts." In *Mediation Research*, ed. K. Kressel and D. G. Pruitt, 91–114. San Francisco: Jossey-Bass.

Kolb, Deborah M., and Jeffrey Z. Rubin. 1991. "Mediation through a Disciplinary Prism." *Research on Negotiation in Organizations* 3: 231–57.

Kozan, M. K. 1997. "Culture and Conflict Management: A Theoretical Framework." *International Journal of Conflict Management* 8 (4): 338–60.

Kozan, M. K., and C. Ergin. 1999. "The Influence of Intra-Cultural Value Differences on Conflict Management Practices." *International Journal of Conflict Management* 10 (3): 249–67.

Kressel, Kenneth. 1972. *Labor Mediation: An Exploratory Survey*. New York: Association of Labor Mediation Agencies.

Kressel, Kenneth, and Dean G. Pruitt, eds. 1989. *Mediation Research: The Process and Effectiveness of Third-Party Intervention*. San Francisco: Jossey-Bass.

Kriesberg, L. 1982. *Social Conflicts*, 2d ed. Englewood Cliffs, N.J.: Prentice-Hall.

Laure, J. H. 1990. "The Emergence and Institutionalization of Third Party Roles in Conflict." In *Conflict: Readings in Management and Resolution*, ed. J. Burton and F. Dukes. New York: St. Martin's.

Lewicki, R. J., and J. Litterer. 1985. *Negotiation*. Homewood, Ill.: Richard D. Irwin.

Meyer, Arthur. 1960. "Functions of the Mediator in Collective Bargaining." *Industrial and Labour Relations Review* 13 (June): 159–65.

Mitchell, Christopher R. 1981. *The Structure of International Conflict*. London: Macmillan.

————. 1993. "The Process and Stages of Mediation: The Sudanese Cases." In *Making War and Waging Peace: Foreign Intervention in Africa,* ed. David Smock. Washington, D.C.: United States Institute of Peace Press.

Moore, Christopher W. 1986. *The Mediation Process: Practical Strategies for Resolving Conflict.* San Francisco: Jossey-Bass.

Northedge, Fred S., and Michael D. Donelan. 1971. *International Disputes: The Political Aspects.* London: Europa Publications.

Ott, Mervin C. 1972. "Mediation as a Method of Conflict Resolution." *International Organization* 26 (4): 595–618.

Pearson, J., and N. Thoennes. 1984. "A Preliminary Portrait of Client Reactions to Three Court Mediation Programs." *Mediation Quarterly* 1 (3): 21–40.

Princen, Thomas. 1992. *Intermediaries in International Conflict.* Princeton, N.J.: Princeton University Press.

Provencher, R. 1968. *Two Malay Communities in Selangor.* Ann Arbor, Mich.: University Microfilms.

Regan, P. M., and A. C. Stam. 2000. "In the Nick of Time: Conflict Management, Mediation Timing, and the Duration of Interstate Disputes." *International Studies Quarterly* 44 (2): 239–60.

Roehl, J. A., and R. F. Cook. 1985. "Issues in Mediation: Rhetoric and Reality Revisited." *Journal of Social Issues* 41: 161–78.

Rubin, Jeffrey Z. 1980. "Experimental Research on Third-Party Intervention in Conflict." *Psychological Bulletin* 87 (2): 379–91.

————, ed. 1981. *Dynamics of Third-Party Intervention: Kissinger in the Middle East.* New York: Praeger.

Sawyer, Jack, and Harold Guetzkow. 1965. "Bargaining and Negotaitions in International Relations." In *International Behavior: Social Psychological Approaches,* ed. Herbert Kelman, 393–432. New York: Holt, Rinehart and Winston.

Schelling, Thomas. C. 1960. *The Strategy of Conflict.* Cambridge, Mass.: Harvard University Press.

Sheppard, B. H. 1984. "Third-Party Conflict Intervention: A Procedural Framework." *Research in Organization Behavior* 6: 141–90.

Simkin, William E. 1971. *Mediation and the Dynamics of Collective Bargaining.* Washington, D.C.: Bureau of National Affairs.

Singer, Linda R. 1990. *Settling Disputes: Conflict Resolution in Business, Families, and the Legal System.* Boulder, Colo.: Westview.

Slim, Randa. 1992. "Small-State Mediation in International Relations: The Algerian Mediation of the Iranian Hostage Crisis." In *Mediation in International Relations,* ed. Jacob Bercovitch and Jeffrey Z. Rubin. New York: St. Martin's.

Spencer, Doyle E., and Huang Yang. 1993. "Lessons from the Field of Intra-National Conflict Resolution." *Notre Dame Law Review* 67: 1495–1512.

Stein, Janice Gross. 1985. "Structure, Strategies and Tactics of Mediation." *Negotiation Journal* 1 (4): 331–47.

Stevens, Carl M. 1963. *Strategy and Collective Bargaining Negotiations*. New York: McGraw-Hill.

Stulberg, Joseph B. 1981. "The Theory and Practice of Mediation: A Reply to Professor Susskind." *Vermont Law Review* 6: 85–117.

———. 1987. *Taking Charge/Managing Conflict*. Lexington, Mass.: D.C. Heath.

Susskind, Lawrence, and Jeffrey Cruickshank. 1987. *Breaking the Impasses: Consensual Approaches to Resolving Public Disputes*. New York: Basic Books.

Touval, Saadia. 1985. "Context of Mediation." *Negotiation Journal* 1: 373–78.

———. 1992. "The Superpowers as Mediators." In *Mediation in International Relations*, ed. Jacob Bercovitch and Jeffrey Z. Rubin. New York: St. Martin's.

Touval, Saadia, and I. William Zartman. 1985. "Mediation in Theory." In *International Mediation in Theory and Practice*, ed. Saadia Touval and I. William Zartman. Boulder, Colo.: Westview.

Vasquez, J. A. 1983. *The Power of Power Politics: A Critique*. London: Frances Pinter.

Wall, James A. Jr. 1981. "Mediation: An Analysis, Review and Proposed Research." *Journal of Conflict Resolution* 25 (1): 157–80.

Wall James A. Jr., and Ann Lynn. 1993. "Mediation: A Current Review." *Journal of Conflict Resolution* 37 (1): 160–94.

Wall, J. A., John B. Stark, and R. L. Standifer. 2001. *Journal of Conflict Resolution* 45 (3): 370–91.

Walton, Richard E. 1969. *Interpersonal Peacemaking: Confrontations and Third-Party Consultation*. Reading, Mass.: Addison-Wesley.

Wilkenfeld, Jonathan, David Quinn, and David Smarick. 2003. "Mediating International Crises: Cross National and Experimental Perspectives." *Journal of Conflict Resolution* 47 (3): 279–301.

Yarrow, C. H. 1978. *Quaker Experiences in International Conciliation*. New Haven, Conn.: Yale University Press.

Young, Oran R. 1967. *The Intermediaries: Third Parties in International Crises*. Princeton, N.J.: Princeton University Press.

Zacher, Mark W. 1979. *International Conflicts and Collective Security, 1946–1977: The United Nations, Organization of American States, Organization of African Unity, and the Arab League*. New York: Praeger.

Zartman, I. William. 1985. *Ripe for Resolution: Conflict and Intervention in Africa*, 2d ed. New York: Oxford University Press.

5

ADJUDICATION

International Arbitral Tribunals and Courts

Richard B. Bilder

International adjudication is a method of dispute settlement that involves the referral of the dispute to an impartial third-party tribunal—normally either an arbitral tribunal or an international court—for binding decision, usually on the basis of international law. In contrast with so-called political means of settlement, international adjudication usually involves a legal obligation on the part of the parties to the dispute to accept the third party's decision as settling the dispute. This chapter describes the general nature and role of international adjudication, some of its advantages and disadvantages as compared with other dispute-settlement techniques, and its prospects.

The vision of a legal order in which all international disputes are subject to binding and impartial adjudication has strongly influenced thinking about international law and governance. Not surprisingly, national legal systems have furnished the model for people's expectations about a legally regulated international society. National experience and jurisprudence have traditionally accorded adjudication a preeminent status among dispute-settlement techniques. Indeed, it has generally been assumed that the hallmark and sine qua non of an effective domestic legal system is the compulsory settlement of disputes by permanent courts. Consequently, many have set the compulsory settlement of disputes by permanent courts as the goal for the international legal system as well. Subjecting nations to the rule of law has often been equated with subjecting their behavior to the judgment of impartial international tribunals. For Americans in particular, the historical experience in which courts have played an important role in forging and maintaining an effective federal system shapes the view that international courts might play a similar role in helping to establish an effective international system.

By this standard, the achievement of an effective international legal order remains elusive. It is a fundamental principle of international law that no state need submit its disputes to impartial adjudication unless it wishes; unless all states involved in a particular dispute have given their consent, an international arbitrator or court has no jurisdiction to decide the dispute. Yet states have generally been reluctant to give such consent. While nations often pay lip service to the ideal of judicial settlement, in practice they have established only a few international courts—most notably, the International Court of Justice (ICJ), or the World Court—and have entrusted relatively few significant disputes to international arbitral tribunals or courts. Much thought has been devoted to ways to encourage nations to make more use of international tribunals, but none have proved very successful.

Although this discussion encourages and urges strengthening the role of adjudication in international dispute settlement, it may be useful to keep several caveats in mind.

First, as the other chapters in this book demonstrate, adjudication is only one of many possible ways of dealing with disputes. The usual and accepted methods of peaceful settlement are listed in Article 33 of the UN Charter—negotiation, conciliation, arbitration, judicial settlement, resort to regional agencies or arrangements, and resort to UN or other international organization dispute-settlement procedures. A full list of methods reflects a spectrum of techniques that range from so-called diplomatic means, such as negotiation, consultations, good offices, mediation, and conciliation, which give control of the outcome primarily to the parties themselves, to so-called legal means, such as arbitration or judicial settlement, which give control of the outcome primarily to a third party (or parties). The various dispute-settlement techniques are not mutually exclusive, and a particular process of dispute resolution will often combine different methods. Indeed, negotiation—which is the predominant and preferred method of resolving disputes—typically plays at least some part in any dispute-settlement effort, including one ultimately resolved through adjudication. Thus, in deciding whether to use adjudication to resolve a particular international dispute, the states involved will have to weigh its advantages and disadvantages carefully against those of alternative available methods.

Second, it is open to question whether national legal systems, overseeing a wide variety of relations among millions or hundreds of millions of individuals coexisting in a close-knit society, are appropriate models for an international legal system, designed to meet very different problems of order and cooperation among less than two hundred nation-states. The special characteristics of the international political order—and in particular the inevitability of continuous interactions and relations among its members—may suggest the appropriateness of legal institutions, techniques, and responses very different from those found in national legal orders. In short, we are beginning to realize that there is no one way in which a legal system must work; instead, there are a number of ways of organizing a legal order, more than one of which may be effective.

Moreover, although adjudication plays a significant role in national legal orders, there is growing evidence that this role is probably different than commonly assumed. Recent studies, at least in the United States, suggest that the great majority of disputes are settled by means other than formal court decisions. Indeed, much of the evidence suggests that lawsuits function primarily as a spur to private settlement and that judges function significantly as mediators in encouraging such settlements, in addition to their more formal role as deciders of disputes. Consequently, legal scholars and practitioners have been devoting more attention to the role of nonadjudicatory techniques in the functioning of the legal order and to devising innovative alternative dispute-resolution techniques to meet the needs of an overburdened and often expensive judicial system.

Third, one may argue that a focus on adjudication reflects a particularly Western bias toward methods of dispute settlement. For example, it has been said that Chinese, Japanese, and certain other non-Western societies traditionally emphasize nonadversarial techniques of mediation and mutual accommodation to deal with disputes and are generally reluctant to use adjudication or other adversarial or "legally oriented" methods. This perceived Western bias suggests a need for sensitivity in any international dispute to the particular cultural attitudes and responses toward conflict and dispute settlement of the parties involved. Certainly, any conflict-management strategy must take into account differing cultural perspectives in deciding on the appropriateness of adjudicatory versus other dispute-settlement approaches in particular contexts.

Finally, the U.S. position toward international adjudication has been and remains ambivalent, reflecting fluctuations in U.S. foreign policy between messianism, a belief that the United States should lead nations toward acceptance of the rule of law in international affairs, and chauvinism, or the distrust of international law and institutions and the belief that only realpolitik can safeguard the national interest. As we will see, although the United

States pioneered the idea of international arbitration and was long one of the strongest advocates of international adjudication, its recent policy has been less clear—particularly in the wake of the ICJ's 1984 and 1986 judgments against the United States in the *Nicaragua* case.

THE NATURE OF INTERNATIONAL ADJUDICATION

What are international arbitral tribunals and courts, what do they do, and how do they work?

In contrast to the compulsory jurisdiction normally exercised by courts in national legal systems, the jurisdiction of international arbitral tribunals and courts is solely consensual. Absent special agreement, a state is under no international obligation to submit a dispute with another state—or, *a fortiori*, with an individual or non-governmental organization—to legally binding settlement by an international court, arbitral tribunal, or other third party. Consequently, under international law, an international court or arbitral tribunal can render a binding decision regarding a dispute only in situations where the state or states concerned have expressly or implicitly consented to that court or tribunal exercising jurisdiction over the particular dispute or category of dispute. A state may give its consent either by special agreement at the time of the dispute or by agreement in advance in some other treaty or instrument. If a state does consent to arbitration or judicial settlement of a dispute with another state, it is bound by that consent, and the appropriate tribunal may exercise jurisdiction according to the terms of such consent.

In view of states' reluctance to relinquish control over the outcomes of their disputes to third parties, it is not surprising that, in general, international arbitral tribunals and courts have played a rather limited role in the settlement of international disputes. States have been particularly reluctant to obligate themselves in advance to the compulsory binding adjudication of potential disputes with other countries—especially over issues that may involve what they consider vital national interests. In general, they have been willing to do so only when their commitment to such compulsory jurisdiction is restricted in terms of subject matter or otherwise carefully circumscribed.

There are essentially two methods of international adjudication: arbitration and judicial settlement by an international court. The differences between the two methods lie principally in the permanence of the tribunal to which the dispute is referred, the scope of its jurisdiction or authority, and the extent to which the parties to the dispute can control the selection of the third parties —arbitrators or judges—who will rule on their dispute and the tribunal's jurisdiction and procedures.

Arbitration

Arbitration is a form of adjudication that involves the referral of a dispute or disputes to an ad hoc tribunal, rather than to a permanently established court, for binding decision. In this case, the parties, by their agreement (usually called a *compromis*), establish the tribunal, which will decide their dispute "from scratch." The agreement defines the issue to be arbitrated and determines the method for selecting the arbitrator or arbitrators, the machinery and procedure of the arbitral tribunal, and the way of paying for the tribunal's costs. The arbitral tribunal is constituted to address only the particular issue or issues entrusted to it by the parties' agreement and is bound strictly by the terms of that agreement. Once the tribunal's work is completed, it ceases to exist. While arbitration tribunals typically are constituted to deal only with a single dispute, some important arbitral tribunals (sometimes called claims commissions) have been established to address a number of related disputes over a period of time, particularly involving claims by individuals or corporations that are nationals of one state against another state. An example is the Iran-U.S. Claims Tribunal, which was established at The Hague under the 1981 Algiers Accords between the two countries to deal with several thousand claims arising mostly out of the U.S.-Iran hostage crisis. As of May 2007, the tribunal had still not completed its work.

Typically, an arbitral tribunal is composed of three arbitrators, one chosen by each party and the third, or "neutral," arbitrator selected by agreement of the two "national" arbitrators, or failing the parties' agreement, by an impartial third party such as the president of the ICJ. (It is important to provide some "fallback" impartial appointment mechanism, because otherwise a recalcitrant party might try to block the arbitration process by refusing to agree to the selection of any particular neutral arbitrator.) However, the parties may wish to select a single arbitrator, such as the UN secretary-general; a tribunal of five, with three neutral arbitrators; or, as in the case of the nine-member Iran-U.S. Claims Tribunal, a larger number of arbitrators. The parties typically choose highly reputable judges, diplomats, former prominent government officials, international lawyers, or academics to serve as arbitrators. The parties and arbitrators also must decide upon the tribunal's procedure, including its meeting times and places. In 1958, the UN General Assembly recommended to states a set of Model Rules of Arbitral Procedure, developed by the UN International Law Commission, which has provided a very useful and widely accepted basis for agreement on arbitral procedures. States may also draw upon other model procedural codes, such as the Arbitration Rules of the UN Commission on International Trade Law, which govern the procedure of the Iran-U.S. Claims Tribunal.

Because the parties must specifically agree to any arbitration—and are not likely to do so unless they believe that they can "live with" an adverse decision—it is not surprising that most states comply with arbitral decisions (usually called awards). However, disputes may occasionally arise with respect to arbitral judgments, particularly where a losing party claims that the tribunal exceeded its authority or failed to do what was asked under the compromis and that, consequently, its award is a nullity. A study of the execution of three hundred arbitral awards between 1794 and 1936 uncovered only twenty cases of noncompliance, although there have been several more since that time.

Arbitration is one of the oldest forms of international adjudication, dating back to the time of the early Greeks—indeed, some scholars say, to early Mesopotamia. More modern forms of international adjudication date back to the Jay Treaty of 1794 and the 1814 Treaty of Ghent between the United States and Great Britain, both of which established several arbitral commissions. The concept of international arbitration was broadly endorsed by the international community at the Hague Peace Conference of 1899, which, among other things, approved a Convention for the Pacific Settlement of International Disputes and the establishment of the so-called Permanent Court of Arbitration at The Hague. Despite its name, this institution is not really a court, but rather a bureau that maintains a roster of potential international arbitrators and, on request, provides services to an arbitral tribunal.

According to a scholarly survey (Stuyt 1990), in the past two centuries about 450 international arbitrations were conducted between or among states. During this same period, the United States alone was involved in some 115 such international arbitrations, including the famous 1871–72 *Alabama Claims* arbitration with Great Britain, in which the tribunal decided that Great Britain had to pay compensation for damage caused by a Confederate warship that was built in Great Britain and permitted to sail from that country in violation of its obligation as a neutral during the American Civil War.

There have been at least several dozen significant arbitrations since 1945. They include the 1965 *Gut Dam* arbitration (United States and Canada); the 1968 *Rann of Kutch* arbitration (India and Pakistan); the 1977 *Beagle Channel* arbitration (Argentina and Chile); the 1986 *Rainbow Warrior* arbitration (France and New Zealand); the 1988 *Taba* arbitration (Egypt and Israel); three arbitrations involving air transport agreements between the United States and, respectively, France, Italy, and the United Kingdom; decisions of the Eritrea-Ethiopia Boundary and Claims Tribunals established under the December 2000 peace agreement between those two countries; and the continuing series of decisions handed down by the still-functioning Iran-U.S. Claims Tribunal, which, as of March 2007, had issued some 600 awards involving over $3 billion.

International arbitration has assumed an important role in the adjustment of trade and investment disputes through specialized arbitrations occurring under the auspices and dispute-settlement procedures of the General Agreement on Tariffs and Trade (GATT, now the World Trade Organization, or WTO), the World Bank–sponsored International Centre for the Settlement of Investment Disputes, the Canada-U.S. Free Trade Agreement, and, more recently, the North American Free Trade Agreement. Mention should also be made of the UN Compensation Commission, established by the United Nations to address claims against Iraq arising from Iraq's 1990–91 invasion and occupation of Kuwait. As of March 2007, the commission had approved awards of over $52 billion to pay more than 1.5 million claims. There has also been a significant growth in the settlement of international commercial disputes through private international arbitration; under the provisions of the 1958 New York Convention on the Recognition and Enforcement of Foreign Arbitral Awards, such awards are now recognized and enforced in more than 142 countries.

Judicial Settlement

Judicial settlement is a form of adjudication that involves the referral of a dispute or disputes to a permanent judicial body for binding settlement. In the case of judicial settlement, the machinery and procedure of the tribunal, including the method of selecting the judges of the court, are already established by existing international instruments, such as the statute and the rules of the ICJ. A permanent judicial tribunal is typically established to deal with a broad number and range of disputes submitted by a variety of states and continues in existence beyond its judgment in any particular case.

The first permanent international court was the little-known Central American Court of Justice, which was established by the Washington Peace Conference of 1907 as part of its settlement of the conflict among Guatemala, El Salvador, and Honduras; between 1908 and 1918 the court heard ten cases. The first truly global international court was the Permanent Court of International Justice (PCIJ), which was formally inaugurated in 1922 at The Hague, Netherlands, under the aegis of the League of Nations as part of the post–World War I peace settlements. The PCIJ, housed in an elaborate building donated by Andrew Carnegie called the "Peace Palace," functioned from 1922 to 1940; it ceased to exist when the League was formally dissolved in 1946. The present World Court, the ICJ, was established by the UN Charter as the principal judicial organ of the United Nations and also has its seat in the Peace Palace. The ICJ is the legal successor to, and is in most respects similar to, the PCIJ, with a comparable statute and a shared and continuing jurisprudence. In view of the ICJ's importance, it is discussed in greater detail in the next section.

Although the ICJ is the most prominent international court and at present the only one with a general and global jurisdiction, several other important international courts have more specialized functions and jurisdictions. They include the European Union's Court of Justice and the Court of First Instance (the latter established in 1989), operating in Luxembourg, Belgium, under the provisions of the Treaty of Rome and the Single European Act, respectively; the European Court of Human Rights, with its seat in Strasbourg, France, which operates under the European Convention for the Protection of Human Rights and Fundamental Freedoms and its various protocols; the Inter-American Court of Human Rights, with its seat in San José, Costa Rica, which was established by the Organization of American States and functions under the American Convention on Human Rights; and the African Court on Human and Peoples' Rights, functioning under the African Union and ruling on compliance with the African Charter on Human and Peoples' Rights. Each of these specialized courts plays a major role in its respective regional system, and each has addressed important cases and developed a significant jurisprudence. Moreover, each of these courts has unique and interesting jurisdictional and procedural features. For example, each of these courts can in certain circumstances hear cases brought by individuals—unlike the ICJ, which has jurisdiction solely over cases brought by states. Under Part XV of the UN Law of the Sea Convention, which entered into force in 1994, an International Tribunal for the Law of the Sea was established, with its seat in Hamburg, Germany. Other continuing international tribunals include the administrative tribunals of the United Nations' specialized agencies, such as the International Labor Organization, the World Bank, and the International Monetary Fund, which deal with disputes between these organizations and their staff members.

Neither the ICJ nor any of the other international courts is authorized to exercise criminal jurisdiction over individuals. Although international criminal courts are not, strictly speaking, primarily directed at resolving disputes between or among states, a brief survey of them may be relevant. The most important experiment in this respect was the post–World War II Nuremberg and Tokyo International Military Tribunals, established by the victorious Allied powers to try major Axis war criminals. Since that time, proposals for the establishment of a permanent international criminal court have been made repeatedly, both in the United Nations and by a number of unofficial bodies. Until recently, such proposals had little result. However, the atrocities of the conflict in Bosnia have led to several significant developments in this regard. In May 1993, the UN Security Council established a sixteen-judge ad hoc International Tribunal for the former Yugoslavia, with its seat in The Hague and with jurisdiction to prosecute persons responsible for serious violations of international humanitarian laws committed in the region since 1991. As of May 2007 this tribunal had indicted 161 persons, of whom 50 have to date been convicted and sentenced.

In November 1994, the UN Security Council established an ad hoc International Tribunal for Rwanda, with its seat in Arusha, Tanzania, to prosecute violations of humanitarian law that occurred in that country in 1994. Although largely separate, the Rwanda tribunal shares some elements with its counterpart for the former Yugoslavia, in particular its chief prosecutor, some of the prosecutor's staff, and some appellate judges. As of April 2007, the Rwanda Tribunal had handed down twenty-seven judgments involving thirty-three accused individuals.

Experience with these two ad hoc tribunals has led to renewed interest in establishing a permanent international court. As a consequence, in the summer of 1998 a diplomatic conference meeting in Rome negotiated and approved a treaty (called the "Rome Statute") establishing an International Criminal Court, which became effective on July 1, 2002, having been ratified by 70 states and signed by more than 140 states. The International Criminal Court (ICC) has its seat in The Hague, the Netherlands; is composed of eighteen judges and a prosecutor; and has broad jurisdiction over the most serious crimes of international concern—genocide, crimes against humanity, and war crimes. The ICC's jurisdiction is subject to a number of conditions and procedural safeguards and is based on the principle of complementarity, according to which the ICC can exercise its jurisdiction only when a national court is unable or unwilling genuinely to do so itself. In March 2005, the UN Security Council referred to the ICC crimes allegedly occurring in the Darfur region of Sudan, and in mid-2005 the ICC issued its first arrest warrants against five Ugandan rebel leaders for atrocities against civilians in northern Uganda, which is a contracting state to the Rome Statute. As of May 2007, 104 countries were parties to the Rome Statute and the ICC. However, as of this writing, the United States has indicated that it has no intention of ratifying the Rome Statute.

Choosing between Arbitration and Judicial Settlement

Assuming that states are willing in principle to submit their dispute to binding third-party settlement, or that they are both parties to a treaty that contains a compromissory clause allowing a choice between arbitration and judicial settlement, how do they decide whether to submit their dispute to arbitration or judicial settlement? A relevant compromissory clause in a prior agreement expressly specifying only one or the other method of settlement, or submission of the dispute to a tribunal, will usually determine the matter. If not, the parties' choice will depend on considerations such as their particular attitudes and preferences, the relative physical convenience or cost of a particular method, the parties' past experience and familiarity with one or the other method, the relative expertise of potential arbitrators or judges to handle the particular issue, and other circumstances.

The principal advantage of arbitration is that it offers the parties maximum control and flexibility over the selection of the arbitrators who will hear the case, the scope of the issue before the tribunal, and the tribunal's procedures. In other words, by negotiating their own compromis, the parties can tailor the adjudicative process to meet their particular needs and concerns, which may be particularly useful when the issues to be placed before the tribunal are highly technical, as in disputes involving international trade, aviation, the law of the sea, and so forth; the parties may sometimes prefer that such issues be decided by an arbitrator or arbitrators with special background and expertise. States may sometimes prefer arbitration because one or both parties, or their relevant national constituencies, lack confidence in the competence or impartiality of an international court, such as the ICJ. Although there appear to be few, if any, recent cases in which states have agreed to allow an arbitral tribunal or court to decide a *dispute ex aequo et bono* (i.e., on the basis of what they consider a fair and reasonable solution rather than strictly on the basis of legal rights), some commentators have suggested that it might be easier to ask an arbitral tribunal than a court to do so; indeed, some believe that arbitral tribunals inherently tend to decide disputes this way, seeking compromise solutions. Arbitration can sometimes, if the parties wish, be conducted less expensively, less formally, and with less publicity than international court proceedings. Finally, because the jurisdiction of the ICJ is limited solely to disputes between states, any dispute in which one of the parties is not a state (i.e., an international organization, a corporation, or an individual) must be referred to arbitration for binding settlement. (Under traditional international legal principles of state responsibility and diplomatic protection, individuals or corporations may persuade the state of their nationality to espouse or "take up" their claim against a foreign state and thus bring it within the ICJ's jurisdiction.)

Arbitration also has its drawbacks. The fact that parties must agree on both the constitution and the jurisdiction of the arbitral tribunal and on the selection of the arbitrators may involve considerable additional effort and delay and perhaps create even more controversy between the parties. Part-time arbitrators may have less judicial experience and be less insulated from out-side influence than permanent judges. Arbitration may sometimes involve greater expense, because the parties themselves must share an arbitral tribunal's costs, which can be substantial. Finally, some commentators have suggested that, because arbitral tribunals are generally less prestigious than international courts, states may feel less pressure to comply with an arbitral award than a court judgment, and the award may be less enforceable as a consequence.

Conversely, the principal advantage of an international court is that it is already in existence and therefore readily available to states wishing to sub-mit their dispute to impartial settlement. Moreover, the international com-munity pays the court's costs. Finally, the judges on a court are usually full-time professionals who presumably have considerable judicial experience, a special commitment to impartiality, and an interest in the court's development of a consistent jurisprudence. On the other hand, a court has its disadvantages as well. One or both parties may lack confidence in the expertise, general com-petence, or impartiality of a particular international court or its judges. They may consider the court's location, traditions, or procedures inappropriate for the case. Finally, one or both parties might conceivably be concerned that a court would constitute too prestigious and conspicuous a forum; it may be more politically awkward for a losing party to fail to comply with a court's judgment than with an arbitral tribunal's award.

In practice, the differences between arbitration and judicial settlement may be narrower than portrayed here, and particular adjudicative procedures may incorporate elements of both methods. Thus, the Iran-U.S. Claims Tri-bunal, while technically an arbitral tribunal, has assumed many of the charac-teristics of a permanent international court, including the development of its own unique and significant jurisprudence. Conversely, pursuant to the ICJ's rules, several recent cases have been submitted by the parties to a special chamber of the court consisting of a limited number of judges (usually five), who are, in effect, selected with the approval of the parties.

"Legal" versus "Political" Disputes

In discussions of international disputes, a distinction is sometimes drawn between so-called legal or justiciable disputes and so-called political, non-legal, or nonjusticiable disputes. The implication is that certain disputes, such as those involving national honor, "vital" national interests, or the use of force, have inherent characteristics that make them particularly inappropri-ate for the use of adjudication as a dispute-settlement technique. Iran made such an argument in the *Tehran Hostages* case, as did the United States in the later *Nicaragua* case—both unsuccessfully.

A number of early treaties generally providing for the arbitration of disputes, in fact, made such distinctions. Certainly, nations are less willing to agree to binding third-party settlement of very politically sensitive disputes; in these cases, adjudication may indeed not be the most effective technique. However, because international law is, at least in theory, a complete system, it is difficult to argue that any particular type of dispute is inherently beyond the jurisdiction or capacity of a court or arbitral tribunal to decide, even if the parties so desire and have given the tribunal their consent to do so. Thus, at least in theory, all international disputes seem to be "justiciable" in this sense. Indeed, the World Court has never yet rejected a case on the grounds that it involved nonlegal issues or that it could more appropriately be resolved by a political organization such as the UN Security Council.

Nevertheless, this supposed distinction may be helpful in reminding the world community that some disputes are better settled through negotiations and decisions by the states directly concerned or by political bodies, and that effective adjudication of disputes requires both parties' genuine political acceptance and consent to such settlement. The hard fact remains that absent more effective international governance and enforcement mechanisms, it is very difficult for any international tribunal—or the international community at large—to impose an adverse judgment on an unwilling state.

THE INTERNATIONAL COURT OF JUSTICE

The most prominent and important international judicial institution—and the only one that presently exercises a general global jurisdiction—is the International Court of Justice (ICJ), sometimes referred to as the World Court. Indeed, when most people talk about international adjudication, they usually have the ICJ in mind. Consequently, it may be useful to look more closely at this court and its work.

The ICJ was established in 1945 by the UN Charter as the principal judicial organ of the United Nations and is governed by a special treaty called the "Statute of the Court," which is annexed to the UN Charter and to which all members of the United Nations are also parties. Under the charter, nonmember states may under certain conditions become parties to the court's statute; Switzerland became a party pursuant to this provision before becoming a member of the United Nations in 2002. The court is composed of fifteen judges from different countries, elected for staggered terms of nine years each by the UN General Assembly and the Security Council, with a view to obtaining judges from diverse regions and with different ethnic and cultural backgrounds. (As of May 2007, the court was composed of judges from the

United Kingdom, Jordan, Madagascar, China, Sierra Leone, Venezuela, the United States, Japan, Germany, Slovakia, France, New Zealand, Mexico, Morocco, and the Russian Federation. Beginning in July 1995, the court for the first time included a woman judge, Rosalyn Higgins of the United Kingdom, who in 2006 was elected president of the court.) Because each party to a case is entitled to choose an ad hoc judge if no judge of its nationality is otherwise on the court, more than fifteen judges may sit on a particular case.

The judges serve as jurists rather than as representatives of their countries and are supposed to act impartially in deciding cases according to the rules of international law. As already mentioned, under the court's rules, the parties to a case may also, by agreement, submit their dispute to a special chamber or panel of judges (usually five) rather than the full court—with the court "consulting" the parties as to the membership of the chamber; several cases have been heard by such chambers. In response to the growing importance of international environmental issues, the court has established a special Chamber on Environmental Matters; however, as of this writing, no cases have been referred to it.

The Court's Jurisdiction

The court's most important job is to deliver legally binding judgments in so-called contentious cases involving disputes between states. Only states can bring contentious cases before the court; the United Nations, other intergovernmental organizations, non-governmental organizations, or individuals cannot do so. Under the court's statute, the ICJ is required to decide such disputes in accordance with international law, applying treaties and other international agreements accepted by the parties, customary international law, and general principles of law recognized by the international community, unless the parties expressly agree that the court should decide the case *ex aequo et bono*. The ICJ does not exercise any criminal jurisdiction and has no authority to try or punish individuals for violations of international criminal law.

The court is also authorized by the UN Charter and its statute to give advisory opinions in response to requests from the UN General Assembly, the Security Council, or other organs of the United Nations or its specialized agencies so authorized by the General Assembly; currently, neither states, other intergovernmental organizations, non-governmental organizations, nor individuals can request such opinions from the court. The court's delivery of such an advisory opinion is discretionary; it may refuse to give an opinion, for example, if it believes that the request is, in effect, an attempt by one party to obtain the court's legal ruling on a dispute over which it does not have the other party's consent to the court's jurisdiction. However, in almost all cases the court has complied with such requests. The court has, in fact, delivered a number of very important advisory opinions, including the 1949 opinion on *Reparation for Injuries*, the 1962 opinion on *Certain Expenses of the UN*, the 1971 *Namibia* opinion, and the 1975 opinion on the *Western Sahara*. Responding to a request by the UN General Assembly, the court issued an advisory opinion in July 1996 on the *Legality of the Threat or Use of Nuclear Weapons* stating that the threat or use of nuclear weapons would generally be unlawful (i.e., contrary to the rules of international law applicable to armed conflict), except possibly in extreme circumstances of self-defense in which the very survival of a state was at stake.

Like all international arbitral and judicial bodies, the court can hear and decide disputes only with the consent of the states involved. As set out in Article 36 of the court's statute, states can consent to the court's jurisdiction over a contentious case in several ways. First, they may conclude a special agreement providing for the court to decide an existing dispute, the most common way for states to submit cases and the method, for example, by which the United States and Canada submitted the 1984 *Gulf of Maine* maritime boundary case to the court. Second, states may agree in advance, in a treaty's "compromissory clause," that the court shall have jurisdiction to decide any future dispute involving the interpretation or application of that treaty. As of July 2006, there were approximately 130 multilateral treaties and conventions, and 180 bilateral treaties, providing for the jurisdiction of the court. As of 2006, the United States was party to approximately seventy treaties including such compromissory clauses. This was the basis on which the United States, for example, persuaded the court to assert jurisdiction over Iran in the 1980 *Tehran Hostages* case, because Iran was a party to several relevant treaties with the United States containing such compromissory clauses. Finally, under the provisions of the "optional clause" of Article 36(2) of the court's statute, any state may, by filing a declaration to this effect in advance, give the court "compulsory jurisdiction" to decide any dispute it may have in the future with any other nation that has also made such a declaration. As of July 2006, 67 of the 192 states currently members of the United Nations had accepted the compulsory jurisdiction of the court under the optional clause, although some of them had done so with significant reservations. Usually these reservations concern disputes involving "national security" or those arising before the declaration was filed; more recently, states have reserved the right under the optional clause to exclude "any given category or categories of dispute" upon making an appropriate notification to the UN secretary-general. In such cases, the court will have jurisdiction only to the extent that the parties' declarations are, in fact, reciprocal and coincide. Such parallel declarations were involved in the *Nicaragua* case, brought in 1984 by Nicaragua against the United States.

Where the parties to the dispute have specifically agreed to submit the dispute to the World Court, there is rarely any question as to the court's jurisdiction to hear the case. However, where one state seeks to bring another before the court on the basis that they both are parties to a compromissory clause in a particular treaty or that they have both filed declarations under the optional clause, the respondent state may challenge the court's jurisdiction to hear the case by arguing, for example, either that it did not consent in advance to the court's jurisdiction over the particular type of dispute or that the applicant state has not so consented. In this event, the court will typically deal with the case in two stages: first, a "jurisdictional" phase, in which the court determines whether both states have, in fact, consented to its hearing the case, and then, if it determines that it does have jurisdiction, a "merits" phase, in which the court proceeds to decide the substance of the dispute. Sometimes an unwilling respondent state believes so strongly that the court is not entitled to hear a case brought against it that it refuses even to appear before the court. For example, Iceland refused to appear in the 1974 *Fisheries Jurisdiction* case brought against it by the United Kingdom and the Federal Republic of Germany; France refused to appear in the 1974 *Nuclear Tests* case brought against it by Australia and New Zealand; Iran refused to appear in the 1980 *Tehran Hostages* case brought against it by the United States; and, as we will see, the United States refused to appear in the "merits" phase of the *Nicaragua* case, after the court held that it had jurisdiction to hear Nicaragua's claims. However, the court may hear a case even if the respondent state fails to appear, provided the court finds that it has jurisdiction. Under the court's statute, the court's own decision on whether it has jurisdiction is final and binding.

The ICJ has various other powers necessary to the performance of its functions. For example, even at the initial stages of a case, if the court believes the circumstances so require, it may "indicate" any provisional measures the parties should undertake in order to preserve their respective rights. Thus, as occurred in both the *Tehran Hostages* and the *Nicaragua* cases, the court may request one or both parties to avoid actions that might add to the tensions between them or make it more difficult for the court to resolve the dispute. In its decision in 2001 in the *LaGrand* case (Germany v. United States), the ICJ held that such a provisional measures order could be legally binding. Again, the court may, under certain circumstances, permit third parties to intervene in contentious cases to which they are not initially a party.

Under the UN Charter and the court's statute, the ICJ's judgment is legally binding upon the parties. However, the court's statute makes clear that its decision has no binding force except between the parties and in regard to that particular case; that is, the ICJ has no doctrine of precedent binding on other parties, as is the case in the U.S. legal system. Article 94 of the UN Charter expressly provides that "Each Member of the United Nations undertakes to comply with the decision of the International Court of Justice in any case to which it is a party," and states have usually complied with this international obligation. Notable exceptions are Albania, which failed to comply with the judgment against it in the 1949 *Corfu Channel* case; Iran in the 1980 *Tehran Hostages* case; and the United States in the 1986 *Nicaragua* case. Each indicated that it would not comply with the court's adverse judgment. However, the United States, pursuant to the 1981 Algiers Accords, subsequently withdrew the *Tehran Hostages* case. And the Chamorro government in Nicaragua, which replaced the Sandinista regime in 1990, withdrew the *Nicaragua* case in 1991. Consequently, neither Iran nor the United States is now in noncompliance.

Article 94 also stipulates, "If any party to a case fails to perform the obligations incumbent upon it under a judgment rendered by the Court, the other party may have recourse to the Security Council, which may, if it deems necessary, make recommendations or decide upon reasons to be taken to give effect to the judgment." There has thus far been little recourse to this provision, because states usually do comply with the court's judgments. Presumably, Article 94 permits the Security Council to decide on measures that are legally binding on all UN members, possibly including the use of sanctions or even military force, to bring about compliance with a judgment. However, any such decision by the Security Council would, of course, be subject to a permanent member's veto. As yet, the Security Council has never made a decision under Article 94.

The Court's Work

Over their history, the ICJ and its predecessor, the PCIJ, have decided relatively few cases. During the quarter-century of its existence, the PCIJ issued thirty-two judgments and twenty-seven advisory opinions. During the period 1946–2006, the ICJ handed down ninety-two judgments on disputes concerning, among other things, land frontiers and maritime boundaries, territorial sovereignty, the nonuse of force, noninterference in the internal affairs of states, diplomatic relations, hostage taking, the rights of asylum, nationality, guardianship, rights of passage, and economic rights. During this same period, the ICJ gave twenty-five advisory opinions concerning, among other things, the legal consequences of the construction of a wall in the occupied Palestinian territory, admission to the United Nations, reparation for injuries suffered in the service of the United Nations, territorial status of South-West Africa (Namibia) and Western Sahara, judgments rendered by international administrative tribunals, expenses of certain UN operations, applicability of the United Nations Headquarters Agreement, the status of human rights rapporteurs, and the legality of the threat or use of nuclear weapons. Although some of these cases were of fairly minor importance, a number were of major significance both in terms of their usefulness in settling very troublesome disputes between the parties and for their impact on the development of international law. During the past few years there has been an apparent resurgence of interest among states in the ICJ, and the court has never been busier. As of February 2007, the court had twelve contentious cases pending on its docket.

The United States and the Court

What is the attitude of the United States toward the court? Although it has long supported the broad concept of the peaceful settlement of disputes, the United States has often been ambivalent in its policy toward international adjudication and the court. In 1946, President Truman accepted the court's compulsory jurisdiction under the optional clause, albeit with broad reservations. Before 1984, the United States had been involved as both applicant and respondent in several cases before the court. The most significant of these was its suit against Iran in the 1980 *Tehran Hostages* case, in which the court ruled in favor of the United States. But the most important U.S. involvement with the court has been Nicaragua's 1984 suit against the United States, charging that U.S. support of the contras and other activities directed against the Sandinista regime violated international law.

Because the *Nicaragua* case has had considerable effect on U.S. policy regarding the court, it is worth describing briefly. Despite strong U.S. arguments to the contrary, the court decided in 1984 that it had jurisdiction over Nicaragua's claim against the United States and that the matter was admissible and appropriate for judicial consideration. The United States vigorously protested the court's jurisdictional decision and announced that it would not participate further in the case. Moreover, in view of its strong disagreement with the court's holding, the United States announced in October 1985 that it was terminating its acceptance of the court's compulsory jurisdiction under the optional clause, to take effect one year from that date. Despite U.S. nonappearance in the final phase of the *Nicaragua* case, the court proceeded to a hearing on the case's merits, as its statute permitted. In June 1986, the court issued its judgment, finding that U.S. support of the contras, as well as certain other actions, were in violation of international law; however, it withheld for further consideration a determination of damages. The Reagan administration again protested the court's Nicaragua decision, announced that the United States would not recognize the judgment, and vetoed a Security Council resolution calling upon the United States to do so. Thereafter, the case remained inactive until 1991, when Nicaragua's Chamorro government withdrew the case.

Since that time, the United States has been involved with the court on several other occasions. During 1987–89, the United States brought the so-called ELSI case against Italy—with the parties agreeing that the case should be heard by a special chamber of the court—and lost. It has also appeared before the court as respondent in two cases brought by Iran arising from U.S. actions in the Persian Gulf during the Iran-Iraq war (one of which it won and the other of which was discontinued following settlement); in a case brought by Libya involving U.S. efforts to obtain extradition of two Libyan intelligence agents alleged to have participated in the bombing of Pan American Flight 103 over Lockerbie, Scotland (which was discontinued); and in several cases involving the duty of the United States to inform foreign nationals detained by law enforcement officials of their right to consular assistance under consular treaties and conventions (which the United States lost). The United States has also participated in proceedings relating to several requests for advisory opinions by the court.

As of this writing, the George W. Bush administration had not yet clearly stated its policy regarding U.S. use of the court—or, more specifically, regarding reacceptance of the court's compulsory jurisdiction, as some groups and commentators have urged.

ARE THERE TOO MANY INTERNATIONAL TRIBUNALS?

There has been a significant increase in the number of international courts and arbitral tribunals in recent years, particularly those established to deal with specialized treaty regimes concerned with regional human rights, trade and investment, and law of the sea issues. As the international system is presently constituted, each of these tribunals acts and reaches its decisions independently, and they are generally not (as is typically the case with different courts within national judicial systems) arranged in a hierarchical structure or even required to take each other's decisions into account. Thus, unlike the U.S. Supreme Court, for example, the ICJ will normally have no jurisdiction to hear appeals from or overrule the decisions of other tribunals within the international legal system.

Some commentators have expressed concern that the proliferation of international tribunals may lead to problems of overlapping jurisdiction, or "forum-shopping" by litigating states, and differing decisions on similar issues by different tribunals, thus threatening the unity, cohesion, and universality of international law. However, commentators seem to agree that, at least thus far, the multiplication of international tribunals has been, for the most part, a beneficial and healthy development, creating more diverse and flexible dispute settlement options for states, increasing resort to and the effectiveness of international dispute settlement, and generally contributing to the development of international law. Moreover, the multiplication of international tribunals does not appear thus far to have threatened the primary role of the ICJ as the leading and most authoritative interpreter of international law. However, it is also apparent that, with the growing number and diversity of international tribunals, there is an increased need for the development of a "judicial dialogue" among the various tribunals and for each to become more aware of and take account of what others are doing.

SOME PROS AND CONS OF ADJUDICATION

When is adjudication likely to be the most appropriate or sensible way of trying to resolve an international dispute, and when is it unlikely to be helpful? From the standpoint of the international community and the interests of the states involved in a dispute, adjudication offers both potential advantages and disadvantages compared with other methods of dispute settlement. Because national leaders and other state officials usually weigh these pros and cons carefully in deciding whether to use adjudication or other techniques to deal with a particular dispute, they are worth spelling out in some detail.

Some Advantages of Adjudication

Advantages of adjudication include the following:

- *Adjudication is dispositive.* At least ideally, an arbitral or judicial decision puts an end to the dispute. Sometimes it is important to the parties that a dispute simply be settled, regardless of how it is done. When negotiations are for some reason unsuccessful, adjudication provides a way for the parties to put the matter behind them and move on to other issues.

- *Adjudication is impartial and principled.* The basic idea of third-party adjudication is that an impartial arbitrator or judge will decide the dispute in a fair and just way, on the basis of neutral legal or equitable rules or principles— "the rule of law"—rather than the parties' respective power or the judges' bias or arbitrary whim. Decisions reached by impartial processes assert a strong claim to acceptability and legitimacy, both by the parties themselves and by the international community at large.

- *Adjudication is authoritative.* To the extent the parties have genuinely consented to third-party adjudication of a dispute, the tribunal is respected, and its procedures are perceived as fair, the decision is likely to be viewed by the international community as authoritative and entitled to respect, buttressing expectations of and pressures for compliance with the judgment.

- *Adjudication is impersonal.* Because the decision is rendered by a neutral third party, the governments of the parties themselves cannot be held directly responsible for the outcome. Consequently, third-party settlement is a politically useful way foreign offices can dispose of certain politically sensitive issues without taking responsibility for losses or concessions. They can "pass the buck" for not "winning" a dispute submitted to a third-party tribunal, saying, in effect, "Don't blame us, blame the judge!"

- *Adjudication is serious.* Because adjudication is generally understood to be a complex, expensive, and somewhat intimidating process involving significant costs and risks for those involved, a state's proposal to submit a dispute to adjudication shows the other party and the international community that it takes the matter seriously and that it is prepared to go to considerable lengths to pursue its claim. Consequently, simply threatening or bringing an action in an international court may in itself buttress a party's credibility and bargaining strength in further negotiations. Such an act may make the other party pay more serious attention to the claim and increase pressure by other nations or by the international community at large on the other party to settle the dispute.

- *Adjudication is orderly.* The well-established structure of the adjudicative process provides a framework for the orderly presentation and development of the opposing parties' respective claims concerning the dispute. Consequently, adjudication may lead to both a better understanding by the parties themselves of the respective merits of each other's positions and possibly their own negotiation of a settlement.

- *Adjudication may reduce tensions and buy time.* Agreeing to submit a dispute to adjudication demonstrates the parties' commitment to a peaceful and fair settlement and may "depoliticize" the dispute or serve as a politically acceptable way of buying time for the parties to make further attempts to seek a negotiated solution.

- *Adjudication can be precedential and help develop international law.* An authoritative arbitral or judicial decision not only settles the particular dispute before the tribunal, but may also provide guidance to both the parties and other states as to how they should conduct themselves in the future— that is, it serves as a guide to the relevant rules and expectations of the international community concerning particular kinds of international behavior.

- *Adjudication reinforces the system.* Impartial adjudication is widely viewed as symbolizing the international rule of law, and a nation's willingness to submit a dispute to judicial settlement is generally taken as a test of its respect for and commitment to international law. To the extent that many or most states demonstrate a commitment to international adjudication, international law and the international legal system are strengthened.

Some Risks of Adjudication

Adjudication also poses a number of risks and potential disadvantages, which parties considering arbitration or judicial settlement will also need to consider carefully. These include the following:

- *Adjudication involves the risk of losing.* Adjudication necessarily involves the possibility of an adverse decision. In contrast to other "nonlegal" or "political" methods of dispute settlement, submission to binding third-party settlement means that parties give up their ultimate control over outcomes, which foreign policy officials and their political masters are loath to relinquish. Many nations are simply unwilling to take the chance that they may lose, particularly when the dispute involves what they consider important or "vital" national interests.

- *Adjudication may not be impartial.* The premise of adjudication is that the arbitrator or judge will be impartial. However, the process of selecting international judges may be influenced by political factors, and international tribunals typically include judges of one or both of the parties' nationalities; thus, some judges may be predisposed toward one party's position. International arbitration is less likely to raise this problem, because the parties have more control over selection of the tribunal's members and the party-appointed arbitrators must usually agree on selection of the neutral arbitrator.

- *Adjudication is unpredictable.* The outcome of adjudication may be difficult to predict, either because no relevant rules of international law exist or because, as is often the case, existing rules are ambiguous or uncertain. Moreover, apart from the problem of deliberate bias by the tribunal, letting a third party decide a matter always involves an element of chance. No matter how careful the parties are in selecting an arbitrator or judge, and regardless of the judge's reputation, any judge may simply fail to understand the issue, have unconscious biases, try to avoid responsibility or criticism by compromising or "giving something to each side," or simply reach a wrong decision through incompetence or faulty reasoning.

- *Adjudicative settlement is imposed.* In contrast to a settlement reached by the parties themselves through negotiated agreements, a judicial tribunal imposes its own settlement on the parties. Even when a state has initially consented to adjudication, traditional notions of sovereignty and national pride may make it resist the idea that an international arbitrator or court can appropriately rule on its behavior or tell it how to behave or what to do.

- *Adjudicative settlement may be illusory or superficial.* A tribunal must focus narrowly on the immediate "legal" issue before it, which may have little to do with the underlying causes of the dispute or the true source of contention between the parties. In cases where the legal issue is only the symptom or symbol of a far more complex problem, the tribunal's judgment may not really settle, and may even exacerbate, the dispute.

- *Adjudication is adversarial and potentially escalatory.* Despite efforts by the international community to encourage judicial settlement, being "taken to court" may be regarded as a hostile and unfriendly act—something that nations wanting to continue doing business together are generally loath to do. When one party to a dispute does not want impartial adjudication, efforts by the other party to force judicial settlement upon it may increase ill will, discourage further negotiation, and sidetrack alternative attempts to reach solutions.

- *Adjudication may freeze the dispute and the parties' options.* Once a dispute is brought to court, the dispute will move, at least to some extent, outside the control of the parties. The case may acquire its own dynamic, and "winning" the case may become the only goal. In some cases, the tribunal may permit the matter to drag on, locking the parties into long-term contention and further exacerbating tensions. In other cases, the tribunal may have little choice but to move swiftly and remorselessly toward a decision, even if it is in the parties' mutual interest to let the dispute sit a while in the hopes that, with time and changing circumstances and perceptions, it will fade away. Moreover, the fact that adjudication is usually public and often newsworthy may freeze the parties' positions, give the dispute a public prominence and significance that neither party desires, and obstruct possibilities for a compromise settlement.

- *Adjudication is inflexible.* In theory, adjudication is a zero-sum game—one party wins, the other party loses. But many problems are intrinsically resistant to such all-or-nothing solutions, or may be better resolved by compromise than by a "win-lose" decision. Where two states are necessarily engaged in continuous interaction, a decision that legally disposes of a particular dispute but leaves one party feeling it has been treated unfairly may ultimately do more harm than good. In this case, feelings of resentment and attempts to compensate in other areas for what is perceived as an unjust decision may hamper future relationships between the parties or even alienate the losing party from the legal or political system. If such a result is likely, techniques that permit reaching mutually acceptable and politically viable compromise settlements may be more useful and appropriate.

- *Adjudication is conservative.* Because adjudication is, at least in theory, only applied law, it looks for principles of what the law is rather than what the law ought to be. Thus, when one party is really demanding a change in the law—perhaps with good reason—judicial tribunals may have difficulty providing an adequate or acceptable resolution of the dispute. While states may, in theory, instruct a tribunal to decide cases according to its sense of what is most reasonable and fair—*ex aequo et bono*—states have rarely chosen to do so. However, consistent with relevant customary international law, which indicates that states should settle their maritime delimitation disputes on equitable principles, the ICJ has generally tried to reach "an equitable result" in maritime boundary cases, and its decisions have been accepted by the parties.

- *Adjudication may be inconvenient and costly.* Arbitral or judicial proceedings may be complex, time-consuming, and expensive and may divert the energies of high-level officials from other important duties. For poorer nations, the legal costs of hiring sophisticated counsel (usually from Western countries) may be significant. (However, as discussed below, the UN secretary-general has established a special fund to help poorer nations in this respect.) Moreover, delays may be substantial; it is not uncommon for the decision of a case to take a number of years.

- *Adjudication may be too precedential.* The precedential nature of adjudication can pose risks as well as advantages. A party may be relatively indifferent to the outcome of a particular minor dispute, but not indifferent to the potentially precedential effect of a decision on similar or analogous disputes, either with the same or other parties, that may be of much greater and more lasting significance.

- *Adjudication may be used for propaganda or harassment purposes.* A nation may be concerned that adjudication may encourage other, unfriendly nations to abuse any available judicial processes by bringing frivolous suits in order to embarrass or harass it. However, it is not always easy to make a clear distinction between a "proper" and an "improper" use of international adjudication. Certainly, nations often seem to have a largely political or propaganda purpose in mind when resorting to the ICJ, in the sense that they usually hope, by legitimating their claim, to bring the force of the international community's opinion to bear on the other party's actions.

- *Adjudication may be ineffective.* Absent more effective international procedures for the enforcement of international arbitral or judicial decisions, a nation may be uncertain whether a favorable judgment will be carried out, particularly if one party is an unwilling litigant before the tribunal and has indicated in advance that it will not recognize either the tribunal's jurisdiction or its judgment.

THE CASE FOR INTERNATIONAL ADJUDICATION

This discussion suggests that international adjudication is not likely to play a major part in the settlement of international disputes for some time to come. Given the alternatives, the parties to a dispute often prefer to use negotiation and other nonadjudicative methods of settlement that entail fewer risks and allow them a greater degree of control. However, even if relatively few international disputes are actually resolved through international adjudication, international adjudication is not insignificant, nor can we afford to ignore it. International adjudication deserves the international community's encouragement and support for a number of reasons.

First, although adjudication may not be the best way of resolving every dispute, arbitration or judicial settlement may be the best way of handling the problem in a number of situations and can perform a very useful dispute-settlement function. In practice, most disputes do not involve issues of significant or "vital" national concerns. In these cases, while each party may prefer to win the dispute, the stakes involved are limited and each can afford to lose; adjudication is a good way for the parties to achieve their most important objective—disposing of the dispute. Among the types of disputes particularly conducive to adjudication are the following:

- disputes that do not involve significant national interests and in which the governments concerned, for political or other reasons, are unable to make concessions or compromises in negotiations (e.g., substantively unimportant but emotionally volatile minor border disputes or issues of sovereignty over small or insignificant areas of territory or maritime boundaries);
- disputes involving difficult and complex factual or technical questions in which the parties may be prepared for a compromise solution but cannot themselves develop a basis for arriving at a viable compromise (e.g., certain complex border or related issues, such as delimitation of maritime areas, continental shelves, fisheries, or the deep seabed); and

- certain particularly awkward or dangerous disputes, in which the resort to judicial settlement may be a politically acceptable way of buying time and containing a volatile situation while solutions continue to be worked out.

As these categories suggest, a significant number of arbitrations and World Court judgments have, in fact, concerned territorial or maritime delimitation disputes.

Second, the very availability of international tribunals may help avoid disputes or induce their settlement. Even if states choose only infrequently to invoke the compromissory clauses in relevant agreements or the ICJ's jurisdiction under the optional clause, such commitments are not useless. On the contrary, because each party to a dispute covered by such provisions knows that the other can resort to the World Court, a state that wishes to avoid adjudication will have more incentive to act reasonably and to reach a negotiated settlement. That is, where the parties have conferred potential jurisdiction on an international tribunal, their decisions and bargaining, like those of parties to domestic disputes, are more likely to occur "in the shadow of the law." As one prominent international scholar notes, "The value of arrangements for dispute settlement is not to be judged solely by the cases decided under these arrangements; a provision for compulsory arbitration, by its very existence, can discourage unreasonable behavior and so may be useful even if it is never invoked" (Merrills 2005, 123).

Finally, it is important to note that, for many people throughout the world, international adjudication symbolizes civilized and ordered behavior and the rule of law in international affairs. Whatever the truth may be as to how the international legal system actually works, the public's perceptions of the relevance and effectiveness of international law are at least partly based on whether it sees impartial international tribunals, and particularly the ICJ, as playing a significant role in international dispute settlement. If many states (particularly powerful ones) are willing to submit their disputes to impartial settlement by international arbitral tribunals and courts, the public will deem international law relevant and worthy of respect. If, on the other hand, powerful states show indifference or contempt for international adjudication and the World Court, the public is likely to conclude that international law has little significance or relevance and to withhold its support from efforts to promote international law and its institutions. Indeed, these public attitudes may over time reflect back on official and bureaucratic attitudes toward respect for international law; if the public believes international law "counts," public officials will be under political pressure to act accordingly. Consequently, if a state believes that its national interest will be furthered by wider global respect for international law, it will also have an interest in doing what it can to strengthen and support the role of international adjudication.

In sum, because adjudication can be a particularly useful device in the international community's toolbox of dispute-settlement techniques, it is important that it be readily available and employed to the fullest whenever its use is warranted. Even if adjudication is not a panacea for problems of world order, it makes sense to do all that we can to strengthen and encourage the greater use of judicial institutions and to improve their ability to respond in flexible ways to nations' dispute-settlement needs.

PROPOSALS TO ENCOURAGE ADJUDICATION

What kinds of steps might we take to facilitate and encourage the use of adjudicative techniques to resolve international disputes? Several have been proposed and are worth considering, including the following:

- Establish new courts or other judicial mechanisms with jurisdiction over disputes arising in specialized contexts or particular regions, for example: a new global International Human Rights Court or a new International Environmental Tribunal, operating within the UN framework and composed of judges with special expertise in those areas; and a new regional African International Court or International Court for Latin America, dealing with disputes arising between states on these continents, perhaps with the ICJ serving an appellate function.

- Expand the number and scope of compromissory clauses—that is, provisions for the compulsory judicial settlement of disputes—in treaties. This goal could be accomplished by amending existing international agreements to add compromissory clauses where they presently lack such provisions and by ensuring that most new treaties include such provisions. Alternatively, states could consider developing a new "umbrella" Treaty on the Peaceful Settlement of Disputes, designed expressly to commit states to the compulsory judicial settlement of their disputes, either generally or perhaps where they are also parties to treaties lacking such compromissory clauses.

- Expand the advisory jurisdiction of the ICJ by, for example, (1) granting authority to seek advisory opinions from the court to additional UN-related bodies, such as the Human Rights Committee functioning under the International Covenant on Civil and Political Rights or the Committee on Racial Discrimination functioning under the UN Convention on the Elimination of Racial Discrimination; (2) amending the court's statute to permit additional applicants, such as the UN secretary-general, regional organizations, or even member states or national courts, to seek advisory opinions directly on questions of international law; and (3) establishing some procedure whereby states or national courts can indirectly obtain advisory opinions through an intermediary special committee of the UN General Assembly.

- Amend the court's statute to grant it jurisdiction over contentious cases brought by the UN secretary-general; other important international officials, such as the new UN high commissioner for human rights; other public international organizations, such as the European Union or the Organization of American States; and perhaps major non-governmental organizations, or possibly even individuals. A general suggestion along these lines would be to broaden access and participation by concerned international and non-governmental organizations and even individuals through provisions for filing *amicus curiae* ("friend of the court") briefs in cases brought before the court.

- Make existing courts and arbitral arrangements more "user friendly," particularly for newer, smaller, or poorer states, by simplifying and expediting procedures, broadening the parties' range of choice over arbitrators and judges, expanding available remedies, and reducing costs. One initiative along these lines is the ICJ's revision of its rules expanding the availability and use of its chamber procedure and expediting and focusing its other procedures. Another is the UN secretary-general's 1989 action establishing a trust fund to assist states seeking settlement of their disputes through the ICJ—designed to provide financial assistance to poorer states for expenses incurred in bringing cases before the court by special agreement. Other proposals of this type include providing for more prompt and effective interim measures of relief; further developing standardized rules of arbitral procedure and authoritative and usable lists of experienced and competent arbitrators; and providing "legal aid" to newer and poorer states under the auspices of the International Law Association, national societies of international law, or the UN Institute for Training and Research.

- Encourage more states, including the United States, to accept the compulsory jurisdiction of the World Court under the optional clause of Article 36(2) of the court's statute—and to do so without crippling reservations. The American Society of International Law, the American Bar Association, and other concerned groups have made or are currently studying proposals for such U.S. reacceptance. Some proposals along this line suggest arrangements that would permit states to accept the court's compulsory jurisdiction on a step-by-step basis, starting with less risky obligations and gradually extending their commitment as their confidence in the court develops.

CONCLUSION

In concluding this chapter, let me suggest why support of international adjudication seems very much in the U.S. national interest. Since the foundation of the republic, the principle of respect for law has been a firm tenet of U.S. foreign policy. The American public has generally believed that its country's and its children's future will be brighter and more secure in a world governed by law than in one where disputes are resolved solely through power and coercion. Moreover, considering the importance of the United States in international affairs, there seems little likelihood of achieving an effective international legal order without firm U.S. commitment and participation.

One of the most vital ways the United States can demonstrate a commitment to international law is by supporting impartial dispute settlement and the role and work of the World Court and other international tribunals. Such a policy would recognize not only the potential practical usefulness of international adjudication in advancing immediate U.S. foreign policy interests—as in its use of the ICJ in the Iran hostage crisis—but also the broader contribution that arbitration and judicial settlement can make in resolving international disputes, developing international law, and symbolizing the ideal of international order.

In his September 11, 1990, address to a joint session of Congress during the Persian Gulf crisis, President George H. W. Bush noted,

> A hundred generations have searched for this elusive path to peace, while a thousand wars raged across the span of human endeavor. Today that new world is struggling to be born. A world quite different from the one we have known. A world where the rule of law supplants the rule of the jungle. A world in which nations recognize the shared responsibility for freedom and justice. A world where the strong respect the rights of the weak.
>
> . . . .
>
> America and the world must support the rule of law. And we will.

A policy of strong U.S. support for international adjudication and the World Court could very well be an important step toward implementing this vision.

LIST OF CASES CITED

Case concerning Elettronica Sicula (ELSI)
United States v. Italy. 1989 ICJ 15.

Certain Expenses of the UN
(Advisory opinion) 1962 ICJ 151.

Corfu Channel Case
United Kingdom v. Albania. 1949 ICJ 4.

Fisheries Jurisdiction
United Kingdom v. Iceland; Federal Republic of Germany v. Iceland. 1974 ICJ 3, 175.

Gulf of Maine
Canada v. United States, 1984 ICJ 246.
LaGrand case
Germany v. United States. 40 ILM 1069 (2001).

Legality of the Threat or Use of Nuclear Weapons
(Advisory opinion) 1996 ICJ 226.

Namibia
(Advisory opinion) 1971 ICJ 16.

Nicaragua
Case concerning Military and Paramilitary Activities in and against Nicaragua
Nicaragua v. United States. 1984 ICJ 392 (judgment of November 26, 1984, on juris-diction and admissibility), 23 ILM 468 (1984); 1986 ICJ 14 (judgment of June 27, 1986, on merits), 25 ILM 1623 (1986).

Nuclear Tests
Australia v. France; New Zealand v. France. 1974 ICJ 253, 457.

Reparation for Injuries
(Advisory opinion) 1949 ICJ 174.

United States Diplomatic and Consular Staff in Tehran (Tehran Hostages)
United States v. Iran. 1980 ICJ 3.

Western Sahara
(Advisory opinion) 1975 ICJ 12.

REFERENCES

Merrills, John G. 2005. *International Dispute Settlement,* 4th ed. Cambridge University Press.

Stuyt, Alexander M., ed. 1990. *Survey of International Arbitrations, 1794–1989,* 3d updated ed. Dordrecht, Netherlands: Martin Nijhoff.

ADDITIONAL READINGS

This chapter draws on some of the author's other writings on this subject, in particular *Managing the Risks of International Agreement* (Madison: University of Wisconsin

Press, 1981); "An Overview of International Dispute Settlement," *Emory Journal of International Dispute Resolution* 1 (1986): 1–32; "International Dispute Settlement and the Role of International Adjudication," *Emory Journal of International Dispute Resolution* 2 (1987): 131–73, and in *The International Court of Justice at a Crossroads*, ed. Lori F. Damrosch (Dobbs Ferry, N.Y.: Transnational, 1987), 155–80; "International Third-Party Dispute Settlement," *Denver Journal of International Law and Policy* 17 (1989): 471–503, and in *Approaches to Peace: An Intellectual Map*, ed. W. Scott Thompson and Kenneth M. Jensen (Washington, D.C.: United States Institute of Peace Press, 1991), 191–226; "The United States and the World Court in the Post–'Cold War' Era," *Catholic University Law Review* 40 (1991): 261–62; and "International Law in the 'New World Order': Some Preliminary Reflections," *Florida State University Journal of Transnational Law and Policy* 1 (1992): 1–21.

I

Some useful writings on the general topic of international adjudication are:

Bernhardt, Rudolf, ed. 1992. *Encyclopedia of Public International Law*. Amsterdam: North Holland. See especially the entries on "Arbitration," "The International Court of Justice," "International Courts and Tribunals," and "Judicial Settlement of International Disputes."

Collier, J., and V. Lowe, 1999. *The Settlement of Disputes in International Law: Institutions and Procedures*. New York: Oxford University Press.

Janis, Mark W., ed. 1992. *International Courts for the Twenty-First Century*. Dordrecht, Netherlands: Martin Nijhoff.

Merrills, John G. 2005. *International Dispute Settlement*, 4th ed. Cambridge University Press. See especially chapters 5, 6, 7, and 11.

Schachter, Oscar. 1960. "The Enforcement of International Judicial and Arbitral Decisions." *American Journal of International Law* 54: 1–24.

United Nations. 1992. *Handbook on the Peaceful Settlement of Disputes between States*. New York: United Nations. See especially pages 55–80 and 146–54.

For current information on international tribunals generally, see the website maintained by the Project on International Courts and Tribunals, www.pict-pcti.org.

II

Some useful writings on international arbitration are:

Carlston, Kenneth S. 1946. *The Process of International Arbitration*. New York: Columbia University Press.

Lillich, Richard B., and Charles N. Brower, eds. 1993. *International Arbitration in the 21st Century: Towards "Judicialization" and Uniformity*. Irvington, N.Y.: Transnational.

Petrochilos, Georgios. 2004. *Procedural Law in International Arbitration*. New York: Oxford University Press.

Schwebel, Stephen. 1987. *International Arbitration: Three Salient Problems*. Cambridge, Mass.: Grotius.

Simpson, John L., and Hazel Fox. 1959. *International Arbitration: Law and Practice*. London: Stevens.

Waldock, C. M. H., ed. 1972. *International Disputes: The Legal Aspects*. London: Stevens. See chapter 2.

Wetter, J. Gillis. 1979. *The International Arbitral Process: Public and Private*, 5 vols. Dobbs Ferry, N.Y.: Oceana.

III

Some useful writings on the International Court of Justice are:

Damrosch, Lori F., ed. 1987. *The International Court of Justice at a Crossroads*. New York: Transnational.

Franck, Thomas M. 1986. *Judging the World Court*. New York: Priority Press.

Gill, Terry D. 2003. *Rosenne's The World Court: What It Is and How It Works*, 6th rev. ed. Leiden, Netherlands: Martinus Nijhoff.

Jennings, Robert. 1995. "The International Court of Justice After Fifty Years." *American Journal of International Law* 89: 493–505.

Rosenne, Shabtai. 2006. *The Law and Practice of the International Court 1920–2005*, 4 vols., 4th ed. Leiden, Boston: Martinus Nijhoff.

Shulte, Constanze. 2005. *Compliance with Decisions of the International Court of Justice*. New York: Oxford University Press.

Zimmerman, Andreas, Christian Tomuschat, and Karin Oellers-Frahm. 2006. *The Statute of the International Court of Justice: A Commentary*. Oxford, New York: Oxford University Press.

The International Court of Justice has an excellent website: www.icj-cij.org.

IV

Some useful writings on some of the more specialized international courts and arbitral procedures discussed in this chapter are:

(1) On the Court of Justice of the European Union:

Brown, L. N., and T. Kennedy. 2000. *The Court of Justice of the European Communities*, 5th ed. London: Sweet and Maxwell.

De Búrca, Gráinne, and Jason D. Brueschke, eds. 2002. *The European Court of Justice*. New York: Oxford University Press.

(2) On the European Court of Human Rights:

Kempees, Peter, ed. 1999. *A Systematic Guide to the Case-Law of the European Court of Human Rights*. The Hague, Netherlands: Martinus Nijhoff.

Merrills, John G. 1995. *The Development of International Law by the European Court of Human Rights*, 2d ed. Manchester, UK: Manchester University Press.

Van Dyk, Peter, and G. J. H. Van Hoof. 1998. *Theory and Practice of the European Convention on Human Rights*, 3d ed. Boston: Kluwer.

(3) On the Inter-American Court of Human Rights:

Buergenthal, Thomas. 1982. "The Inter-American Court of Human Rights." *American Journal of International Law* 76: 231–45.

Davidson, Scott. 1992. *The Inter-American Court of Human Rights.* Brookfield, Vt.: Gower.

Pasqualucci, Jo M. 2003. *The Practice and Procedure of the Inter-American Court of Human Rights.* Cambridge, UK: Cambridge University Press.

(4) On the Iran-U.S. Claims Tribunal:

Aldrich, G. 1996. *The Jurisprudence of the Iran-United States Claims Tribunal.* New York: Oxford University Press.

Brower, C. N., and J. Brueschke. 1998. *The Iran-United States Claims Tribunal.* Boston: Kluwer.

Caron, David, and J. Crook, eds. 2001. *The Iran-United States Claims Tribunal and the Process of International Claims Resolution.* Irvington, N.Y.: Transnational.

Lillich, R., D. Magraw, and D. Bederman. 1998. *The Iran-United States Claims Tribunal.* Irvington, N.Y.: Transnational.

(5) On the International Tribunal for the Law of the Sea:

Klein, Natalie. 2005. *Dispute Settlement in the UN Convention on the Law of the Sea.* Cambridge UK: Cambridge University Press.

6

INTERACTIVE CONFLICT RESOLUTION

Ronald J. Fisher

Interactive conflict resolution (ICR) involves problem-solving discussions between unofficial representatives of groups or states engaged in violent protracted conflict. Since 1965, various academic-based initiatives have sought to increase mutual understanding and encourage movement toward the resolution of many destructive intercommunal and international conflicts. The analysis of the conflict and the development of alternative solutions or directions toward resolution are facilitated by a skilled and impartial team of scholar-practitioners who organize and manage the discussions. More recently, non-governmental organizations working in applied conflict resolution have added to the scope and variety of interactive work, typically directed toward destructive ethnopolitical conflict. Objectives have ranged from simple education in terms of increased understanding and improved attitudes, to shared realizations about the sources and nature of the conflict, to the joint generation of creative solutions that can and have been put into operation (Fisher 1993a).

This chapter reviews various applications of ICR, from seminal contributions to ongoing initiatives at both the international and the intercommunal levels. Major contributions to a theory of practice are identified before the present state of the field is briefly assessed. The chapter concludes with challenges that ICR must meet to attain its unique potential in contributing to the resolution of international conflict.

Although ICR is a multidisciplinary effort, the method is rooted primarily in social-psychological assumptions about international disputes (Fisher 1997; Kelman and Fisher 2003). Conflict is generally seen to be a mix of objective interests and subjective factors, the latter having greater influence as the conflict intensifies. Thus, subjective aspects—such as misperceptions, negative attitudes, unwitting commitments, and miscommunication—need to be addressed, as must the relationship issues—such as mistrust, win-lose orientations, and unrecognized basic needs—to which they contribute. Although ICR is initially directed toward changes in individuals, it recognizes that these changes must be transferred and integrated into policy formulation and decision making at the political level in order to influence the de-escalation of a conflict. Thus, ICR is based on the assumption that conflict systems, like social systems, comprise interacting individuals, and that influence processes move both ways. The more influential and representative the individual participants in ICR workshops are, the greater the potential impact on the political process and policymaking.

In line with the objective and subjective mix of factors involved in a conflict, ethnopolitical conflicts are increasingly being recognized as involving both instrumental, resource-based concerns and psycho-social, identity-based elements; both of these need to be dealt with in ICR (Pearson 2001; Ross 1993). In fact, when conflict is predominantly identity based, with concerns over recognition and survival, methods designed to address instrumental issues, such as traditional mediation, may exacerbate and prolong the conflict (Rothman 1997a).

ICR is often implemented through workshops. Some are primarily educational; that is, they focus on changing individual perceptions, attitudes, and ideas. Others are more political, concerned with transferring these changes via influential participants to decision-making bodies. Many interventions combine both these aspects (Kelman 1986). Foltz (1977) distinguishes process-promoting workshops from problem-solving ones: the former provide participants with new knowledge and abilities that they can take back so they can function more effectively in their conflict-torn societies; the latter facilitate a better understanding of the differences between the parties, a distinction between negotiable and immutable issues, and an examination of creative and even radical solutions.

Workshops can play a role in several phases of the ICR process:

- *prenegotiation*, in which the workshop helps the parties examine the barriers to negotiation, including relationship issues, create conditions conducive to negotiations, and develop actions to promote negotiations (Fisher 1989; Kelman 1982);
- *paranegotiation*, in which a continuing workshop provides a parallel track to official negotiations where unofficial representatives can examine obstacles

in the negotiating process, formulate shared principles underlying negotiations, analyze particularly thorny issues, and consider topics that are not yet on the table (Kelman 1993b); and

* *peacebuilding,* in which workshop interactions among antagonists occur at different levels in various sectors (e.g., education, business, media) and focus on ways of de-escalating the conflict and planning joint activities to improve the relationship (Fisher 1993b). In a postsettlement phase, ICR can continue to play a peacebuilding role by helping to reestablish cooperation among past enemies so that reconciliation and reconstruction go hand in hand.

ICR assumes that dialogue and problem solving between adversaries are most likely to be brought about through the efforts of a trusted, knowledgeable, skilled intermediary. The term "third-party consultation" emphasizes the facilitative and diagnostic role of the scholar-practitioners who manage the sessions (Fisher 1972, 1990). The third party improves communication using a range of human relations skills and encourages analysis of the conflict by providing a variety of relevant concepts from the study of conflict. Participants are invited to engage in a common analysis of their situation before exploring the joint development of creative ideas for its improvement. Third-party consultation further assumes that only authentic and effective face-to-face interaction among the parties themselves can lead to the de-escalation and resolution of destructive, intractable conflicts. The ultimate goals are deep understanding, mutual recognition and respect, and jointly acceptable and sustainable solutions—in sum, an improved relationship between the parties.

As a form of third-party intervention, ICR or "consultation" needs to be distinguished from other intermediary activities, including conciliation, mediation, and arbitration and adjudication (Fisher and Keashly 1988). Whereas the more established methods generally accept an adversarial and/or judgmental approach to settling the substantive issues in a conflict, ICR (and some forms of conciliation and mediation) attempts to induce an analytical and collaborative reorientation of the parties, which may ultimately transform their relationship in the conflict—and thus the conflict itself—into a more positive social reality. ICR may thus play a useful premediation role by reducing the negative effects of subjective factors so that other third parties can more effectively address the substantive elements of the conflict (Fisher and Keashly 1991).

ICR is an unofficial approach that is not seen as a replacement for official diplomatic and governmental activities, but as a complement to them. The rationale is to provide an informal, low-risk, noncommittal, and neutral forum in which unofficial representatives of the parties may engage in exploratory analysis and creative problem solving, free from the usual constraints of official policy and public scrutiny. But ICR is more than simple citizen-to-citizen contact, because delegates are often selected with the approval of official decision makers and are chosen in part for their ability to influence policy.

ICR's focus has generally been on complex and destructive conflicts between communal identity groups defined in racial, religious, cultural, linguistic, or ethnic terms. Azar (1983, 1990) coined the term "protracted social conflict" to denote seemingly irresolvable and hostile interactions with sporadic outbreaks of violence that are based on communal and ethnic cleavages rooted in the denial of fundamental human needs for individual and social development. These needs include security; the establishment, maintenance, and recognition of a distinct identity; effective participation in social and political decision making; and the promotion of distributive justice to overcome inequality. In a similar vein, Burton (1987) uses the term "deep-rooted conflict" to refer to differences that are based not on interests that can be negotiated, but on underlying needs that cannot be compromised—needs that, paradoxically, are not in short supply. Such conflicts tend to occur in situations of profound and pervasive social inequality, where needs for identity and participation are frustrated; and they are most violent where communities or nations resort to extraordinary means to mobilize their members in the cause of preserving their identity, culture, and values. The central element of ethnopolitical conflict is that group identity is highly related to the degree of collective advantage or disadvantage that the society provides (Gurr, 1993). Thus, the primary foci for ICR scholar-practitioners have been on the world's seemingly intractable conflicts, from Cyprus to Northern Ireland, from Sri Lanka to Afghanistan, from Lebanon to the Horn of Africa, and from Cambodia to the Middle East.

REVIEW OF APPLICATIONS

Initiatives in Interactive Conflict Resolution

The creation of ICR is attributed to the work of John Burton and his colleagues at University College London, who arranged informal but officially sanctioned discussions with high-level representatives of factions and countries engaged in violent conflict. Burton, an Australian diplomat turned academic, was able to use his connections and practical understanding of diplomacy in combination with his nontraditional approach to international relations to create a unique methodology for conflict-resolution activities (Burton 1969; Mitchell 2001). Burton's idea of a third-party panel of social scientists established the use of skilled and impartial facilitators who controlled communication to foster an open and supportive climate for the representatives to examine their perceptions, analyze the conflict, and create innovative directions toward resolution. The rationale came partly from an understanding of small-group dynamics provided by colleagues like Anthony de Reuck (1974), who had experience in facilitating multinational problem-solving discussions.

The escalating conflict among Indonesia, Malaysia, and Singapore, which defied continued attempts at mediation in the early to mid-1960s, was the Burton group's first focus. Delegates from the three countries were invited to London for a five-day workshop, followed by a series of briefer sessions over the next six months. After some initial confusion, the workshop moved toward correcting mutual misperceptions, redefining the conflict, reassessing the costs of the parties' objectives, and envisaging new policy options (de Reuck 1974). The parties reestablished diplomatic relations and developed the overall understanding and framework that was represented in the 1966 peace agreement.

On the crest of this success, Burton and his colleagues moved on to address the deadlocked intercommunal conflict in the Republic of Cyprus. Representatives from the Greek and Turkish Cypriot communities met in London with Burton's group for five days of discussions in late 1966 at a point when UN mediation had broken down. The two sides shared their perceptions of the political situation on the island, considered new directions for resolving the conflict, and developed fresh insights. As judged by follow-up contacts, these discussions in part led to a resumption of the UN-sponsored negotiations (Mitchell 1981). Thus, both initiatives had an important influence on international conflict resolution.

Also during the mid-1960s, American social psychologist Leonard Doob sought to explore whether the analytical basis of modern social science had anything to offer the world of practice in terms of addressing destructive conflicts. Doob and his colleagues organized workshops based largely on human-relations training models (see Shaffer and Galinsky 1974) that brought together influential members of parties engaged in violent conflicts, specifically in the Horn of Africa and Northern Ireland (Doob 1970; Doob and Foltz 1973). A two-week workshop with participants from Ethiopia, Somalia, and Kenya held in 1969 met with some success in applying sensitivity training and other workshop methods, but was unable to achieve a consensus or have any apparent influence on the conflict. A ten-day workshop with Catholic and Protestant community leaders from Belfast in 1971 employed the Tavistock method and other exercises, and had considerable impact on the participants in both positive and negative terms. In fact, an acrimonious conflict emerged among members of the organizing team over the workshop's appropriateness and outcomes, obscuring the legacy of the workshop with a cloud of confusion and concern to this day. Doob attempted to intervene in the Cyprus conflict, but his plans for a workshop were cut short by an Athens-sponsored coup and a military intervention by Turkey in 1974, and a series of discussions in 1985 was terminated by authorities of one of the Cypriot communities (Doob 1974, 1987).

Herbert Kelman, an American social psychologist with interests in international relations, was a member of the third-party panel for Burton's Cyprus workshop. Kelman's encounter with Burton's work led him to conclude that this social-psychological approach to international conflict resolution was potentially useful (Kelman 1993b). His initial comparison of the Burton and Doob approaches helped prepare the way for a 1971 prototype workshop, co-designed with Canadian social psychologist Stephen Cohen, on the Israeli-Palestinian conflict (Kelman 1972; Cohen et al. 1977). Subsequently, Kelman and his colleagues organized more than thirty workshops with Palestinian and Israeli influentials, contributing positively to the peace process between the two entities, which culminated in the Oslo Accords, before deteriorating as a result of mutual instransigence and hostility (Kelman 1979, 1986, 1993a, 1995). The typical workshop begins with separate preworkshop sessions with each side to allow the third party to understand each side's concerns and build familiarity within each national team. The workshop proper starts with participants expressing their views of the conflict and their central concerns (needs and fears) about it, followed by an exploration of the overall shape of a mutually acceptable solution. The workshop ends with a discussion of the constraints hindering movement toward resolution and how to overcome them. Over time, Kelman's workshops have been tailored to ongoing relations in the region and have involved representatives of increasing political influence.

Edward Azar, an American political scientist of Lebanese origin, was a third-party member in one of Kelman's early workshops and later teamed up with Cohen to make further contributions to peace in the Middle East. Azar and Cohen served as facilitators for discussions beginning in 1976 and culminating in a two-day problem-solving workshop in 1979 with Egyptian and Israeli intellectuals that covered a number of the conflict's central issues. Combined with in-depth interviews with decision makers, this experience enabled Cohen and Azar (1981) to provide a social-psychological description and evaluation of the peace process that culminated in the peace treaty between Israel and Egypt. In 1985, Azar invited Burton to help launch the Center for

International Development and Conflict Management at the University of Maryland. In addition to studies in conflict and development, the center began specializing in a conflict-resolution method Azar termed "problem-solving forums."

Azar drew on the work of Burton, Doob, Kelman, and others in developing the forum model, which he saw as the most appropriate applied intervention for addressing protracted social conflicts (Azar 1990). The forum uses a panel of third-party facilitators to help create an analytical, nonadversarial environment in which representatives of the groups in conflict can discuss identity-related needs and explore the alternatives necessary to achieve a breakthrough from intractable conflict to peace. Azar, Burton, and their colleagues carried out a series of problem-solving forums during the early to mid-1980s, focusing on three intractable conflicts:

- Three forums addressed the conflict between Argentina and the United Kingdom over the Falkland/Malvinas Islands, which led to military confrontation in 1982. Influential representatives, including parliamentarians from both countries, searched for directions toward mutually agreeable definitions of sovereignty over the disputed islands. The meetings produced a set of principles that balanced the question of sovereignty with that of self-determination. The principles served as a basis for negotiations, carrying over into official meetings between the parties, but without any apparent effects (Little and Mitchell 1989).

- Two forums were held on the civil war in Lebanon, bringing together representatives nominated by the country's various religious and political leaders. The first meeting produced a consensual agreement on an integrated and independent Lebanon, while the second worked on principles for a united country and established an ongoing network that produced the 1988 National Covenant Document that was integrated into the 1989 Taif Accords, bringing peace to Lebanon.

- In 1985, a forum on the conflict in Sri Lanka brought together Tamil and Sinhalese influentials. This session resulted in joint realizations about the conflict and a commitment to develop tension-reducing measures to address it. The forum was followed by two briefer seminars in 1986 and 1987.

Unfortunately, Azar had to discontinue his work in the late 1980s because of ill health. Following his death in 1991, no further forums were held, although the center continues to sponsor activities in international conflict resolution, including an interest in unofficial intervention (Davies and Kaufman 2002).

Continuing Contributions to Theory and Practice

Many individuals have contributed to ICR in theory and practice. Because it is impossible to acknowledge them all in this brief overview, the following sections highlight the work of a select number of scholar-practitioners who have contributed to both.

Christopher Mitchell, a British specialist on international relations, was an original member of Burton's group and served as a panel member in the Cyprus meetings (Mitchell 1966). Along with A. J. R. Groom, de Reuck, and others, he helped Burton found the Centre for the Analysis of Conflict (CAC) in London in 1965, which proposed to conduct research on conflict and offer reconciliation services to various parties. Mitchell (1973) was a staunch defender of the new methodology, countering a slate of criticisms raised by Yalem (1971). Mitchell served as a primary field worker, attempting to arrange further problem-solving sessions on various destructive international conflicts, and was a panel member in a workshop involving trade unionists from Northern Ireland, of which no report has been published. In 1978, the CAC moved to the University of Kent at Canterbury with Groom and Burton as codirectors. Following Burton's departure for the United States in 1982, the CAC continued as a forum for research, engaging in no direct problem-solving applications until a successful project on the Moldova conflict, whose results have yet to be fully published (see below). In 1989, the CAC was reorganized as the Centre for Conflict Analysis to recognize the incorporation of a new generation of scholars whose interests focus on international mediation as well as problem solving.

On the basis of his varied experiences, Mitchell (1981) argues for a subjective approach to understanding conflict, which underlies the need for a shift from traditional, often ineffective third-party methods to that of problem solving. He proposes the development of third-party consultancy as a means of providing professional services to parties in a voluntary and nondirective manner so that all sides can gain through innovative solutions. Mitchell counters criticisms that the problem-solving approach is impractical, ineffective, and untestable, and maintains that there are no a priori reasons to preclude its further development. However, he does conclude that strenuous efforts will be required to convince decision makers and policy specialists of the new methodology's potential.

In the early 1980s, Mitchell took part in the initiatives organized by Azar and Burton at the University of Maryland and coedited a collection of papers on the Falklands/Malvinas conflict in the wake of the Maryland workshops (Little and Mitchell 1989). In the late 1980s, he joined Burton at George Mason University, where both contributed to the development of the Institute for Conflict Analysis and Resolution (ICAR), initially established in 1981 by the late Bryant Wedge and his colleagues to train professional practitioners in conflict management (Wedge and Sandole 1982). Working with a former CAC colleague, Michael Banks of the London School of Economics and Political Science, Mitchell produced a practical handbook on the problem-solving approach that is useful for training graduate students and others in the methodology of organizing and facilitating workshops (Mitchell and Banks 1996). ICAR has become a major center for promulgating the problem-solving approach to complex and persistent conflicts in a multifaceted fashion, offering a master's degree and the world's first interdisciplinary doctoral program in conflict analysis and resolution. An innovative aspect of ICAR is its Applied Practice and Theory program (formerly the Conflict Clinic, founded by the late James Laue), which engages in various interventions and involves graduate students through working groups and practicums. Internationally, ICAR has worked on several protracted conflicts, including those in Northern Ireland and Spain's Basque country, although no reports have been published.

Herbert Kelman has used his academic base at Harvard's Center for International Affairs to make a continuing contribution to the peace process in the Israeli-Palestinian conflict. Kelman's workshops have involved influentials of increasingly greater stature over more than thirty years, beginning with graduate students and young professionals, and moving to academics, parliamentarians, former government officials, policy advisors, and political activists. Kelman (1979) casts this work as a program of action research that integrates efforts at conflict analysis and resolution with opportunities to learn about Middle East conflict and international conflict in general. Action research was created in part by Kurt Lewin, a founder of applied social psychology, and typically involves a social scientist collaborating with a group of people experiencing a problem (such as a conflict) to collect data on the problem, develop interventions to deal with the problem, and evaluate the interventions through further data collection (Fisher 1982). In Kelman's program, workshops are the unique action component (intervention), but they are combined with various other activities, including contacting and interviewing decision makers and policy advisors, training third-party panel members, and developing detailed policy analyses of the conflict. Kelman (1986) emphasizes that the action component requires a research context to provide rationale and legitimacy, and the research aspect requires action to learn about and contribute to the resolution of the conflict.

Over time, Kelman (1978, 1982) came to see his work as helping to identify the psychological prerequisites for mutual acceptance of the parties in a conflict and to create the conditions for negotiations. Thus, the workshop approach became primarily a prenegotiation process between Palestinians and Israelis that helped create the psychological and political conditions for negotiations, particularly a mutual recognition of each other's identity and rights and a differentiated rather than monolithic image of the adversary (Kelman 1987). Kelman (1991) has consistently maintained that problem-solving workshops are not a substitute for official negotiations but can help prepare the way for, supplement, and feed into negotiations by helping to create an atmosphere of mutual reassurance and giving parties an opportunity to explore elements of a solution that can be fed into the formal negotiation process.

One unique aspect of Kelman's contributions is an ongoing series of policy analyses of the Israeli-Palestinian conflict based on his workshop and related experiences. He has articulated the psychological prerequisites for mutual acceptance, portrayed prenegotiation as a series of successive approximations toward mutual reassurance, and identified ways of overcoming barriers to a negotiated solution (Kelman 1978, 1982, 1987). In this way, he has provided a powerful and balanced statement of the directions required to move toward settlement and resolution, which are reflected whenever movement occurs in the Israeli-Palestinian peace process.

In 1990, Kelman and Nadim Rouhana, then based at Boston College, initiated a continuing workshop in which the same high-level influentials participated in an ongoing series of sessions tailored to developments in the conflict itself (Kelman 1992; Rouhana and Kelman 1994). Kelman and Rouhana were joined on the third-party panel by Christopher Mitchell and Harold Saunders (the latter now at the Kettering Foundation). The continuing workshop design has the unique potential of developing joint ideas on an iterative basis and building pronegotiation coalitions across the lines of the conflict (Kelman 1993b). The advent of formal peace talks in 1991 required a reformulation of the continuing workshop toward paranegotiation, exploring obstacles to progress and helping to create a supportive political climate. The breakthrough of the Norwegian-sponsored back-channel talks of 1993 affirmed many of the principles that Kelman saw as essential for progress in negotiations. The continuing workshop was superseded by a joint working group that met regularly with third-party facilitation to explore particularly difficult political issues in preparation for the final-status negotiations (Kelman 1995). A number of the negotiators and advisors on both sides in both the formal talks and the back-channel meetings had participated in Kelman's workshops. Their participation is just one tangible indicator of how the work has helped build a network of influentials who have contributed to a constructive political dialogue and to the conditions necessary for peace in the Middle East.

Kelman and his associates formalized their longtime working group as the Program in International Conflict Analysis and Resolution (PICAR), which is now defunct. PICAR was devoted to understanding protracted intergroup conflict and the processes for resolving it. In particular, PICAR worked on developing interactive problem-solving approaches, with the Israeli-Palestinian conflict as its primary focus. Other efforts centered on Northern Ireland, Sri Lanka, racially diverse communities in the United States, and indigenous communities in Canada. Protégés of Kelman also developed and evaluated innovative extensions of the methodology, including a women's workshop on the Israeli-Palestinian conflict (d'Estree and Babbitt 1998).

Fisher has made a continuing contribution to ICR over the years by developing the approach of third-party consultation, a term coined by Richard Walton (1969) to describe interpersonal "peacemaking" among corporate executives. An initial review (Fisher 1972) drew on the work of Burton (1969) and Doob (1970) but was also informed by the intergroup methodology of Blake, Shepard, and Mouton (1964). A later review focused on intergroup interventions in a number of spheres, including organizational, community, and international (Fisher 1983). This assessment identified limitations in both guiding theory and evaluative research, and therefore cautioned against premature conclusions of effectiveness. A review focusing exclusively on intercommunal and international interventions introduced the broader concept of interactive conflict resolution and cautioned that the field needs to address a number of critical issues for its continued development (Fisher 1993a). Fisher's (1997) comprehensive treatment of ICR provides an overview of its history, its current expressions, and its potential as a major method of conflict analysis and resolution.

The initial focus of Fisher's work was on intergroup conflict in community settings (Fisher 1976; Fisher and White 1976a, 1976b). Moving to the international level, a pilot workshop was organized in 1976, bringing together representatives of the Indian and Pakistani communities in Canada to discuss the conflict between their two countries. The workshop resulted in more positive—and more complex—intergroup attitudes among participants and provided an analysis of the conflict's major issues. Analyses of tape-recorded discussions documented the problem-solving process and the facilitative role of the third-party consultants (Fisher 1980). In 1984, international conflict resolution in Canada acquired an institutional base with the establishment of the Canadian Institute for International Peace and Security (CIIPS), which organized a series of seminars focusing on the protracted conflict on Cyprus (LaFreniere and Mitchell 1990; Salem 1992).

During 1989–91, a follow-up project was organized, using conflict analysis workshops to bring together influential Greek and Turkish Cypriots. The first event in 1990 included Turkish and Greek Cypriots living in Canada who maintained close ties with Cyprus and in some cases had connections with decision makers on the island. The session engendered intense dialogue, with some new realizations on both sides and some consensus on the nature of a renewed relationship to help resolve the conflict (Fisher 1991). A second workshop was held in England in 1991, bringing together influential unofficial representatives from the two communities on the island. The agenda covered the underlying fears and needs of the two communities, the assurances and acknowledgments required to address them, the principles and qualities of a renewed relationship, potential peacebuilding activities, and ways of overcoming the barriers to them (Fisher 1992). The agenda was influenced by the work of Kelman, a member of the third-party panels along with Fisher, Mitchell, Groom, and Brian Mandell. Evaluations indicating high levels of satisfaction and usefulness were reported to the leadership of the two communities. Also, participants subsequently were able to undertake a number of concrete peacebuilding activities, including bicommunal art exhibits, cross-community visits by business leaders, and creation of a joint committee to foster intercommunal contact.

CIIPS was abolished in 1992, but two workshops were held on Cyprus in 1993 with alternate funding and the assistance of the UN peacekeeping force. These workshops brought together influential specialists in education from the two communities to focus on potential confidence-building activities. Following an analysis of issues, fears, and needs, the participants discussed the role of education in sustaining the conflict and its possible role as a peacebuilding mechanism for de-escalating the conflict and rebuilding the intercommunal relationship. Joining the two third-party panels were Louise Diamond, Loraleigh Keashly, Christopher Mitchell, and Jay Rothman. Subsequently, two bicommunal planning meetings were held in which workshop graduates formed mixed task forces to develop and implement specific projects (Fisher 1994). These efforts were frustrated by an intense media campaign by Greek Cypriot nationalists against all forms of intercommunal interaction, particularly a North American-based training program in conflict resolution. This attack was ultimately countered by both official and unofficial efforts, and the peacebuilding movement emerged stronger than before. Diamond and Fisher (1995) describe how the consultation workshops were supportive of a subsequent multiyear training program in conflict resolution for peacebuilders on the island. Fisher (2001) considers both official and unofficial interventions in the Cyprus conflict and concludes that a sustained effort in ICR is necessary to overcome the trauma and hostility of the past and help move the conflict toward resolution.

Vamik Volkan, an American psychiatrist of Turkish Cypriot origin, has led a continuing effort to develop a psychodynamic approach to interactive conflict resolution (Volkan 1991). Volkan applies concepts based in psychoanalytic theory to understand the underpinnings of violent intercommunal conflict and invokes other concepts to explain intergroup behavior in workshop interactions. For example, the defense mechanism of projection, by which unacceptable ingroup characteristics are transferred to an outgroup, is seen as playing an important role in forming negative attitudes between conflicting groups, while the mechanism of displacement often creates a "miniconflict" at the beginning of a workshop, that is, a challenge to the third-party organizers through transferring aggression toward the enemy onto the third party. Regardless of the validity one attributes to psychoanalytic theorizing, the strategies and mechanisms for organizing and facilitating workshops appears similar to those of other scholar-practitioners in the field, and therefore form an important part of its theory of practice.

The first major intervention carried out by Volkan and his colleagues, notably Julius Demetrius and Joseph Montville, was a series of workshops hosted by the American Psychiatric Association focusing on the Middle East conflict. Between 1979 and 1984, the third-party team or "catalyst group" brought together Israelis, Egyptians, and later Palestinians to explore the psychological aspects of the conflict (Julius 1991; Volkan 1988). Six workshops were held over this period, with numerous smaller support meetings, bringing together a variety of influential professionals (psychiatrists, politicians, journalists, retired generals) to analyze the conflict, discuss painful aspects of it, and work on areas of potential cooperation. In addition to the understanding and trust that was developed through the series of meetings, a number of practical projects were also initiated, including collaboration among scholars and the revision of Arab images in Israeli textbooks.

To provide institutional support for his conflict resolution work, Volkan founded the Center for the Study of the Mind and Human Interaction (CSMHI) at the University of Virginia in 1988; one of its first projects brought together influential professionals from the Soviet Union and the United States to discuss the psychological aspects of the conflict between their two countries. These meetings led to cooperation between CSMHI and Russian institutions that paved the way for a series of workshops focusing on the conflict between Russia and the Baltic republics following the end of the Cold War. Each of the three Baltic republics—Estonia, Latvia, and Lithuania—has a significant Russian minority, and difficulties arose in each case between this recently powerful and protected minority and the majority ethnic group of the republic. Volkan and his colleagues, some of whom had worked on the Middle East project, organized a series of workshops that brought together both unofficial and official delegates from the countries involved to discuss the grievances and issues between them and to work toward practical action possibilities. Because some of the delegates were in official positions, "critical junctures," whereby unofficial ideas are transferred to the official realm, could be explored and evaluated immediately (Volkan and Harris 1992, 1993). The later meetings focused primarily on Estonia and Russia, particularly the situation of the Russian minority in Estonia, with a view to linking the reduction of ethnic tensions to the broader processes of democratization and institution building (Volkan 1995). The culmination of the Baltics work involved the sponsorship of community development projects in three locations in Estonia, where cooperation and relationship building between the Estonian and Russian ethnic groups were the mechanism and the intended outcomes of the projects (Volkan 1998). In a similar vein, CSMHI continued its focus on ethnopolitical conflict and organized a project bringing together mental health caregivers from Georgia and South Ossetia for dialogue and other training, and collaborated with Joseph Montville, then at the Center for Strategic and International Studies (CSIS), on a dialogue project involving Greek and Turkish influentials. Following Volkan's retirement, CSMHI closed its doors in 2005.

Joseph Montville, a former U.S. foreign service officer and former director of the now defunct Preventive Diplomacy Program at CSIS, also represents the psychodynamic approach to ICR and is acknowledged as the creator of the term "track-two diplomacy," which refers to unofficial, unstructured interaction, that is, problem-solving workshops, between members of adversarial groups or nations directed toward conflict resolution by addressing psychological elements of the conflict. Montville (1987) includes macrolevel strategies to affect public opinion to reduce the sense of victimhood and rehumanize the enemy, and cooperative economic activities to rebuild war-torn societies and provide continuity to relationships. As a practitioner, Montville has served as a member of third-party teams in a number of intractable conflicts, including the Middle East and Northern Ireland. He has also worked on a project bringing together influential Greeks and Turks in a series of problem-solving workshops, wherein a political psychology analysis is applied to issues of historical loss, group identity, the Aegean islands, and the Cyprus conflict. As a theoretician, he has used the psychoanalytic base to emphasize the importance of mutual victimization, the legacy of a violent and traumatic history, and the need for reconciliation and healing through contrition and forgiveness (Montville 1993).

Most of the primary contributors to ICR are academics who have developed their own interests in unofficial diplomacy. Harold Saunders is one of a small number of diplomats, along with John McDonald and Joseph Montville, who have moved in the other direction, from official diplomatic work to unofficial conflict resolution efforts. Saunders served on the National Security Council in the White House and then in various roles with the U.S. State Department. He was involved in the Kissinger shuttle diplomacy efforts in the Middle East and in the Carter mediation team that brought about the Camp David accords and the Egyptian-Israeli peace treaty. On the unofficial side, Saunders was on the third-party panel in one of the workshops involving Egyptians, Israelis, and Palestinians organized by Vamik Volkan and his colleagues. However, Saunders made his most extensive contributions through his role in the Dartmouth Conference, sponsored in the United States by the Kettering Foundation and in the Soviet Union by the Soviet Peace Committee and the Institute of USA/Canada Affairs.

Since 1960, the Dartmouth Conference has annually invited Soviet (now Russian) and U.S. influentials, primarily foreign policy specialists, to an unofficial, policy-relevant, citizen-to-citizen dialogue on relations between the two countries (Saunders 1991; Stewart 1987). In 1981, two task forces were set up, one on arms control and one on regional conflicts, that Saunders was asked to cochair along with a Soviet counterpart, Evgeny Primakov and later Gennady Chufrin (Chufrin and Saunders 1993). Over the course of more than ten years and twenty biannual meetings, the task force analyzed and developed a conceptual framework for addressing difficult regional situations—Afghanistan, the Middle East, Central America—and shared its insights with official decision makers. Discussions also focused on the overall relationship between the superpowers as reflected in their interaction over regional conflicts. Analyses of interests were used to probe the motivations behind each side's actions and to understand more deeply how each side viewed the other. In the late 1980s, a number of the Soviet participants served as policy advisors to Gorbachev, and many of the principles and approaches articulated in the Soviet leader's "new political thinking" had their genesis in the Dartmouth discussions (Chufrin and Saunders 1993). Saunders and his colleagues attribute part of the success of the Dartmouth task force to the mutual ownership of the process, including the cochairing of sessions as a balanced third party.

Saunders, as director of international affairs at the Kettering Foundation, has applied the sustained dialogue process to other conflicts. He and colleague Randa Slim organized a series of dialogue sessions with representatives of the factions involved in the Tajikistan conflict (Slim and Saunders 1996). In these sessions, a third-party team of three Americans was joined by three

Russian colleagues who were also graduates of the Dartmouth experience. The dialogue was initiated in 1993, bringing together representatives of the various factions and regions, and has continued meeting about every two months. Representation is roughly divided between government supporters and members of the opposition. When formal negotiations were started in 1994 under UN auspices, some dialogue participants became formal delegates. According to Saunders (2002), the dialogue process made a number of useful contributions to the initiation of negotiations and then turned its attention to future concerns, including reconciliation, implementation of the 1997 peace agreement, and the building of a civil society. The strategies, stages, and techniques of the method of sustained dialogue have been comprehensively described in the context of a public peace process with applicability to both domestic and international conflicts (Saunders 1999).

Intercommunal Dialogues

Many applications of ICR deal not with highly influential representatives but simply with interested members of the groups or individual citizens of the countries involved, members of their diaspora communities in other countries, or others associated with their cause. These interventions are generally concerned not so much with directly influencing policy processes as with instituting dialogue and increasing understanding among the wider publics, which may eventually affect policy.

Given the significance of the Middle East conflict and ICR's development primarily in the United States, it is not surprising that a number of interventions pertain to the Arab-Israeli conflict and have often involved Jewish Americans as organizers and/or facilitators. Illustrations of dialogue projects focusing on this conflict are described before various other examples are considered. The sampling of the field's diversity provided here is illustrative rather than representative, because many dialogue interventions are likely to go unreported.

An early example of applying sensitivity training supplemented by other exercises in a mixed group of Israeli Jews and Arabs is provided by Lakin, Lomranz, and Lieberman (1969). The objectives of improving communication and reducing intergroup suspicion were assessed with a variety of techniques, which generally indicated mildly positive outcomes. A number of problem-solving workshops bringing together Arabs and Jews living in Israel were carried out by Levi and Benjamin (1976) following a systematic and iterative task model of conflict resolution. Although many "mine fields" must be dealt with in the process, participants generally make progress, and in one workshop agreed on a mutually acceptable peace plan (Benjamin and Levi

1979). Based on his innovative work in prenegotiation, Rothman (1991, 1993) implemented a problem-solving intervention, bringing together Jews and Arabs living in Jerusalem to explore and promote functional cooperation between the two communities in such areas as economic development, education, and safety. Facilitated seminars were used to engage participants in a joint analysis of the problems and to produce cooperative solutions and recommendations. Participants from the two groups developed implementation plans and coauthored policy papers.

In the United States, a number of dialogue sessions have been organized between Jewish and Arab Americans who identify with the conflict in the Middle East. Reena Bernards coordinated a dialogue project bringing together American Jewish and Palestinian women in positions of leadership who represent mainstream organizations in their respective communities. Reports on three workshops held during 1989–91 indicate a challenging and useful process in which the two groups explored the major issues in the Israeli-Palestinian conflict, identified areas of agreement and disagreement, and created options for the future of the region. A working relationship between the groups was established, proposals for separate and joint actions to promote peace were developed, and a joint coordinating committee was formed to oversee activities, including two joint trips to Israel and the occupied territories. In a similar vein, a team from Kelman's group at Harvard facilitated a series of meetings involving a mixed Arab-Israeli political group (Hicks et al. 1995). A variety of difficult issues was discussed, and the participants came to realize the basic hopes and ultimate fears on both sides, thus building a stronger base for their joint political actions. Hicks and her colleagues also provide a candid analysis of the process within the third-party team that is valuable for educating others about the challenges of ICR.

Louis Kriesberg and Richard Schwartz at Syracuse University have played a central role in helping to organize the Syracuse Area Middle East Dialogue (SAMED). This grassroots initiative, beginning with a core group of Jews, Palestinians, and interested Americans, produced a consensus statement on the Israeli-Palestinian conflict through numerous interactions. Subsequently, SAMED initiated contacts with other dialogue groups, leading to the formation of a national coalition to share support and influence U.S. policy on the Middle East. Schwartz (1989) concludes that grassroots reconciliatory dialogue across adversarial lines can be successful in creating mutual understanding and generating ideas that help counteract the influence of pressure groups working to block conciliatory policies.

Dialogue and problem-solving forums of various kinds have been applied to a variety of conflicts around the world during the past few decades. Many of these meetings, such as those organized by the Society of Friends or the International Peace Academy, are not publicly reported because of the sensitivity of the situation and concern about risks to the participants. In one early example, American sociologist A. Paul Hare describes a private intervention in the escalating political conflict on the island nation of Curaçao (Hare, Carney, and Osview 1977). Following preliminary interviews with informal leaders on the two sides, Hare identified important issues in economic development and governance, and organized a series of joint seminars in which impartial experts provided their input into mutual problem solving. The impending crisis was defused over time, and development work was undertaken to address the conflict's underlying issues.

A similar intervention at a different point in a conflict was a workshop on Cambodian reconstruction held in 1991 and chaired by Peter Wallensteen (1991), founder of the Department of Peace and Conflict Research at Uppsala University. During a critical period in the peace process, the workshop brought together mostly Cambodian experts and influentials, from both inside Cambodia and abroad, with outside development experts to discuss in a nonpolitical forum the strategies necessary for reconstruction. After exploring various aspirations for and images of the country's future, participants discussed strategies to move from the current reality to the desired future and then worked on proposals in key development sectors, such as agriculture, health, and education. The sessions rebuilt trust among participants from various factions and stimulated ongoing dialogue within the Cambodian community.

An intervention focusing on the question of national unity in Canada provides a unique example of a dialogue process that was sponsored by and reported in a national newsmagazine (*Maclean's* 1991). The publisher engaged Roger Fisher and two colleagues from his Conflict Management Group to facilitate a weekend workshop to bring together participants from all parts of Canada representing important clusters of conflicting opinions on national issues—the primary one being the separation of the province of Quebec. The consultants facilitated the sharing of concerns and the development of strategies for action on major problems, using a single-text procedure to guide the participants toward producing a mutually acceptable set of suggestions for the country's future. A follow-up workshop six months later produced a restatement of shared Canadian values and a compromise formula for renewed federalism (*Maclean's* 1992). The outcomes were communicated to politicians involved in the ongoing process of constitutional reform, which failed in a national referendum some months later.

The development of a structured dialogue process and its application to various intergroup and international conflicts was initiated by the Center for

Psychology and Social Change, affiliated with Harvard Medical School. The center's projects on facilitating dialogue have adapted techniques of family systems therapy to promote dialogue between groups with differing ideologies or cultures whose intergroup perceptions are distorted by hostility. One example is a 1987 workshop in which participants from forty countries, primarily Americans, Soviets, and citizens of countries allied with each superpower, exchanged and clarified their assumptions about one another (Chasin and Herzig 1988). The exchange resulted in a wide range of useful confrontations and realizations on all sides. Similar techniques have been applied in workshop formats to a variety of intergroup cleavages, including whites and Asians in Australia, peace activists and defense analysts in the United States, and supporters and opponents of abortion rights (Chasin and Herzig 1993). The center's highly professional approach to dialogue facilitation is now carried forward by the Public Conversations Project of Cambridge, Massachusetts, which has produced a guide and other resource materials and organizes dialogues on a number of issues, including reactions to the September 11 terrorist attacks (www.publicconversations.org).

Another example comes from an application of the decision seminar, developed by Harold Lasswell, to the question of postwar governance in Afghanistan (Willard and Norchi 1993). Conducted in 1990, this seminar involved a diverse group of influential Afghan refugees in Pakistan who represented a range of political and other affiliations. The American seminar leaders provided input on a number of topics, including the tasks of decision making, basic values and human rights, and an interactive approach to problem solving. The participants applied these concepts to the Afghan situation through seminar-wide and small-group discussions. The seminar provided a unique opportunity for a diverse group of Afghan influentials to engage in mutual inquiry to clarify their common interest in the postwar governance of their country.

Since the mid-1990s, there has been a virtual dialogue explosion, as numerous U.S. and European-based non-governmental organizations have adopted ICR methods for engaging members of conflicting groups and factions. Some of these interventions have been carried out in countries that have experienced or are experiencing violent conflict, while others have taken place with members of diasporas living in the United States or elsewhere. Much of this work is not well documented, with brief reports occurring in agency newsletters or on web pages. What follows is a very selective sampling of this work designed to give a sense of its flavor.

The Institute for Multi-Track Diplomacy instituted a dialogue project on Ethiopia in 1993, bringing together members of different groups and factions living in the Washington, D.C., area. The dialogue sessions, designed to improve understanding and identify common concerns, lasted for a number of years, and were replicated with a similar project on Somalia (www.imtd.org). Subsequently, the Institute for Conflict Analysis and Resolution at George Mason University carried out a series of dialogue sessions on the continuing differences in Ethiopia (www.gmu.edu/departments/ICAR).

The National Peace Foundation instituted the Transcaucasus Women's Dialogue in 1994, bringing together women leaders from Georgia, Armenia, and Azerbaijan following a successful women's forum held in Armenia in 1991. The dialogue meetings were held approximately once a year and focused on peace-building through regional cooperation. Women's councils were established in each country and projects were developed to work on areas such as democracy building and the rehabilitation of refugees (www.nationalpeace.org).

Search for Common Ground established the Centre for Common Ground in Angola in 1996 to help that war-ravaged country move toward national reconciliation following thirty years of violent conflict. The center has organized numerous dialogues in communities of displaced persons, estimated at more than three million, to reduce hostility, rebuild harmony, and deal with a range of community issues using creative problem solving (www.sfcg.org).

The Institute of World Affairs began a community dialogue project in Lebanon's Bekaa Valley in 1999 to assist members of Christian and Druze communities address intercommunal issues and work toward reconciliation. Some of the dialogues tackled the difficult question of how to reintegrate displaced people back into their once-mixed villages and how to reestablish harmony with neighbors (www.iwa.org).

Conciliation Resources in the United Kingdom teamed up with the Berghof Center for Constructive Conflict Management in Germany to create the Georgian-Abkhazian Dialogue Seminar, which brings together politicians, officials, and members of civil society from the two sides for constructive engagement on issues relating to the conflict between them. Several meetings were held beginning in 1993 to provide an informal channel of communication for joint analysis geared toward reestablishing mutual trust. A more recent focus of the effort brings together journalists from Georgia and Abkhazia to discuss how to improve the transmission of information across the divide of the conflict (www.c-r.org).

PROBLEM-SOLVING WORKSHOPS AND FACILITATED DIALOGUES

A number of more recent interventions have followed the basic approach taken by the initiators of ICR, that is, bringing together influential but unofficial representatives of conflicting parties to analyze the current expression of the conflict and jointly search for ways to move toward a peaceful outcome. However, there has also been a growing involvement of official participants who come in an unofficial capacity, that is, they do not speak for their governments or leaders and they are not committed to any policy options that are discussed. Thus, the discussions are off the record and are without prejudice to existing or future policy. These types of sessions tend to go beyond simple dialogue for understanding toward laying a basis for negotiations. There is also a trend to combine traditional ICR activities of analysis and problem solving with other methods such as training in conflict resolution or facilitated brainstorming of options. Thus, there is a healthy but sometimes confusing eclecticism growing in the field of ICR in which combinations of methods are adapted to the needs of specific situations. As long as clear goals and clear linkages between methods and goals are maintained, eclecticism can be a positive development. This section briefly describes some cases that illustrate the expanding variety of ICR interventions.

In the critical prenegotiation period of the longstanding conflict in South Africa between proponents of apartheid and the African National Congress (ANC), a variety of meetings occurred between representatives of the two sides. Daniel Lieberfeld (2002) describes and evaluates the contributions of these track-two initiatives and generally concludes that they made positive contributions to the initiation of negotiations and the changes in party politics and public opinion that supported talks. Of particular interest to ICR, Lieberfeld reports on a series of six workshops held in England between 1987 and 1990 that brought together prominent members of the Afrikaner Broederbond (League of Brothers), closely linked to the ruling National Party, and high-ranking leaders of the ANC. These quiet, unofficial meetings were organized and facilitated by executives and consultants of a British mining company with interests in South Africa. The participants used the opportunity to seek information on each side's intentions, options, and priorities; discuss political and security issues; and propose reciprocal confidence-building measures. Overall, the meetings contributed to the perceptions that the other side was reasonable and that a negotiated settlement was possible.

The Project on Ethnic Relations (PER), founded by Allen Kassof, has played a central role in promoting dialogue, analysis, and problem solving on issues of majority-minority relations in a number of Eastern European states since the 1990s. The earliest and most extensive work of PER occurred in Romania, where interethnic violence broke out in the Transylvania region in 1990. PER organized meetings with officials of the Romanian majority and leaders of the Hungarian community with a view to replacing confrontation

with dialogue on critical issues, such as minority education and language policies. Roundtables in 1993 led to PER-mediated negotiations resulting in an
agreement on a number of items, including the establishment of a Council of
National Minorities. In 1995, further dialogue led to outcomes such as the creation of 300 new spaces in teacher training for Hungarian language secondary
schools. Partly as an indirect effect, moderate Hungarian politicians who had
gained prominence through PER activities were elected, which led to the first
interethnic coalition government in Romania's history (1997–2000). Following the next election, cooperative activity also led to a formal agreement on
political cooperation between the governing party and the ethnic Hungarian
party (now in opposition), thus continuing the thrust of interethnic accommodation. In 2001, a major conference was held to review and analyze ten
years of efforts to build interethnic harmony and consider ways to preserve it
(www.per-usa.org). The overall theme of PER's efforts is that persistent and
deliberate dialogue can encourage moderates from majority and minority
communities to take part in constructive activities that promote the interests
of both groups, thus supporting interethnic coexistence. PER has also been
active in similar situations, for example, in Slovakia, and is highly engaged in
the wider regional context, for example, by facilitating meetings of the leaders
of Hungarian communities from several East European countries to encourage them to enter into dialogue with their host governments. PER also organized unofficial discussions between Romanian and Hungarian policy makers
that led to the official talks that produced the first state treaty between the
two countries.

In 1995, the Conflict Management Group, founded by Harvard Law Professor Roger Fisher, partnered with the Norwegian Refugee Council to initiate a
series of facilitated joint brainstorming sessions involving a mix of unofficial
and official influentials from the Republic of Georgia and the breakaway
region of South Ossetia, the focus of a violent internal conflict. The violence
erupted in 1990, was halted by a Soviet military intervention, and was being
held in check by a peacekeeping force. In addition to open discussion sessions
to cover perceptions and interests and to brainstorm options, the workshops
included training in negotiation concepts and skills. The first workshop, held
in Norway, dealt with practical problems, such as restoring communications,
while the second moved to political issues, particularly the constitutional status of South Ossetia and the design of a negotiating framework. Following
the start of negotiations, a third workshop, held in the United States, brought
together individuals connected to the negotiations to focus on economic cooperation, the repatriation of refugees, and public support for reconciliation and
eventual settlement. Fitzgerald (1998) concludes that the first phase of the

intervention helped establish the official bilateral process and prepared key individuals to take part. Based on further research, including interviews with participants, Nan (2002) concludes that these three workshops established relationships and instilled a constructive negotiation process that allowed the two sides to address substantive issues more effectively. In the second phase of the project, from 1998 to 2000, a core group of participants formed a local steering committee, which met frequently to share perspectives on the issues relevant to negotiations. Although as of this writing, negotiations had yet to reach a mutually acceptable outcome, participants generally were enthusiastic about the workshops, seeing theses as providing for a real exchange of views, the creation of new ideas, the clarification of each side's approach to the conflict, and the development of a structured and constructive strategy of negotiation. According to Nan, these experiences led to an improved relationship between negotiators, more effective negotiation processes, and a number of concrete ideas for statements and steps to help talks move forward.

The now defunct Preventive Diplomacy Program at CSIS sponsored a multiyear project directed by David Steele to provide conflict resolution seminars for religious leaders from the different faiths in the former Yugoslavia. Between 1995 and 2002, more than thirty workshops provided a combination of dialogue, conflict analysis, and training in conflict resolution leading to peacebuilding activities at the local level and to the creation of interreligious institutions. The overall goal of the project was to develop support among religious people to overcome the ethnic divisions that shattered Yugoslavia. Over time, Steele developed three levels of seminars. The first focuses on interethnic community building, that is, the development of trust and solidarity, by sharing grievances through story telling, examining the cycle of victimhood and aggression, discussing shared responsibility for the traumatic history, and moving toward reconciliation through expressions of apology and forgiveness. Religious elements play an important role in reconciliation, through information on the grief process, the respectful acknowledgment of grievances, the confession of evil acts performed by some of one's own group, and the admission of bias found in sinful attitudes. The second-level seminars built on the trust of the first level to provide training in communication, problem solving, negotiation, and mediation, which helped shift the adversarial approach to conflict toward a joint search for mutually acceptable solutions, and resulted in cooperative initiatives, such as mediation programs. The third-level seminars assisted the religious communities to develop local peacebuilding initiatives to address structural issues underlying the conflict. Based on several years' experience, Steele (2002) has theorized about guidelines for effective dialogue and strategies for building supportive institutional structures.

He maintains that interfaith dialogue involves identifying basic human needs for security, identity, and community and the fears that these needs will not be met, that is, the fears that typically drive violent interethnic conflict. To ensure follow-up on peacebuilding activities, Steele engaged local consultants from the beginning of the project, and these individuals working across conflict lines have now created interreligious institutions in each country to foster ongoing communication and cooperation. Based on these successes in the former Yugoslavia, the project held seminars in Kosovo and Montenegro with similar goals of restoring or maintaining peace between conflicting religious communities. When CSIS abolished the Preventive Diplomacy Program, Steele moved his projects under the aegis of the Conflict Management Group.

During the 1990s, the former Soviet Republic of Moldova experienced severe internal conflict, which was the focus of a series of problem-solving workshops in the Burton style. Immediately before and during the dissolution of the Soviet Union, the Romanian majority adopted language and other laws that alienated ethnic minorities, particularly the Slavic (Russian and Ukrainian) peoples, who constituted the majority in the Transniestria region. Shortly after Moldova declared independence, armed conflict ensued, but it was soon controlled by Russian troops and then a multinational peacekeeping force. Before the cease-fire in July 1992, Joe Camplisson, a Northern Ireland community worker with interests in conflict resolution, had visited the region to assess needs and organize conferences focusing on community development. In response to pleas to help find a way to peace, Camplisson contacted John (A. J. R.) Groom at the Centre for Conflict Analysis at the University of Kent to help plan a conflict resolution intervention (Camplisson and Hall 1996). With the support of the political leaderships of Moldova and Transniestria, three problem-solving workshops were held in the 1994–96 period, bringing together political advisors, parliamentarians, government officials, and members of the negotiating teams working for a constitutional solution, all in an unofficial capacity. These workshops were devoted primarily to conflict analysis, whereby the third-party team asked questions and identified themes from the discussions in order to help the parties gain a deeper understanding of each other's perspectives, concerns, and preferred directions toward resolution. The challenge was to develop a shared vision as to how the two entities could exist in a common political community (Williams 1999). The later workshops in the series focused on the constitutional options that could provide a mutually acceptable basis for reintegration. Although the parties remained committed to a peaceful resolution of their conflict, the interplay of political, economic, and identity issues made it difficult to find one.

In concert with its Balkans Initiative, designed to promote peace and pre-vent further conflict in this troubled region, the United States Institute of Peace has organized a series of facilitated dialogues and training seminars in-volving a range of leaders, officials, and influentials from war-ravaged Kosovo. Under the stewardship of Daniel Serwer, director of the initiative, and George Ward, director of training at the Institute, the work began after the North Atlantic Treaty Organization military intervention in late 1999 with separate workshops for Albanian and Serbian leaders. The session with Albanians produced the "Lansdowne Declaration" (named for the meeting place in Vir-ginia), an extensive statement of principles and practices supporting a plural-istic society and designed to guide Kosovo toward democratic self-rule. The session with Serbian leaders produced a declaration calling for the end to all violence and dialogue between Serbs and Albanians leading to the rule of law and equal rights for all.

In May 2000, a joint workshop was organized for local community leaders living in an area under the control of the U.S. Army and focused on coexis-tence in a multiethnic society. At the national level, the separate sessions in 1999 culminated in a July 2000 workshop on coexistence, the first face-to-face interaction among top leaders since the end of the war. This session of dia-logue and discussion produced the "Airlie Declaration" (again named for the meeting place), which outlined the steps necessary to implement the earlier separate declarations. Included in this comprehensive vision was a plan for a campaign against violence, mechanisms for the return of displaced persons, and procedures for choosing municipal councils. Taken together, these vari-ous statements amount to a practical vision for achieving a shared, peaceful future for Kosovo.

In February 2001, the Institute organized a four-day training workshop for mayors and municipal officials in negotiation and mediation skills to support cooperation at the local level. Dialogue at this session also produced an agree-ment to initiate a variety of measures to support good governance, including equal rights for minorities and a code of ethics for municipal officials. In June 2002, a workshop on good governance brought together members of the Kosovo Assembly, representing different groups, for a combination of dia-logue and training designed to increase mutual understanding and build skills in conflict management and consensus building. This meeting produced a con-sensus statement on a number of major areas of concern, including protecting human rights, improving education to European standards, establishing a social welfare system, and making the assembly more effective. There was also a call for dialogue between politicians and civil society and for the development of multiethnic non-governmental organizations. The innovative sessions organized by the United States Institute of Peace (www.usip.org) are contributing to a broad international effort to stabilize the current situation and improve the quality of life for both the majority Albanian population and the different ethnic groups living in Kosovo.

Contributions to a Theory of Practice

ICR is not a body of strategies and activities based on a set of lofty ideals, hidden assumptions, and unspoken principles. It is a field of professional practice with a value base and a conceptual rationale that underlie a social technology of conflict analysis and resolution. A number of contributors have articulated an understanding of this practice, thus adding to a body of theory that is related and somewhat cumulative. However, there has been no comprehensive distillation of the various pieces into a widely accepted model; thus, there is no single statement of the essential principles and techniques of the method. This section draws attention to the various contributions.

Burton, the field's intellectual pioneer, produced his first practice model of "controlled communication" through inductive theorizing based on the Malaysia-Indonesia and Cyprus workshops (Burton 1969). This model stressed the role of the third party in creating a nonthreatening, analytical atmosphere in which the parties could mutually examine their misperceptions about the conflict and each other, and then jointly explore functional avenues toward resolution. According to Burton (1969), successful reperception enables the parties to understand the subjective elements of their conflict and thus paves the way for developing broad directions toward resolution and, ultimately, successful negotiations on administrative arrangements to manage the objective differences. The problem-solving aspect of the method was emphasized by de Reuck (1974), who saw parallels between the conflict analysis workshops and other small-group problem-solving sessions. Mitchell (1981) provided a broad treatment of the consultant's role, situating the method in the domain of peacemaking and inducing from various applications a positive and yet realistic assessment of its potential. Groom (1986), another member of the initial London group, presented a concise statement of problem solving in international relations that identified many common features of the method and adapted it to the international level.

For his part, Burton continued to grapple with the nature of the approach and its place within the political system. He came to see the basis of "deep-rooted conflict" not so much in the subjective difficulties of dealing with differences as in the pursuit of fundamental human needs that are irrepressible and nonnegotiable, such as the needs for identity, security, and distributive justice (e.g., Burton 1985). Concurrently, he articulated a systematic process to analyze deeper motivations and explore the means to address basic needs (Burton 1987). Burton (1987) provides an explicit, although somewhat rigid, statement of the "rules" for facilitated conflict resolution and the professional and ethical obligations of facilitators. A wider context for the method is found in a four-volume series in which Burton (1990) details the case for problem solving—not just for conflict resolution but for conflict "provention," where the sources of conflict are removed through the promotion of environmental conditions that create collaborative relationships. Thus, Burton (1992) sees conflict resolution not simply as a method for dealing with specific cases, but as a new approach to political decision making that is based on human needs and requires institutions to embody problem solving rather than adversarial procedures. This thinking requires all institutions to constantly reassess the relevance of their assumptions, goals, and procedures, and for conflict resolution to be incorporated into all aspects of their functioning.

Doob's contributions to a theory of practice are less well known, but nonetheless significant. He discusses the major components (goals, participants, methods, and so forth) involved in unofficial interventions in destructive conflicts and concludes that the work is useful although highly risky (Doob 1975). Doob (1976) considers the question of evaluating interventions in detail and concludes that the complexities of the process make assessment an immense challenge. In his broader work on the pursuit of peace, Doob (1981) considers the unique role of unofficial diplomacy and notes the potential of workshops as a prelude to negotiations. In a comprehensive treatment of intervention, which includes intermediary activities in situations of two-party conflict, Doob (1993) covers important considerations in the planning, selection, timing, implementation, and evaluation of interventions. Thus, Doob's cumulative contributions have provided useful input for the conceptual basis underlying the social technology of interactive conflict resolution.

Kelman has made major ongoing contributions to the conceptual underpinnings of the problem-solving approach, not the least of which is his promotion of the term "problem-solving workshop" to emphasize its experiential, participatory nature and the process of problem solving, distinguishing it from human relations training (Kelman 1972). In this approach, discussions are facilitated by social scientists serving as special third parties who induce norms of respectful and sustained analysis rather than debate and accusation (Kelman and Cohen 1976, 1979, 1986). In addition, the third party provides observations on the process to improve communication as well as problem solving and provides theory-based interventions to increase understanding of the conflict and the participants' interactions, which often mirror the conflict. According to Kelman (1979), the power of the method lies in its social-psychological nature, which emphasizes the centrality of social interaction in conflict processes, and the simultaneous interplay of individual and institutional factors in intergroup conflict. Social-psychological assumptions consider international conflict as occurring between societies rather than states. Thus, conflict must be addressed through face-to-face interactions of the parties, which result in new realizations and, eventually, a transformation in their relationship (Kelman 1992).

Fisher (1972, 1983) was the first to review and integrate a variety of applications and develop a generic model of third-party consultation that specifies the essential components of ICR practice. As shown in figure 6.1, the model includes the identity and role of the third party, the setting, the core strategies and related tactics, and the objectives of the method (Fisher 1976). In terms of identity, the third party must be a skilled and impartial intermediary who can facilitate productive confrontation and is not seen by either party as biased. At the international level, the intervenor typically is a team of conflict resolution specialists with unofficial status and a national or group identification that is neutral or at least balanced. The team needs skills in human relations, group processes, and problem solving as well as knowledge about conflict processes in the context of the international system. A working knowledge of the conflict in question is essential, although a high degree of substantive knowledge can bias the team toward preconceived solutions, thus inhibiting the problem-solving process. The team's identity lays the basis for a respectful, understanding, and trusting relationship between the third party and the parties to the conflict that is characterized as a helping or consulting relationship. Given that the approach operates from a base of low power, the intervenor has influence primarily through a combination of expertise and rapport with the parties.

The social structure of the method is expressed in the third-party role and the situation. The role (i.e., appropriate pattern of behavior) of the consultant is primarily facilitative and diagnostic and somewhat parallels that of mediator; yet its emphasis and focus differs in that it is designed to facilitate creative problem solving on the basic relationship, rather than a negotiated settlement on specific issues (Fisher 1983; Fisher and Keashly 1988). The consultant works to diagnose the conflict in direct and open interaction with the representatives of the parties, using substantive knowledge of conflict processes and skills in group facilitation. In contrast, mediators often work around relationship issues such as hatred and mistrust, assuming that an acceptable settlement will ultimately take care of such problems. The situation embodies the essential physical and social arrangements in which the consultant arranges the problem-solving discussions, typically following a workshop

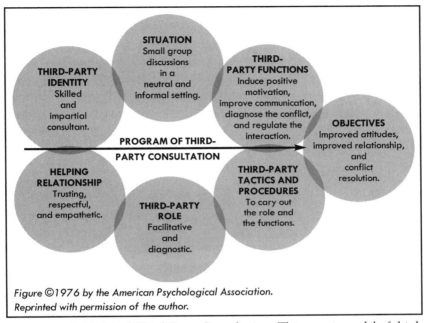

Figure ©1976 by the American Psychological Association.
Reprinted with permission of the author.

Figure 6.1. A Model of Third-Party Consultation. This generic model of third-party consultation specifies the essential components of ICR practice and their integration.

format. The informal meetings are usually held in secluded yet accessible locations on neutral territory. The agendas for the group sessions themselves must be flexible and yet directed at key aspects of the conflict. The rationale for the role and situation is to enable the parties to focus directly on the nature of their conflict, mutually understand its deeper elements, and jointly search for ways to de-escalate and resolve it.

The core strategies of the method are captured in the four functions of (1) inducing mutual positive motivation for problem solving, (2) improving the openness and accuracy of communication, (3) diagnosing the issues and processes of the conflict, and (4) regulating the interaction through the sequence of joint problem solving. Of course, these strategies must be operationalized through specific behaviors, referred to as tactics and procedures, that the third party implements when appropriate. Motivation, for example, can be increased by emphasizing the costs of nonresolution; communication is aided by skills such as paraphrasing or empathy; diagnosis is induced by drawing concepts from conflict theory into the discussions; and regulation is assisted by balancing the time allotted to the parties for discussion and moving problem solving from differentiation to integration when appropriate. Procedures refer to broader, structured activities in which participants engage in order to increase mutual understanding or joint problem solving. For example, to induce greater motivation and provide direction, the conflict's two sides might be asked to independently develop their images of an ideal future relationship, which are then shared and discussed.

All previous components of the model are directed toward a set of objectives, the priority of which varies with different interventions. At a minimum, the third party looks for positive changes in attitudes among the participants, in the sense that they now have a more realistic (i.e., accurate and complex) and favorable predisposition toward the other side. Concurrently, the orientation of participants toward the interparty relationship should shift from adversarial and destructive to cooperative and constructive, and the potential for these changes should be transferred to the relationship itself. Finally, the intervention should produce innovative proposals for peacebuilding or conflict resolution that have been jointly created and are mutually supported.

The critical issue facing ICR, however, is whether any of these changes, assuming they occur, can be transferred back to the political decision-making venues of the parties. No clearly articulated model of transfer exists, and until recently only impressionistic evidence for such effects could be found (Fisher 1997). Nonetheless, the model depicted in Figure 6.1 has guided practice and been evaluated in terms of interaction process, participant outcomes, and unique effects on attitudinal and relationship variables in comparison to mediation (e.g., Fisher 1980, 1990; Fisher and White 1976a; Keashly, Fisher, and Grant 1993).

A different, yet related, description by Azar (1990) covers preparation, nature of the interaction, identity of participants, competency and role of the facilitators, and manner of follow-up. Jay Rothman, who initially worked as one of Azar's student associates, has produced groundbreaking work in the area of prenegotiation, developing a systematic model based on the problem-solving approach that includes the stages of framing the issues, inventing integrative options, and structuring the process and substance of negotiations (Rothman 1992). The model has been used for training diplomats and complements a wider framework for moving ethnic conflict from confrontation to cooperation through dialogue and problem solving, illustrated by its application to conflicts in the Middle East. More recently, Rothman (1997a) developed a comprehensive approach for addressing identity-based conflict through his Antagonism, Resonance, Invention, Action (ARIA) framework, which provides a structured process for analyzing and resolving such struggles.

The framework provides a guide for third-party facilitators to assist the parties to understand their deep, human needs and to construct cooperative ways for managing their differences.

Based on his Dartmouth experience, Saunders has come to emphasize the concept of relationship for understanding and improving the international system and has articulated a framework for public, intercommunal problem solving (Saunders 1992). Building on this framework, Chufrin and Saunders (1993) describe the Dartmouth work in terms of a "public peace process" whereby adversaries can analyze their relationship and develop new ways of thinking and acting together. Saunders (1999) broadens and deepens his description of the public process based on sustained dialogue through application to the Tajikistan case as well as to race relations in the United States. His systematic five-stage model provides a comprehensive conceptualization that is useful for both describing and evaluating interventions in ICR. Saunders's work is compatible with previous thinking about unofficial diplomacy (e.g., Berman and Johnson 1977) and in particular with Joseph Montville's (1987) concept of track-two diplomacy, which denotes unofficial, informal interaction directed toward conflict resolution among members of adversarial groups or nations.

John McDonald, president of the Institute for Multi-Track Diplomacy, has been a primary contributor to track-two thinking (e.g., McDonald and Bendahmane 1987). After initially expanding the distinction to five tracks, McDonald collaborated with Louise Diamond to produce a typology consisting of nine tracks of interaction. In Diamond and McDonald's conceptualization of multitrack diplomacy, track one is official government-to-government interaction, whereas tracks two through nine are various unofficial activities that contribute to international peacebuilding and peacemaking (Diamond and McDonald 1991; McDonald 1991). Track two involves non-governmental activities by professionals in conflict resolution, roughly corresponding to ICR. Tracks three through nine involve various unofficial actors' (individuals, groups, organizations) interaction in different sectors of international society such as business, research, training and education, peace and environmental activism, religion, and the media and public opinion. This typology highlights the potential power of unofficial processes for transforming situations of destructive conflict into peaceful and cooperative relations.

ASSESSING THE STATE OF THE FIELD

One review of third-party consultation efforts (Fisher 1983) concluded that the realm of practice demonstrates potential, but the underlying theory is rudimentary and supporting research lacks rigor and sophistication. Unfortunately, not much has changed in ICR since the early 1980s, although some positive developments have occurred.

With respect to theory, most models are inductive descriptions of core components of practice, with some prescriptive guidelines for interventions. The need to move from this normative theory to a scientific or predictive theory still exists (Hill 1982). Most conceptualizations of the method are static pictures of practice, rather than dynamic representations of the links and flow among components and outcomes, although stage models of the process do now exist (e.g., Rothman 1997a; Saunders 1999). Thus, we still lack a comprehensive and systematic theory that captures the static and dynamic complexity of the method and serves as a basis for practice and a guide for research (Fisher 1983).

Each major approach has its strengths and limitations. Burton's innovative thinking was in part based on the experiences of the first workshops and developed alongside his pluralist, systems approach to international relations that called for a paradigm shift in the discipline (Banks 1984; Burton 1968). At the same time, his rules of practice (Burton 1987) can be seen as overly restrictive and lacking adequate explanation (Warfield 1988). Doob's adaptation of group training methods to social intervention in destructive conflicts, while creative, resulted in controversies severe enough to call into question its basic approach (Fisher 1997). Among the pioneers, Kelman's work stands as the most impressive—carefully crafted interventions with a solid conceptual base carried out over the long term with ongoing connections to the complexity of the conflict. Azar's contribution is a succinct statement of the problem-solving method wedded to the characteristics of protracted social conflict. However, in terms of a theory of practice, his model adds little to previous work. In substantive terms, the same can be said of Fisher's model, although it may stand as the most systematic and comprehensive statement of the essence of the method, as articulated by a variety of other contributors. Rothman's ARIA framework captures the flow of conflict analysis and resolution as experienced by the participants in a successfully facilitated intervention. Saunders's approach gains strength because it is consistently sensitive to the processes of policymaking that must be understood and influenced if ICR interventions are to have any utility.

Among the trends in theory development is the growing contribution of scholar-practitioners who are primarily diplomats to descriptions of practice, increasing the richness and validity of ICR theory. In addition to Montville's and McDonald's concepts of track-two and multitrack diplomacy, Saunders's articulation of a public peace process is most useful. A second trend is the continual broadening of the scope of theory. Burton's own view shifted from one primarily directed to the subjective aspects of particular conflicts to one of seeing conflict analysis and resolution as grounded in a concept of basic human needs and as an essential element in decision making at all levels of society.

Mitchell (1993) considers how problem-solving exercises are useful for developing theory about conflict and its resolution, and identifies different types or domains of theory that are necessary to fully understand problem solving and its outcomes. Microlevel theories posit relations among aspects of the practice (e.g., third-party functions) and their impact on individual perceptions, attitudes, expectations, and so on. Macrolevel theories deal with the sources and dynamics of social conflict and are used in workshops to stimulate analysis and help produce useful outputs in terms of proposals. Mesolevel theories involve hypotheses about the design and outcomes of workshops in relation to characteristics of the particular conflict in question. As Mitchell notes, the ultimate goal for the ICR community is to discover how ICR can be adapted to the stages of a conflict and coordinated with other methods of conflict management to be maximally effective in particular situations.

Research remains the weakest link in the theory-research-practice loop (Fisher 1983, 1997). Case-study analysis continues to be the predominant form of documentation, and many projects go unpublished, with only brief, laudatory accounts available. While these descriptions provide a context for understanding specific interventions, they do not yield a rigorous evaluation of workshop processes or outcomes, nor do they provide a base for meta-analyses. Quantitative measures having adequate psychometric properties in before-and-after or control-group designs would enable inferences about immediate effectiveness to be drawn. Longitudinal field research in the wider community is necessary to assess transfer effects to political decision making where appropriate. Recently, Fisher (2005) took a step in this direction by collecting nine cases of ICR interventions from practitioners and researchers and performing a comparative case analysis to assess transfer effects in relation to characteristics of the interventions and qualities of the conflicts being addressed. The analysis indicates that the interventions brought about a variety of useful transfer effects that made contributions to the official peace processes, particularly in the prenegotiation phase. Measuring and tracking process variables in relation to both short- and long-term outcomes would allow for the study of theoretical relationships and the development of more scientific models. Thus, the potential for useful research is extremely high.

Unfortunately, as is the case with any third-party intervention, a number of factors render research evaluations of ICR, especially on transfer effects, highly problematic (Keashly and Fisher 1996). Professional intervenors guarantee anonymity and confidentiality and are therefore opposed to follow-up evaluations that might identify participants and place them at risk. In addition, a concern about interfering with the practice side of the work prevents many third parties from collecting systematic research data, either during or after interventions. For intervenors who want to assess outcomes, a daunting array of methodological and practical constraints present themselves. A simple pre/postevaluation of a workshop is a major research effort in itself, and many practitioners do not have the time or money to complete one. Long-term evaluations of transfer effects would require an even larger-scale effort, involving multiple methods (interviews, observation, content analysis) and would in some cases run into restrictions on access to sensitive information. Finally, even if data on political effects were collected, placing and evaluating the contribution of an ICR intervention within the complexity of multiple factors that affect policymaking would be an immense and uncertain task.

In working to improve the evaluation of ICR, practitioners may first need to improve the state of their practice. In a provocative statement, Rouhana (1995) claims that some programs in the conflict resolution field, including ICR interventions, have vague or unspecified goals, provide a limited description of their activities, or involve questionable activities given their goals. In addition, there is often no rationale provided for how the activities should result in the goals or outcomes that are intended or claimed. These problems are well known in the field of program evaluation and have led to methods to assist practitioners in clearly articulating the goals of their interventions, linking them plausibly and logically to the program activities, and ensuring that the activities have been implemented as intended before trying to assess outcomes. To improve the evaluation of ICR interventions (and thereby confidence in the field), Rouhana (2000) proposes that practitioners need to formulate the linkages between their methods and the objectives of their interventions. For example, if reducing mutual stereotypes is a workshop goal, then activities need to be implemented, such as jointly examining and challenging intergroup attitudes, that would be expected on the basis of theory to change stereotyped images. Rouhana maintains that workshop activities and objectives need to be linked to the larger goals of changing the dynamics of the conflict. Thus, if a practitioner claims that new ideas will be injected into policymaking, the creation of such insights in the workshop must be documented, and the linkages by which these will be communicated need to be identified and assessed through follow-up research. Although such documentation and assessment is rarely if ever done directly, Rouhana conceptualizes a number of plausible effects of longer-term ICR interventions, such as legitimizing problem-solving interactions between adversaries and the accumulation of public opinion supporting negotiation.

Seasoned practitioners of ICR, such as Kelman and Saunders, also take a long-term, complex view of the evaluation question. Kelman (1996) proposes nonintrusive, respectful methods of gathering data, such as written transcripts of sessions and interviews with participants and their peers, as opposed to methods (such as tape recording) that would compromise the process or threaten privacy or confidentiality. Rather than using standard social science research techniques, Kelman recommends accumulating pieces of evidence to demonstrate the feasibility and effectiveness of the method. Some of the links in this theoretical chain include involving participants with the appropriate characteristics (e.g., political influentials), demonstrating appropriate activities (e.g., joint analysis of conflict dynamics), showing intended changes in individuals (e.g., more complex images), documenting their subsequent behavior affecting others (e.g., writings, speeches), tracking effects on policymaking (e.g., pronouncements, legislation), and describing the negotiation of a high-quality, lasting agreement. Saunders (1996) also proposes a careful approach to evaluation that protects the process and the welfare of participants. He suggests that evaluation should document goals as they develop and assess their attainment so that the course of the intervention can be adjusted accordingly. Goal assessment should be in terms of what participants value in relation to achieving a sustainable peace.

The participative approach to evaluation is voiced even more strongly in Rothman's (1997b) action evaluation strategy, in which the role of the evaluator is to gather information from participants and other stakeholders on goals. Differences and similarities are identified, and this information is fed back to stakeholders for comment, so that ongoing refinement of goals can occur. The overall effect is to engage participants and others in documenting, monitoring, and evaluating the intervention, with outcome assessment occurring at the end of the process. Ross and Rothman (1999) discuss the applicability of the action evaluation model in relation to a diversity of intervention cases from the wider domain of conflict resolution.

D'Estree and her colleagues (2001) offer a broad framework for evaluation, based on the premise that different forms of intervention (dialogue, problem solving, reconciliation) have different and equally legitimate intended outcomes. D'Estree and her colleagues posit that it is important to specify the criteria for success and to identify the linkages from micro- to macro-objectives, that is, the transfer effects of the intervention. Their framework includes four sets of changes, ranging from new cognitive representations (e.g., attitude change), to changes in relations (e.g., increased empathy), to foundations for transfer (joint statements), to foundations for outcome (e.g., reforms in political structures). It thus offers a comprehensive schema for conceptualizing the effects of ICR, on the assumption that identified effects can be evaluated. The challenge for the field is to integrate these many good prescriptions for evaluation into ongoing practice.

The actual practice of ICR creates the most satisfaction and optimism. Applications continue to grow in number and variety, addressing an expanding range of complex and intense conflicts. Fisher (1997) reviews more than seventy-five interventions from the previous three decades, most of which claim positive results, while Fisher (2005) provides a comparative case analysis of nine successful interventions from 1965 to 2000. The method has been successfully operationalized in numerous contexts, has generally had positive effects on participants' perceptions and attitudes, and has resulted in concrete forms of interparty cooperation. In addition, a number of politically focused interventions have apparently had useful inputs and effects on the wider interaction that contributed to conflict de-escalation and resolution. At the same time, the number of well-documented cases is relatively small, especially when one considers the seriousness of the problem. One important development is the move to continuing workshops, such as in the work of Kelman and Saunders and their colleagues, which can make a sustained contribution to conflict analysis and management by complementing other methods, such as negotiation or mediation. On the whole, ICR can be seen as a promising social technology to help address protracted social conflicts.

CHALLENGES FOR THE FIELD

To fulfill its rich potential, ICR must overcome a number of challenges (Fisher 1993a, 1997). The degree of applicability of this individually focused, small-group method to the complex, power-driven, and relatively anarchical realm of global politics remains a concern. Although there may be no a priori reasons for dismissing ICR's applicability, there is a need to develop and test theoretically sophisticated models of linkage to political processes. Kelman's ongoing articulation of workshop outcomes in relation to political processes, and his policy analyses based in large part on workshop interaction, are good examples of movement in this direction.

The question of effectiveness needs to be addressed through the increased operationalization of high-quality demonstration research projects that are systematically and rigorously evaluated and do not compromise ethics. However, because some funders and decision makers question applicability, they will not provide the resources and support to assess effectiveness in a more sophisticated manner, thus trapping the method in a perplexing catch-22. In addition, increased applications require skilled professionals with assured support and a secure and flexible institutional base.

Although growing, the pool of available, well-trained talent in ICR is small and needs to be nurtured. Interdisciplinary, doctoral-level training programs for scholar-practitioners, following an apprenticeship model, are required. This training must stress the linkages among theory, research, and practice and must place a high premium on ethical considerations. Although there are a few bright lights, such as George Mason University's ICAR, adequate training is not generally available; thus, the concern remains that well-meaning but naive practitioners are marketing their services to enthusiastic but uninformed, and ultimately disappointed, clients.

The low funding level is a central concern for ICR, especially in comparison with the money available for more traditional methods of studying and improving international security. Even senior practitioners often must scramble from one grant to the next, making it virtually impossible to mount continuous programs for maximal effect. Those new to the field have trouble acquiring enough funding to mount adequately powerful interventions, which predetermines their ineffectiveness. This situation is created in part because of a particular further set of perplexities that trouble funders and applicants (Fisher 1993a). For example, funders appear reluctant to support the large amount of necessary preintervention work, and yet without it, projects may be inappropriate or misguided. Also, funders often want detailed action plans from the intervener or public commitments from the parties, both of which are incompatible with the adaptable and unofficial nature of the enterprise. Therefore, a clear need exists for dialogue between funders and applicants. However, the need for such communication largely goes unaddressed despite some good intentions on both sides.

The final issue is the need for strong institutional bases to support ICR. The pioneers in the field tend to be academics who blend the unpredictable requirements of the work into the constant demands and limited resources of a faculty member's role. Many requests for interventions have been declined because of a lack of funding and an inflexible and unsupportive institutional base. Much of the practice has now shifted to non-governmental organizations in applied conflict resolution, and these are meeting with mixed success in providing institutional bases for long-term programs of intervention. Cooperation between academic and applied organizations is one way to create a stronger footing for the work. A solid institutional foundation for ICR would provide greater flexibility, credibility, and consistency of practice; more resources for research and theorizing; and a stronger base for training. While the disadvantages of institutionalization need to be considered, the ideal base appears to be a university-affiliated, nonprofit, interdisciplinary center for research and practice in which scholar-practitioners at different levels of competence could interact on agendas of professional development.

The challenges facing ICR can be partly addressed through a movement toward professionalization focusing on educational and associational activities; regulatory mechanisms would best be left to a later stage of development. Thus, the continuing development of the Alliance for Peacebuilding (www.allianceforpeacebuilding.org), a network of applied conflict resolution organizations, should be encouraged. Through various kinds of developmental activities, the field should find its useful and legitimate place in the domain of international conflict management and resolution.

The point here is that ICR in some form is essential if the world is to shift from power-coercive and adversarial approaches to ways of dealing with conflict in an effective and multifaceted fashion. The social technology that ICR brings to the field is uniquely designed to enable parties to diagnose their dilemma more fully and jointly, create flexible options for de-escalation and resolution, and to develop mutually collaborative actions that address their basic needs. This technology in some ways parallels approaches being developed to address complex, multiparty policy and environmental disputes, which have been advanced by individuals such as James Laue, Thomas Scott, Lawrence Susskind, and Barbara Gray. The goal is to find mutually beneficial ways to solve problems and collaborate rather than compete and attack. Nothing inherent in the international system should preclude this change as a necessary element in the social evolution of humankind.

REFERENCES

Azar, Edward E. 1983. "The Theory of Protracted Social Conflict and the Challenge of Transforming Conflict Situations." *Monograph Series in World Affairs* 20 (M2): 81–99.

———. 1990. *The Management of Protracted Social Conflict*. Hampshire, UK: Dartmouth.

Banks, Michael, ed. 1984. *Conflict in World Society: A New Perspective on International Relations*. New York: St. Martin's.

Benjamin, A. J., and A. M. Levi. 1979. "Process Minefields in Intergroup Conflict Resolution: The Sdot Yam Workshop." *Journal of Applied Behavioral Science* 15 (4): 507–19.

Berman, Maureen R., and Joseph E. Johnson, eds. 1977. *Unofficial Diplomats*. New York: Columbia University Press.

Blake, Robert R., Herbert A. Shepard, and Jane S. Mouton. 1964. *Managing Intergroup Conflict in Industry*. Houston: Gulf.

Burton, John W. 1968. *Systems, States, Diplomacy, and Rules*. London: Cambridge University Press.

————. 1969. *Conflict and Communication: The Use of Controlled Communication in International Relations*. London: Macmillan.

————. 1985. "The Facilitation of International Conflict Resolution." *Research in Social Movements, Conflicts, and Change* 8: 33–45.

————. 1987. *Resolving Deep-Rooted Conflict: A Handbook*. Lanham, Md.: University Press of America.

————. 1990. *Conflict: Resolution and Provention*. New York: St. Martin's.

————. 1992. "Conflict Prevention as a Political System." Paper presented at George Mason University, Institute for Conflict Analysis and Resolution, June, Fairfax, Va.

Camplisson, Joe, and Michael Hall. 1996. *Hidden Frontiers: Addressing Deep-Rooted Violent Conflict in Northern Ireland and the Republic of Moldova*. Newtownabbey, UK: Island.

Chasin, Richard, and Margaret Herzig. 1988. "Correcting Misperceptions in Soviet-American Relations." *Journal of Humanistic Psychology* 28 (Summer): 88–97.

————. 1993. "Creating Systemic Interventions for the Sociopolitical Arena." In *The Global Family Therapist: Integrating the Personal, Professional, and Political*, ed. B. Berger Gould and D. Hilleboe DeMuth. Boston: Allyn and Bacon.

Chufrin, Gennadi I., and Harold H. Saunders. 1993. "A Public Peace Process." *Negotiation Journal* 9 (2): 155–77.

Cohen, Stephen P., and Edward E. Azar. 1981. "From War to Peace: The Transition between Egypt and Israel." *Journal of Conflict Resolution* 25 (1): 87–114.

Cohen, Stephen P., Herbert C. Kelman, Frederick D. Miller, and Bruce L. Smith. 1977. "Evolving Intergroup Techniques for Conflict Resolution: An Israeli-Palestinian Workshop." *Journal of Social Issues* 33 (Winter): 165–89.

Davies, John, and Edward Kaufman, eds. 2002. *Second Track/Citizens' Diplomacy: Concepts and Techniques for Conflict Transformation*. Lanham, Md.: Rowman and Littlefield.

de Reuck, Anthony V. S. 1974. "Controlled Communication: Rationale and Dynamics." *The Human Context* 6 (Spring): 64–80.

d'Estree, Tamra P., and Eileen F. Babbitt. 1998. "Women and the Art of Peacemaking: Data from Israeli-Palestinian Problem-Solving Workshops." *Political Psychology* 19 (1): 185–209.

d'Estree, Tamra P., Larissa A. Fast, Joshua N. Weiss, and Margaret S. Jacobsen. 2001. "Changing the Debate about 'Success' in Conflict Resolution Efforts." *Negotiation Journal* 17 (1): 101–13.

Diamond, Louise, and Ronald J. Fisher. 1995. "Integrating Conflict Resolution Training and Consultation: A Cyprus Example." *Negotiation Journal* 11 (3): 287–301.

Diamond, Louise, and John McDonald. 1991. *Multi-Track Diplomacy: A Systems Guide and Analysis*. Grinnell: Iowa Peace Institute.

Doob, Leonard W., ed. 1970. *Resolving Conflict in Africa: The Fermeda Workshop*. New Haven, Conn.: Yale University Press.

———. 1974. "A Cyprus Workshop: An Exercise in Intervention Methodology." *Journal of Social Psychology* 94 (December): 161–78.

———. 1975. "Unofficial Intervention in Destructive Social Conflicts." In *Cross-Cultural Perspectives on Learning*, ed. Richard W. Brislin, Stephen Bochner, and Walter J. Lonner. New York: Wiley.

———. 1976. "Evaluating Interventions: An Instance of Academic Anarchy." In *Aboriginal Cognition: Retrospect and Prospect*, ed. G. E. Kearney and D. W. McElwain. Canberra: Australian Institute of Aboriginal Studies.

———. 1981. *The Pursuit of Peace*. Westport, Conn.: Greenwood.

———. 1987. "Adieu to Private Intervention in Political Conflicts?" *International Journal of Group Tensions* 17 (1): 15–27.

———. 1993. *Intervention: Guides and Perils*. New Haven, Conn.: Yale University Press.

Doob, Leonard W., and William J. Foltz. 1973. "The Belfast Workshop: An Application of Group Tensions to a Destructive Conflict." *Journal of Conflict Resolution* 17 (3): 489–512

Fisher, Ronald J. 1972. "Third-Party Consultation: A Method for the Study and Resolution of Conflict." *Journal of Conflict Resolution* 16 (1): 67–94.

———. 1976. "Third-Party Consultation: A Skill for Professional Psychologists in Community Practice." *Professional Psychology* 7 (3): 344–51.

———. 1980. "A Third-Party Consultation Workshop on the India-Pakistan Conflict." *Journal of Social Psychology* 112 (2): 191–206.

———. 1982. *Social Psychology: An Applied Approach*. New York: St. Martin's.

———. 1983. "Third-Party Consultation as a Method of Conflict Resolution: A Review of Studies." *Journal of Conflict Resolution* 27 (2): 301–34.

———. 1989. "Prenegotiation Problem-Solving Discussions: Enhancing the Potential for Successful Negotiations." *International Journal* 64 (Spring): 442–74.

———. 1990. *The Social Psychology of Intergroup and International Conflict Resolution*. New York: Springer-Verlag.

———. 1991. *Conflict Analysis Workshop on Cyprus: Final Workshop Report*. Ottawa: Canadian Institute for International Peace and Security.

———. 1992. *Peacebuilding for Cyprus: Report on a Conflict Analysis Workshop, June 1991*. Ottawa: Canadian Institute for International Peace and Security.

———. 1993a. "Developing the Field of Interactive Conflict Resolution: Issues in Training, Funding, and Institutionalization." *Political Psychology* 14 (1): 123–38.

———. 1993b. "The Potential for Peacebuilding: Forging a Bridge from Peacekeeping to Peacemaking." *Peace and Change* 18 (3): 247–66.

————. 1994. *Education and Peacebuilding in Cyprus: A Report on Two Conflict Analysis Workshops*. Saskatoon: University of Saskatchewan.

————. 1997. *Interactive Conflict Resolution*. Syracuse, N.Y.: Syracuse University Press.

————. 2001. "Cyprus: The Failure of Mediation and the Escalation of an Identity-Based Conflict to an Adversarial Impasse." *Journal of Peace Research* 38 (3): 307–26.

————, ed. 2005. *Paving the Way: Contributions of Interactive Conflict Resolution to Peacemaking*. Lanham, Md.; Lexington Books.

Fisher, Ronald J., and Loraleigh Keashly. 1988. "Third-Party Interventions in Intergroup Conflict: Consultation Is Not Mediation." *Negotiation Journal* 4 (4): 381–93.

————. 1991. "The Potential Complementarity of Mediation and Consultation within a Contingency Model of Third Party Intervention." *Journal of Peace Research* 28 (1): 29–42.

Fisher, Ronald J., and James H. White. 1976a. "Reducing Tensions between Neighborhood Housing Groups: A Pilot Study in Third-Party Consultation." *International Journal of Group Tensions* 6 (1–2): 41–52.

————. 1976b. "Intergroup Conflicts Resolved by Outside Consultants." *Journal of the Community Development Society* 7 (Spring): 88–98.

Fitzgerald, Keith. 1998. "Georgian-Ossetian Joint Brainstorming." In *Private Peacemaking*. Peaceworks no. 20, ed. David Smock. Washington, D.C.: United States Institute of Peace Press.

Foltz, William J. 1977. "Two Forms of Unofficial Conflict Intervention: The Problem-Solving and Process-Promoting Workshops." In *Unofficial Diplomats*, ed. Maureen R. Berman and Joseph E. Johnson. New York: Columbia University Press.

Groom, A. J. R. 1986. "Problem Solving in International Relations." In *International Conflict Resolution: Theory and Practice*, ed. Edward E. Azar and John W. Burton. Brighton, Sussex, UK: Wheatsheaf.

Gurr, Ted R. 1993. *Minorities at Risk: A Global View of Ethnopolitical Conflicts*. Washington, D.C.: United States Institute of Peace Press.

Hare, A. Paul, Frank Carney, and Fred Osview. 1977. "Youth Responds to Crisis: Curaçao." In *Liberation without Violence*, ed. A. Paul Hare and Herbert H. Blumberg. London: Rex Collings.

Hicks, Donna, Hugh O'Doherty, Pamela Pomerance Steiner, Winifred Taylor, Maria Hadjipavlou-Trigerorgis, and William Weisberg. 1995. "Addressing Intergroup Conflict by Integrating and Realigning Identity: An Arab-Israeli Workshop." In *Group Process and Political Dynamics*, ed. Mark F. Ettin, Jay W. Fidler, and Bertram D. Cohen. Madison, Conn.: International Universities Press.

Hill, Barbara J. 1982. "An Analysis of Conflict Resolution Techniques: From Problem-Solving Workshops to Theory." *Journal of Conflict Resolution* 26: 109–38.

Julius, Demetrios A. 1991. "The Practice of Track Two Diplomacy in the Arab-Israeli Conferences." In *Unofficial Diplomacy at Work*, vol. 2 of *The Psychodynamics of*

International Relationships, ed. Vamik D. Volkan, Joseph V. Montville, and Demetrios A. Julius. Lexington, Mass.: Lexington Books.

Keashly, Loraleigh, Ronald J. Fisher, and Peter R. Grant. 1993. "The Comparative Utility of Third Party Consultation and Mediation within a Complex Simulation of Intergroup Conflict." *Human Relations* 46 (3): 371–93.

Keashly, Loraleigh, and Ronald J. Fisher. 1996. "A Contingency Perspective on Conflict Interventions: Theoretical and Practical Considerations." In *Resolving International Conflicts: The Theory and Practice of Mediation*, ed. Jacob Bercovitch. Boulder, Colo.: Lynne Rienner.

Kelman, Herbert C. 1972. "The Problem-Solving Workshop in Conflict Resolution." In *Communication in International Politics*, ed. Richard L. Merritt. Urbana: University of Illinois Press.

———. 1978. "Israelis and Palestinians: Psychological Prerequisites for Mutual Acceptance." *International Security* 3 (Summer): 162–86.

———. 1979. "An Interactional Approach to Conflict Resolution and Its Applications to Israeli-Palestinian Relations." *International Interactions* 6 (2): 99–122.

———. 1982. "Creating the Conditions for Israeli-Palestinian Negotiations." *Journal of Conflict Resolution* 26 (1): 39–75.

———. 1986. "Interactive Problem Solving: A Social-Psychological Approach to Conflict Resolution." In *Dialogue toward Interfaith Understanding*, ed. William Klassen. Jerusalem: Ecumenical Institute for Theological Research.

———. 1987. "The Political Psychology of the Israeli-Palestinian Conflict: How Can We Overcome the Barriers to a Negotiated Solution?" *Political Psychology* 8 (3): 347–63.

———. 1991. "Interactive Problem Solving: The Uses and Limits of a Therapeutic Model for the Resolution of International Conflicts." In *Unofficial Diplomacy at Work*, vol. 2 of *The Psychodynamics of International Relationships*, ed. Vamik D. Volkan, Joseph V. Montville, and Demetrios A. Julius. Lexington, Mass.: Lexington Books.

———. 1992. "Informal Mediation by the Scholar-Practitioner." In *Mediation in International Relations: Multiple Approaches to Conflict Management*, ed. Jacob Bercovitch and Jeffrey Z. Rubin. New York: St. Martin's.

———. 1993a. "Coalitions across Conflict Lines: The Interplay of Conflicts within and between the Israeli and Palestinian Communities." In *Conflict between People and Peoples*, ed. Jeffry Simpson and Stephen Worchel. Chicago: Nelson-Hall.

———. 1993b. "Social-Psychological Approaches to Peacemaking in the Middle East." Address to the Third Symposium on the Contributions of Psychology to Peace, Randolph-Macon College, August 16, Ashland, Va.

———. 1995. "Contributions of an Unofficial Conflict Resolution Effort to the Israeli-Palestinian Breakthrough." *Negotiation Journal* 11 (1): 19–27.

———. 1996. "An Approach to Evaluation of NGO Contributions to the Resolution of Ethnonational Conflicts." Paper presented at the Carnegie Corporation Conference on the Role of International NGOs in Ethnic and National Conflicts, November 15–16, New York.

Kelman, Herbert C., and Stephen P. Cohen. 1976. "The Problem-Solving Workshop: A Social-Psychological Contribution to the Resolution of International Conflict." *Journal of Peace Research* 13 (2): 79–90.

————. 1979. "Reduction of International Conflict: An Interactional Approach." In *The Social Psychology of Intergroup Relations*, ed. William G. Austin and Stephen Worchel. Monterey, Calif.: Brooks/Cole.

————. 1986. "Resolution of International Conflict: An Interactional Approach." In *The Social Psychology of Intergroup Relations*, 2d ed., ed. Stephen Worchel and William G. Austin. Chicago: Nelson-Hall.

Kelman, Herbert C., and Ronald J. Fisher. 2003. "Conflict Analysis and Resolution." In *Handbook of Political Psychology*, ed. Donald O. Sears, Leonie Huddy, and Robert R. Jervis. New York: Blackwell.

LaFreniere, Francois, and Robert Mitchell. 1990. *Cyprus: Visions for the Future*. Working Paper no. 21. Ottawa: Canadian Institute for International Peace and Security.

Lakin, Martin, Jack Lomranz, and Morton A. Lieberman. 1969. *Arab and Jew in Israel: A Case Study in a Human Relations Approach to Conflict*. Washington, D.C.: NTL Institute.

Levi, A. M., and A. Benjamin. 1976. "Jews and Arabs Rehearse Geneva: A Model of Conflict Resolution." *Human Relations* 29 (11): 1035–44.

Lieberfeld, Daniel. 2002. "Evaluating the Contributions of Track-Two Diplomacy to Conflict Termination in South Africa." *Journal of Peace Research* 39 (3): 357–74.

Little, Walter, and Christopher R. Mitchell. 1989. "The Maryland Workshops." In *In the Aftermath: Anglo-Argentine Relations since the War for the Falklands/Malvinas Islands*, ed. Walter Little and Christopher R. Mitchell. College Park: Center for International Development and Conflict Management, University of Maryland.

Maclean's. 1991. "The People's Verdict: How Canadians Can Agree on Their Future." July 1, 10–76.

————. 1992. "An Action Plan for Canada." January 6, 8–45.

McDonald, John W. 1991. "Further Exploration of Track Two Diplomacy." In *Timing the De-escalation of International Conflict*, ed. Louis Kriesberg. Syracuse, N.Y.: Syracuse University Press.

McDonald, John W., and Diane B. Bendahmane, eds. 1987. *Conflict Resolution: Track Two Diplomacy*. Washington, D.C.: Foreign Service Institute.

Mitchell, Christopher R. 1966. *Cyprus Report*. London: Centre for the Analysis of Conflict.

————. 1973. "Conflict Resolution and Controlled Communication: Some Further Comments." *Journal of Peace Research* 10 (1–2): 123–32.

————. 1981. *Peacemaking and the Consultant's Role*. Westmead, UK: Gower.

————. 1993. "Problem-Solving Exercises and Theories of Conflict Resolution." In *Conflict Resolution Theory and Practice: Integration and Application*, ed. Dennis J. D. Sandole and Hugo van der Merwe. Manchester, UK: Manchester University Press.

————. 2001. "From Controlled Communication to Problem Solving: The Origins of Facilitated Conflict Resolution." *International Journal of Peace Studies* 6 (1): 59–67.

Mitchell, Christopher, and Michael Banks. 1996. *Handbook of Conflict Resolution: The Analytical Problem-Solving Approach*. New York/London: Pinter.

Montville, Joseph V. 1987. "The Arrow and the Olive Branch: The Case for Track Two Diplomacy." In *Conflict Resolution: Track Two Diplomacy*, ed. John W. McDonald and Diane B. Bendahmane. Washington, D.C.: Foreign Service Institute.

————. 1993. "The Healing Function in Political Conflict Resolution." In *Conflict Resolution Theory and Practice: Integration and Application*, ed. Dennis J. D. Sandole and Hugo van der Merwe. Manchester, UK: Manchester University Press.

Nan, Susan Allen. 2002. "Unofficial Conflict Resolution as a Complement to Diplomacy: A Case Study of the Georgian-South Ossetian Peace Process Highlighting 'Track One and a Half Diplomacy.'" Paper presented at the annual convention of the International Studies Association, March 24–27, New Orleans.

Pearson, Frederic S. 2001. "Dimensions of Conflict Resolution in Ethnopolitical Disputes." *Journal of Peace Research* 38 (3): 275–87.

Ross, Marc H. 1993. *The Management of Conflict: Interpretations and Interests in Comparative Perspectives*. New Haven, Conn.: Yale University Press.

Ross, Marc H., and Jay Rothman, eds. 1999. *Theory and Practice in Ethnic Conflict Management: Theorizing Success and Failure*. London: Macmillan.

Rothman, Jay. 1991. "Negotiation as Consolidation: Prenegotiation in the Israeli-Palestinian Conflict." *The Jerusalem Journal of International Relations* 13 (1): 22–44.

————. 1992. *From Confrontation to Cooperation: Resolving Ethnic and Regional Conflict*. Newbury Park, Calif.: Sage.

————. 1993. "Defining and Evaluating Success and Failure in an Action-Research Conflict-Resolution Project with Israelis and Palestinians." Paper presented at the Annual Scientific Meeting of the International Society of Political Psychology, July 4–8, Cambridge, Mass.

————. 1997a. *Resolving Identity-Based Conflict in Nations, Organizations, and Communities*. San Francisco: Jossey-Bass.

————. 1997b. "Action Evaluation and Conflict Resolution Training: Theory, Method and Case Study." *International Negotiation* 3 (3): 451–70.

Rouhana, Nadim N. 1995. "Unofficial Third Party Intervention in International Conflict: Between Legitimacy and Disarray." *Negotiation Journal* 11 (3): 255–70.

————. 2000. "Interactive Conflict Resolution: Issues in Theory, Methodology, and Evaluation." In *International Conflict Resolution after the Cold War*, ed. Paul C. Stern and Daniel Druckman. Washington, D.C.: National Academies.

Rouhana, Nadim N., and Herbert C. Kelman. 1994. "Promoting Joint Thinking in International Conflict: An Israeli-Palestinian Continuing Workshop." *Journal of Social Issues* 50 (Spring): 157–78.

Salem, Norma, ed. 1992. *Cyprus: A Regional Conflict and Its Resolution*. London: Macmillan.

Saunders, Harold H. 1991. "Officials and Citizens in International Relationships: The Dartmouth Conference." In *Unofficial Diplomacy at Work*, vol. 2 of *The Psychodynamics of International Relationships*, ed. Vamik D. Volkan, Joseph V. Montville, and Demetrios A. Julius. Lexington, Mass.: Lexington Books.

———. 1992. "Thinking in Stages: A Framework for Public Intercommunal Problem-Solving from Experience in the Dartmouth Conference Regional Conflicts Task Force, 1982–92. Paper presented at the Annual Scientific Meeting of the International Society of Political Psychology, San Francisco, July.

———. 1996. "The Case of the Inter-Tajikistani Dialogue: A Process for Evaluating Sustained Dialogue." Paper presented at the Carnegie Corporation Conference on the Role of International NGOs in Ethnic and National Conflicts, New York, November.

———. 1999. *A Public Peace Process: Sustained Dialogue to Transform Racial and Ethnic Conflicts*. New York: St. Martin's.

———. 2002. "Sustained Dialogue in Tajikistan." Paper presented at the Annual Convention of the International Studies Association, March 24–27, New Orleans.

Schwartz, Richard D. 1989. "Arab-Jewish Dialogue in the United States: Toward Track II Tractability." In *Intractable Conflicts and Their Transformation*, ed. Louis Kriesberg, Terrell A. Northrup, and Stuart J. Thorson. Syracuse, N.Y.: Syracuse University Press.

Shaffer, John B. P., and M. David Galinsky. 1974. *Models of Group Therapy and Sensitivity Training*. Englewood Cliffs, N.J.: Prentice-Hall.

Slim, Randa M., and Harold H. Saunders. 1996. "Managing Conflict in Divided Societies: Lessons from Tajikistan." *Negotiation Journal* 12 (1): 31–46.

Steele, David. 2002. "Contributions of Interfaith Dialogue to Peacebuilding in the Former Yugoslavia." In *Interfaith Dialogue and Peacebuilding*, ed. David R. Smock. Washington, D.C.: United States Institute of Peace Press.

Stewart, Philip D. 1987. "The Dartmouth Conference: U.S.-USSR Relations." In *Conflict Resolution: Track Two Diplomacy*, ed. John W. McDonald and Diane B. Bendahmane. Washington, D.C.: Foreign Service Institute.

Volkan, Vamik D. 1991. "Psychological Processes in Unofficial Diplomacy Meetings." In *The Psychodynamics of International Relationships*. Vol. 2, *Unofficial Diplomacy at Work*, ed. Vamik D. Volkan, Joseph V. Montville, and Demitrios A. Julius. Lexington, Mass.: Lexington Books.

———. 1995. "Developing Institutions to Reconcile Groups in Conflict in Estonia." Paper presented at the Annual Scientific Meeting of the International Society of Political Psychology, Washington, D.C., July.

———. 1998. "The Tree Model: Psychopolitical Dialogues and Promotion of Coexistence." In *Handbook of Interethnic Coexistence*, ed. Eugene Weiner. New York: Abraham Fund.

Volkan, Vamik D., and Max Harris. 1992. "Negotiating a Peaceful Separation: A Psychopolitical Analysis of Current Relationships between Russia and the Baltic Republics." *Mind and Human Interaction* 4 (1): 20–39.

———. 1993. "Vaccinating the Political Process: A Second Psychopolitical Analysis of Relationships between Russia and the Baltic States." *Mind and Human Interaction* 4 (4): 169–90.

Wallensteen, Peter. 1991. "Report from the Workshop Chairman." Cambodian Workshop on Reconstruction and Development, Penang, Malaysia, August 18–25, Penang, Malaysia.

Walton, Richard E. 1969. *Interpersonal Peacemaking: Confrontations and Third-Party Consultation.* Reading, Mass.: Addison-Wesley.

Warfield, John N. 1988. "Do as I Say: A Review Essay of John W. Burton's Resolving Deep-Rooted Conflict: A Handbook." *International Journal of Group Tensions* 18 (3): 228–36.

Wedge, Bryant, and Dennis Sandole. 1982. "Conflict Management: A New Venture into Professionalization." *Peace and Change* 8 (Summer): 129–38.

Willard, Andrew R., and Charles H. Norchi. 1993. "The Decision Seminar as an Instrument of Power and Enlightenment." *Political Psychology* 14 (4): 575–606.

Williams, Andrew. 1999. "Conflict Resolution after the Cold War: The Case of Moldova." *Review of International Studies* 25 (1): 71–86.

Yalem, Ronald J. 1971. "Controlled Communication and Conflict Resolution." *Journal of Peace Research* 8 (3): 263–72.

7

RELIGION AND PEACEBUILDING

Cynthia Sampson

Religion and spirituality offer vital, dynamic, and creative resources for peace-building. Religious communities made significant contributions to conflict transformation in the past century and are mobilizing even more effectively in the new millennium. From the anticolonial nonviolence movements of Mahatma Gandhi and Abdul Ghaffar Khan on the subcontinent in the 1920s to 1940s, to the proliferation of denominational and interreligious efforts today, religiously based peacebuilding is an increasingly important, though often untold, story behind headlines heralding political diplomatic peace initiatives.

Religious involvement in the work of peace, which in the past occurred sporadically, episodically, and sometimes seemingly by happenstance, is giving way to commitments by many religious communities and multireligious bodies to institutionalize their efforts and prepare themselves for more proactive peace-building roles. Growing numbers of religious actors of many sorts—laypersons, individual religious leaders, denominational structures, ad hoc commissions and delegations, and interdenominational and multireligious bodies—have been involved in a range of peacebuilding efforts during the past several decades. Still, the recent record but hints at the great potential inherent in a more systematic and coordinated mobilization of the spiritual and sociological resources of religion for conflict transformation and peacebuilding.

Today, religious practitioners are found at every level of the peacebuilding process, from top-level peace negotiations to grassroots-level initiatives in conciliation, mediation, trauma healing, reconciliation, and reconstruction. Their conflict transformation activities include education for peace, reconciliation,

and democracy; advocacy for nonviolent sociopolitical change; conflict resolution processes such as conciliation, facilitation, and mediation; election
monitoring; and post-conflict trauma healing and reconciliation, to name but
some of the major categories. In addition, many of the relief and development
non-governmental organizations (NGOs) operating in conflict zones, her-
alded as the "new conflict managers" (a major theme of the 1994 Managing
Chaos conference, sponsored by the United States Institute of Peace), operate
from a religious affiliation and resource base. A noteworthy new trend in interreligious conflict transformation is the introduction of religious meanings
as the medium and not just the motivation for peacebuilding practice, with
prayer, meditation, and religious discourse and rituals increasingly finding a
place at the dialogue—and sometimes the bargaining—table or being advocated as integral to transforming conflict systems, particularly those in which
religious dynamics are at play.

This chapter differs from others in this volume in that its focus is not on one
particular approach to conflict intervention, but rather on a particular category of actor. It provides an overview of a diverse array of peacebuilding roles
performed by a wide variety of actors, with a religious impetus serving as the
common thread. In describing and situating this multiplicity of roles and actors, the chapter also makes use of a broader conceptual framework than that of
conflict resolution and peacemaking. The proper framework for understanding the motivations, activities, and potentials of religious actors is that of
conflict transformation and peacebuilding.

WHY RELIGION, AND WHY NOW?

What accounts for the high salience of religion and religiously motivated ap-
proaches in contemporary conflicts? To begin with, religion is often an im-
portant defining characteristic of communities in conflict, whether they be
Catholics, Orthodox, and Muslims in Bosnia; Buddhists and Hindus in Sri
Lanka; Christians and Muslims in Nigeria; or Catholics and Protestants in
Northern Ireland.

Although religion may at times be directly implicated in justifying and fuel-
ing intergroup violence, what appear to be "religious conflicts" often have more
to do initially with how a people and a culture define themselves than with religious doctrine. Even in cases where the roots of the conflict may be economic
or political, "the revolt against the status quo may express itself in religious
terms or appeal to religious sensibilities" (Appleby 2000, 169). Some analysts
are increasingly placing responsibility for politicizing and igniting intergroup
tensions on leaders seeking personal political gain. "War is often used as an

instrument of politics in the hands of willful leaders," asserts the Carnegie Commission on Preventing Deadly Violence, which takes the "strong view . . . that the words 'ethnic,' 'religious,' 'tribal,' or 'factional'—important as they may be in intergroup conflict—do not, in most cases, adequately explain why people use massive violence to achieve their goals" (Carnegie Commission 1997, 29). Nonetheless, once religious passions are aroused and politicized, they tend to be fiercely prosecuted.

The politicization of religion in conflicts is often facilitated by contradictions found in sacred texts and other doctrinal sources of religions as they relate to war and peace (Vendley and Little 1994; Gopin 1997, 2000a; Appleby 2000; Johnston 2003). Most religions, for example, have two distinctly contrasting cultures: the "holy war" and the "peaceable kingdom" (Boulding 1986). Ambiguities in religious teachings have found parallels in the social behavior of believers. Thus, despite clear religious mandates for peacemaking in a given tradition, the record of action is likely to be mixed. Until recently, religiously motivated peacemaking efforts had their greatest impact in conflicts in which religion was not an important defining characteristic.[1]

Many religions possess social and moral characteristics that give them the potential to act as constructive forces for peace and conflict transformation. Dispersed throughout societies, religious communities are often organized at the national and international levels, representing significant channels for communication and action. Religious traditions establish ethical visions that can summon those who believe in them to powerful forms of committed action. Many religions provide moral warrants for resistance against unjust conditions, including those that give rise to conflict, and thus provide an impetus for adherents to take responsibility for preventing, ameliorating, or resolving conflicts nonviolently (World Conference on Religion and Peace n.d.).

Not only are religious communities located in and on all sides of contemporary conflicts, but

> the primary arena of church activity and faith—that of the spiritual, emotional, and relational well-being of people—lies at the heart of contemporary conflict. . . . [W]here neighbor fears neighbor and blood is shed by each, the emotive, perceptual, social-psychological, and spiritual dimensions are core, not peripheral, concerns. (Lederach 1993, 11–12)

Indeed,

> [r]eligions are capable of providing a cultural foundation for peace in their respective societies. Drawing on their intimate knowledge of the myths, beliefs, and deepest feelings of people shaped by religious cultures—including people who may no longer practice the religion in question—religious leaders are poised

to promote peace-related values, including friendship, compassion, humility, service, respect for strangers, repentance, forgiveness, and the acceptance of responsibility for past errors. (Appleby 2000, 169)

Although conflict management techniques designed to end hostilities and separate the parties might be adequate in conflicts between states, in internal conflicts, where antagonists living in close proximity serve as constant reminders of the bitter fighting and atrocities that have occurred, it is necessary to move beyond conflict management to reconciliation and healing in order to arrest the recurring cycles of violence and revenge and restore the torn fabric of human relationships and community. Until recently, these processes have tended to fall outside the purview of traditional diplomacy and have tended to be viewed as soft or naive by the secular social science field of conflict resolution (Assefa 1993b).

On the other hand, conflict resolution is natural terrain for religious peacebuilders; the processes associated with reconciliation—confession, repentance, forgiveness, mercy, compassion, and conversion based on self-reflection and acceptance of personal responsibility—have emerged from religious, not secular, contexts. Many religiously motivated peacemakers have a natural predisposition to working on reconciliation—the restoration of relationships—as well as personal and social transformation. Moreover, it is easier for religious figures to talk about repentance and forgiveness—and they are more likely to be viewed as the legitimate actors to do so—than many secular leaders, for whom such talk does not come naturally or whose motives might be questioned (Sampson 1987; Nhat Hanh 1987b; Kraybill 1988; Hamlin 1991; Assefa 1993a, 1993b, 1994, 1999, 2004; Sivaraksa n.d.; Henderson 1996, 1999; Gopin 2001; Henderson 1996, 1999; Lederach 1997, 1999; Appleby 2000; Hart 2000; Johnston 2003).

A religious actor that is perceived as impartial and apolitical may qualify as an honest broker and mediator in a peace process. Religious groups, active in most settings through works of charity and social relief, often lend legitimacy to negotiations. Religious communities are both on the ground in conflict situations and part of an extensive and constantly growing transnational network (Carnegie Commission 1997, 114–18). In societies in which the government is widely viewed as illegitimate or centralized authority has broken down altogether, organized religion may be the only institution retaining some measure of credibility, trust, and moral authority among the population at large. Perhaps most significant, because they are long-term players who come from and work with the people and groups in the conflict throughout its life cycle, religious actors can work effectively in the peacebuilding process.

CONCEPTUAL FRAMEWORK

Building peace in a fractured world at the start of the twenty-first century involves a broad range of functions and tasks designed to transform social conflict and construct the conditions and infrastructure necessary to support a dynamic, sustainable peace. Although most early pioneers in religious peacebuilding were not formally schooled in the concepts and theories of conflict resolution, two particularly active religious practitioners contributed significantly to the development of theory. These contributions provide a framework for understanding the broader body of work in the religious sector, particularly as it relates to the relationship and interplay of two distinct but interdependent conflict intervention roles: advocate and intermediary.

In an early conceptual work, Quaker conciliator Adam Curle identified "peacemaking approaches appropriate for different sorts or stages of conflict" (1971, 186). A key variable in determining the approach, according to Curle, is the distribution of power between adversaries. In a situation of balance, where the conflict parties are roughly equal in terms of resources and capabilities, conciliation and negotiation may be applied to end a conflict and reach a settlement. In a situation of imbalance, education is needed to increase awareness of the structural inequities. With greater awareness, confrontation can be employed as necessary to reduce the imbalance and enable the weaker party(ies) to negotiate on the basis of greater equality. Curle saw this restructuring of the relationship as essential to achieving the ultimate goal of stable, peaceful relations.

Mennonite peacebuilder John Paul Lederach builds on Curle's work in describing conflict as a progression and elaborating the roles that emerge in the transformation of conflict from violent and destructive to constructive and peaceful manifestations (see figure 7.1). Lederach notes that, according to this framework, "education, advocacy, and mediation share the goal of change and restructuring unpeaceful relationships. . . . They share the vision of justice, of substantive and procedural change. . . ." The roles do differ, however. "Advocacy, for example, chooses to stand by one side for justice's sake. Mediation chooses to stand in connection to all sides for justice's sake" (1995, 14–15). Yet Lederach sees these roles as mutually supportive and dependent:

> Negotiation becomes possible when the needs and interests of all those involved and affected by the conflict are legitimated and articulated. This process happens most often through confrontation and advocacy. . . . On the other hand, restructuring the relationship toward increased equality and justice does not emanate automatically from confrontation. . . . Mediation can and should facilitate the articulation of legitimate needs and interests of all concerned into fair, practical, and mutually acceptable solutions.

. . . [T]he former [advocacy] is experienced as increasing conflict and the latter [mediation] as reducing conflict, creating the impression of incompatibility. This framework, however, suggests the inverse: that the longer-term progression of conflict toward justice and peaceful relations must integrate and view these activities as necessary and mutually interdependent in the pursuit of just change and peaceful transformation. (14–15)

The interplay of these two roles in the experience of several religious actors in conflict situations seems to defy the conventional wisdom that advocacy and intermediary roles are mutually exclusive and therefore cannot be performed by the same individual, or at least not concurrently. In South Africa and the former East Germany (both discussed below), church leaders moved in and out of advocacy and mediation roles, the latter taking the form of an insider/partial third party (Wehr and Lederach 1991, 90–91). The mediators were clearly aligned with groups that were challenging repressive regimes, but their position of trust and connectedness with the opposition made it possible for them to serve as third parties in those contexts.

Several key points should be emphasized with regard to advocacy in the religious sector. The first is that the type of advocacy prescribed by Curle and Lederach, both members of historic peace churches, is nonviolent activism. Moreover, advocacy by religious actors tends to be oriented more toward defending human rights and empowering disenfranchised parties than toward taking sides in the conflict, even though such advocacy may end up favoring one side. In fact, several types of roles discussed below—truth-teller, observer, and educator—although conceived as neutral by the religious actor, may be perceived as partisan by the dominant power in the conflict whose actions are being spotlighted.

In addition to a predisposition toward empowering weak parties to restructure the conflictual relationship, as noted earlier, many religiously motivated peacemakers naturally gravitate toward the work of reconciliation. Here again the focus is on a relationship—the restoration of relationship and community severed by war and dislocation. These two aspects of conflict transformation seek to restore or build conditions that can help achieve and sustain peace. They are, in short, peacebuilding dimensions, and they are appropriate at every stage of conflict transformation, not only in the period following a peace accord. Thus, "peacebuilding," as used in this chapter, spans the entire continuum of activity in and is virtually synonymous with conflict transformation. Throughout the various stages of the conflict progression (latent, confrontation, negotiation, and post-conflict), conflict transformation or peacebuilding may involve education, advocacy, conflict resolution, reconciliation, rehabilitation, reconstruction, and socioeconomic development.

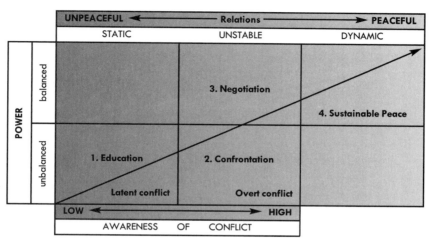

Figure from Lederach (1995). ©1995 by Syracuse University Press. Reprinted with permission.

Figure 7.1. The Progression of Conflict. Appropriate roles for advocates and intermediaries in a conflict transformation process can be seen in the graphic representation of a conflict progression above. Advocates have a role to play at a conflict's earliest stages (lower left) in educating the less powerful about the prospects of changing the static conflict system's power imbalance. Advocates are also active during the phase when the weaker party confronts the more powerful party (lower middle) to have its grievances acknowledged and to gain more power. Once the distribution of power becomes more balanced and parties can negotiage on a roughly equal basis (upper middle), mediation can be employed to assist the parties in finding ways of ending hostilities and redressing grievances. Peace becomes sustainable if the settlement succeeds in maintaining the parties in a dynamic, balanced relationship (upper right).

Religion is a pervasive social institution. As such, religious actors potentially can be—and in many cases already are—active in the full range of peacebuilding activities within a process of conflict transformation, operating at different levels of society and from different levels of organization within the religious community. Several actor typologies are used in this chapter:

- type of religious affiliation (single denomination or religion, interdenominational body within a religious tradition, multireligious body, or spiritually motivated nondenominational organization);

- organizational structure of the religious actor (individual layperson or cleric; religious institution, body, or ad hoc grouping); and

- organizational level (local, subnational, national, regional, or international).

As an overarching organizing framework, the case examples are grouped according to four broad categories of conflict intervention roles: advocate, intermediary, observer, and educator. Religiously motivated advocates are primarily concerned with empowering the weaker party(ies) in a conflict situation, restructuring relationships, and transforming unjust social structures. Intermediaries devote themselves to the task of peacemaking, focusing their efforts on bringing the parties together to resolve their differences and reach a settlement. Observers offer themselves as a physical and moral presence in a conflict setting, in hopes of preventing violence and transforming the conflict dynamics. Educators lay the groundwork for conflict transformation by conveying to others—whether in the classroom, the training seminar, or experientially—the knowledge and skills of conflict transformation and peacebuilding. In practice, the roles most associated with—but not restricted to—the different stages of conflict are advocate during the confrontation stage; intermediary during the negotiation stage; observer during the confrontation, negotiation, and post-conflict stages; and educator during the entire conflict progression, including the latent stage—before a conflict has come to full awareness and become manifest in society.

In this chapter, each of the four roles is illustrated with a number of site-specific examples of conflict interventions by religiously motivated actors. A detailed sketch of South Africa is presented as a case of significant social and political transformation to illustrate the multiplicity of religious actors that may be involved in a conflict's progression over time. Finally, the chapter takes a more generic look at the body of work of certain institutional actors—religious communities or spiritually motivated groups that have worked over a sustained period across role categories. These actors include the Roman Catholic Church, the Society of Friends (Quakers), the Mennonites, Initiatives of Change (formerly Moral Re-Armament), and the engaged Buddhists. The chapter concludes with a look at the emerging trends in and future directions of the religious sector. This chapter should be viewed not as an exhaustive survey but, rather, as suggestive of a larger body of experience yet to be acknowledged, documented, and better understood through more systematic research and analysis.

ROLES PLAYED BY RELIGIOUS ACTORS

Advocates

Moving beyond Curle's (1971) typology, Laue and Cormick (1978) identified two partisan conflict-intervention roles: the activist, who is closely aligned with the powerless or nonestablishment party, and the advocate, who supports the goals of one conflict party but is not directly affiliated with that party and therefore can promote its cause to opponents and to the wider community. The dichotomy is useful for distinguishing the functions of internal and external religious actors in several cases in which the conflict is national in scope and involves massive social change. Internal religious actors, particularly those representing institutional religion, are integral to the society and may play critical activist roles as catalysts for change. External religious actors, as in the cases of South Africa and Rhodesia/Zimbabwe, play the role of advocate in promoting the cause of the proponents of change beyond national borders, serving to help internationalize the conflict and bring to bear on the ruling regime the pressures of world opinion and of powerful state and multilateral actors. However, given that both the internal activist and the external advocate are essentially partisan roles, they are treated together in this chapter under the common heading of "advocate."

A further subset within the advocate role is that of "truth-teller" (Kraybill 1994), which involves raising a voice of moral outrage against what are seen as systemic injustices or wrongful acts committed by a party to the conflict. Truth-telling is not intended to be an act of taking sides in the conflict, although it is likely to be perceived as such by the party whose actions are being exposed. In any case, it is distinctly an act of moral advocacy on the part of the religious actor.

When a moral message serves to mobilize mass action, or when the moral messenger backs its words with effective leadership of its own, the religious actor can become a significant catalyst for change. In most of the examples that follow, institutional religion functions in this way—for example, the church (or churches) in predominantly Christian societies or the *sangha* (the religious order of monks) in predominantly Buddhist societies. The institutional religion represents a substantial portion of the population and possesses moral legitimacy as well as temporal power, or at least the capacity to reach and mobilize adherents and others throughout the society.

Antecedents: Gandhi and the "Frontier Gandhi." The grandfather of nonviolence movements and the inspiration for many that have followed, Mahatma Gandhi is seen as the father of independent India. Less well-known, though with an equally compelling story, is Abdul Ghaffar Khan, Gandhi's Muslim counterpart in the Northwest Frontier Province of colonial India.

Gandhi (1983) developed his spiritual and ethical philosophy and action technique known as satyagraha, or "truth force," in fighting oppression while working as a barrister in apartheid South Africa. Although satyagraha did not spring whole cloth from Gandhi's native Hindu tradition—and has been practiced by believers of diverse faiths and nonbelievers alike—it has deep roots in Hinduism. Gandhi believed that the only means of knowing God—truth—was nonviolence rooted in *ahimsa*, an ancient Hindu, Jain, and Buddhist ethical precept meaning refusal to do harm, which Gandhi refined to mean a positive state of love, of doing good even to the evil-doer. The test of love and the essence of nonviolence in satyagraha is *tapasya*, or self-sacrifice, which is directed toward the moral persuasion of the one because of whom it is undertaken. Far from cowardice or a weapon of the weak, self-sacrifice is seen as resulting in the least loss of life over the long run and ennobles those who do lose their lives (Bondurant 1988).

Gandhi's objectives in the anticolonial struggle were *swaraj*, which included political independence and individual self-rule (Gandhi 1997), and *sarvodaya* (literally, "uplift of all"), which described the ideal society. The goal of satyagraha was to win a victory over the conflict situation, to discover further truths, and to persuade the opponent not to triumph (Bondurant 1988).

There were hundreds of satyagraha movements in the struggle leading to Indian independence in 1947. Among the major cases and those most representative of satyagraha principles were:

- the twenty-five-day Ahmedabad Labor satyagraha, a 1918 campaign in which five thousand to ten thousand textile workers participated in a strike, demonstrations, and a fast in the successful attempt to increase textile workers' rate of pay (Bondurant 1988, 65–73);

- a seven-week, nationwide campaign in 1919 against the Rowlatt bills, drafted to strengthen the government's control of crime and sedition, in which millions of Indians—Hindus and Muslims, men, women, and children—participated in shop closings, demonstrations, and the contravention of laws to achieve withdrawal of the bills and mobilize popular support for the nationalist struggle (Bondurant 1988, 73–88);

- the sixteen-month Vykom Temple Road satyagraha of 1924–25 in the state of Travancore, in which hundreds of Hindus succeeded in removing the prohibition against use by untouchables of roadways passing this and other temples in India, a campaign that also proved to be a major turning point in the fight against untouchability (Bondurant 1988, 46–50);

- the six-month Bardoli peasants' campaign in 1928, in which Hindus, Muslims, Parsis, and Kaliparaj (aboriginals), with women leading some of the central action, opposed a land-tax levy by petitioning, refusing to pay the tax increase, not cooperating with tax collectors, trespassing, submitting to arrest, resigning from offices, and protesting at the national level (Bondurant 1988, 53–64); and

- the yearlong Salt satyagraha, a national civil disobedience movement in 1930–31, in which Gandhi led a two-hundred-mile march to the sea to protest the Salt Acts, which gave the government a monopoly on the production and sale of salt (Bondurant 1988, 88–102).

A contemporary of Gandhi and a Muslim partner in the independence struggle who was deeply admired and valued by Gandhi was Abdul Ghaffar Khan. Ghaffar Khan's social-reform-cum-radical-nonviolence movement against local authoritarianism and British imperialism involved the Pashtuns (also known as Pathans) of the Northwest Frontier Province, a region now located in northwestern Pakistan and parts of Afghanistan. Because of the strategic importance of the Khyber Pass as a vital transit point in East-West trade, this region had suffered invasion and occupation for centuries. British colonialists brutally suppressed a people considered backward and violent, whose unwritten law, pakhtunwali, and its strict code of revenge, badal, often resulted in blood feuds as the means of handling disputes (Easwaran 1984; Johansen 1997).

Ghaffar Khan surrendered his land holdings for an ascetic life of service to God and the impoverished people of the Northwest Frontier Province, basing his movement on the ancient Islamic principles of universal brotherhood, submission to God's will, and serving God through service to His creatures. An early influence was Ghaffar Khan's peace-loving father, who tried to make no enemies and avoided feuds, but it was through Gandhi's teachings that Ghaffar Khan embraced nonviolence as a way of life and a path to social transformation and independence for his people, earning him the name of "Frontier Gandhi" (Easwaran 1984). Ghaffar Khan also found justification for this nonviolent path in the Prophet Mohammed's example, fourteen hundred years earlier, and in his reading of the prophet: "That man is a Muslim who never hurts anyone by word or deed, but who works for the benefit and happiness of God's creatures" (quoted in Easwaran 1984, 55).

In 1910, Ghaffar Khan embarked on a path of social reform in education, agriculture, hygiene, and sanitation. Claiming that "God makes no distinction between men and women," he encouraged women to come out from behind the veil and to become active in the movement for social reform and political independence. He began to hear about Gandhi's nonviolent campaigns, and his own reform work took on new meaning as a path not only out of poverty and ignorance but also to freedom. He traveled throughout the province with a message of sacrifice, work, and forgiveness (Easwaran 1984).

Ghaffar Khan arose as a leader of bold political action aimed at self-determination, socioeconomic development, democratization, and opposition to corruption, while adhering to strictly nonviolent means despite extreme and violent provocation by the British. Repeatedly imprisoned for his efforts, he spent fifteen years in prison under the British, much of the time in solitary confinement (Johansen 1997).

His most powerful social innovation was the creation, in 1929, of the Khudai Khidmatgar, a nonviolent army (literally, "servants") of God. In a creative fusion of religiously rooted mandates for nonviolence and selfless service and the powerful Pashtun cultural code of honor and courage, the Khudai Khidmatgar was a drilled and disciplined army of volunteer nonviolent soldiers—with officers, platoons, red-shirted uniforms, flag, and bagpipe corps—that pledged to fight with their lives rather than with guns (Easwaran 1984). The Khudai Khidmatgar oath, which a person committed to honor with his or her life, had nonviolence at its heart and was directed not only at the British but also against the pervasive violence of Pashtun life. Its tenets included serving humanity in the name of God (Easwaran 1984; Johansen 1997).

When the National Congress Party declared independence from Britain on New Year's Eve 1930, the Khudai Khidmatgar embarked on an intensive campaign of education and organization throughout the frontier. When, in April 1931, Ghaffar Khan exhorted a mass meeting to join in the civil resistance, he was arrested and imprisoned for three years (Easwaran 1984). The Khudai Khidmatgar's efforts continued unabated, with hundreds of nonviolent actions taken against the British; its numbers swelled to more than 100,000 (Pyarelal 1950, as cited in Johansen 1997, 58). By 1932, the Khudai Khidmatgar had gained political parity for the province with the rest of British India and an indigenous head of the regional government.

In the 1930s and 1940s, the Muslim activists refused to cooperate with the British and remained resolutely nonviolent in the face of recurrent British provocation and violence. The Khudai Khidmatgar suffered some of the most severe repression of the Indian independence movement. At times, the entire province was sealed off from the outside world to leave the British military free to destroy the movement in any way it could. Whole villages were decimated; repeated mass firings on unarmed groups resulted in hundreds of casualties; members of the Khudai Khidmatgar were flogged and arrested sometimes by the thousands; troops herded members of the Khudai Khidmatgar into icy streams in the winter, forced them at gunpoint to remove their clothes in public, confiscated property, burned their fields, and destroyed winter food supplies. There is no evidence of any Khudai Khidmatgar killing an adversary, despite the organization's large membership and repeated provocations by the British (Easwaran 1984; Johansen 1997; Ackerman and Kruegler 1994, 175–77).

When independence came to India in 1947, the two great independence leaders, Gandhi and the Frontier Gandhi, declined to take part in the celebrations. Both men had resolutely opposed partition of Indian into two states, one predominantly Hindu and the other predominantly Muslim. Ghaffar Khan lived to see the end of his movement and endured still further persecution, this time at the hands of his coreligionists, mainly leaders of the Muslim League, who were now governing the new state of Pakistan. Suspicious of Ghaffar Khan's popularity, influence, and nonviolent methods, and seeing him as "too Hindu," they feared his continued advocacy for regional autonomy within the new state. Ghaffar Khan spent another fifteen years in prison and seven in exile during the first thirty years of Pakistan's existence (Easwaran 1984; Johansen 1997).

Truth-Telling and the Transition from Rhodesia to Zimbabwe. A significant example of truth-telling to both a nation and the world is that of the Roman Catholic Church during the war of independence in Rhodesia (Linden 1980; Kraybill 1994, 212–22). Through a long-distance liaison between two Catholic institutions—the Justice and Peace Commission (JPC) in Rhodesia and the London-based Catholic Institute for International Relations (CIIR)—the church was active from 1975 until the war ended in 1979 in exposing wartime atrocities committed by the Rhodesian security forces. As government censorship tightened, the church became the only reliable source of information about life in the war zones, often through the accounts of deported missionaries and church workers (some eighteen Catholics were expelled by the government for speaking out). The JPC and CIIR also lobbied the British and other Western governments, arguing against both accepting the compromise Internal Settlement government and lifting sanctions against Rhodesia. Rhodesia's Catholic bishops issued ten pastoral statements between 1961 and 1980, calling for racial justice and principled behavior on the part of the combatants. Catholic bodies also challenged the liberation fronts on several occasions, deploring both publicly and privately reported atrocities by guerrilla forces.

In 1977, recognizing an impasse in the war and the devastation of the country's economy and social welfare, the JPC and Catholic hierarchy shifted to active, high-level peace-process advocacy in hopes of getting the parties to the bargaining table. In a final initiative just months before a negotiated settlement would end the war, the JPC enlisted the pope to urgently pressure five Western governments to intervene in an attempt to stop the suffering.

Pronouncements and "People Power": The Catholic Church in the Philippines. The world was held spellbound in February 1986 as two million Filipinos massed in Manila to provide a cordon of protection around soldiers rebelling against the repressive and corrupt regime of Ferdinand Marcos. Many of these citizens responded to a call by Cardinal Jaime Sin, the archbishop of Manila, "to all the children of God" to protect "our idealist friends" (Wooster 1994, 163; Wise and Cardel 1991).

The Second Vatican Council of 1962 and subsequent papal encyclicals stressed that efforts to eradicate injustice and economic inequality were integral to preaching the gospel. Since the imposition of martial law in the Philippines in 1972, the Catholic Church had led the religious opposition to the Marcos regime. Through frequent pastoral letters, the church was able to reach parishes throughout the country with calls for the defense of human rights, social justice, and rejection of violence, and with increasingly direct attacks against the Marcos regime's repression, corruption, and economic mismanagement. Many priests and nuns served as monitors in the election that Marcos fraudulently claimed as a victory over Corazón Aquino and that was subsequently denounced in a Bishops Conference declaration that the regime had lost its mandate to govern. As the four-day "People Power" revolution unfolded, the Catholic-owned Radio Veritas was instrumental in mobilizing the popular defense of the military that proved decisive in expelling Marcos nonviolently and bringing Aquino to power (International Observer Delegation 1986, 19–20; Wooster 1994, 159–66; Appleby 2000, 227–29).

Turning East Germany Around. During *die Wende* (the turnaround), East Germany's nonviolent revolution of 1989–90, the churches, particularly the Evangelische Kirche, played a central role in the overthrow of the communist system. Initially providing support, meeting space, and protection from harassment to the independent peace movement, in 1988 the church became more actively involved in protesting government actions, defending human rights, and holding prayer services that became the rallying points for mass demonstrations. As tensions heightened, and especially with the fall of the regime of Erich Honecker, the church's role in East Germany became a blend of continued activism on the one hand and facilitation of dialogue between protesters and the government and security forces on the other. Many individual church leaders were instrumental in moderating roundtables that were formed at the national and local levels to allow for popular participation in establishing a new political order and that served in some locations as de facto governments during the turbulent transition to democracy and unification with West Germany (Steele 1994).

A "Subtle Protest" in Burma. In the closed country of Burma (Myanmar), the Buddhist *sangha* is the only nationally organized institution other than the army. More than 90 percent of the population is Buddhist. Monks hold strong moral authority, enjoying popular support for their asceticism, and monasteries have often served as both launching pads for mass protests and sanctuaries for political outlaws (Jones 1989a). For five weeks in 1988, during the country's brief period of prodemocracy protests just before the army's imposition of martial law, hundreds of thousands of protesters led by Buddhist monks took over Burma's second-largest city of Mandalay, home to some 260 monasteries and 100,000 monks. Upon the imposition of martial law, hundreds of monks and lay people were arrested, and many others fled or went underground. One year later and still under martial law, thousands of monks, lacquer begging bowls in hand, walked single file past Mandalay's military installations in a "subtle protest" of silent defiance, marking the anniversary of the start of massive killings of prodemocracy protesters (Jones 1989b).

During this period, Aung San Suu Kyi, daughter of Aung San, who had led Burma to independence in 1947, emerged as the most visible and influential leader of the nonviolent prodemocracy movement. She advocated self-responsibility rooted in the Buddhist principles of *cetna* (right intention) and *metta* (compassion). The ruling military council placed her under house arrest in 1989. Despite intimidation, imprisonment, torture, and witnessing the execution of prodemocracy activists, Aung San Suu Kyi, who was awarded the Nobel Peace Prize in 1990, rejected retaliatory violence. After her release in 1995, she continued to articulate the connection between Theravada Buddhism, Burma's religious and cultural heritage, and the democratization movement (Appleby 2000, 214).

Intermediaries

Intermediary roles played by religious actors have included fact finding, good offices, peace-process advocacy, facilitation, conciliation, and mediation, usually in some combination. Religious actors have mediated high-level peace talks and have also been active nonofficially at all levels of peacemaking in advocating for negotiated settlement and trying to improve the climate and prospects for peace. Their means of entry into conflict situations and their methodologies have varied widely, including one particular characteristic that outwardly distinguishes them from secular counterparts: the degree to which explicit religiousness is or is not expressed during the peace process.

Peacemaking in Sudan, Then and Now. In 1972, peace talks between the government of Sudan and rebels from the country's southern insurgency, the Southern Sudan Liberation Movement, ended the civil war between the two sides and brought a decade of peace to the war-ravaged country. The negotiations—which featured prayers and sermons as part of the proceedings and produced tears of remorse among Muslim and Christian generals alike— were successfully mediated by a three-man team: Reverend Burgess Carr, secretary-general of the All-Africa Conference of Churches (AACC); Leopoldo Niilus, director of the World Council of Churches' (WCC) Commission of the Churches on International Affairs; and Kodwo Ankrah, WCC refugee secretary (Assefa 1987). The WCC/AACC delegation's access to the Khartoum government came through a meeting called to discuss aid, although the members went prepared to provide their good offices, an offer that was readily accepted (Rees 1977). Also influential in gaining the government's confidence was a WCC-commissioned report on the background and issues of the conflict that was considered knowledgeable, fair, and objective.

The 1972 agreement gradually eroded over the following decade because of problems with its implementation. It was finally abrogated in 1983, when the Sudanese government imposed Islamic *sharia* law over the entire country, including the non-Muslim south. Civil war again broke out between the northern and southern regions. After eight years of fighting, a split occurred in the leadership of the south's Sudanese People's Liberation Army, and interfactional fighting ensued. Concerned about the impact on civilians of this conflict within a conflict, and aware that peace with the north could not be achieved without southern unity, the National Council of Churches of Kenya, the Kenyan Catholic Secretariat, and the largely church-supported Nairobi Peace Initiative decided to back a 1991 mediation attempt by a group of church leaders from southern Sudan. Significant agreement was reached on a number of contentious issues, but the process broke down in 1992, followed by further splintering of the southern insurgency movement (Assefa 1993c).

More recently, efforts at faith-based diplomacy between the Muslim and Christian communities have paralleled secular diplomatic efforts to end the civil war. Over several years, the Washington, D.C.-based International Center for Religion and Diplomacy (ICRD) interacted with the Christian and Muslim communities in the north, including the government of Sudan. In 2000, the ICRD, together with the Sudan Council of Churches, convened a conference of religious leaders and scholars in Khartoum to address the religious aspects of the conflict and of social tensions more generally. The religious dimensions of the gathering included an informal prayer breakfast each morning; prayer and readings and meditations from the Qur'an and Bible at the sessions; and several members of the facilitation team who attended for the sole purpose of praying and fasting for the success of the deliberations. The conference produced seventeen consensus recommendations for interreligious cooperation in the areas of human rights, education, employment, and humanitarian assistance (Johnston 2003, 11–14).

Conciliation in Nicaragua. In Nicaragua, a process of negotiations between the Sandinista government and a coalition of exiled Indian groups from the country's east coast was mediated by a Conciliation Commission of religious figures, which brokered a preliminary agreement between the two sides in 1988 (Nichols 1994). Commission members included a minister, Andy Shogreen, and three other representatives of the Moravian Church (the predominant denomination in the country's east coast provinces); a Baptist pastor and director of an ecumenical relief and development agency, Gustavo Parajón; and an American Mennonite, John Paul Lederach, who served as a conflict resolution consultant. The agreement opened the way for a substantial number of Indian refugees living in exile to return to Nicaragua (Nichols 1994, 82).

Although subsequent rounds of talks failed to resolve the remaining issues at the time, a final agreement was brokered by former U.S. president Jimmy Carter in 1989 on a trip to arrange for monitoring of the upcoming Nicaraguan election, thus opening the way for the remaining Indian leaders to return and participate in the elections. That agreement was signed in a Moravian church on the east coast, with the Conciliation Commission members present (Lederach 1989).

Peacemaking in the Punjab. Jainism, a religion of India that dates from the sixth century B.C., was the earliest historical expression of *ahimsa*, the philosophy of nonviolence. For adherents living a life of strict asceticism, absolute nonviolence is considered the highest virtue (Sharma 1990). Mahavira, an early Jain reformer, is said to have instructed his followers not to preach Jainism but to "go from village to village and maintain peace among mankind" (*Free Press Journal, Sunday Press*, May 24, 1987, as cited in Hall 1987, 4).

One example of the religion's active embrace of nonviolence is the work of a Jain monk, Acharya Sushil Kumar, who was active in Hindu-Sikh conciliation in the Indian state of Punjab. In 1987, Kumar opened channels of communication and mediated between the government of India and Sikh militants who had been occupying the Golden Temple at Amritsar in the Punjab since 1984. Before each of his meetings in the temple, the monk was successful in securing the withdrawal of the heavily armed Indian police guard, which had encircled the shrine continuously for three years. Some of the most militant Sikh leaders participated in the meetings. The dialogue produced a four-point peace plan, which faltered, apparently owing to the lack of support from the Punjab state government (*Patriot* 1987; *Siddhachalam Newsletter* 1987; Hall 1987).

In 1988, Kumar arranged a meeting for Sikh leaders from the Punjab to try to settle their differences, but the meeting was canceled when one of the leaders was assassinated. However, Kumar's final initiative, an appeal to the central government for the release of imprisoned priests from the Golden Temple, met with success (*Siddhachalam Newsletter* 1988).

Interreligious Councils. In 1994, the World Conference of Religions for Peace (WCRP; formerly World Conference on Religion and Peace, which since its founding in 1974 has pursued a holistic peace agenda in the areas of disarmament, development, human rights, conflict resolution, refugees, and children; Braybrooke 1992, 159–64; Jack 1993), launched a conflict transformation program to explicitly engage the "meaning structures"—the moral and spiritual resources—and the social structures of religions for peacebuilding. Capitalizing on the WCRP's strength as a global association of world religions, the program builds on the premises that multireligious efforts can often be more powerful than those of a religious community acting alone and that cooperation across religions can promote tolerance and an understanding of pluralism in circumstances where religion is a divisive factor in conflict (World Conference on Religion and Peace n.d.). A leading WCRP approach has been to support the development of national interreligious councils to work at peacemaking and conflict transformation in war-afflicted countries. In Bosnia-Herzegovina, for example, WCRP helped local religious leaders establish an interreligious council through which the four major religious communities issued a Statement of Shared Moral Commitment opposing ethnoreligious violence. The Interreligious Council of Sierra Leone, whose work was facilitated by WCRP, assisted with the mediation that helped end the civil war in that country and helped implement the resulting peace agreement, for example, obtaining the release of significant numbers of child soldiers (Lampman 1999; Appleby 2000, 152–55; Smock 2001b, 5–6).

Observers

In a conflict situation, the observer provides a watchful, compelling physical presence that is intended to discourage violence, corruption, human rights violations, or other behavior deemed threatening and undesirable. Far from being passive, religiously motivated observers have, for example, actively monitored and verified—and even ensured—the legitimacy of elections.

In the observer's more activist form of providing a presence, civilian peacekeeping groups, or peace teams, have positioned themselves between sides in active conflict situations—becoming a "living wall," as Gandhi termed it—to stop violence and transform the conflict dynamics (Schirch 1995, 3). This form of interpositionary peacekeeping involves taking an impartial stance toward all parties. In situations where parties are not easily separated or violence is perpetrated primarily by one party against another, intercessionary peacekeeping may be used to deter violence, either through accompanying individuals or groups believed to be in danger or by maintaining a presence in a threatened community (Schirch 1995, 24–29).

Election Monitoring in Zambia. In Zambia, a predominantly Christian country, the churches played a central role in carrying out the 1991 national election. About a month before the election, the churches pulled out of a national coalition of NGOs after they lost confidence that the coalition could ensure a free and fair election. Then, using the infrastructures of three denominational networks working in close cooperation—a Protestant evangelical association, the national council of churches, and the Catholic Bishops Conference—the churches recruited, trained, and deployed monitors for three thousand polling sites (Vendley 1995). Several months earlier, in a political impasse with President Kenneth Kaunda's government, the Movement for Multiparty Democracy, the party of the leading presidential contender (and soon to be elected president), Frederick Chiluba, threatened to boycott the election. The two men agreed to meet in the Anglican cathedral in Lusaka. Their meeting, set within a shared faith context and begun with prayer, resulted in a redrafting of the constitution that opened the way for the elections to proceed (Carter 1994, vi).

Civilian Peacekeeping. Two religiously motivated groups have been involved in ongoing civilian peacekeeping work. Witness for Peace (WFP), an ecumenical organization formed in the early 1980s, has provided a nonviolent presence in Nicaragua, Guatemala, El Salvador, Mexico, Haiti, South Africa, and the Middle East. Its principal engagement was in Nicaragua, where more than four thousand North Americans from various religious traditions visited for periods of several weeks to more than a year between 1983 and 1991. WFP's primary objective was activist in nature: to change U.S. foreign policy in the region. Members' activities in Nicaragua included living among and working with the Nicaraguan people, reporting on Nicaraguan living conditions upon their return home, documenting human rights violations, fostering dialogue and reconciliation, documenting the conflict and peace initiatives, and providing nonviolence training (Schirch 1995, 103–05).

Christian Peacemaker Teams (CPT), sponsored by the Mennonites, Church of the Brethren, and Quakers, have pursued nonviolent direct action as human rights monitors since 1986, focusing attention on issues of violence and militarism in Iraq, Palestine, Israel, and Haiti, as well as in the United States and Canada. CPT sees its role as proclaiming the gospel of repentance, salvation, and reconciliation, and its mandate as a new dimension of the churches' ongoing peace and justice ministries. It believes that if justice does not accompany peace, practical steps such as nonviolent direct action should be taken in the spirit of loving the enemy, as taught in the Bible (Christian Peacemaker Teams n.d.; Schirch 1995, 105–07; Kern 2000; Appleby 2000, 146, 149–50).

Educators

Education and training play a role during each stage of conflict transformation, whether to sensitize a society to inequities in the system; to foster an understanding of and build the skills of advocacy, conflict resolution, democracy, or living with diversity; or to promote healing and reconciliation. The key to this activity is the dimension of preparation—of teaching or in some way providing a learning experience for others from a position one step removed from direct involvement in conflict intervention.

Nonviolence Training. Three religiously motivated actors have been particularly active in the area of nonviolence training. Continuing the legacy of the grandfather of all modern nonviolence movements, the Gandhi Peace Foundation, headquartered in Delhi with thirty-three field centers across India, conducts research, field work, and educational programs on the nonviolent alternative in conflict situations and in relation to nature and the environment (Gandhi Peace Foundation n.d.).

The International Fellowship of Reconciliation, founded in 1919 in the Netherlands, is represented on every continent through a network of organizations, branches, and affiliated groups of people working for active nonviolence from a faith perspective. In 1992, it established the Nonviolence Education and Training Project as a grassroots movement to train people in peace and social change movements and to develop cross-cultural and interfaith training resources (Nonviolence Education and Training Project n.d.).

Nonviolence International (NI) was founded by Mubarak Awad, a Palestinian Christian who was schooled in Quaker and Mennonite beliefs, trained in the techniques of Gandhi, and further inspired by the work of Martin Luther King Jr. (Ingram 1990, 28–53). Headquartered in Washington, D.C., NI provides training in nonviolent action; coordinates international teams; provides legal support to activists and campaigns; and cooperates internationally with other programs, including resource centers in Moscow, Bangkok, Jerusalem, and Johannesburg (Nonviolence International 1995).

Learning Communities in Northern Ireland. In Northern Ireland, where the Catholic and Protestant communities have historically lived, worshipped, and even been educated separately, a faith-based response to the conflict has been the emergence of "intentional communities of reconciliation" (Morrow and Wilson 1994, 23). These communities provide a chance for experiential learning so that their members may "rediscover each other as human beings" (Morrow n.d., 4). Best known among them is the ecumenical Corrymeela Community, founded in 1965, whose direct work with local community groups is supported by an all-age residential program (Hinton 1993, 94–110; Morrow n.d.; Morrow and Wilson 1994, 23; Appleby 2000, 180–81). Other examples are the Cornerstone and Curragh communities in Belfast, which work with community development programs; the Columbanus Community, which offers courses in ecumenics; and the Rostrevor Centre, which specializes in renewal and healing. Most people in these communities are "dispersed" members, who live and work outside the communities but join together through them for work on particular projects (Morrow and Wilson 1994).

Preparing People for Peace in Mozambique. The Christian Council of Mozambique (CCM), an ecumenical body of Protestant churches, launched its Preparing People for Peace Program in 1991 (Brubaker 1993)—a year before peace came to that country—to help a population that had known almost thirty years of war prepare for the transition. CCM's Peace and Reconciliation Commission, under the leadership of Anglican Bishop Dinis Sengulane, had been active during the conflict in bringing the warring sides together (Appleby 2000, 161, 218). Now it turned its attention to the pressing needs of building peace and resettling a massively dislocated population. The program proceeded in two phases. The first was a five-week training seminar held in Maputo for CCM and church representatives (including those from non-CCM churches) from all ten provinces, using material from the Bible as an instrument of peace and including sessions on conflict resolution and the "three r's" (reconciliation, repatriation, and rehabilitation), public health, the family, child development, trauma treatment, nonviolence, human rights, the Mozambican Constitution, disarmament, and amnesty. The second phase consisted of two-week training seminars in the provinces, delivered by the people trained in Maputo, for church and district representatives (Brubaker 1993).

Academic and Training Programs. Of the many religiously affiliated colleges and universities around the world with programs related to peace and conflict studies, three leading examples are Eastern Mennonite University's (EMU) Center for Justice and Peacebuilding and associated Summer Peacebuilding

Institute, which draw participants from around the world to academic and training programs targeted principally at religious communities and NGO personnel involved in developing peacebuilding programs in settings of protracted conflict; the Joan B. Kroc Institute for International Peace Studies at the Catholic University of Notre Dame, which has a graduate program, summer institute, visiting fellows program, and a research program in religion, conflict, and peacebuilding; and Duquesne University, a Catholic institution that hosted an "African Church as Peacemaker" colloquium in 1994 and instituted a Conflict Resolution and Peace Studies program as part of its Graduate Center for Social and Public Policy.

Modeled on the EMU's Summer Peacebuilding Institute, the Mindanao Peacebuilding Institute in the Philippines, with funding from Catholic Relief Services and the Mennonite Central Committee; the Africa Peacebuilding Institute in Zambia, with funding from the Mennonite Central Committee; and the West Africa Peacebuilding Institute largely serve religiously affiliated constituencies. A Center for Strategic and International Studies (CSIS) project on religion and conflict resolution in 1995 conducted some three dozen interreligious dialogue and training seminars in various parts of the former Yugoslavia. The CSIS project also nurtured the creation of two indigenous peacebuilding centers now carrying out training—the Centre for Peace, Nonviolence and Human Rights in Osijek, Croatia, and the Centre for Religious Dialogue in Sarajevo, Bosnia (Appleby 2000, 242–43; 294, 297; Smock 2001b, 6–7; Steele 2002). The Plowshares Institute, which conducts faith-based training in the skills of conflict transformation from a spiritual and moral perspective, has been intensively involved in southern Africa and other parts of the world (Smock 2001b, 3).

A CONSTELLATION OF ACTORS: THE CASE OF SOUTH AFRICA

The multiplicity of religious actors that participated in South Africa's transformation from apartheid to majority democratic rule illustrates the myriad types of religious actors at the societal and international levels that can contribute to social change and peacebuilding. Although admittedly a difficult undertaking, constructing a map of all possible religious actors in a religiously diverse society might be aided by looking at the multiple intersections of three typologies:

- the organizational structure of the religious actor, be it an individual member of the laity or clergy, an institution (church, mosque, synagogue, temple), an established body (a collective entity, such as a youth group or a federation), or an ad hoc body (such as a commission, delegation, or gathering);

- the religious or spiritual base of the religious actor, be it a single religious denomination or tradition, an interdenominational body within a single tradition, a multireligious body working across religions, or a nondenominational body comprising people who operate from a religious or spiritual motivation; and

- the organizational level represented by the religious actor, be it local, subnational, national, regional, or international.

South Africa's antiapartheid struggle included more than twenty such types of actors. This list is incomplete, to be sure. A cursory review of individual action, provided for illustrative purposes only, does not do credit to the large number of spiritually impelled and courageous individuals at all levels of South African society who actively opposed apartheid at great personal risk. Suffice it to say that beginning with the period of confrontation and struggle against apartheid, religious actors of many sorts were involved, some more deeply than others, and some whose role evolved through the transition to the post-conflict phase.

Looking first at the level of individual action, many laypersons at the local church level repudiated the proapartheid position of the Dutch Reformed Church (DRC), and numerous local clergy were defrocked for their opposition to apartheid. Within the Islamic community, arrests and detentions of individual Muslims occurred in numbers out of proportion to their share of the population (Esack 1994).

Among the most prominent national denominational leaders who took courageous stances were Anglican Archbishop Desmond Tutu, whose championing of nonviolent resistance won him the Nobel Prize in 1984 (he also at times served as a mediator and was called upon to chair the National Truth and Reconciliation Commission in the immediate postapartheid period; Ingram 1990, 272–84; Tutu 1994; Appleby 2000, 197–201); Reverend Allan Boesak, the colored leader of the Dutch Reformed Mission Church and president of the World Alliance of Reformed Churches (Claiborne 1989); and Beyers Naudé, an influential DRC minister who forsook his position by repudiating the church's role in sanctifying apartheid and founded the Christian Institute for Nonracial Christianity, the first religious institution established to criticize and act against apartheid (Johnston 1994, 186–93). Other prominent national religious leaders included Reverend Frank Chikane, general secretary of the South African Council of Churches (Claiborne 1989), and Michael Cassidy, a Christian evangelist and head of African Enterprise (Cassidy 1995; Lean 1995).

Also working at the level of individual action was Methodist Bishop Stanley Mogoba. During the 1991–94 transition period leading to the national election, Mogoba chaired the National Peace Committee, a body charged with overseeing implementation of the National Peace Accord, to which key political parties agreed as a response to the violence that threatened to engulf the country. As part of this process, many pastors (denominational leaders working at local and regional levels) were deeply involved in peace committees as chairs, organizers of committee activities, mediators, and violence monitors (Kraybill 1995).

Finally, in a dramatic feat that may have saved the national election in 1994 and prevented an outbreak of violence, Professor Washington Okumu, a former Kenyan diplomat and layperson acting internationally, brokered the agreement among Zulu Chief Mangosuthu Buthelezi, African National Congress (ANC) leader Nelson Mandela, and President F. W. de Klerk that brought Buthelezi's Inkatha Freedom Party into the election in the final hour. Okumu and Buthelezi had met twenty years earlier at a White House prayer meeting (Keller 1994; Cassidy 1995; Lean 1995; Henderson 1995, 1996, 124–31).

At the institutional level, many white churches, both local and national denominational institutions, opposed apartheid. At the Rosettenville Conference in 1949, the first national interdenominational gathering following the National Party's victory in 1948, the English-speaking churches came out in clear opposition to apartheid. In time, as other groups opposed to apartheid were effectively nullified through banning and arrests, churches assumed the leadership in the defense of human rights and became virtually the only place where antiapartheid activists could meet for discussion and to organize protests (Johnston 1994, 190). Within the DRC, the Cape Province Synod, a subnational denominational body, broke ranks with the church on apartheid, as did one of the DRC "daughter" churches, the colored Dutch Reformed Mission Church, a national denominational institution (Johnston 1994, 192). The Muslim youth organization Call of Islam, a national denominational body, was the most visible organization through which Islamic resistance to apartheid was galvanized (Esack 1994, 1997). An external church actor, the Mennonite Central Committee placed North American Mennonites in South Africa over three decades, in roles that shifted with the changes in the struggle—from advocacy for victims of apartheid, to support for nonviolent struggle, to providing support for reconciliation (Herr and Herr 2000).

The South African Council of Churches, a national interdenominational body, took strong and sometimes confrontational stances against the government. Its 1968 "Message to the People of South Africa" underscored the incongruity between the teachings of Christianity and the concepts of apartheid (Johnston 1994, 191–200). The evangelical Christian group African Enterprise, a continental or regional interdenominational body, worked at building bridges across the lines of division in South African society. In 1992, it began a series of weekend retreats for political leaders across the political spectrum, not all of them Christians (Cassidy 1995; Lean 1995). The National Initiative for Reconciliation, a national ad hoc interdenominational body, was initiated at a 1994 conference attended by church leaders and theologians from a wide range of denominations. Its Statement of Affirmation rejected apartheid but avoided further social analysis and criticism. Immediately following this statement came the publication by 153 predominantly black church leaders and theologians of the Kairos Document, a theological critique calling for decisive action against apartheid (Winkler 1986; Johnston 1994). At the Rustenburg Conference of 1990, the largest national interdenominational gathering of black and white South African churches in history, representatives of ninety-seven denominations and forty organizations endorsed a declaration confessing responsibility for the wrongs perpetrated by apartheid (Johnston 1994, 199; Battersby 1990). The Ecumenical Monitoring Programme in South Africa, a national ad hoc interdenominational body organized by the South African Council of Churches (SACC) and the Catholic Bishops Conference, played an active role in the country's first national nonracial election in 1994.

Christian and Muslim individuals and bodies were not the only religious actors involved in the antiapartheid struggle. The South African chapter of the World Conference of Religions for Peace (WCRP-SA), a national multireligious body, was founded as a result of the Interfaith Colloquium on Apartheid, an international multireligious gathering held in London in 1984 (Lubbe 1994, 2–8). Active in promoting interfaith dialogue and cooperation, WCRP-SA held prayer and protest meetings in various parts of the country; in 1987, it held a consultation with the ANC in Zambia on religion in a postapartheid South Africa; and in 1988, it waged a campaign against the racial municipal elections. National denominational bodies representing seven religious traditions that actively associate with WCRP-SA include the South African Catholic Bishops Conference, the South African Hindu Maha Sabha, the South African Tamil Federation, the Jewish Board of Deputies, Jews for Social Justice, Call of Islam, the Muslim Judicial Council, the Spiritual Assembly of Baha'is, the Pretoria Buddhist Group, the Sikh Council of South Africa, and the Federation of Indigenous Churches in South Africa, in addition to the interdenominational SACC (Lubbe 1994, 2–8). Prompted by the 1990 Johannesburg National Interfaith Conference, a national multireligious gathering, WCRP-SA took up the issue of religious freedom during the transition period as its contribution to South African democracy (Lubbe 1994, 2–8). Starting in late 1994, at the request of the National Truth and Reconciliation Commission, it worked to coordinate religious participation in the commission's work.

At the global level, two international interdenominational bodies were active as advocates on behalf of the antiapartheid struggle. The WCC held a consultation to protest apartheid in 1960, began to provide humanitarian support to the liberation movements in 1970, called on its members to press for comprehensive sanctions against South Africa in 1985, and organized a 1987 conference in Zambia for SACC representatives and exiled members of the ANC (Johnston 1994, 190–91, 195, 196). The World Alliance of Reformed Churches, a grouping of some one hundred fifty Reformed, Presbyterian, and Congregational churches, declared apartheid a heresy in 1987, suspended two proapartheid Afrikaans-language churches, and elected Allan Boesak as its president (Johnston 1994, 192). Dating from the 1960s, the International Fellowship of Reconciliation, an international nondenominational body, was the group that worked in the most systematic manner to advocate the concept of nonviolent struggle (see, e.g., Wink 1987). The Vatican, an international denominational institution, also denounced apartheid, and Pope John Paul II added his voice to the call for strict sanctions (Johnston 1994).

INSTITUTIONAL ACTORS

We return now to take a closer look at the work of several religious communities and other institutional actors that have long-established records of peacebuilding over many years and in diverse roles.

Roman Catholic Church

The most consistent role played by the Catholic Church in countries around the globe has been that of "prophetic voice," making pronouncements from the pulpit and in the public square about injustice, corruption, authoritarianism, and other social ills; calling for moral rectitude and courage in elections and at times of national crisis; and at times helping mobilize mass movements for social change, as in the case of the Philippines, described above. Roman Catholic prelates have also often played intermediary roles in countries where the church has a significant presence.

At the international level, Pope John Paul II officially mediated the process leading to the signing of a 1984 treaty that ended a century-old border dispute between Chile and Argentina over the Beagle Channel (Princen 1987, 1992a, 133–85). The day-to-day mediation process took more than six years to reach an agreement and was conducted by a team of clerics headed by Cardinal Antonio Samore, a career Vatican diplomat. The mediation was leveraged by messages from the pontiff and occasional audiences with him. The

Vatican attributed its success largely to the pope's moral authority as the spiritual sovereign of the two Catholic nations and its ability to make demands on the parties that no other third party could have made; for example, the pope couched his urgings for reconciliation in religious terms, and the Vatican periodically called on local parishes to pray for peace (Princen 1987, 348–50).

In teamwork that spanned international, national, and local levels of the Roman Catholic Church, Mozambican Archbishop Jaime Gonçalves and the lay Catholic Community of Sant'Egidio—supported by encouragement and strategically applied pressure from the Vatican—played the lead mediation role in two years of peace talks that ended Mozambique's civil war in 1990 (United States Institute of Peace 1993; Schneidman 1993; Hume 1994; Gonçalves 1993, 1994; Appleby 2000; Bartoli 2001a, 2001b). Sant'Egidio is headquartered in a sixteenth-century former Carmelite convent in Rome, where ten rounds of peace talks were held from 1990 to 1992, and has communities in several Italian cities and some forty countries. Joining Archbishop Gonçalves on the mediation team were two Sant'Egidio representatives: Andrea Riccardi, its founder and leader, and Don Mateo Zuppi, a parish priest in Rome. (A fourth team member, Mario Raffaelli, represented the Italian government.) Building on the success in Mozambique, Sant'Egidio has subsequently been active in mediation in Algeria, Kosovo, Albania, and elsewhere (Drozdiak 1995; Pierre and Quandt 1995; Impagliazzo 1998; Morozzo della Rocca 1998; Appleby 2000; Bartoli 2001a, 2001b).

Frequently, individual bishops are thrust into national leadership roles as conciliators and mediators in civil conflicts. Some leading examples identified by Christiansen (2001, 10–13) include Bishop Samuel Ruiz of Mexico, who mediated for a time between the government and Zapatista rebels in the Mexican state of Chiapas and was also a staunch defender of human rights (see also Robberson 1994; Scott 1994a, 1994b; LaFranchi 1995); Bishop Carlos Felipe Ximenes Belo, who won the Nobel Peace Prize for his nonviolent leadership in the struggle for human rights and independence for East Timor (Shiner 1998; Kohen 1999); Jerusalem's Roman Catholic Patriarch Michel Sabbah, who has been central in overcoming centuries-long rivalries among Jerusalem's Christian churches to form a common ground on issues of justice, peace, and human rights; and Congolese Archbishop Monsengwo, for many years the official conciliator in the former Zaire (see also Richburg 1993; Reuters News Service 1993). Other examples from Central America include mediation in Nicaragua by Cardinal Obando y Bravo, head of the Nicaraguan National Reconciliation Commission (Wehr and Lederach 1991, 90–91; Larmer 1988); in Guatemala by Bishop Rodolfo Quezada, head of the Guatemalan National Reconciliation Commission (*Washington Post* 1992); in

Panama by Archbishop Marcos McGrath (Germani 1988); and in El Salvador by Archbishop Arturo Rivera y Damas. And elsewhere in Africa, in the Republic of Congo, Archbishop Ernest Nkombo presided at sessions of the Supreme Council of the Republic, a 153-member legislative body established in 1991 to govern for twelve months and organize elections for the following year (*Africa News* 1991; Shiner 1992); and in Benin, Archbishop Isidore de Souza served as president of a national conference that prepared the country's transition from Marxist dictatorship to democracy (de Souza 1994; *Washington Post* 1993).

Society of Friends

The early case literature of religiously motivated peacemaking focused on the intermediary work of the Society of Friends, or Quakers, between India and Pakistan in 1965 (Yarrow 1977, 1978); in Nigeria during the Biafran war (Yarrow 1978; Princen 1992a; Sampson 1994); during the war of independence in Rhodesia (Kraybill 1994); in Sri Lanka (Princen 1992b); and personal accounts or reflections of experienced Quaker conciliators involved in these initiatives (Curle 1971, 1981, 1986a, 1986b, 1990, 1995; Warren 1987) or in the Middle East (Bolling 1977, 1987; Jackson 1983; Bailey 1979, 1985, 1993).

One of the historic peace churches, the Society of Friends traditionally coupled its refusal to fight with efforts to "bind up the wounds of the victims of war" through war-relief activities that date from the mid-1850s (Bailey 1993, 37–61). Quakers have also historically pursued advocacy—referred to as "speaking truth to power"—at the local, national, and international levels on behalf of the peaceful settlement of disputes and over a wide variety of issues, including disarmament and human rights (Bailey 1993, 65–75, 122–26). Quaker humanitarian and conciliation efforts are motivated by the belief "that of God in every one" (Curle 1981, 5), which imbues its adherents with a deep respect for all those involved in a conflict and a desire to relieve the suffering it creates on all sides.

Quakers foster a distinctive intermediary role—a blend of conciliation and mediation—that characterizes much of their work (Bailey 1993). They capitalize on the "power of the powerless" in doing for the parties in conflict what the parties could not do on their own (Princen 1992b). Often initiated through a fact-finding process of seeking to gain a sympathetic, yet balanced, understanding of each party's perspective ("balanced partiality"; Yarrow 1977), Quaker involvement typically evolves quickly into a good offices function of carrying messages among the parties. Working in teams of two or three, the Quakers move at the highest levels of decision making, interacting with heads of state or high officials in governments, liberation movements, and international organizations. Their access at this level often is facilitated by the leaders' prior exposure to Quaker humanitarian programs, conferences for diplomats, or other service activities (Yarrow 1978; Sampson 1994; Kraybill 1994).

In carrying messages for parties in conflict, the Quaker conciliator is not simply a passive messenger but an active participant in the peace process who tries to remove obstacles to a negotiated settlement by reducing suspicions, misperceptions, and fears (Curle 1990, 61). Sometimes this role has evolved into mediation, when teams became involved in conveying or themselves proposing the substantive terms of a possible settlement. Quakers also actively engage in peace-process advocacy and support of other intermediaries and initiatives in the course of an extended peace process (Yarrow 1978; Sampson 1994; Kraybill 1994).

Another area of Quaker intermediary work is in reconciliation, which involves a long-term, open-ended effort to build bridges of understanding between peoples (Bailey 1993, 126–32). Reconciliation takes two principal forms. One is the work of Quaker international affairs representatives stationed on the ground in areas of conflict, such as that between East and West Germany during the 1960s (Yarrow 1977, 51–143; Warren 1987) or in the Middle East (Young 1987). The other form is convening and facilitating informal, off-the-record meetings that bring parties face to face in nonofficial settings, for example, Russians and Americans during the Cold War, Jews and Arabs, Indians and Pakistanis in the Kashmir dispute, and Greeks and Turks in the conflict over Cyprus (Bailey 1979).

Mennonites

Rooted in the traditional Anabaptist values of nonviolence, social justice, and reconciliation, Mennonite peacebuilding has evolved a distinctive orientation and form that builds on more than eighty years of direct involvement in international relief and development work by the Mennonite Central Committee (MCC). Although conciliation had been an MCC concern over the decades, its proactive pursuit of peace-related activity began with the formation of the MCC Peace Section in 1960. Next came the founding of the Pennsylvania-based Mennonite Conciliation Service in 1978, one of the earliest entries in the nascent North American alternative dispute resolution field. In the mid-1980s, acting on the growing recognition of the links between relief, development, and conciliation work in settings of protracted conflict, the MCC began to formulate specific conciliation assignments in its international programs (e.g., community-level conflict resolution training in Central America). In 1990, it established the International Conciliation Service to strengthen the peacebuilding capacities of overseas volunteers, churches, and local "partner" organizations (e.g., local NGOs) through consultancy, training, and occasional direct mediation services (Driedger and Kraybill 1994; Appleby 2000, 143–50). Because of their long tradition of experience on the ground in situations of protracted conflict, Mennonite practitioners have pioneered "elicitive" approaches that tailor conflict resolution training and practice to fit particular cultural contexts (Lederach 1995).

Though individual Mennonite peacebuilders work at higher levels of the process, most Mennonite peacebuilding supported by MCC or Mennonite mission boards is focused at the grassroots level, working "from the ground up." Examples include the reconciliation work of North American Mennonites in Northern Ireland spanning more than thirty years (Liechty 2000; Campbell 2000; Sampson 2000); conflict resolution training, mediation, and support for reconciliation in Central America dating from the mid-1980s (Lederach 2000a; Chupp 2000); reconciliation work in Somalia and Somaliland, including support for indigenous conferences of elders (Lederach 2000b; Bergey 2000); advocacy for victims in apartheid South Africa, support for the nonviolent struggle in that country, and then support for postapartheid reconciliation (Kraybill 2000; Herr and Herr 2000); education, advocacy, and conciliation work carried out by the indigenous Mennonite peacebuilding center, Justapaz, in Colombia (Esquivia 2000; Sampson 2000); and resourcing for trauma-healing and reconciliation workshops carried out by the indigenous Christian Health Association during Liberia's civil war (Hart 1993, 1995, 2000; Hart and Gbaba 1993).

Applying a cultural analysis to these cases, anthropologist Sally Merry has identified key practices of Mennonite peacebuilding: (1) the emphasis on empowering local peacebuilders to control the process rather than taking charge; (2) the commitment to long-term involvement, which "is related to the commitment of presence, to 'being there' as a Mennonite religious community, and to the political practice of standing with the vulnerable and oppressed"; (3) the strategy of "working with ordinary, often poor, and powerless people as a route to peace," a practice she calls "working from the edge"; (4) the attention given to confronting social inequalities and helping the weakest; and (5) the "central tenet of Mennonite peacebuilding . . . that entry depends upon forming relationships of trust with the parties in conflict as the basis for negotiations or other interventions" (Merry 2000; see also Mitchell 2000).

The establishment of a master's degree program in conflict transformation and an associated Practice Institute at Eastern Mennonite University in Harrisonburg, Virginia, further underscores the growing Mennonite involvement in the theoretical and practical dimensions of conciliation (Charles 1994, 21). Targeting religious communities and NGO personnel involved in developing peacebuilding programs in settings of protracted conflict, this program also illustrates the denomination's distinctive niche in the field.

Initiatives of Change

Founded at Oxford University in the 1920s by Frank Buchman, an American Lutheran minister (Lean 1983), Initiatives of Change (IofC), until 2002 known as Moral Re-Armament, is nondenominational in approach, interreligious in participation, and is organized in some forty countries as a loosely structured global network. IofC's work is founded on a spiritual philosophy that stresses moral regeneration and personal transformation as a precursor to reconciliation in relationships, peacemaking, and constructive social change. The IofC approach involves seeking God's guidance in all aspects of daily living and striving to live according to four absolute moral standards: honesty, purity, unselfishness, and love. It emphasizes personal responsibility and the role of repentance and forgiveness in relationships, whether personal, intergroup, or international (Piguet 1985; Hamlin 1992; Henderson 1996).

Large international assemblies have long been an important vehicle for advancing IofC's ideas. Since its opening in 1946, the IofC conference center in Caux, Switzerland, has been a venue for encounter, relationship building, and genuine transformation and reconciliation among people from different sides of conflicts, as have other Moral Re-Armament centers around the world. Caux was an important site for Franco-German reconciliation following World War II (Piguet 1985; Luttwak 1994; Henderson 1996), and also provided a venue for a 1968 meeting of Austrian and Italian political figures to discuss the two countries' dispute of more than two decades over the South Tyrol (Henderson 1992, 1996, 148–60).

IofC involvement during Rhodesia's war of independence illustrates the broad range of approaches that characterize the group's work. Such involvement included a major international conference attended by more than a thousand participants in Salisbury; a confession of guilt at the conference from Alec Smith, an IofC worker and son of the prime minister, for his complicity in the country's oppressive white-minority rule and his expressed personal commitment to work for a solution; visits by individuals from other countries and different walks of life whose personal stories of moral regeneration and change were deemed to have parable-like relevance for those enmeshed in the Rhodesian conflict; the promotion of reconciliation among key individuals in the society by involving them in conferences at Caux, regional meetings in Africa, small gatherings in Rhodesia, and one-on-one encounters; the facilitation of moral discourse with public figures; the provision of personal support to members of negotiating teams during peace talks; and attempts to reach the larger society with a moral message through publications, newspaper ads, open meetings, and educational films (Kraybill 1994, 222–33; Henderson 1996, 131–46).

Engaged Buddhism

Adherents of the generally introspective tradition of Buddhism have tended to pursue social action and conflict resolution under the rubric of "engaged Buddhism" (Nhat Hanh 1987c; Eppsteiner 1988; Ingram 1990, 74–97; Queen and King 1996). The philosophy was developed in the 1960s by the Vietnamese Zen master Thich Nhat Hanh, who founded the Tiep Hien Order in Vietnam to pursue social action to relieve the suffering on both sides during the Vietnam War. Writes Appleby:

> During the Vietnam war, Thich Nhat Hanh became convinced of the futility of preaching compassion and self-control to individuals subjected to the most trying of circumstances, in which social chaos made inner serenity impossible to achieve. His Tiep Hien Order reversed the traditional Buddhist teaching that pacifying the self would bring peace to the world: pursuing social justice in the world, he instructed the monks, will bring peace to the self. (2000, 137)

More recently, much Buddhist writing and action has been directed specifically to peace and peacebuilding (Nhat Hanh 1987b; Ghosananda 1992; Chappell 1999), and most of it draws direct connections between Buddhist teachings and behavior that promotes peace.

The social activism of engaged Buddhism is based on the fundamental Buddhist precept that meaningful outward change cannot occur without inner transformation. It holds that peace work begins with an inner process of "being peace," which then proceeds outward to all parts of an individual's personal, social, and political life (Nhat Hanh 1987a). Two key tenets constitute Nhat Hanh's peace framework. The first is *nondualism*, which rejects the categories of "them" and "us" in favor of the "we" of a common humanity united against a common enemy of hatred, ignorance, and violence. The second tenet is *interbeing*, which stresses the interconnectedness of everything and the interwoven nature of relationships. Seeing an intimate interconnection between all beings, Nhat Hanh believes that peaceful and happy people will not create suffering in others and that working to alleviate hunger, war, oppression, and injustice makes an individual peaceful and happy. Reconciliation is to understand both sides and to describe to each side the suffering being endured by the other side (Nhat Hanh 1987a, 1987c, 1988; Perry [1989?]). Nhat Hanh's Fourteen Precepts of the Order of Interbeing include specific guides to individual and group behavior, among them admonishments or prohibitions against attachment to any doctrine, theory, ideology (including Buddhism), or personal views; ignoring or losing awareness of suffering; pursuit of wealth, fame, or sensual pleasure; maintaining anger or hatred or uttering words that create discord; and killing or living with a vocation that is harmful to humans or nature (1987c).

Elaborating on these themes, Sulak Sivaraksa of Thailand, a founder of the International Network of Engaged Buddhists, writes that the causes of conflict are essentially spiritual and psychological. Critical self-awareness is key to bringing out an individual's anger, greed, or delusion, and it is then Buddhism's task "to find ways in which the destructive cycle of greed, hate, and delusion may be transformed into that of renunciation, compassion, and wisdom" (Sivaraksa n.d., 5). Maha Ghosananda of Cambodia, in justifying social engagement, suggests that one of Buddha's most courageous acts was to walk onto a battlefield to stop a conflict, an act that today we would call "conflict resolution": "We Buddhists must find the courage to leave our temples and enter the temples of human experience, temples that are filled with suffering. If we listen to the Buddha, Christ, or Gandhi, we can do nothing else. The refugee camps, the prisons, the ghettos, and the battlefields will then become our temples" (1992, 62). The rest of this section highlights the manifestations of engaged Buddhism found within the stages of conflict transformation: latent, confrontation, negotiation, and post-conflict. The first example discussed below, the Sarvodaya Shramadana Movement of Sri Lanka, actually dates from before the concept of engaged Buddhism was articulated by Thich Nhat Hanh.

Sri Lanka has experienced almost continuous ethno-religious violence since 1983 between the politically dominant Sinhalese Buddhist majority and the minority Tamil Hindu community (Little 1994). Since 1958, long before the fissures in Sri Lankan society had erupted into open warfare—and therefore during the latent-conflict stage—the Sarvodaya Shramadana Movement has applied a model of social transformation through people-centered development at the grassroots level (Ariyaratne 1989, 170–71; Macy 1985). Headed by A. T. Ariyaratne, a devout Buddhist who was also inspired by Gandhi (a Hindu), Sarvodaya Shramadana means literally "the awakening of all in society by the mutual sharing of one's time, thought, and energy" (Ariyaratne n.d., 23–43). Spiritual and cultural patterns of Sri Lankan life, including meditation, devotional songs, and traditional customs, have played a major role in Sarvodaya development programs, as have morality, self-discipline, and service to the community (Perera and Ariyaratne 1989, 3). Organized in almost one-third of all Sri Lankan villages, Sarvodaya Shramadana has sought not only to attack the causes of poverty and disease—contributors to conflict—but also to build bridges of collaboration across Sinhalese and Tamil communities. Once communal violence between the two communities did break out (confrontation stage), Ariyaratne, a well-known figure throughout Sri Lankan society, organized peace meetings and seminars around the country and led a number of peace marches and meditations for peace (Liyanage 1988).

Thich Nhat Hanh's actions during the confrontation stage of the Vietnam War reflected two core principles. One principle is "nonseparation from all parties involved in conflict" and therefore the refusal to take sides, but instead to work toward reconciliation and healing. Success, then, is defined as "the overcoming of distrust, antipathy, blame . . . and the creation of harmonious community in which the former enemies all participate" (King 1996, 344–45). The other principle "is always to stop all killing and acute suffering as quickly as possible and to ameliorate suffering when stopping it is impossible." In spite of his policy of not taking sides between north and south, Nhat Hanh's work for peace during the Vietnam War involved "unswerving efforts to end U.S. bombing and to bring about a cease-fire"(King 1996, 342).

In addition to being an inspiration and teacher to many through his poetry, books, public lectures, and meditation workshops, Nhat Hanh's post-conflict peacebuilding in the years since the Vietnam War reflects the nonseparation principle. In working to heal the legacy of the Vietnam War—and viewing American soldiers as well as the Vietnamese as victims of the war—he is forging reconciliation between American Vietnam veterans and Vietnamese refugee communities in the United States, Australia, and France (Perry n.d., 11–12).

The International Network of Engaged Buddhists (INEB) has conducted training in a variety of conflict situations, including programs in nonviolence, mediation, and reconciliation for exiled Burmese prodemocracy students living in camps along the Burmese-Thai border (in confrontation with Burma's military dictatorship). INEB and Quakers have collaborated on training workshops in mediation, reconciliation, and nonviolent approaches to democratization for people from Cambodia, Sri Lanka, Burma (Myanmar), Nepal, India, and Thailand. The INEB-Quaker collaboration has been fostered by the minimal role of doctrinal beliefs in the two traditions and the shared emphasis on the quality of goodness and sacredness in every human being (Sivaraksa n.d.). A British Quaker wrote a handbook on mediation for Buddhist peacemakers (McConnell 1995) and has used this method in conjunction with the work of INEB and other groups in Thailand between Thais and non-Thais who are mostly Buddhist.

The peacebuilding work of Cambodian Buddhist monk Maha Ghosananda began in 1978 amid the "walking skeletons," as the Cambodian survivors of the Khmer Rouge killing fields were called as they streamed across the border into refugee camps in Thailand. (Studying Buddhism in Thailand when the Khmer Rouge seized power, Ghosananda escaped the devastation, but lost his entire family in the genocide.) Ghosananda's peace philosophy might be summed up in a verse from the Dhammapada, which he passed out on slips of paper to refugees and chanted in camps with those yearning to reclaim their lost Buddhist heritage (Kornfield 1992; Channer 1994, 13): "Hatred is never appeased by hatred. Hatred is appeased by love. This is an eternal law" (Buddha, quoted in Ghosananda 1992, 27).

Both before and after the peace accord, Ghosananda worked in the refugee camps at reconciliation, education, cultural restoration, and beginning the work of reinstating Buddhism in Khmer society. His Interreligious Mission for Peace in Cambodia established a temple in each camp, ordained new monks, and trained them in Buddhism and the skills of democracy, human rights, nonviolence, and conflict resolution (Cambodian Mission for Peace 1989, 1994; Ghosananda 1992; Channer 1994; Pond 1995).

During the peace process, Ghosananda led a small contingent of monks to all the top-level Cambodian peace talks held in various capital cities, to be on hand as a spiritual presence, meditate, and conduct symbolic rituals of unity (Channer 1994). Taking a strictly neutral stance, they brought a calm presence to the meetings, proposed compromise, implored the leaders to recall their Buddha nature, and reminded everyone of the power of nonviolence (Ghosananda 1992, 19–20).

In 1992, with other Buddhist monks and nuns, Ghosananda led what would become the first annual Dhammayietra, or peace march. Cambodians from Thai refugee camps marched across the battlefields of northwestern Cambodia to areas where they could settle again among their own people. In 1993, in the run-up to UN-sponsored elections for a new national government, Ghosananda led hundreds of monks, nuns, and laity in a month-long, cross-country march through war-torn regions still controlled by the Khmer Rouge to the capital Phnom Penh. Their purpose was to build popular confidence in the elections and overcome the fear of Khmer Rouge violence and disruption. More than 10,000 Cambodians had joined their ranks by the time they reached the capital, where they held meditations for peace at various monuments. In the 1994 Dhammayietra, held in support of national reconciliation, marchers planted trees as a symbol of rebirth and reconciliation in vast tracts of deforested land and areas made perilous by land mines. Caught in crossfire between Cambodian soldiers and Khmer Rouge guerrillas near the

Thai border, a Buddhist monk and a nun were killed and four other marchers were injured. The theme of the Dhammayietra in 1995 was the need to end global landmine production; in 1997, the theme was peace and reconciliation with the Khmer Rouge (Kim Teng Nhem 1993, 34–41; Appleby 2000, 12, 123–24).

TRENDS IN RELIGIOUS PEACEBUILDING AND CONCLUSIONS

What trends are suggested by this survey and other recent developments?

First, religious communities are increasingly adopting a more intentional and systematic approach to peacebuilding. Not only are communities and denominations that are already involved more actively seeking out training and opportunities to serve, but new entrants have appeared. These include Baptists, active in parts of Asia, Africa, Europe, and Latin America (Buttry 1997; United States Institute of Peace 2001); Methodists, active in Bosnia; and Christian Scientists, active in bringing the ideas of positive approaches to peacebuilding to the fore. Brahma Kumaris have been a close partner with the United Nations in promoting the development of a culture of peace. The United Religions Initiative, a global interfaith association of grassroots organizations, emerged out of Episcopalian circles in San Francisco (Gibbs 2002). Jews, Muslims, and Christians are deeply involved in Middle East peacemaking. Baha'is, Sikhs, and Zoroastrians join the other major world religions, indigenous sacred traditions, and countless smaller religious and spiritual communities in interfaith forums around the world. Other examples abound.

Second, in addition to the growing case literature on religious and interreligious peacebuilding, much of it cited in this chapter, there is a veritable blossoming of writings that look generically at specific religious traditions and identify the religious and sociological resources that have been used to justify or might be mobilized in support of pacifism, nonviolent social action, conflict resolution, forgiveness and reconciliation, democratization, ecumenism, or interfaith dialogue and cooperation.[2] More than a mere theoretical exercise, this genre of searching and discerning research and writing nurtures ever-broadening levels of awareness, acceptance, and the opening of new possibilities for engagement by these religious communities.

Third, recognizing that international development is often undermined or undone by conflict—and also that development can at times unwittingly contribute to conflict—religiously affiliated relief-and-development NGOs have increasingly sought out consultation and training for headquarters and field staff in conflict transformation and peacebuilding. The U.S.-based Catholic Relief Services has incorporated conflict transformation into its official mandate (Headley 2001). Other examples include World Vision, American Jewish Joint Distribution Committee, American Jewish World Service, Mercy Corps, Church World Service, and Lutheran World Relief (Appleby 2000; Smock 2001a, 2001b). The World Conference of Religions for Peace assisted in creating an Interreligious Development Action Committee composed of major humanitarian agencies from the Islamic, Christian Orthodox, Catholic, and Protestant communities (Steinfels 1995).

Fourth, as with individual religious communities, the ecumenical and interreligious sphere is expanding and adopting a more intentional approach to peacebuilding. In addition to the conflict transformation initiatives of the World Conference of Religions for Peace with national interreligious councils, detailed above, numerous national and regional councils of churches and interreligious bodies of many kinds are active in or newly entering the peacebuilding arena. The United Religions Initiative, a rapidly growing global network of some 275 grassroots member "cooperation circles," is active in interfaith dialogue throughout its network; has published an *Interfaith Peacebuilding Guide* (Abu-Nimer et al. 2004); and, inspired by the ideas of John Paul Lederach (2005) on the moral imagination as the "art and soul of building peace," is increasingly proactive in developing on-the-ground peacebuilding.

Fifth, whereas previously religious peacebuilding had the greatest impact in conflicts in which religion was not a major factor in the conflict dynamics, some religious actors are now boldly asserting and pursuing a role for religion in even the most tenacious conflicts involving religious differences, as evidenced in titles such as *Holy War, Holy Peace: How Religion Can Bring Peace to the Middle East* (Gopin 2002) and *Faith-Based Diplomacy: Trumping Realpolitik* (Johnston 2003). The latter volume proposes as yet unrealized (or underrealized) possibilities for religious communities in specific conflict settings (Hinduism in Kashmir, Buddhism in Sri Lanka, Judaism in Israel-Palestine, Christianity in Bosnia-Herzegovina and Kosovo, and Islam in Sudan). Newly conceptualized (but referencing prior cases of religious peacemaking, such as Sudan, Mozambique, Nicaragua), faith-based diplomacy recognizes religion as a defining element of national security in many conflicts and therefore seeks to engage the transcendent, reconciling aspects of religion in overcoming secular obstacles to peace, assisting parties and societies to overcome historic grievances, muting religious fanaticism, and facilitating forgiveness and reconciliation.

Sixth, some secular foreign affairs practitioners are beginning to recognize the salience of religion and religious practitioners in peacemaking. Both an evidence of and a contributor to this trend is the Religion and Peacemaking Initiative of the congressionally funded United States Institute of Peace. Since the initiative was founded in 2001, it has convened workshops and published reports on the contributions of individual religious communities and faith-based NGOs to peacebuilding (Smock 2001a, 2001b); documented interfaith dialogue and peacebuilding (Smock 2002a); facilitated information exchange and networking among religious and interreligious peacebuilders and initiatives (United States Institute of Peace 2001); and been active in facilitating interreligious dialogue among the Abrahamic faiths and between Muslims and Christians in the Philippines, Macedonia, and in Indonesia.

What does this add up to for conflict transformation and peacebuilding overall? For one thing, it implies a pluralism of actors, roles, and methodologies in the religious sector. The sheer diversity of possible actors within and across religious communities is clear. The roles that religious actors define or develop for themselves, too, are necessarily manifold, for they are a function of various temporal factors, among them size, organizational level, and organizational structure of the religious actor; base of operation (inside or outside the conflict setting); degree of power and/or moral authority in the society; history of past programs (humanitarian assistance, educational, and so on); and familiarity with the conflict parties or level of recognition in the society at large.

At least as important in shaping these roles, however, are the moral and spiritual—the theological and philosophical—resources motivating and informing the work of religious peacebuilders. These resources affect the way a given religious actor defines the fundamental problem in the conflict—what is wrong and what needs changing, be it structural, spiritual, moral, or psychological. The way the problem is defined shapes the way an intervention is conceived, its goals, and the methodologies and activities chosen to achieve the goals. Although religious actors are increasingly pursuing training in specific skill areas (active nonviolence, conflict resolution, trauma healing, reconciliation, and the like), because of the inherent differences in the meaning structures of religious communities, it is likely that broad methodological diversity in the overall character of religiously motivated interventions in conflict situations will continue.

If active engagement and pluralism on the part of religious actors are here to stay, then other conclusions certainly follow: that it behooves us to continue to identify, encourage, develop, mobilize, and empower the special resources and potentials of religious actors for constructive conflict transformation—and to coordinate their contributions as integral to the larger peacebuilding enterprise.

ACKNOWLEDGMENTS

The author wishes to express appreciation to the Niwano Peace Foundation for a research grant that supported research on the religious roots of Buddhist, Gandhian, and Islamic peacebuilding. She also wishes to acknowledge the Catalyst Fund for its support during the writing of this chapter. Parts of this chapter, updated and revised from the original 1997 volume, draw on a document the author prepared for the World Conference on Religion and Peace (WCRP; Sampson 1999), which in turn was enriched by the thinking and wisdom of WCRP Secretary-General William Vendley.

REFERENCES

Abbad, Abdul El-Rahman. 1996. "Peace and Pacifism in Islam." *International Journal of Nonviolence* 3: 60–70.

Abu-Nimer, Mohammed. 2000–01. "A Framework for Nonviolence and Peace-building in Islam." *The Journal of Law and Religion* 15 (1 and 2): 217–65.

———. 2003. *Nonviolence and Peace Building in Islam: Theory and Practice.* Gainesville: University Press of Florida.

Abu-Nimer, Mohammed, Barbara Hartford, Claudia Liebler, Susanna McIlwaine, and Cynthia Sampson. 2004. *Interfaith Peacebuilding Guide.* San Francisco: United Religions Initiative.

Ackerman, Peter, and Christopher Kruegler. 1994. *Strategic Nonviolent Conflict: The Dynamics of People Power in the Twentieth Century.* Westport, Conn.: Praeger.

Africa News. 1991. "Bits and Pieces: Church and State" 35, no. 2 (summer): 8.

Appleby, R. Scott. 2000. *The Ambivalence of the Sacred.* Lanham, Md.: Rowman and Littlefield.

Arabi, Oussama. 1997. "Constitutional Aspects of Conflict Resolution in Classical Islam." In *Conflict Resolution in the Arab World: Selected Essays,* ed. Paul Salem. Beirut: American University of Beirut.

Ariyaratne, A. T. n.d. *Collected Works,* vol. I. Netherlands: n.p.

———. 1989. *Collected Works,* vol. IV. Moratuwa, Sri Lanka: Vishva Lekha.

Assefa, Hizkias. 1987. *Mediation of Civil Wars: Approaches and Strategies—The Sudan Conflict.* Boulder, Colo.: Westview.

———. 1993a. *Peace and Reconciliation as a Paradigm.* Nairobi, Kenya: Nairobi Peace Initiative.

———. 1993b. "On Healing and Reconciliation: A Dialogue." In *Pilgrim Voices: Citizens as Peacemakers,* ed. Ed Garcia. Manila: Ateneo de Manila University Press.

———. 1993c. "The Sudan: Peacemaking in a Conflict within a Conflict." In *Pilgrim Voices: Citizens as Peacemakers,* ed. Ed Garcia. Manila: Ateneo de Manila University Press.

————. 1994. "Relevance of Religion to Peacemaking." Paper presented at the sixth world assembly of the World Conference on Religion and Peace, November 5, Riva del Garda, Italy.

————. 1999. "The Meaning of Reconciliation." In *People Building Peace: 35 Inspiring Stories from Around the World*. Utrecht, Netherlands: European Centre for Conflict Prevention.

————. 2004. "Peacebuilding in a Globalizing Africa: The Roles of Religious Institutions and Leaders." *Peace Colloquy* 6: 5–12.

Bailey, Sydney. 1979. "The Christian Vocation of Reconciliation." In *Crucible: The Journal of the Board of Social Responsibility of the General Synod of the Church of England* (July–September): 205–22.

————. 1985. "Non-official Mediation in Disputes: Reflections on Quaker Experience." *International Affairs* 61 (2): 205–22.

————. 1993. *Peace Is a Process*. London: Quaker Home Service and Woodbrooke College.

Bartoli, Andrea. 2001a. "Mediating Peace in Mozambique: The Role of the Community of Sant'Egidio." In *Herding Cats: Multiparty Mediation in a Complex World*, ed. Chester Crocker, Fen Osler Hampson, and Pamela Aall. Washington, D.C.: United States Institute of Peace Press.

————. 2001b. "Catholic Peacemaking: The Experience of the Community of Sant'Egidio." Talk delivered at the United States Institute of Peace, February 5, Washington, D.C.

Battersby, John. 1990. "South Africa's Churches Move Toward Conciliation." *Christian Science Monitor*, November 13.

Bergey, Bonnie. 2000. "The Bottom-Up Alternative in Somali Peacebuilding." In *From the Ground Up: Mennonite Contributions to International Peacebuilding*, ed. Cynthia Sampson and John Paul Lederach. New York: Oxford University Press.

Bolling, Landrum. 1977. "Quaker Work in the Middle East Following the June 1967 War." In *Unofficial Diplomats*, ed. Maureen R. Berman and Joseph E. Johnson. New York: Columbia University Press.

————. 1987. "Strengths and Weaknesses of Track Two: A Personal Account." In *Conflict Resolution: Track Two Diplomacy*, ed. John W. McDonald Jr. and Diane B. Bendahmane. Washington, D.C.: Foreign Service Institute.

Bondurant, Joan V. 1988. *Conquest of Violence: The Gandhian Philosophy of Conflict*. Princeton, N.J.: Princeton University Press.

Boulding, Elise. 1986. "Two Cultures of Religion as Obstacles to Peace." *Zygon* 21 (December): 501–18.

Braybrooke, Marcus. 1992. *Pilgrimage of Hope: One Hundred Years of Global Interfaith Dialogue*. London: SCM Press.

Brubaker, Alta. 1993. "Preparing People for Peace: Program of Work by the Peace and Reconciliation Committee of the Christian Council of Mozambique." Report to the Mennonite Central Committee, March 18, Nampula, Mozambique.

Buttry, Daniel L. 1997. "Gospel New Wine and the Gabel Fund." Plenary address at Baptist Peace Fellowship summer conference, Eastern Mennonite University, Harrisonburg, Va., July 13.

Cambodian Mission for Peace. 1989. Press release, May 12, Bangkok.

———. 1994. "The Cambodian Mission for Peace: Description of Strategic Program Development." Cambodian Mission for Peace, Providence, R.I., May 10.

Campbell, Joseph. 2000. "Partnering with the Mennonites in Northern Ireland." In *From the Ground Up: Mennonite Contributions to International Peacebuilding*, ed. Cynthia Sampson and John Paul Lederach. New York: Oxford University Press.

Carnegie Commission on Preventing Deadly Violence. 1997. *Preventing Deadly Conflict*. New York: Carnegie Corporation.

Carter, Jimmy. 1994. Foreword. In *Religion, The Missing Dimension of Statecraft*, ed. Douglas Johnston and Cynthia Sampson. New York: Oxford University Press.

Cartwright, Michael G. 1996. "Conflicting Interpretations of Christian Pacifism." In *The Ethics of War and Peace*, ed. Terry Nardin. Princeton, N.J.: Princeton University Press.

Cassidy, Michael. 1995. *A Witness for Ever: The Dawning of Democracy in South Africa, Stories Behind the Story*. London: Hodder and Stoughton.

Channer, Alan. 1994. "Cambodia's Nobel Nominee." *For a Change* 7 (October/November): 12–13.

Chappell, David W., ed. 1999. *Buddhist Peacework: Creating Cultures of Peace*. Somerville, Mass.: Wisdom Publications.

Charles, J. Robert. 1994. *Mennonite International Peacemaking During and After the Cold War*, Occasional Paper no. 21. Akron, Penn.: Mennonite Central Committee.

Christian Peacemaker Teams. n.d. "Christian Peacemaker Teams." Informational brochure of Mennonite, Church of the Brethren, and General Conference Mennonite Churches, Chicago.

Christiansen, Drew. 2001. "Catholic Peacemaking: From Pacem in terris to Centesimus annus." Talk delivered at the United States Institute of Peace, February 5, Washington, D.C.

Chupp, Mark. 2000. "Creating Space for Peace: The Central American Peace Portfolio." In *From the Ground Up: Mennonite Contributions to International Peacebuilding*, ed. Cynthia Sampson and John Paul Lederach. New York: Oxford University Press.

Claiborne, William. 1989. "De Klerk, Tutu Group to Meet." *Washington Post*, October 7.

Curle, Adam. 1971. *Making Peace*. London: Tavistock.

———. 1981. *True Justice: Quaker Peace Makers and Peace Making*. London: Quaker Home Service.

———. 1986a. *In the Middle: Non-official Mediation in Violent Situations*. New York: St. Martin's.

———. 1986b. "Mediation: Steps on the Long Road to Negotiated Settlement of Conflicts." *Transnational Perspectives* 12 (1): 5–7.

————. 1990. *Tools for Transformation: A Personal Study*. Stroud, UK: Hawthorn.

————. 1995. *Another Way: Positive Response to Contemporary Violence*. Oxford: Jon Carpenter.

de Souza, Isidore. 1994. "African Churches as Peacemakers." Presentation at the African Church as Peacemaker Colloquium, October 2–6, Duquesne University, Pittsburgh, Penn.

Driedger, Leo, and Donald B. Kraybill. 1994. *Mennonite Peacemaking: From Quietism to Activism*. Scottdale, Penn.: Herald.

Drozdiak, William. 1995. "Algerian Parties Unite in Call for Peace Talks." *Washington Post*, January 14.

Easwaran. Eknath. 1984. *A Man to Match His Mountains: Badshah Khan, Nonviolent Soldier of Islam*. Petaluma, Calif.: Nilgiri.

Eppsteiner, Fred, ed. 1988. *The Path of Compassion: Writings on Socially Engaged Buddhism*. Berkeley, Calif.: Buddhist Peace Fellowship and Parallax.

Esack, Maulana Faried. 1994. Presentation on Muslim participation in the antiapartheid struggle, at the Magaliesburg Consultation of the World Conference on Religion and Peace, August 8, Magaliesburg, South Africa.

————. 1997. *Qur'an, Liberation and Pluralism: An Islamic Perspective of Interreligious Solidarity Against Oppression*. Oxford, UK: Oneworld.

Esquivia, Ricardo, with Paul Stucky. 2000. "Building Peace from Below and Inside: The Mennonite Experience in Colombia." In *From the Ground Up: Mennonite Contributions to International Peacebuilding*, ed. Cynthia Sampson and John Paul Lederach. New York: Oxford University Press.

Finger, Thomas. 1994. "A Mennonite Theology for Interfaith Relations." Prepared for N.C.C.C. Consultation, "Discovering Christian Resources for a Theology of Interfaith Relations," October 13–14, Elizabeth, N.J.

Fisk, Timothy D. 1992. *Islam and Democracy: Religion, Politics, and Power in the Middle East*. Washington, D.C.: United States Institute of Peace Press.

Gandhi, Mohandas K. 1983. *Mohandas K. Gandhi Autobiography: The Story of My Experiments with Truth*. New York: Dover.

————. 1997. *Hind Swaraj and Other Writings*. Cambridge, UK: Cambridge University Press.

Gandhi Peace Foundation. n.d. "Gandhi Peace Foundation." Informational brochure. Delhi, India.

Germani, Clara. 1988. "Panama's Reluctant Church: Conservative Catholic Clergy Uneasy in Political Role." *Christian Science Monitor*, April 12.

Ghosananda, Maha. 1992. *Step by Step: Meditations on Wisdom and Compassion*, ed. J. S. Mahoney and P. Edmonds. Berkeley, Calif.: Parallax.

Gibbs, Charles. 2002. "The United Religions Initiative at Work." In *Interfaith Dialogue and Peacebuilding*, ed. David R. Smock. Washington, D.C.: United States Institute of Peace Press.

Gonçalves, Jaime. 1993. "Peace in Mozambique Today." Presentation at the Carnegie Endowment Center, Washington, D.C., February 17.

————. 1994. Presentation on Catholic peacemaking during the Mozambique war of independence, at the African Church as Peacemaker Colloquium, October 2–6, Duquesne University, Pittsburgh, Pennsylvania.

Goodman, Naomi. 1996. "The Jewish Tradition of Nonviolence." *International Journal of Nonviolence* 3: 53–59.

Gopin, Marc. 1997. "Religion, Violence, and Conflict Resolution." *Peace and Change* 22 (January): 1–31.

————. 2000a. *Between Eden and Armageddon: The Future of World Religions, Violence, and Peacemaking.* New York: Oxford University Press.

————. 2000b. "The Religious Component of Mennonite Peacemaking and Its Global Implications." In *From the Ground Up: Mennonite Contributions to International Peacebuilding,* ed. Cynthia Sampson and John Paul Lederach. New York: Oxford University Press.

————. 2001. "Forgiveness as an Element of Conflict Resolution in Religious Cultures." In *Reconciliation, Justice, and Coexistence: Theory and Practice,* ed. Mohammed Abu-Nimer. Lanham, Md.: Lexington Books.

————. 2002. *Holy War, Holy Peace: How Religion Can Bring Peace to the Middle East.* New York: Oxford University Press.

Hall, Mitchell. 1987. "In the Lion's Mouth: The Non-Violent Mission of Acharya Muni Sushil Kumarji Maharaj." Unpublished manuscript. Warren, Vt.

Hamlin, Bryan. 1991. "The Role of Religiously Motivated Peacemakers in International and Intercommunal Conflict." Paper presented at the National Conference on Peacemaking and Conflict Resolution, June 3–8, Charlotte, N.C.

————. 1992. *Forgiveness in International Affairs.* Salem, Ore.: Grosvenor Books.

Hart, Barry. 1993. *Trauma Healing and Reconciliation Training Manual: A Handbook for Trainers and Trainees.* Monrovia, Liberia: Christian Health Association of Liberia.

————. 1995. Telephone interview, January 28.

————. 2000. "Trauma-Healing and Reconciliation in Liberia." In *From the Ground Up: Mennonite Contributions to International Peacebuilding,* ed. Cynthia Sampson and John Paul Lederach. New York: Oxford University Press.

Hart, Barry, and Joe Gbaba. 1993. *UNICEF Training Manual of Conflict Resolution, Reconciliation, and Peace.* Monrovia, Liberia: UNICEF.

Hashmi, Sohail H. 1996. "Interpreting the Islamic Ethics of War and Peace." In *The Ethics of War and Peace,* ed. Terry Nardin. Princeton, N.J.: Princeton University Press.

Headley, William. 2001. "Catholic Relief Services' Contribution to International Peacemaking." Talk delivered at the United States Institute of Peace, February 5, Washington, D.C.

Henderson, Michael. 1992. "South Tyrol's Example." *Christian Science Monitor,* July 1.

————. 1995. "Africa's Quiet Peace-Maker." *For a Change* 8 (June/July): 13.

————. 1996. *The Forgiveness Factor: Stories of Hope in a World of Conflict*. Salem, Ore., and London: Grosvenor Books.

————. 1999. *Forgiveness: Breaking the Chain of Hate*. Wilsonville, Ore.: Book Partners.

Hillman, Eugene. 1989. *Many Paths: A Catholic Approach to Religious Pluralism*. Maryknoll, N.Y.: Orbis.

Herr, Robert, and Judy Zimmerman Herr. 2000. "Building Peace in South Africa: A Case Study of Mennonite Program." In *From the Ground Up: Mennonite Contributions to International Peacebuilding*, ed. Cynthia Sampson and John Paul Lederach. New York: Oxford University Press.

Hinton, Jeanne. 1993. *Communities: Stories of Christian Communities in Europe*. Guildford, Surrey, UK: Eagle.

Hume, Cameron. 1994. *Ending Mozambique's War: The Role of Mediation and Good Offices*. Washington, D.C.: United States Institute of Peace Press.

Impagliazzo, Marco. 1988. "The St. Egidio Platform for a Peaceful Solution of the Algerian Crisis." In *Private Peacemaking: USIP-Assisted Peacemaking Projects of Nonprofit Organizations*, Peaceworks no. 20, ed. David Smock. Washington, D.C.: United States Institute of Peace Press.

Ingham, Michael. 1997. *Mansions of the Spirit: The Gospel in a Multi-Faith World*. Toronto: Anglican Book Centre.

Ingram, Catherine. 1990. *In the Footsteps of Gandhi: Interviews with Spiritual Social Activists*. Berkeley, Calif.: Parallax.

International Observer Delegation. 1986. "A Path to Democratic Renewal: A Report of the February 7 Presidential Election in the Philippines." Washington, D.C.: National Democratic Institute for International Affairs.

Jack, Homer. 1993. *WCRP: A History of the World Conference on Religion and Peace*. New York: World Conference on Religion and Peace.

Jackson, Elmore. 1983. *Middle East Mission*. New York: Norton.

Johansen, Robert C. 1997. "Radical Islam and Nonviolence: A Case Study of Religious Empowerment and Constraint Among Pashtuns." *Journal of Peace Research* 34 (1): 53–71.

Johnston, Douglas. 1994. "The Churches and Apartheid in South Africa." In *Religion: The Missing Dimension of Statecraft*, ed. Douglas Johnston and Cynthia Sampson. New York: Oxford University Press.

————, ed. 2003. "Introduction: Beyond Realpolitik." In *Faith-Based Diplomacy, Trumping Realpolitik*, ed. Douglas Johnston. New York: Oxford University Press.

Johnston, Douglas, and Cynthia Sampson, eds. 1994. *Religion: The Missing Dimension of Statecraft*. New York: Oxford University Press.

Jones, Clayton. 1989a. "Mending Broken Burma." *World Monitor* (August): 4 4–51.

————. 1989b. "Monks March in Subtle Protest." *Christian Science Monitor*, August 14.

Keller, Bill. 1994. "Zulu Party Ends Boycott of Vote in South Africa." *New York Times*, April 20.

Kern, Kathleen. 2000. "From Haiti to Hebron with a Brief Stop in Washington, D.C.: The CPT Experiment." In *From the Ground Up: Mennonite Contributions to International Peacebuilding,* ed. Cynthia Sampson and John Paul Lederach. New York: Oxford University Press.

Kim Teng Nhem. 1993. "Walking Slowly Towards Peace in Cambodia." In *Pilgrim Voices,* ed. Edward Garcia. Manila: Ateneo de Manila University Press.

King, Sallie B. 1996. "Thich Nhat Hanh and the Unified Buddhist Church: Nondualism in Action." In *Engaged Buddhism: Buddhist Liberation Movements in Asia,* ed. Christopher S. Queen and Sallie B. King. Albany: State University of New York.

Kohen, Arnold S. 1999. *From the Place of the Dead: The Epic Struggle of Bishop Belo of East Timor.* New York: St. Martin's.

Koontz, Theodore J. 1996. "Christian Nonviolence." In *The Ethics of War and Peace,* ed. Terry Nardin. Princeton, N.J.: Princeton University Press.

Kornfield, Jack. 1992. Preface. In *Step by Step by Maha Ghosananda.* Berkeley, Calif.: Parallax.

Kraft, Kenneth, ed. 1992. *Inner Peace, World Peace: Essays on Buddhism and Nonviolence.* Albany: State University of New York Press.

Kraybill, Ronald. 1988. "From Head to Heart: The Cycle of Reconciliation." *Conciliation Quarterly* 7 (Fall): 2–3, 8.

———. 1994. "Transition from Rhodesia to Zimbabwe: The Role of Religious Actors." In *Religion: The Missing Dimension of Statecraft,* ed. Douglas Johnston and Cynthia Sampson. New York: Oxford University Press.

———. 1995. Interview with the author, February 13, Harrisonburg, Va.

———. 1996. Peacebuilders in Zimbabwe: An Anabaptist Paradigm for Conflict Transformation. PhD diss., University of Cape Town.

———. 2000. "Reflections on Twenty Years in Peacebuilding." In *From the Ground Up: Mennonite Contributions to International Peacebuilding,* ed. Cynthia Sampson and John Paul Lederach. New York: Oxford University Press.

LaFranchi, Howard. 1995. "How a Year Changed Chiapas." *Christian Science Monitor,* January 3.

Lampman, Jane. 1999. "Faith's Unbreakable Force." *Christian Science Monitor,* December 3.

Landau, Yehezkel. 2003. "Healing the Holy Land: Interreligious Peacebuilding in Israel/Palestine." Peaceworks no. 51. Washington, D.C.: United States Institute of Peace Press.

Larmer, Brook. 1988. "Cardinal Throws the Contras a Lifeline: Mediator's Plan Gives Rebels New Negotiating Power." *Christian Science Monitor* (Weekly International Edition), February 29–March 6.

Laue, James, and Gerald Cormick. 1978. "The Ethics of Intervention in Community Disputes." In *The Ethics of Social Intervention,* ed. Gordon Bermant, Herbert C. Kelman, and Donald P. Warwick. Washington, D.C.: Halsted.

Lean, Garth. 1983. *Frank Buchman: A Life*. London: Constable and Company.

Lean, Mary. 1995. "Did God Intervene in South Africa?" *For a Change* 8 (June/July): 10–11.

Lederach, John Paul. 1989. Interview with the author, June 13, Washington, D.C.

———. 1993. "Pacifism in Contemporary Conflict: A Christian Perspective." Paper presented at the United States Institute of Peace Symposium on Religious Perspectives on Pacifism, July 28, Washington, D.C.

———. 1995. *Preparing for Peace: Conflict Transformation Across Cultures*. Syracuse, N.Y.: Syracuse University Press.

———. 1997. *Building Peace: Sustainable Reconciliation in Divided Societies*. Washington, D.C.: United States Institute of Peace Press.

———. 1999. *Journey Toward Reconciliation*. Scottdale, Penn.: Herald.

———. 2000a. "Journey from Reconciliation to Transformative Peacebuilding." In *From the Ground Up: Mennonite Contributions to International Peacebuilding*, ed. Cynthia Sampson and John Paul Lederach. New York: Oxford University Press.

———. 2000b. "Mennonite Central Committee Efforts in Somalia and Somaliland." In *From the Ground Up: Mennonite Contributions to International Peacebuilding*, ed. Cynthia Sampson and John Paul Lederach. New York: Oxford University Press.

———. 2005. *The Moral Imagination: The Art and Soul of Building Peace*. New York: Oxford University Press.

Liechty, Joseph. 2000. "Mennonites and Conflict in Northern Ireland, 1970–1998." In *From the Ground Up: Mennonite Contributions to International Peacebuilding*, ed. Cynthia Sampson and John Paul Lederach. New York: Oxford University Press.

Linden, Ian. 1980. *The Catholic Church and the Struggle for Zimbabwe*. London: Longman.

Little, David. 1994. *Sri Lanka: The Invention of Enmity*. Washington, D.C.: United States Institute of Peace Press.

Liyanage, Gunadasa. 1988. *Revolution under the Breadfruit Tree*. Nugegoda, Sri Lanka: Sinha Publishers.

Lubbe, Gerrie. 1994. *A Decade of Interfaith Dialogue*. Johannesburg: South African Chapter of the World Conference on Religion and Peace.

Luttwak, Edward. 1994. "Franco-German Reconciliation: The Overlooked Role of the Moral Re-Armament Movement." In *Religion: The Missing Dimension of Statecraft*, ed. Douglas Johnston and Cynthia Sampson. New York: Oxford University Press.

Macy, Joanna. 1985. "In Indra's Net: Sarvodaya and Our Mutual Efforts for Peace." In *The Path of Compassion: Writings on Socially Engaged Buddhism*, ed. Fred Eppsteiner. Berkeley, Calif.: Parallax.

McConnell, John A. 1995. *Mindful Mediation: A Handbook for Buddhist Peacemakers*. Bangkok: Buddhist Research Center, Mahachula Buddhist University.

Merry, Sally. 2000. "Mennonite Peacebuilding and Conflict Transformation: A Cultural Analysis." In *From the Ground Up: Mennonite Contributions to International*

Peacebuilding, ed. Cynthia Sampson and John Paul Lederach. New York: Oxford University Press.

Mitchell, Christopher. 2000. "Mennonite Approaches to Peace and Conflict Resolution." In *From the Ground Up: Mennonite Contributions to International Peacebuilding*, ed. Cynthia Sampson and John Paul Lederach. New York: Oxford University Press.

Morrow, Duncan, and Derick Wilson. 1994. "Churches and Chaos in Northern Ireland: From Religion and Conflict to Freedom in Faith?" Paper prepared for the World Conference on Religion and Peace, September 6–11, Bellagio, Italy.

Morrow, John. n.d. "The Corrymeela Community." Informational brochure. Belfast, Northern Ireland.

Morozzo della Rocca, Roberto. 1998. "Community of St. Egidio in Kosovo." In *Private Peacemaking: USIP-Assisted Peacemaking Projects of Nonprofit Organizations*, Peaceworks no. 20, ed. David Smock. Washington, D.C.: United States Institute of Peace Press.

Moussalli, Ahmad S. 1997. "An Islamic Model for Political Conflict Resolution: Tahkim (Arbitration)." In *Conflict Resolution in the Arab World: Selected Essays*, ed. Paul Salem. Beirut: American University of Beirut.

Nhat Hanh, Thich. 1987a. *Being Peace*. Berkeley, Calif.: Parallax.

———. 1987b. "Seven Steps to Reconciliation." *Fellowship* (July/August): 4–5.

———. 1987c. *Interbeing: Fourteen Guidelines for Engaged Buddhism*. Berkeley, Calif.: Parallax.

———. 1988. *The Heart of Understanding*. Berkeley, Calif.: Parallax.

Nichols, Bruce. 1994. "Religious Conciliation between the Sandinistas and the East Coast Indians of Nicaragua." In *Religion: The Missing Dimension of Statecraft*, ed. Douglas Johnston and Cynthia Sampson. New York: Oxford University Press.

Nonviolence Education and Training Program. n.d. "The Nonviolence Education and Training Program." Informational brochure. Alkmaar, Netherlands: International Fellowship of Reconciliation.

Nonviolence International. 1995. "Nonviolence International." Informational brochure, Washington, D.C.

Paige, Glenn D., Chaiwat Satha-Anand, and Sarah Gilliatt, eds. 1993. *Islam and Nonviolence*. Honolulu: University of Hawaii.

Patriot (New Delhi). 1987. "Punjab Talks Gaining Momentum," May 9.

Perera, D. A., and A. T. Ariyaratne. 1989. "Sarvodaya as a Movement." Occasional paper. Moratuwa, Sri Lanka: Sarvodaya Shramadana.

Perry, Patricia Hunt. n.d. "Opening the Cone and Harvesting the Seeds: Thich Nhat Hanh, Buddhism, and the Peace Movement." Unpublished paper. Ramapo College of New Jersey, Mahwah, N.J.

Pierre, Andrew J., and William B. Quandt. 1995. "The 'Contract' With Algeria: One Last Chance for the West to Help Stop the Civil War." *Washington Post*, January 22.

Piguet, Jacqueline. 1985. *For the Love of Tomorrow: The Story of Irene Laure*. London: Grosvenor Books.

Pond, Peter. 1995. Telephone interview with the author, February 8.

Pran, Dith. 1992. Foreword. In *Step by Step by Maha Ghosananda*. Berkeley, Calif.: Parallax.

Princen, Thomas. 1987. "International Mediation—The View from the Vatican: Lessons from Mediating the Beagle Channel Dispute." *Negotiation Journal* 3 (4): 347–66.

———. 1992a. *Intermediaries in International Conflict*. Princeton, N.J.: Princeton University Press.

———. 1992b. "Quiet Peacemaking in a Civil War." In *When Talk Works: Profiles of Mediators*, ed. Deborah M. Kolb and Associates. San Francisco: Jossey-Bass.

Pyarelal, Nayar. 1950. *A Pilgrimage of Peace: Gandhi and Frontier Gandhi among N.W.F. Pathans*. Ahmedabad, India: Navajivan.

Queen, Christopher S., and Sallie B. King, eds. 1996. *Engaged Buddhism: Buddhist Liberation Movements in Asia*. Albany: State University of New York.

Rees, Elfan. 1977. "Exercises in Private Diplomacy: Selected Activities of the Commission of the Churches on International Affairs." In *Unofficial Diplomats*, ed. Maureen R. Berman and Joseph E. Johnson. New York: Columbia University Press.

Reuters News Service. 1993. "Zaire's Ruler Returns after Trip to France." *Washington Post*, February 28.

Richburg, Keith. 1993. "Mobutu Clings to Power in Violence-Torn Zaire." *Washington Post*, February 23.

Robberson, Tod. 1994. "Mexico Says Catholic Church Fomented Peasant Rebellion." *Washington Post*, January 1.

Said, Abdul Aziz, Nathan C. Funk, and Ayse S. Kadayifci, eds. 2001. *Peace and Conflict Resolution in Islam: Precept and Practice*. Blue Ridge Summit, Penn.: University Press of America.

Sampson, Cynthia. 1987. *A Study of the International Conciliation Work of Religious Figures*. Working Paper Series 87–6. Cambridge, Mass.: Harvard University Program on Negotiation.

———. 1994. "To Make Real the Bond Between Us All: Quaker Conciliation During the Nigerian Civil War." In *Religion: The Missing Dimension of Statecraft*, ed. Douglas Johnston and Cynthia Sampson. New York: Oxford University Press.

———. 1999. "Conflict Transformation Commission Seventh WCRP World Assembly: Preparatory Document," November 25–29, Amman, Jordan.

———. 2000. "Local Assessments of Mennonite Peacebuilding." In *From the Ground Up: Mennonite Contributions to International Peacebuilding*, ed. Cynthia Sampson and John Paul Lederach. New York: Oxford University Press.

Schirch, Lisa. 1995. *Keeping the Peace: Exploring Civilian Alternatives in Conflict Prevention*. Uppsala, Sweden: Life and Peace Institute.

Schneidman, Whitney W. 1993. "Conflict Resolution in Mozambique." In *Making War and Waging Peace: Foreign Intervention in Africa*, ed. David R. Smock. Washington, D.C.: United States Institute of Peace Press.

Scott, David Clark. 1994a. "Mexico Bishop at Center of Crisis." *Christian Science Monitor*, January 24.

———. 1994b. "Rebels Win Rights for Indians, Spur Ballot Reforms for Mexico." *Christian Science Monitor*, March 4.

Sharma, I. C. 1990. "The Ethics in Eastern Philosophy and Religion." In *Nonviolence in Theory and Practice*, ed. Robert L. Holmes. Belmont, Calif.: Wadsworth.

Siddhachalam Newsletter. 1987. "Guruji's Peace Mission in Punjab." July.

Siddhachalam Newsletter. 1988. "Punjab." June.

Shiner, Cindy. 1992. "Zaire's Weighty Crisis Persists." *Africa News* 36, no. 1 (May): 11–24.

———. 1998. "E. Timor Sees Church in Role of Protector." *Washington Post*, June 25.

Sivaraksa, Sulak. n.d. "Buddhism and Peace: A Buddhist Approach to Mediation and Reconciliation." Paper presented at the Sixth World Assembly of the World Conference on Religion and Peace, November 5, Riva del Garda, Italy.

Smock, David, ed. 2001a. *Catholic Contributions to International Peace*. United States Institute of Peace Special Report 69, April 9.

———. 2001b. *Faith-Based NGOs and International Peacebuilding*. United States Institute of Peace Special Report 76, October 22.

———. 2002a. *Interfaith Dialogue and Peacebuilding*. Washington, DC: United States Institute of Peace Press.

———. 2002b. *Islam and Democracy*. United States Institute of Peace Special Report 93, September.

Steele, David. 1994. "At the Front Lines of the Revolution: East Germany's Churches Give Sanctuary and Succor to the Purveyors of Change." In *Religion: The Missing Dimension of Statecraft*, ed. Douglas Johnston and Cynthia Sampson. New York: Oxford University Press.

———. 2002. "Contributions of Interfaith Dialogue to Peacebuilding in the Former Yugoslavia." In *Interfaith Dialogue and Peacebuilding*, ed. David R. Smock. Washington, D.C.: United States Institute of Peace Press.

Steinfels, Peter. 1995. "Two World Conferences and Two Very Different Roles for Religion: One Quiet, the Other Noisy." *New York Times*, March 18.

Tanko, Bauna Peter. 1991. *The Christian Association of Nigeria and the Challenge of the Ecumenical Imperative*. Jos, Nigeria: Fab Anieh Nigeria.

Tibi, Bassam. 1996. "War and Peace in Islam." In *The Ethics of War and Peace*, ed. Terry Nardin. Princeton, N.J.: Princeton University Press.

Tutu, Desmond. 1994. *The Rainbow People of God: The Making of a Peaceful Revolution*. New York: Doubleday.

United States Institute of Peace. 1993. *Conflict and Conflict Resolution in Mozambique: Report from a Conference on "Discussions from Dialogues on Conflict Resolution," July 13–15, 1992.* Washington, D.C.: United States Institute of Peace Press.

———. 2001. Survey on religion and peacemaking, conducted by USIP Religion and Peacemaking Initiative, email messages, June 12, 25.

Vendley, William F. 1995. Telephone interview with the author, February 8.

Vendley, William, and David Little. 1994. "Implications for Religious Community." In *Religion: The Missing Dimension of Statecraft*, ed. Douglas Johnston and Cynthia Sampson. New York: Oxford University Press.

Walzer, Michael. 1996. "War and Peace in the Jewish Tradition." In *The Ethics of War and Peace*, ed. Terry Nardin. Princeton, N.J.: Princeton University Press.

Warren, Roland L. 1987. "American Friends Service Committee Mediation Efforts in Germany and Korea." In *Conflict Resolution: Track Two Diplomacy*, ed. John W. McDonald Jr. and Diane B. Bendahmane. Washington, D.C.: Foreign Service Institute.

Washington Post. 1992. "Guatemalans Find Limited Accord in Peace Talks," August 9.

———. 1993. "Pope Touring Africa," February 4.

Wehr, Paul, and John Paul Lederach. 1991. "Mediating Conflict in Central America." *Journal of Peace Research* 28 (February): 85–98.

Wink, Walter. 1987. *Violence and Nonviolence in South Africa: Jesus' Third Way.* Philadelphia: New Society.

———. 1992. *Engaging the Powers.* Minneapolis: Fortress.

Winkler, Renate. 1986. "Recent Church Initiatives for Peace and Justice in South Africa." Mimeograph. Centre for Intergroup Studies, Cape Town, South Africa.

Wise, Gordon, and Alice Cardel. 1991. "The Cardinal and the Revolution." *For a Change* 4 (April): 12–13.

Wooster, Henry. 1994. "Faith at the Ramparts: The Philippine Catholic Church and the 1986 Revolution." In *Religion: The Missing Dimension of Statecraft*, ed. Douglas Johnston and Cynthia Sampson. New York: Oxford University Press.

World Conference on Religion and Peace project summary. n.d. World Conference on Religion and Peace. New York: WCRP/International.

Yarrow, C. H. 1977. "Quaker Efforts toward Reconciliation in the India-Pakistan War of 1965." In *Unofficial Diplomats*, ed. M. R. Berman and J. E. Johnson. New York: Columbia University Press.

———. 1978. *Quaker Experiences in International Conciliation.* New Haven, Conn.: Yale University Press.

Young, Ronald. 1987. Interview with the author, March 23, Cambridge, Mass.

NOTES

1. See, for example, the seven case studies in Johnston and Sampson (1994), as well as the Catholic mediation between Chile and Argentina, the Catholic mediation of the Mozambique civil war, and interreligious peacemaking in Sierra Leone, all discussed in this chapter. A notable exception is the successful mediation of Sudanese peace talks in 1972 by religious figures, also discussed in this chapter.

2. Some examples include on Islam, Fisk (1992), Paige, Satha-Anand, and Gilliatt (1993); Tibi (1996), Hashmi (1996), Abbad (1996), Arabi (1997), Moussalli (1997), Esack (1997), Said, Funk, and Kadayifci. (2001), Abu-Nimer (2000–01, 2003), Landau (2003); on Judaism, Walzer (1996), Goodman (1996), Gopin (2000a, 2001), Smock (2002b), Landau (2003); on Christianity, Wink (1992), Koontz (1996), Cartwright (1996), Ingham (1997), Landau (2003); on Anabaptism/Mennonitism, Finger (1994), Kraybill (1996), Lederach (1999), Gopin (2000a, 2000b); on Roman Catholicism, Hillman (1989) and Tanko (1991); on Buddhism, Kraft (1992), McConnell (1995), Nhat Hanh (1987a, 1987b, 1987c).

PART THREE

EDUCATION AND TRAINING

8

ADDRESSING CONFLICT THROUGH EDUCATION

Pamela R. Aall, Jeffrey W. Helsing, and Alan C. Tidwell

This chapter focuses on two aspects of the relationship between education and conflict. The first part examines some of the developments in the past fifteen years in higher education curriculum and course offerings, especially in the United States, related to the study of conflict and its management. This period has seen a dramatic growth in the numbers of courses and programs in this area, and an equally dramatic expansion of the subject matter that these courses treat. Much of the attention is a result of faculty research in fields as diverse as political science, international relations, psychology, sociology, anthropology, biology, economics, mathematics, and law. It has also developed out of the experience of practitioners, both within and outside of government, in mediation and negotiation. Some of this expansion is student driven. Especially since the end of the Cold War, students have demanded courses that not only analyze the causes of conflict but also give some insight into the means of resolving those conflicts.

This chapter uses "conflict resolution" as a catch-all phrase that encompasses conflict prevention, management, resolution, and transformation. This is to avoid burdening the reader with a long list of conflict terms that would only get in the way of grasping the larger meaning of the text. The term is not used, however, as a synonym for peace studies or peace education, which, as the chapter discusses, incorporate an element of social activism that is not as prevalent in conflict resolution. Peace studies programs—both internationally and domestically focused—have multiplied at the undergraduate level, and many institutions have established master's-level courses in conflict management, resolution, or transformation. The consequence of this growth in interest in addressing conflicts is not clear. Will it produce a cadre of people who are capable of sustaining complex negotiations and reaching settlements on issues affecting inter- and intrapersonal, group, institution, and state relations? Will it breed a large new group of social activists, dedicated to changing society both at home and abroad? Will it inspire young people to become involved in international relations or political life in order to influence issues of war and peace? Or will it simply form the background for whatever careers these students choose, providing one framework for analysis among many others that the students will employ throughout life?

The answer to all these questions is probably yes: the growth in interest in this field will produce more scholars and practitioners who make conflict prevention, management, and resolution their lives' work or at least an important part of their worldview. Education plays a vital role in preparing individuals, institutions, and states to address conflict in constructive ways. There is another side to this picture, however, because the mix of education and conflict can be explosive as well as constructive. An education system can act as a repository for a conflict, keeping alive memories and interpretations of history that support one side of a conflict and denigrate the other. Because education shapes and transmits values, it can serve as a battleground where different communities compete over history and the society's narratives. As the field of conflict resolution grapples with the deeper causes of and possible solutions to conflict, education is increasingly being recognized as an important factor in conflict. It can inflame but it can also provide a fertile ground for creating an environment that will sustain peace over time and over generations. The second part of the chapter examines the emergence of "peace education"—a term that encompasses new approaches to using the educational experience to change attitudes, foster healing and tolerance of diversity, and decrease violence in a number of countries around the world.

TEACHING ABOUT PEACE AND CONFLICT IN THE UNITED STATES

Transformation in the Nature and Study of Conflict

Understanding the origins, dynamics, and outcomes of violent conflict has formed a core of the study of history since Thucydides wrote about the Peloponnesian Wars. Generations of students have learned about how wars begin and end, focusing on the political and military strategies that determined outcomes and the technological developments that gave advantage to one side or another. As the field of political science developed, students learned about the primacy of national security concerns in the functioning of the state; about the resources—that is, revenue and manpower—and institutions needed to protect or promote national security; and about the fluid world of alliances and counteralliances that allow states to leverage their power against a common enemy and sometimes—in pursuit of their own interests—to mortgage their future to another sovereign entity. Because most conflicts came to an end on the battlefield, the focus was on the consequences of the treaty arrangements, for example, the degree to which the 1871 Treaty of Frankfurt led to the outbreak of World War I or how the Treaty of Versailles contributed to the outbreak of World War II. Until the creation of the European Coal and Steel Community in 1952, established as a post–World War II effort to bind Germany and France together to make future war unlikely between the two nations, little attention was given in the classroom to the origins, dynamics, and outcomes of coexistence and cooperation or—more practically—to how to prevent or resolve conflicts.

The end of the Cold War brought changes that affected how conflict and conflict resolution is taught. The most significant has been the increase in intrastate and intergroup conflicts, which seem to grow in number day by day. Not only were long-standing unresolved conflicts in the Middle East, Northern Ireland, Cyprus, and the Korean peninsula left over from the previous era, but they were joined by vicious wars in Somalia, Bosnia, Algeria, Rwanda, Burundi, both Congos, Georgia, Afghanistan, Kosovo, Liberia, Sierra Leone, and East Timor. No matter what their original cause, many of these conflicts developed an identity-based aspect, pitting religion against religion, ethnic group against ethnic group. In addition to affecting their own societies, these conflicts also had a destabilizing effect on their regions, spreading or threatening to spread beyond their borders into surrounding countries, as occurred with the 1994 Rwandan conflict. The complexity challenged faculty to broaden their perspectives, to look both vertically and horizontally at large-scale violent conflicts—that is, within as well as between societies and states.

The proliferation of internal conflicts—all with their own causes, state of play, key players, and contexts—led many to the conclusion that these cases were unique, that factors that mattered in case A would not, and could not, be applied to case B. What could the experience in Ethiopia and Eritrea contribute to the understanding of why conflict broke out in East Timor? What relevance did the settlement in Cambodia in the early 1990s have to the conflict in the Balkans? The conflict parties themselves were among the most resistant to comparing their conflict to others, closely followed by area experts whose in-depth knowledge of a conflict confirmed their belief that conflicts grow out of a set of special circumstances. As identity-based conflicts continued to flare up in the 1990s, however, both academics and practitioners began to focus on some generalizations that seem to hold true across cases and conflicts. Research on the nature of democratic peace, the sizable body of scholarship on the nature and dynamics of ethnic conflict, the exploration of the theory and practice of conflict prevention, the investigation of perceptions of ripeness and mutually hurting stalemate as necessary ingredients to start negotiations, and the examination of conflict transformation all laid the groundwork for a new set of theories and generalizations about peace and conflict (see, e.g., Russet 1993; Mansfield and Snyder 1995; Brown 1993; Lund 1996; Jentleson 1999; Zartman 1989; Lederach 1997). These generalizations were in turn tested against the evidence presented by case studies, leading to the modification of concepts and theories and new avenues for research. Even parties deeply involved in their own conflicts started to seek out others who had had similar experiences. People from Northern Ireland sought the counsel of South Africans; the Basque sought the advice of experts from Northern Ireland; the Tamil Tigers sought guidance on the nature of federalism from Switzerland, a country that has successfully avoided identity-based conflict. In the post–Cold War period, a dynamic relationship emerged between scholars, third-party practitioners, and, in some cases, combatants, all directed at building a greater conceptual understanding of the nature of conflict and, most important, the conditions, nature, and timing of attempts to prevent, manage, settle, resolve, and transform conflict.

It also became clear that understanding the variety of actors that play a role in promoting inter- and intrastate conflict is important. Academics and practitioners must be able to explain how opportunistic political leaders, like Slobodan Milosevic, could mobilize support for their leadership by creating ethnic fear and animosity. But they also must explain how local leaders—both official and nonofficial—help such causes, as well as how transnational illicit trade in arms, drugs, and other materials fuel the conflict. It is important to understand how mobilization works on individuals so that they turn on their neighbors and engage in wholesale slaughter. In order to grasp the multicausal nature of conflict, students must understand the nature of the informal economy that grows up around conflict—or even sometimes spawns rebellions—producing a whole class of actors whose interests in promoting the continuation of the conflict is tied to economic rather than political ends.

On the response side of the equation, there has been an explosion of institutions engaged in conflict management and resolution. Once the domain of major states, peacemaking is now an activity of many institutions with different mandates, rules of engagement, decision-making structures, and capabilities.

The very nature of the "new" conflicts has forced changes in these institutions. Government officials wrestle with changes in the meaning and practice of sovereignty as both global and subnational forces challenge the status quo. The military has undergone changes as it has taken on new roles in peacekeeping and humanitarian assistance while maintaining its ability to fight wars. Roles for nonofficial actors have opened up, bringing many more individuals and institutions into the complex emergency process and allowing private people and groups to intervene as third parties, as the Community of Sant'Egidio did in Mozambique, Algeria, and Burundi, and the Carter Center did in Northern Uganda, Congo-Brazzaville, and Liberia. Humanitarian organizations such as Catholic Relief Services and CARE have established conflict resolution programs as components of their relief and development work. The complexity itself has become a factor in determining the success or failure of a third-party intervention, as institutions have launched competing initiatives or failed to support efforts by other peacemakers (see Crocker, Hampson, and Aall 1999).

Along with the increase in the numbers of players, the methods of intervening in a conflict have expanded. Track-one and track-two mediation are covered in other chapters of this volume; other techniques include facilitation, problem solving, and dialogue. The relative import of when and how one intervenes is a hotly debated issue; local capacity building, governance or rule of law training, improved health and environmental conditions, and media training have become more significant contributors to lasting peace settlements. Just as many specialists in the United States and other major powers thought that they had begun to understand this new world, the terrorist attacks on New York and Washington, D.C., on September 11, 2001, by nonstate actors with no fixed address added another layer to this complicated world environment. The challenge to the academic profession to teach in this rapidly changing milieu is enormous.

Criticisms: Too Abstract and Too Narrow

Teachers are trying to respond to changing student perspectives and needs as well as to changes in the global environment. Undergraduate and graduate students of international affairs have voiced two principal concerns about how the subject is taught: the field is too abstract and it is too narrow (see Aall, Crocker, and Hampson 1997). These critical comments reflect student concerns about applying what students learn to their future jobs in international affairs or other areas that will involve international exposure (see, e.g., Kacowicz 1993; Fox and Keeter 1996; Mann 1996; Cox 1993).

Students complain that the study of international conflict (and international relations, in general) is marked by too much theorizing about the world and the sources of international conflict. It is certainly true that much scholarly writing is about theoretical matters and the validity of different theoretical models (e.g., realism versus liberalism; structuralism versus postmodernism; see Maghroori and Ramberg 1982; Smith 1987; Taylor 1978; also note the high dosage of theory in leading introductory textbooks such as Holsti 1995; Light and Groom 1985; Russett and Starr 1996; and Spanier 1992). Professional rewards and academic promotion for young scholars continue to be based on theoretical rather than empirical contributions to new knowledge.

Although methodological rigor and theoretical development are essential to any academic discipline, the strong emphasis on theory in course readings and teaching of international affairs at the undergraduate level sits uncomfortably with the academic and training needs of the majority of students who do not intend to go on to do doctoral work in political science and international affairs. What these students generally look for is not more theory but more history and geography and a better understanding of the role of their country as well as the roles of international organizations, non-governmental organizations (NGOs), and private individuals in world affairs. Without a historical, geographical, and diplomatic context, most students get lost in debates about appropriate theories, methodologies, or suitable taxonomies. Without an understanding of the capabilities and limitations of various actors, students fail to grasp what can and cannot be done. Although this is especially true of undergraduates who may take only one or two courses in international politics, it is also true of graduate students in professionally oriented master's programs in international affairs, who often see little relevance or applicability of international relations theory to real-world problems and situations (Cassidy 1996).

The other set of concerns expressed by undergraduates and graduate students targets the lack of interdisciplinarity in the study and teaching of international conflict. A common complaint is that the field is dominated by political science, unlike related areas in which other disciplines have a stronger presence, for example, economics in political economy and anthropology, sociology, and economics in development studies. Political science has dominated the security studies literature, although political psychology has made some important contributions to the literature on decision making and deterrence theory, as has history to the study of international conflict processes (see, e.g., Lebow and Stein 1994; Jervis 1976; Larson 1989).

A Merging of Approaches

How have academic institutions and faculty reacted to the challenges of teaching about conflict and peacemaking? The most apparent response has been a dramatic growth in the field. As Louis Kriesberg documents in chapter 1, the conflict resolution field traces its roots to research done in the 1930s and 1940s on revolutions and other large-scale conflicts and on social and psychological sources of intergroup and interstate conflict. Interest in the field grew throughout the second half of the twentieth century, and the years since 1986 have seen a strong growth in institutions devoted to nonviolent means of addressing conflict, from peer mediation programs in secondary schools to the creation of non-governmental and international organizations devoted specifically to peacemaking. The European Platform for Conflict Prevention and Transformation keeps a tally of organizations active in the field of conflict prevention and resolution worldwide. In 1998, it identified 475 organizations; by 2003, the list numbered 1,300 (see European Platform 1998, 2003).

This institutionalization of the practice of conflict resolution has been accompanied by a rapid growth in academic programs on conflict resolution and peace studies. When the Consortium of Peace Research, Education and Development (COPRED) issued its first directory of peace and conflict resolution studies programs in 1981, it identified thirty-six universities that housed courses or programs that fit their definition. By 1995, the directory listed 288 universities in 30 countries around the world, and by 2000, the list had grown to 381 colleges and universities in 42 countries (see Wien 1984; Consortium on Peace 1995, 2000; Harris, Fisk, and Rank 1998). Although many of these courses are at the undergraduate level, there has been a rapid rise in the number of graduate-level courses. A survey commissioned by the United States Institute of Peace in 2002 identified nearly one hundred U.S. and Canadian universities that grant master's degrees or graduate certificates in conflict management/resolution, international peacemaking, and related subjects (Kovacs 2002). This expansion is not confined to higher education: more than 10 percent of American public schools (K–12) have some type of conflict resolution component, such as peer mediation programs.

If the objective of education in the conflict resolution field is to prepare students to respond constructively to conflict, the list of required knowledge and skills is alarmingly long. Practitioners must have a strong analytical capacity, sharp political sense, and finely honed skills in relating to other people. They must have a working knowledge of such topics as the sources and changing nature of conflict; preventive action and the tools of conflict prevention; negotiation, mediation, and third-party capabilities and limitations; the consequences of intervention and failure to intervene; the economics and politics of protracted wars; political, economic, and ethical problems of post-conflict reconstruction; and legal issues related to constitution building and reconciliation. Understanding and preparing to respond to these different issues requires the mobilization of several disciplines: political science, law, psychology, sociology, history, literature, economics, and, in the case of the game theory's contribution to negotiation, mathematics.

To capture this complexity and broaden the approach to the field, several higher education institutions have established interdisciplinary programs. Interdisciplinarity has not always been the case, however. For example, in 1975, social psychologists Jeffrey Z. Rubin and B. R. Brown wrote *The Social Psychology of Bargaining and Negotiation*. The next year, political scientist I. William Zartman wrote *The 50% Solution: How to Bargain Successfully with Hijackers, Strikers, Bosses, Oil Magnates, Arabs, Russians, and Other Worthy Opponents in this Modern World*. Each book deals with negotiation, each book has approximately one thousand references, and *none* of the references overlap. As Zartman observes, this lack of reference to pertinent books from other disciplines would never happen today.[1]

An example of growing interdisciplinarity can be found in the shifting alliances and occasional collaboration of core approaches to the study of conflict: conflict resolution, peace studies, and security studies. Security studies, with a focus on state capacity and national security concerns, is conceptually the most distinct, although with the introduction of such concepts as human security—as contrasted with state security—this approach encompasses material that previously had been the province of peace-oriented approaches. Although some programs continue to focus on arms control and national and international security affairs, others have broadened their curriculum to address both substate and global threats to security as well, bringing in countries and regions of the world that would not have been considered in security studies courses in the 1980s. The Program in Arms Control, Disarmament, and International Security at the University of Illinois at Urbana-Champaign, for instance, concentrates on "understanding the way force is used in the modern era," but this focus includes "the growth of identity politics, security problems in Africa, Asia, and Latin America; the intersection of advanced technology with arms control and the pursuit of power; and the emergence of new, politically and militarily powerful states" (Arms Control, Disarmament, and International Security 2002). The recognition of the central role of security in post-conflict reconstruction has highlighted overlapping concerns of security studies and conflict resolution. The two approaches have converged around a common set of issues in the analysis and discussion of intrastate security dilemmas as obstacles to conflict resolution—problems of guarantees, credible commitment, and the impact of conflict parties' need to satisfy the demands of their own constituencies as well as deal with the demands of their adversaries (i.e., two-level games).

Turning to conflict resolution and peace studies, an outside observer might well ask whether real differences between them exist. Many experts in the field assert that they do. Simona Sharoni writes in the foreword to COPRED's 2000 directory, "Despite their growing convergence in the academy, there have been serious tensions, both conceptual and political, between 'peace studies' and 'conflict resolution'" (COPRED 2000). A principal difference centers on the final objective of the activity. Peace studies are based on the belief that conflict is the result of social, economic, or political inequities and that, in order to end conflict, the injustices that underlie the conflict must be rectified. Consequently, peace studies place great importance on developing the analytical and personal skills necessary to act as an agent of change in a conflictual situation. As an example, the peace and justice subconcentration at Fordham University in New York provides "an awareness of individual and social experiences of persons in the world, especially as they relate to issues such as poverty, economic justice, world hunger and world peace. It also engages students in social analysis of societal structures that impede the achievement of justice and peace; examines models of social ministry and social justice; and encourages student involvement in community of church efforts in peace and justice ministry and education" (see Fordham University 2004).

Conflict resolution emphasizes the need to arrive at a settlement of differences between the parties to the conflict so that they can build a nonviolent and constructive relationship that will form the foundation for a sustainable peace. Conflict resolution emphasizes the importance of recasting the conflict so that both parties develop interests in reaching a negotiated solution, and it focuses on building analytical and personal skills to act as an effective third party in pursuit of this end. George Mason University's Institute for Conflict Analysis and Resolution describes its program as "the study of serious, deep-rooted social conflicts and the development of processes leading to their peaceful resolution or transformation" through research, third-party facilitation, and conflict resolution practices (see Institute for Conflict Analysis and Resolution 2004).

This distinction between peace studies and conflict resolution is useful mainly to establish that discernable differences between the two fields exist. However, this discussion does not start to capture the rich array of activities studied or practiced under the headings of peace studies or activism and conflict resolution. Nor does it capture the myriad ways in which the two fields overlap, especially in the area of defining what is necessary to establish a sustainable peace, as opposed to an end to violence. In fact, most of the teaching and research programs of the two fields emphasize similar objectives: to give students conflict analysis skills and a strong grasp of tools available to address conflicts in a nonviolent manner. The Conflict Management Program at Johns Hopkins University's School of Advanced International Studies in Washington, D.C., teaches graduate students destined for NGO and government policy careers how to analyze conflict situations and how to apply theory to improve performance in conflict prevention and regime building, bilateral and multilateral negotiation, and post-conflict institution building, as well as teaching conflict management to local middle-school students.

Looking at the titles of courses and programs dedicated to these issues supports the observation that these fields are converging. American University's major graduate program in the area is the International Peace Studies and Conflict Resolution Program; the University of California at Berkeley hosts the Peace and Conflict Studies Program. The University of California at Santa Barbara is home to the Global Peace and Security Program, while San Diego State's institution devoted to these topics is called the Institute for International Security and Conflict Resolution. The same phenomenon occurs in university settings outside the United States. The Catholic University of Leuven houses the Centre for Peace Research and Strategic Studies and King's College London has the international peace and security concentration, sponsored jointly by the Department of War Studies and the School of Law. These titles do not reflect muddy thinking on the part of these institutions or an attempt to be all things to all people. Nor do they represent the "war and peace" curriculum of days past, which focused almost exclusively on war. On the contrary, in a field whose dimensions are changing rapidly, academic institutions are breaking down the borders between formerly distinct entities—peace studies, conflict resolution, security studies—in an attempt to provide teaching and research appropriate to the field's complexity.

The drive toward interdisciplinary approaches goes beyond these core approaches to include such innovations as the Health Science and Human Survival Program of the University of California at San Francisco, which draws from anthropology, history, social medicine, nursing, epidemiology, and biostatistics to focus on the relationship between health and international politics and to examine the links between poverty, human rights, violence, peace, and health. Similar programs with an emphasis on responding to complex emergencies are found at Harvard, Tulane, and Johns Hopkins Universities. These interdisciplinary schools are spawning teaching and research materials on conflict management tools and techniques ranging from formal mediation by governments and international organizations to second-track or "informal" mediation and conflict resolution initiatives by non-governmental actors. Much of the literature is rooted in such diverse disciplines as law, psychology, peace studies, history, and sociology.[2]

However, interdisciplinary approaches are not easy to foster in an academic world governed by disciplines. It is still difficult for faculty trained in one discipline to master the approaches of other disciplines, and there is still some distance to travel in terms of developing a genuine interdisciplinary approach in the classroom that delves into different literatures and disciplines in more than just a superficial way. Team teaching with scholars from a variety of disciplines is one solution. Another is to use texts and course materials that explicitly adopt an interdisciplinary approach to international conflict. But we clearly need to develop a much better understanding about the difficulties of interdisciplinary teaching and the problems of combining diverse social science literatures that have their own vocabularies and methodological assumptions about the sources of conflict and approaches to intervention.

Bringing Practice into Peace and Conflict Studies

The experience of the turbulent years since the end of the Cold War also highlights the need for well-prepared practitioners in the field of conflict management and peacemaking. Like interns in the field of medicine, students of conflict management need a structured opportunity to put into practice the knowledge they have gained in class before they start operating on a real conflict. Many academic institutions focus on providing an analytic framework for conflict management and peacemaking, but they do not provide instruction on applying that framework to an actual situation. For instance, students may learn that there is an active debate about the causes of conflict—whether primordial ethnic differences or political manipulation of ethnic differences cause conflict—but they do not have a chance to apply their knowledge before they leave school.

Central questions are how to make the subject less theoretical and how to further students' appreciation of the intricate nature of the field without adding to their sense of overwhelming complexity.[3] One approach is to emphasize the role of experience in teaching about conflict and conflict management, either through student exposure to practitioners who have worked in conflict or through the use of simulations, case studies, and training exercises that allow students to gain and apply experience in a classroom setting. Some schools establish professorships in the practice of diplomacy, for instance, in an attempt to bring the practitioner experience on board. However, these appointments are generally short term and not well integrated in academic life. An added problem is that bringing practice into the classroom, whether through simulations or testimonies, is always secondhand. Arranging for direct experience through internships may provide a solution, but most internship programs place students far away from the day-to-day action of peacemaking. Even in the case of internships, the academic and experiential components tend to be separated. A school's contribution to the application of peacemaking is helping students find internship or fieldwork, but there is little time or inclination to integrate real-life experience into the analytic framework. Although a number of institutions have taken steps to increase the amount of experiential education they provide for their students, this area clearly should be expanded.

Bringing experience into the classroom has several educational objectives. One objective is to broaden students' understanding of conflict and peacemaking by exposing them to the complexities that real life imposes on any theoretical approach. Another objective is to help students absorb important lessons about the subject matter by applying their knowledge to actual situations. A third objective—and probably the least practiced in a nonprofessional academic setting—is to provide students with skills that will serve them in their future lives and jobs. The fundamental reason for bringing experience into courses on conflict management, however, is to round out and complement theory with direct exposure to the world of possibilities and constraints: the difficulty of developing international will to prevent conflict; the challenge of building coalitions; the impact of political pressure; inescapable ethical ambiguities; and unintended consequences—in short, the complexities of making peace in the fog of war.

TEACHING ABOUT PEACE AND CONFLICT IN ZONES OF CONFLICT

Education about conflict changes dramatically when one moves from a largely peaceful theoretical environment to the heart of a violent conflict. As Ofelia Durante, cofounder of the Notre Dame University Peace Education Program in Mindanao, notes:

> A major impulse for peace education in North, advanced industrialized regions was undoubtedly the disarmament movement. . . . However, for Third World peoples in South societies, the daily realities of conflict, violence and grim human suffering related directly to problems and crises other than a potential nuclear holocaust. A framework for educating for peace in the Philippines hence needed to emerge from the firm terrain of Filipino peacelessness. (Toh, Floresca-Cawagas, and Durante 1992, 114)

In many societies in conflict, youth under the age of thirty carry out most of the violence. When young people in places such as Congo, Nigeria, or Indonesia are excluded or feel alienated from their political, economic, and/or social structures, they can easily become attracted to causes that promise to bring about change, albeit through violent means. In any society, education is a major vehicle for the transmission of ideas, attitudes, and beliefs, raising the question of whether the schools, education systems, and curriculum harbor the seeds for future conflict. In other words, have the seeds of the most recent terrorism been planted in the madrassas of Pakistan? Lack of educational opportunities fuels anger and resentment among Palestinians in the West Bank and Gaza. The divided school system impedes the progress of post-conflict reconstruction and peacebuilding in the Balkans. The Dayton peace process did not focus on rebuilding relationships; as a consequence, Bosnian schools were often segregated or marginalized and unable to contribute to a reconciliation process.

The content and pedagogy of education can contribute to or precipitate violent conflict—particularly if education reinforces social cleavages or is combined with social and economic inequities, poor governance, perceived threats to cultural identity, or an absence of the rule of law. A number of UN Education, Scientific, and Cultural Organization (UNESCO) studies have concluded that weaknesses in educational structure and content often contribute to civil conflict. The mix of education and conflict can be explosive as well as constructive. An education system can act as a repository for a conflict, keeping alive memories and interpretations of history that support one side of a conflict and denigrate the other. There is considerable evidence that education is critical to development, and thus an important factor in reducing some key sources of conflict. Collier makes the point that "a country that has ten percentage points more of its youth in school—say 55 percent instead of 45 percent—cuts its risk of conflict from 14 percent to around 10 percent" (2001, 149). Increasingly, research has demonstrated that a significant investment in education—particularly for girls—in the world's poorest countries produces greatly improved health results and significant economic returns.

In a war-torn society, education can also provide a means out of the war, fostering attitudes of openness, tolerance, and responsibility and creating the skills necessary for a lasting peace. Education has become recognized as an important component of conflict prevention, post-conflict reconstruction, and the rebuilding of war-torn societies. Education is also viewed as critical to fostering social values necessary for sustainable peace. A vital issue for post-conflict societies is whether their schools can play a role in diffusing tensions, helping disenfranchised young people find a place in their communities and changing attitudes about their conflict and the other groups involved in the conflict. It is important to grasp the role that education in zones of conflict can play in promoting conflict resolution and reconciliation at the grassroots level as a means of building a supportive environment in the wider society for a peace settlement or its implementation.

The Interaction between Conflict and Education and the Emergence of Peace Education

To appreciate how constituencies may use peace education, we will examine the interaction between conflict and education. Conflict is ultimately a social enterprise; so is education. These two social activities interact in ways that one might predict, but also in ways that might be unexpected. Although conflict has a negative impact on education, at times the impact has been positive.

The negative consequences of conflict are not hard to find, particularly because education suffers from societal violence; learning cannot take place and schools are often destroyed. Schools in the territory of Aceh in Indonesia have been put to the torch, though both the government and the Free Aceh Movement deny involvement in the destruction. Even more extensive physical destruction of schools was experienced in Mozambique when Renamo forces destroyed some 45 percent of the nation's physical infrastructure. Why are schools destroyed? In Aceh and Mozambique, one explanation is the intimidation of the local population. In addition, schools and education are often identified with the values and beliefs of a certain group or groups in society. The values of the academic curriculum in schools are seen as reinforcing the beliefs or values of an ethnic or religious minority or a government ruling elite.

Other examples can be found of conflict interacting with education, including physical violence in the classroom. This might include the teacher physically abusing students, students attacking teachers, or students attacking one another. Students may become targets for military recruitment. Recruiters of child soldiers may come to a school to kidnap new recruits. The area surrounding the school may be a combat zone, forcing students to dodge bullets or avoid landmines. Often, when conflict erupts, government allocations to schools decline or cease, leaving schools underfunded and ill equipped. A society's productive capacity is profoundly affected by civil strife and conflict; as gross domestic product (GDP) declines, so, too, does the government's capacity to contribute to the school system. Declining GDP also causes unemployment and may place greater pressure for children to contribute, however modestly, to the family income and thus leave school. Finally, some forces may use education to foster hate against others. A. H. Nayyar and Ahmed Salim (2003) detail how the Pakistani educational system indoctrinates Pakistani students against Hindus and Christians in the guise of education.

Educational institutions are "a powerful mechanism that can sustain an infrastructure to promote post-accord peacebuilding"; the failure of institutions and structures to meet people's inherent needs is one of the major reasons for their resort to violence (Cilliers 2006, 176). In Bosnia, educators were excluded from most of the processes associated with the implementation of the Dayton Peace Accords. Transformation of the education system was dominated by international actors and agencies and hampered by the corruption of local elites. Local people felt no ownership and were apathetic about involvement. Thus, in the first few years after the Dayton Accords, education undermined the peace process. After the overthrow of Iraq's Saddam Hussein, the U.S. government and international donor agencies put millions into rebuilding schools, but often with little thought about to the content that would be taught in those schools.

On the other hand, exposure to conflict in the home environment has spurred teachers and scholars to create new approaches to conflict resolution through pedagogy and curricula. This approach to conflict through education is often called peace education. In these early years, when much experimentation in using education as an intervention point in a conflict is occurring, there is no hard and fast definition of peace education. However, some generalizations are possible. For instance, in addition to the analytical approach of many conflict resolution courses, peace education incorporates two other components: values and beliefs such as tolerance, respect, multiculturalism, and human rights; and skills building, often related to management tools such as mediation or facilitation. As Rosandic, a Serbian psychology professor who headed an agency for training and research in constructive conflict resolution, noted about peace education, there are two underlying approaches: "(1) a more cognitive, fact-oriented education *about* peace; and (2) a broader approach found in the *education for peace*, oriented to informal learning of attitudes, values, and behavior" (2000, 10).

The Peace Education Working Group at UNICEF defines peace education as

> the process of promoting the knowledge, skills, attitudes and values needed to bring about behavior changes that will enable children, youth and adults to prevent conflict and violence, both overt and structural; to resolve conflict peacefully; and to create the conditions conducive to peace, whether at an intrapersonal, interpersonal, intergroup, national or international level. (Fountain 1999, 1)

In societies experiencing violent conflict, "peace education often embodies an activist orientation whereby education is seen as a powerful engine of social change" (Burns and Aspeslagh 1996, 7). However, there is a difference between programs that promote peace as a culture, focused generically on enhancing peace between people in the abstract, and programs that focus concretely on how to achieve peace between specific groups or communities of people. One Israeli education scholar sees another set of approaches that distinguishes the different types of peace education:

> changes on the local, microlevel, for example, learning to settle conflicts and to cooperate on an inter-personal level, versus desired changes on a more *global*, macrolevel, for example, changing perceptions, stereotypes, and prejudices pertaining to whole collectives. Although in both cases individuals are the targets for change, the change itself pertains to two different levels: more positive ways of handling other *individuals* versus handling other collectives. Still another possible distinction is between the political, economic, and social status of peace education participants: racial or ethnic majority versus minority, conqueror versus conquered, and perpetrator versus victim. Clearly, peace education for the weak and dominated is not the same as for the strong and dominating. (Salomon 2002, 5)

Marc Sommers, a UN consultant on development and education issues, makes a distinction between peace education and conflict resolution initiatives: "Peace education initiatives tend to teach about how to prevent conflicts before they take place. Its teachers often present overarching peace-related themes to a wide range of students, from school-age children in formal schools to adults in non-formal settings." He contrasts this with conflict resolution initiatives, which "typically address specific, context-based issues about conflicts that already exist. Adults are the primary target" (2004, 166).

Peace education aims to impart knowledge, affect attitudes and behavior, and develop specific skills. The skills include communication, active listening, and assertive or persuasive speech, as well as problem-solving methods such as brainstorming or consensus building. In addition, skills development may include cultural awareness, demonstrating empathy, and nonviolent methods of problem solving and dispute resolution. As do other kinds of values education programs, such as human rights education, antibias training, and tolerance education, peace education shares a commitment to enhancing the quality of life by emphasizing the dignity and sanctity of life. The best examples of peace education also emphasize analytic thinking about how to unpack hatred's roots and penetrate into actor motivations, inculcating sensitivity to the other and awareness of motives of political actors living from polarized behaviors.

Finally, a significant contribution of peace education is pedagogical. Like its counterparts in other parts of the world, peace education is interdisciplinary, drawing on communication, sociology, political science, law, international relations, anthropology and ethics, to name a few disciplines. Many of the core principles of conflict resolution (elicitive engagement and interaction, suspension of judgment, inclusive and pluralist problem-solving approaches) are in fact principles of good teaching. Just as certain conflict resolution techniques embody the principle of conflict transformation and redressing a power imbalance between protagonists, teaching methodology in conflict resolution and peace education helps transform the teacher's role from a dominating to a facilitating one and the student's role from a passive to an active one (Rosandic 2000). In societies in conflict, empowering students for peace can help to counteract the prevalent pull of conflict that seeks to empower for violence.

Peace Education in Zones of Conflict

Examples of government or privately sponsored efforts to promote peace through education can be found in conflict areas around the world. Educators in Lebanon adopted a peace education curriculum developed for schools throughout the country with the support of UNICEF. Education officials in Azerbaijan, Armenia, and Georgia unveiled a common history textbook that is intended to promote peace through understanding the perspective of the other in that region of the Caucasus. A peace curriculum has been developed in Liberian schools. Mediation and alternative dispute resolution centers were established throughout Albania because citizens had little faith in the legal system. Student and teacher workshops on human rights in Kosovo have introduced conflict resolution education because the Kosovar organizers believe that the principles and values embodied in conflict resolution will enhance respect for human rights and develop good citizen behavior among young people by developing the tools and values to "live peace" as they deal with each other within, and between, their communities (Helsing 2002). The Rwandan Ministry of Higher Education played a strong role in reconciliation efforts there, developing seminars on tolerance and teacher training and creating radio messages that emphasize cultural diversity. Peace education and human rights curricula and training workshops are growing in Lebanon, even in Shi'ite schools in the south. In addition, the Lebanese Conflict Resolution Network holds training workshops in Lebanon, Syria, and Armenia, in addition to recent work with the Iraqis. The Center for Anti-Violence Education and Human Rights in Sierra Leone views its peace education and conflict resolution education as critical components of the reconciliation process in that war-torn country. In Northern Ireland, in an effort to create the conditions for a lasting and structurally embedded peace in a society with a strong culture of violence and a weak culture of peace, the Department of Education established a program of Education for Mutual Understanding in every sector of the elementary school curriculum (Gallagher 2004).

Another example of how peace education can play a role in promoting conflict prevention, conflict resolution, nonviolence, and reconciliation comes from the Philippines. Peace education is used in Mindanao as a means of preventing further outbreak of conflict between Christians and Muslims. The conflict in Mindanao springs from several different sources: religion, poverty, and contested power relations. Mindanao has resisted central authority from Manila for some five hundred years; the conflict has been particularly violent and seemingly intractable since the early 1970s. The peace education program at the University of Notre Dame in Cotabato City was founded in 1987 under the tutelage of Dr. Toh Swee-Hin and Dr. Ofelia Durante. The content of programs like the Notre Dame program varies, but these programs generally include courses such as conflict resolution, peacemaking, and religion and peacemaking. Such programs emphasize the development of a hierarchy of peace, beginning with inner or personal peace and moving upward through family, neighborhood, community, and national peace. Offering courses at the undergraduate and graduate level, the peace education program strives to provide students with both analytical tools so that conflict can be better diagnosed and peacebuilding strategies that can be used in formal and informal educational settings. Graduates of the program go on to work in a number of educational and community contexts. It is the intention of the Notre Dame program that these peace educators spread the word of peace education and incorporate the pedagogy in their places of employment.

Peace educators are also interested in healing the wounds and trauma caused by violent conflict. For example, Karen refugees, an ethnic group located in Burma and currently in conflict with the ruling government in Yangon (Rangoon), have been living in camps in Thailand for some years. A workshop in trauma healing was organized for primary school teachers, library staff, and community volunteers. The workshop elicited from participants their views on the nature of the conflict and began to examine ways in which they could recover from conflict-induced trauma. Not only did the workshop address conflict-induced trauma, it also provided an opportunity for participants to investigate ways in which their community could be rebuilt and demonstrated that targeting teachers can be an effective strategy; teachers can impart what they learn from a peace education workshop to their students.

Working within zones of conflict sometimes requires taking people out of the conflict. Education NGOs have brought together students from different sides of a conflict in an effort to contribute to the peacemaking process and break down barriers. The late John Wallach, a journalist, developed a program for young Palestinian and Israeli children called Seeds for Peace. The program runs a summer camp that brings together some four hundred Israeli and Arab children annually. The summer camp is an informal peace education program, where the objective is to teach methods of dialogue and understanding.

Wallach described Seeds of Peace as "making real peace in the real world. It is about changing attitudes, ending the fears and prejudices that have prevented entire generations from getting to know one another" (2000, 13). These relationships connect people from different sides of the conflict. Not only are images of the enemy replaced with images of at least the known, if not a friend, but participants gain insights that they bring back to their own communities. For Seeds of Peace to succeed, several Arab governments and the Israeli government had to cooperate in identifying likely candidates for participation: the very act of putting together the summer camp was an exercise in cooperation. Furthermore, Seeds of Peace demonstrates that peace education principles and pedagogies can contribute to building peace between perceived enemies as well as show how peace education objectives can be achieved in informal settings. Similar programs exist in Northern Ireland and Cyprus.

CHALLENGES TO EDUCATION-BASED PEACE EFFORTS

As peace education programs have become increasingly popular, some criticisms have emerged. Peace itself cannot be defined in the same way for everyone—it is context bound. For an Israeli in 2007, peace would be the absence of terror and an enhanced security in one's daily life. True peace would secure the right of Israel to exist as a Jewish homeland. For Palestinians, peace would be the elimination of humiliation in one's daily life; peace would embody justice and equality, with less emphasis on security than for an Israeli. Empathy for displaced Palestinian refugees might be perceived by Israelis as legitimating a right of return of Palestinian refugees to homes or communities in Israel that would threaten the perception or definition of peace for most Israelis, whereas empathy for Holocaust victims might be seen by Palestinians as legitimating the Israeli settlements in Palestinian territory.

There are also pedagogical issues to consider. Peace education is an activity or activities aimed at bringing about changes in the way people—especially young people—behave. The question emerges, however, of how this process can be mounted when the educational system itself is failing. Conflict brings about tremendous stresses and strains on the provision of education. It can destroy an educational system so that not only is peace education not offered, but literacy is impossible. In these circumstances, peace education cannot replace the basic educational needs of a community or society.

Even where the conflict does not close down schools, other problems exist. The opportunity to change the way teachers teach or are trained, particularly in resource-poor countries, may be impossible or limited. Many teachers in poor countries have little training in the subjects they teach and have received little pedagogical instruction. In most poor countries, significant numbers of children drop out of school, often early in the formal education process. And many zones of conflict are not conducive to direct peace education. Wounds are too fresh and time is necessary to rebuild trust. Many mixed communities in Bosnia and in Vukovar in Croatia promote the reintegration of schools, but in some places that means Croat students go to school in the morning and Muslim students in the afternoon; in other cases, one group holds classes in the top floor, the other on the bottom floor, reinforcing ethnic or identity divisions. Yet, in some communities, the classroom or educational settings may be the first place where divided communities can come back together or begin the process of bridging the community divide.

Working for peace through education brings risks to both faculty and students who engage in the activity. There is often resistance to peace education, among both political authorities and the local populace. In Northern Ireland, some viewed peace education as a form of indoctrination, and peace educators as "agents of the government who wanted to pacify the people" (Duffy 2000, 22). At the University of Ulster, it became important for the acceptance of peace studies to name the program Peace and Conflict Studies. Students in peace studies often complained that "they were ashamed to say they were doing 'Peace Studies' in their neighbourhoods as their friends assumed that they had 'sold out' to the British government" (Duffy 2000, 24). There is also a risk of social ostracism. Both Israeli and Palestinian teachers report that their own communities view their attempts to engage in joint projects with cynicism or suspicion, dismissing the effort as naive and idealistic, or worse, as a treacherous act in this deeply divided conflict.

Many argue that conflict resolution too often replicates the existing power structure or power relationship. Even the best-intentioned conflict resolution and education efforts between Israeli Jews and Israeli Arabs have been hampered by distrust, language barriers, and a belief by many Palestinians that Jews want to work with Palestinians primarily out of a sense of charity or even pity, not on a basis of equality. In the Neve Shalom/Wahat al Salam ("Oasis of Peace") community, in which Israeli Jews and Arabs live together, many Palestinians have chafed at the reluctance of their Jewish colleagues to learn Arabic. Almost all discourse, therefore, is in either Hebrew or English, thus reinforcing existing inequities and a disparity in power. In this case, however, there is a recognition that these inequities may disappear in the next generation, because the community supports a school in which children do learn each other's languages and have grown up together.

The language of peace education can become politically charged. The term "tolerance," a goal of many conflict resolution programs, "might be interpreted by some as ignoring the atrocities of the 'other side'" (Duffy 2000, 25). The words "justice" and "human rights" may be interpreted by many members of a majority group in a conflict as cover for a separatist agenda on the part of the minority group. For many Israelis, for example, to hear a Palestinian call for a "just peace" conjures up images of a desire to destroy the state of Israel and revert to the pre-1948 status quo. And in fact, in a war, talking about peace often appears banal, even nonheroic, when juxtaposed with the language of violence and war, where heroism is dying for honor and glory, sacrificing for the nation, and celebrating victory or martyrdom.

Thus, patience is important. Change will not occur at once, but a commitment to education is critical, beginning during periods of emergency relief. There is usually an immediate reward for education efforts in crises, particularly in providing young people skills, knowledge, and hope; creating a culture and expectation of education can pay off in the long term. Thus, creating effective teachers by helping them develop good teaching skills, as well as skills to deal with trauma and conflict, has become an increasingly critical priority for those engaged in humanitarian relief and development efforts.

At the same time, many teachers are not comfortable as agents of social change and are skeptical that anything they teach can counter the history that students learn at home. In the most extreme cases, in highly charged political contexts where adopting new teaching approaches or texts may lead to threats against teachers' physical safety, teachers are especially likely to shy away from innovation. In zones of conflict, therefore, "when one considers that peace educators [work] against a background of a political and ethnic barometer which is constantly shifting, it is clear that their task is difficult indeed" (Duffy 2000, 22). Too often, faculty in education programs that bring students from opposing communities together find that the students have meaningful interaction when they are together but revert to their original attitudes when back in their neighborhoods or homes. A major obstacle to education efforts lies in the resistance of parents and other members of the students' larger communities. Parents, in particular, can reinforce the positive lessons that education programs are promoting or they can prevent their children from establishing relationships with students from the other side. Marc Sommers argues that "peace education positions itself between schoolchildren and adults in the same community making it virtually impossible for education to inculcate peaceful values in children when adult role models are built on conflict. In fact, cultivating a disjunction between values promoted at home and in school may cause 'anxiety and distress in children' rather than optimism and peacebuilding." He also repeats a fundamental question posed by an aid worker who wonders why agencies should "teach peace to victims of aggression and not to their aggressors" (2004, 180). In an effort to engage parents as partners in opening students' minds, some education programs have expanded beyond the schoolyard. A school-based human rights education program in Southern Lebanon, for instance, has developed programs for the pupils' mothers, teaching them about human rights but being careful to observe local customs in doing so, and that these human rights are not foreign concepts but grow naturally out of Lebanese and Islamic culture.

Finally, there is often little analysis and evaluation of the impact of peace education programs. Are the behavior and attitudes of individuals transformed? Is learning overall enhanced by a different type of pedagogy in the classroom? What are the contributions of peace education to the mitigation or resolution of conflict in the daily lives of students, teachers, and others affected by conflict?

The success of programs emphasizing the development of a culture of peace is at the moment indeterminate. The development of a culture of peace is more than simply the culmination of an academic experience. The creation of a culture of peace, like any other sort of culture, depends on the creation of shared experiences, meanings, and beliefs as well as on the educational experiences of individuals. Thus, the development of a culture of peace takes a long time—making evaluation somewhat problematic in the short term. More evaluation of peace education programs and the degree to which the principles and methodologies of peace education impact young people, teachers, the community, and the well-being of a particular society is needed. Such evaluation must focus not only on whether a given program was successful in its own terms, but also whether and how it contributes to a sustainable peace.

CONCLUSION

The end of the Cold War profoundly affected teaching and learning about conflict and its management in U.S. colleges and universities, as we sought to understand the capabilities and limitations of peacemaking in international conflict. Over the same period, teachers and professors in zones of conflict were seeking to understand the constructive role that education could play in dampening violence and promoting dialogue in their own societies. Although there was much interaction between the two streams (especially between U.S. peace studies curricula and the growth of peace education in conflict zones), there was a distinct difference of perspective. In the United States, the principal concern focused on third-party roles—on mediation and facilitation, peacekeeping, and peace enforcement—because this was the role that the United States played or was asked to play in conflicts around the world.

Inside those conflicts, however, the focus was on building the peacemaking capacities of parties that were directly involved in or affected by the conflict.

The events of September 11, 2001, changed the U.S. perspective; the United States joined the war on terrorism and engaged in war in Afghanistan and Iraq. Now, instead of focusing on third-party roles, U.S. policymakers, students, and scholars grapple with the difficult question of whether and how it is possible to engage in peacemaking while fighting a war with an elusive enemy and unclear borders. At the same time, the targeting of civilians as a tactic of war in conflict-prone or post-conflict situations has led educators in zones of conflict to question the utility—or the morality—of establishing any sort of dialogue with the combatants. As after the end of the Cold War, educators will have to redouble their efforts to bring an understanding of the causes, nature, and resolution of conflict. More than ever, education must address both conflict resolution and security, understanding the other and protecting one's own. The next challenge for the educational community—and an area in which U.S. academics should work in tandem with educators in zones of conflict—will be to create an education that can truly address the conflicts of the twenty-first century.

REFERENCES

Aall, Pamela, Chester A. Crocker, and Fen Osler Hampson. 1997. "Bridging the Teaching Gap in International Conflict Analysis and Management." Paper presented at the Thirty-Eighth Annual International Studies Association Convention, *Coping with Insecurity: Threats More than Enemies*, March 18–22, Toronto, Canada.

Akhavan, Payam. 1996. "The Yugoslav Tribunal at a Crossroads: The Dayton Peace Agreements and Beyond." *Human Rights Quarterly* 18 (2): 259–85.

Arms Control, Disarmament, and International Security (ACDIS). 2002. http://www.acdis.uiuc.edu (accessed August 2).

Beer, Francis A., Grant P. Sinclair, Alice F. Healy, and Lyle E. Bourne Jr. 1995. "Peace Agreement, Intractable Conflict, Escalation Trajectory: A Psychological Laboratory Experiment." *International Studies Quarterly* 39 (3): 297–312.

Brown, Michael, ed. 1993. *Ethnic Conflict and International Security: The International Dimensions of Internal Conflict*. Princeton, N.J.: Princeton University Press.

Burns, Robin J., and Robert Aspeslagh, eds. 1996. *Three Decades of Peace Education around the World*. New York: Garland.

Cassidy, John. 1996. "The Decline of Economics." *New Yorker* 72 (37): 50–60.

Cilliers, Jaco. 2006. "Transforming Post-Accord Education Systems: Local Reflections from Bosnia-Herzegovina." In *Troublemakers or Peacemakers? Youth and Post-Accord Peace Building*, ed. Siobhán McEvoy-Levy. Notre Dame, Ind.: University of Notre Dame Press.

Collier, Paul. 2001. "Economic Causes of Civil Conflict and Their Implications for Policy." In *Turbulent Peace: The Challenges of Managing International Conflict*, ed. Chester A. Crocker, Fen Osler Hampson, and Pamela Aall. Washington, D.C.: United States Institute of Peace Press.

Consortium on Peace Research, Education and Development. 1995. *Peace Studies Directory*. Fairfax, Va.: COPRED.

————. 2000. *Global Directory of Peace Studies and Conflict Resolution Programs*. Fairfax, Va.: COPRED.

Cox, Robert. 1993. "Why It Is Difficult to Teach Comparative Politics to American Students." *PS: Political Science and Politics* 26 (1): 68–72.

Crocker, Chester A., Fen Osler Hampson, and Pamela Aall, eds. 1999. *Herding Cats: Multiparty Mediation in a Complex World*. Washington, D.C.: United States Institute of Peace Press.

Damrosch, Lori Fisler, ed. 1993. *Enforcing Restraint: Collective Intervention in International Conflicts*. New York: Council on Foreign Relations Press.

Duffy, Terence. 2000. "Peace Education in a Divided Society: Creating a Culture of Peace in Northern Ireland." *Prospects* 30 (1): 22.

European Platform for Conflict Prevention. 1998. *Prevention and Management of Violent Conflicts: An International Directory*. Leiden, Netherlands: European Platform for Conflict Prevention.

————. 2003. *Prevention and Management of Violent Conflicts: An International Directory*, 2d ed. Leiden, Netherlands: European Platform for Conflict Prevention.

Fordham University. 2004. www.fordham.edu (accessed May 31).

Fountain, Susan. 1999. "Peace Education in UNICEF." www.unicef.org/programme/education/peace_ed.htm (accessed October 13, 2003).

Fox, J. Clifford, and Scott Keeter. 1996. "Improving Teaching and Its Evaluation: A Survey of Political Science Departments." *PS: Political Science and Politics* 29 (2): 174–80.

Gallagher, Tony. 2004. *Education in Divided Societies*. New York: Palgrave Macmillan.

George, Alexander L. 1993. *Bridging the Gap: Theory and Practice in Foreign Policy*. Washington, D.C.: United States Institute of Peace Press.

Harris, Ian M., Larry J. Fisk, and Carol Rank. 1998. "A Portrait of University Peace Studies in North America and Western Europe at the End of the Millennium." *International Journal of Peace Studies* 3 (1): 91–112.

Helsing, Jeffrey W. 2002. Interview with Dr. Neshad Aslani (director, Kosova Center for Human Rights, Dayton, Ohio), September 11.

Hermann, Margaret G., and Charles W. Kegley Jr. 1995. "Rethinking Democracy and International Peace: Perspectives from Political Psychology." *International Studies Quarterly* 39 (4): 511–33.

Holsti, K. J. 1995. *International Politics: A Framework for Analysis*, 7th ed. Englewood Cliffs, N.J.: Prentice-Hall.

Howard, Signe, and Roy Willis, eds. 1989. *Societies at Peace: Anthropological Perspectives*. New York: Routledge.

Institute for Conflict Analysis and Resolution (George Mason University). 2004. http://icar.gmu.edu (accessed May 31).

Jentleson, Bruce. 1999. *Opportunities Missed, Opportunities Seized: Preventive Diplomacy in the Post–Cold War World*. Lanham, Md.: Rowman and Littlefield.

Jervis, Robert. 1976. *Perception and Misperception in International Politics*. Princeton, N.J.: Princeton University Press.

Joas, Hans. 1991. "Between Power Politics and Pacifist Utopia: Peace and War in Sociological Theory." *Current Sociology* 39 (1): 47–66.

Kacowicz, Arie M. 1993. "Teaching International Relations in a Changing World: Four Approaches." *PS: Political Science and Politics* 26 (1): 76–80.

Kovacs, Monique. 2002. Unpublished survey conducted for the United States Institute of Peace. August.

Kriesberg, Louis, Terrell A. Northrup, and Stuart J. Thorson, eds. 1989. *Intractable Conflicts and Their Transformation*. Syracuse, N.Y.: Syracuse University Press.

Larson, Deborah Welch. 1989. *Origins of Containment: A Psychological Explanation*. Princeton, N.J.: Princeton University Press.

Lebow, Richard Ned, and Janice Gross Stein. 1994. *We All Lost the Cold War: Can We Win the Peace?* Princeton, N.J.: Princeton University Press.

Lederach, John Paul. 1997. *Building Peace: Sustainable Reconciliation in Divided Societies*. Washington, D.C.: United States Institute of Peace Press.

Light, Margot, and A. J. R. Groom, eds. 1985. *International Relations: A Handbook of Current Theory*. London: Frances Pinter.

Lund, Michael. 1996. *Preventing Violent Conflicts*. Washington, D.C.: United States Institute of Peace Press.

Maghroori, Ray, and Bennett Ramberg, eds. 1982. *Globalism versus Realism: International Relations' Third Debate*. Boulder, Colo.: Westview.

Mann, Sheilah. 1996. "Political Science Departments Report Declines in Enrollments and Majors in Recent Years." *PS: Political Science and Politics* 29 (3): 527–33.

Mansfield, Edward, and Jack Snyder. 1995. "Democratization and War." *Foreign Affairs* 74, no. 3 (May–June): 79–97.

Nayyar, A. H., and Ahmed Salim. 2003. *The Subtle Subversion: The State of Curricula and Textbooks in Pakistan*. Islamabad, Pakistan: Sustainable Development Policy Institute.

Ratner, Steven R. 1993. "The Cambodia Settlement Agreements." *American Journal of International Law* 87 (1): 1–41.

Rosandic, Ruzica. 2000. *Grappling with Peace Education in Serbia*, Peaceworks no. 33. Washington, D.C.: United States Institute of Peace Press.

Rubin, Jeffrey Z., and B. R. Brown. 1975. *The Social Psychology of Bargaining and Negotiation*. New York: Academic Press.

Russet, Bruce M. 1993. *Grasping the Democratic Peace: Principles for a Post–Cold War World*. Princeton, N.J.: Princeton University Press.

Russett, Bruce M., and Harvey Starr. 1996. *World Politics: The Menu for Choice*. New York: W. H. Freeman.

Salomon, Gavriel. 2002. "The Nature of Peace Education: Not All Programs Are Created Equal." In *Peace Education: The Concept, Principles, and Practices Around the World*, ed. Gavriel Salomon and Baruch Nevo Mahwah. Mahwah, N.J.: Erlbaum.

Smith, Steve. 1987. "The Development of International Relations as a Social Science." *Millennium* 16 (2): 189–206.

Sommers, Marc. 2004. *Co-ordinating Education during Emergencies and Reconstruction: Challenges and Responsibilities*. New York: UNESCO.

Spanier, John. 1992. *Games Nations Play: Analyzing International Politics*, 8th ed. Washington, D.C.: Congressional Quarterly.

Stein, Janice Gross. 1991. "Reassurance in International Conflict Management." *Political Science Quarterly* 106 (3): 431–51.

Taylor, Trevor, ed. 1978. *Approaches and Theory in International Relations*. New York: Longman.

Toh, Swee-Hin, Virginia Floresca-Cawagas, and Ofelia Durante. 1992. *Building a Peace Education Program*. Peace Education Reprints no. 38. Malmo: School of Education, Lund University.

Wallach, John. 2000. *The Enemy Has a Face: The Seeds of Peace Experience*. Washington, D.C.: United States Institute of Peace Press.

Wien, B. J., ed. 1984. *Peace and World Order Studies: A Curriculum Guide*. New York: World Policy Institute.

Zartman, I. William. 1976. *The 50% Solution: How to Bargain Successfully with Hijackers, Strikers, Bosses, Oil Magnates, Arabs, Russians, and Other Worthy Opponents in this Modern World*. Garden City, N.Y.: Anchor.

————. 1989. *Ripe for Resolution*. New York: Oxford University Press.

NOTES

1. Remarks at "Seminar on the State of the Art in Peace and Conflict Studies" (Joan B. Kroc Institute for Peace and Justice, University of San Diego, October 24, 2004).

2. For a sampling of the literature, see Damrosch (1993), Akhavan (1996), Ratner (1993), Howard and Willis (1989), Beer et al. (1995), Hermann and Kegley (1995), Stein (1991), Joas (1991), Kriesberg, Terrell, and Thorson (1989).

3. On the challenges of marrying international relations theory with public policy practice, see George (1993).

9

DEALING WITH CONFLICT

The Contributions of Training

George F. Ward Jr. and J. Michael Lekson

Much has been written about whether—and, if so, how—the nature of conflict has changed with the end of the Cold War or in response to the terrorist attacks of September 11, 2001. At some point in the future, all will doubtless be much clearer, including the outcomes of the post-9/11 interventions by the United States and others in Afghanistan and Iraq. What does seem clear even now is that, to a greater degree than ever before in history, outside actors—motivated both by humanitarian concerns and by strategic interests—are intervening to forestall, resolve, and clean up after violent intrastate, often identity-based, conflicts. The increased frequency of large-scale international peace and humanitarian operations has presented a new set of challenges for peacemaking practitioners even while the traditional requirements for preparing conflict managers remain. How long this trend will last is yet to be determined.

This chapter focuses on how trainers in the field of conflict prevention, management, and resolution are adapting and working toward a new training synthesis. "Training" here refers to the craft of helping practitioners of conflict prevention, management, and resolution acquire and improve the skills they need to be more effective in their roles. Although training in conflict management skills and education about conflict draw on a common conceptual base, training and education differ in several respects, including purpose, audience, and mode of presentation. In general, educators seek to help students understand concepts, whereas trainers work with practitioners to develop skills. There are many similarities between education and training in the conflict field. For example, both educators and trainers often employ role-play exercises and simulations. In the case of education, these are usually meant to illustrate the applicability of concepts, while in training they are settings for exercising skills. Training often takes place in the context of an ongoing conflict, thereby becoming a form of direct or indirect third-party intervention.

Long before the end of the Cold War, practitioners dealing with identity-based conflicts began to mine the conflict resolution field for instruments and techniques that might be useful in improving communication between parties and uncovering new options for nonviolent settlements. There was a concerted and somewhat successful effort to transfer techniques of alternative dispute resolution (ADR) from their traditionally domestic context to the international arena (McHugh 1996; USAID 1998). New training programs sought not only to teach skills such as analysis, problem solving, negotiation, and third-party services, but also to use the training experience to promote dialogue among parties in conflict. The facilitation of problem-solving dialogues became an important ancillary skill for conflict resolution trainers. Promotion of problem-solving dialogue has become a genre of third-party intervention often referred to as "facilitation," "moderation," or "consultation." (In its initial phase, conflict resolution training often focused on track-two rather than on track-one dialogue. In the context of multitrack diplomacy, "track one" refers to official governmental actions, whereas "track two" describes methods of diplomacy that exist outside the formal governmental system, including "nongovernmental, informal, and unofficial contacts and activities between private citizens or groups of individuals" [Diamond and McDonald 1996, 1–2].)

Governments as well as international organizations and non-governmental organizations (NGOs) have changed their approaches to complex emergencies involving violence and humanitarian disasters in recent years. Deployments of forces by ad hoc coalitions and intergovernmental organizations have become more frequent. The record of these operations has been mixed. One lesson learned (and sometimes relearned) through bitter experience has been the need for better cooperation and coordination in every phase of operations among the organizations involved—military and civilian, governmental and non-governmental. Too often, the key players in an operation encounter each other only after the operation has begun and fateful decisions have been made. There are often gaps of organizational culture, goals, values, and even vocabulary between governmental and non-governmental organizations.

The training community has a role in filling these gaps. Ongoing research by David Davis of George Mason University's Peace Operations Policy

Program identifies, in the Conceptual Model of Peace Operations, 222 high-level objectives, subdivided into hundreds of tasks, for successfully implementing a peace operation. In 2005, the U.S. State Department's Office of the Coordinator for Reconstruction and Stabilization (S/CRS) developed the essential task matrix, which categorizes reconstruction operations "into five technical sectors (security, governance and participation, humanitarian assistance and social well-being, economic stabilization and infrastructure, and justice and reconciliation)" (U.S. Department of State, iii). Within the matrix are 54 overarching objectives, with 193 high-level tasks that contain hundreds of individual assignments to accomplish stability. Other researchers have devised similar compendiums. There is substantial agreement on what needs to be done, though some divergence on how best to portray this agreement. The United States Institute of Peace has developed the Framework for Success for Societies Emerging from Conflict, which consolidates most of the tasks into a small number of elements that support five mutually reinforcing desired end states (safe and secure environment, rule of law, stable democracy, sustainable economy, and social well-being). Analogous frameworks in other phases of conflict are in preparation.

In his examination, Davis found more than 533 courses and programs at 137 separate institutions worldwide that endeavor to provide education or training in these essential tasks for peace and stability operations (Coliero 2002). There seems to be fairly complete coverage of all tasks by these training providers; what is lacking is a central catalog detailing the level and extent of coverage these training and educational institutions offer. As of 2007, efforts are under way to fill that gap.

Exact numbers aside, these complex contingencies involve the integration of a large number of skills. Many of these skills, such as humanitarian demining and the delivery of food and clean water, are outside the boundaries of training in conflict prevention, management, and resolution. Others, such as the rule of law and human rights, are in a gray area. They are clearly relevant to peace operations, but whether they should be addressed in conflict skills courses for generalists is another question. In practice, the limitations of time are likely to be dispositive: technical topics may have to be reserved for advanced courses or workshops for specialists or addressed in general terms as part of a concentrated training effort, perhaps to be followed up online.

Joint training programs that bring civilian and military practitioners together deserve priority. For these programs, a new training synthesis is needed and may already be developing. This new synthesis should incorporate the combination of training in "microskills"—derived from the conflict resolution and ADR fields and including, for example, conflict analysis, interpersonal communications, negotiation, and mediation—with "macrotechniques" of operational planning, coordination, and logistics. The objective of the new synthesis would be for civilian government agencies, the military, intergovernmental organizations, and NGOs to discover jointly how to deal most effectively with complex peace and humanitarian challenges.

COMPONENTS OF A TRAINING PROGAM

In practitioner training, the presentation and study of concepts can contribute to the primary goal of helping the practitioners acquire and improve skills. With a solid conceptual understanding of the background of conflict prevention, management, and resolution, training participants will more likely succeed in transferring skills learned in role-playing and simulations to problems they face in their professional lives.

Effective training requires a working partnership between the trainers and the trained. Although this partnership needs to function at every stage in the training process, it is never more important than in the planning phase, when objectives are set. Training objectives should meet the following criteria:

- Objectives should relate the training to the conflict or conflicts in which the participants are, or are likely to be, involved. What phase is the conflict in? Are the participants working for prevention, for resolution, or for stabilization and reconstruction?
- Objectives should be specific in terms of outcomes. Is the purpose of the training program primarily to improve skills? If so, which skills? Or is the training focused on strengthening relationships among the participants?
- Objectives should be few in number. Proliferation in the number of objectives can lead to superficial coverage of each.
- Objectives should be achievable. Modesty is called for in setting objectives. A single training program is unlikely to produce a dramatic conceptual or practical breakthrough.

Once training objectives have been established, the next step is to formulate content. At least five elements should be considered when determining the content of any training program:

- The program should help participants establish effective interpersonal relationships.
- The program should present the concepts of conflict prevention, management, and resolution.

- The program should help participants acquire and improve skills related to conflict prevention, management, and resolution.
- The program should give participants the chance to practice skills through simulation.
- The program should guide participants in applying skills to concrete problems related to the conflict or conflicts in which participants are involved.

The relative weight of each of these elements will depend on training objectives. For example, if the training program is aimed at improving dialogue among representatives of contending ethnic groups, establishing effective interpersonal relationships becomes paramount. If, on the other hand, the objective is to improve the negotiation skills of diplomats who will be assigned in various zones of conflict, then the interpersonal element, although not omitted, should be subordinate to the acquisition, improvement, and practicing of skills.

In general, the order in which the training elements are listed above is an effective schematic for organizing training programs. We do not mean to imply that each training program should progress in a linear fashion, from one element to another; in fact, the most effective programs incorporate feedback loops, in which concepts are presented and practiced and then become the basis for learning additional concepts and skills. To understand this practice, it may be helpful to look at each element in the training process in greater depth.

Help Participants Establish Effective Interpersonal Relationships

Shortly after the end of hostilities in Kosovo in 1999, a group of five Serb and Albanian leaders in the region of Gnjilane, a major town within the sector for which U.S. forces had responsibility, made the courageous decision to open a cross-ethnic dialogue in the pursuit of mutual benefits.[1] With physical security and facilities provided by the U.S. military force in the area, the group gradually expanded its reach, consciously bringing in leaders, both women and men, from diverse occupational fields and ethnicities. After a few months, the core group felt confident enough to contemplate expansion both in numbers and in level of activity, and requested that the United States Institute of Peace facilitate a training workshop focused on coexistence and coalition building.

Most of the thirty-five participants in the initial workshop facilitated by the Institute were well acquainted with one another but had not met since the war. At the outset, the Serb and Albanian groups gathered separately, with individuals darting furtive glances at members of the other group. The facilitation team, having anticipated this situation, opened the workshop by dividing the participants into small groups of mixed ethnicity. In these groups, each participant was asked to relate his or her firsthand experiences during the conflict. Horrific tales of killing, torture, and rape emerged. But not all the stories were of cruelty. Here and there, vignettes emerged that told of Serbs who sheltered fleeing Albanians, and of Albanians who protected Serbs during the latter stages of the conflict. Emotions ran high during these story-telling sessions, but they served several useful purposes:

- The sessions were cathartic. Once participants told their stories, many appeared visibly relieved and less tense.
- The sessions presented issues early, when there was time to process them.
- The sessions helped participants understand that everyone, Albanian and Serb, had suffered in the conflict.

During another Institute workshop involving municipal officials from Kosovo, the facilitators made a different decision and dispensed with an initial exchange of personal experiences on the assumption that most of the participants already knew each other (United States Institute of Peace 1999). This assumption proved to be an error when, at a crucial point in a problem-solving working group, one of the Albanian Kosovar participants felt compelled to recount the murder of her husband and sons by ethnic Serb paramilitaries. This terrible account galvanized Albanian hostility toward Serbs, aroused Serbian defensive reactions, and interrupted progress toward agreement on programs of interethnic cooperation. The facilitators were able to get the discussion back on track, but at a considerable cost in time. Had participants been afforded the opportunity to relate their personal experiences early in the workshop, the emotions related to this woman's personal tragedy might not have been a factor as participants sought closure on concrete steps toward coexistence.

Present the Concepts of Conflict Prevention, Management, and Resolution

Because the length of practitioner training programs is usually limited by participants' busy schedules, time is at a premium. Moreover, studies have shown that the attention span of adult learners in lecture situations is very brief (Knowles 1980; Masek 2000). Twenty- to thirty-minute presentations, with participatory activities, are the most effective learning mode. In that context, it is usually preferable to present thoroughly a few key concepts that are directly related to conflict management skills rather than to survey the broad range of conflict management theory. Following are some essential conceptual areas in a typical training session:

- Conflict analysis, including understanding the life cycle of a conflict and the importance of systematic analysis of key conflict factors;

- Modes and styles of dealing with conflict situations, including the impact of personal styles on negotiating behavior;
- Cross-cultural communication, including understanding the importance of nonverbal behavior;
- Interest-based negotiation, especially the distinction between negotiating positions and interests;
- Third-party roles, including differentiation among conciliation, facilitation, mediation, and arbitration; and
- Peace and humanitarian operations, especially the differences among peace enforcement, peacekeeping, and post-conflict peacebuilding; the roles of the various organizations and entities involved in these operations; the cultures of these organizations; and the mechanisms for coordination and management.

Help Participants Acquire Essential Skills

The process of acquiring and improving skills for conflict prevention, management, and resolution begins with conceptual understanding but succeeds only if effective use is made of more participatory techniques, such as role-play exercises and case studies. Let us look at this process in the context of a few essential skills for conflict managers.

The discipline of looking at conflict in a systematic, dispassionate manner does not come naturally. Participants in conflict tend to look at their situation and evaluate the actions of the other side through the optic of their own identity group. They will not generally succeed in "putting themselves in the other's shoes" unless they are exposed to the rudiments of conflict analysis. The training team that facilitated the coalition-building workshops for the Initiative for Inclusive Security (formerly known as Women Waging Peace), a project of the Hunt Alternatives Fund, put this lesson into practice. During ongoing annual colloquia, which began in 1999, women leaders and delegates from both sides of a variety of international conflicts are brought together to share their views. In 2007, the colloquium hosted women from Iran, Iraq, Nepal, Colombia, Uganda, and Sudan. Despite the fact that participants were all community leaders, the ability of most to articulate a sophisticated, multidimensional view of their societal difficulties was limited before the training they received at the colloquium.

Many frameworks for conflict analysis exist. Some trainers ask participants to map their conflicts visually. Others use acting and role-playing. The International Institute for Democracy and Electoral Assistance has proposed a more traditional framework for analysis of conflict based on nine elements:

actors, issues, underlying factors, scope, previous attempts at settlement, phases and intensity, balance of power, capacity and resources, and state of the relationship between the adversaries (Harris and Reilly 1998, 41–43). The United States Institute of Peace tends to combine some of these to produce a shorter list of basic elements. Whereas the more visual or action-oriented forms of analysis may be best adapted to grassroots leaders, written forms of analysis may appeal to representatives of governments and political parties. In a sense, learning the discipline of using any reasonable form of analysis is more important than the specific analytical framework chosen. Analytical exercises are usually most effective when performed by small groups of five to eight participants and, to the extent possible, each group has the opportunity to report its analytical findings to the larger group.

Most participants come to training without having consciously reflected on their own and others' **conflict styles**, or **modes**. Several interesting instruments for assessing conflict modes exist. One that is particularly well suited for use in practitioner training workshops is the Thomas-Kilmann Conflict Mode Instrument. As stated in the instrument's introductory text,

> This exercise introduces participants to five basic conflict-handling modes. They learn how and when each mode is typically more appropriate and gain eye-opening insights about how over- or under-using any one mode can create unwanted situations for themselves and for the people around them. (Thomas and Kilmann 1974, 2002)

The instrument makes participants aware of the mode or conflict modes that they use unconsciously, providing them with insight into how their personal styles may cause or fuel conflict. A virtue of the Thomas-Kilmann approach, unlike some other conflict mode inventories, is that it avoids labeling any style as best or worst. The relative effectiveness of each style is discussed in situational terms. Because the conflict modes in Thomas-Kilmann nearly coincide with the five basic bargaining styles cited by scholars in the field of negotiation theory and practice, including G. Richard Shell (1999), trainers may find the Thomas-Kilmann instrument a useful transition from work on conflict modes to negotiations.

In the area of **communications**, active listening is one of the most difficult skills to teach effectively. The North American style of active listening, which involves frequent oral feedback by the listener to encourage, restate, reflect, and summarize, does not generally transfer well to other cultures. In Asian societies, for example, frequent interruption of the speaker is seen as disrespectful (Gesteland and Seyk 2002). Some societies find constant feedback by the listener to be annoying and distracting. Successful experiences with Balkan audiences suggest that a three-part approach to teaching active listening skills may be effective. The first step involves a short conceptual presentation aimed at making participants aware that much communication is nonverbal. Second, two facilitators engage in a role-play to illustrate effective and ineffective listening skills. The display of ineffective skills is exaggerated so that they stand out clearly for participants. Finally, participants are divided into groups of eight or so. Within each small group, participants are paired, ideally with someone from another ethnic group, and each individual is asked to relate a firsthand experience involving conflict to his or her counterpart. After each participant has spent about five minutes recounting the experience, the small group reconvenes, and each participant relates what he or she has heard, focusing on facts, values, and emotions.

Although time and other constraints often favor a more sustained presentation of **negotiation and third-party skills**, followed by a comprehensive role-play, another effective method of teaching these skills is through an iterative progression of minilectures, short exercises, and role-plays, each of which illustrates a single aspect of negotiating practice. Programs conducted by Linda Singer of the Center for Dispute Settlement in Washington, D.C., follow this pattern (Singer 1990). The Harvard Program on Negotiation has prepared an excellent series of progressive negotiation exercises.[2] These are primarily oriented to business negotiations but could be easily adapted to international conflict situations.

In many cases, negotiation skills are taught as only one part of a conflict management or resolution workshop, and insufficient time is available for a full series of lectures and exercises. In that event, the time available should be spent on helping participants become comfortable with the identification of interests and differentiation between interests and positions. The works of Roger Fisher and William Ury are especially useful in teaching these concepts (Fisher and Ury 1991; Ury 1993). Many short and effective role-play exercises effectively illustrate the concepts of interests and positions.

Provide the Opportunity to Practice Using Simulations

Facilitators at the United States Institute of Peace and elsewhere, including the U.S. State Department's Foreign Service Institute and the National Defense University, have increasingly turned to multirole simulations as course capstones. Simulations have several advantages: First, if properly crafted, they can exercise most, and sometimes all, of the skills learned during workshops, from conflict analysis to the coordination of large-scale peace operations. Second, simulations place participants under time pressure—a key factor that decision makers experience in actual practice. Third, simulations force participants to make decisions on the basis of incomplete information, just as they would in actual conflict situations. Fourth, simulations take participants out of the context of their own conflicts, thereby removing many of the emotions and tensions inherent in those situations. At the same time, because they can pose problems similar to those that the participants actually face, simulations are powerful settings for learning. Inevitably, participants "read into" simulation scenarios identifying aspects of their own conflicts, sometimes to the point of insisting that the only difference is that the conflict has been given a fictitious name. (One United States Institute of Peace simulation that was originally designed for use with Africans has been identified as "clearly about us" by Latin Americans, South Asians, and South Central Europeans.) As a consequence, workshop participants almost invariably take the simulation scenarios very seriously and play their assigned roles as realistically as possible. Postcourse evaluations almost always rate a simulation as the most effective and useful aspect of a skills workshop. Finally, simulations, when conducted simultaneously by several small groups, illustrate a range of outcomes and provide valuable opportunities to compare different approaches to conflict.

The Institute for Defense Analyses (IDA) has developed a very effective simulation technique. Strategic Economic Needs and Security Exercise (SENSE) is a large-scale simulation based on a computer model of a society and economy in transition from violent internal conflict. During simulation play, participants must deal with issues of ethnic antagonisms, transition from a command economy to a market economy, modernization of the defense establishment, environmental degradation, social unrest, health, and education— in a realistically pressured and time-constrained environment. In three training days, ten years of simulated experience can be gained. While simulation play is very much person-to-person, the requirement to feed resource allocation and other decisions into the computers, and then to see the tangible results of those decisions as they interact with those of all the other players, provides a "reality check": actions have consequences, problems are not solved by assuming them away, and wishing does not make it so.

More than fifty participant roles have been written for the simulation, including ones for all the typical internal and external players in a post-conflict environment. SENSE has excellent potential for training civilian-military teams working together on post-conflict problems and for use in helping decision makers in both donor and recipient countries model different policy approaches to key problems. It was originally designed for Bosnia, to facilitate Dayton Agreement implementation; it has since been used elsewhere in the Balkans and the Caucasus, as well as with American officials and academics. At the request of the United States Institute of Peace, IDA has revised

SENSE to include a potentially large oil sector vulnerable to terrorist disruption and a substantially augmented element of monetary policy. The Institute has used this version of SENSE extensively with Iraqis. Via intensive training efforts, the Institute has transferred a SENSE-delivery capability to an Iraqi NGO and to the Polish government, both of which were then licensed by IDA to conduct this simulation. The Iraqi NGO (the Iraq Institute for Economic Reform) has used it for a domestic audience; the Poles have used it in programs for neighboring countries.

Return to Reality: The Problem-Solving Element

As in the Gnjilane program, any conflict management training program that involves members of opposing groups is in effect a third-party intervention in the conflict. Protagonists in conflict gain the opportunity to look at problems through the eyes of the other and to learn new skills for dealing with issues. Training activities also offer opportunities for members of opposed groups to work together toward common objectives. In some instances, participants work together chiefly in exercises and simulations. Increasingly, however, training programs take advantage of the opportunity to facilitate work among members of opposed groups on the issues central to their conflict. The vehicle most often chosen is the problem-solving working group.

How should problem-solving working groups be structured as elements of conflict management training? The role of the facilitator is key. Almost always, facilitation is a task for the trainers rather than the participants. The facilitator's role is not simply to chair the working group but to keep the focus on the future rather than on the past. The facilitator must act impartially, countering the inevitable tendency of participants to rehash past grievances and to appeal to the power of the chair rather than to deepen dialogue with each other. One useful technique is to challenge the participants to look five to ten years into the future and describe their hopes. The balance of the workshop is then spent striving for consensus on steps that could be taken to make this vision a reality. In the process, the communication, negotiation, and third-party skills that the participants have learned can be exercised. Experience has demonstrated that problem-solving workshops are most effective when group size is relatively small. Eight may be the minimum number for maintaining a fruitful discussion. In groups greater than about fifteen, some members may feel that they are denied the opportunity to express their views.

In choosing working group topics, facilitators should select themes broad enough to capture the attention and imagination of the participants, but narrow enough to permit the group to arrive at concrete recommendations within the time available. One or more rapporteurs should be designated for each working group. Each group should be required to prepare a report and deliver it to the workshop in plenary session. Often the reports of working groups are interesting enough to merit further dissemination, either in print or on the web. Of course, facilitators should be careful to obtain participants' consent before disseminating the results of working groups. As a general rule, it is much more important that participants have confidence in the process and are able to express themselves candidly and constructively than that the end products of their discussions be made public. This was the case in intergroup training programs conducted in 2004 with Iraqis, as well as with a cross-sectoral program in 2003 with Colombians. The decision to publish results must be a decision of the participants, facilitated by the trainers. In the case of some United States Institute of Peace work with leaders from Kosovo, working group reports have become benchmarks for measuring progress in reducing interethnic tensions and improving prospects for coexistence. For one Institute interethnic program in Northern Iraq, working group reports effectively recorded progress on assigned problem-solving projects, but they also served as a vehicle to increase the collaboration among the interethnic team members. In this case, the projects addressed local problems, such as increasing wheat exports, improving technology education in middle schools, and reducing juvenile crime, that were not specific to any one community and cut across all such boundaries. These specific themes were identified by the participants themselves after receiving general guidelines from the workshop facilitators. The key is for working groups to address questions in a way that responds to the concerns of the training participants themselves.

MEETING TRAINING NEEDS

Before addressing the significant topic of joint training for peace and humanitarian operations, let us look briefly at the categories of practitioners who might benefit from training in conflict prevention, management, and resolution, briefly commenting on the training opportunities available to them. We will consider groups internal to the conflict and outside intervenors.

Indigenous Parties

Training for persons indigenous to conflicts is rarely undertaken in time to be useful during the prevention stage, although the United States Institute of Peace is trying to focus more training and other work on this neglected area. Most training begins after significant violence has already taken place. When they are undertaken, training activities tend to focus on single segments of society, such as government officials, high-level leaders, or grassroots organizations, rather than taking a cross-sectoral approach. The Institute has increasingly tried to undertake cross-sectoral training programs (e.g., in a new program in Colombia in 2007).

Once a conflict gains the attention of the international community, considerable resources for training are sometimes made available. Although individual training efforts can have valuable results even in intractable conflicts (e.g., the Seeds of Peace program for Palestinian and Israeli youth in the 1990s), they also can become part of an overall stalemate (Seeds of Peace 2007).[3] Without detracting from the appropriateness or effectiveness of individual training activities, it is fair to say that a better balance between postconflict and preconflict training would be beneficial.

There are few examples of effective single-country conflict prevention training programs; the cases that can be cited are therefore notable. In Nigeria, women leaders founded a group called Women for Democracy and Leadership. With funding from a United States Institute of Peace grant, over a two-year period it conducted conflict prevention workshops and roundtables in two of Nigeria's federal states beset by interethnic strife.[4] Although the effort did not end the danger of conflict escalation, it successfully defused several nascent problems. The project also demonstrated the ability of a group of dedicated women to win recognition as impartial peacemakers in a male-dominated society.

When training programs succeed in bringing together cross-sections of societies on a sustained basis, they can become vehicles for positive change. As noted earlier in this chapter, in the aftermath of the 1999 war in Kosovo, the United States Institute of Peace organized a series of training programs and problem-solving workshops aimed at promoting coexistence (United States Institute of Peace 1999). The first of these meetings occurred in September 1999 and created an atmosphere in which political leaders were obliged to talk with and listen to representatives of those parts of Kosovo society outside their immediate political factions.

The Lansdowne meeting set the pattern for subsequent training programs in Kosovo. Perhaps the most successful involved a multiethnic group of leaders from various sectors of society in the region of Gnjilane; this meeting led to a commitment by leaders of the two sides to enter into dialogue for the mutual benefit of their ethnic groups. After almost two years of dialogue supported by the U.S. Army, the U.S. diplomatic office in Kosovo, and the United States Institute of Peace, the Lansdowne Group in Gnjilane transformed itself into the Council of Professionals a registered NGO promoting cooperation at the professional level among members of the various ethnic groups. Within the council, committees of physicians, teachers, lawyers, and agricultural engineers were formed. Although the council has by no means solved the interethnic problems that exist in the Gnjilane region, it has contributed significantly to the limited resumption of cooperation between Serbs and Albanians and to a decrease in cross-ethnic violence.

The Military

In the early days of peace operations, outside interventions in conflicts were matters mainly for soldiers and UN officials. During the current generation of peace operations, however, the cast of characters has become much larger and more diverse. Soldiers and UN officials remain central players, but they have been joined by many others, including representatives of hundreds of international and single-country NGOs, other intergovernmental organizations and agencies, regional intergovernmental organizations, and police officers from dozens of countries. Each group possesses a unique organizational culture and tends to apply its own peculiar vocabulary to peace and humanitarian operations.

Of these groups, only the military trains in anything approaching a comprehensive manner for peace and humanitarian operations. Yet, many countries provide their forces with little such training. Others stand out as examples of excellence. Canada has historically treated peace operations as a primary mission of its armed forces. The Lester B. Pearson Peacekeeping Centre (PPC), an independent nonprofit organization formerly operated by the Canadian government, provides training and simulation exercises for various military headquarters throughout Africa, Eastern Europe, and Latin America. Domestically, the PPC operates in Cornwallis, Nova Scotia, and Ottawa, offering residential courses on modern peacekeeping operations. The Swedish armed forces present peacekeeping training courses for their own members, members of other countries' forces, civilian government officials, and NGO representatives; they have trained individuals and groups from more than sixty-five countries. The Australian Defence Force Peacekeeping Training Centre conducts an annual two-week seminar on peace and humanitarian operations that is open to allied, regional, and Australian personnel.

Within the U.S. defense establishment, units alerted for duty in peace operations go through a training cycle similar to that used to prepare for combat deployments. The training program is adjusted somewhat to emphasize skills needed in peace operations, such as negotiating and mediating, quelling civil disturbances, operating checkpoints, understanding rules of engagement in different settings, conducting risk assessments, civil-military relations, interagency planning, and multinational operations.

In 1995, U.S. Marine Corps General Anthony Zinni initiated a series of exercises, called the Emerald Express, designed "to bring together senior representatives from military, relief, political, and diplomatic communities to address issues that arise during humanitarian and peace operations" (Center for Naval Analyses 1996, 1). Since General Zinni's pioneering efforts, the U.S. Army and the Marine Corps have adopted such training scenarios, which are used regularly at a number of locales to conduct realistic field exercises based on previous peace operations. The Joint Readiness Training Center, housed at Fort Polk, Louisiana, conducts field training in peace operations at a variety of unit levels. To simulate real-world conditions, scenarios integrate civilian role-players from host nations, representatives of NGOs, news media organizations, and other elements of the challenging environments that units may face during a mission (Joint Readiness Training Center 2007, par. 4).

Additionally, peace operations topics—often as part of a broader operational spectrum extending to counterinsurgency and irregular warfare—are taught to a full range of military students, including commanders, general staff, and company-grade officers, at an equally wide range of Department of Defense institutions. These include the National Defense University as well as the individual service academies and war colleges. At the Army War College in Carlisle, Pennsylvania, the Peacekeeping and Stability Operations Institute (PKSOI) trains and educates mid- to senior-level audiences, teaching the full spectrum of decision making through all phases of a stability operation: "Audiences include U.S. military services, interagency programs, civilian organizations, foreign militaries, and IOs/NGOs" (PKSOI 2007, par. 1). The Center for Stabilization and Reconstruction Studies is a teaching institute located at the Naval Postgraduate School in Monterey, California. It provides educational opportunities for the full spectrum of actors who become involved in stabilization and reconstruction activities and a wide variety of practitioner-oriented programs, including games/tabletop exercises, short courses, workshops, conferences, and applied research initiatives.

Non-Governmental Organizations

Even though the military itself recognizes the need to continue to improve its training efforts for peace operations, these efforts are at an entirely different level from what has been done on the civilian side. The consensus at a 2001 United States Institute of Peace conference on best practices in training for peace and humanitarian operations was that the crisis-oriented nature of NGOs works against the development of an effective learning culture (Schoenhaus 2002). Lessons are most often learned on an ad hoc, personal level.

Few NGOs have developed organizational cultures that highly value training. Experiential learning at the individual level is not generally compiled or analyzed at the organizational level. There are several obstacles to improving training for NGO personnel:

- Demand from the NGO community is weak. Most NGOs are too busy "getting the job done" in a compartmentalized, donor-oriented world.
- Because demand is weak, the supply of training is limited and tends to follow donor fads rather than addressing fundamental needs.
- Supply is limited by the lack of funds for training, as NGOs struggle to minimize their organizational overhead in order to maintain donor appeal.
- The reservations about program evaluation and verification standards that have characterized some parts of the NGO community have tended to reduce the interest in, or even the existence of, training or other means of identifying and inculcating "lessons learned." (Attitudes appear to be evolving in this area.)

Given this situation, it is not surprising that training opportunities for NGOs are relatively few. The American Council for Voluntary International Action, or InterAction, is the largest alliance of U.S.-based international development and humanitarian NGOs, with 163 members operating worldwide. InterAction has offered courses on relief operations and security for NGO workers. The American Red Cross provides extensive training in a wide range of skills relevant to domestic and international emergencies for its own employees and volunteers. Caritas offers training in peacebuilding to its own employees and those of other NGOs. Other large NGOs provide similar training.

There have been a limited number of other training opportunities for NGO personnel. The United States Institute of Peace offers weeklong workshops twice annually on conflict management and negotiations skills for personnel working for NGOs and other institutions in the humanitarian and relief areas, and there is increasing interest in this community in seeking to make more such cross-sectoral training opportunities available. The UN Institute for Training and Development, through its Program of Correspondence Instruction, offers a Certificate of Training in UN Peace Support Operations. This program combines classroom training, correspondence courses, and individual student research. One of the correspondence courses is "The Conduct of Humanitarian Relief Operations."

Civilian Police

To build a stable and durable peace, reestablishment (or, perhaps more frequently, establishment) of the rule of law is fundamental to success. This process requires a range of capabilities, all of which are essential, though none is more crucial—or more glaring in its absence or failure—than effective civilian police. Much progress has been made in learning how to develop these capabilities, but a great deal more needs to be done.

Reestablishment of police services poses a difficult challenge. Indigenous police personnel are often discredited and morally compromised. Military peacekeeping units are ill equipped to perform civilian functions and are reluctant to do so on more than a temporary basis. Although international civilian police officers under UN jurisdiction are often the most logical choice for post-conflict situations, these personnel are perpetually in short supply.

> While their number and authority have increased, UN Police missions have been troubled by problems with recruiting, training, logistics, and timely deployment. . . . Unlike military forces that are trained and kept in a state of "readiness" to deploy abroad, police are usually occupied serving their communities. (Perito 2007, 37)

Yet, international civilian police operations have become a growth industry. According to Perito (2007, 35), "the UN Police Division is now a separate independent unit within the UN Department of Peace Keeping Operations. In May 2006, 7,500 UN Police were engaged in seventeen UN operations, an increase from one mission with 35 officers twenty years ago." The UN Police Division has strengthened its ability to respond to these operations by creating a small standing police capacity for rapid deployment in emergency situations (Perito 2007, 35). The Group of Eight recognized the growing need for better-trained police and, in 2005, established the Center of Excellence for Stability Police Units (CoESPU), located in Vicenza, Italy (CoESPU 2007). Originally, CoESPU placed emphasis on capacity development for stability police from African countries, but its students now come from countries around the world.

During a peace operation, civilian police functions often include patrolling, providing training, advising local police services, and helping to ensure compliance with human rights standards. Although officers are provided a limited amount of training on arrival in the operational area, the preparation of police officers for their missions is generally a national responsibility. A few countries, including Canada and some members of the European Union, provide fairly extensive in-residence training to civilian police officers before their assignment to the United Nations. However, there are wide differences among contributing nations in police training and the duties performed (Perito 2007, 37). The United States, which currently contracts with three private companies to recruit, train, and prepare civilian police officers, provides significantly less training than its European and Canadian counterparts. To enhance U.S. capacity and capability, the Department of State, which has responsibility for the civilian police program, is developing a Civilian Response Corps that will include experts in policing and in rule of law.

Civilian Officials

As already noted, research and study on conflict prevention has advanced significantly in recent years. Much of this research is relevant to the work of diplomats and intergovernmental organization officials, to whom falls a great deal of the work of prevention. Unfortunately, formal training in the skills needed for preventive diplomacy—analysis, communications, negotiations, and mediation—is seldom offered. Attendance at the few existing training programs is often disappointing. In the case of the U.S. Department of State, this lack of attendance reflects a self-reinforcing vicious cycle of relative understaffing (unlike in the Department of Defense, there is no significant personnel "float") and a culture in the foreign service that sees any training aside from foreign languages as unlikely to have a positive impact on either promotion prospects or assignment selection. Top management at the State Department has often addressed this problem but has yet to solve it. The United Nations offers courses to humanitarian workers, staff, and other people interested in global peace and security through its Institute for Training and Research, Program of Correspondence Instruction in Peacekeeping Operations. However, these courses rarely provide specific in-depth training in conflict prevention, management, or resolution. The Organization for Security and Cooperation in Europe (OSCE) maintains a vigorous training program that draws on the organization's own resources and outside expertise.

Quo Vadimus?

In summary, despite the proliferation of conflict-related training programs worldwide, few potential peacebuilders (aside from those in military programs) get training when it is really needed, before violence occurs. Most training takes place after the outbreak of violence, when those most in need of it are too busy to take it. Efforts are under way to redress this problem by increasing the amount of joint training that brings together professionals from across the spectrum of the conflict management community.

TRAINING AND THE CYCLE OF CONFLICT

In *Preventing Violent Conflicts*, Michael S. Lund (1996) defines five stages in the life span of a conflict. These are, in ascending order of tension, durable peace, stable peace, unstable peace, crisis, and war. The cycle of conflict may

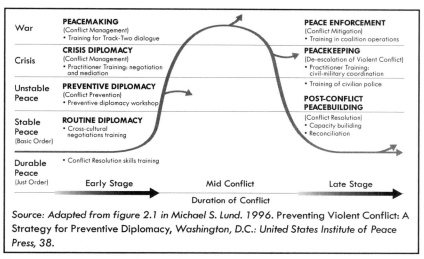

Source: Adapted from figure 2.1 in Michael S. Lund. 1996. Preventing Violent Conflict: A Strategy for Preventive Diplomacy, Washington, D.C.: United States Institute of Peace Press, 38.

Figure 9.1. Life History of a Conflict.

be thought of as a curve that connects these stages. In idealized form, this curve resembles a sine wave, escalating from the various kinds of peace through crisis to war at the top, followed by a descent from crisis to some kind of peace.

Figure 9.1, which derives from Lund's "life history of a conflict," illustrates these ideas. Different versions of this curve have been developed since Lund's original work.

The United States Institute of Peace has grown to see "stable peace" as somewhat more cordial than in Lund's original concept, where he used "cold peace" as an alternative title. Indeed, in some of its more recent work, the Institute has combined "durable peace" and "stable peace" and focused instead on the conflict-prevention challenges of "unstable peace." (For a fuller discussion of the underlying concepts, as well as applications of the curve to two actual conflicts [Rwanda and Kosovo], see the Institute's online Conflict Analysis Certificate Course, www.usip.org/training/online/analysis.html.) Experience has demonstrated that specific types of training interventions are appropriate for each stage of the cycle of conflict. The discussion that follows largely employs Lund's original terminology but is intended to apply to any comparable means of distinguishing different stages of conflict.

As the small arrows in figure 9.1 demonstrate, there is nothing automatic about how a given conflict evolves. The actions of both protagonists and outsiders can cause a conflict to deescalate, escalate further, or stall at a particular level of violence. Lund identified specific types of interventions as appropriate at each stage of the cycle of conflict. In categorizing interventions, Lund (1996, 40) referred to "the 'C' series (conflict prevention, crisis management, conflict management, conflict mitigation, conflict termination, and conflict resolution)" and "the 'P' series (preventive diplomacy, peacemaking, peace enforcement, peacekeeping, and peacebuilding)."

On both the ascending and the descending slopes of the curve, training in both micro- and macroskills is required. The following paragraphs provide examples (by no means exhaustive) of training appropriate to the various stages of conflict.

At the stage of **durable peace**, when there is a virtual absence of self-defense measures among parties, training has the luxury of leaning toward the generic. This stage is the moment to equip as many international practitioners as possible with conflict resolution skills in order to strengthen the reserve of experts available for timely intervention.

In 1999, the government of Romania campaigned successfully to become the OSCE chair-in-office for the year 2001. To prepare for the experience, Romania requested assistance from the United States Institute of Peace. Teaming with P. Terrence Hopmann of Brown University, the Institute presented a weeklong workshop to a group of professionals from the Romanian executive and legislative branches and NGOs.[5] The seminar used a case study and simulation exercise to explore typical challenges that the OSCE presidency would encounter. The Romanian government later evaluated the workshop as having been very helpful in preparing its staff for an eventful year as chair of the OSCE.

Another example of the effective use of times of relative peace for training is the Rapid Expert Assistance and Co-operation Teams (REACT) initiative of the OSCE. Adopted by the OSCE Ministerial Council in December 2000, this initiative is targeted at reducing, through advance training and orientation, the delays often experienced in deploying civilian experts to peace and humanitarian operations. The OSCE has established specific REACT training standards in eighteen skills, ranging from conflict management and human rights to the more mundane but essential skills of first aid and map reading. Implementation of REACT training remains a national responsibility and has been approached in different ways. The Austrian Study Center for Peace and Conflict Resolution offers a two-week residential course that covers all the REACT skill sets. In the case of the United States, the Department of State asked the United States Institute of Peace to prepare a distance-learning program that covers OSCE history, OSCE operations, conflict management, and area studies. The course, known as REACT and available at http://www.usip.org/training/online/osce.html, is required for Americans seeking positions in OSCE field missions and had been taken and passed by more than 1,400 individuals as of June 2007.

At the stage of **stable peace**, there is "wary communication and limited cooperation" between the parties in conflict (Lund 1996, 39). Lund also calls this stage "cold peace"; he uses the U.S.-Soviet relationship during much of the Cold War as an example. During this phase, training that helps practition ers on both sides overcome barriers posed by culture and identity is particularly relevant.

Gary Weaver of American University's Intercultural Management Institute has, for more than thirty years, helped prepare American diplomats, military personnel, and private sector executives to negotiate effectively across cultures. His work draws on a contrast-culture simulation developed in the mid-1960s as part of a project for improving the interpersonal communication skills of U.S. military advisors (Weaver 2007).[6] Usually referred to as the Khan exercise, the simulation uses a role-playing technique based on scenarios with specific problems or tasks involving a participating American, often representing his or her particular organization and job, and Mr. Khan as the person's counterpart in a country overseas. The scenario always takes place in a generic non-American and non-European culture, and Mr. Khan is always culture-general. He represents no particular culture but is instead a contrast to the mainstream American culture. Firsthand encounters with "Mr. Khan" teach more in minutes than could be learned in hours of reading.

In order to help negotiators prepare for encounters with representatives of specific countries, the United States Institute of Peace has published several studies on negotiating behavior during the past few years. These have included works on American, Chinese, French, German, Israeli and Palestinian, Indian and Pakistani, Japanese, North Korean, and Russian negotiating behavior (Quinney 2002; Solomon 1995 and 1999; Cogan 2003; Smyser 2002; Wittes 2005; Kux 2006; Blaker 2002; Snyder 1999; Schecter 1998, respectively). Additional country-specific studies are planned.

Perhaps more than any other scholarly endeavor in recent years, the work of the Carnegie Commission on Preventing Deadly Conflict, during the late 1990s, focused the minds of practitioners on the possibilities for conflict prevention (Carnegie Commission 1998). Preventive action is particularly important at the stage Lund calls **unstable peace**, in which "tension and suspicion among parties run high but violence is either absent or only sporadic" (Lund 1996, 39).

The twenty-three-nation Regional Forum of the Association of Southeast Asian Nations (ARF) is one intergovernmental organization that has elevated preventive diplomacy to the status of a primary objective (ASEAN Regional Forum 2007).[7] A relatively new security organization, the ARF made a decision at its first meeting in 1994 that it would strive to make significant contributions to efforts toward confidence-building and preventive diplomacy in the Asia-Pacific region. In cooperation with its track-two counterpart, the Council on Security Cooperation in the Asia Pacific, the ARF has pursued this goal through a policy dialogue supported by a series of training workshops for diplomats, military officers, and think-tank personnel. Over a period of three years, successive ARF policy-level meetings progressively deepened the organization's commitment to preventive diplomacy. In parallel, a series of training programs facilitated by the United States Institute of Peace has sought to help diplomats, defense officials, and NGO activists deepen their understanding of preventive diplomacy. The workshops have included multirole simulations, real-world case studies, skills training in analysis, negotiations, and mediation, and intensive problem-solving working groups.

Situations involving **crisis and war** pose formidable obstacles to effective training. With respect to the actual protagonists in a conflict, physical and psychological barriers to bringing people together may prove insurmountable. When dangers and barriers can be overcome, however, training provides a useful vehicle for preserving the remnants of intercommunal relationships and laying the basis for postwar peacebuilding.

David Steele of the Conflict Management Group and Mercy Corps in Washington, D.C., conducted two interfaith training workshops in Bosnia during the latter stages of the war in 1995 (United States Institute of Peace 1997). When he discovered that his initial objective of active problem solving was beyond the participants' capabilities, he focused instead on building relationships. During the training, participants were equipped to look more objectively at the role of their own ethnic groups in the conflict and to understand the needs of other groups. The relationships built during these seminars were crucial to the success of Steele's postwar endeavors, one of which resulted in a successful intercommunal project to facilitate the return of refugees to their homes.

Opportunities for training present themselves during the peace enforcement, peacekeeping, and post-conflict peacebuilding phases—the downward slope of Lund's curve of conflict. Two of the most intractable problems of modern peace operations have been the failure to deploy integrated civilian-military teams of peacekeepers rapidly enough, and delays in the transition to civilian control of peace operations once the primary military tasks have been completed. To a significant degree, these difficulties are due to training deficits.

In June 2001, the United States Institute of Peace convened a symposium on best practices in training for peace and humanitarian relief operations (Schoenhaus 2002). Drawing on his experiences as a military leader in Bosnia and a civilian administrator in Kosovo, Major General William Nash, U.S. Army (ret.), underlined the stark contrast between the capabilities of military and civilian components during predeployment. For civilians, predeployment team training was almost unheard of, and there was little individual training. Nash asserted that until the civilian components involved in peace operations attained the same level of competence and comparable levels of resources as the military, the objectives of peace operations would not be efficiently attained. Other participants in the symposium, including civilian government and NGO representatives, broadly agreed with Nash.

Following the interventions in Afghanistan and Iraq, the manifest disparities in training between the military and civilian agencies gave impetus to efforts to change how the civilian government and military coordinate and operate together. In November 2005, the U.S. Department of Defense issued Directive 3000.05, "Military Support for Stability, Security, Transition, and Reconstruction (SSTR) Operations," giving equal priority to SSTR operations and conventional war fighting. Further complementing the military's new role in peace operations was the December 2005 National Security Presidential Directive (NSPD)-44, "Management of Interagency Efforts Concerning Reconstruction and Stabilization." NSPD-44 gives the secretary of state the authority to coordinate all stabilization and reconstruction activities throughout federal agencies, including the Department of Defense, in all U.S. military operations spanning the conflict spectrum. NSPD-44 led to the creation of the State Department's Office of the Coordinator for Reconstruction and Stabilization.

Since the implementation of Directive 3000.05 and NSPD-44, the importance of joint civilian-military training has been universally recognized, but training programs still require greater effort and cooperation across the interagency community and beyond. Training for provincial reconstruction teams in Iraq and Afghanistan has been implemented in a variety of ways, largely ad hoc. Efforts are under way to make training for civilians in such future missions much more systematic. As of mid-2007, S/CRS, in accordance with NSPD-44, was working within the interagency community to develop training and education plans for the prospective Civilian Response Corps.

CHALLENGES FOR THE FUTURE

Training for conflict prevention, management, and resolution has been a growth industry in the post–Cold War world. Even so, training offerings and participation do not yet meet the needs of practitioners. Many groups in conflict never have the opportunity to acquire skills that might help them avoid violence. Peace operations forces continue to be deployed without proper training for key civilian and military personnel.

Given the number of violent conflicts and threats to peace that exist around the world today, it is unlikely that any foreseeable increase in resources for training will materially alter the reality described above. Traditional in-residence seminars are simply too expensive and time consuming to reach many potential audiences. Even "training of trainers" seminars will not extend the reach sufficiently. If we aspire to broaden skills training for practitioners in this field, we need to explore new technologies and new means of delivery.

Given the widespread availability of computers connected to the Internet, distance learning, is a leading option for training. A review undertaken by Science Applications International Corporation for the United States Institute of Peace indicated that most distance learning in the field consists of university-level courses. Practitioner training is offered by a few institutions. These include the Inter-American Defense College; the University of Wisconsin Disaster Management Center, under contract with the UN High Commissioner for Refugees; the European Network University; and the Conflict Research Consortium at the University of Colorado. Under a contract with the U.S. Department of State, the United States Institute of Peace created a course of predeployment training and orientation for American civilian volunteers for service with the OSCE.

"Blended learning," which combines distance learning with traditional face-to-face courses, is another viable alternative. The Program of Correspondence Instruction of the UN Institute for Training and Research offers a Certificate of Training in UN Peace Support Operations, which is based on twelve self-paced correspondence courses and an in-residence classroom course at any of several recognized national peacekeeping training centers or universities worldwide. Another potential application of blended learning would be to require prospective participants in residential workshops to complete a Web- or CD-based preparatory course. For example, a distance-learning module on conflict analysis could be used to help level the playing field for participants coming from diverse backgrounds to a residential training workshop.

Computer-based distance learning opportunities in this field are beginning to be more common as the demand for training in the peace operations community grows. While the electronic equivalents of paper-based correspondence courses are still available online (and still serve a valid purpose), increasingly the focus is on dynamic presentation methods, taking advantage of broadband and other advances in connectivity. Self-paced courses, which can be taken by anyone with a computer and at times convenient to the student, will continue to play a unique and irreplaceable role in the overall training effort. Use of the Internet to facilitate virtual classrooms, in which genuine teacher-student and student-student exchanges take place, as well as to conduct multiparticipant exercises and simulations, offers unparalleled potential for instructional interaction.

The next stage of development for training conflict prevention, management, and resolution will face two important challenges. The first is to bridge existing gaps between scholars and practitioners, governments and NGOs, and soldiers and civilians in order to develop common vocabularies, conceptual approaches, operating guidelines, and training goals. The second is to summon forth the creativity necessary to exploit the new training possibilities being opened up by advances in communications and media technology. These are difficult and critical tasks, and worthy of our common efforts.

ACKNOWLEDGMENTS

The authors gratefully acknowledge the outstanding contributions of Sarah Jakiel and Aaron Teeter, both for much of the research that underpins this chapter and for their sage editorial assistance and advice. Deepest thanks also go to Noor Kirdar for her great work in producing figure 9.1.

REFERENCES

ASEAN Regional Forum. 2007. www.aseanregionalforum.org/AboutUs/tabid/57/Default.aspx (accessed July 5).

Blaker, Michael. 2002. *Case Studies in Japanese Negotiating Behavior.* Washington, D.C.: United States Institute of Peace Press.

Carnegie Commission on Preventing Deadly Conflict. 1998. "Preventing Deadly Conflict: Final Report." New York: Carnegie Corporation of New York.

Center of Excellence for Stability Police Units. 2007. Home page. http://coespu.carabinieri.it (accessed June 28).

Center for Naval Analyses. 1996. "Emerald Express '95: Analysis Report." Alexandria, Va.: Center for Naval Analyses.

Cogan, Charles. 2003. *French Negotiating Behavior: Dealing with La Grande Nation.* Washington, D.C.: United States Institute of Peace Press.

Coliero, Christine. 2002. "Training and Education for Peace Operations Evaluation Research Project." Unpublished report.

Diamond, Louise, and John McDonald. 1996. *Multi-Track Diplomacy: A Systems Approach to Peace*. West Hartford, Conn: Kumarian.

Fisher, Roger, and William Ury. 1991. *Getting to Yes: Negotiating Agreement without Giving In*. Boston: Houghton Mifflin.

Gesteland, Richard, and George Seyk. 2002. *Marketing across Cultures in Asia: A Practical Guide*. Copenhagen: Copenhagen Business School Press.

Harris, Peter, and Ben Reilly, eds. 1998. *Democracy and Deep-Rooted Conflict: Options for Negotiators*. Ljubljana, Slovenia: International Institute for Democracy and Electoral Management.

Joint Readiness Training Center. 2007. "Forging the Warrior Spirit." www.jrtc-polk .army.mil/AboutJRTC.htm (accessed June 6).

Knowles, Malcolm S. 1980. *The Modern Practice of Adult Education: From Pedagogy to Andragogy*. Chicago: Follett.

Kux, Dennis. 2006. *India-Pakistan Negotiations: Is Past Still Prologue?* Washington, D.C.: United States Institute of Peace Press.

Lund, Michael. 1996. *Preventing Violent Conflicts: A Strategy for Preventive Diplomacy*. Washington, D.C.: United States Institute of Peace Press.

Masek, Linda E. 2000. "Advice for Teaching Hands-On Computer Classes to Adult Professionals." *Computers in Libraries* 20 (3): 32–36.

McHugh, Heather. 1996. *Alternative Dispute Resolution: The Democratization of Law?* Washington, D.C.: Center for Development of Information and Evaluation, USAID.

Peacekeeping and Stability Operations Institute. 2007. *Training and Education*. www.carlisle.army.mil/pksoi/training.aspx?action=training&sideNavNum=1 (accessed July 5).

Perito, Robert, ed. 2007. *Guide for Participants in Peace, Stability, and Relief Operations*. Washington, D.C.: United States Institute of Peace Press.

Quinney, Nigel. 2002. *U.S. Negotiating Behavior*. Washington, D.C.: United States Institute of Peace Press.

Schecter, Jerrold. 1998. *Russian Negotiating Behavior: Continuity and Transition*. Washington, D.C.: United States Institute of Peace Press.

Schoenhaus, Robert. 2002. "Training for Peace and Humanitarian Relief Operations: Advancing Best Practices," *Peaceworks* no. 43. Washington, D.C.: United States Institute of Peace Press.

Seeds of Peace. 2007. www.seedsofpeace.org (accessed July 5).

Shell, G. Richard. 1999. *Bargaining for Advantage: Negotiation Strategies for Reasonable People*. New York: Penguin.

Singer, Linda. 1990. *Settling Disputes: Conflict Resolution in Business, Families, and the Legal System*. Boulder, Colo.: Westview.

Smyser, W. R. 2002. *How Germans Negotiate: Logical Goals, Practical Solutions.* Washington, D.C. : United States Institute of Peace Press.

Snyder, Scott. 1999. *Negotiating on the Edge: North Korean Negotiating Behavior.* Washington, D.C.: United States Institute of Peace Press.

Solomon, Richard. 1995. *Chinese Political Negotiating Behavior 1967–1984.* Washington, D.C.: United States Institute of Peace Press.

———. 1999. *Chinese Negotiating Behavior: Pursuing Interests through "Old Friends."* Washington, D.C.: United States Institute of Peace Press.

Thomas, William, and Richard Kilmann. 1974, 2002. "Thomas-Kilmann Conflict Mode Instrument." New York: Xicom.

U.S. Department of State, Office of the Coordinator for Stabilization and Reconstruction. 2005. "Post-Conflict Reconstruction: Essential Tasks." www.state.gov/documents/organization/53464.pdf (accessed June 26, 2007).

United States Institute of Peace. 1997. "Religion and the Future of Intercommunal Relations in Bosnia-Herzegovina and the Former Yugoslavia" (Chairman's Report and Concluding Observation). Workshop, Central European University, Budapest, October 12–14. www.usip.org/religionpeace/rehr/bosniaconf.html#participants.

———. 1999. "Democratic Coalition Building." Workshop, September 10–13, Lansdowne Conference Center, Leesburg, Va. The following link provides a media release on the conference as well as a link to the Lansdowne Declaration: www.usip.org/newsmedia/releases/pre2002/nb990914.html (accessed July 17, 2007).

Ury, William. 1993. *Getting Past No: Negotiating Your Way from Confrontation to Cooperation.* New York: Bantam.

USAID Center for Democracy and Governance Technical Publication Series. 1998. *Alternative Dispute Resolution Practitioner's Guide.* Washington, D.C.: United States Agency for International Development.

Weaver, Gary. 2007. www.imi.american.edu/conf_sessions_khan_simulation.htm, March 15–16 (accessed August 23, 2007).

Wittes, Tamara Cofman. 2005. *How Israelis and Palestinians Negotiate: A Cross-Cultural Analysis of the Oslo Peace Process.* Washington, D.C.: United States Institute of Peace Press.

NOTES

1. The workshop "Building Skills for Peace and Co-existence in a Multiethnic Society" took place May 3–6, 2000, at Gnjilane, Kosovo. The "Gnjilane Papers," which resulted from this workshop, were not published and were not formally adopted by the workshop as a whole but were accepted by the various working groups without dissent.

2. According to the program's Web site, "The Program on Negotiation at Harvard Law School (PON) is an interdisciplinary research center on negotiation and conflict resolution. Drawing from numerous fields of study, including law, business, government, psychology, economics, anthropology, and education, PON works to connect rigorous research and scholarship with a deep understanding of practice. PON presents lectures, discussions, classes, and conferences in addition to producing publications and teaching materials" (www.pon.harvard.edu/about.php).

3. Seeds of Peace began in 1993 with forty-six Israeli, Palestinian, and Egyptian teenagers. Since then it has grown to include several Middle East delegations, as well as young leaders from Cyprus, the Balkans, and the United States. The Seeds of Peace International Camp in Maine now hosts eight delegations from the Middle East (Egyptians, Israelis, Jordanians, Moroccans, Palestinians, Qataris, Yemenis, and Tunisians), two from Cyprus (Greek and Turkish Cypriots), five from the Balkans (Bosnia, Croatia, Kosovo, Macedonia, and Serbia), and others from Greece, Turkey, India, Pakistan, and Afghanistan. The camp also hosts two domestic programs: Beyond Borders and Maine Seeds.

4. In 2000–2001, a Nigerian organization called Women for Democracy, led by Ayoka Lawoni, conducted the project "Training of Women in Western Nigeria in Peacemaking." The group was awarded $35,000 under grant number USIP 099-99F to complete its work.

5. "The OSCE Chairmanship-in-Office: A Professional Development Seminar" took place January 17–21, 2000, at the Crowne Plaza Hotel, Bucharest, Romania. No formal publication or report issued from this seminar.

6. The Khan exercise was designed by Gary Weaver, founder and executive director of the Intercultural Management Institute (IMI) at American University. The simulation continues to be used in Professor Weaver's Cross Cultural Communications Course as well as at the IMI annual conference.

7. The ASEAN Regional Forum, in its first chairman's statement, in 1994, outlined the following goals: (1) to foster constructive dialogue and consultation on political and security issues of common interest and concern; and (2) to make significant contributions to efforts toward confidence-building and preventive diplomacy in the Asia-Pacific region.

PART FOUR

Positive and Negative Inducements in Foreign Policy

10

SANCTIONS AND STABILITY PACTS

The Economic Tools of Peacemaking

David Cortright

The power of trade has long been recognized as an important force in shaping political affairs. Throughout history, regimes have sought to influence each other's policies by offering or withholding economic benefits. Classic studies such as Albert Hirschman's *National Power and the Structure of Foreign Trade* (1980) and David Baldwin's *Economic Statecraft* (1985) confirm the vital role of economic incentives and sanctions in the conduct of international affairs. A distinctive feature of the post–Cold War era has been the increased use of multilateral economic incentives and sanctions. By one count, there were fifty cases of sanctions use during the decade of the 1990s, compared to one hundred sixteen such cases in the previous seventy-five years (Elliott and Hufbauer 1999). As the UN Security Council has become more active in international affairs and the European Union and other regional organizations have emerged as major political actors, the opportunities for interstate collaboration have multiplied, resulting in a greater use of economic tools of statecraft.

Incentives and sanctions may be applied for a broad range of peacemaking purposes: to promote democracy and human rights, to condemn or prevent military aggression, to curb terrorism and weapons proliferation, and to encourage military demobilization and post-conflict reconstruction. By their very nature, inducement strategies are persuasive and are often intended to promote reciprocity and cooperation. Sanctions are a means of applying pressure on wrongdoers. They offer governments an option for responding forcefully to abusive policies without incurring the costs and risks of war. Incentives and sanctions are often employed together, and in combination they form the very essence of diplomacy. Economic tools of persuasion and pressure have the potential to serve as effective means of resolving international conflict and promoting peaceful political relations.

This chapter examines the role of economic incentives and sanctions in international peacemaking. It begins by providing a typology of incentives and sanctions and highlights the trend in recent years toward the use of more targeted forms of economic statecraft. It then reviews recent cases of sanctions imposed by the UN Security Council, assesses the relative effectiveness of these measures, and examines the factors that account for success or failure. The chapter then examines the use of inducement strategies and the factors that account for their success or failure, emphasizing the importance of combining incentives with sanctions. It concludes with an examination of regional economic integration as a strategy for conflict prevention and resolution, and an analysis of the role of the European Union (EU) and its Stability Pact for Southeastern Europe as models for international peacemaking through cooperative economic development.

DEFINING TERMS

The tools of economic statecraft are the means by which a nation or group of nations, defined as the sender, seeks to influence the policies of another regime, defined as the recipient or target. The intended policy change can range from modest objectives, such as encouraging support for human rights, to more sweeping goals, such as halting military aggression or overthrowing a regime. Sanctions can be instrumental, designed to bring about a specific policy change, or symbolic, expressing a message of political disapproval for abusive policies. Incentives and sanctions are often analyzed separately, but they are closely related. Baldwin (1985) combines the two under the general heading of sanctions, distinguishing between "positive" and "negative" sanctions. In economic theory, incentives and sanctions are often interchangeable. The withholding of an incentive can be a sanction, and the removal of a sanction can be considered an incentive.

The range of policy instruments that can be subsumed under the heading of incentives is extensive. It includes an array of economic, political, and military benefits:

- providing foreign assistance;
- offering loans on concessional terms;

- providing preferential trade agreements;
- giving diplomatic and political support;
- offering military assistance and cooperation;
- granting access to advanced technology;
- facilitating private investment;
- offering debt relief;
- providing security assurances;
- offering membership in international or regional economic organizations or security alliances; and
- lifting negative sanctions.

Incentive measures seek to influence the recipient regime through persuasion. Their goal, according to Robert Keohane, is to encourage other parties to "adjust their behavior to the actual or anticipated preferences of others" (1998, 51).

Economic sanctions are sometimes associated with general trade embargoes, but the dominant trend in recent decades has been toward the use of targeted and selective measures. Targeted sanctions apply pressure on decision-making elites, while seeking to avoid unintended consequences for third parties and vulnerable populations. Targeted sanctions are designed to deny wrongdoers the resources that are needed to carry out objectionable policies. Targeted sanctions include:

- arms embargoes, which ban the supply of weapons, military-related technology, and other forms of military assistance;
- financial sanctions, which freeze the assets of and block financial transactions with designated individuals and entities;
- travel sanctions, which ban the travel of designated individuals or prohibit travel on designated airlines or to targeted regimes;
- commodity sanctions, which prohibit imports or exports of commodities such as diamonds, oil, or timber; and
- diplomatic sanctions, which deny participation in international events or organizations or withdraw the diplomatic privileges of designated individuals or regimes.

ASSESSING SANCTIONS

Although sanctions have been employed with increasing frequency in recent years, doubts about their effectiveness are widespread. Margaret Doxey, the dean of sanctions scholars, wrote that "sanctions will not succeed in drastically altering the foreign and military policy of the target" (1987, 92). Gary Hufbauer and his colleagues at the Institute for International Economics (IIE) stated that "sanctions are seldom effective in impairing the military potential of an important power, or in bringing about major changes in the policy of the target country" (Hufbauer, Schott, and Elliot 1990, 94). The assessment of impact is complicated by the multiple purposes sanctions serve. As Alan Dowty emphasized, "the 'success' of sanctions depends on what goals they are measured against" (1994, 192). When sanctions serve symbolic or expressive purposes, such as reinforcing international norms, they can exert influence even when their instrumental impact is minimal. Sanctions may have implicit objectives that are not stated in official resolutions but are widely shared in the international community. A major goal of sanctions against Iraq, for example, was the political isolation and military containment of the regime of Saddam Hussein. For this purpose, the Iraq sanctions were quite successful, although they failed as instruments of persuasion and bargaining.

Sanctions can be unilateral or multilateral. They can be imposed by a single government, a regional organization, or the entire international community through the UN Security Council. The United States has imposed unilateral sanctions frequently, almost fifty cases between 1990 and 1996 (O'Sullivan 2003). With the rise of international trade and the increasing globalization of the world economy, however, unilateral sanctions generally have become less effective. Regimes subjected to unilateral sanctions usually can find substitute trade options, as Iran has done in circumventing U.S. oil and trade embargoes. Multilateral measures imposed through the United Nations are more likely to be effective, provided there is broad international compliance and enforcement. Since the end of the Cold War, the Security Council has imposed sanctions with increasing frequency, seventeen episodes between 1990 and 2006, compared with only two cases in the preceding forty-five years. The European Union has become a significant practitioner of economic statecraft, employing sanctions dozens of times between 1989 and 2006, consisting primarily of arms embargoes and the suspension of development aid as part of its Common Foreign and Security Policy (Hazelzet 2001).

Meghan O'Sullivan (2003) identified three broad categories of goals for which sanctions are applied: behavior change, containment, and regime change. Sanctions can be effective in changing the policy preferences and political behavior of a regime, or in containing the political and military power of a particular government or nonstate actor, but sanctions by themselves are not capable of achieving regime change. O'Sullivan and other analysts have also noted that multiple or conflicting goals can undermine the success of sanctions.

Attempting to measure the effectiveness of sanctions is an uncertain enterprise subject to a widely varying range of interpretations. The most authoritative empirical study of sanctions, conducted by the IIE, examined 116 sanctions episodes between 1914 and 1990 and found an overall success rate of 34 percent. Sanctions made a significant contribution to the purpose for which they were imposed in approximately one-third of the cases (Hufbauer, Schott, and Elliot 1990). The IIE study found that sanctions are most effective when the economic costs are high for the target but low for the sender, when the gross domestic product of the sender is much larger than that of the target, and when the target and the sender have extensive trade relations. Sanctions also take time to achieve their political effects, on average nearly three years. Sanctions are more likely to be effective when the sender and the target have amicable political relations (Drezner 1999).

George A. Lopez and I (Cortright and Lopez 2002; Cortright, Lopez, and Gerber-Stellingwerf 2007) examined effectiveness issues in the following seventeen cases of sanctions imposed by the UN Security Council from 1990 to 2006:

- Iraq, 1990–2003
- Yugoslavia, 1991–95
- Somalia, since 1992
- Libya, 1992–99
- Liberia, 1992, expanded in 2001, progressively lifted in 2006–7
- Haiti, 1993–94
- Angola/UNITA, 1993–2002
- Rwanda, since 1994
- Sudan, 1996–2001
- Sierra Leone, since 1997
- Yugoslavia/Kosovo, 1998–2001
- Afghanistan, 1999, revised since 2001
- Ethiopia/Eritrea, 2000–01
- Democratic Republic of Congo, 2005
- Sudanese officials and rebel group leaders, 2004
- Côte d'Ivoire, 2004
- Iran, 2006

In our assessment of the effectiveness of these sanctions, we considered three pragmatic, rather modest criteria. Did sanctions help to convince a targeted regime to comply at least partially with Security Council demands? Did sanctions contribute to an enduring, successful bargaining process leading to a settlement of conflict? Did sanctions help to isolate or weaken the military and political power of an abusive regime? We readily admit the subjective nature of these criteria. Analysts will disagree about the degree of partial compliance or political isolation and containment in a particular case. The definition of what constitutes partial compliance or successful bargaining does not lend itself to precise measurement or quantification. Nonetheless, we believe that our criteria reflect the objectives policy makers have in mind when they impose sanctions and that these criteria provide a basis for making judgments about political effectiveness.

Of the seventeen cases under examination, we concluded that sanctions had at least partial impact in several instances. In Iraq, the pressure of sanctions helped to produce significant concessions in 1993 (the acceptance of ongoing weapons monitoring) and 1994 (the acceptance of the redrawn border with Kuwait). Sanctions also prevented the regime from substantially rebuilding its military machine and impeded the development of weapons of mass destruction. In Yugoslavia during the Bosnian War, sanctions exerted bargaining leverage on the Milosevic regime that helped to produce the Dayton Peace Accords. In Libya, sanctions were a central factor in negotiations that eventually brought suspected terrorists to trial and convinced the regime to reduce its support for international terrorism. In Sierra Leone, sanctions combined with military pressures to isolate and weaken the Revolutionary United Front (RUF) military rebels. In Angola, sanctions that were initially ineffective became stronger over the years and combined with military pressures to weaken the National Union for the Total Independence of Angola (UNITA) rebel movement. In Liberia more vigorous sanctions imposed in 2001 helped to isolate and weaken the Charles Taylor regime, and the lifting of these measures, starting in 2006, helped to facilitate the transition to a new democratically elected government. In no case did sanctions achieve full and immediate compliance, but in six of the episodes—Iraq, Yugoslavia, Libya, Sierra Leone, Angola, and Liberia—sanctions achieved modest to considerable success in attaining UN objectives.

In the eleven other cases, the impacts of UN sanctions were more limited. In Haiti and Somalia, sanctions had a temporary impact in sparking negotiations, but they were not successful in achieving UN objectives. In the cases in which the Security Council imposed arms embargoes alone—Sudan, Liberia (until 2001), Rwanda, Yugoslavia (1998–2001), and Ethiopia/Eritrea—UN sanctions had little or no impact. In Afghanistan, UN sanctions imposed on the Taliban government in 1999–2001 had little or no discernible impact on that regime. In the more recent cases of Congo, Sudan, Côte d'Ivoire, and

Iran, sanctions' initial impacts were limited. The partial success of six out of seventeen cases translates into a 35 percent rate of effectiveness. This performance record is equivalent to that found in the IIE analysis of a much larger set of cases over a longer period of time.

The effectiveness of the various types of targeted sanctions is more difficult to assess. As noted, stand-alone arms embargoes have been ineffective. They may signal international disapproval of a target regime's policies, but generally they have had little or no instrumental impact on the military capabilities or policy preferences of the targeted regimes. Financial sanctions, on the other hand, seem to have had considerable impact. One of the interesting findings of the IIE study is that financial sanctions have a higher success rate (41 percent) than general trade sanctions (25 percent; Hufbauer, Schott, and Elliot 1990). Financial sanctions are often imposed in combination with other forms of sanctions and add powerful leverage against the targeted regime.

The impact of travel sanctions is less certain. The economic effects of restricting travel are very limited, although quite concentrated. These measures primarily affect privileged elites who travel internationally. In this sense, travel sanctions are the quintessential example of a targeted sanction. When combined with financial sanctions, travel restrictions prevent government leaders and designated elites from conducting business abroad. Aviation sanctions may impose similar forms of targeted pressure on governments and ruling elites. Such restrictions are not likely to have an immediate policy impact, but over time, as in the case of Libya, they may contribute to the isolation and weakening of a target regime and change the cost-benefit calculus of those responsible for objectionable policies.

Boycotts of specific commodities (diamonds, oil, and lumber products) were used in six of the seventeen cases of Security Council sanctions between 1990 and 2006. Oil embargoes were imposed in the cases of Iraq, Angola, and Sierra Leone. Diamond embargoes are a relatively new and innovative development in UN sanctions policy and have been applied in Angola, Sierra Leone, and Liberia. The diamond sanctions imposed against UNITA in Angola and the RUF in Sierra Leone initially had little discernible impact. As enforcement efforts strengthened in 1999 and 2000, however, aided by a more energetic UN Sanctions Committee process and the monitoring efforts of special UN investigative panels, the effectiveness of the diamond sanctions increased. Similar pressures were applied to Liberia when sanctions were strengthened in 2001. Diamond sanctions have been combined with other targeted measures, including arms embargoes and travel sanctions, to exert focused pressure on targeted regimes.

HOW SANCTIONS WORK

The conventional theory of how sanctions are supposed to work assumes that political change is directly proportional to economic hardship. The greater the economic pain caused by sanctions, the higher the probability of political compliance. Johan Galtung (1983) termed this the "naïve theory" of sanctions because it fails to account for the efforts of the targeted regime to adjust to or counteract the impact of sanctions. The naive theory assumes that the population in a targeted regime will react to the pain of sanctions by forcing political leaders to change policy. As Baldwin observed, however, "the economic effects of sanctions do not necessarily translate into political impact" (1985, 63). There is no direct transmission mechanism by which economic and social pain is translated into political gain, especially in the authoritarian or dictatorial regimes that are the usual targets of sanctions.

Sanctions may actually strengthen a targeted regime or reactionary forces within it and generate a "rally 'round the flag" effect. The targeted regime may adopt defensive measures enabling it to withstand the pressures of economic coercion. It may redirect the hardships onto isolated or repressed social groups while insulating itself and its supporters. Rather than causing political disintegration, sanctions may evoke nationalist sentiments and generate greater autarchy in the targeted regime. In some cases, sanctions may enrich and enhance the power of political elites who organize and profit from smuggling and illegal trade activities. In Yugoslavia during the Bosnian War, hard-line militia groups used their control of checkpoints and smuggling routes to enrich themselves and enhance their political power. When sanctions thus strengthen the forces of nationalism and enhance the power of abusive rulers, political objectives are undermined.

On the other hand, sanctions sometimes enhance the prospects for compliance by generating an "internal opposition" effect. Sanctions may empower internal political forces and render more effective their opposition to a regime's objectionable policies (Eland 1995). A report by the U.S. General Accounting Office observed, "If the targeted country has a domestic opposition to the policies of the government in power, sanctions can strengthen this opposition and improve the likelihood of a positive political response" (1994, 12). Kim Richard Nossal (1999) found that sanctions are most likely to be successful against states with a functioning multiparty electoral system. Sanctions are more likely to be effective when there is some degree of political pluralism in the targeted regime and when the sender can appeal to reform-minded constituencies within the target.

The prospects for arousing internal opposition depend on the degree of support for sanctions within the targeted regime. When credible opposition constituencies and political movements within the targeted regime support the goals of the sanctioning authorities, the moral legitimacy and likely political effectiveness of sanctions are enhanced. In a 1993 study, *Dollars or Bombs*, the American Friends Service Committee argued that sanctions are morally justified when there is "significant support for sanctions within the targeted country among people with a record of support for human rights and democracy, or by the victims of injustice" (9). One reason the international sanctions against South Africa were effective in helping to end the apartheid regime is that they enjoyed widespread political support from the African National Congress in South Africa. In her review of the ethics of sanctions, Lori Fisler Damrosch emphasized the importance of internal support for sanctions in the South African and Rhodesian cases: "I attach great significance to the fact that the authentic leadership of the majority populations called for the imposition, strengthening, and perpetuation of sanctions" (1993, 302).

Targeted sanctions have the potential to reinforce internal opposition effects while minimizing the prospect of a "rally 'round the flag" effect. By avoiding harmful impacts on vulnerable populations, targeted measures deny political elites the opportunity to rally broad political support. Instead of punishing the general population, targeted measures apply pressure to political and military elites who are responsible for wrongdoing. Combining targeted measures with support for democratic opposition constituencies is likely to be the most effective strategy for achieving the desired political changes within the targeted regime while minimizing adverse humanitarian consequences.

The Bargaining Model

The naive theory of sanctions is based on what might be called the punishment model of economic statecraft. In this approach, sanctions serve as means to coerce and isolate, to force a targeted regime into submission. The means of influencing the target and the criteria for lifting pressure are cast in terms of demand, capitulation, and ostracism. Bargaining and negotiation are discouraged, and compliance is considered the only legitimate response from the target. If concessions are not forthcoming, the usual response is further punishment in the form of continued or stronger sanctions, or in some cases the use of military force.

An alternative approach is the bargaining model of sanctions. In this approach, sanctions are considered a form of persuasion, a tool for encouraging targeted regimes to reevaluate the costs and benefits of their policy options. The aim of economic statecraft is not to punish but to impose costs for defiance while offering benefits for compliance. This approach places sanctions within the broader context of diplomacy. It combines positive and negative measures in a strategy of persuasion, not punishment. It views the implementation of sanctions not as a policy unto itself, but as part of a continuum of policy instruments, both positive and negative, designed to encourage political compromise and bring about a negotiated settlement. Of course bargaining and punishment are related. Punishment, or at least its threat, can be an important element in stimulating a bargaining process. It often takes the threat or actual carrying out of coercive action to create a willingness to negotiate. But coercive pressure becomes dysfunctional when it is unconditional, when it demands total submission as the price for an easing of pressure. For bargaining to be successful, punitive measures must be eased as well as imposed.

In the bargaining model of sanctions, effectiveness does not derive primarily from the ability to punish or coerce. The impact of sanctions comes not from the severity of the economic damage they cause but from their ability to encourage dialogue and bargaining. From this perspective, sanctions can be considered at least partially successful if they contribute to a bargaining process and become the basis around which a negotiated settlement is reached. It is not necessary to impose draconian economic hardship to have persuasive influence. Sanctions need cause only sufficient discomfort to motivate the targeted authorities to enter into a bargaining process. The bite of sanctions is determined not by an objective measure of economic pain but by the subjective response of targeted political leaders, often expressed as a willingness to negotiate. Sanctions work when the desire for avoiding or lifting coercive pressure serves as an inducement for compliance and negotiation.

The Power of a Threat

A review of sanctions cases shows that the threat of sanctions is often a powerful inducement for bargaining. In a number of instances, targeted regimes responded to the mere threat of sanctions with conciliatory gestures and offers of partial compliance. Merely by deciding to impose sanctions, the Security Council prompted targeted regimes to make gestures of conciliation in several cases:

- In Somalia, the imposition of sanctions in January 1992 led to a cease-fire agreement among warring factions in Mogadishu, although the accord did not last.
- In Libya, the Qaddafi regime made several partial offers before and immediately after sanctions were imposed in March 1992 to turn over suspected terrorists for trial in international or Arab tribunals.

- In June 1993, just as sanctions were being imposed against Haiti, the military junta in Port-au-Prince agreed to enter negotiations that led to the Governors Island agreement.
- The government of Sudan responded to diplomatic sanctions in April 1996 by informing the Security Council that Osama bin Laden had been asked to leave the country.
- In Sierra Leone, the military junta responded to the imposition of sanctions in February 1997 by signing an agreement in Conakry to restore the elected government.
- In Afghanistan, the Taliban responded to the threat of sanctions in 1999 by offering to present the bin Laden case to an Islamic tribunal.
- In Liberia, the Taylor government announced a series of measures in early 2001, before sanctions went into force, purporting to comply with UN demands.

In some cases, the initial offers made by targeted regimes were partial and limited, falling far short of Security Council demands. In Libya and Afghanistan, the targeted regimes offered to turn over suspected terrorists to Islamic or international tribunals that were unacceptable to the Security Council. These gestures may have been intended merely as delaying tactics or as attempts to weaken the political resolve of the Security Council. In other cases, though, such as the signing of the Governors Island accord in Haiti or the Conakry agreement in Sierra Leone, the response of the targeted regime led to a negotiated agreement that, although initially unenforced, eventually became the basis for a political agreement.

The initial response to sanctions may be an attempt to float options for a negotiated agreement. The gesture may reflect a genuine effort by the targeted regime, or at least a faction within it, to find a diplomatic solution. In these instances, it may be appropriate to engage in a negotiating process, and perhaps even to postpone the implementation of sanctions in exchange for concrete gestures of compliance. If a process of reciprocity can be established through such interactions, further compliance and a possible settlement of the dispute may follow. At the very least, an initial bargaining offer or conciliatory gesture from a targeted regime should occasion an attempt at dialogue to determine the prospects for further movement toward compliance.

This pattern of early response to sanctions indicates the way in which economic measures can influence the decision-making calculus of a targeted regime. It illustrates how sanctions create possibilities for resolving a dispute and confirms the importance of combining negative measures with positive inducements to maximize the effect of economic statecraft.

The Role of Inducements

Along with the increased use of multilateral sanctions in recent years has come a greater reliance on inducement strategies to resolve and prevent conflict. Powerful states such as the United States and Germany, regional organizations such as the European Union, and international financial institutions such as the World Bank have used economic leverage and security assurances to influence the policies of recipient regimes. In 1996, a task force of the Carnegie Commission on the Prevention of Deadly Conflict examined fifteen cases in which incentives figured prominently in international peacemaking efforts. Among the cases examined were the use of incentives to prevent nuclear weapons proliferation in North Korea, the Ukraine, and other countries; the use of trade and technology incentives in U.S. relations with China; U.S. efforts to prevent weapons proliferation in India and Pakistan; the role of multilateral economic assistance in the Bosnian peace process; the use of U.S. foreign assistance to facilitate the peace process in El Salvador; U.S. and European community incentives to improve Baltic-Russian relations; and the role of international financial institutions in conflict prevention and post-conflict reconstruction (Cortright 1997).

Several important successes in recent years demonstrate the potential value of incentives-based bargaining. In 1994, the United States joined with Japan and South Korea to provide inducements to North Korea in exchange for Pyongyang's agreement to shut down plutonium production and reprocessing and accept on-site monitoring to verify compliance. Although the Pyongyang government later violated the spirit of that agreement by acquiring uranium enrichment production capability, North Korea continued to adhere to the 1994 agreement for several years, thus maintaining a freeze on at least one element of its nuclear weapons program. In the early 1990s, the United States joined with Russia and Great Britain to provide security assurances and economic assistance to Ukraine in exchange for Kiev's agreement to transfer the nuclear weapons on its soil to Russia and join the Nuclear Nonproliferation Treaty as a nonnuclear state. Throughout the 1990s, the European Union and the North Atlantic Treaty Organization (NATO) used the offer of membership to encourage postcommunist states in Central and Eastern Europe to resolve border disputes, guarantee the rights of ethnic minorities, participate in international nonproliferation regimes, and strengthen democratic institutions. The creation of the European Union's Stability Pact for South Eastern Europe in 1999 was an important part of this process, as is examined in more detail below. These and other examples demonstrate the utility of incentives-based bargaining as a tool of international peacemaking.

In his study of German foreign policy toward Poland and Russia, Randall Newnham (2000) found that economic inducements were highly effective in achieving Germany's policy objectives. Germany used its considerable economic leverage with Russia to encourage détente in the 1970s and the end of the Cold War in the 1990s. The German-Russian treaty of 1990 offers a particularly striking example of the use of economic inducements. In the 1990 treaty, Germany offered the Soviet Union 16 billion deutsche marks to facilitate the withdrawal of Soviet forces from East Germany. The funds were earmarked for the construction of housing for returning troops and support of their families in Russia. In exchange, Moscow accepted German unification, previously considered anathema by Soviet leaders, and pledged to maintain peaceful relations with Germany. According to Newnham, this and other examples from German foreign policy confirm that "positive sanctions can be more effective than negative sanctions" (2000, 88).

Positive Reciprocity

Incentives can be either specific or general. They can be conditional, with the sender seeking a specific policy response in exchange for the benefits provided, or they can be unconditional, in which no explicit reciprocal action is required. In the real world of international politics, pure unconditionality probably does not exist. All political actors expect at least some degree of cooperation and goodwill in exchange for the benefits and assistance they provide. Rather than distinguishing between conditional and unconditional incentives, I find it more accurate to speak of degrees of conditionality. Benefits can be offered in a strictly conditioned manner or as part of a more open-ended long-range process in which no immediate response is requested or expected. The latter form of general incentive seeks to build a basis for cooperation and development in the future rather than to achieve a specific near-term response.

Newnham (2000) has observed that economic inducements can help to create interdependence and cooperation. Although the international order is inherently anarchic, inducement policies may be used to establish a basis for mutual cooperation and reciprocity. An emphasis on incentives can change the setting in which states interact. By creating an expectation of reciprocity and cooperation, inducement strategies can help to tame the conflictual tendencies of interstate competition. By making offers rather than issuing threats, states may alter a recipient nation's image of itself and its perception of potential friends and adversaries (Forsberg 1996). Incentive strategies thus shape the subjective motivations that determine policy preferences and enhance the prospects for cooperation.

Cooperation theorists emphasize the power of positive reciprocity—the ability of cooperative gestures to induce similar responses from others. Robert Axelrod's pioneering work in game theory explored the conditions that facilitate cooperation. Axelrod (1980) demonstrated that the simple tit-for-tat process, in which one party responds in kind to the gestures of the other, is a highly stable form of cooperation. He tested a number of different strategies for attempting to solve the familiar prisoners' dilemma puzzle. Responding in kind to the positive gestures of another proved to be the most effective strategy for winning the game. Axelrod's research confirmed that positive responses to conciliatory gestures offer the best prospect for mutually beneficial cooperation.

Numerous historical examples may be cited to lend credibility to these game theory findings. In relations between the United States and the Soviet Union during the Cold War, conciliatory gestures often led to reduced tensions, while hard-line policies usually produced a mirror response of heightened animosity. Lloyd Jensen (1984) found in his review of American-Soviet arms negotiations that concessions by one side tended to be reciprocated by the other. William Gamson and André Modigliani (1971) examined patterns of interaction between the West and the Soviet Union from 1946 to 1963. When Western nations made accommodative gestures to the Soviet Union, Moscow tended to respond with conciliatory behavior. By contrast, there was a tendency toward "refractory" actions when one side was confronted by belligerence from the other. Martin Patchen's review of the literature on this subject likewise found that "the usual tendency is for one side in a dispute to reciprocate the moves of the other, to match incentives if offered with return incentives" (1998, 262).

A dramatic example of the power of positive reciprocity occurred in September 1991, when U.S. President George H. W. Bush announced the unilateral demobilization of U.S. tactical nuclear weapons from ships and submarines and the removal of nuclear artillery and short-range missiles in Europe. This bold initiative was promptly reciprocated by Soviet President Mikhail Gorbachev, who announced a similar and even more sweeping withdrawal and dismantlement of Soviet tactical nuclear weapons. These actions, which came to be known as the Presidential Nuclear Initiatives, led to significant reductions, estimated at 7,165 weapons on the U.S. side and more than 11,000 weapons on the Soviet side (Millar and Ipe 2007, 134). The 1991 experience shows the ability of positive gestures to reduce nuclear dangers and facilitate arms reduction. This example corroborates the wisdom of offering concessions as a strategy for achieving mutual benefit and reducing mistrust. As Alexander Wendt observed, "positive reciprocation can foster a sense of common identification and help to create mutual interests between former adversaries" (1992, 420–22). Deborah Welch Larson (1987) similarly emphasized the importance of conciliatory action as a way of establishing the foundations for cooperative behavior.

Charles Osgood (1962) pioneered the consideration of risk reduction initiatives with his concept of Graduated Reciprocation in Tension Reduction (GRIT). The GRIT strategy was designed to go beyond simple tit-for-tat reciprocity. Under the GRIT strategy, the initiating side offers a series of accommodating steps and continues even in the absence of a reciprocal response. If the other side exploits the situation or acts in a hostile manner, the initiating side responds in kind, but only to the limited extent necessary to restore the status quo ante. If the other side reciprocates positively, the pace of conciliatory action is accelerated. Amitai Etzioni (1967) interpreted the de-escalation of U.S.-Soviet tension in the early 1960s that led to the Limited Test Ban Treaty as an example of the GRIT strategy in action. The Bush-Gorbachev nuclear reductions of 1991 and other East-West mutual concessions at the end of the Cold War also partially followed the GRIT concept.

HOW INDUCEMENTS WORK

The Carnegie Commission Working Group on Incentives (Cortright 1997, 272–90) examined variables that account for the success or failure of inducement strategies. Among the factors identified were the nature of the sender's objectives, the perceived value of the incentives package, the credibility of the sender, and political dynamics between and within the sender and recipient regimes. In his study of appeasement in international affairs, Stephen Rock (2000) identified two additional factors: the nature of the recipient regime and the presence or absence of exogenous incentives.

As with sanctions or any other attempt to exert external influence, incentives are most likely to succeed when they are employed in pursuit of limited objectives. The smaller the change sought, the greater the likelihood of success (Rock 2000). Economic inducements will be more effective in changing minor elements of policy than in changing fundamental issues of security. According to Wolfers (1962), incentives will be most effective in the area of "low politics," where national sovereignty and territorial integrity are not at stake. It is extremely difficult to persuade a state to trade territory or alter its security policies in exchange for economic benefits. On the other hand, if security assurances and the benefits of political alliance are included in an inducement package, more far-reaching political changes may be achievable. The denuclearization of Ukraine in the early 1990s is a case in point. The newly sovereign government of Ukraine was persuaded to give up nuclear weapons on its soil in exchange for an inducements package that included broad security guarantees and political assurances. The pursuit of major political objectives may be possible through the use of incentives, but this requires a large-scale and comprehensive inducements package with benefits that outweigh the costs of compliance. If security issues are at stake, the inducements package must include security guarantees and compensating forms of protection.

The perceived value of an inducements package is crucial to its effectiveness. In economic theory, an incentive is calibrated to increase the value of the option preferred by the sender over what the recipient would otherwise choose. An incentive offer seeks to change a recipient's calculation of cost and benefit. It raises the value of cooperation and increases the cost of defiance. The scale of the incentive depends on the magnitude of the desired change in policy. The greater the change, the larger the required inducements package. The value of the incentive offered must match or exceed the value the recipient attaches to maintaining the status quo.

The effectiveness of economic inducements also depends on the credibility of the sender. A reputation for fulfilling pledges and a demonstrated ability to deliver the promised rewards are crucial to success (Fisher 1969). Promptness in delivering rewards is also important. The swift fulfillment of a pledge increases the influence of the offer and raises the likelihood of positive reciprocation. A delay in the implementation of an incentive tends to impede cooperation. According to Axelrod (1984), the quicker the response to a conciliatory gesture, the more predictable and enduring the ensuing cooperation.

Focus and consistency are important to the effectiveness of inducement strategies. Incentives are more successful when they are sustained over time and employed in pursuit of a single objective. In the real world of politics, however, competing interests and cross-cutting purposes are common. Senders often pursue multiple or even conflicting objectives. In such circumstances, attempts to influence a targeted regime become more difficult. U.S. policy toward Pakistan is a classic case of conflicting and inconsistent purposes. Washington has sought Pakistan's cooperation in battling Soviet influence and now terrorism in Afghanistan, while urging Islamabad to refrain from weapons proliferation. Since September 11, 2001, counterterrorism goals have taken precedence, and nonproliferation pressures have largely disappeared.

As William Zartman notes in the introduction to this volume, exogenous factors often play a significant role in the success or failure of peacemaking efforts. Conditions and developments beyond the control of those attempting to influence a targeted regime may significantly affect such efforts. These exogenous factors may be at the international level, such as the target regime's loss or gain of an ally, or they may be internal to the sender or recipient, such as a sudden change in domestic political alignments. These international or domestic factors are often unpredictable and may significantly determine whether a conflict is "ripe" for resolution. Political change depends on the right opportunity structure. A keen sensitivity to such opportunities is key to determining whether an incentives offer is likely to succeed.

As with sanctions, the effectiveness of inducement strategies depends on how they affect the internal political dynamics of the target regime. As Denis Goulet observed, "An incentive system can only sway a subject who is disposed to respond" (1988, 11). The intended beneficiary of an offer will be the final judge of its effectiveness. Baldwin (1985) made the same point in noting that the effectiveness of an incentive depends on a recipient's perceptions and expectations. Inducement strategies seek to influence the political preferences of important actors within the recipient regime by delivering benefits to particular stakeholders and constituencies within the recipient regime who may then exert leverage on behalf of the desired policy change. Understanding and shaping the likely internal responses to an incentives offer can significantly enhance the prospects for policy success.

The nature of the recipient regime affects the appropriateness of inducement strategies and the manner in which incentives are offered. Rock (2000) argued that aggressive war-seeking states cannot be appeased. Some regimes are so abusive that inducement strategies will not work. In cases of overt military aggression or extreme violations of human rights, incentives are inappropriate morally and counterproductive politically. In other settings, where a regime is hostile but not actively belligerent, incentives may be appropriate, but only if they are strictly conditioned. When the recipient regime is hostile and there is mistrust between the parties, the delivery of incentives must be tied directly to specific concessions. In such settings, the incentives package can be broken down into component elements, with each reward delivered in response to specific actions from the other side. The process begins slowly with small steps and builds steadily toward larger and more significant gestures as the process of reciprocity becomes established. A strictly conditioned step-by-step process makes it possible to offer incentives as a peacemaking strategy even with abusive or hostile regimes.

COMBINING CARROTS AND STICKS

Incentives and sanctions are spoken of separately, but in practice they are often combined. States employ a variety of policy approaches simultaneously. They may shift back and forth between positive and negative measures, depending on the flow of events and the responses of the recipient. Baldwin

(1971) argued that negative and positive sanctions can be mutually reinforcing. George, Hall, and Simons (1971) and George and Smoke (1974) also emphasized that coercive diplomacy may require persuasion as well as pressure to achieve success. Many attempts to influence the affairs of other nations have involved a mix of positive and negative measures.

A number of scholars have attempted to measure the relative effectiveness of sanctions and incentives and the benefits of combining the two. A study at the Center for International Relations at the University of California at Los Angeles examined twenty-two cases of compellence that featured the use of sanctions and incentives either alone or in combination (Amini 1997). The study found that positive measures were more successful than negative sanctions, and that the combination of incentives and sanctions was more effective than the use of incentives alone. According to the study, "as one moves from the exclusive use of threats and punishments to the use of rewards and promises, the likelihood for success in a compellence situation increases by thirty-four percent. Additionally, as one opts to use both carrots and sticks over the use of carrots alone, one is again thirty-four percent more likely to succeed . . . There is a definite correlation between success and inclusion of positive sanctions, either alone or in conjunction with negative ones" (27–28).

A study at the Department of Sociology and Political Science at the Norwegian University of Science and Technology came to similar conclusions (Dorussen and Mo 1999). The authors analyzed the role of incentives in the 116 cases examined in the IIE study, *Economic Sanctions Reconsidered*. By focusing on the cases in which positive inducements were applied along with sanctions, Dorussen and Mo (1999) were able to document the benefits of inducement strategies. The authors found that the cases in which incentives were applied had a higher success rate than those in which sanctions alone were used. They concluded that incentives increase the effectiveness of sanctions and that "the simultaneous use of incentives and sanctions is more effective than the use of sanctions or incentives separately" (2).

Combining sanctions with incentives helps to avoid the problem of appeasement and the moral hazard of seeming to reward wrongdoing. When incentives are offered unconditionally to an aggressive or bellicose state, they may have the effect of encouraging further aggression. If inducements are offered pusillanimously as a substitute for decisive action, the recipient may interpret this strategy as a sign of weakness and attempt to exploit the situation. Researchers have found that incentives work best when they are offered from a position of strength rather than one of weakness. According to Patchen (1998), inducement strategies are more effective when they flow from strength and are accompanied by a latent threat capacity. Russell Leng observed that offers "are more likely to be effective when the influencer has the requisites for the effective use of negative inducements as well" (1993, 115). When carrots are mixed with sticks, or at least the threat of sticks, the dangers of appeasement can be diminished.

The decision to emphasize incentives or sanctions in a given situation depends on the nature of the problem and the objectives being served. When there is an urgent crisis, especially a conflict involving mass suffering or posing a danger to international security, a more coercive response may be necessary. When the policies of the targeted regime are especially abusive, such as apartheid in South Africa, or the transgression is a threat to international security, such as Iraq's 1990 invasion of Kuwait, incentives must give way to more coercive policies. Sanctions and military force may be a necessary response to crises involving overt aggression. When the transgression does not pose an immediate threat to peace, however, inducement strategies may be more appropriate. Incentives are preferable for creating the long-term foundations for peace and cooperation and for ameliorating conflict situations before they reach the crisis stage. They may also help to rebuild a society ravaged by conflict as a way of avoiding the recurrence of violence.

The suitability of sanctions or incentives in a given situation depends on the type of change being sought. The objective may be persuading the other party to initiate a new policy or convincing the party to halt an existing policy. According to Louis Kriesberg (2003), positive incentives are more suitable for the former objective because they provide a concrete benefit for the change of policy, whereas coercive measures are more appropriate for the goal of changing an existing policy. Offering incentives for the latter purpose might be seen as providing a "recurrent bribe" that would lose effectiveness and political credibility.

The choice of carrots and sticks also depends on the relationship between the parties. When political relations between initiator and recipient are distant or highly conflictual, it may be difficult to craft an effective incentives policy. The communication and bargaining aspects of an inducement process are more uncertain when the two sides are hostile and distrustful of one another. According to Wolfers (1962), inducements tend to be more effective in cooperative contexts, when relations between the actors are friendly. The same holds true for sanctions. As Drezner (1999) noted, sanctions are more likely to be effective when the sender and targeted regime have friendly political relations. The targeted regime will not want to lose the benefits derived from such a relationship, and as a result it will be more likely to bend its policies to the sender's will. Political communications are also clearer and more effective under conditions of cordial relations. The paradox, of course, is that nations enjoying friendly political relations are less likely to face the kind of sharp political differences and conflict that give rise to the use of coercive measures.

Even when political relations are unfriendly, sanctions and incentives policies can be successful in contributing to the resolution of conflict. The 1994 Agreed Framework between the United States and North Korea is an example. Despite the lack of diplomatic relations between the United States and North Korea, and notwithstanding hostile rhetoric and military mobilization on both sides, incentives-based bargaining proved to be successful in diffusing the crisis and facilitating a negotiated agreement to freeze North Korea's plutonium production program. It may be hard to initiate a constructive bargaining process when relations between the two countries are adversarial, but once the process of dialogue begins, mutual accommodation becomes possible. Even in the most contentious circumstances, incentives-based diplomacy can be successful, especially when it is combined with the threat of coercive action.

COMPARING INCENTIVES AND SANCTIONS

Although sanctions and incentives have much in common, they also have significant differences. The financial costs and benefits of the two differ considerably. Sanctions do not impose direct costs on governments, and they do not show up as a line item in national budgets. The financial burden of sanctions falls instead on private companies and local communities that lose jobs or income because of the interruption of trade. Where sanctions impose costs on particular industries and communities, trade incentives can bring benefits to such groups. The economic benefits generated by the use of trade and technology incentives can help to create political constituencies within the recipient nation that favor the changes sought by the sender. Domestic constituencies in the sender and recipient states may gain a stake in maintaining trade and technology inducements and strengthening cooperative relations. William Long (1996) identified this mutuality of interest as a crucial factor in the political effectiveness of inducement policies. In contrast to sanctions, which can cause economic hardships for both sender and recipient, trade and technology incentives bring benefits to both. They are a classic win-win proposition.

Incentive strategies also differ significantly from sanctions in their relation to overall market forces. When sanctions are imposed, pressure is generated for smuggling and the circumvention of trade restrictions. A successful embargo will raise the price of imports, and in turn generate powerful incentives for black marketeering. Sanctions may also create a "black knight" phenomenon, in which the targeted regime turns to another country for the economic and political support lost because of sanctions. Cuba's Cold War turn toward the Soviet Union is the classic example of this phenomenon. When incentives are employed, there is no natural tendency for third parties to come to the aid of the recipient regime. Nor is there pressure for smugglers and other economic actors to step in. As Eileen Crumm (1995, 326) observed, "Where market forces work against negative sanctions they can reinforce positive ones." Incentives work in harmony with the natural forces of the market and thus have a significant advantage over sanctions.

Sanctions and incentives also have differing impacts on international trade and global economic development. One of the most significant characteristics of recent history has been the dramatic worldwide expansion of free markets and the substantial increase in international commerce. As is emphasized below, the greater interdependence and communication that result from expanded trade can establish a long-term foundation for peace and enhanced international cooperation. Richard Rosecrance (1987) identified the "trading state" phenomenon as an antidote to war and armed conflict. Peter van Bergeijk (1994) argued that the use of negative sanctions can threaten the expansion of trade, thereby weakening incentives for greater political cooperation. By contrast, positive incentives and trade benefits increase commercial interaction and interdependence and thereby contribute to the long-term prospects for greater political cooperation. Incentives provide a basis for improved cooperation and understanding and thus create the foundation for international stability and peaceful political relations.

One of the greatest differences between incentives and sanctions lies in their impact on human behavior. Drawing on the insights of behavioral psychology, Baldwin (1971, 32) identified key distinctions between the two approaches. Incentives foster cooperation and goodwill, whereas sanctions create hostility and separation. Threats tend to generate reactions of fear, anxiety, and resistance, whereas the normal responses to a promise or reward are hope, reassurance, and attraction. Threats send a message of "indifference or active hostility" while promises "convey an impression of sympathy and concern" (Baldwin 1971, 32). Incentives tend to enhance the recipient's willingness to cooperate with the sender, whereas negative measures tend to impede such cooperation. Where threats and punishment generate miscommunication, promises and rewards tend to foster cooperation and dialogue (Fisher 1969). Because incentives create less resistance in the recipient, communication is likely to be clearer, and negotiations have a greater chance for success. Punitive measures may be effective in expressing disapproval of a recipient's policies, but they are not conducive to constructive dialogue. Where sanctions generate communications gridlock, incentives open the door to greater interaction and understanding.

DEVELOPMENT, DEMOCRACY, AND PEACE

One of the most powerful inducements for peacemaking in the world today is access to the system of cooperative security and economic development that exists within the Euro-Atlantic community and beyond. A zone of relatively prosperous and secure nations now stretches from Japan and Australia across North America through much of Europe. The states in this zone are characterized by democratic governance, relative security, and high levels of economic development. The EU and NATO are core institutions in this zone of prosperous security, and they have become powerful inducement engines for encouraging political cooperation. In their political relations with one another and the rest of the world, the countries of the European Union have espoused multilateral cooperation and the rule of law as essential principles. The prospect of political and economic integration into the European Union has proved to be a highly effective incentive. By establishing standards of membership, European officials have encouraged governments in Central and Eastern Europe to make substantial changes in their domestic and foreign policies. Paul Schroeder (1994) described this process as "association-exclusion." The greatest inducement for cooperation lies not in the power to punish, according to Schroeder, but in the creative use of association to reward those who abide by agreed-upon standards of behavior, while excluding those who do not. Participating countries are persuaded to change their policies, not through coercive pressure, but through the lure of membership in a beneficial community of nations.

Political and economic integration is widely recognized as a peacemaking strategy. Integration increases the tendency toward cooperative problem solving among participating states. It provides a basis for resolving conflicts through negotiation and bargaining rather than armed violence. The enhanced levels of communication and social interaction that are characteristic of integrated communities provide a basis for understanding and resolving differences before they become active conflicts (Kriesberg 2003). In the 1950s, Karl Deutsch and his colleagues (1957) analyzed the emergence of "security-communities" in the North Atlantic area and found several essential conditions for their success in reducing the incidence of armed conflict: (1) a compatibility of values regarding political decision making, (2) the capacity of participating parties to respond to each other, and (3) the mutual predictability of behavior.

The very existence of the European Union is predicated on the linkage between cooperative economic development and peace. From its beginnings in the 1950s as the European Coal and Steel Community to its present evolution as an expanding political community, the European Union has sought to use cooperative economic development to help resolve disputes and tame political differences among and within member states. In the process, the participating countries face a more stable and secure future. On a continent once ravaged by war, a new community of cooperating nations has emerged. Robert Kagan described this process as a "blessed miracle . . . a continent free from nationalist strife and blood feuds, from military competition and arms races" (2003, 97). The new Europe has rejected the principle of military dominance in favor of a new order based on mutuality, economic interdependence, and conflict prevention.

The peacemaking potential of the European Union is based on the assumption that economic interdependence, democracy, and the rule of law reinforce preferences for cooperation and peaceful development. Classic liberal theory holds that the expansion of trade reduces the likelihood of war, while protectionism and autarchy lead to greater conflict. Immanuel Kant (1948) argued at the end of the 18th century that the expansion of trade, what he called the "spirit of commerce," would encourage nations to avert war. Rosecrance (1987) and other writers have emphasized the role of economic interdependence in strengthening the preference for political cooperation. According to Lloyd Dumas (1990, 163), "generating sustained economic development is one of the most important elements in creating greater security."

Empirical evidence tends to confirm the linkage between commercial interdependence and peace. In his extensive survey of the relationship between economic interaction and war, Edward Mansfield (1994) found that the level of international trade among nations is inversely related to the incidence of armed conflict. The higher the level of commercial interdependence, the lower the likelihood of war. William K. Domke (1988) examined dozens of wars between 1870 and 1975 and found that countries with extensive trading relations were less likely to make decisions for war. Other studies of patterns of conflict between pairs of states have found a similar relationship between high levels of commercial interdependence and reduced levels of armed conflict. According to Louis Kriesberg (2003, 152), the relationship between increased trade and reduced conflict is "quantitatively large and statistically significant."

A shared commitment to democratic decision making is another factor that increases the likelihood of peaceful political relations among nations. Democratic peace theory holds that democratic nations seldom if ever wage war on one another (Russett 1993). One of the most solidly documented

findings of social science is that democratic societies tend to avoid armed conflict with one another. Two states that are democratic are much less likely to
wage war on one another than nondemocratic dyads (Kriesberg 2003). As
Michael Mandelbaum (2002) observed, the conditions that are associated with
democracy—freedom, civil society, and the rule of law—are also the basis of
market economies and successful international commerce. Democracy, economic prosperity, and peaceful political relations are thus mutually reinforcing.

Policy makers and scholars increasingly recognize the links between economic development and conflict prevention. Impoverished countries that
lack economic opportunity are prone to lawlessness and violent conflict. Wars
retard economic development and destroy the human and material foundations of production and trade. Resolving or preventing conflict is necessary
for sustainable economic development. Policies that reduce poverty and create economic opportunity reduce the likelihood of armed conflict. These connections are acknowledged in the development assistance strategies of international financial institutions. According to the Development Assistance
Committee (DAC) of the Paris-based Organization for Economic Cooperation and Development, "development cooperation . . . must play its role in
conflict prevention and peace building alongside a full range of other instruments available to the international community" (1997, 2).

It is not economic growth per se, but equitable and balanced development
that reduces the risk of violence. When the benefits of economic development are shared broadly, they contribute to the strengthening of civil society.
The DAC emphasized the importance of economic development that can
"strengthen democratic systems toward the structural stability that allows for
the nonviolent resolution of conflicts." Development should take into account
"the distribution and the transfer of power, as well as the protection and
inclusion of minorities and marginalized groups" (1997, 2). Economic development is most effective as a peacemaking strategy when it promotes power
sharing and democracy.

The empowerment of women is of particular importance to the dual dynamic
of development and conflict prevention. The DAC observed that women
play a central role in conflict resolution throughout the world. According to
DAC guidelines, "Emphasis should be given to the empowerment of women
in peace efforts and in the mobilization of support for conflict resolution, mitigation, and prevention. Integrating women fully into all phases of the process
will enhance the opportunities for building a just and equitable society" (1997,
2). Empirical studies of war-making tendencies among nations show a correlation between the empowerment of women and more peaceful foreign policies.
In his classic study *Development as Freedom*, economist Amartya Sen noted

that the political empowerment of women is directly related to such variables as a woman's literacy and education and her ability to find employment and income outside the home (Sen 1999, 191). Caprioli and Boyer (2001) found that countries where women are relatively empowered, as measured by education, professional employment, and participation in government, are less likely to use military force in international relations. According to the authors, "States that are characterized by higher levels of gender equality use lower levels of violence during crises than those with lower levels of gender equality," according to Caprioli and Boyer. These findings suggest that "the pursuit of gender equality in societies throughout the world may have positive effects for the lessening of violence." A similar study by Monty Marshall and Donna Ramsey Marshall in 1999 found strong support for the proposition that "gender empowerment is closely associated with a state's willingness to use force: the gender factor is negative and significant in all of the analyses" (Marshall and Marshall 1999, 22). Strategies that elevate the social, economic, and political status of women are likely to increase the prospects for preventing and resolving conflict.

The European Union: Regional Integration for Democracy and Peace

The economic development of Western Europe and the peaceful political relations that have accompanied this growth seem to confirm the connections between development and cooperation. European nations have developed a conscious strategy of encouraging harmony between and within states by using cooperation in the economic sphere to build peaceful political relations. As European Commission president Romano Prodi explained, by "making a success of integration we are demonstrating to the world that it is possible to create a method for peace" (quoted in Kagan 2003, 60). As the European Union has evolved economically, the participating states have deepened their political integration. They have codified the principles of democracy, the rule of law, respect for human rights, tolerance for minorities, and peaceful relations as conditions for membership. They have encouraged states to strengthen civil society and facilitated cross-border collaboration. States that wish to enjoy the economic benefits of the integrated European market must cooperate and abide by agreed-upon standards of political behavior. The presence of NATO as a parallel security structure offers a powerful additional benefit for the countries that are members of both organizations. NATO and the European Union are separate structures, but they have worked in concert to promote political and economic cooperation.

The European community has achieved some success in encouraging aspiring member states in Central and Eastern Europe to resolve conflicts and protect the rights of national minorities. As the countries of Eastern Europe have sought to join the European Union and NATO, they have had to accept specified policies and take concrete steps toward resolving local disputes. In Estonia and Latvia, significant tensions developed in the early 1990s over the citizenship rights of Russian-speaking minorities. The newly sovereign governments in these countries initially denied rights to Russian-speaking residents, arousing nationalist concerns in Russia and leading to the slowing of Russian troop withdrawals. The Organization for Security and Cooperation in Europe (OSCE) stepped in to help mediate the dispute, and the Council of Europe encouraged the Baltic states and Russia to find a political solution. The Baltic states were offered membership in the major European organizations— the Council of Europe, the OSCE, and the European Union—in exchange for liberalizing their citizenship laws and residency requirements for nonethnic Balts. Russia was offered financial support and membership in the Council of Europe to encourage the withdrawal of Russian troops. These inducement policies produced results. The Baltic states altered their citizenship laws, and Russian troops completed their withdrawal (Hurlburt 1997).

In Slovakia, a similar dispute emerged over the rights of minorities. The nationalist government in newly sovereign Slovakia initially denied Hungarian-speaking minorities the right to use their native tongue in official communication with government authorities. Once again the OSCE stepped in to mediate the dispute, and the European Union insisted that Slovakia provide protections for the rights of minorities as a condition of membership. The Slovak government responded by changing its laws to allow minorities to communicate with local authorities in their mother tongue (Kopanic 1999), removing the obstacles to Slovakia's integration into the European Community. Similar developments occurred in Hungary, Romania, and other EU candidate states. Throughout the region, human rights protections and democratic procedures were strengthened as nations prepared themselves to join the EU and NATO.

In addition to offering membership as a peacemaking inducement, the European Union has used direct economic assistance to encourage regional cooperation. Through funding for economic development, the EU has sought to strengthen social stability and prevent deadly violence (Eavis and Kefford 2002). These assistance efforts have been designed to promote political cooperation, improve government accountability, and resolve specific disputes that have the potential of escalating into violent conflict. Several specific aid programs have been created for these purposes. The Poland and Hungary: Action for Rehabilitating the Economy program began as a specific initiative to help Poland and Hungary, but the program has been extended to cover fourteen countries throughout eastern and southeastern Europe. It provides financial and technical assistance to countries aspiring to EU membership so that they have the necessary legal and institutional infrastructure for democratic, market-based societies. The Technical Assistance for the Commonwealth of Independent States (TACIS) program provides similar assistance to former Soviet republics in the Caucasus and central Asia. TACIS programs provide training and technical assistance for the transition to a market economy and offer low-interest loans to local entrepreneurs. These and other EU programs are facilitating democracy and market-based development as a strategy for cooperation and conflict prevention (Eavis and Kefford 2002).

The Stability Pact for Southeastern Europe

The wars and political violence that erupted in former Yugoslavia in the 1990s profoundly challenged the EU vision of a peaceful community of democratic nations. The savagery displayed in Bosnia, Croatia, and elsewhere in the Balkans shocked European officials and dispelled any facile optimism about the ability to guarantee a peaceful continent. European institutions and the wider international community were ill prepared for dealing with the conflicts. The many policy tools that were employed—diplomacy, sanctions, and peacekeeping—seemed incapable of containing the carnage. In 1993, the European community created the Stability Pact, also known as the Balladur Plan, which was designed to encourage the countries of central and eastern Europe to resolve their grievances through negotiation. The initial Stability Pact had little impact in stemming violence in the Balkans, however. It lacked sufficient resources and political commitment from the major European powers, and it suffered from what one analyst described as "poor coherence at the EU level in the planning and execution of programs" (Eavis and Kefford 2002, 5). The initial pact also came at a time when the conflicts were not yet ripe for resolution, as the warring parties continued to pursue their agendas through military means. Out of this experience came a recognition of the need for a more coordinated effort among a larger network of institutions, a greater commitment of resources and political will, and a more timely effort to resolve disputes before they descend into full-scale war.

In June 1999, the EU created a new Stability Pact for Southeastern Europe. The program emerged as the crisis in Kosovo intensified in late 1998 and early 1999. It was an attempt to contain the spread of violence there and in Macedonia and to encourage cooperation and integration throughout the region. The Stability Pact was intended as a mechanism for providing positive assistance to states in the region. It was created at a time when negative pressures were also being applied against Serbia, including EU and U.S. sanctions and NATO military action. The strategy thus combined carrots and sticks—offers of economic assistance along with targeted sanctions and military action. It embodied what could be called a two-hands policy: one hand applying coercive pressure to end violence and repression, the other hand offering assistance and support for peaceful cooperation.

Although initiated by the European Union, the Stability Pact for Southeastern Europe has been supported by more than forty nations, regional bodies, and international organizations working in partnership under the auspices of the OSCE. The EU has played the dominant role and is the major donor supporting the pact's conflict prevention programs. Germany's leadership and sponsorship of the Stability Pact has been an important asset. Most countries of the region do not wish to offend the EU's largest member and the region's dominant trading partner and investor. The Stability Pact has three general purposes: to promote democracy, to protect human rights, and to facilitate economic development. It has three major working groups that focus on democratization and human rights, economic reconstruction and cooperation, and security issues. The Stability Pact works in conjunction with the EU's Stabilization and Association Process to offer the nations of the region the prospect of accelerated accession to the European Union, in exchange for a greater commitment to regional cooperation in fulfillment of EU political standards. The prospect of eventual membership in the EU, combined with offers of technical assistance and financial aid, serve as powerful inducements for compliance. The Stability Pact (2004) described the process as follows:

> In the implementation of the Stability Pact, important lessons are being drawn from post World War II reconstruction programs, as well as the Helsinki process (CSCE/OSCE). The Stability Pact works as a two-way street. In order to receive support from the international community, the recipient countries must implement appropriate reforms. South Eastern European governments have undertaken to carry out economic reforms (dismantling of trade and investment barriers) and to fight corruption and organised crime within the context of the Stability Pact. In exchange, donors support the reconstruction process in a co-ordinated way through assistance and credits.

The Stability Pact has initiated projects to mediate specific disputes, improve interethnic relations, and support government reform efforts. It has been a useful mechanism for encouraging the countries of southeastern Europe to cooperate on a diverse range of issues, from trade facilitation and crime fighting to specific regional problems. The pact secured 5.4 billion euros in funding for a Quick Start Package of 244 projects. Nearly half of these funds have been committed for infrastructure development efforts, with the rest devoted to a variety of programs to facilitate refugee return and assist regional cooperation. Under the auspices of the Stability Pact, the governments of Bosnia, Croatia, and Yugoslavia signed the June 2001 Agenda for Regional Action, pledging to resolve the situation of 1.2 million refugees and displaced persons. Other accomplishments include negotiations among Bosnia, Croatia, Slovenia, and Yugoslavia on the joint management of the Sava River basin, leading to an international treaty on the Sava River. The Stability Pact has also negotiated a regional implementation plan on controlling the spread of small arms in southeastern Europe and launched a Support of Defense Reform initiative to provide financial assistance for Bulgaria and Romania as they restructure their armed forces.

The essential requirement for these and all other Stability Pact programs is the active participation of the countries in the region. The Stability Pact seeks to create broader regional identities and demonstrate the benefits of cooperation by building cross-border partnerships. It involves countries of the region in the planning and development process and requires mutual cooperation as a condition for support. By fostering interstate collaboration, the Stability Pact builds a foundation for long-term cooperation. The Stability Pact is not a panacea, however. Many of the integration and partnership programs begun under its auspices have been tentative and limited in scope and have not resolved underlying political differences. Some disputes in the region have not been amenable to resolution even with the most generous offers of assistance. The Stability Pact has also suffered from the problem of raised expectations, leading to disillusionment when the anticipated levels of support did not materialize. When initial expectations of a massive infusion of resources were not met, there was considerable disappointment and criticism in the region. Notwithstanding these limitations, the Stability Pact has been a positive experiment in the use of regional integration and economic assistance to create a more stable and secure political environment. The pact has applied a holistic approach that links economic development with various reform issues—democracy, human rights, government reform, enhanced security, and cooperation—to address the root causes of conflict and prevent future outbreaks of armed violence.

CONCLUSION

Not only in Europe but in many parts of the world, economic tools of statecraft have proven to be effective means of pressuring and persuading regimes to resolve conflicts and respect international norms. Whether the emphasis is on negative sanctions, as in the civil wars of Angola and Sierra Leone, or on positive measures, as in the denuclearization of Ukraine, the application of economic statecraft has been a key element of international peacemaking efforts. Political theory and empirical evidence suggest that inducements have advantages over sanctions, and that political effectiveness is enhanced when positive and negative measures are combined. In many settings, sanctions and incentives have been essential elements in a bargaining process that has led to the negotiated resolution of conflict. The strategy of applying pressure in the face of defiance and offering concessions in response to cooperation has been effective in helping to prevent and resolve conflict.

The European model of regional integration offers important lessons for the use of inducement strategies to strengthen international peacemaking. The EU and NATO have used the powerful incentives of prosperity and security to promote democracy, free markets, tolerance, and regional cooperation. In Central and Eastern Europe, EU policy makers have been particularly active in attempting to resolve disputes and encourage democratic reform, launching the Stability Pact for Southeastern Europe as a comprehensive initiative to use economic assistance to encourage cooperation. By facilitating economic interdependence and interstate cooperation to solve regional problems, European officials hope to increase understanding and establish a firmer foundation for peaceful relations.

The EU model is not fully transferable to other parts of the world, but the general strategy of encouraging regional cooperation as a means of preventing conflict is broadly applicable. Although the EU and NATO are unique in the degree of prosperity and security they can provide for member states, the broader principle of supporting economic development and offering security assurances to encourage political cooperation is valid generally. In the European model, the benefits of economic development and trade cooperation are combined with security assurances and guarantees of democracy. To the extent that other regional organizations can link economic development, security cooperation, and democratization, the prospects for resolving and preventing conflict will increase. A strategy that offers integration into a system of democracy, development, and security in exchange for adherence to the rule of law and agreed standards of cooperation and tolerance has the potential to advance international stability and peace.

ACKNOWLEDGMENTS

My partner, George A. Lopez, helped to develop much of the material in this chapter, especially the first half. I am also indebted to Linda Gerber-Stellingwerf for valuable research and editing assistance.

REFERENCES

American Friends Service Committee, Working Group on International Economic Sanctions. 1993. *Dollars or Bombs: The Search for Justice Through International Sanctions*. Philadelphia: American Friends Service Committee.

Amini, Gitty M. 1997. "A Larger Role for Positive Sanctions in Cases of Compellence?" Working Paper 12. Los Angeles: Center for International Relations, University of California.

Axelrod, Robert. 1984. *The Evolution of Cooperation*. New York: Basic Books.

Baldwin, David A. 1971. The Power of Positive Sanctions. *World Politics* 24 (1): 18–38.

———. 1985. *Economic Statecraft*. Princeton, N.J.: Princeton University Press.

Caprioli, Mary, and Mark A. Boyer. 2001. "Gender, Violence, and International Crisis." *Journal of Conflict Resolution* 45 (August): 503–18.

Cortright, David, ed. 1997. *The Price of Peace: Incentives and International Conflict Prevention*. Lanham, Md.: Rowman and Littlefield.

Cortright, David, and George A. Lopez, eds. 2002. *Smart Sanctions: Targeting Economic Statecraft*. Lanham, Md.: Rowman and Littlefield.

Cortright, David, George A. Lopez, and Linda Gerber-Stellingwerf. 2007. "Sanctions." In *The Oxford Handbook on the United Nations*, ed. Thomas Weiss and Sam Daws. New York: Oxford University Press.

Crumm, Eileen. 1995. "The Value of Economic Incentives in International Politics." *Journal of Peace Research* 32 (3): 313–30.

Damrosch, Lori Fisler. 1993. "The Civilian Impact of Economic Sanctions." In *Enforcing Restraint: Collective Intervention in Internal Conflicts*, ed. Lori Fisler Damrosch, 274–315. New York: Council on Foreign Relations.

Deutsch, Karl W., et al. 1957. *Political Community and the North Atlantic Area*. Princeton, N.J.: Princeton University Press.

Development Assistance Committee, OECD. 1997. "Policy Statement: Conflict, Peace and Development Cooperation on the Threshold of the 21st Century." Paris: Development Assistance Committee. www.oecd.org/dataoecd/15/54/1886146.pdf (accessed August 24, 2007).

———. 2001. "Helping Prevent Violent Conflict, (Executive Summary)." DAC Guidelines. Paris: Development Assistance Committee. webnet1.oecd.org/EN/document/0,,EN-document-notheme-2-no-24-5782-0,FF.htm.

Domke, William K. 1988. *War and the Changing Global System*. New Haven, Conn.: Yale University Press.

Dorussen, Han, and Jongryn Mo. 1999. "Sanctions and Incentives." Paper presented at the annual meeting of the American Political Science Association, Atlanta, Ga.

Dowty, Alan. 1994. "Sanctioning Iraq: The Limits of the New World Order." *The Washington Quarterly* 17 (3): 179–98.

Doxey, Margaret P. 1987. *International Sanctions in Contemporary Perspective*. New York: St. Martin's.

Drezner, Daniel W. 1999. *The Sanctions Paradox: Economic Statecraft and International Relations*. Cambridge, UK: Cambridge University Press.

Dumas, Lloyd J. 1990. "Economics and Alternative Security: Toward a Peacekeeping International Economy." In *Alternative Security: Living Without Nuclear Deterrents*, ed. Burns Weston, 137–75. Boulder, Colo.: Westview.

Eavis, Paul, and Stuart Kefford. 2002. "Conflict Prevention and the European Union: A Potential Yet to Be Realized." In *Searching for Peace in Europe and Eurasia*, ed. Paul van Tongeren, Hans van deVeen, and Juliette Verhoven, 3–14. Boulder, Colo.: Lynne Rienner.

Eland, Ivan. 1995. "Economic Sanctions as Tools of Foreign Policy." In *Economic Sanctions: Panacea or Peacebuilding in a Post–Cold War World?* ed. David Cortright and George A. Lopez, 29–42. Boulder, Colo.: Westview.

Elliot, Kimberly Ann, and Gary C. Hufbauer. 1999. "Same Song, Same Refrain? Economic Sanctions in the 1990s." *American Economic Review* 89 (2): 403–8. Papers and Proceedings of the One Hundred Eleventh Annual Meeting of the American Economic Association, May 1999.

Etzioni, Amitai. 1967. "The Kennedy Experiment." *Western Political Science Quarterly* 20: 361–80.

Fisher, Richard. 1969. *International Conflict for Beginners*. New York: Harper and Row.

Forsberg, Toumas. 1996. "The Efficacy of Rewarding Conflict Strategies: Positive Sanctions as Face-savers, Payments and Signals." Paper prepared for the Annual Meeting of the International Studies Association, April, San Diego, Calif.

Galtung, Johan. 1983. "On the Effects of International Sanctions." In *Dilemmas of Economic Coercion: Sanctions in World Politics*, ed. Miroslav Nincic and Peter Wallensteen. New York: Praeger.

Gamson, William, and André Modigliani. 1971. *Untangling the Cold War*. Boston: Little, Brown.

George, Alexander L., David K. Hall, and William R. Simons. 1971. *The Limits of Coercive Diplomacy: Laos-Cuba-Vietnam*. Boston: Little, Brown.

George, Alexander L., and Richard Smoke. 1974. *Deterrence in American Foreign Policy: Theory and Practice*. New York: Columbia University Press.

Goulet, Denis. 1988. *Incentives for Development: The Key to Equity*. New York: Horizons.

Hazelzet, Hadewych. 2001. Carrots or Sticks? EU and US Reactions to Human Rights Violations (1989–2000). PhD diss., European University Institute.

Hirschman, Albert. 1980. *National Power and the Structure of Foreign Trade*, expanded ed. Berkeley: University of California Press.

Hufbauer, Gary C., Jeffrey Schott, and Kimberly Ann Elliot. 1990. *Economic Sanctions Reconsidered: History and Current Policy*, 2d ed. Washington, D.C.: Institute for International Economics.

Hurlburt, Heather F. 1997. "Gaining Leverage for International Organizations: Incentives and Baltic-Russian Relations, 1992–1994." In *The Price of Peace: Incentives and International Conflict Prevention*, ed. David Cortright, 225–41. Lanham, Md.: Rowman and Littlefield.

Jensen, Lloyd. 1984. "Negotiating Strategic Arms Control: 1969–1979." *Journal of Conflict Resolution* 28: 535–59.

Kagan, Robert. 2003. *Of Paradise and Power: America and Europe in the New World Order*. New York: Alfred A. Knopf.

Kant, Immanuel. 1948. "Essay on Eternal Peace." Reprinted in *Inevitable Peace*. ed. Carl Joachin Fredrich. Cambridge, Mass.: Harvard University Press.

Keohane, Robert. 1998. *After Hegemony: Cooperation and Discord in the World Political Economy*. Princeton, N.J.: Princeton University Press.

Kopanic, Michael J. 1999. The New Minority Language Law in Slovakia. *Central Europe Review* 1 (2). www.ce-review.org/99/2/kopanic2.html (accessed August 24, 2007).

Kriesberg, Louis. 2003. *Constructive Conflicts: From Escalation to Resolution*, 2d ed. Lanham, Md.: Rowman and Littlefield.

Larson, Deborah Welch. 1987. "Crisis Prevention and the Austrian State Treaty." *International Organization* 41 (1): 27–60.

Leng, Russell. 1993. "Influence Techniques Among Nations." *Behavior, Society and International Conflict*, vol. 3, ed. Philip E. Tetlock et al. Oxford: Oxford University Press.

Long, William J. 1996. *Economic Incentives and Bilateral Cooperation*. Ann Arbor: University of Michigan Press.

Mandelbaum, Michael. 2002. *The Ideas that Conquered the World: Peace, Democracy and Free Markets in the Twenty-First Century*. New York: Public Affairs.

Mansfield, Edward D. 1994. *Power, Trade, and War*. Princeton, N.J.: Princeton University Press.

Marshall, Monty G., and Donna Ramsey Marshall. 1999. "Gender Empowerment and the Willingness of States to Use Force." Paper presented at the annual meeting of the International Studies Association, Washington, D.C., February 19.

Millar, Alistair, and Jason Ipe. 2007. "Cutting the Deadly Nexus." In *Uniting against Terror: Cooperative Nonmilitary Responses to the Global Terrorist Threat*, ed. David Cortright and George A. Lopez. Cambridge, Mass.: MIT Press.

Newnham, Randall E. 2000. "More Flies with Honey: Positive Economic Linkages in German Ostpolitik from Bismark to Kohl." *International Studies Quarterly* 44 (1): 73–96.

Nossal, Kim Richard. 1999. "Liberal Democratic Regimes, International Sanctions, and Global Governments." *Globalization and Global Governments*, ed. Raimo Väyrynen, 127–49. Lanham, Md.: Rowman and Littlefield.

O'Sullivan, Meghan. 2003. *Shrewd Sanctions: Statecraft and State Sponsors of Terrorism*. Washington, D.C.: Brookings Institution Press.

Osgood, Charles E. 1962. *An Alternative to War or Surrender*. Urbana: University of Illinois Press.

Patchen, Martin. 1998. *Resolving Disputes Between Nations: Coercion or Conciliation?* Durham, N.C.: Duke University Press.

Rock, Stephen R. 2000. *Appeasement in International Politics*. Lexington: University of Kentucky Press.

Rosecrance, Richard. 1987. *The Rise of the Trading State*. New York: Basic Books.

Russett, Bruce M. 1993. *Grasping the Democratic Peace*. Princeton, N.J.: Princeton University Press.

Schroeder, Paul W. 1994. "The New World Order: A Historical Perspective." *The Washington Quarterly* 17 (2): 25–43.

Sen, Amartya. 1999. *Freedom as Development*. New York: Anchor Books.

Stability Pact for Southeastern Europe. 2004. "About the Stability Pact." www.stabilitypact.org/about/default.asp (accessed August 24, 2007).

U.S. General Accounting Office. 1994. *International Trade: Issues Regarding a Position of an Oil Embargo Against Nigeria*. Report no. GAO/GGD-95-24 prepared for the Chairman, Subcommittee on Ethics, Committee on Foreign Affairs, U.S. Cong., House. 103rd Cong., 2d. Sess.

van Bergeijk, Peter A. 1994. *Economic Diplomacy, Trade and Commercial Policy: Positive and Negative Sanctions in a New World Order*. Aldershot, UK: Edward Elgar.

Wendt, Alexander. 1992. "The Anarchy is What States Make of It: The Social Construction of Power Politics." *International Organization* 46 (2): 391–425.

Wolfers, Arnold. 1962. "Power and Influence: The Means of Foreign Policy." In *Discord and Collaboration: Essays on International Politics*, ed. Arnold Wolfers, 103–15. Baltimore: Johns Hopkins University Press.

11

THE ROLE OF FORCE IN PEACEMAKING

Jane Holl Lute

In 2003, Iraq's notorious leader Saddam Hussein could not have had many friends in the world. Chief architect of the eight-year war with Iran in the 1980s, leader of a precipitous invasion of Kuwait in 1990, and author of unspeakable crimes against his own citizens for more than thirty years, Saddam held a decades-long grip on Iraq, overseeing a regime that was characterized by aggressive brutality at home and abroad. Yet when the United States undertook to unseat this acknowledged tyrant and regional menace, it found itself all but isolated in its determination to use force to do the job. Indeed, Washington came under sharp criticism from nearly every corner of the globe—including from some of its closest allies—for its unwavering march toward war.

This criticism was remarkable for seeming, at times, to defend Saddam against the United States. It was also remarkable coming, as it did, so soon in the wake of the terrorist strikes of September 11, 2001. In the months following the attacks, the world had largely shared solidarity with the United States, extending genuine sympathy as well as agreeing with the U.S. plan for dealing with the newly appreciated threat of global terrorism—in which, Washington argued, Saddam played a central part. Terrorist networks with a global reach would be broken, and states that harbored such groups, including Iraq, were put on notice to end their sanctuary.

In making its case for war against Baghdad, the United States emphasized a familiar argument about Saddam—that he represented a latter-day Hitler with nuclear and other weapons of mass destruction—and Washington also made claims that linked Saddam's Iraq to the world's most dangerous terrorist group, Osama bin Laden's al-Qaeda. These claims would later be proved wrong, but when the invasion of Iraq was under operational development in 2002, the rationale for using force to bring Saddam to heel could hardly have appeared more potent. The United States argued that in the interest of regional—indeed, global—peace and security, Saddam was a threat that could be eradicated only through the use of force. Moreover, ending his hold on Iraq—Americans argued—would open space for Arab democracy in the Middle East; put other states such as Syria on notice to cease support for terrorist groups; ease pressure on Israel to, in turn, create better prospects for peacefully settling its dispute with the Palestinians; and permit a clearer global focus on Iran as a state sponsor of terror and determined seeker of nuclear weapons. It would also free an important source of global oil (the second largest known reserves in the world) from Saddam's control.

Yet as worthy as these goals might have been, they failed to move the vast majority of the world's states to share U.S. enthusiasm for forceful action. Why? Part of the explanation can be attributed to the complex interaction of the regional stakes and equities of major states—including not only the United States and Great Britain, but also Russia, France, Germany, Turkey, Saudi Arabia, and others. The answer also lies, in part, in what many viewed as the high-handed way in which the Bush administration had pursued its foreign policies during its first years in office. But much of the reluctance can be traced to how, at the end of the twentieth century, many states had come to view the use of force for any purpose other than self-defense with the deepest misgivings.

Such disagreement arises, in part, because of the sheer cost of using force; nations send their young men—and increasingly their young women—off to dangerous situations with a high chance that these lives will be lost. Countless money is spent, thousands of lives are displaced, and vast infrastructures are destroyed. Particularly in an age when so much destructive power is so readily available to such great numbers of potential belligerents, people the world over have become increasingly uneasy at the prospect of violent conflict—especially given its inherent ability to spread.

Moreover, the costs of using force cannot be reliably predicted and are often seen to outweigh any expected gains, thus adding to the concerns. Beyond that are the inherent risks of unintended consequences, making the use of force an extremely unpredictable exercise. Thus, many have come to believe that it ought to be hard to use force; it ought to be hard to go to war.

Occasionally, however, there is a justified resort to the use of force. For example, forceful measures may be the only effective means to counter aggression, end atrocities, halt genocide, or bring peace and stability. But just what is the rightful role of force to make or keep peace? This chapter considers this central issue in the international relations of making peace—that is, the use of force to secure, maintain, and restore peace. It discusses how international norms have developed for these purposes and how these norms have been reinforced through the evolved habits of the international community to prevent, manage, and resolve the conflicts of its members.

But first, some semantic housekeeping. The terms "war" and "force" are used throughout this chapter, but it is useful to be mindful of the distinction. War is used here in its familiar sense as traditionally large-scale, organized violence; force, although including war, contemplates threats and other forms of armed coercion.[1] Peace is not the total absence of conflict but rather the state of affairs in which breaches are more properly thought of as law-and-order problems rather than as fundamental challenges to security.

PEACE WILL NOT KEEP ITSELF

Peace begins with war, or so history of the human experience tells us. The *pax Romana*—lasting 207 years—followed the Roman Civil Wars. The end of the Thirty Years War inaugurated the Peace of Westphalia in 1648, which persisted for 144 years until the onset of the French Revolution and the Napoleonic Wars in 1792. Napoleon's defeat at Waterloo in 1815 gave rise to the Congress of Vienna, which, arguably, maintained peace among the major powers for nearly one hundred years. And the defeat of Germany and Japan in 1945 ended World War II, inaugurating the "long peace" or *pax Americana*, which, again arguably, has persisted ever since (Gaddis 1989).[2] Some authors assert that *Pax Americana* has long ceased to exist (Huntington 1988–89; Nye 1990).

But more than the simple product of war, peace has, in many respects, come to depend for its very existence on the force of arms. Law is upheld, aggression is thwarted, and evils are destroyed—ultima ratio—through force. It may not be too much to say that the only legitimate use of force today, aside from essential acts of self-protection, is to bring about peace.

Indeed, in the modern era, the use of force in international relations is, for the most part, illegal. Powerful norms, with roots reaching back over half a millennium, have emerged in international law and from the political practice of states to repudiate the use of force for offensive purposes. No longer can title be claimed through conquest. No longer can states adventure with impunity to secure political, economic, social, or other advantage through force of arms. No longer are states able to sustain limitless indifference as people are coerced into submission by their sovereigns. Today, the only legal—and legitimate—use of force other than self-defense is to bring about peace.

Using force in this way is not without controversy. Some observers hold the view that the use of force has no place in civilized relations among people and that it is, indeed, a distortion of our moral compass to convey legitimacy to some uses of force while denying it to others (see, e.g., Moskos and Whiteclay 1993; Hermann 1992). Others believe that military forces should be preserved for fighting and winning a nation's major wars in defense of vital interests. Yet, the dominant perspective today among scholars and practitioners of international relations is that force is legitimate, appropriate, and indeed often necessary to manage international relations and maintain peace (see, e.g., Peterson 1998).

Our ability to distinguish between legitimate and illegitimate uses of force in international relations proceeds from a long historical experience. All the modern principles at issue today regarding the legitimate use of force—for example, last resort, necessity, proportionality, immunity for noncombatants—and many of the fundamental tenets of international peacekeeping—for example, neutrality, impartiality, participation through consent—have historical antecedents that trace back through centuries; some tenets have roots going back to before the modern state system was formed. The basic conviction that the use of force is, under certain circumstances, "just" for the purpose of peace dates to the Middle Ages. Thus, this discussion begins with a brief review of the history of the main ideas that lie beneath today's notions regarding the legitimate use of force to secure and uphold peace.

In tracing the well-worn paths of state interaction that have led to modern norms and practice, and in examining the uses to which force is legitimately put today, this chapter reaffirms the proposition that the governments of states still—as they have for centuries—constitute the only legal and legitimate authority to use force. Some scholars have taken note of the rise of supranational institutions such as the United Nations (UN), the European Union (EU), and the Organization of American States (OAS), as well as the development of subnational forces rendering states incapable of effective governance, signaling the demise of the state system. Most commentators, however, believe that these judgments are premature (Mearsheimer 1994–95, 2001; Weiss 1998; Evans 1997; Finnemore 1996).

Yet states are not unconstrained in the use of power. Through their political, economic, social—and yes, military—engagements with one another, states have conditioned each other to expand their mutual tolerance and devise alternative ways to deal with their differences. As the international system has changed from a multipolar distribution of power to a bipolar division, or even now to unprecedented unipolarity, states ultimately remain the primary source of legitimate authority when using force. Yet, over time, through international agreements, treaties, institutions, organizations, and practice, states have become increasingly circumscribed, even circumspect, in the deployment of forces and the use of force to deal with complex international problems.[3]

Moreover, the conditions under which this authority is legitimately exercised have become more restrictive through the ages. As a result, today there are just three conditions for which there seems to be international consensus on when force may be legitimately used: first, if one is attacked; second, if one is asked, as part of a collective defense effort; or third, if one is otherwise allowed under the provisions of international law, that is to say, under the provisions of Chapter VII of the UN Charter, "Action with Respect to Threats to the Peace, Breaches of the Peace and Acts of Aggression." In addition, force is recognized in the service of peace when it is put to three purposes: first, as the ultimate means to uphold the rule of law; second, as a decisive way to draw clear limits against unacceptable behavior (i.e., to deny the malintentioned and therefore illegitimate offensive use of force); and third, to destroy or eliminate a pernicious evil.

This discussion concentrates on these permissible and practiced uses of force and is organized around these questions: What are the peaceful uses of force? When is such use legitimate or justified? Who decides the foregoing? What international processes exist to determine when, how, and to what purpose force may legitimately be used? In other words, what conditions trigger the call for force? Should other means to alleviate the situation—for example, political or economic measures—be tried first? Should force always be a last resort? Once a determination has been made that force should be used, what missions should military forces be given? What limits are put on the use of force? Who ultimately determines that conditions warrant the use of force? Who deploys the forces? How is it determined what they do and how long they stay?

In addition to these questions, the following discussion also touches briefly on the ethical issues implicated in the use of force to counter force. What are the moral repercussions of threatening or using force to make peace? For issues as important as the ones under examination here, it is important to raise the question, even if one must accept that a complete answer may not be possible. Finally, this examination concludes with a brief discussion of the extent to which the legitimate uses of force should be stretched: although a customary right to use force may exist under certain conditions, for example to keep or restore peace, is there ever a duty to do so?

THE EVOLUTION OF NORMS REGARDING THE LEGITIMATE USE OF FORCE

We live in a world awash in violent conflict. In the early years of the twenty-first century, some three dozen active conflicts were under way (Smith 2002a,

2002b). Tragic, destructive, and in many cases chronic, these conflicts and those of the last years of the twentieth century are estimated to have taken in excess of six million lives, displaced more than thirty-five million people from their homes and livelihoods, and cost untold billions of dollars. As a result of conflict, several states have more than a million internally displaced persons (see also Gurr and Harff 1998; Gurr and Moore 1997). Grown from a tradition of hatred and capacity for destruction, these conflicts play out in an era when the ability to destroy life and property seems to be without limit.

These kinds of conflicts do not spring up in an instant, like a sudden storm, but can be seen forming in their earliest stages. In an era of nearly instantaneous communications, we know often before victims do that they will be victims. For example, although news sources citing eyewitness accounts of missionaries and aid workers reported the widespread massacres engulfing Rwanda as early as April 1994, there is little evidence that the victims themselves had any warning of their encroaching fate until mid-June (Cahill 1996; Carlson, Sung-Joo, and Kupolati 1999; Holman 1994). And in Colombia, human rights violations became so widespread that the government developed the Early Warning System, which allows local mayors or regional leaders to alert the central government—often before the potential victims themselves know of the danger—about impending violations of human rights (see Human Rights Watch 2002; UN Commission on Human Rights 2001).

These wars have certain, if often complex, causes—they stem from traditional competition for territory, resources, or wealth or represent newer struggles for recognition, political space, power, and wealth. Characteristically, they involve neighbor fighting neighbor. In these ways, many of today's wars resemble past wars. Yet at least two things distinguish many of today's conflicts from those of the past: first, more of these conflicts occur within states than between them; and second, the international community has become ever more active—indeed, intrusive—in dealing with the violence these wars generate.

Although international engagement has often exacerbated the violence, prolonged the fighting, and widened the destruction, many efforts are also under way (nearly two dozen as of this writing), to bring these conflicts to an end using some measure of counterforce. Today, the international community, largely under the auspices of the UN Security Council, has taken on a new willingness to use force to separate belligerents, disarm warring factions, oversee lines of demarcation, implement peace agreements, and provide some degree of security so that people in armed struggle can put down their arms, pursue other means to resolve their differences, and emerge from conflict to begin the political, economic, and social processes of healing.

Moreover, international forces deployed to keep the peace have often been asked to do much more than simply patrol demilitarized zones, separate warring parties, or collect weapons. It is not uncommon to find these "third-generation" peacekeeping missions with the mandate to organize and conduct elections, establish institutions to maintain law and order, reestablish financial systems and open markets, help maintain dialogues to reconcile former enemies, safeguard human rights, and even establish basic health and education systems.

These international operations to bring peace have two unique features: first, the use of force is a deliberate component in the mix; second, the force is deployed and used with a high degree of international legitimacy. Without the deployment of armed forces prepared to use force to discharge a mandate, these operations would be hardly more than traditional development efforts; without the wide degree of political legitimacy they enjoy, they would be little more than old-style occupations—unilateralist impulses magnified by multilateral capabilities.

How did this international practice of using force to bring peace come into prominence? How did the modern sensibility evolve regarding the use of force as the means of war and the use of force as a means of peace?

If today, war between states is generally viewed as illegal and the use of force thought to be more generally constrained, it was not always so. For thousands of years, war and other uses of force were a principal means by which territory and wealth were accumulated. For hundreds of years, the ability to declare war was the special province of kings (and the occasional queen) with license to wage it so long as wealth, skill, and luck held out, and that depended, in part, on the success of their campaigns. Yet today, sovereigns have largely lost the right to wage wars on whim or for profit. What stands in their way is the collective weight of international opinion—given heft by the strength of history and the complex evolution of interstate economic, political, social, and military interactions—and that opinion has its clearest expression in the UN Charter.

Ascribed to by 192 independent states in the international system today, the Charter starkly precludes war as an acceptable instrument of statecraft. The relevant article, 2(4), holds that, "All members shall refrain in their international relations from the threat or use of force against the territorial integrity or political independence of any state, or in any other manner inconsistent with the Purposes of the United Nations."

Those purposes, above all, include the peaceful relations of states. And since the formal adoption of the Charter in 1945, states have taken pains to justify how their uses of force have not violated Charter principles. For example,

Israel launched a preemptive attack against Iraq in 1981, destroying its nuclear reactor at Osirak. Advancing an argument based on necessity and self-defense, Israel sought to establish the consistency of its actions with Charter principles, yet Israel was publicly condemned by the Security Council in Resolution 487 on June 19, 1981 (see Arend and Beck 1993, 71–79). In 1999, the United States argued that bombing Belgrade was consistent with prior Security Council action on Kosovo. In 2003, however, the United States took action without express authorization from the UN Security Council for its invasion of Iraq, though it did rely on previous UN Security Council resolutions on Iraqi disarmament.

Behind the short lines of Article 2(4) lies a rich and storied history of thought, literature, law, and practice in the Western tradition that reaches principally back to the thirteenth century and the Christian doctrine of "just war." From this tradition, peace emerged as a collective value—more highly prized than sovereign prerogative, economic progress, or even justice.[4] In addition, the basic principles of necessity, proportionality, restraint, and discrimination (i.e., avoiding noncombatants and nonmilitary targets) that exist to regulate war and to constrain lesser uses of force have their origins in the just war tradition.

The Just War Tradition

More than seven centuries ago, Catholic theologian Thomas Aquinas, building on ideas originally developed by Augustine (354–480 AD), outlined the notion of just war, reflecting the maturation of a view within Christianity that had come to reject the absolute pacifism prevalent in the early church (see Cahn 2002; Boucher 1998; Keen 1965). Adhering to the precepts of natural law, Aquinas legitimized the view that, at times—to right a grievous wrong, for example—the use of force was not only necessary but justified (Grotius 1949; Strauss and Cropsey 1987).

To be considered just (*jus ad bello*)—and as such to reflect divine will—the act of war had to satisfy several criteria. First, the action had to spring from rightful intention for a right cause, that is, to counter a wrongful aggression— self-aggrandizing purposes were not considered legitimate—and the ultimate aim had to be to restore peace. Second, the right to wage war belonged only to legitimate authority, that is, the sovereign—armed gangs or individuals acting on their own could not claim to wage a just war. Third, likely victory had to be in the offing—war could not be considered just if the use of force would foreseeably result only in wasted effort, wanton destruction, or hopeless cause. Moreover, reflecting the early Christian pacifism, war could be undertaken only as a means of last resort; all means of peaceful resolution had first to be tried before the choice to wage war could be considered rightful. And finally, only that force necessary to right the wrong and restore peaceful order was justified. In other words, the forceful means had to be proportional to the ends sought.

A corresponding doctrine—*jus in bello*—prescribed the ways in which wars were justly waged. Noncombatants—innocents—could not be attacked, means had to correspond to ends, and ends had to be judged more valuable than the costs incurred to achieve them. From these beginnings, a number of modern-day principles regarding the use of force can be seen, such as last resort, the exclusion of noncombatants, and the imperative of proportionality. The right to use force in self-defense was not, at its core, altered by the just war doctrine. Stemming from the fundamental right to exist, the right of self-defense reflected the widespread acknowledgment of a deep existential need for self-preservation. It is the near universal recognition of the primordial need to preserve self that generated the doctrine of necessity—that is, the justified use of force when the preservation of life and limb warrant (see Grotius 1949). The inherent right to self-defense and the doctrine of necessity were codified in the 1930 Hague Convention and are also embodied in Article 51 of the UN Charter, confirming the right of self-defense in the face of an armed attack (see Scott 1915; Walzer 1977; Coady and Ross 2000).

In the centuries following Aquinas, the increasing reality of Christian states at war with one another—each, of course, claiming the justness of its cause—clarified an unpleasant truth that perhaps not all wars could be just, and strengthened the idea that force was the means of last resort and that other means for resolving a dispute had to be pursued before a state was justified in resorting to war. Moreover, preserving a general peace among the principal actors within the newly developing state system surfaced as an increasingly important value even over others, including an unlimited right of self-defense. Sovereigns were becoming obliged to pursue means other than simply resorting to force of arms to broker their differences. More than a justified response to correct a wrongful act, force was seen in its highest and best use as a rightful means of preserving peace or restoring general order where it had been breached.

Yet the natural law tradition that had given rise to the concepts and doctrine of just war began to come under strain as an ever more complex international system began to take shape.

Sovereignty Constrained

The searing experience of the Thirty Years' War in the seventeenth century led to the creation of the Westphalian system of states in Europe with the mutual realization that each state enjoyed sovereign equality with every other and the associated recognition that, in the absence of any supranational (not to say supernatural) authority, no state could pass judgment on the legitimacy or justness of another's cause for war. As part of their sovereign right, states needed nothing other than their own rationale or determination of need when resorting to force to pursue their interests (see Tilley 1975; Strang 1991; Howard 2000; Mann 1988).

Dutch legal scholar Hugo Grotius gave voice in the seventeenth century to a rethinking of the principles and values used to justify war. In the view of Grotius and others who followed in this positivist tradition, law sprung not from God or nature, but rather from states' prerogatives as sovereign entities, and decisions to use force fell clearly within the scope of their sovereign authority. Yet, given its distraction, expense, and destructiveness, war could be rationalized best only in self-defense (including the protection of property) or for retribution in the face of a patent wrong done. This sensibility led to an emphasis less on the legitimate causes for war than on the importance of limiting the need to resort to war, minimizing damage through more careful conduct in war, and accelerating the achievement of a durable peace. In addition to Grotius, other notable writers included Emer de Vattel and Giovanni de Legnano (see Tuck 1999; O'Brien 2001).

In this context, and as a pragmatic matter, early notions of neutrality began to emerge as states endeavored to hold themselves apart from conflicts involving other states and to refrain (at least in principle) from interfering in others' internal affairs, especially in the face of an armed internal uprising. Dealing impartially with all belligerents would give way over time, however, if an insurgency proved successful and gained parity with those in power; outsiders would then feel less constrained to join whichever side served their interests (see Orvik 1953). As a practical matter, no sovereign wanted to set an example that would provide others with the capacity or incentive to interfere in its own internal affairs. These principles of nonparticipation and nondiscrimination (remaining impartial) came to form the basis for the modern international presumption—absent the obligations of specific treaty commitments—against engagement and in favor of impartiality when dealing with the armed disputes of others. The Hague Peace Conferences of 1899 and 1907 gave rise to the modern codification of the rights of neutrals (see Lauterpacht 1970; Henkin 1979).

As a general peace settled in among the great powers in the first half of the nineteenth century and democracy spread slowly throughout the continent of Europe, gradual increases in life expectancy, education, and commerce and a growing sensitivity to the disruptions of war forced governments to work harder to justify their wars and clarify the necessity of fighting to the death for the causes at stake (see Howard 1976; Stern 1977; Weston, Falk, and Charlesworth 1997). States began to recognize that their competing interests could not play out inexhaustibly through the force of arms, especially as their world expanded through multiple colonial ambitions. Indeed, any change in the status quo would depend for its durability on recognition and acceptance by other states, and this recognition would not be forthcoming if the gains were deemed ill gotten through illegitimate means. Thus, the great states came to value peace, particularly among themselves, as a primary interest.

To avoid full-scale warfare where possible, governments began in the nineteenth century to take greater pains to develop ways to use force, short of war, to secure their aims. Through evolving practice with such measures as reprisals, blockades, limited occupations, detentions, and other forms of forceful demonstrations, states submitted themselves to a slowly developing international legal doctrine of restraint while justifying actions that were taken on the basis of necessity and rightness of cause. And indeed, even in self-defense, states were constrained to justify their actions. In an exchange of letters concerning the famous *Caroline* case, U.S. Secretary of State Daniel Webster contended that there must be a "necessity of self-defense, instant, overwhelming, leaving no choice of means and no moment for deliberation," and that the act should involve "nothing unreasonable or excessive, since the act justified by the necessity of self-defense must be limited by that necessity and kept clearly within it" (Moore 1906, 409–12). This case is often cited as an important codification of the doctrine of self-defense, with a state's obligation to demonstrate that the forceful actions taken were overwhelmingly necessary. In seeking means short of war to achieve their aims, leaders found it relatively easy to avoid the term "war" to describe even large-scale hostilities that were increasingly seen as costly if not wasteful of resources, lives, money, and time.

Thus, in part to avoid domestic opposition and in part to avoid the upheaval brought on by large-scale violence (e.g., loss of trade, cessation of normal diplomatic and political interaction, suspension of treaty obligations, not to say opprobrium) that inevitably accompanied the declaration of full war, states pursued and, in the process, institutionalized lesser means of using force to achieve their international goals. Customary law grew up around these coercive alternatives to war to protect nationals or property in the territory of another. Practices such as the use of sanctions, naval blockades, coercive diplomacy, and the deployment of small military contingents to secure the interests of the state, short of war, emerged in an environment growing increasingly opposed to the outbreak of large-scale conflicts. Peace (however superficial) became valued over war, and states undertook efforts not to be cast as transgressors of this emerging norm (see Macfarlane 2002; Howard 2000,

34–59). Thus, by the end of the nineteenth century, states' unconstrained use of force had given way both to the practical difficulties of doing so and to the political efforts under way to place increasing limits on the use of force. The most prominent of these efforts were the Hague Conventions of 1899 and 1907 (see also Caron 2000). Indeed, the Hague Conventions changed attitudes toward warfare that would, over the course of the coming century, give rise to less tolerance for warfare within states. In addition, the restraints on war established the foundation upon which modern sensibilities regarding the role of force in keeping peace would be developed over the next one hundred years.

Institutionalizing Peace: Early Efforts

The wholesale destruction of World War I—or more precisely, the failure of the system to avert it—demonstrated that the great power system could not function under pressure to maintain a general peace. It was clear that new ways had to be found to prevent any such future disaster. In just such an effort, world leaders came together to forge a new consensus regarding ways to manage their differences and established the League of Nations, following the lead, principally, of U.S. President Woodrow Wilson.

The League of Nations represented a major effort to execute a clean break from the notion of war as right—to war as wrong. Signatories obliged themselves to observing cooling-off periods when in crisis and to submit disputes to arbitration or judicial settlement. The League's charter also justified the use of collective measures—economic, political, and military—to thwart aggression.

Articles 10 through 19 of the Covenant of the League of Nations dealt with threats to international peace, collective action, and methods of arbitrating the peaceful resolution of conflicts. Remarkably, however, nowhere was the use of force prohibited, perhaps because no state could muster the willingness or imagination necessary to take such a dramatic step in the wake of the catastrophic violence of World War I, when superior force ultimately carried the victory.[5] Although some states hoped that the League would represent an important institutionalized international authority (principally through its intended role in the administration of selected European colonies under the mandate system), the League early on became preoccupied largely with the political oversight of several contested territories in Europe (namely Danzig, Upper Silesia, and the Saar Basin—areas under German control during the war). The League was instrumental in achieving some success in these cases, for example, in brokering a solution mutually agreeable to Germany and Poland regarding Upper Silesia; however, it was all but completely undermined in its engagement with the mandatories (where its efforts were quickly overwhelmed by the sheer size of the challenge and by noncooperation from states). In the end, pressures in Europe and the renewed German capacity for war spelled the League's demise (see Chesterman 2004; Wright 1930).

The failure of the League—seen only in part as a result of the United States' ultimate unwillingness to join—did not mark the end of efforts to strengthen international norms against war. The Kellogg-Briand Pact of 1928 embodied for the first time a total, global prohibition on the use of war. Yet, this effort too was held at arms length by a number of states and never fully exercised. The pact, signed in Paris on August 27, 1928, and ratified by the United States, Australia, Canada, Czechoslovakia, Germany, Great Britain, India, Ireland, Italy, New Zealand, South Africa, Poland, Belgium, France, and Japan, called for the full renunciation of war as an instrument of national policy. But the pact fell far short of the aspirations of its proponents and ultimately succumbed under the weight of the coming world war (see also Fiorina, Peterson, and Voss 2002).

Perhaps the failure of these efforts made it inevitable that only major catastrophe could fully turn the tide of sensibilities. The aggression of Adolph Hitler, the unspeakable atrocities of the Holocaust, and the wider destruction of a second world war so soon after the first crystallized the imperative for action and infused the great states with a determination to change course. The Nuremberg trials also affected the development of international law related to war, its conduct, and the culpability of participants (see Ehard 1949; International Law Commission 1950). The influence of the tribunal can also be seen in proposals for a permanent international criminal court and the draft international criminal codes prepared by the International Law Commission (see Yale University School of Law 1924, 2006).

The United Nations

With the stirring words in which the members of the United Nations assert their collective determination to "save succeeding generations from the scourge of war . . . which has brought untold sorrow to mankind," the UN Charter outlines the basic principles of modern state interaction. The Charter reaffirms the sovereign independence of states, but also details a number of obligations for states living in an international environment of cosovereignty—especially with respect to the maintenance of international peace and security.

Contemporary views on the prohibitions of Article 2(4) against the use of force fall into two general camps. The legalist view advocates strict adherence to the terms laid forth in the language of Article 2(4), and thus precludes forceful measures even for humanitarian purposes. A more liberal perspective summons the spirit of the Charter to subordinate restrictions on the use of force in favor of overarching aims such as the pursuit of justice, the protection of human rights, and the preservation of international peace and stability (see Walzer 1977; Schachter 1986, 1991, 110–13). Overall, however, the prohibition on the use of force has been construed relatively strictly since the Charter's adoption in 1945 (see Henkin 1991, 37–71; Franck 1970; and Damrosch and Scheffer 1991). Consequently, states have been criticized in the international community for unilaterally using force outside their territorial borders (see Arend and Beck 1993, 71–79).

Moreover, additional measures have been enacted to reinforce this prohibition. In 1970, the UN General Assembly unanimously adopted the Declaration of Principles of International Law Concerning Friendly Relations Among States in Accordance with the Charter of the United Nations. And in 1981, it adopted the Declaration on the Inadmissibility of Intervention and Interference in the Internal Affairs of States to detail those actions contemplated within the general proscription, including, for example, the impermissibility of providing sanctuary and support for mercenary groups, terror organizations, or even those seeking to exploit the media of another state.

Yet, self-defense remains an important exception to the prohibition on the extraterritorial use of force. Article 51 of the UN Charter provides that "[n]othing in the present Charter shall impair the inherent right of individual or collective self-defense if an armed attack occurs against a Member of the United Nations." Even here, the right is not unconstrained. Although states can use force, even preemptively, to respond to an armed attack, and can act to protect citizens in another state, they must demonstrate the condition of necessity and observe the constraint of proportionality. Two notable cases are the Israeli raid on Entebbe in 1975, in which Israeli commandos stormed an Air France plane to free Jewish hostages who had been hijacked en route to Paris, and the U.S. invasion of Grenada in 1983, undertaken to ensure the safety of American medical students studying on the island who were reportedly threatened by a coup (see Onyango-Obbo 1997; Ronzitti 1985). In another example, tensions flared between Venezuela and Colombia as accusations surfaced that Venezuela provided sanctuary to Colombian guerrillas, especially the Revolutionary Armed Forces of Colombia. In 2001, Venezuela recalled its ambassador from Colombia over the dispute (see Fleischer 2001).[6]

Yet, these declaratory prohibitions on the use of force have not obscured the appreciation within the United Nations that to keep peace among its members there is a need, at times, to use forceful means for that purpose. Hence, an imperative emerged to craft sustainable positions regarding the legitimate use of force—for purposes other than self-defense.

THE ROLE OF FORCE IN KEEPING PEACE

One of the principal ways in which the member states of the United Nations have used that institution to maintain peace and security is through the deployment and management of peacekeeping operations. Traditional peace-keeping missions—minimally armed and authorized to use force only in self-defense, neutral with respect to the parties and issues in dispute, deployed with the consent of the belligerents, and limited in their scope and duration—have historically functioned as an interpositional buffer force to bring a meas-ure of stability and security to situations heretofore marked by open conflict between parties. These operations were typically mounted only once a peace accord of some type had been achieved, and provided the necessary physical—and political—support to help the parties observe the terms. Over the course of nearly sixty years, the international community employed such peace-keeping operations dozens of times, with ever greater frequency.

In the past two decades, however, circumstances have not always permit-ted the consensual introduction of peacekeeping forces in an environment of agreed cease-fire. The international community has had to confront situations of chronic violence that have generated widespread destruction and flows of refugees, inducing an even wider instability or explosive fighting that has threatened to engulf neighboring countries. In these circumstances, more ro-bust peacekeeping operations have been mounted. These so-called Chapter VII operations (referring to that section of the UN Charter that permits the use of "all necessary means" to address a threat to international peace and se-curity) have been deployed with increasing frequency, and many questions surround their use: What is the purpose of such international interventions? What grounds justify them? What is the scope of permissible action? How long will international forces stay in these situations? By what authority are these and other decisions regarding the use of force made? It is to these broader questions that I now turn.

Force and the Purpose of Peace

Over time, a number of peaceful processes and institutions have been estab-lished to help maintain and restore peace, and today the use of forceful measures is embedded in a complex political context. Through the use of confidence-building measures, risk-reduction strategies, good offices, fact-finding or ob-server missions, and conciliation and mediation efforts, states have worked collectively to help manage the volatile international environment, and they have also come together repeatedly to deploy international forces to help keep or restore peace.

Undertaken principally through the United Nations (with important regional contributions and exceptions), both the rate of such deployments and the complexity of their missions have intensified since the end of the Cold War. International forces have been inserted to patrol lines of demarcation between warring parties (e.g., Côte d'Ivoire); to secure borders with neighboring states to prevent conflict spillover (e.g., the former Yugoslav Republic of Macedonia); to stop ethnic cleansing, mass killings, and other atrocities or crimes against humanity (e.g., the former Yugoslavia, Rwanda, Liberia); to deliver humanitarian aid (e.g., Somalia, the former Yugoslavia, Rwanda); to uphold ceasefire agreements (e.g., the former Yugoslavia, Cambodia, Liberia, East Timor); and to respond to the collapse of civil order (e.g., Somalia, Haiti, Liberia).

Collective measures to maintain or restore peace generally fall into one of four areas: peacemaking, peacekeeping, peace enforcement, and peacebuilding. Although these terms have often been used interchangeably, they do have established meanings that reflect their distinct function in helping to manage international disputes.[7]

Peacemaking constitutes peaceful measures, for example, negotiation, mediation, arbitration, and fact finding, undertaken by third-party individuals, groups, or organizations to help contending parties resolve their conflict by nonviolent means. Peacemaking efforts are designed to help prevent an ongoing dispute from turning violent or escalating in violence by offering alternative ways for the parties to resolve their differences. Threats or use of force have sometimes been employed at the same time peacemaking efforts are under way to help bolster their effectiveness.

Peacekeeping traditionally involves the consensual deployment of a lightly armed international military and/or civilian presence, usually under UN Chapter VI auspices, to help the parties adhere to an agreement to end active hostilities. Typically inserted in the aftermath of a conflict once a peace agreement of some type has been agreed to by the parties, peacekeeping operations of this nature have also been used to a limited degree as a preventive measure—in Macedonia in 1992 (United Nations Preventive Deployment Force, or UNPREDEP), and authorized (but never deployed) in Liberia in 1993 and in Sierra Leone in 1999.

Peace enforcement operations authorized under the provisions of Chapter VII of the Charter constitute a major commitment by the international community to use active forceful measures to compel warring parties to observe the terms of a standing peace agreement. The first such enforcement operation was in Congo in 1963.

Peacebuilding activities are complex operations conducted by the international community—usually in the aftermath of active hostilities once a peace accord has been achieved—to help the parties recover from violent conflict and put a permanent end to hostilities. These operations consist of a combination of political, economic, social, and security measures designed to stabilize a situation and to help create the necessary political space and time needed to strengthen local institutions, permit the repatriation of refugees and the displaced to recover from the violence, and create the conditions and opportunities for reconciliation and reconstruction to occur.

Peacemaking and peacebuilding emphasize nonmilitary approaches and the importance of political, economic, social, and other measures in creating stable conditions for peace, whereas peacekeeping and peace enforcement highlight the use of military or police forces and the prospect of forceful measures. Because the lines between these undertakings have often become blurred, the entire field has come, in some circles, to be known generically as "peace operations."

Peacemaking. Peacemaking comprises largely political and diplomatic efforts to bring contending parties to a peaceful resolution of their dispute. By its definition, peacemaking does not contemplate measures involving the use of force. The United Nations has undertaken peacemaking efforts in Afghanistan, Cambodia, Cyprus, the Middle East, and Mozambique, among other places.[8] Yet, the threat or the actual use of forceful measures can contribute to the parties' willingness to seek accommodation through peaceful measures. Peacekeeping forces have been deployed during the course of negotiations for various purposes, including verifying positions on the ground, securing neutral or sensitive sites, and standing ready to assume additional missions once a peace document is signed. In 1999, for example, ground forces were positioned along the Serbian-Macedonian border as part of the negotiation strategy designed to persuade the Serbs to halt their campaign of ethnic cleansing in Kosovo (see Freedman 1999; U.S. State Department 1999).

Used in this way to support international political and diplomatic efforts, the insertion of a peacekeeping force—and sometimes simply its prospect—has helped parties reach agreement to cease active hostilities and pursue a resolution to their differences through dialogue and negotiation. In 1992, for example, Serbia and Croatia were locked in a bitter struggle following Croatia's unilateral declaration of independence from the former Yugoslavia. It was only when the special representative of the UN secretary-general, former U.S. secretary of state Cyrus Vance, began negotiations backed up by the promise of thousands of UN peacekeepers to oversee an agreement between Zagreb and Belgrade that the violence finally ended (see Woodward 1995).

The specter of international force can also support peacemaking or other efforts to negotiate a way out of prospective or ongoing violence. Haiti in

1994 provides a clear example. In the same moments that a high-level team from the United States was sitting down to negotiate with the military government of Raoul Cédras which had illegally seized power, U.S. military planes were launched with airborne forces to conduct an invasion of the island. Armed with an ultimatum from the United States supported by the UN Security Council, former U.S. president Jimmy Carter and his delegation were outlining the terms for a peaceful return to democracy in Haiti when they got word that the planes were—literally—in the air. In relatively short order, Cedras and his associates had decamped from the Haitian capital en route to asylum in Panama (see Bermeo 2001; Robyn 2001).

Although these examples do not conform to the strict interpretation of peacemaking, they do constitute instances where the primary vehicle to secure agreements among warring parties—that is, negotiations—was supported by the threat or use of stronger measures to encourage cooperation (see George and Simons 1991; George 1994; Schelling 1966). Moreover, these instances also illustrate how the combination of forceful and nonforceful measures can render the need to resort to open conflict unnecessary.

What distinguishes these efforts from mere coercion is the legitimacy with which force is threatened. In the cases above, the threat of force was supported by Security Council determination and a formal resolution that the circumstances had deteriorated to such a point that international peace and security were threatened and more assertive measures to counter that threat were authorized if necessary.

Traditional Peacekeeping. Although never explicitly referred to in the Charter, peacekeeping operations are almost as old as the United Nations itself—the first peacekeeping mission, United Nations Truce Supervision Organization (UNTSO), was authorized in 1948 to supervise the truce between the new state of Israel and its Arab neighbors. Typically authorized by the Security Council under the provisions of either Chapter VI or Chapter VII of the Charter and overseen by the UN secretary-general, these operations have traditionally consisted of lightly armed or unarmed observers whose principal job is to oversee a peace agreement between formerly warring factions. These missions are usually inserted only with the consent of the belligerents and remain impartial with respect to the issues and parties in dispute.

Charged with responsibilities, for example, to monitor cease-fire lines (in Cyprus in 1964 and Croatia in 1992), to maintain separation between factions (in the Middle East in 1948), to supervise the withdrawal of forces (in Egypt/Israel in 1956 and 1973, in Lebanon in 1978), and to report on compliance with peace agreements (in the Golan Heights in 1974), these forces, usually lightly armed, operate under restrictive rules of engagement that are limited to permitting the use of force or deadly measures only in self-defense.

In the forty-five years between 1945 and 1990, some fourteen traditional peacekeeping missions were mounted to deal with a diverse array of challenges that threatened international security. In the following thirteen years, an additional nineteen operations were initiated under a Chapter VI mandate.

Operations ranged from monitoring cease-fires (in West New Guinea in 1962; in Somalia in 1992), to supervising the withdrawal of forces (in India/Pakistan in 1965; in Libya/Chad in 1994), disarming or demobilizing irregular military units (in the former Yugoslavia in 1996), serving as a military damper between hostile factions (in the Middle East in 1948), monitoring paramilitary activities (in Central America in 1989), and providing an armed presence on the ground to observe and monitor compliance with a peace agreement (in Mozambique in 1992). In one important development, a Chapter VI mission in the former Yugoslav Republic of Macedonia was deployed as a preventive measure before open hostilities broke out. This mission succeeded in managing the tense situation along the border between Macedonia, Albania, and Serbia for several years until its mandate was terminated. Indeed, this mission was viewed as an important example of how traditional peacekeeping operations might better be thought of by the international community as a preconflict measure—as means to help stabilize a situation before violence breaks out, deployed while there is still a peace to keep—rather than strictly as a post-conflict response in the wake of destructive violence.

Perhaps reflecting the complexity of the conflicts they are deployed to help manage, the missions of traditional peacekeeping operations have increasingly expanded beyond the relatively straightforward military duties of monitoring cease-fire terms, patrolling buffer zones, and maintaining an international presence to help prevent a resumption of hostilities. Missions now include a wide variety of what might be termed "civilian" tasks, such as the ongoing provision of humanitarian assistance (in Liberia in 1992 and 1993), repatriating refugees and other displaced persons (in Rwanda in 1993, in Croatia in 1998), the establishment of local medical and other public health services (in the Democratic Republic of Congo in 1960 and 1999, in Sierra Leone in 1999), supervision of elections and their supporting political processes (in Namibia in 1989, in the Central African Republic in 1998, in East Timor in 2002, in the Democratic Republic of Congo in 2003), reform of the judicial, law enforcement, and penal systems (in Haiti in 1997), and the establishment of a stable financial system and recreation of functioning markets (in Haiti in 1996).

Nearly all military operations have conducted their work alongside public and private sector civilian agencies with chief responsibility to manage these nonmilitary aspects of peace operations. And, notwithstanding a desire to limit the duration and scope of their engagement, military units have often experienced "mission creep" as civilian agencies proved unable to manage the challenges they faced. For example, while thousands of North Atlantic Treaty Organization (NATO) forces marched into Bosnia to begin implementing the military aspects of the Dayton Peace Accords in 1996, the international community's high representative charged with overseeing the bulk of the agreement—Carl Bildt of Sweden—was by all accounts equipped with little more than, as one anonymous observer put it, "a cell phone, a secretary, and a suitcase." As the civilian side of implementation of the accords foundered, expectations mounted in capitals and publics for NATO forces to assume more of those responsibilities. Bildt warned that the Dayton Peace Accords were tenuous from the start, arguing that while the military side was moving ahead well, the civilian aspects of the accords had barely begun (see Whitney 1996; Bildt 1996, 1999).

Moreover, beyond tasks necessary to keep peace in the immediate aftermath of a cease-fire, new missions associated with what many have termed "nation building" have crept into the peacekeeping repertoire. Such tasks as overseeing the reduction and reform of former belligerents' armed forces, creating a new police force (in El Salvador in 1991), supervising parts of civil administration (in Western Sahara in 1991, in Cambodia in 1992, in East Timor in 2002), and overseeing the clearing of land mines (in Cambodia in 1991, in Bosnia and Herzegovina in 1995) have all become missions for these international forces deployed to help keep the peace.

Peace Enforcement. Since the end of the Cold War, the Security Council has "determined," "recognized," or expressed "concern," that nearly three dozen circumstances of ongoing conflict have constituted threats to international peace and security, warranting strong measures in response. In some of these cases, a cease-fire had been agreed to between warring parties, but terms were not met with compliance in whole or in part by the main or fringe elements of each side. In other cases, the parties have shown little independent inclination to end their fighting without strong urging and action by outside states.

In these situations, the international community has often elected to insert more heavily armed military forces equipped with more sweeping mandates than traditional peacekeepers to restore or maintain order. These operations are not to be confused with such actions as have been undertaken to counter international acts of aggression (e.g., Korea in 1950 and Iraq in 1991). But several categories of circumstances have risen to this urgent need for forceful management: for example, massive flows of refugees across borders

(Iraq in 1991, Yugoslavia in 1992, Liberia in 1993, Haiti in 1994, Rwanda in 1994), widespread violence that has defied repeated attempts to defuse (Liberia, Somalia, Haiti, Angola, Rwanda, Sudan, Congo [Zaire], Angola, Sierra Leone, East Timor, Afghanistan), and the total collapse of internal order (Somalia, Sierra Leone, Liberia, Haiti).

In the early 1990s, robust peacekeeping missions—lying somewhere between traditional Chapter VI activities and the peace enforcement missions of Chapter VII—were sometimes referred to as "Chapter VI?." These circumstances were far too violent to conform to the traditional environment for UN peacekeeping where parties agree to pursue more peaceful strategies for managing their disputes. Yet they were not violent enough to prompt the Security Council to invoke its strongest measures (see Mackinlay and Chopra 1992; Berdal 2000). These operations and other experiences of the past decade have led to a near-universal call for all peace operation missions to be supported by consistent, clear, and practicable mandates, the cooperation of the parties in implementing that mandate, the continuing support of the Security Council, and the readiness of member states to contribute the necessary resources and personnel to help maintain momentum (see United Nations 2000).

Peacebuilding. Peacebuilding efforts emphasize the overarching political and economic factors necessary to sustain societies emerging from conflict. These efforts often depend on a mix of military and what might be termed civilian tasks to bring a permanent end to violence. Based in part on agreement between the formerly warring parties to end their violence, peacebuilding efforts often go well beyond those agreements to help create the conditions for a durable peace and sustainable development (see Evans 1993; Joulwan and Shoemaker 1998). Tasks that usually require the use of military troops prepared to use force include disarming factions, taking custody of and destroying weapons, repatriating refugees, reforming the security sector, and strengthening institutions of central government to permit a full return to local control.

The scope and ambition of international efforts to help rebuild a country in massive disarray can be seen in the case of Cambodia and the implementation of the Paris Accords of October 1991. The United Nations Transitional Authority in Cambodia (UNTAC), established in 1992, was given broad authority to oversee the demobilization of armed forces, supervise the withdrawal of Vietnamese troops, monitor the return of refugees, collect and destroy weapons, monitor the human rights situation, and oversee other terms of the cease-fire. But UNTAC was also given sweeping authority to assert control over civil agencies responsible for running the country. In effect, UNTAC became the government of Cambodia (see Blood and Sinai 1995, 381–98; Alagappa 1993; Doyle, Johnstone, and Orr 1997; Griffin and Jones 2000).

In fact, peacebuilding operations functioning with robust mandates that constitute, in effect, peace enforcement, really represent far more than simple efforts to keep people from killing each other over their differences. They represent efforts by the international community to help create "capable societies," that is, societies able to provide and manage the basic security, well-being, and justice needs for all their citizens and to conduct their affairs—at home and with their neighbors—in relative peace (see Carnegie Commission 1997; Association of the United States Army 2002).

Of course, peace operations of all types are not cost or error free. Severe problems have plagued nearly every peace operation ever mounted and deployed. These problems include inordinate delays in getting forces to the ground, the provision of inappropriately trained or unskilled soldiers for the tasks at hand, lack of funding, lags in assuming appropriate duties due to mission confusion, and lack of cultural, regional, or historical expertise (see Dellaire 2004; Rose 1999; O'Hanlon and Solarz 1999; U.S. Army Peacekeeping Institute 2000).

Yet, a number of general principles governing the use of force in missions to help restore or keep peace have emerged. Perhaps not surprisingly, many of these principles reflect some of the well-developed ideas that have emerged not just in the period since the end of the Cold War, but over centuries. Today, reflecting in part these evolved traditions, it is generally agreed that these missions must have clear and achievable objectives that are designed to maintain or restore general order and reduce the threat posed to international peace and security. They must do more good than harm, the level of force must be proportionate to the need, and the force package must be configured and resourced to succeed. In addition, to help ensure success, these missions must be part of a broader political approach to resolving the underlying issues of dispute that also includes appropriate social and economic elements, and be linked to the priorities and objectives of the people on whose behalf the forces are deployed (see Fund for Peace 2001a; 2001b; 2002a; 2002b; United Nations 2000). At least as important, the missions must be deployed by an authority with the legitimacy to take such action.

In short, the purpose of peacekeeping operations is to protect and strengthen fragile peace—that means, first and foremost, that there must be a peace (however fragile) to keep.

Force and Legitimacy

Perhaps no other question in international relations has generated as much thought, scholarship, controversy, and intellectual angst as the issue of legitimate force. Since ancient times, statesmen, soldiers, jurists, and scholars have struggled to define criteria and clarify circumstances that unambiguously warrant—and hence justify—the use of force. (In this context, measures taken in self-defense do not rise to the same level of disagreement as do measures taken for humanitarian purposes or on behalf of others.)

The just war tradition outlines several criteria that must be met before the use of force can be considered justified: rightness of cause, rightful authority, likely victory, proportionality, and last resort. To these criteria have been added necessity, discrimination, and restraint—that is, the use of force must be considered necessary to deal effectively with the challenge at hand, and the efforts undertaken must not target noncombatants or engage in wanton destruction. Of these criteria for just war and just conduct in war, rightness of cause comes closest to resolving the issue of when force should be used, although it served originally to characterize war undertaken to right a grievous wrong or to restore the general peace.

A number of major efforts have been undertaken in the modern era to clarify the circumstances that would give rise to a right cause for using force, although nearly without exception, they have fallen short of doing so—principally because of their lack of specificity in declaring just when international action is required and what form that action should take; of course, it is just such specificity that would likely preclude the adoption of any measure. Of these efforts, perhaps the most well-known is the Convention on the Prevention and Punishment of the Crime of Genocide, commonly referred to as the genocide convention.

The genocide convention defines genocide—whether committed in times of peace or war—as a crime under international law. Article 2 lists the following acts committed with the intent to destroy, in whole or in part, a national, ethnic, racial, or religious group as constituting genocide: killing members of the group; causing serious bodily or mental harm to members of the group; deliberately inflicting on the group conditions of life calculated to bring about its physical destruction in whole or in part; imposing measures intended to prevent births within the group; and forcibly transferring children of the group to another group.

In addition, the convention identifies any act of genocide, conspiracy to commit genocide, incitement or attempt to commit genocide, and complicity in genocide as punishable under the statute.

Yet, the genocide convention has not operated with the clarity and force necessary to compel states to intervene when genocidal conditions have been present. The genocide convention was not invoked in Cambodia in 1975, when an estimated 1.7 million people were slaughtered or forcibly displaced and imprisoned by the Pol Pot regime; or in Rwanda in 1994, when nearly one million people were killed in just over ninety days; nor is it being decisively invoked to aid the people of Sudan's Darfur in 2007.

Other efforts to put in place criteria for action have generated similar lists of crimes and abuses that warrant an international response. The Rome Statute of the International Criminal Court identifies the crime of genocide, crimes against humanity, war crimes, and the crime of aggression as within the jurisdiction of the court.

The statute defines the crime of genocide consistent with the genocide convention, and war crimes as those acts that constitute grave breaches of the Geneva Convention. It leaves the crime of aggression to be defined in the future in accordance with statutory procedures. It does, however, elaborate crimes against humanity as any of the following acts when committed as part of a widespread or systematic attack directed against any civilian population: murder, extermination, enslavement, deportation or forcible transfer, imprisonment or other severe deprivation of physical liberties in violation of fundamental rules of international law, torture, rape and other forms of comparable sexual violence, enforced disappearances, apartheid, and other inhumane acts.

The UN General Assembly has defined aggression as the use of armed force by any state or group of states in any other manner inconsistent with the Charter of the United Nations. This definition is designed to be exhaustive and includes invasion or attack, unlawful military occupation, bombardment, blockade, any attack on another's military forces, any use of forward-stationed armed forces in contravention of agreements governing their presence, allowing one's territory to be used to perpetrate an act of aggression, and supporting insurgent groups, irregulars, or mercenaries that carry out acts of armed force against others.

Yet, although these documents detail the characteristics of unlawful acts, they do not prescribe any clear remedy. That is to say, no provisions exist for the permissible, much less automatic, use of force—or any other measures for that matter—to end or limit these transgressions. Moreover, while the General Assembly definition of aggression does specifically note that force for offensive purposes constitutes a crime against international peace that gives rise to international responsibility, no course of action in response to such use is specified. However, international public consensus has begun to coalesce around the legitimacy of protecting innocents from massive slaughter, displacement, and gross human rights abuses.[9] In addition, recent experience has begun to shape a variety of "peace operations" in which the use of forces and the use of force have been deployed for these purposes.

Mandating the Use of Force: Who Decides?

It is probably nothing short of remarkable that so much consensus now exists around the question of who mandates the use of force. Whereas in the past states were accustomed to making their own determination of when and where to deploy force, even for humanitarian purposes, today most observers agree that with the important exception of self-defense, only multilateral decisions to use force carry sufficient legal weight and political legitimacy in the international system. Among these multilateral actions, the ones considered most legitimate are those taken in accordance with the principles and procedures of the UN Charter.

In the view of many legal scholars and policy practitioners around the world, the UN Charter represents the definitive statement regarding the legitimacy of the use of force in international relations (see Chayes and Chayes 1995, 191–220; Damrosch and Scheffer 1991). And, consistent with international practice reaching back centuries, the Charter does so in such a way as to elevate peace yet again as the value of highest order among the international community of states—superior even to legitimate claims of national sovereignty, interest, or grievance. In other words, even as the Charter reaffirms the sanctity of national sovereignty and precludes the general interference of individual states of the United Nations in the internal affairs of member states, such a presumption does not "prejudice the application of enforcement measures under Chapter VII of the Charter." However, the idea that sovereignty constitutes an impermeable barrier to other international priorities—never true in reality—has been under strain for some time (see, e.g., Perez de Cuellar 1991a, 1991b; Boutros-Ghali 1992, 1995; Annan 1998a, 1998b, 2000; Helton 2000). When circumstances warrant, as they have with increasing frequency over the past dozen years, the international community has shown that it will act.

As part of UN-authorized action, forces have been deployed, among other places, to former Yugoslavia, Iraq, Cambodia, Liberia, Rwanda, Mozambique, Angola, Sierra Leone, Haiti, and Chechnya. The roles of these forces have ranged from upholding cease-fire agreements and delivering humanitarian aid to limiting ethnic cleansing and the forcible dislocation of whole populations and filling the void created by the collapse of civil order.

In this context, it is interesting to note that although originally designed to help manage relations between states, the United Nations and its Security Council have been called upon increasingly, in fact overwhelmingly, since the end of the Cold War to regulate behavior within states. As a crude but nevertheless persuasive indicator of this migration of international responsibility, and the broader trend in international relations, a simple count of UN

Security Council Resolutions since the fall of the Berlin Wall in 1989 (more than seventeen hundred at this writing) reveals a remarkable ratio of almost three to one for nontraditional—that is, intrastate—matters over those that are interstate, or broadly transnational, in nature. To illustrate the degree of international involvement, between 1991 and 2001 the Security Council passed 136 resolutions to deal with the situation in the former Yugoslavia, 23 in Haiti, 38 in Iraq, 17 in Somalia, and 29 in Rwanda. By comparison, during the period between its founding and the 1991 Gulf War, the Security Council passed fewer than 700 resolutions in total, on all matters. Interestingly, by this and other means, the United Nations has functioned to help establish customary law among states—in this case, to facilitate international engagement in affairs within troubled states as well as between them (see Hehir 1995, 2002; Wedgewood 1991).

Matters that require Security Council action come to its attention via various means. For example, any member state has the right to bring forward any dispute or situation that might lead to "international friction" or give rise to conflict under the provisions of Article 35 of the UN Charter. Similarly, the General Assembly has such rights under Article 11(3). In addition, under Article 11(1), the General Assembly may discuss any question relating to the maintenance of international peace and security brought before it by any member or nonmember, and the General Assembly, in turn, can refer the matter to the Security Council. The General Assembly also may act under the Uniting for Peace resolution when the Security Council cannot or does not act because of a lack of consensus among its permanent members. Moreover, under the provisions of Article 99, the secretary-general has broad independent powers to "bring to the attention of the Security Council any matter which in his opinion may threaten the maintenance of international peace and security."

Once a potential problem is identified, the Security Council may implement various tools to monitor the situation to determine whether the parties to the dispute can be persuaded to pursue their differences through nonviolent means or whether conditions warrant stronger measures. States involved in a dispute are instructed by the Charter to seek a solution by various peaceful means, including enquiry, mediation, conciliation, arbitration, judicial settlement, the resort to regional arrangements, or other peaceful means of their own choosing (see also Sweden Ministry for Foreign Affairs 2001). In addition, the Security Council can investigate the dispute, task the secretary-general to pursue an independent inquiry, or call on states acting alone or through regional arrangements (under Chapter VIII of the Charter) to intensify monitoring and make recommendations for additional measures to help ensure that conditions do not worsen (see also Murphy 1996, 11–13). If the situation does deteriorate, the Security Council can declare the matter a threat to international peace and security, and thereby open the way for "all measures necessary" to deal more effectively with the situation.

Note that nowhere does the Charter require or explicitly permit the use of force for any purpose, not even to prevent or curtail genocide or to protect or uphold human rights. Nor, moreover, may any state make such a unilateral determination. States may only legitimately respond to such situations with force under conditions of self-defense that, as discussed earlier, is itself subject to international constraint, or when called upon by the Security Council to do so. Under the authority of Article 39 of the Charter, the Security Council may determine that a growing problem does constitute a threat to the broader peace and, determining that such a threat exists, may, under the provisions of Article 42, authorize "all measures necessary," including such military actions that may be required to restore international peace and security. As former secretary-general Kofi Annan (1998c) observed, "Can we really afford to let each state be the judge of its own right, or duty, to intervene in another state's internal conflict? Most of us would prefer to see such decisions taken collectively, by an international institution whose authority is generally respected. And surely the only institution competent to assume that role is the Security Council of the United Nations."

The Role of Regional Organizations. Although this discussion has focused on multilateral action taken under UN auspices, it is worth noting that regional organizations or arrangements have often taken on a role to maintain or restore peace within their regions. Regional organizations have certain advantages for coping with local disputes. Their members usually are deeply familiar with the parties or issues in contention and, because they have vested interests in seeing conflicts resolved quickly, are often able to reach rapid consensus that strong measures are required to deal with a deteriorating situation. On the other hand, their very proximity and familiarity can be a source of compromised equities that preclude impartiality or delay rapid action.

Nevertheless, regional organizations have stepped in numerous times with forces prepared to use force to keep peace. For example, the Organization of African Unity (now the African Union), the League of Arab States, and the Organization of the Islamic Conference joined efforts with the United Nations in 1992 (prior to the U.S. engagement later that year) to deal with the desperate circumstances in Somalia. The Economic Cooperation Organization of West African States (ECOWAS) deployed a ten-nation peacekeeping force (ECOMOG) to Liberia in 1990 to bring an end to civil war and provide a stabilization force.[10] In 1997, ECOWAS, under Nigerian leadership, went into Sierra Leone to restore order, reverse a coup d'état, and protect human rights. Indeed, in Liberia and Sierra Leone, ECOWAS intervened with force before it had secured either local consent or a Security Council resolution. It was only after the interventions that the United Nations established the UN Observer Mission in Liberia and the UN Observer Mission in Sierra Leone, respectively. In the case of the United States' invasion of Grenada, a request was made by the Organization of Eastern Caribbean States (OECS) for U.S. intervention following a coup by an extreme leftist group. Some observers doubt the legitimacy of the OECS request (see Burrowes 1998). The United Nations gave retroactive approval for regional operations in three cases: the ECOWAS intervention in Liberia in August 1990, via UN Security Council Resolution 1116; the ECOWAS intervention in Sierra Leone; and the intervention in Kosovo. Although Operation Allied Force began on March 24, 1999, it was not until June 10, 1999 (via UN Security Council Resolution 1244) that the Security Council authorized member states and relevant international organizations to establish an international security presence in Kosovo.

Multilateral organizations play key diplomatic and political roles as well. In Latin America, the end of the war in Nicaragua involved a highly complex effort that was initiated by leaders of the region and conducted jointly with the United Nations. In addition, under the UN Security Council Resolution 1080 in 1990, the Santiago Commitment to Democracy and Renewal of the Inter-American System, the OAS secretary-general has the responsibility and authority to activate OAS members for consultation and action if a determination is made that the constitutional order of a regional state is in jeopardy. Since its adoption, Resolution 1080 has been enacted six times: in Haiti in 1991, in Peru in 1992, in Guatemala in 1993, in Paraguay in 1996, in Ecuador in 2000, and in Peru in 2000.

In Asia, the members of the Association of South East Asian Nations (ASEAN) aided the parties in Cambodia working with the United Nations. The UN-sanctioned operation on the ground, UNTAC, received a significant portion of the forces and logistics from ASEAN states, a move that opened a dialogue on the expansion of the role of the ASEAN Asia Regional Forum to deal with regional threats to peace and play a larger role in peacekeeping operations in the region (see Alagappa 1992, 1993).

In Europe, the European Union, the Organization for Security and Cooperation in Europe, and NATO joined with the United Nations to deal with the crisis in former Yugoslavia following the 1995 Dayton Peace Accords, which provided for a 60,000 member, NATO-led implementation force in Bosnia (later replaced in 1996 by a smaller stabilization force). In 1999, following the adoption of UN Security Council Resolution 1244, a NATO-led international force was established in Kosovo (see Rose 1994).[11] In 2003, the European Union mounted a French-led force in Congo to stabilize a rapidly deteriorating situation, and more recently NATO has worked side by side with the United Nations in Afghanistan.

Partly as a result of these experiences, and partly in recognition of the need to pool strengths and share burdens, a consensus has emerged in the international community regarding the legitimacy of authority when deploying forces for humanitarian purposes, to thwart aggression, or more generally in the service of peace. Force is considered most legitimate when authorized by multilateral institutions—ideally the United Nations. Regional organizations are also seen as acceptable but must accord their decisions with the principles and provisions of the UN Charter (see Fund for Peace 2001a, 2001b, 2002a, 2002b; Locke and Ladnier 2001).

Nearly without exception, unilateral action to use force even for humanitarian purposes is seen as illegitimate, except in cases of self-defense. Yet even under legitimate authority, for just cause, and as a last resort, the use of force to preserve peace raises poignant questions that seek to balance the tensions that adhere in these issues.

ETHICAL CONSIDERATIONS

What moral hazard exists when using force to prevent the use of force? How do we reconcile the instinctive sense that the use of coercive measures to prevent or limit coercion somehow undermines the very objective to which those measures are put?

Just war prescribes a set of criteria for the legitimate use of force. But do the provisions of right authority, just cause, proportionate means, and prospects for success (meaning, in effect, that force is deemed the right tool for the job) address all or even the major ethical concerns? There have been attempts to confront some of these issues directly. The Geneva Conventions, for example, established the modern standards for ethical conduct in war. Yet, some of the very principles that help guide the justified use of force—last resort, proportionality, and likely success, for example—may present ethical dilemmas that defy easy resolution.

For example, when force is reserved as a last resort, decision makers usually defer action—fearing a slippery slope—until circumstances have deteriorated so badly as to be amenable to solution only through dramatic force. Yet, under such conditions, it seems almost guaranteed that the level and intensity of force required will be higher than that perhaps needed earlier in a crisis, when more measured uses or threats of force might constructively reinforce diplomatic and political efforts to defuse a crisis. The dilemma is that early in a crisis, the relative costs of such interventions are relatively low, and so, too, usually are the stakes. Yet, the political risks of premature engagement are high—especially if conditions continue to worsen after action is taken. As a practical matter, leaders contemplating the use of force to help alleviate a crisis are less inclined to balance the risks of action with the risks of inaction than they are to balance the prospect of failure with the hope that things might improve either on their own or without the need for military intervention.

Thus, in part because of the strong impulse that force should be a last resort as a matter of principle and in part because the consequences of mounting a major military undertaking that might fail are so great, leaders feel best advised to defer such decisions until there is no other course. The ethical tension results when massive loss of life, displacement, and destruction mount as a result of the decision not to intervene.

In a similar way, the principle of proportionality—to apply only that level of force necessary and appropriate to achieve the desired outcome—requires decision makers to strike a balance. Applying the minimum force necessary may generate the desired effect, but it might also lead to a trial-and-error strategy when it fails to achieve results. For many states—not just the United States—the specter of Vietnam and the paradigmatic case of gradual escalation is a nightmare to avoid at all costs. One reaction to this dilemma has been the development of the doctrine of "overwhelming force," both as an antidote to gradualism and as a means to bring hostilities—should they ultimately prove necessary—to a rapid end. In the United States, the doctrine of overwhelming force is also known as the Powell doctrine, named for Colin Powell, senior military assistant to former secretary of defense Caspar Weinberger, and chairman of the Joint Chiefs of Staff under presidents George H. W. Bush and Bill Clinton. This doctrine is attributed to Powell because he helped both to craft and, later, to enlarge the "Weinberger principles" for using force (see Powell 1992–93; Weinberger 1984). Although some have argued that the principle of overwhelming force does not coexist easily within the just war parameters—such as proportionality or last resort—others believe that in fact a willingness to use preponderant force makes it morally sustainable to wait until a crisis has reached its most acute phase before taking action.[12]

The principle that the use of force is justified only if success is likely poses a different ethical challenge. Success is often defined quite differently for those inside a crisis and those more removed. Usually those most able to intervene to stop a slaughter are not directly involved in the fighting. Yet, those most in need of the intervention are precisely those least able to help themselves. When one is not fighting on one's own behalf, such as in these cases, what constitutes success? Who decides? In Rwanda in 1994, if the international community had intervened with force to stop the genocide, how many hundreds of thousands of lives would have been saved? In evaluating chances for success, how important are the needs of the victims when compared to the interests and expectations of those who would intervene? Moreover, if the intervention succeeds, does a long-term obligation for the victims' recovery ensue? No easy answers to these difficult questions readily suggest themselves.

Yet, international experience has yielded the essential judgment that force is a legitimate instrument when used proportionately, as a last resort, and by rightful authority. Moreover, the international community has manifested greatest comfort when force is deployed for three main purposes: first, to uphold the rule of law; second, to thwart unlawful aggression and to deny belligerents the illegitimate use of offensive force; and finally (although I have not examined this purpose in depth), where the elimination or destruction of a pernicious evil and threat to international peace and security is the only remedy. For some problems—defeating Adolf Hitler's Germany or eliminating ruthless dictators such as Pol Pot, for example—force may be the only adequate response left to the international community and the broader peace it seeks to maintain.

For some observers, the inherent tensions that exist when using force for even consensus cases will never be reconciled. It is interesting to note that in two major post–Cold War cases regarding the international community and the use of force—Iraq in 1990–91 and former Yugoslavia in 1993–94—Pope John Paul II issued strongly worded statements to the Catholic faithful and the world at large saying that the use of force was not justified to deal with Saddam Hussein, but it was justified in dealing with Serbian aggression. Remarkably, the international community manifested unprecedented agreement on precisely the opposite view in both cases: states agreed on the use of force against Iraq and refused to undertake forceful action at the time in Bosnia (see Haberman 1990, 1991; Cowell 1994). But for the majority of practitioners and scholars of modern humanitarian disasters, the major ethical issues lie not in acting, but in failing to act (see Hamburg 2002; Lund 1996; Rubin 2002).

SHOULD THERE BE AN INTERNATIONAL DUTY TO USE FORCE?

Never before in the history of the world have so many rights for so many of the world's peoples been so well-defined, while so many remain imperiled by the very authorities designated to preserve those rights. Today more people die at the hands of their own governments and their fellow citizens than from the invasions and attacks of foreigners. Political scientist R. J. Rummel (1997, 1999) has termed the mass killing of citizens by their own government or its agents "democide." He views democide as distinct from genocide because people are killed for reasons other than ethnicity or nationality, such as political or cultural reasons. Although some human rights activists have begun to use this term, many view it as representing an extreme position. Striking though it may seem, many people can no longer turn to their governments for protection from foreigners; rather, they must increasingly turn to foreigners for protection from their own governments. The plight of the Kurds at the end of the Gulf War in 1991 provides a poignant illustration of this dilemma. With Saddam bearing down on the Kurdish population in the north of Iraq as part of Baghdad's effort to quell an incipient rebellion in the aftermath of hostilities in Kuwait, Kurds fled to the mountains and into neighboring Turkey. The Turkish military responded forcefully, stationing troops at critical points to prevent Kurds from coming into the country. Thus, the world witnessed bizarre images of Kurdish peasant women and children, confronted by Turkish soldiers brandishing Western weapons, fleeing back into Iraq. Western countries had to cope with the fact that defenseless refugees had just fled a NATO ally for the relative safety of a pariah state. Intense advocacy by from such groups as Refugees International and Save the Children suggest that the core problem of governments menacing or failing to protect their own populations remains a current one.[13]

The notion that the international community should have, if not a duty, then at least the right to intervene in complex humanitarian disasters has generated a good deal of discussion not only in legal circles, but in international policy and academic communities as well.[14] The range of opinion on the matter varies widely, with many observers cynically viewing an aspirational duty to rescue as hopelessly naive while other steadfastly believe that intervention is a moral imperative for responsible governments. Sean D. Murphy (1996, 216–38) suggests that applying such a duty to states both individually and through international organizations might be a means to ensure that international action is taken when conditions warrant.

While the humanitarian catastrophes that have characterized the post–Cold War period may give added impetus to the calls for such a duty, states have long recognized the value and necessity of responding to other states in need. Indeed, relations between states have always featured alliances and defense pacts to ensure mutual expectations of aid if attacked. The argument now is whether to extend that willingness to act to protect not just states but the people who live in them.

Under international treaty law, the closest thing to a duty to rescue is the genocide convention, which permits states to call upon the United Nations to take action under the Charter as deemed necessary to prevent or stop the genocide. Explicit action under the genocide convention has never been undertaken, although three cases stand out: India in East Pakistan in 1971, Tanzania in Uganda in 1978, and Vietnam in Cambodia (Kampuchea) in 1978.

It is important to note that the genocide convention was explicitly not invoked in the episodes discussed above (in fact, its use apparently was never contemplated). But even in a circumstance of clear genocide—for example, in Rwanda in 1994, where nearly one million people were slaughtered in three months—states refuse to call the carnage genocide or to activate the response mechanism envisaged in the genocide convention. In the case of Rwanda, official UN and government statements acknowledged for the first time in 1998 what was patently clear in 1994: that the world had witnessed genocide but had failed to act (see Scales 1998; Kempster 1997; McKinley 1998). Could this genocide have been prevented? Canadian General Romeo Dallaire, commander of United Nations Assistance Mission for Rwanda, the UN peacekeeping operation in Rwanda at the time, claimed then and continues to assert that a robust brigade of five thousand troops, properly trained and equipped, could have made a difference. A panel of senior active-duty military officers from the United States, NATO, Africa, and the United Nations convened to consider Dellaire's claims and agreed (see Feil 1998).

The principal shortcoming of the genocide convention as a catalyst for international action may be its failure to trigger automatic international action in the face of clear evidence that a genocide is ongoing. As noted earlier, although the convention requires that signatory states take the necessary steps to fulfill its provisions, states are by this very obligation reluctant to classify a situation as genocide, because to do so would require them to act. States have proved themselves unable or unwilling to undertake effective action to counter a genocide—especially if it occurs halfway around the globe (see Gutman 1992a, 1992b; Gourevitch 1998; Steering Committee 1996).

However, perhaps at least as great an obstacle to applying the genocide convention to many contemporary circumstances is that, in fact, no clear guidelines exist for calling a killing genocide. Notwithstanding the criteria noted earlier, no number of dead or displaced, no amount of wounded or raped, have emerged to trigger unambiguously the international community to act.

Over the past one hundred years, and indeed, in the post–World War II era alone, dozens of international treaties, declarations, and statements on human rights have been enacted. The Universal Declaration on Human Rights, joined by the International Covenant on Economic, Social, and

Cultural Rights, and the International Covenant on Civil and Political Rights, with its two Optional Protocols, form the International Bill of Human Rights. The International Covenant on Civil and Political Rights outlines minimum standards for governments to observe to ensure the fundamental human rights of citizens, while prohibiting torture, inhumane punishment, slavery, and other abridgements of those rights. The International Covenant on Economic, Social, and Cultural Rights outlines measures to improve the human condition. In addition to these international declarations, states have enacted dozens of regional human rights treaties, initiatives, and laws. In Europe, for example, the European Convention for the Protection of Human Rights and Fundamental Freedoms was entered into force in 1953 and established the European Commission of Human Rights and the European Court of Human Rights. In Latin America, the Charter of the Organization of American States and the American Declaration of the Rights and Duties of Man (adopted in 1948) combine with the American Convention on Human Rights to undergird the operations of the Inter-American Commission on Human Rights and the Inter-American Court of Human Rights (see Newman and Weissbrodt 1979). In Africa, the member states of the African Union enacted the African Charter on Human and People's Rights in 1981, creating the African Commission on Human and People's Rights.

Yet, a number of difficulties exist in trying to adapt a notion of humanitarian duty to circumstances that require the use of the strongest measures—that is, the use of force—to remedy. Who determines what extreme humanitarian need is and the nature and scope of action to be taken? What actions are most effective? Who retains political control of the intervention? How is the action terminated? These questions and others have been raised by the International Commission on Intervention and State Sovereignty (International Development Research Centre 2001). There are no easy answers to these questions, but when governments refuse to provide human rights protections, or worse, when governments actively abuse the rights of some or all citizens, states must have a clear system of response and, if necessary, penalties to forestall or halt such action.

CONCLUDING OBSERVATIONS

This discussion makes the point that although the use of force for most offensive purposes has been repudiated, forceful measures are sometimes justified. Force is certainly a legitimate response if attacked. The right to use force in self-defense has been preserved through millennia, and the dominant normative framework calls for the response to be necessary, proportionate, and limited in scope. Preemptive action for self-defense is permissible if an impending armed attack is obvious and imminent. The 2002 National Security Strategy of the United States (White House 2002) makes the preemptive use of force a central feature of American foreign policy in cases of self-defense. States may also use force as part of a collective defense regime when assisting a state under imminent threat or experience of armed attack. However, states are limited in the nature and scope of the help they render. Finally, they may use force if otherwise allowed under provisions of the UN Charter.

Yet, in the twenty-first century, the principles that have evolved regarding the legitimate use of force have also come under strain. For example, what exactly do the traditional criteria of clear, imminent, or armed mean in an age when terrorists fly commercial passenger airplanes into buildings and kill thousands? What should be the appropriate response to governments that persist in using coercive measures to suppress their populations or governments (such as Saddam Hussein's) that use weapons of mass destruction in wholesale slaughter? How should established states respond in an era of increasing lawlessness, where no order (anarchy), contested order (insurgency), and alternative order (global terrorism and organized crime) pose grave threats to international stability? Collective force may be necessary to deal with such threats, but there are limits to what force can achieve.

In the 1991 coalition war with Iraq, the United States and its partners won a decisive victory. Yet Saddam Hussein did not experience decisive defeat, and he continued to suppress Iraq's citizens and provoke wider unease for more than a dozen years afterward. In 2003, by contrast, the U.S.-led coalition achieved Saddam's decisive defeat, but as of this writing in 2007, it could not yet claim decisive victory. Simply put, force cannot do all that needs doing.

Yet, surely forceful measures will continue to prove necessary at times to maintain international peace and security. Indeed, the greatest military campaigns are known not just by what they destroy, but also by what they create—a new land, a better order, a more durable peace. Indeed, war begets peace, just as it is ultimately peace that distinguishes war.

ACKNOWLEDGMENTS

The author would like to thank Benjamin Hemingway, Jo Anna Sellen, Beth Hetzler, Hyung Hak Nam, Robert Art, Renata Dwan, Roxanna Ghiciu, Paula Souverijn-Eisenberg, and several anonymous readers for their help in the preparation of this manuscript. The views expressed here are the author's and do not reflect the official position of the United Nations or any of its agencies, funds, or programs.

REFERENCES

Alagappa, Muthiah. 1992. *United Nations Transitional Authority in Cambodia*. New York: United Nations Department of Peacekeeping Operations.

———. 1993. "Regionalism and the Quest for Security: ASEAN and the Cambodian Conflict." *Journal of International Affairs* 46 (Winter): 439–67.

Alao, Abiodun. 1993. "ECOMOG in Liberia: The Anemic Existence of a Mission." *Jane's Intelligence Review* 5 (September): 429–31.

Annan, Kofi. 1998a. "Speeches Made to the Non-Aligned Summit." UN Doc. SG/SM/668.

———. 1998b "The U.N. Should Intervene before Force Is Needed." *International Herald Tribune*. June 29, sec. A, 23.

———. 1998c. "Secretary-General Reflects on Intervention in Thirty-Fifth Annual Ditchely Foundation Lecture." UN Doc. SG/SM/6613.

———. 2000. "Sustaining Our Future." In *We the Peoples: The Role of the United Nations in the 21st Century*. New York: United Nations. www.un.org/millennium/sg/report/summ.htm (accessed September 11, 2007).

Arend, C. A., and R. Beck. 1993. *International Law and the Use of Force: Beyond the U.N. Charter Paradigm*. New York: Routledge.

Association of the United States Army and the Center for Strategic and International Studies. 2002. "The Post Conflict Reconstruction Project." www.pcrproject.com (accessed September 11, 2007).

Berdal, Mats. 2000. "Lessons Not Learned: The Use of Force in 'Peace Operations' in the 1990s." *International Peacekeeping* 7 (4): 55–74.

Bermeo, Sarah. 2001. *Clinton and Coercive Diplomacy*. Princeton, N.J.: Princeton University, Woodrow Wilson School.

Bildt, Carl. 1996. "Bosnia Can Have Free Elections." *Financial Times*. June 13.

———. 1999. "Beyond Protectorates: Possibilities for Peace in Southeastern Europe." Remarks made at the United States Institute of Peace, March 16, Washington, D.C. www.usip.org/oc/cibriefing/bildt_cib.html.

Blood, Peter, and Joshua Sinai. 1995. "United Nations Transition Authority in Cambodia (UNTAC)." In *United Nations Peace Operations: Case Studies*, ed. Joshua Sinai. Washington, D.C.: Library of Congress.

Boucher, David. 1998. *Political Theories of International Relations—From Thucydides to the Present*. New York: Oxford University Press.

Boutros-Ghali, Boutros. 1992. "An Agenda for Peace: Preventive Diplomacy, Peacemaking, and Peacekeeping." Report of the secretary-general pursuant to the statement adopted by the Summit Meeting of the Security Council on 31 January 1992. June 17 (A/47/277-S/24111).

———. 1995. "Supplement to an Agenda for Peace." Position paper of the secretary-general on the occasion of the fiftieth anniversary of the United Nations. January25 (A/50/60-S/1995/1).

Boutwell, Jeffrey. 1999. *Report from the Pugwash Study Group on Intervention, Sovereignty, and International Security.* Venice. www.pugwash.org/reports/rc/rc5.htm (accessed September 11, 2007).

Brownlie, Ian. 1963. *International Law and the Use of Force by States.* Oxford, UK: Clarendon.

Burrowes, Reynold A. 1998. *Revolution and Rescue in Grenada: An Account of the U.S.-Caribbean Invasion.* Westport, Conn.: Greenwood.

Cahill, Kevin M., ed. 1996. *Preventive Diplomacy: Stopping Wars before They Start.* New York: Basic Books.

Cahn, Stephen M. 2002. *Classics of Political and Moral Philosophy.* New York: Oxford University Press.

Carlson, Ingvar, Han Sung-Joo, and Rufus M. Kupolati. 1999. *Report of the Independent Inquiry Into the Actions of the United Nations During the 1994 Genocide in Rwanda.* S/1999/1257, http://documents-dds-ny.un.org/doc/UNDOC/GEN/N99/395/47/img/N9939547-pdf?OpenElement.

Carnegie Commission on Preventing Deadly Conflict. 1997. *Preventing Deadly Conflict.* New York: Carnegie Corporation.

Caron, David. 2000. "War and International Adjudication: Reflections on the 1899 Peace Conference." *American Journal of International Law* 94 (1): 4–30.

Chayes, Abram, and Antonia H. Chayes. 1995. "Alternatives to Escalation." *The United States and the Use of Force in the Post–Cold War Era.* Queenstown, Md.: Aspen Institute.

Chesterman, Simon. 2004. *You, the People: The United Nations, Transitional Administration, and State-Building.* New York: Oxford University Press.

Clark, Anthony, and Robert J. Berk, eds. 1993. *International Law and the Use of Force: Beyond the UN Charter.* New York: Routledge.

Coady, C. A. J. 2002. *The Ethics of Armed Humanitarian Intervention,* Peaceworks, no. 45. Washington, D.C.: United States Institute of Peace. www.usip.org/pubs/peaceworks/pwks45.html.

Coady, C. A. J., and Jeff Ross. 2000. "St. Augustine and the Ideal of Peace." *American Catholic Philosophical Quarterly* 74 (1): 153–61.

Cowell, Alan. 1994. "Pope Seeks a Disarming of 'Aggressor' in Bosnia." *New York Times.* January 12.

Damrosch, Lori Fisler, and David Scheffer, eds. 1991. *Law and Force in the New International Order.* Boulder, Colo.: Westview.

Danish Institute of International Affairs. 1999. *Humanitarian Intervention: Legal and Political Aspects.* Copenhagen: DUPI. www.dupi.dk.591/en1224.html#download.

Dellaire, Romeo. 2004. *Shake Hands with the Devil.* New York: Avalon.

Deng, Francis M., Sadikiel Kimaro, Terrence Lyons, Donald Rothchild, and I. William Zartman. 1996. *Sovereignty as Responsibility: Conflict Management in Africa.* Washington, D.C.: Brookings Institution Press.

Dinstein, Yoram. 1988. *War, Aggression and Self-Defence*. Cambridge, UK: University of Cambridge Press.

Doyle, Michael, Ian Johnstone, and Robert Orr, eds. 1997. *Keeping the Peace: Multi-Dimensional U.N. Operations in Cambodia and El Salvador*. New York: Cambridge University Press.

Ehard, Hans. 1949. "The Nuremberg Trial against the Major War Criminals and International Law." *American Journal of International Law* 43 (April): 223–45.

Evans, Gareth. 1993. *Cooperating for Peace: The Global Agenda for the 1990s and Beyond*. St. Leonards, Australia: Allen and Unwin.

Evans, Peter. 1997. "The Eclipse of the State? Reflections on Stateness in an Era of Globalization." *World Politics* 50 (1): 62–87.

Feil, Scott. 1998. *Preventing Genocide: How the Early Use of Force Might Have Succeeded in Rwanda*. Washington, D.C.: Carnegie Commission on Preventing Deadly Conflict.

Finnemore, Martha. 1996. *National Interests in International Society*. Ithaca, N.Y.: Cornell University Press.

Fiorina, Morris, Paul Peterson, and D. Voss. 2002. *America's New Democracy*. New York: Penguin.

Fleischer, Lowell R. 2001. "Pastrana, Chávez Seek to Calm Tensions." In *CSIS Hemisphere Report* IX, no. 2. Washington, D.C.: Center for Strategic and International Studies.

Franck, Thomas M. 1970. "Who Killed Article 2(4)?" and "Changing Norms Governing the Use of Force by States." *American Journal of International Law* 64 (4): 809–37.

Freedman, Lawrence. 1999. "Comment: The Road to a Diplomatic Settlement with Serbia." *London Independent*. April 14.

Fund for Peace. 2001a. "African Perspectives on Military Intervention." *Regional Responses to Internal War* 1 (December). www.fundforpeace.org (accessed September 11, 2007).

———. 2001b. "Criteria for Military Intervention in Internal Wars: The Debate." *Regional Responses to Internal War* 2 (December). www.fundforpeace.org (accessed September 11, 2007).

———. 2002a. "Perspectives from the Americas on Military Intervention." *Regional Responses to Internal War* 3 (June). www.fundforpeace.org (accessed September 11, 2007).

———. 2002b. "Perspectives from Asia on Military Intervention." *Regional Responses to Internal War* 4 (September). www.fundforpeace.org (accessed September 11, 2007).

Gacek, Christopher M. 1994. *The Logic of Force: The Dilemma of Limited War in American Foreign Policy*. New York: Columbia University Press.

Gaddis, John Lewis. 1989. *The Long Peace: Inquiries into the History of the Cold War*. London: Oxford University Press.

Gallant, Judy A. 1992. "Humanitarian Intervention and Security Council Resolution 688: A Reappraisal in Light of a Changing World Order." *American University
Journal of International Law and Policy* 7: 501–30.

George, Alexander. 1994. *The Limits of Coercive Diplomacy*. Boulder, Colo.:
Westview.

George, Alexander, and William F. Simons, eds. 1991. *Forceful Persuasion: Coercive Diplomacy as an Alternative to War*. Washington, D.C.: United States Institute of
Peace Press.

Gourevitch, Philip. 1998. *We Wish to Inform You that Tomorrow We Will Be Killed
with Our Families*. New York: Farrar, Straus, and Giroux.

Griffin, Michele, and Bruce Jones. 2000. "Building Peace through Transitional
Authority: New Directions, Major Challenges." *International Peacekeeping* 7 (4): 75–90.

Grotius, Hugo. 1949. *The Law of War and Peace*, trans. Louise R. Loomis. New
York: Walter J. Black.

Gurr, Ted Robert, and Will H. Moore. 1997. "Ethnopolitical Rebellion: A Cross-
Sectional Analysis of the 1980s with Risk Assessment for the 1990s." *American Journal of Political Science* 41 (4): 1079–103.

Gurr, Ted Robert, and Barbara Harff. 1998. "Systematic Early Warning of Humanitarian Emergencies." *Journal of Peace Research* 35 (5): 551–79.

Gutman, Roy. 1992a. "Death Camps: Survivors Tell of Captivity, Mass Slaughters
in Bosnia." *Newsday*. August 2.

———. 1992b. "U.S. Aide Quits over Yugoslavia; Calls Bush Policy Unrealistic."
Newsday. August 27.

Haberman, Clyde. 1990. "Pope in Christmas Message, Warns on a Gulf War."
New York Times. December 25.

———. 1991. "Pope Denounces the Gulf War as 'Darkness.'" *New York Times*.
April 1.

Hamburg, David A. 2002. *No More Killing Fields: Preventing Deadly Conflict*. Lanham, Md.: Rowman and Littlefield.

Hehir, J. Bryan. 1995. "Intervention: From Theories to Cases." *Ethics and International Affairs* 9: 1–13.

———. 2002. "The Limits of Loyalty." *Foreign Policy* 132 (September/October):
38–9.

Helton, Arthur C. 2000. "Forced Migration, Humanitarian Intervention, and
Sovereignty." *SAIS Review* 20 (1): 61–86.

Henkin, Louis. 1979. *How Nations Behave*, 2d ed. New York: Columbia University Press.

———. 1989. "Use of Force: Law and U.S. Policy." In *Right v. Might: International
Law and the Use of Force*, ed. Louis Henkin, Stanley Hoffmann, Jeane J. Kirkpatrick,
Allan Gerson, William Rogers, and David Scheffer. New York: Council on Foreign
Relations.

————. 1991. "Use of Force: Law and U.S. Policy." In *Right v. Might: International Law and the Use of Force*, 2nd ed., ed. Louis Henkin, Stanley Hoffmann, Jeane J. Kirkpatrick, Allan Gerson, William Rogers, and David Scheffer. New York: Council on Foreign Relations.

Hermann, Tamar. 1992. "Contemporary Peace Movements: Between the Hammer of Political Realism and the Anvil of Pacifism." *Western Political Quarterly* 45: 869–93.

Holman, Michael. 1994. "Oxfam Warns of Rwanda Genocide." *Financial Times*. April 29, sec. A, 3.

Howard, Michael. 1976. *War in European History*. New York: Oxford University Press.

————. 2000. *The Invention of Peace: Reflections on War and International Order*. New Haven, Conn.: Yale University Press.

Human Rights Watch. 2002. *2001 Report on Columbia*. New York: Human Rights Watch. www.hrw.org/wr2K2/americas.html (accessed September 13, 2007).

Huntington, Samuel. 1988–89. "The U.S.—Decline or Renewal?" *Foreign Affairs* 67 (2): 76–96.

International Commission on Intervention and State Sovereignty. 2001. "The Responsibility to Protect: Report of the International Commission on Intervention and State Sovereignty." Ottawa: International Development Research Centre. www.iciss-ciise.gc.ca/report-en.asp (accessed September 11, 2007).

International Court of Justice. 1984. *Case Concerning Military and Paramilitary Activities In and Against Nicaragua: Nicaragua v. United States of America* no. 70 (June 27), www.icj-cij.org/docket/index.php?p1=3&p2=3&code=nus&case=70&k=66 (accessed September 12, 2007).

International Development Research Centre. 2001. *Responsibility to Protect*. Ottawa: International Development Research Centre.

International Law Commission. 1950. "Formulation of the Principles of International Law Recognized in the Charter of the Nuremberg Tribunal and in the Judgment of the Tribunal." In *Yearbook of the International Law Commission* vol. 1. New York: United Nations Publication http://untreaty.un.org/ilc/publications/yearbooks/ 1950.htm (accessed September 11, 2007).

International Peace Academy/Organization of African Unity. 1996. *Civil Society and Conflict Management in Africa*. Cape Town, South Africa: International Peace Academy.

Joulwan, George A., and Christopher C. Shoemaker. 1998. *Civilian-Military Cooperation in the Prevention of Deadly Conflict: Implementing Agreements in Bosnia and Beyond*. Washington, D.C.: Carnegie Commission on Preventing Deadly Conflict.

Keen, Maurice. 1965. *The Laws of War in the Late Middle Ages*. London: Routledge and K. Paul.

Kempster, Norman. 1997. "In Africa, Albright Vows 'New Chapter' in Ties; Diplomacy: It's Time for the U.S. to Work With Budding Democracies to Transform the Continent, Secretary of State Says." *Los Angeles Times*. December 10, sec. A, 4.

Krasner, Stephen D. 1985. *Structural Conflict*. Berkeley: University of California Press.

———. 1999. *Sovereignty: Organized Hypocrisy*. Princeton, N.J: Princeton University Press.

Lauterpacht, H. 1970. *International Law*. Cambridge, UK: Cambridge University Press.

Locke, Mary, and Jason Ladnier. 2001. *Criteria for Military Intervention in Internal War: The Debate*. New York: Fund for Peace.

Lund, Michael. 1996. *Preventing Violent Conflicts: A Strategy for Preventive Diplomacy*. Washington, D.C.: United States Institute of Peace Press.

Macfarlane, S. Neil. 2002. *Intervention in Contemporary World Politics*. New York: Oxford University Press.

Mackinlay, John, and Jarat Chopra. 1992. "Second Generation Multinational Operations." *Washington Quarterly* 15 (3): 113–31.

Mann, Michael. 1988. *States, War and Capitalism*. Oxford: Basil Blackwell.

McKinley, James C. Jr. 1998. "Ugly Reality in Rwanda." *New York Times*. May 10, sec. A, 4.

Mearsheimer, John. 1994–95. "False Promise of International Institutions." *International Security* 19 (3): 5–49.

———. 2001. *The Tragedy of Great Power Politics*. New York: Norton.

Moore, John Bassett. 1906. "Letter from Daniel Webster, Secretary of State, to Lord Ashburton, August 6, 1842." *A Digest of International Law* 2: 409–12.

Moskos, Charles, and John Whiteclay II, eds. 1993. *The New Conscientious Objection: From Sacred to Secular Resistance*. New York: Oxford University Press.

Murphy, Sean D. 1996. *Humanitarian Intervention: The United Nations in an Evolving World Order*. Procedural Aspects of International Law 21. Washington, D.C.: PAIL Institute Publications.

Newman, Frank, and David Weissbrodt. 1979. *International Human Rights: Law, Policy and Process*. Boston: Little, Brown.

Northedge, F. S. 1946. *The League of Nations: Its Life and Times, 1920–1946*. Leicester, UK: Leicester University Press.

———. 1974. *The Use of Force in International Relations*. London: Faber and Faber.

Nye, Joseph S. Jr. 1990. *Bound to Lead: The Changing Nature of American Power*. New York: Basic Books.

———. 2002. "What New World Order?" *Foreign Affairs* 71 (2): 82–96.

O'Brien, Jasonne. 2001. *The Communal Law of War: Giovanni de Legnano's De Bello and the Medieval Origins of International Public Law*. Lawrence: University of Kansas Press.

O'Hanlon, Michael, and Stephen Solarz. 1999. "Deciding When to Go." *Washington Post.* February 7, sec. B, 1.

Onyango-Obbo, Charles. 1997. "Entebbe Raid of 1976 Recalled." *The East African,* July 7–13. www.charlesobbo.com/article95.html (accessed September 11, 2007).

Orvik, Nils. 1953. *The Decline of Neutrality, 1914–1941.* Oslo: J. Tanum.

Perez de Cuellur, Javier. 1991a. United Nations, Department of Public Information. 1991. "Secretary-General's address at University of Bordeaux." April 24 (UN Press Release: SG/ SM/4560).

———. 1991b. United Nations, General Assembly. 1991. Report of the Secretary-General on the work of the Organization. 1991 (A/46/1: G.A. Official Records, 46th sess. Supplement no. 1).

Peterson, Frederick. 1998. "The Facade of Humanitarian Intervention for Human Rights in a Community of Sovereign Nations." *Arizona Journal of International Comparative Law* 15: 871–904.

Powell, Colin. 1992–93. "U.S. Forces: Challenges Ahead." *Foreign Affairs* 71 (5): 32–45.

Robyn, Paul. 2001. *The United States and Haiti (1992–1993): A Case Study in Coercive Diplomacy.* Princeton, N.J.: Princeton University, Woodrow Wilson School. www.wws.princeton.edu/~cases/papers/haiti.html (accessed September 11, 2007).

Rodley, Nigel. 1992. "Collective Intervention to Protect Human Rights and Civilian Populations: The Legal Framework." In *To Loose the Bands of Wickedness: International Intervention in Defense of Human Rights,* ed. Nigel Rodley, 14–42. London: Bassey's.

Ronzitti, Natalino. 1985. *Rescuing Nationals Abroad Through Military Coercion and Intervention on Grounds of Humanity.* Boston: Martinus Nijhoff.

Rose, Michael. 1994. "Bosnia Herzegovina 1994: NATO Support for UN Wider Peacekeeping Operations." *NATO Sixteen Nations* 39: (3–4): 8–11.

———. 1999. *Fighting for Peace: Lessons from Bosnia.* London: Warner.

Rubin, Barnett R. 2002. *Blood on the Doorstep.* Washington, D.C.: Brookings Institution Press.

Rummel, R. J. 1997. *Death by Government.* New Brunswick, N.J.: Transaction.

———. 1999. *Statistics of Democide: Genocide and Mass Murder Since 1900.* London: Lit Verlag.

Scales, Ann. 1998. "Clinton Concedes U.S. Erred in Rwanda; Cites Inadequate Response to Killing, Calls It Genocide." *Boston Globe.* March 26.

Schachter, Oscar. 1986. "In Defense of International Rules on the Use of Force." *University of Chicago Law Review* 53 (1): 113.

———. 1991. *International Law in Theory and Practice.* Dordrecht, Netherlands: Martinus Nijhoff.

———. 1995. *United Nations Legal Order.* Cambridge, UK: Cambridge University Press.

Schelling, Thomas C. 1966. *Arms and Influence*. New Haven, Conn.: Yale University Press.

Schermers, Henry. 1991. "The Obligation to Intervene in the Domestic Affairs of States." In *Humanitarian Law of Armed Conflict: Challenges Ahead—Essays in Honour of Frits Kalshoven*, ed. Astrid Delissen and Gerard J. Tanja. Norwell, Mass.: Kluwer.

Scott, James Brown, ed. 1915. *The Hague Conventions and Declarations of 1899 and 1907, Accompanied by Tables of Signatures, Ratifications and Adhesions of the Various Powers and Texts of Reservations*. New York: Oxford University Press.

Smith, Daniel. 2002a. "War and Peace." *Defense Monitor* 31 (3): 1–3.

———. 2002b. "The World at War—January 2002." *Defense Monitor* 31 (1):1–18.

Steering Committee on the Joint Evaluation of Emergency Assistance to Rwanda. 1996. *The International Response to Conflict and Genocide: Lessons from the Rwanda Experience*. Denmark: DANIDA.

Stern, Fritz R. 1977. *Gold and Iron: Bismarck, Bleichroder, and the Building of the German Empire*. New York: Knopf.

Strang, David. 1991. "Anomaly and Commonplace in European Political Expansion: Realist and Institutionalist Accounts." *International Organization* 45 (Spring): 145–62.

Strauss, Leo, and Joseph Cropsey, eds. 1987. *The History of Political Philosophy*. Chicago: University of Chicago Press.

Stremlau, John. 1998. *People in Peril: Human Rights, Humanitarian Action, and Preventing Deadly Conflict*. Washington, D.C.: Carnegie Commission on Preventing Deadly Conflict.

Sweden Ministry for Foreign Affairs. 2001. *Preventing Violent Conflict: Swedish Policy for the 21ˢᵗ Century*. Stockholm: Ministry for Foreign Affairs.

Tilley, Charles, ed. 1975. *The Formation of National States in Western Europe*. Princeton, N.J.: Princeton University Press.

Tuck, Richard. 1999. *The Rights of War and Peace—Political Thought and the International Order from Grotius to Kant*. New York: Oxford University Press.

United Nations. 2000. *Report of the Panel on United Nations Peace Operations* (Brahimi Report). UN Doc A/55/305-S/2000/809 (August 21). www.un.org/peace/reports/peace_operations (accessed September 11, 2007).

United Nations, Commission on Human Rights. 2001. Report of the United Nations High Commissioner for Human Rights on the human rights situation in Colombia. February 8 (E/CN.4/2001/15).

U.S. Army Peacekeeping Institute. 2000. *Challenges of Peacekeeping and Peace Support Into the 21st Century*. Carlisle, Penn.: Center for Strategic Leadership.

U.S. State Department. 1999. "Understanding the Rambouillet Accords." www.state.gov/ www/regions/eur/fs_990301_rambouillet.html (accessed September 12, 2007).

Van Evera, Stephan. 1999. *Causes of War: Power and the Roots of Conflict*. Ithaca, N.Y.: Cornell University Press.

Walzer, Michael. 1977. *Just and Unjust Wars: A Moral Argument with Historical Illustrations*. New York: Basic Books.

Ware, Glenn T. 1997. "The Emerging Norm of Humanitarian Intervention and Presidential Decision Directive." *Naval Law Review* 25 (44): 372–407.

Wedgewood, Ruth. 1991. "The Intervention by Invitation." In *Law and Force in the New International Order,* ed. Lori Fisler Damrosch and David J. Scheffer. Boulder, Colo.: Westview.

Weinberger, Caspar. 1984. "The Uses of Power." Speech to the National Press Club, November 28, Washington, D.C.

Weiner, Robert O., and Fionnuala Ni Aolain. 1996. "Beyond the Laws of War: Peacekeeping in Search of a Legal Framework." *Columbia Human Rights Law Review* 293 (1996): 293–354.

Weiss, Linda. 1998. *The Myth of the Powerless State*. Ithaca: Cornell University Press.

Weston, Burns H., Richard A. Falk, and Hilary Charlesworth. 1997. *International Law and World Order*. St. Paul, Minn.: West Group.

White House. 2002. *The National Security Strategy of the United States of America*. Washington, D.C.: Government Printing Office.

Whitney, Craig R. 1996. "As Carl Bildt Sees Things, Bosnia Has a Shaky Future." *New York Times*. March 26, sec. A, 21.

Woodward, Susan L. 1995. *Balkan Tragedy: Chaos and Dissolution After the Cold War*. Washington, D.C.: Brookings Institution Press.

Wright, Quincy. 1930. *Mandates under the League of Nations*. Chicago: University of Chicago Press.

———. 1941. *A Study of War*. Chicago: University of Chicago Press.

Yale University School of Law. 1924. *Avalon Project: The Covenant of the League of Nations*. www.yale.edu/lawweb/avalon/leagcov.htm (accessed September 11, 2007).

———. 2006. *The Avalon Project: The Charter of the International Military Tribunal*. www.yale.edu/lawweb/avalon/imt/proc/imtconst.htm.

NOTES

1. For a fuller discussion of the force spectrum, see Northedge (1974, 99–123), Wright (1941), and Van Evera (1999).

2. Reference works cited in this chapter are illustrative and are cited to reinforce the author's points but are by no means exhaustive.

3. For a criticism of the future of the state system, see Krasner (1985, 1999). For a discussion of the evolution of the state system, see Nye (2002).

4. For a discussion of Charter values—peace, self-determination, respect for human rights, and economic and social development—and the primacy of peace among these, see Henkin (1989, 37–71).

5. For an account of the League, its aspirations, and its ultimate undoing—mainly by its inability to manage a resurgent Germany, rising Italy, and increasingly bellicose Japan—see Northedge (1946).

6. For an introduction to the essential arguments on the international doctrine of self-defense, see Brownlie (1963), Dinstein (1988), and Chayes and Chayes (1995). For a discussion of the constraints on states acting as part of a collective defense regime, see International Court of Justice (1986), in which the International Court of Justice found against the United States.

7. A related concept, preventive diplomacy, seeks to resolve disputes before they turn violent—see Boutros-Ghali (1992, 1995).

8. For additional information on the United Nations' role in peacemaking, see peacemaker.unlb.org.

9. For a sample of more recent work, see the Danish Institute of International Affairs (1999), Boutwell (1999), Fund for Peace (2001a, 2001b, 2002a, 2002b), and International Commission on Intervention and State Sovereignty (2001).

10. For an overview of ECOMOG, see International Peace Academy/Organization of African Unity (1996) and Alao (1993).

11. For discussion of the increasing activism of regional organizations, with a special emphasis on the OSCE, see Wedgewood (1991), Schachter (1995), Weiner and Ni Aolian (1996), Ware (1997), and Gallant (1992).

12. For a discussion of American attempts to come to grips with these and other tensions regarding the appropriate use of force, see Gacek (1994) and Coady (2002).

13. See, for example, the open letter by Kenneth H. Bacon, president of Refugees International, to (incoming) UN Secretary-General Ban Ki-moon, www.refugeesinternational.org/content/article/detail/9721; and Save the Children, "Protecting Children in Emergencies," policy brief, Spring 2005, vol. 1, no. 1,

14. For post–Cold War reflections on the subject, see Schermers (1991), Clark and Berk (1993), Damrosch and Scheffer (1991), Rodley (1992, 14–42), Stremlau (1998), and Deng et al. (1996).

CONCLUSION

The Use of Methods and Techniques in a Conflict's Lifespan

I. William Zartman

The previous chapters in this book have laid out an array of methods and techniques for peacemaking in international conflicts. However, a toolbox that contains users' instructions but not construction plans for the final product may produce more of a workers' convention than a building project. Both analysts and practitioners of peacemaking need help answering the most important research questions: which, when, and by whom is peacemaking conducted? This chapter is by no means a mail-order blueprint, nor could it be: there is too much in the practice of peacemaking that is idiosyncratic and case specific to give firm general instructions. The best that can be offered is more in the way of building tips and substitutes. This conclusion draws out some general guidelines about when to use direct negotiation, mediated negotiation, adjudication, and workshops; when to call on states, international organizations, or non-governmental organizations, including religious agencies, in order to make peace; and where carrots and sticks—incentives and constraints—can best be used in the process. It includes insights drawn from the preceding chapters, seeking to answer the all-important questions: which, when, and by whom?

Negotiation is the first line of conflict resolution. It can be used when parties are ready to seek a solution for their conflict or to resolve a problem through cooperation over principles, norms, rules, or procedures in a given issue-area. Sometimes, official efforts need informal assistance. Workshops are useful when formal negotiations need to be prepared, relaxed, unblocked, or reinforced. But parties may not be ready to negotiate at the same time and conflicts rarely ripen on their own; when this situation occurs, mediation may be required. Mediation is used when the parties to a conflict cannot negotiate their solution directly. Mediation is not adjudication, however. Adjudication is used when any solution is preferred to a particular solution or when a particular solution is salient and an authority is needed to enunciate it. In addition to or in conjunction with these methods, sanctions and inducements often help parties arrive at a successful conclusion. Positive and negative incentives are used to sweeten the process and outcome of peacemaking and to sour alternatives. In extremis, forceful dissuasion and enforcement are sometimes necessary to block alternatives or implement agreements. The tools for making peace are summarized in the following discussion.

NEGOTIATION

Negotiation is used in two very different types of situations: bi- or plurilateral conflicts, involving two or a few parties, and multilateral cooperation, involving many. Conflicts—not necessarily violent—among two or a few parties are best resolved by the parties themselves under the defining conditions of negotiation: when the decision rule is unanimity (i.e., not majority or authority) and when the parties need to set the terms of trade to conduct a transaction. These conditions in themselves have implications. They mean that the parties must recognize and accept each other as legitimate parties to a conflict and hence to its solution and as formally equal partners in the search for a solution. Although parties are likely to be unequal—even very unequal—in their respective power in the conflict, they are equal in their possession of a veto over the negotiated agreement. For example, neither North Korea and the international community nor the Palestine Liberation Organization (PLO) and Israel could make an agreement without mutual recognition and legitimization of the other as an equal and valid party.

The question of when should a party avail itself of negotiation has two answers. One is when the moment is ripe—that is, when the parties feel themselves to be in a mutually hurting stalemate and perceive the possibility of a way out. Only when the parties feel they cannot escalate their way out of the stalemate and on to victory at an acceptable cost will they have an interest in negotiation. For example, Joe Slovo, head of the South African Communist Party, said of the South African freedom struggle, "Neither side won the war.

The National Party couldn't rule any longer, and we [the African National Congress] couldn't seize power by force. So that means both sides have to compromise. That's the reality" (Taylor 1992). This perception does not guarantee a successful outcome to the negotiations, but it does have to persist to the end if there is to be one.

The other answer to when should a party avail itself of negotiation is the other side of the same coin: when both parties feel they are better off with a possible agreement than without; in other words, when each feels it can gain something from an agreement compared to nonagreement. Both answers depend on the parties' perception of "pain" in the absence of an agreement and their perception of comparative benefit from an agreement; the answers further depend on each party's perception that the other feels the same way—a situation termed "requitement"—and so is ready to participate in an agreement—a way out—that is acceptable to the other.

These conditions may sound highly theoretical, but they are the basis of some very practical calculations that parties make when deciding whether or not to negotiate. The calculations concern a party's own costs and gains and, equally important, its estimates of the other party's calculations. Parties may make a computerized log sheet of their own and the other's costs and gains, as decision analysts would have them do, or they may simply do their reckoning in their head and in brainstorming sessions; in either case, the calculations are integral to the decision-making process.

Calculations to engage in multilaterally negotiated cooperation are similar, although they translate somewhat differently. The defining characteristics are loosely the same: there must be consensus in defining the option and the parties must be acceptable as formally equal and legitimate participants. Ripeness is still required, not in the form of a painfully stalemated conflict, but in the form of conflicts and inefficiencies in the conduct of transactions or the need to create a good that cannot be created unilaterally. The efficient attainment of joint goals is blocked, and so the parties need to negotiate. Without the need for cooperation, negotiations are unattractive or unnecessary. Cooperative negotiations are problem-solving efforts, impelled by a need for some order—norms, rules, expectations, agreements—in new or existing transactions; without negotiations, cooperation is stalemated and the stalemate is uncomfortable. The parties feel they can create a better outcome only by coordinating their cooperation, and they perceive the others to feel the same way. Most simply, when parties feel they need each other, negotiation to form a response to the need is essential.

In regard to cooperation, the considerations indicating negotiation may sound commonplace. They point quite simply to the estimations parties make before engaging and focus on the core elements of the decision: the existence of a disturbing problem or conflict and the need for several-party agreement rather than unilateral action to resolve it.

MEDIATION

For negotiations to occur, the parties must perceive the pressing need for negotiation as well as the attractive possibilities it presents—that is, they must see both the mutually hurting stalemate and a way out. These conditions do not necessarily lead to successful negotiations, however. At this point—when negotiations are difficult to accomplish—the parties might consider mediation. This simple judgment contains a powerful distinction; for example, very few conflicts during and after the Cold War were resolved by direct negotiation and most resolved conflicts were handled by mediation.

The conditions for mediation can be grouped into three categories, each requiring a specific type of mediation. Sometimes parties cannot communicate with each other, calling for a mediator who facilitates the exchange of messages, a communicator. Other times parties cannot conceive of solutions that will meet their separate and joint needs—a way out—and so need a mediator who can propose new types of solutions, a formulator. Finally, sometimes parties do not see adequate benefits in an agreement or are in too weak a position to be able to precipitate or participate in negotiations—a mutually hurting stalemate—and they require mediation that can sweeten the pot or strengthen the players: a manipulator. Mediation helps the parties do what they cannot do by themselves to come to an agreement.

Mediation therefore carries the same defining conditions as negotiation but also helps obtain them. Other elements enter into the calculation to seek or accept mediation. Third parties are unlikely to offer mediation in conflicts that are intractable, involve superpowers, or involve nonstate disputants, but the conflict's intensity increases the likelihood that the parties will accept mediation (Bercovitch and Gartner 2006; Terris and Maoz 2005). The parties must accept each other as legitimate and equal, and the mediator may serve as the crutch of that recognition. Parties talk when they feel stalemated; if that perception is absent, the mediator can work to create it. Certainly, the mediator should not just sit around and wait until ripeness occurs on its own. Parties seek mediation when each or both feel that they can get a better deal with a mediator, when rejection of mediation would have its own costs, or when they seek to improve their relations with the mediator. For example, former secretary of state James Baker, referring to the process of reviving the Mideast Peace Process through the 1991 Madrid talks, writes, "It was our job as mediator to push and pull the region toward peace. One of our strongest points of leverage . . . was the threat to . . . lay the dead cat on their doorstep. No one wanted to accept the blame for scuttling the process" (1999, 188).

But not all parties are equal, and so their interest in invoking mediation is subject to different calculations. In interstate conflicts, sovereign equality among the parties may hide real differences in power and therefore produce different calculations on either side, but in intrastate conflicts, government and rebel movements reckon differently. Because mediation generally strengthens the weaker party, it tends to favor the rebellion by giving it status and recognition. By the same token, mediation requires interference in internal affairs, implying that the state is unable to handle its problems by itself, and so tends to be resisted by the state. Interest in mediation is therefore asymmetrical, unless the state sees mediation as a way to unburden itself of the problem of the rebellion, for example, by obliging the rebels to engage in political talks rather than in violence.

Reasons for mediation must also be considered from the mediator's side. Mediation is not a disinterested business; mediators have their reasons for acting, even if it is only to bring peace or to maintain one's reputation as a mediator or to exercise a capability or a responsibility that others do not possess. But mediation can present advantages for the mediator: through it, the mediator can extend its influence, build its role, or protect its own interests. A mediator will consider intervening when the conflict hurts its interests, by spilling over into its domestic politics, for example, or by affecting one of its allies, or by attracting the attentions of a rival. A final element of becoming a mediator is that the mediator must be invited or accepted by the parties. Thus, the answer to the question, "Who should mediate?" is complex.

It might appear that direct negotiation is a better policy alternative than mediated negotiations for conflicting parties (and possibly for a potential mediator, too, who is subject to suspicion and charges of meddling for its pains). Negotiation gives ownership and control over the outcome to the parties themselves; they can always refuse and veto the result, because their agreement is required. But for that very reason, mediation may at times be preferable, even when the parties might be able to come to an agreement by themselves. The mediator is not only a meddler, it is a crutch, something the parties can lean on in their search for an acceptable outcome. A party can always blame the mediator for the need to accept the results, and the ability to put the burden on a respected third party may be crucial to the agreement. Alternatively, a party or parties may expect to gain a better agreement with the help of a mediator than it or they could obtain alone. Or a party may want better relations with the mediator as an additional benefit of mediated negotiations.

Meddling has its advantages, as well as its price, making mediation preferable to direct negotiation on occasion.

Although these calculations are particularly relevant to conflict mediation, mediation is also functional in instances of multilateral problem-solving cooperation. Here mediation is a softer concept, because all parties are potential mediators in the negotiations among their partners. But specific third-party roles can be useful in conference diplomacy. Multilateral cooperation negotiations tend to need a conductor, a party without direct interests in a particular substantive outcome but with a concern for effective procedures to produce an outcome to which the interested parties can agree—in other words, a conference chair or general secretary. Mediation can keep the proceedings going, provide trust, serve as a crutch or alibi, provide ideas and formulas, and facilitate communications. When these functions are lacking, mediation is needed for cooperation to occur.

DIALOGUE

There is a growing awareness that peacemaking involves two levels and the space between them as well: the formal agreement and the underlying relationships. The formal agreement tends to be an official compact, whereas the underlying relationships involve a broader public. But informal personal relationships are involved even in a formal agreement. Diplomats have long worked at the informal level, seeking to meet their counterparts, talking in corridors and delegates' lounges and bars, taking walks in the woods. Any negotiation and mediation requires combining the formal process with human contacts, relationship building, and informal meetings. This type of dialogue is an integral part of a successful negotiation and mediation processes.

There is also a large space before, around, and after negotiation and mediation that can often be filled with scheduled dialogue. Dialogue workshops can be utilized before negotiations take place, to pace or punctuate negotiations during their course, or in the implementation period. In general, any negotiation can benefit from pre-, para-, and postnegotiation dialogues, but dialogues are especially useful when official negotiations show a need for relaxing, unblocking, supporting, and reinforcing. Dialogues are not an alternative to official peacemaking but rather an adjunct to the formal process. They may be directed at the official negotiators themselves or at components of the context in which they take place, from public leaders' brainstorming sessions to citizens' discussion groups. Thus, to be effective, dialogue workshops must be linked to the official process, lest they become merely detached exercises.

ADJUDICATION

Fewer disputes are submitted to and resolved by judicial means—that is, by binding decision of an authoritative third party—than are resolved by the parties themselves in negotiation or mediation. The reasons for seeking adjudication or arbitration and thereby giving up control over the outcome are an extension of the reasons for mediation and are inherent in the nature of the adjudication process. Parties turn to judicial means when an authoritative decision maker is needed in one of two types of situations: when finding a solution is more important than finding a particular solution or when the correct solution is obvious (at least to the parties). In both cases, an authority is needed to decree it. As in any recourse to the law, these conditions may produce surprises (the parties might not agree on the "correct" solution, each expecting its own solution to prevail).

In the first situation, where any likely solution is acceptable to a party or the parties, judicial recourse is a path to peacemaking that will lift the burden of the conflict. The other situation, where a particular result is expected, is typical of any judicial pleading, and the parties must be ready to abide by surprises.

The assumptions for adjudication are similar to those for negotiation and mediation. Parties are equal before the law and the judge and must admit each other's legitimacy and standing in order to appear in court. They turn to the courts when the conflict hurts, and the act of submission implies that the parties both feel there is a way out. In adjudication, however, parties give up their decision power and the possibility of a veto over the outcome. States in international conflicts are often reluctant to forgo this authority. Major powers, who bear a burden of responsibility in conflict resolution as well as in conflict and who may be the subject of suits motivated by their status rather than by their actions in a conflict, are particularly reluctant to hand over their fate to a court.

INDUCEMENTS

Associated with the various approaches to peacemaking is an array of inducements that any approach (except adjudication) can use to make peaceful outcomes more attractive and continued conflict less so. Such inducements can be positive gratifications or negative deprivations, values added to the possible outcome that make it more or less attractive. Inducements are limited by the goals or the nature of the parties themselves. When goals are absolute or concern perceived vital interests, neither negative nor positive inducements are likely to have much effect; when a party is a spoiler, it is beyond the reach of inducements. At the same time, there is no absolute threshold to any of these elements, and peacemaking involves pushing back the apparent limits to conciliation. The potential usefulness of inducements should never be defined a priori.

Gratifications are useful simply when the proposed outcome is not large or attractive enough to sway a party from its present behavior. Side payments, the introduction of new items into the exchange, and compensation for losses are all aspects of building agreement beyond discussion of the basic items in conflict. At a greater level of complexity, gratifications can be used to overcome uncertainty and risk inherent in the commitments that characterize negotiation and mediation. Gratifications may be used to establish relations beyond the elements in the agreement and to improve the image of the giver. Finally, tactical gratifications have a place in initiating or responding to concessions from the other side, a basic element in the ethos of equality (procedural equality in this aspect) that underlies the expectation of reciprocal concessions and is fundamental to negotiation and peacemaking.

Deprivations also have their use when it becomes necessary to render the current situation or a competing proposal less attractive than a proposed solution. Direct or mediated negotiation always takes place in competition with the parties' security points (their situation in the absence of negotiations), and worsening a party's security point is a standard way of making a proposed solution appear more attractive. Thus, deprivations are important tools in ripening a conflict for resolution so as to make peacemaking efforts possible, just as they are useful adjuncts to those efforts themselves in the course of peacemaking. Sanctions, a particular form of deprivation, are most useful when used in conjunction with present or potential internal pressure—in other words, when they heighten the pressure of the conflict and impel the parties toward resolution.

The most extreme inducement is the deepest deprivation, the use of force, first contingent or threatened and then actually used. The conditions for the legitimate use of force are clear, if interpretable: unilaterally to check an unprovoked use of force by defeating or stalemating it, or multilaterally to engage in an effort of collective security or collective defense. These conditions contain the functional limits of the use of force in peacemaking: to obtain a stalemate to start talks, to contain efforts to break out of talks or to restrain spoilers, to monitor and enforce peacemaking steps such as cease-fires, and to implement agreements. The threat of returning to conflict always hovers over peacemaking and can be helpful in keeping negotiators active and on track.

The decision to use one inducement or another must be considered comparatively. Gratifications are positive elements that improve the atmosphere and the prospects of peacemaking; deprivations sour it. The two create opposite effects, yet must be used together. Deprivations are better suited to ripening the conflict for peacemaking by increasing the push factor of a mutually hurting stalemate toward talks, but ripeness also involves requitement and a way out, a belief that the other party is willing to search for a solution and that there is a solution on which both parties can agree. Once talks have begun, that push factor and thus the potential use or threat of deprivations need to be maintained, but the emphasis needs to shift to the pull factor of a mutually enticing opportunity and hence the potential use of associated gratifications. During cooperation negotiations, gratifications are the subject of the discussion, but deprivations are frequently involved in the bargaining, even though they run counter to the ostensibly creative atmosphere of the talks. During peacemaking, gratifications have been shown to be more powerful than deprivations, especially in asymmetrical situations when used by the stronger party, and gratifications combined with deprivations have been shown to be more effective than either used alone. Yet, a counterthesis, expressed in prospect theory, notes that people react more strongly to losses than to gains. Thus, it is unclear whether carrots are stronger than sticks, but it is clear that carrots and sticks are best when used together.

More specifically, threats and promises must be credible, so each can be used only when they can be delivered. However, successful threats need not be delivered, whereas successful promises need to be kept, which introduces a tension in the use of threats, which are more costly to the user when they fail, whereas promises are more costly when they succeed. An additional distinction can be drawn between voluntary inducements, such as threats and promises, and involuntary ones such as warnings and predictions. It is preferable to use the latter because they do not involve any action by the inducer and so do not look like menaces or bribes. Although insights into when to use inducements can be further fine-tuned in regard to particular conflicts, these guidelines are generally useful.

EDUCATION

Education, if it is considered at all, is usually considered the broadest action to be taken toward peacemaking. Yet the actions discussed above could not be undertaken—or at least not well—if the parties had not been trained to do so, and they would not receive public support if peacemaking were not socially valued. Whereas diplomatic skill was once thought to be an inherent characteristic (and some diplomats still feel that their skills are genetic and not transmissible), most people today agree that good negotiators are made, not just born. Effective practices from the past are conceptualized and transmitted to future diplomats and peacemakers through education and training. Unlike the other tools in the toolbox, education and training are primarily generic, not specific to any one peacemaking effort, and prepare the practitioner and the public for all eventualities, although education and training can also be applied to specific conflicts and occasions. The agents for such work are teachers and trainers in a broad spectrum of institutions, as well as the media, who have a special role to play in understanding and supporting efforts to overcome conflict and induce cooperation. Educators see themselves as one ingredient in the broadest effort to present peacemaking skills and tools to future users.

AGENTS

Peacemaking involves an array of actors, from states to private parties, acting alone or in concert. Although the tools and techniques of peacemaking can be applied to any type of conflict or cooperation, down to the daily interpersonal level, nearly all the situations covered here involve states. In the end, in nearly all instances, it takes states to deal conclusively with states. States have the resources, legitimacy, and authority to deal with other states. Mediation, negotiation, cooperation, and inducements are part of regular diplomacy conducted by states on both a routine and an ad hoc basis, and states have dedicated resources for such activities. This work includes state participation in and use of international organizations; other actors have limited budgets and ad hoc capabilities. States alone possess the internationally recognized sovereign standing to make official representations to other sovereign states, to make commitments and exchange obligations, and to witness official engagements; other actors can engage only in informal conversations and temporary relations. States alone are authorized to sign treaties to commit their publics, pursuant to both international and domestic law, to impose sanctions and, ultimately, to make war; others are moral observers and informal persuaders.

States increase these capabilities by working together. Resources are added, or even multiplied; legitimacy is raised to a higher level; and authority becomes paramount when expressed in international treaties, regimes, and organizations. Cooperation is particularly important when the use of force, usually expressed through the UN Security Council or a regional organization, is deemed necessary. Similarly, coordinated cooperation through multilateral engagements combines legitimacy with effectiveness. This does not mean that the trumps that international organizations hold over unilateral action are always effective; in the anarchic international systems, states ignore international organizations as they ignore international law. On occasion, and, more frequently and more positively, mediation, dialogue, and inducements are more effectively carried out by individual states than by multistate agencies. As in any type of activity, multiactor decisions and implementations are cumbersome and, when achieved, inflexible. They involve compromises and inefficiencies and lean toward the lowest common denominator. Although they may combine the advantages of their various members, multiactor cooperation may inhibit special relationships, helpful biases, and bilateral understandings. With peacemaking agents, more may be better, but fewer is often best.

When should states make peace unilaterally and when should they work cooperatively? The answer is not correlated to particular tools, but rather to the particular demands of the situation. When peacemaking takes the form of cooperative agreements, multilateral action is needed by definition, but it generally involves unilateral initiatives and strategies, both to start the discussions and to lead them to fruition. In dealing with conflict, when rapid and decisive action is required, when special relationships (including productive biases) are involved, when a state holding a particular role (superpower, neighbor, diaspora host) is required, unilateral practice of negotiation, mediation, and inducements is indicated. When the weight of the international community is needed, when a fully neutral actor is required, when broadly available resources are necessary, multilateral peacemaking through international organization agencies is preferable. Between the two is international community support for unilateral actions through enabling resolutions, assistance by other states, coalitions of "friends of the mediator or of the parties" and the like. But when multiple actors are involved, coordination is absolutely necessary, lest the parties trip over each other's efforts and open themselves to competitive mediation and one-upmanship or even to undercutting mediation with conflict support. In peacemaking, unilateral action with multilateral support still seems to be the more frequent and most effective practice.

That said, nonstate actors play important ancillary roles. As informal agents, they have an advantage in informal activities and in dealing with other nonstate actors (including rebels and insurgents). Non-governmental organizations (NGOs) can go where states cannot and can reach conflicting parties without the commitments involved in state contacts. As such, they can loosen the constraints of conflict and encourage creativity and flexibility. Second- or even multitrack diplomacy can prepare, support, and implement track-one, or official, diplomacy; with rare exceptions, it cannot replace it. It can, on occasion, operate in cooperation with official efforts, taking the apparent lead with state backing, which is known as track-one-and-a-half diplomacy, as the Norwegian Institute for Applied Social Science did in facilitating the Oslo Accords between Israel and the PLO in 1993 or as the Catholic lay organization Sant'Egidio did in mediating the end to civil war in Mozambique in 1990–92.

A particular type of NGO involvement comes in the form of faith-based agencies, such as Sant'Egidio, which have a limited but special role in peacemaking. Faith-inspired agencies often have a difficult time separating advocacy from peacemaking; the former is an important and laudable endeavor, but in religious as in political organizations it can impede mediation. The other limitation comes from the context: the ministrations of religious agencies may or may not be welcome to parties in conflict. Yet, faith-based agencies can be useful in peacemaking, for the very reasons of their limitation. On one hand, such agencies can provide special access when a non-governmental intervenor is needed and the particular religious character provides an entrée into the conflict. The religious nature can provide a special authority that is either shared by the parties or external to them. On the other hand, such agencies can be useful when a neutral, powerless, moral voice is needed, a voice for the voiceless or for the downtrodden.

No general rule applies as to which, when, and by whom peacemaking tools should be implemented. Force and adjudication both stand as the last resort, an ever-present alternative to goad the multifaceted tools of "alternative dispute resolution" through dialogue, negotiation, mediation, and inducements. Which of these latter methods and techniques to try first is impossible to recommend; the soundest approach would be to try—or at least to evaluate—them all, for they can reinforce each other. Similarly, there is no sequencing among agents. NGOs can prepare the ground for official actions and be particularly useful in goading slow-moving diplomatic bureaucracies into gear. When states undertake peacemaking, exercising unilateral initiatives first and then gathering multilateral support, NGOs have a role to play as part of the team. When the efforts succeed, both states and NGOs need to stay involved, each playing to their strengths. Peacemaking is a collective and ongoing business.

CONCLUSION

Peacemaking rests squarely in the hands of third parties. The very fact of conflict inhibits the parties involved from finding their own way out: they need help. Help may take the form of direct negotiation or it may take the form of some kind of mediation—communication, formulation, or manipulation. It may involve the utilization of inducements, both negative and positive, to push the parties into a process of peacemaking and then to pull them successfully out of the process into peace. Methods, techniques, and agents have their own conditions for utilization and effectiveness; the best-intentioned efforts at peacemaking ignore guidelines on when to use which of these at their peril.

But these are only guidelines. Just as there is no single theory of negotiation and mediation, there is no handbook for the practice of peacemaking. The discussion in this book can facilitate the task of trial and error by providing tools and descriptions of how to use them, but it does not instruct users on how to make peace. The process of making peace is a circular one, a learning curve that draws lessons from good practice and generalizes them for further improvement. What we know comes from the best practice of practitioners, extrapolated by analytical thinking, inductively produced guidelines for deductive testing, correcting, and further use. The toolbox and instructions are here for all actors in peacemaking to employ; the answers to the questions of which tools to use, who should use them, and when they should be used are offered here for thoughtful application according to the needs of a variety of situations.

ACKNOWLEDGMENT

The author is grateful to the participants in a workshop organized by Osnabrück University for the preparation of these ideas: Günter Bierbrauer, Kristina Baumert, Jutta Cohausz, Christopher Cohrs, Ivor Dikkers, Anne Geniets, Barbara Gruss, Heidi Ittner, Ulrich Schoop, Christina Schwenck, Corinna Vigier, Luc Vocks, and Bettina von Helversen.

REFERENCES

Baker, James. 1999. "The Road to Madrid." In *Herding Cats: Multiparty Mediation in a Complex World*, ed. Chester A. Crocker, Fen O. Hampson, and Pamela Aall. Washington, D.C.: United States Institute of Peace Press.

Bercovitch, Jacob, and Scott Gartner. 2006. "Do Conflicts Matter? Analyzing the Conditions and Occurrence of Third Party Management." Paper presented at the annual conference of the American Political Science Association, Philadelphia.

Taylor, Paul. 1992. "South African Communist Sparks an Explosive Debate." *Washington Post*, November 22, sec. A, 32.

Terris, Leslie G., and Zeev Maoz. 2005. "Rational Mediation: A Theory and a Test." *Journal of Peace Research* 42 (5): 563–72.

CONTRIBUTORS

Pamela R. Aall is vice president for education at the United States Institute of Peace. Her research interests include mediation in inter- and intrastate conflicts, the role of nonofficial organizations in conflict management and resolution, and the role of education in exacerbating conflict or promoting reconciliation. Before joining the Institute in 1993, she was a consultant to the President's Committee on the Arts and the Humanities and to the Institute of International Education. She also held a number of positions at the Rockefeller Foundation and has worked for the European Cultural Foundation (Amsterdam and Brussels) and the International Council for Educational Development (New York). She is a past president of Women in International Security. Aall holds a B.A. from Harvard University and a master's from Columbia University and attended the London School of Economics, where she conducted research on political and economic integration in Scandinavia and Europe. Her published books include *Leashing the Dogs of War*, *Grasping the Nettle*, *Taming Intractable Conflicts*, *Turbulent Peace*, and several other volumes and papers.

Jacob Bercovitch is a professor of international relations at the University of Canterbury in Christchurch, New Zealand. He received a doctorate from the London School of Economics in 1980 and has since written extensively on international conflict resolution and mediation. He was senior fellow at the United States Institute of Peace in 2002, was elected vice president of the International Studies Association in 2003, and was a fellow of the Royal Society in New Zealand in 2005. In 2007, he was a senior fellow at Georgetown University.

Richard B. Bilder is Foley and Lardner-Bascom Emeritus Professor of Law at the University of Wisconsin-Madison. He was educated at Williams College and Harvard University Law School, and as a Fulbright scholar at the University of Cambridge. He served for some years as an attorney in the Office of Legal Adviser at the U.S. Department of State before moving to the University of Wisconsin, where he has taught in the areas of international and foreign relations law. Bilder has served as vice president, honorary vice president, and counselor of the American Society of International Law; member of the board of editors of the *American Journal of International Law*; executive board member of the Law of the Sea Institute; chair of the International Courts Committee of the American Bar Association; U.S. delegate to international conferences; and as an arbitrator in international and domestic disputes. He is the author of *Managing the Risks of International Agreement* and of a number of articles and other scholarly publications on international and foreign relations law.

David Cortright is a research fellow at the Joan B. Kroc Institute for International Peace Studies at the University of Notre Dame and president of the Fourth Freedom Forum. He has served as consultant or adviser to agencies of the United Nations, international think tanks, and the foreign ministries of Canada, Japan, and several European countries. He has written widely on nuclear disarmament, multilateral counterterrorism, and the use of incentives and sanctions as tools of international peacemaking. He is the author or editor of fifteen books, including *Uniting Against Terror: Cooperative Nonmilitary Responses to the Global Terrorist Threat*, coedited with George A. Lopez; and *Gandhi and Beyond: Nonviolence in an Age of Terrorism*.

Daniel Druckman is a professor in the Department of Public and International Affairs at George Mason University and at the University of Queensland in Brisbane, and a faculty member at Sabanci University in Istanbul. He has held senior positions at several consulting firms and at the U.S. National Academy of Sciences. He has published widely on negotiating behavior, nationalism and group identity, human performance, peacekeeping, political stability, nonverbal communication, and research methodology. His book *Doing Research: Methods of Inquiry for Conflict Analysis* received the best book award from the International Association for Conflict Management (IACM) in 2006. He also received the 1995 Otto Klineberg award for Intercultural and International Relations from the Society for the Psychological Study of Social Issues for his work on nationalism, and a Teaching Excellence award in 1998 from George Mason University. His 2001 article on turning points in negotiation, in the *Journal of Conflict Resolution*, was the IACM outstanding article of the year. He received the 2003 Lifetime Achievement Award from the IACM.

Ronald J. Fisher is a professor and director of the international peace and conflict resolution program in the School of International Service at American University in Washington, D.C., and was previously the founding coordinator of the Applied Social Psychology Graduate Program at the University of Saskatchewan, Saskatoon, Canada. His primary interest is interactive conflict resolution, which involves informal third-party interventions in protracted and violent ethnopolitical conflict. Fisher's publications include *Social Psychology: An Applied Approach*, *The Social Psychology of Intergroup and International Conflict Resolution*, *Interactive Conflict Resolution*, *Paving the Way: Contributions of Interactive Conflict Resolution to Peacemaking*, and numerous articles in the field of peace and conflict resolution. In 2003, he received the Morton Deutsch Conflict Resolution Award from the Peace Psychology Division of the American Psychological Association, and he has been elected as a fellow in both the American and the Canadian psychological associations. He holds an M.A. in psychology from the University of Saskatchewan and a doctorate in social psychology from the University of Michigan.

Jeffrey W. Helsing, deputy director of education at the United States Institute of Peace, is responsible for many of the Institute's faculty and teacher workshops and for curriculum development. He often leads workshops on teaching about war and peace. Helsing also works with many groups in Israel and the Palestinian Authority to train educators, non-governmental organization (NGO) workers, students, and young leaders in developing skills in conflict resolution, nonviolence, human rights, and communication and facilitation. He has twenty years' experience as an educator, having taught courses on conflict resolution and peacebuilding, international relations, and foreign policy analysis. Helsing coedited a book on conflict and human rights and has written articles and book chapters on American policy in the Middle East and on Middle East conflicts. He holds a doctorate in political science from Columbia University and a B.A. from Stanford University.

Herbert C. Kelman is Richard Clarke Cabot Professor of Social Ethics, Emeritus, and cochair of the Middle East Seminar at Harvard University. A pioneer in the development of interactive problem solving—an unofficial third-party approach to the resolution of international and intercommunal conflict—he has been engaged for more than thirty years in efforts toward the resolution of the Israeli-Palestinian conflict. His writings on interactive problem solving received the Grawemeyer Award for Ideas Improving World Order in 1997. His major publications include *International Behavior: A Social-Psychological Analysis* (editor and coauthor), *A Time to Speak: On Human Values and Social Research, and Crimes of Obedience: Toward a Social Psychology of Authority and Responsibility* (with V. Lee Hamilton).

Louis Kriesberg is a professor emeritus of sociology, Maxwell Professor Emeritus of Social Conflict Studies, and founding director of the Program on the Analysis and Resolution of Conflicts at Syracuse University. In addition to more than 125 book chapters and articles, his published books include *Constructive Conflicts, International Conflict Resolution, Timing the De-Escalation of International Conflicts* (coeditor), *Intractable Conflicts and Their Transformation* (coeditor), *Social Conflicts, Social Inequality, Mothers in Poverty, Social Processes in International Relations* (editor), *and Research in Social Movements, Conflicts and Change* (editor, vols. 1–14). He was president of the Society for the Study of Social Problems, and he lectures, consults, and provides training on conflict resolution, security issues, and peace studies.

J. Michael Lekson is vice president for professional training at the United States Institute of Peace. He joined the Institute as a training program officer in 2003 following a twenty-six-year career in the Department of State. His final position at the State Department was deputy assistant secretary of state for arms control, where he oversaw all multilateral arms control negotiations and treaty implementation and for which he received the Secretary's Distinguished Service Award. Before that, he was deputy to the special representative of the president and the secretary of state for implementation of the Dayton Peace Agreement. During his Foreign Service career, he served at a number of posts in Latin America and Western Europe. His final overseas assignment was as deputy U.S. representative to the Organization for Security and Cooperation in Europe (OSCE) in Vienna. Lekson has a B.A. in English from Princeton University and an M.A. in linguistics from Stanford University.

Jane Holl Lute is UN assistant secretary-general and officer in charge, Department of Field Support, responsible for UN field-based peace operations worldwide. She joined the United Nations from the UN Foundation and Better World Fund, where she served as executive vice president and chief operating officer. Previously, she directed the Role of American Military Power project for the Association of the United States Army and was senior public policy fellow at the Woodrow Wilson International Center for Scholars.

She was executive director of the Carnegie Commission on Preventing Deadly Conflict and director for European affairs on the National Security Council staff at the White House, serving under presidents Bush and Clinton. A career Army officer, she held command, served in the Persian Gulf during Operation Desert Storm, and taught political science at the U.S. Military Academy at West Point. Lute retired from the Army in 1994. She holds a PhD in political science from Stanford University and a JD from Georgetown University and is a member of the Virginia bar.

Cynthia Sampson is a writer and editor in the areas of religion and the environment. Formerly a scholar and practitioner of religiously motivated peacemaking, she is an author and coeditor (with Douglas Johnston) of *Religion, the Missing Dimension of Statecraft*, an author and coeditor (with John Paul Lederach) of *From the Ground Up: Mennonite Contributions to International Peacebuilding*, and an author and coeditor (with Mohammed Abu-Nimer, Claudia Liebler, and Diana Whitney) of *Positive Approaches to Peacebuilding: A Resource for Innovators*. Sampson worked in program development with the Center for Justice and Peacebuilding, Eastern Mennonite University, and the Conflict Transformation Program of the World Conference on Religion and Peace and has served as an international affairs editor at the *Christian Science Monitor*.

Alan C. Tidwell directs the Center for Australian and New Zealand Studies in the Edmund A. Walsh School of Foreign Service at Georgetown University. From 2001 through 2004, he was a program officer with the United States Institute of Peace, where he focused on conflict resolution and education. He specializes in work on conflict in the Australasian region. Before joining the Institute in 2001, he was a senior lecturer in management at Macquarie Graduate School of Management in Sydney, where he taught courses in conflict resolution and negotiation. Tidwell served as director and deputy director of the Centre for Conflict Resolution at Macquarie University and as acting executive director and research director of the Australian Centre for American Studies at Sydney University. In 1999, he received the Outstanding Teaching Award from Macquarie University. Tidwell holds a doctorate in international relations from the University of Kent at Canterbury, UK, a master's in professional ethics from the University of New South Wales, and a master's in conflict resolution from George Mason University.

George F. Ward Jr. is senior vice president for international programs at World Vision. From 1999 to 2005, he was vice president and director of the

Professional Training Program at the United States Institute of Peace. Ward was a Foreign Service officer for thirty years and served as U.S. ambassador to the Republic of Namibia from 1996 to 1999. From February to June 2003, he served as coordinator for humanitarian assistance in Iraq. In other senior government assignments, he was principal deputy assistant secretary of state for international organizations and deputy chief of mission in Germany. During earlier Foreign Service assignments, he worked extensively on European security questions. Before his Foreign Service career, he was an officer in the U.S. Marine Corps, serving in the United States and Vietnam. Ward holds a B.A. in history from the University of Rochester and an M.P.A. from Harvard University.

I. William Zartman is the Jacob Blaustein Distinguished Professor of International Organization and Conflict Resolution at the Nitze School of Advanced International Studies at Johns Hopkins University, and member of the steering committee of the Processes of International Negotiation at the International Institute of Applied Systems Analysis in Vienna. He was previously all-university head of the Politics Department at New York University. He has been a distinguished fellow of the United States Institute of Peace, Olin Professor at the U.S. Naval Academy, and Elie Halévy Professor at the Institute for Political Studies in Paris, and he received a lifetime achievement award from the International Association for Conflict Management. He has written several books on negotiation, including *The Practical Negotiator*, *Ripe for Resolution*, and *Cowardly Lions: Missed Opportunities to Prevent Deadly Conflict and State Collapse*, and edited other works on the subject, including *Power and Negotiation* and *Elusive Peace*. He is president of the Tangier American Legation Museum Society and past president of the Middle East Studies Association. He received a doctorate from Yale and an honorary doctorate from Louvain.

INDEX

PEACEMAKING IN INTERNATIONAL CONFLICT

METHODS & TECHNIQUES

Revised Edition

This book is set in Goudy; the display type is Twentieth Century. Hasten Design Studio, Inc., designed the book's cover, and Helene Redmond did the page makeup. The text is copyedited by The Editorial Group and proofread by Amy Thompson. The index was prepared by EEI. The book's editor was Michael Carr.